The Bluejackets' Manual

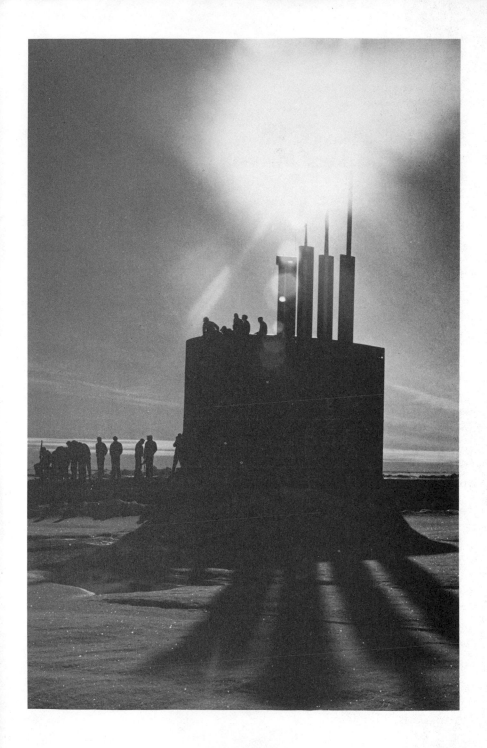

TWENTY-FIRST EDITION

The Bluejackets' Manual

Revised by
Bill Bearden

United States Naval Institute
Annapolis, Maryland

Library of Congress Cataloging-in-Publication Data
ISBN 1-55750-050-9 (pbk)⁻ LC No.: 3-1595

Printed in the United States of America on acid-free paper ⊗
9 8 7 6 5 4 3 2

First printing

This book is dedicated to all those sailors who held a steady helm in the past, those who are steering a straight course today, and those who will plot the Navy's path into the future.

THE UNITED STATES NAVY

GUARDIAN OF OUR COUNTRY

The United States Navy is responsible for maintaining control of the sea and is a ready force on watch at home and overseas, capable of strong action to preserve the peace or of instant offensive action to win in war.

It is upon the maintenance of this control that our country's glorious future depends; the United States Navy exists to make it so.

WE SERVE WITH HONOR

Tradition, valor, and victory are the Navy's heritage from the past. To these may be added dedication, discipline, and vigilance as the watchwords of the present and the future.

At home or on distant stations we serve with pride, confident in the respect of our country, our shipmates, and our families.

Our responsibilities sober us; our adversities strengthen us.

Service to God and Country is our special privilege. We serve with honor.

THE FUTURE OF THE NAVY

The Navy will always employ new weapons, new techniques, and greater power to protect and defend the United States on the sea, under the sea, and in the air.

Now and in the future, control of the sea gives the United States her greatest advantage for the maintenance of peace and for victory in war.

Mobility, surprise, dispersal, and offensive power are the keynotes of the new Navy. The roots of the Navy lie in a strong belief in the future, in continued dedication to our tasks, and in reflection of our heritage from the past.

Never have our opportunities and our responsibilities been greater.

Contents

V. Seamanship, Navigation, and Communication

Appendices

Foreword

There is no greater honor a person can have than to serve his or her country, especially as an American sailor. We are unique professionals, complex and diverse. We must be keenly aware of the importance of each other's specialties in today's highly technical Navy.

The Bluejackets' Manual will give you a broad understanding of our modern Navy as well as the tradition and heritage upon which it is founded. This book is designed to be near at hand—in a seabag, on a work bench or desk—and available for quick reference. It should not be forgotten on a dusty book shelf. The pages should show use. Read it from cover to cover—and read it again.

Your *BJM* will help you become part of the whole Navy and steer you on a proper course. It will remain a cherished possession long after your active service in the United States Navy is over.

Fair winds and following seas!

DUANE R. BUSHEY
Master Chief Petty Officer
of the Navy

Preface

When *The Bluejackets' Manual* first appeared in 1902, there were few sources of information available for the fledgling bluejacket. In that edition the author, Lieutenant Ridley McLean, made available a manual of practical information for recruits as well as a handbook for the use of petty officers who wished to advance themselves.

Today there are literally thousands of different Navy references: textbooks, rate-training manuals, technical manuals, etc. With these available, the twenty-first edition makes no attempt to be a comprehensive textbook. It is, however, a "back-to-basics" handbook that covers a wealth of information for the newest recruit or oldest salt.

Graduation from boot camp does not mean you should discard the twenty-first edition. Its usefulness as a reference aid will continue throughout your Navy career. Although *The BJM* is intended as a "Navy primer," this edition includes a great deal of information of interest to career Navy men and women. It is thus a valuable reference book for all sailors.

Of particular interest is the extensive bibliography (appendix J), which offers additional references, both official and unofficial, on hundreds of subjects. This should be especially useful to ship and station career counselors, retention teams, and other administrators, as well as to division officers and petty officers.

The twenty-first edition of *The BJM* is a blend of the old Navy and new Navy. While the old is reflected in the Navy's time-honored customs and ceremonies, new material has been added to keep *The BJM* current within the technological advances and intricacies of today's Navy.

Acknowledgments

The twenty-first edition of *The Bluejackets' Manual* is the product of considerable time and effort by scores of contributors and reviewers, so many that it is impossible to mention all of their names here. Assistance was sought from numerous ships, other seagoing commands and shore-based activities, as well as individual experts in all areas covered in the *BJM*.

The weapons and weapon systems, ships information, and the navy history appendix are the result of the untiring efforts of Naval Historian John C. Reilly, Jr. The submarine information was checked by Lieutenant Commander A. D. Malcomb. Naval Aviation Historian Roy Grossnick reviewed and updated the current aircraft types and all aviation material, except current numbers of aircraft, which came from Linda Crawford, Office of Naval Operations. The Uniform Code of Military Justice was reviewed and updated by Navy officers of the Judge Advocate General's Office.

All fleet and force master chiefs were consulted. Listed alphabetically, they are: YNCM (SW) Gerald W. Allchin, U.S. Pacific Fleet; HMCM Jeffrey A. Brody, Naval Reserve Force; UCCM Billy Brower, Naval Facilities Engineering Command; OSCM (SW) Emory L. Campbell (Wink), Training Command Atlantic Fleet; ABCM Ronald L. Carter, Naval Air Force Atlantic Fleet; AVCM (AW) Robert W. Dean, Naval Air Training; HMCM William Griffith, Naval Medical Command; AVCM Javier M. Guerrero, U.S. Naval Forces Europe; HTCM (SW) Terry Hammond, Fleet Air Mediterranean; NCCM Floyd E. Harden, Navy Recruiting Command; FCCM (SW) Albert Jackson, Jr., Naval Education and Training Command; TMCM (SS) James A. Kikis, Submarine Force Pacific Fleet; MSCM (SS) Russell E. Malbon, Naval Supply Systems Command; SKCM (SS) Wayne Meyers, Submarine Force Atlantic Fleet; NCCM (SW) Jack R. Mondie, Military Sealift Command; AFCM (AW) Othan N. Mondy, Naval Air Force Pacific Fleet; CTACM (SW) George D. Monroe, Naval Security Group Headquarters; GMCM (SW) Phillip R. Montgomery, Naval Sea Systems Command; AVCM Jon G. Persson, Naval Air Systems Command; BMCM Calvin Lee Rennels, Naval Surface Force Atlantic Fleet; MMCM (SS) Jerry Rose, Training Command Pacific Fleet; MNCM Richard Schommer, Mine Warfare Command; MMCM (SS) Lewis M. Sikes, Jr., U.S. Atlantic Fleet Headquarters; UCCM Wallace A. Sisk, Naval Technical Training; RMCM Thomas E. Ward, Naval Telecommunications Command; and BMCM (SW) Jimmie C. Williams, Naval Surface Force Pacific Fleet. In addition, many command master chiefs were contacted and their response was overwhelming.

Of particular note was the assistance provided by HMC Patricia Cardinale, Navy Medical Command, who reviewed and updated the hygiene, health, and first aid information. Doit Shotts, ETCM (SW) Ken Vencill, and PNCM Stallard, Navy Occupational Development and Analysis Center, verified the classification, rates, and ratings information.

Much of the material contained in chapter 1 on recruit training was verified and updated by YNC Robert Baker.

Other contributors included Connie Pinto and Hank Franhauser, Navy Recruiting Command; George Dornback, Office of the Navy Comptroller; YNC Patsy J. Frank, Office of Information; Robert L. Panek, Director, Navy Budget; Lieutenant Commander Peter J. Reynierse, Naval Reserve; Mr. Nick Sandifer, Coast Guard Headquarters; Gunnery Sergeant Bob Torrez, Headquarters Marine Corps; John P. Devine, Navy Headquarter's Organization; Brenda L. Bruns, Navy Department; and Lieutenant D. Keesler, MMCM (SS) Larry D. Wendland, and Bonnie (Trudy) Allen of the Navy Uniform Board.

This edition would not have been possible without the tremendous across-the-board support from all departments and branches of the Naval Military Personnel Command. Of particular note was the assistance provided by Commander Betty S. Anderson, Commander D. B. Manning, PNCS (SW) Thoerig, and NCC Clippinger.

The continued support of everyone in the Master Chief Petty Officer of the Navy Duane R. Bushey's office is greatly appreciated. They put us in touch with many of the experts—both within and outside the command—who assisted in updating this edition. JO1 Craig D. Grisoli was most helpful.

Other NMPC contributors who did their utmost to answer our questions were the many enlisted detailers we contacted including ENC Roger Large, EMCM Cal Jones, ICC (SW/AW) Chuck Foreman, IC1 (SW) Ken Roebuck, and BMCS Jack Barford.

The photo illustrations for this edition are mostly the products of the creative efforts of the Navy's photographic community. The photographic illustrations of the *BJM* could not have been accomplished without the continuing efforts of Mr. Russ Egnor, Office of Information, and his able staffers.

Special thanks go to Connie Buchanan, who edited the twenty-first edition manuscript, and to Carol Swartz, Naval Institute Press editor, whose able guidance and vast knowledge of publications production pulled all the elements of *BJM* together during its final stages. A great deal of personal time and effort and attention to detail, as well as enthusiastic support, came from Lieutenant Kenneth Cronk, a long-time friend and avid contributor to the *BJM* and other Navy publications.

Many thanks go to my son, Shawn Bearden, who helped with typing, read and proofed manuscripts, categorized and kept track of illustrations, captions, tables and charts. Also, to the many Navy experts—the old salts—who are always eager and willing to take the time to share their knowledge with us so that you might be better informed; without their assistance it would be impossible to keep *BJM* up to date.

I. Welcome Aboard

Introduction to the Navy

Welcome aboard! These words carry a world of significance. They mean that you have made one of the biggest decisions a young person can—you have volunteered to enlist in the United States Navy. By doing so, you have become a member of one of the most famous military services in the world and joined one of the biggest businesses in the United States. Not only have you proved your understanding of citizenship by offering your services to your country, but you have also taken the first step toward an exciting and rewarding career.

Today's Navy is a massive and complex organization, a far cry from the makeshift fleet that opposed the British in the Revolutionary War. For the fiscal period beginning 1 October 1989, the Department of the Navy had budgeted 590,500 Navy and 196,700 Marine Corps officers and enlisted personnel, 347,700 civilian employees, and a total battle force of 551 ships and 5,035 average operating aircraft. It will cost a proposed $97.3 billion to operate the department this year; that's 33.9 percent of the United States defense budget or 8.1 percent of total federal spending.

The Navy plays a vital role in maintaining our national security; it protects us against our enemies in time of war and supports our foreign policy in peacetime. Through its exercise of sea power, the Navy ensures freedom of the seas so that merchant ships can bring us the vital raw material we import from abroad, like petroleum, rubber, sugar, and aluminum. Sea power makes it possible for us to use the oceans when and where our national interests require it, and denies our enemies that same freedom.

First Enlistment

Your introduction to the Navy started at your hometown recruiting station, with interviews and processing conducted by a trained petty officer. Your enlistment (often called a hitch or cruise) may be for three, four, five, or six years. Four years is a normal hitch; five years is for those approved for training in one of twelve specific ratings; and six years is for those qualifying for advanced training. If you enlisted for four years and are a high-school graduate, you may have selected one of the sixty or more Navy technical schools.

All recruits begin their naval careers at a Naval Training Center (NTC) in either Great Lakes, Illinois; San Diego, California; or Orlando, Florida. Women are trained in Orlando; men may be sent to any of the three centers, not necessarily the one nearest their home.

Naval Training Center, Great Lakes

This center, located on Lake Michigan about 40 miles north of Chicago, was opened on 1 July 1911. During World War II, nearly a million men were trained at Great Lakes.

Naval Training Center, San Diego

Located on San Diego Bay, this center was opened on 1 June 1923. San Diego is also homeport for many Pacific Fleet ships.

Naval Training Center, Orlando

The Orlando center, about 50 miles west of the Kennedy Space Center, was opened 1 July 1968. All enlisted women— about 9,000 a year—receive training here.

Each NTC consists of three commands:

Naval Training Station (NTS) maintains buildings and grounds at NTCs and provides housing, clothing, and medical and dental care. NTS also handles recreational and Navy Exchange facilities, communications, postal and transportation service, and police and fire protection.

The Service School Command (SSC) operates the schools that provide technical training for various ratings. These schools train petty officers from the fleet and recruits who have finished boot camp.

The Recruit Training Command (RTC) is where you go first. The RTC helps you make the transition from civilian to military life with a busy schedule of lectures and drills on naval

history, traditions, customs, and regulations. It also gives you instruction in basic military subjects.

The day of arrival at the center is called receipt day, when your initial processing begins. The next three days will be referred to as P-days. The day after P-days is one-one day, indicating the first week and first day of training. The rest of the first week consists of one-two day, one-three day, one-four day, and so on.

First Weeks in the Navy

The procedure may vary from one NTC to another, but in general it goes like this: Report in, turn in orders, and draw your bedding and bunk assignment for your first night on board. Regulations now require that you be given a urinalysis test upon arrival. That same day, or the next, you will begin training. You will also fill out forms: a bedding custody card, a stencil chit, a receipt for a chit book (to be used instead of money for purchases at the Navy Exchange), a safe-arrival card for your parents, a clothing requisition, a packing slip to send your personal gear home (you must pay the shipping costs), and others.

You might have your first meal while still in civilian clothes. Here is a typical menu:

Breakfast	*Dinner*	*Supper*
Hard- or soft-cooked eggs	Spaghetti	Country-style chicken
Grilled hotcakes	Baked lasagna	Chicken gravy
Hot maple syrup	Lyonnaise green beans	Oven-browned potatoes
Beef hash	Pepperoni pizza	Buttered green peas
Broiled ham slices	Toasted garlic bread	Salad bar
Pastry bar	Chilled peach halves	Pineapple pudding
Speed Line	*Speed Line*	
Chilled prunes	Chicken noodle soup	
Chilled fruit juice	Hot fish sandwich	
Assorted dry cereal	Salad bar	
Hot oatmeal	Fruit gelatin	

Male recruits will get a haircut. The barber won't shave the hair off, but they won't leave enough to comb either. Later, at his first duty station, the male recruit will be allowed some choice in hairstyle, as long as it conforms to the Navy's standards for grooming.

Female recruits get haircuts if their hair does not conform to Navy standards. Females cannot wear their hair up while at boot camp.

Your schedule will include the following:

Complete Medical Examination

The exam will cover eyes, teeth, heart, blood, urinalysis, X-rays, inoculation—the works. If you need dental work, it will be scheduled.

Chit Book and Ditty Bag Issue

You will be issued a chit book of coupons to be used in the exchange for toilet articles, sewing kits, shoeshine gear, notebooks, stationery, postage stamps, and pens and pencils. The total cost will be deducted from your pay.

Initial Clothing Issue

This includes enough uniform clothing to make you look like a sailor. Eventually you will receive a complete outfit, or seabag, worth hundreds of dollars, and a marking stencil to put your name on every item.

Training Organization

Soon after reporting in, you will be placed in a company and will meet the people you'll be with for the next several weeks. Then, during a formal commissioning ceremony, an officer will welcome you to the NTC, give a brief talk on the history and mission of the Navy, assign your unit a company number, present a company flag (guidon) bearing that number, and introduce your company commanders (CCs). Two CCs are assigned to each company.

Company Commander

Each company, about eighty-four recruits, is taken through training by its CCs—outstanding leading petty officers who are intimately familiar with instructional techniques, principles of leadership, and administrative procedures. CCs instruct you in military and physical drills and show you how to keep yourself, your clothing, equipment, and barracks in smart, ship-

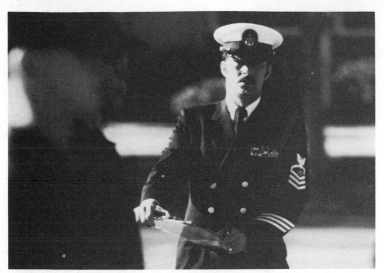

Figure 1–1   A company commander, the most important person in the Navy for the recruit, takes the new sailor through training.

shape condition. For your purposes in RTC, your CCs are the most important people in the Navy. Remember, your CCs also went through recruit training some years ago, and by now they have many years of naval experience. Follow their example and you'll make a good start towards a successful Navy career.

Your CCs are always available to answer questions and help you. They are the only people in the chain of command a recruit can talk to directly without first obtaining permission from someone else.

7

Chain of Command

The Navy is organized like a pyramid, with one person on top and many people (recruits) on the bottom. From highest to lowest, it runs like this:

President   Commander NTC
Vice president   Commanding officer RTC
Secretary of defense   Executive officer RTC
Secretary of the Navy   Military training officer
Chief of naval operations   Assistant military training
  (CNO)   officer

Chief of naval education and
   training (CNET)
Chief of naval technical
   training (CNTECHTRA)

Division officer
Division leading chief petty
   officer
Company commander
Recruits

You may start out at the bottom of the pyramid, but the
Navy will spend a lot of time and money making you into the
kind of sharp, well-trained sailor it needs.

Remember that everyone in the Navy began at the bottom,
and your seniors were once recruits like you. Everyone in the
Navy is junior to someone; but since about 85,000 men and
women enlist every year, there will already be at least a dozen
other people junior to you before you finish reading this.

Recruit Orientation

This is when you're taught the basics about the Navy. First
you have to become familiar with salutes, uniforms, customs
and ceremonies, Navy routine and time, and terminology. In
training, you'll spend many hours learning the details of these
subjects, but this is what you need to know to start.

Salutes: You must salute all officers when addressed by
them or when meeting them. While you're in recruit training,
you must also salute all senior petty officers wearing aiguillettes or ropes (see page 69).

Uniforms: The uniform worn by a Navy person shows at a
glance his or her rank or rate and thus his or her military
authority. You must quickly learn to identify the officers and
enlisted people you see most often during training. Each officer wears a gold cap device made up of a shield, an eagle, and
crossed anchors. The number of gold stripes on the sleeves or
shoulder boards shows the rank—three for commander, two
and a half for lieutenant commander, two for lieutenant, etc.
You should also be familiar with the various collar devices.
(See chapter 3, "Uniforms.")

Customs and Ceremonies: The ceremony of "colors"—the
raising or lowering of the United States flag—is performed
twice a day. "The Star-Spangled Banner" is played at morning
colors by the band, if there is one, and everyone within sight
stops, faces the colors, and salutes—from the first note of the
music or the bugle call "Attention," until the last note or the
call "Secure."

Figure 1–2 Recruits move "on the double" past the frigate mockup *Blue-jacket* during training at the Naval Training Center, Orlando, Florida.

The most impressive ceremony at RTC is graduation, when your company and others take part in a full parade, with band, color guard, and a special company carrying the flags of all fifty states. A senior officer reviews the companies, gives official recognition to outstanding recruits, and presents other awards.

Routine: The daily routine at the training center and else-where in the Navy appears in a bulletin called the plan of the day (POD). It issues the special orders for the day, gives the hours of meals, inspections, parades, and other events; names duty officers and duty petty officers; and, in the fleet, even lists the titles and times of movies. You must read the POD every day.

Time: The Navy runs on a 24-hour day. Aboard ship you will see a clock with a 24-hour dial. Hours of the day are numbered from 1 to 24; at noon, instead of starting again with 1, the Navy goes to 13. The hours, for example 8 A.M. or 7 P.M., are called 0800 (zero eight hundred) and 1900 (nineteen hundred) respectively. Never say "nineteen hundred hours." Hours and minutes in Navy time go like this: 10:45 A.M. is 1045 (ten forty-five), 9:30 P.M. is 2130 (twenty-one thirty).

Terminology: The Navy uses special terminology for many everyday objects and concepts. Beds are bunks, bathrooms are heads, floors are decks, walls are bulkheads, stairways are ladders, and drinking fountains are scuttlebutts. You go top-side for upstairs; below for downstairs. (See appendix K, "Glossary of Navy Terms.") The Navy also uses short abbre-viations in place of long titles, such as these:

AMTO	Assistant military training officer
CC	Company commander
DDPO	Division duty petty officer
DOT	Day of training
EPO	Educational petty officer
FFTU	Firefighting training unit
KOD	Knot of the day
MD	Military drill
MTDPO	Military training duty petty officer
MTO	Military training officer
PI	Personnel inspection
RAB	Recruit aptitude board
RCPO	Recruit chief petty officer
RIF	Recruit in-processing facility
ROD	Rate of the day
RPOD	Recruit plan of the day
STD	Special training division
TG	Training group
TOD	Term of the day
TTO	Technical training officer

Back to School

Recruit training will keep you busier than you've ever been, with a daily schedule of a dozen 40-minute instruction periods, five days a week, and a 10-minute break between the periods. The following, a typical daily schedule, will vary somewhat according to the day of training:

Daily Routine
0530	Reveille
0545	Breakfast (to 0730)
0630	Sick call
0700	Physical training
0755	First call
0800	Colors, sick call
0820	Commence instruction periods
1100	Noon meal (to 1330)
1215	Sick call
1650	Evening meal (to 1900)
	First call to colors 5 minutes prior to sunset
	Sunset—colors

Figure 1–3   Recruits attend one of many training classes during recruit
training at the Naval Training Center, San Diego.

1800	Free period, study time, instruction
2000	Field day
2100	Shower
2130	Taps, bed check

Saturday Routine

0530	Reveille
0545	Breakfast
0755	First call
0800	Colors, sick call
0830	Athletic events as scheduled
1100	Noon meal
1650	Supper
	First call to colors 5 minutes prior to sunset
	Sunset—colors
1800	Free period (to 2000)
2000	Field day (to 2100)
2100	Shower
2130	Taps, bed check

Figure 1-4 "A place for everything and everything in its place" makes sense when you're aboard ship, where space is at a premium, and ashore.

Instruction covers general areas: naval and military training, technical training, administrative training, and processing. Subjects include:

Advancement program	History of the Navy
Aircraft familiarization	Honors and ceremonies
Career incentives/medical benefits	Inspections bill
	Leave and earning statement/pay
CBR warfare/defense	Leave, liberty, and conduct ashore
Chain of command	
Classification	Marlinespike seamanship
Code of conduct/Geneva Convention	Military drill
	Mishap prevention
Deck equipment	Navy mission and organization
Damage control	Officer recognition
Education benefits	Ordnance and weapons
Enlisted service record	Paint and preservation
Financial responsibility	Personal hygiene
Firefighting	Physical conditioning
First aid	Rates and ratings
General orders	Security information
Hand salute and greetings	

Ship familiarization
Small boats
Survival at sea
Telephone talkers
3-M system

Uniform Code of Military
Justice
Watch, quarter, and station bill
Watchstanding

Intro-
duction
to the
Navy

ID Card: The Armed Forces of the United States Identification Card—ID card for short—identifies you as a member of the armed forces. It is not a pass; it remains government property while you have it and must be returned when you're discharged. Altering it, damaging it, counterfeiting it, or using it in an unauthorized manner, such as lending your card to someone or borrowing another person's card, can result in disciplinary action.

Active-duty personnel are issued green ID cards; inactive-duty personnel get a red card; retired personnel get a blue one. An active-duty card shows your name, social security number, photograph, and the date your enlistment expires. Carry your card at all times. It also serves as your Geneva Convention Card; if you are ever taken prisoner of war, your card will identify you as one protected by the provisions of the Geneva Convention.

Cards of those in paygrades E-1 to E-3 are marked "Nonpetty officer." Cards for E-4s to E-9s carry the identification PO3, PO2, PO1, CPO, SCPO, or MCPO, as appropriate. If you lose your card, you will have to sign a statement detailing the circumstances of the loss.

Special Requests: If your request is reasonable, it will probably be granted. Requests are normally made by means of a special request/authorization form (NAVPERS Form 1336/3, often called a request chit), which covers special liberty, special pay, commuted rations, and most other requests not specifically provided for otherwise.

Naval and Military Training

This involves a lot more than learning to march. Military drill will teach you the importance of instant response to orders and the absolute necessity for teamwork. You will see the significance of this later—on the flight deck of an aircraft carrier, in the control tower of a naval air station, or in the nerve center of a nuclear submarine. Few jobs in the Navy are completely independent; you must depend on your shipmates, and they on you.

Figure 1–5 Recruits receive instruction as they sit in the stands at the bow of the training ship *Recruit* (TDE 1) at the Naval Training Center, San Diego.

Training in this area includes instruction in folding and stowing clothing, barracks sanitation, watchstanding, and general orders. You'll also study the Navy's organizational structure, mission, and regulations. All hands in the Navy, no matter what their specialty, must have the same basic knowledge and must be able to perform the same military duties.

Technical Training

Technical training begins at the training center and continues throughout your tour in the Navy. At RTC you will have training sessions covering seamanship, basic swim and survival-at-sea techniques, firefighting, CBR (chemical, biological, and radiological) defense, weapons and ordnance, ships and aircraft, maintenance, and rating duties. You will also study general subjects such as uniforms, salutes, history, discipline and justice, and pay and allowances.

Administrative and Processing

These periods free you up to attend final classification interviews; arrange for pay, uniform fittings, and all medical and dental work; obtain ID cards; mark uniform equipment; and arrange to pick up records, orders, and transportation when you complete training.

Classification

This process helps the Navy select and train the right person for the right job. Classification identifies you in two ways, through your Armed Services Vocational Aptitude Battery (ASVAB) scores, and through Navy Enlisted Classification (NEC) codes. Classification tests measure your basic aptitudes and are designed to find out how much you can *learn* rather than how much you already *know*. The ASVAB testing and classification interviews have already been given to you at the Military Enlistment Processing Station (MEPS) in or near your home town. Besides these tests, a trained Navy classifier has already asked about your hobbies, interests, previous job experience, education, and what you think you would like to do in the Navy.

While in recruit training, you'll be given your final classification. NECs are assigned upon completion of schools or special training.

Schools

The chief objective of Navy enlisted training—which costs millions of dollars a year—is to develop recruits into petty officers who can handle the technical requirements of their ratings. Some men and women may put in two or three tours of sea duty and go through several schools to become tops in their ratings. Recruit training at the Class R school is the first step. Next comes either apprentice training or a Class A school; then assignment to the fleet. The Navy maintains about sixty Class A schools, which train more than 50,000 persons a year. About 60 percent of all recruits are selected for an A school, at Great Lakes, San Diego, or Orlando.

All training in the Navy comes under the control of the chief of naval education and training (CNET), whose headquarters are in Pensacola, Florida. CNET plans and directs training programs for several hundred activities, everything from basic recruit training to postgraduate instruction for officers. CNET also handles dependents' educational programs.

Apprenticeship Training

When your company completes basic military training, some members of the unit will go on to Class A schools, while others will enter apprenticeship programs. Those selected for the latter will receive intensive instruction as seamen, firemen, or airmen. Apprenticeship courses last four weeks.

Competition

The Navy is based on competition. Sailors compete with one another for advancement, and ships compete with each other in gunnery, engineering, and communications. In recruit training, your company will compete for awards in athletic skill, scholastic achievement, military drill, inspection, and overall excellence.

Flags awarded to winning training companies are carried in dress parades and reviews. The training company guidon, bearing the company number, may also carry athletic streamers for awards won in competition in swimming, tug-of-war, volleyball, and various track-and-field events. At the weekly graduation review, one person is selected from all graduating honor personnel and recruit chief petty officers (RCPOs) to receive an outstanding recruit award. Honor graduates also receive special recognition certificates.

16

Personal Affairs

When you report for training, your parents or next of kin will receive notice of your correct address. Your civilian clothing may be donated to charity or sent home at your expense. Because of the tight schedule and the great number of recruits in training, you cannot receive telephone calls; but on occasion, with permission from one of your CCs, you may make long-distance collect calls.

Visitors are not permitted during the first few weeks of training. Later, a visiting time will be scheduled; you may send this information to your family. You will also be given information to send home about graduation review.

Pay

All hands in the Navy are paid twice a month, usually by check. While at RTC you will be paid twice. On transfer from RTC, your pay will be updated, with deductions taken out for allotments and for your chit book and ditty bag.

Liberty and Leave

You may expect liberty at the end of recruit training. After completion of all entry training, including your apprenticeship

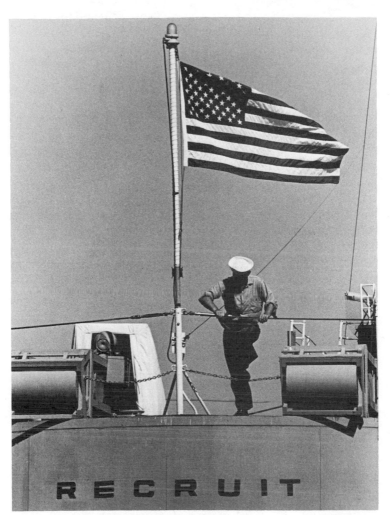

Figure 1–6 A Navy recruit relaxes on the stern of the training ship *Recruit* during a break in the training program at the Naval Training Center, San Diego.

program and A school, you will normally be allowed to take leave en route to your first duty station.

Religion

You will be given full opportunity to attend the church of your choice. All training centers have chapels in which Catholic, Jewish, and Protestant services are conducted by chaplains, who are also available for pastoral counseling and religious education. Recruit choirs are organized and trained to sing at the services.

Orders

Before you know it, recruit training will be over. And it won't be long before you are an apprentice instead of a recruit, with another stripe and higher pay. Some of your "shipmates," those who went through training with you, may go with you to your next assignment; some you will never see again; others you may meet years later.

Being handed a set of orders means going on to new experiences, meeting new people, and moving one step along in your Navy career. Better yet, orders mean a new start in a new job, perhaps even aboard a new ship. No matter how things went before, you have an opportunity to do better. There's even the possibility that, years later, with two or three hashmarks on your sleeve, you may be right back at RTC, training recruits.

Classification, Rates, and Ratings

2

The recruit-training curriculum is a concentrated course in basic naval skills and knowledge. In just a few weeks, this cram course starts everyone off on an equal footing. During basic training you will have a series of tests and interviews that will determine which way you go in the Navy.

Early in recruit training you will be scheduled for a classification interview. This kind of vocational counseling enables the Navy to train and select the right person for the right job. The classification process will identify you in two ways—by the results of the Armed Services Vocational Aptitude Battery (ASVAB) and by your Navy Enlisted Classification (NEC) code.

Navy Classification Tests

The ASVAB test you took before entering the Navy is used to measure your basic aptitudes. In other words, it finds out what you learned in school or civilian jobs, and how you compare with other recruits. It is mainly concerned with how much you can *learn,* rather than how much you *know.*

In addition to the ASVAB, two other tests are administered: the Nuclear Field Qualification Test (NFQT) and the Defense Language Aptitude Battery (DLAB). These tests are used to screen candidates for advanced specialized training. Your eligibility to take these tests is based on your ASVAB scores.

Test scores are important in your Navy career. They determine whether you go to a service school or to the fleet; and they help determine your eligibility for advanced training. Be sure you know your scores in the ASVAB. They show your strong and weak points, they will save you time and effort by eliminating ratings or duties that would be difficult for you, and they will give you a good idea of the ratings and duties for which you are best suited.

Ratings and Rates

A rating is a Navy job—a duty calling for certain skills and aptitudes. The rating of engineman, for example, calls for persons who are good with their hands and are mechanically inclined. A paygrade (such as E-4, E-5, E-6) within a rating is called a rate. Thus an engineman third class (EN3) would have a rating of engineman, and rate of third-class petty officer.

The term *petty officer* (PO) applies to anyone in paygrades E-4 through E-9. E-1s through E-3s are called nonrated personnel. Personnel in general apprenticeships are identified as recruit (E-1), apprentice (E-2), or at the E-3 level by the apprenticeship field, such as seaman, fireman, airman, constructionman, dentalman, or hospitalman. A person training for a specific job in paygrades E-1 through E-3 is called a *striker*—one who has been authorized to "strike" or train for a particular job.

Enlisted seniority is determined by time in rate and time in the Navy. If two POs are in the same paygrade, the one in that grade the longest is considered senior. In the case of two POs in the same paygrade with the same amount of time in grade and in the Navy, the one having the most time in the next lower paygrade is senior.

Ratings

These are divided into three categories: general, service, and emergency.

General ratings are broad occupational fields for paygrades E-4 through E-9. Each general rating has a distinctive badge. General ratings are sometimes combined at the E-8 or E-9 level, when the work is similar, to form even broader occupational fields. For example, senior chief instrumentman (IMCS) and senior chief opticalman (OMCS) can be combined to form the rating of master chief precision instrumentman (PICM). Some general ratings include service ratings; others do not.

Service ratings are subdivisions of a general rating that require specialized training. There are service ratings at any PO level; however, they are most common with E-4s and E-5s. In the higher paygrades, service ratings merge into a general rating, usually at the E-8 level. For example, a chief fire-control technician C (gunfire control) is an FTGC until the E-8 level and then becomes an FTCS. An FTCS must know both guns and missiles.

Emergency ratings are used to identify civilian occupational fields that are only used in time of war, for example, stevedore, transportationman, and welfare and recreation leader. There are no emergency ratings in use today.

Rates

A *rate* identifies the level of your rating. For example, the yeoman rating is broken down into rates E-1 through E-9. *General rates* (not to be confused with general ratings) are the general apprenticeships that identify enlisted personnel in grades E-1, E-2, and E-3. Within these apprenticeships, enlisted personnel receive their recruit training and initial technical training, as preparation for advancement to PO or a service rating. E-1 is generally where recruits start. E-2s (apprentices) perform the routine duties of their occupational groups, but they also perform duties with more responsibility. General rates are identified by various colored stripes.

Title	Color of Stripe
Seaman (SN)	White
Hospitalman (HN)	White
Dentalman (DN)	White
Fireman (FN)	Red
Constructionman (CN)	Blue
Airman (AN)	Green

Stripes are navy blue on a white uniform, except those for FN, CN, and AN, which are the same color as described above on all uniforms.

The following is a basic description of the duties of E-3s:

Seaman (SN): Keeps compartments, lines, rigging, decks, and deck machinery shipshape. Acts as a lookout, member of a gun crew, helmsman, and security and fire sentry.

Hospitalman (HN): Arranges dressing carriages with sterile instruments, dressings, bandages, and medicines. Applies dressings. Gives morning and evening care to patients. Keeps medical records.

Dentalman (DN): Assists dental officers in the treatment of patients. Renders first aid. Cleans and services dental equipment. Keeps dental records.

Fireman (FN): Cares for and operates boilers. Operates pumps, motors, and turbines. Records readings of gauges, and maintains and cleans engineering machinery and compartments. Stands security and fireroom watches.

Constructionman (CN): Operates, services, and checks construction equipment. Performs semiskilled duties in construction battalions. Stands guard watches.

Airman (AN): Performs various duties for naval air activities ashore and afloat. Assists in moving aircraft. Loads and stows equipment and supplies. Maintains compartments and buildings. Acts as member of plane-handling crews.

PO rating groups include paygrades E-4 through E-9, as follows: *E-4,* petty officer third class (PO3); *E-5,* petty officer second class (PO2); *E-6,* petty officer first class (PO1); *E-7,* chief petty officer (CPO); *E-8,* senior chief petty officer (SCPO); and *E-9,* master chief petty officer (MCPO).

Navy Enlisted Classification (NEC) Codes

While the ASVAB measures your basic aptitudes when you enter the Navy, NEC codes show the special knowledge and skills that you have *now.* The rating system is a means of classification; for instance, you probably have a pretty good idea what a quartermaster third class (QM3), a fireman (FN), or a chief yeoman (YNC) does. But there are certain things a rate doesn't show, and this is where NECs come in.

An NEC is a four-digit number or a two-letter classification. Every enlisted person has both a primary and a secondary NEC. Some sailors are identified only by a primary NEC and have an all-zero secondary NEC, such as a 3221/0000. The number 3221 refers to Navy broadcast journalist; the secondary code, 0000, indicates that the individual holds no other qualification beyond the primary code.

NECs help determine where you will work and what you will do. They are invaluable to detailers—the administrative people at the Naval Military Personnel Command (NMPC) in Washington, D.C.—who are responsible for filling the Navy's job requirements. The codes are of five types: entry series, rating series, special series, alphanumeric, and planning.

Entry Series

These NECs are assigned to personnel who are not yet designated as strikers but who have received training, are in train-

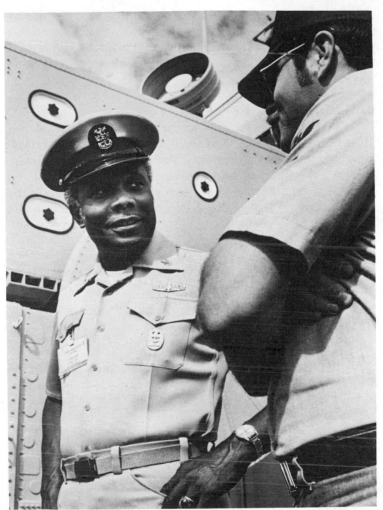

Figure 2–1 Enlisted seniority is determined by time in rate and time in the Navy.

ing, or have the aptitude to be trained for the appropriate rating. There are two types of entry-series NEC codes: defense grouping (DG) codes and rating conversion codes. All DG codes end in 0 and are assigned to personnel in paygrades E-1 through E-3, except for designated strikers and men and women in the ratings of hospital corpsman (HM) and dental technician (DT). The code DG-9700, for example, is assigned to sailors who will become either boatswain's mates (BMs) or quartermasters (QMs). Rating conversion codes, which end either in 99 or a letter plus 9, are assigned to persons in training for conversion to another rating. For example: a PN-2699 is a person converting to the personnelman (PN) rating; a YN-2599 is converting to the yeoman (YN) rating. Entry NECs are always primary codes.

Rating Series

These NECs supplement the general and service ratings. Most rating-series NECs are prefixed by two-letter abbreviations (but there are exceptions). Rating-series NECs may appear as either primary or secondary codes. For example, an HM1 (hospital corpsman first class) who has experience in the preparation and maintenance of eyeglasses would have an NEC of HM-8463, which identifies that person as an optician.

Special Series

These NECs identify secondary skills. They are not usually directly related to a particular rating. Examples of special-series NECs are drug-detector dog-handler, 9542; petroleum specialist, 9561; and locksmith, 9583.

Alphanumeric Series

These NECs identify equipment-specific skills and training levels when management requirements and the complexity of training call for such identification.

Planning NECs

These NECs identify skill requirements for planning purposes only. Planners and personnel managers use the classifications in developing training courses, projecting manpower needs for upcoming projects, and other similar purposes. Planning NECs are not assigned to personnel.

With a few exceptions, all NECs are assigned at NMPC. Changes in your NECs are made only when a training command reports that you have completed a course (earning you a specialty code), when a command shows that your specialty code should be canceled, or when a command reports that you have earned a code through on-the-job training (OJT).

Because NECs identify billets and the personnel qualified to fill them, make sure your NECs actually reflect your qualifications. Not keeping your codes up to date may keep you from getting the duty you want. You may have up to five NECs, although the two most important ones will appear as your primary and secondary codes. All of them are kept in your permanent record at NMPC and are available to the detailers there when you become eligible for reassignment.

Navy Enlisted Occupational Fields

There are twenty-four major occupational-career fields for enlisted personnel. By combining the foregoing information, the Navy can place each person into one of these fields, which are made up of seventy-four general ratings. The purpose of all this is to simplify the identification process, enabling the Navy to match the most qualified person to the job.

A complete analysis of each field may be found in section I of the Manual of Navy Enlisted Manpower and Personnel Classifications and Occupational Standards (NAVPERS 18068). Section II contains a listing of all NECs.

The ratings in which Navy men and women work are described on the following pages. You will notice that these jobs are not all mechanical or technical; in fact, many would be known in civilian life as white-collar jobs. The specialty mark of each rating is included with the rating description. Specialty marks, added to enlisted uniforms in 1866, represented the instrument originally used to perform a particular task. For example, the quartermaster (QM) mark is a ship's helm, while the gunner's mate (GM) mark is two crossed cannons. The custom of representing the type of work with a specialty mark for each rating continues, but many of the designs have been stylized. For instance, the journalist (JO) is represented by a crossed quill and scroll, the cryptologic technician (CT) by a crossed quill and spark.

Occupational Fields
1. General seamanship—BM, SM
2. Ship operations—OS, QM
3. Marine engineering—BT, EM, EN, GS, IC, MM
4. Ship maintenance—HT, IM, MR, ML, OM, PM, DC
5. Aviation maintenance/weapons—PR, AE, AT, AD, AV, AZ, AO, AM
6. Aviation ground support—AB, AS
7. Air traffic control—AC
8. Weapons control—ET, FC, FT
9. Ordnance systems—GM, MN, MT, TM, WT

10. Sensor operations—EW, OT, ST
11. Weapons system support—(none currently assigned)
12. Data systems—DP, DS
13. Construction—BU, CE, CM, EA, EO, SW, UT
14. Health care—DT, HM
15. Administration—LN, NC, PN, PC, YN, RP
16. Logistics—AK, DK, MS, SH, SK
17. Media—DM, JO, LI, PH
18. Musician—MU
19. Master-at-arms—MA
20. Cryptology—CT
21. Communications—RM
22. Intelligence—IS
23. Meteorology—AG
24. Aviation sensor operations—AW

Here's how the general rates of E-2 and E-3 fit into the occupational fields:

SA, SN—1, 2, 4, 8, 9, 10, 12, 15, 16, 17, 18, 20, 21, 22
FA, FN—3, 4
CA, CN—13
AA, AN—5, 6, 7, 16, 17, 23, 24
HA, HN—14
DA, DN—14

Members of the following ratings who are in advanced electronics require a six-year enlistment: AT, AV, CT, DS, ET, EW, FC, FT, OT, RM, and ST.

Members of the following ratings who are in an advanced technical field require a six-year enlistment: BT, GS, HM, HT, IC, and MM.

Enlisted Ratings*†

AB

Cross anchors,
winged

Aviation Boatswain's Mate: ABs operate, maintain, and repair aircraft catapults, arresting gear, and barricades. They operate and maintain fuel- and lube-oil transfer systems. ABs direct aircraft on the flight deck and in hangar bays before launch and after

* The ratings so marked are not available to the incoming recruit.
† The ratings so marked are not available to women.

recovery. They use tow tractors to position planes and operate support equipment used to start aircraft.

AC

Microphone, winged

Air Traffic Controller: ACs assist in the essential safe, orderly, and speedy flow of air traffic by directing and controlling aircraft. They operate field lighting systems, communicate with aircraft, furnish pilots with information regarding traffic, navigation, and weather conditions. They operate and adjust GCA (ground-controlled approach) systems. They interpret targets on radar screens and plot aircraft positions. This is a five-year enlistment.

AD

Two-bladed propeller, winged

Aviation Machinist's Mate: ADs usually maintain jet aircraft engines and associated equipment, or engage in any one of several types of aircraft maintenance activities. ADs maintain, service, adjust, and replace aircraft engines and accessories, as well as perform the duties of flight engineers.

27

AE

Globe, winged

Aviation Electrician's Mate: AEs maintain, adjust, and repair electrical-power generating and converting systems in aircraft, lighting, and control and indicating systems. They also install and maintain wiring and flight and engine instrument systems.

AG

Circle on vertical arrow, winged

Aerographer's Mate: The Navy has its own weather forecasters, AGs, who are trained in meteorology and the use of aerological instruments that monitor such weather characteristics as air pressure, temperature, humidity, wind speed, and wind direction. They prepare weather maps and forecasts, analyze atmospheric conditions to determine the best flight levels for aircraft, and measure wind and air density to increase the accuracy of antiaircraft firing, shore bombardment, and delivery of weapons by aircraft.

AK

Crossed keys,
winged

Aviation Storekeeper: AKs ensure that the materials and equipment needed by naval aviation activities are available and in good order. They take inventory, estimate future needs, and make purchases. AKs store and issue flight clothing, aeronautical materials and spare parts, ordnance, and electronic, structural, and engineering equipment.

AM

Crossed mauls,
winged

Aviation Structural Mechanic: The maintenance and repair of aircraft parts (wings, fuselage, tail, control surfaces, landing gear, and attending mechanisms) are performed by AMs working with metals, alloys, and plastics. AMs maintain and repair safety equipment and hydraulic systems.

AO

Flaming spherical
shell, winged

Aviation Ordnanceman: Navy planes carry guns, bombs, torpedoes, rockets, and missiles to attack the enemy on the sea, under the sea, in the air, and on land. AOs are responsible for maintaining, repairing, installing, operating, and handling aviation ordnance equipment; their duties also include the handling, stowing, issuing, and loading of munitions and small arms.

AS

Crossed maul and
spark, winged

Aviation Support Equipment Technician: ASs perform intermediate maintenance on "yellow" (aviation accessory) equipment at naval air stations and aboard carriers. They maintain gasoline and diesel engines, hydraulic and pneumatic systems, liquid and gaseous oxygen and nitrogen systems, gas-turbine compressor units, and electrical systems.

AT

Helium atom,
winged

Aviation Electronics Technician: ATs perform intermediate-level preventive and corrective maintenance on aviation electronic components supported by conventional and automatic test equipment. They repair weapons-replaceable assemblies (WRAs), shop replaceable assemblies (SRAs), and microminiature (2M) components, and perform test-equipment qualification and associated test-bench preventive and corrective maintenance.

AV

Range finder, winged

Aviation Maintenance Technician: AVs perform organizational-level preventive and corrective maintenance on aviation electronics systems, including equipment used in communications, radar, navigation, antisubmarine warfare, electronic warfare data, fire control, and tactical display.

AW

Spark-pierced electron orbits over wave, winged

Aviation Antisubmarine Warfare Operator: AWs operate airborne radar and electronic equipment used in detecting, locating, and tracking submarines. AWs also operate radars to provide information for aircraft and surface navigation. They perform helicopter-rescue duties and serve as part of the flight crew on long-range and intermediate-range aircraft. This is a five-year enlistment.

AZ

Two-bladed propeller on open book, winged

Aviation Maintenance Administrationman: The many clerical, administrative, and managerial duties necessary to keep aircraft-maintenance activities running smoothly are handled by AZs. They plan, schedule, and coordinate the maintenance workload, including inspections and modifications to aircraft and equipment.

29

BM

Crossed anchors

Boatswain's Mate: BMs are expert seamen who maintain the ship, serve as steersmen, take command of tugs and other small craft, serve as gun captains, look after rigging, paint, handle and care for deck equipment, and serve on working parties and damage-control teams. BMs in upper grades train and supervise others in caring for and handling deck equipment and small boats. There are no Navy technical schools for this rating.

BT

Hero's boiler

Boiler Technician: Because the propelling agent of our large naval ships is steam, the Navy relies on BTs to keep its ships moving. BTs operate and repair marine boilers and fireroom machinery, and they transfer, test, and inventory fuels and water.

BU

Carpenter's square
on plumb bob

Builder: Navy BUs are like civilian construction workers. They may be skilled carpenters, plasterers, roofers, cement finishers, asphalt workers, masons, painters, bricklayers, sawmill operators, or cabinetmakers. BUs build and repair all types of structures, including piers, bridges, towers, underwater installations, schools, offices, houses, and other buildings. This is a five-year enlistment.

CE

Spark on telephone
pole

Construction Electrician: CEs are responsible for the power production and electrical work required to build and operate airfields, roads, barracks, hospitals, shops, and warehouses. The work of Navy CEs is like that of civilian construction electricians, powerhouse electricians, telephone and electrical repairmen, substation operators, linemen, and others. This is a five-year enlistment.

CM

Double-headed
wrench on nut

Construction Mechanic: CMs maintain heavy construction and automotive equipment (buses, dump trucks, bulldozers, rollers, cranes, backhoes, and pile drivers) as well as other construction equipment. They service vehicles and work on gasoline and diesel engines, ignition and fuel systems, transmissions, electrical systems, and hydraulic, pneumatic, and steering systems. This is a five-year enlistment.

CT

Crossed quill and
spark

Cryptologic Technician: CTs control the flow of messages and information. Their work depends on their special career area: *administration* (CTA), administrative and clerical duties that control access to classified material; *interpretive* (CTI), radiotelephone communications and foreign-language translation; *maintenance* (CTM), the installation, servicing, and repair of electronic and electromechanical equipment; *collection* (CTR), Morse code communications and operation of radio direction-finding equipment; and *technical* (CTT), communications by means other than Morse code and electronic countermeasures.

DC

Crossed fire axe and maul

DK

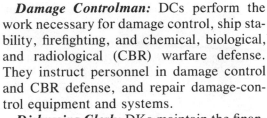

Key on check

DM

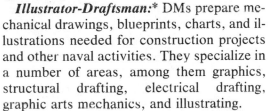

Draftsman's compass on triangle

DP

Quill on gear

DS

Helium atom with input/output arrows

Damage Controlman: DCs perform the work necessary for damage control, ship stability, firefighting, and chemical, biological, and radiological (CBR) warfare defense. They instruct personnel in damage control and CBR defense, and repair damage-control equipment and systems.

Disbursing Clerk: DKs maintain the financial records of Navy personnel. They prepare payrolls, determine transportation entitlements, compute travel allowances, and process claims for reimbursement of travel expenses. DKs also process vouchers for receiving and spending public money and make sure accounting data are accurate. They maintain fiscal records and prepare financial reports and returns.

Illustrator-Draftsman:* DMs prepare mechanical drawings, blueprints, charts, and illustrations needed for construction projects and other naval activities. They specialize in a number of areas, among them graphics, structural drafting, electrical drafting, graphic arts mechanics, and illustrating.

Data-Processing Technician: The Navy needs an extensive accounting system to maintain personnel records, to keep tabs on the receipt and transfer of supplies and the disbursement of money, and to inventory Navy equipment. DPs operate and maintain transceivers, sorters, collators, reproducers, interpreters, alphabetic accounting machines, and digital electronic data-processing (EDP) machines for these purposes. This is a five-year enlistment.

Data-Systems Technician: DSs are electronics technicians who specialize in computer systems, including digital computers, video processors, tape units, buffers, key sets, digital-display equipment, data-link terminal sets, and related equipment. They clean, maintain, lubricate, calibrate, and adjust equipment. They run operational tests, diagnose problems, make routine repairs,

31

DT

"D" on caduceus

EA

Measuring scale
fronting level rod

EM

Globe with
longitude, latitude
lines

EN

Gear

EO

Bulldozer

and evaluate newly installed parts and systems units.

Dental Technician: Navy dentists, like many civilian ones, are assisted by dental technicians. DTs have a variety of "chairside," laboratory, and administrative duties. Some are qualified in dental prosthetics (making and fitting artificial teeth), dental X-ray techniques, clinical laboratory procedures, pharmacy and chemistry, or maintenance and repair of dental equipment. This is a five-year enlistment.

Engineering Aide: EAs provide construction engineers with the information needed to develop final construction plans. EAs conduct surveys for roads, airfields, buildings, waterfront structures, pipelines, ditches, and drainage systems. They perform soil tests, prepare topographic and hydrographic maps, and survey for sewers, water lines, drainage systems, and underwater excavations. This is a five-year enlistment.

Electrician's Mate: The operation and repair of a ship's or station's electrical power plant and electrical equipment is the responsibility of EMs. They also maintain and repair power and lighting circuits, distribution switchboards, generators, motors, and other electrical equipment.

Engineman: Internal-combustion engines, either diesel or gasoline, must be kept in good order; this is the responsibility of ENs. They are also responsible for the maintenance of refrigeration, air-conditioning, and distilling-plant engines and compressors.

Equipment Operator: EOs work with heavy machinery such as bulldozers, power shovels, pile drivers, rollers and graders, etc. EOs use this machinery to dig ditches and excavate for building foundations, to break up old concrete or asphalt paving and pour new paving, to loosen soil and grade it, to dig out treetrunks and rocks, to remove debris from construction sites, to raise girders, and to move and set in place other pieces of equipment or materials needed for a job. This is a five-year enlistment.

ET

Helium atom

Electronics Technician: ETs are responsible for electronic equipment used to send and receive messages, detect enemy planes and ships, and determine target distance. They must maintain, repair, calibrate, tune, and adjust all electronic equipment used for communications, detection and tracking, recognition and identification, navigation, and electronic countermeasures.

EW

Spark through helium atom

Electronics Warfare Technician: EWs operate and maintain electronic equipment used in navigation, target detection and location, and the prevention of electronic spying by enemies. They interpret incoming electronic signals to determine their source. EWs are advanced electronic technicians who do wiring and circuit testing and repair. They determine performance levels of electronic equipment, install new components, modify existing equipment, and test, adjust, and repair cooling systems.

FC

Range finder with inward spark on each side

Fire Controlman:† FCs maintain the control mechanism used in weapons systems on combat ships. Complex electronic, electrical, and hydraulic equipment is required to ensure the accuracy of guided-missile and surface gunfire-control systems. FCs are responsible for the operation, routine care, and repair of this equipment, which includes radars, computers, weapons-direction equipment, target-designation systems, gyroscopes, and rangefinders. FCs are in the advanced electronics field, which requires a six-year enlistment.

FT

Range finder

Fire Control Technician:† FTs maintain advanced electronic equipment used in submarine weapons systems. Complex electronic, electrical, and mechanical equipment is required to ensure the accuracy of guided-

33

missile systems and underwater weapons. FTs are responsible for the operation, routine care, and repair of this equipment. They are in the advanced electronics field, which requires a six-year enlistment.

GM

Crossed cannons

Gunner's Mate: Navy GMs operate, maintain, and repair all gunnery equipment, guided-missile launching systems, rocket launchers, guns, gun mounts, turrets, projectors, and associated equipment. They also make detailed casualty analyses and repairs of electrical, electronic, hydraulic, and mechanical systems. They test and inspect ammunition and missiles and their ordnance components, and train and supervise personnel in the handling and stowage of ammunition, missiles, and assigned ordnance equipment.

34

GS

Turbine with ducting

Gas Turbine System Technician: GSs operate, repair, and maintain gas-turbine engines, main propulsion machinery (including gears, shafting, and controllable-pitch propellers), assigned auxiliary equipment, propulsion-control systems, electrical and electronic circuitry up to printed circuit modules, and alarm and warning circuitry. They perform administrative tasks related to gas-turbine propulsion-system operation and maintenance.

HM

Caduceus

Hospital Corpsman: HMs assist medical professionals in providing health care to service people and their families. They act as pharmacists, medical technicians, food-service personnel, nurses' aids, physicians' or dentists' assistants, battlefield medics, X-ray technicians, and more. Their work falls into several categories: first aid and minor surgery, patient transportation, patient care, prescriptions and laboratory work, food-service inspections, and clerical duties.

HT

Crossed fire ax and
maul with
carpenter's square

IC

French phone over
globe

IM

Calipers

IS

Magnifying glass and
quill

JO

Crossed quill and
scroll

Hull Maintenance Technician: HTs are responsible for maintaining ships' hulls, fittings, piping systems, and machinery. They install and maintain shipboard and shore-based plumbing and piping systems. They also look after a vessel's safety and survival equipment and perform many tasks related to damage control.

Interior Communications Electrician: ICs operate and repair electronic devices used in a ship's interior communications systems— SITE TV systems, public-address systems, electronic megaphones, and other announcing equipment—as well as gyrocompass systems

Instrumentman: The Navy uses many meters, gauges, watches and clocks, typewriters, adding machines, and other office machines. Repairing, adjusting, and reconditioning them is the IM's job. An IM also repairs mechanical parts of electronic instruments, and is often called upon to manufacture parts such as bushings, stems, jewel settings, mainsprings, and spring hooks.

Intelligence Specialist: Military information, especially secret information about enemies or potential enemies, is called intelligence. The IS is one of the people involved in collecting and interpreting intelligence data. An IS analyzes photographs and prepares charts, maps, and reports that describe in detail the strategic situation all over the world.

Journalist: JOs are the Navy's information specialists. They write press releases, news stories, features, and articles for Navy newspapers, bulletins, and magazines. They perform a variety of public relations jobs. Some write scripts and announcements for radio and TV; others are photographers or radio and television broadcasters and producers. The photo work of JOs ranges from

35

LI

Crossed lith crayon
holder and scraper

LN

Vertical millrind
crossing quill

36

MA

Star embossed in
circle within shield

ML

Crossed bench
rammer and stove
tool

administrative and clerical tasks to film processing. This is a five-year enlistment.

*Lithographer:** LIs run Navy print shops and are responsible for producing printed material used in naval activities. LIs print service magazines, newspapers and bulletins, training materials, official policy manuals, etc. They operate printing presses, do layout and design, and collate and bind printed pages. The usual specialties are cameraman, pressman, and binderyman.

*Legalman:** Navy LNs are aides trained in the field of law. They work in Navy legal offices performing administrative and clerical tasks necessary to process claims, to conduct court and administrative hearings, and to maintain records, documents, and legal-reference libraries. They give advice on tax returns, voter-registration regulations, procedures, and immigration and customs regulations governing Social Security and veterans' benefits, and perform many duties related to courts-martial and nonjudicial hearings.

*Master-at-Arms:** Members of this rating help keep law and order aboard ship and at shore stations. They report to the executive officer, help maintain discipline, and assist in security matters. They enforce regulations, conduct investigations, take part in correctional and rehabilitative programs, and organize and train sailors assigned to police duty. In civilian life, they would be detectives and policemen.

Molder: MLs make molds, cores, and rig flasks. They make castings of ferrous and nonferrous metals, alloys, and plastics for the repair of ships, guns, and other machined equipment. MLs identify metals and alloys, heat-treat them, and test them for hardness. They operate furnaces used to melt metals for castings, and they use a variety of special hand and power tools.

MM

Three-bladed propeller

MN

Floating mine

MR

Micrometer and gear

MS

Crossed keys with quill on open ledger

MT

Guided missile and electronic wave

Machinist's Mate: Continuous operation of the many engines, compressors and gears, refrigeration, air-conditioning, gas-operated equipment, and other types of machinery afloat and ashore is the job of the MM. In particular, MMs are responsible for a ship's steam propulsion and auxiliary equipment and the outside (deck) machinery. MMs may also perform duties in the manufacture, storage, and transfer of some industrial gases.

Mineman: MNs test, maintain, repair, and overhaul mines and their components. They are responsible for assembling, handling, issuing, and delivering mines to the planting agent and for maintaining mine-handling and minelaying equipment.

Machinery Repairman: MRs are skilled machine-tool operators. They make replacement parts and repair or overhaul a ship engine's auxiliary equipment, such as evaporators, air compressors, and pumps. They repair deck equipment, including winches and hoists, condensers, and heat-exchange devices. Shipboard MRs frequently operate main propulsion machinery in addition to performing machine-shop and repair duties.

Mess Management Specialist: MSs operate and manage Navy dining facilities and bachelor enlisted quarters. They are cooks and bakers in Navy dining facilities ashore and afloat, ordering, inspecting, and stowing food. They maintain food-service and -preparation spaces and equipment, and keep records of transactions and budgets for the food service in living quarters ashore.

Missile Technician:*† MTs assemble, maintain, and repair missiles carried by submarines. They maintain the specialized equipment used in missile handling. Although missile components and related testing and handling equipment are primarily electrical and electronic, MTs must also work with mechanical, hydraulic, and pneumatic units in launcher, fire-control, and missile flight-control systems.

Musician: MUs play in official Navy bands and in special groups such as jazz bands, dance bands, and small ensembles. They give concerts and provide music for military ceremonies, religious services, parades, receptions, and dances. Official unit bands usually do not include stringed instruments, but each MU must be able to play at least one brass, woodwind, or percussion instrument. Persons are selected for this rating through auditions.

MU

Lyre

Navy Counselor:* NCs offer vocational guidance on an individual and group basis to Navy personnel aboard ships and at shore facilities, and to civilian personnel considering enlistment in the Navy. They assess the interests, aptitudes, abilities, and personalities of individuals.

NC

Anchor crossed with quill

Opticalman: OMs perform organizational- and intermediate-level maintenance on small navigational instruments, binoculars, night-vision sights, rangefinders, turret and submarine periscopes, and other optical instruments. OMs must be highly mechanical, with the ability to perform close, exact, and painstaking work.

38

OM

Lens crossed by lines of light

Operations Specialist: OSs operate radar, navigation, and communications equipment in a ship's combat-information center or on the bridge. They detect and track ships, planes, and missiles. They operate and maintain IFF (identification friend or foe) systems, ECM (electronic countermeasures) equipment, and radiotelephones. OSs also work with search-and-rescue teams.

OS

Arrow through oscilloscope

Ocean Systems Technician: OTs operate special electronic equipment used to interpret and document oceanographic data, such as the depth and composition of the ocean floor and how sound travels through water. They operate tape recorders and related

OT

Neptune's trident crossed by waves

equipment, prepare reports and visual displays, and convert analyzed data for use in statistical studies.

PC

Postal cancellation mark

Postal Clerk: The Navy operates a large postal system manned by Navy PCs, who have much the same duties as their civilian counterparts. PCs collect postage-due mail, prepare customs declarations, collect outgoing mail, cancel stamps, and send the mail on its way. They also perform a variety of record-keeping and reporting duties, including maintenance of an up-to-date directory service and locator file.

PH

Lens pierced by light lines

Photographer's Mate: PHs photograph actual and simulated battle operations as well as documentary and newsworthy events. They expose and process light-sensitive negatives and positives; maintain cameras, related equipment, photo files, and records; and perform other photographic services for the Navy. This is a five-year enlistment.

PM

Wooden jack plane

Patternmaker: In a Navy foundry, PMs are the important link between the draftsmen (DMs), who make the drawings, and the molders (MLs) who produce the castings. PMs make patterns in wood, plaster, or metal from which castings are made. PMs use drafting, carpentry, metalworking skills, and shop mathematics to create their patterns.

PN

Crossed manual and quill

Personnelman: PNs provide enlisted personnel with information and counseling about Navy jobs, opportunities for general education and training, promotion requirements, and rights and benefits. In hardship situations, they also assist enlisted persons' families with legal aid or reassignments. PNs keep records up to date, prepare reports, type letters, and maintain files.

PR

Parachute, winged

QM

Ship's helm

RM

Four sparks

RP

Globe on anchor
within circle

Aircrew Survival Equipmentman: Parachutes are the lifesaving equipment of aircrewmen when they have to bail out. In time of disaster, a parachute may also be the only means of delivering badly needed medicines, goods, and other supplies to isolated victims. PRs pack and care for parachutes as well as service, maintain, and repair flight clothing, rubber life rafts, life jackets, oxygen-breathing equipment, protective clothing, and air-sea rescue equipment.

Quartermaster: QMs are responsible for ship safety, skillful navigation, and reliable communications with other vessels and shore stations. In addition, they maintain charts, navigational aids, and records for the ship's log. They steer the ship, take radar bearings and ranges, make depth soundings and celestial observations, plot courses, and command small craft. QMs stand watches and assist the navigator and officer of the deck (OOD).

Radioman: Naval activities often involve people working at many different locations on land and at sea, and RMs operate the radio communications systems that make such complex teamwork possible. RMs operate radiotelephones and radioteletypes, prepare messages for international and domestic commercial telegraph, and send and receive messages via the Navy system.

Religious Program Specialist: RPs assist Navy chaplains with administrative and budgetary tasks. They serve as custodians of chapel funds, keep religious documents, and maintain contact with religious and community agencies. They also prepare devotional and religious educational materials, set up volunteer programs, operate shipboard libraries, supervise chaplains' offices, and perform administrative, clerical, and secretarial duties. They train personnel in religious programs and publicize religious activities.

SH

Crossed key and
quill

Ship's Serviceman: Both ashore and afloat, SHs manage barbershops, tailor shops, ships' uniform stores, laundries, dry-cleaning plants, and cobbler shops. They serve as clerks in exchanges, soda fountains, gas stations, warehouses, and commissary stores. Some SHs function as Navy club managers.

SK

Crossed keys

Storekeeper: SKs are the Navy's supply clerks. They see that needed supplies are available, everything from clothing and machine parts to forms and food. SKs have duties as civilian warehousemen, purchasing agents, stock clerks and supervisors, retail sales clerks, store managers, inventory clerks, buyers, parts clerks, bookkeepers, and even fork-lift operators.

SM

Crossed semaphore
flags

Signalman: SMs serve as lookouts and, using visual signals and voice radios, alert their ship of possible dangers. They send and receive messages by flag signals or flashing lights. They stand watches on the signal bridge, encode and decode messages, honor passing vessels, and maintain signaling equipment. SMs must have good vision and hearing.

ST

Earphones pierced
by arrow

Sonar Technician: STs are responsible for underwater surveillance as well as assistance in safe navigation and search, rescue, and attack operations. They operate and repair sonar equipment and jam enemy sonars. They track underwater objects and repair ASW fire-control equipment and underwater radiotelephones.

SW

I-beam suspended
from hook

Steelworker: SWs rig and operate all special equipment used to move or hoist structural steel, structural shapes, and similar material. They erect or dismantle steel bridges, piers, buildings, tanks, towers, and other structures. They place, fit, weld, cut, bolt, and rivet steel shapes, plates, and built-up sections used in the construction of overseas facilities. This is a five-year enlistment.

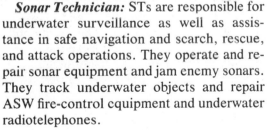

TM

Torpedo

UT

Valve

WT

Spark, Exploding
Shell, and Trident

YN

Crossed quills

Torpedoman's Mate: TMs maintain underwater explosive missiles, such as torpedoes and rockets, that are launched from surface ships, submarines, and aircraft. TMs also maintain launching systems for underwater explosives. They are responsible for the shipping and storage of all torpedoes and rockets.

Utilitiesman: UTs plan, supervise, and perform tasks involved in the installation, operation, maintenance, and repair of plumbing, heating, steam, compressed-air systems, fuel storage and distribution systems, water treatment and distribution systems, air-conditioning and refrigeration equipment, and sewage-collecting and disposal facilities.

Weapons Technician: WTs maintain, store, inspect, test, adjust, repair, and package nuclear-weapon components and associated equipment for surface ships. They also assemble and disassemble nuclear weapons, warheads, and/or components.

Yeoman: YNs perform secretarial and clerical work. They greet visitors, answer telephone calls, and receive incoming mail. YNs organize files and operate duplicating equipment, and they order and distribute supplies. They write and type business and social letters, notices, directives, forms, and reports. They maintain files and service records.

Enlisted Service Record

Your service record contains all the papers and records concerning your Navy career. It is the Navy's official file on you.

Actually, you have two service records, one in the personnel office of your ship or station, which goes with you when you are transferred, and another in the Naval Military Personnel Command (NMPC). At the end of your naval service, the two records are combined and sent to a records-storage center.

Check your record at least once a year to make sure that it is correct and up to date.

When looking it over, remember that it is government property. Do not take anything out, put anything in, or make any changes. If you have comments or questions, the YN or PN on duty will help you.

A look at your service record can be arranged through your division officer or division chief. Some ships and stations have regular hours for sailors to check their service records.

Your record is important during your Navy career and after. When you leave the Navy, you may need information from your record for collecting veterans' benefits, for federal or civilian employment, or for school credits.

Your service record contains copies of such vital documents as birth certificate, school certificates, letters of commendation, etc. But its main contents are the NAVPERS forms that make up the right side of your record and are filed, beginning with the first page listed, from bottom to top. In the early days, you'll have less than half of these pages; more are added as needed.

Enlistment Contract: This is the contract you signed when you joined the Navy.

Agreement to Extend Enlistment: Assignment to and Extension of Active Duty.

Dependency Application/Record of Emergency Data: This page is probably the most important part of your record and should be constantly updated. It contains names and addresses of persons to be notified in case of emergency or death, persons to receive the death gratuity if you have no spouse or child, persons to receive earned pay and allowances, dependents to receive allotment of pay if you're missing or unable to transmit funds, commercial insurance companies to be notified in case of death, and information about government life insurance.

You should make out a new form in the event of any of the following: change of permanent address of those to be notified in case of emergency, change in the names of those to be notified, and any major change in status, such as marriage, an additional child, or divorce.

Enlisted Classification Record: This contains information about aptitude test scores, civilian education and training, personal interests, civilian experience, and recommendations and remarks from your initial classification interview.

Navy Occupation/Training and Awards History: This page provides a complete chronological record of your classification codes and designations, service schools attended, personnel advancement requirements (PARs), performance test scores, personnel qualification standards (PQS), advancement exam results, reductions, changes in rate and rating, and decorations.

History of Assignments: This is a record of your duty assignments, ashore and at sea. It also reflects your record of enlistments, extensions of enlistments, discharges, etc., and the amount of any reenlistment bonuses you've been paid.

Record of Unauthorized Absence: This is used to record unauthorized absences of more than twenty-four hours and lost time due to confinement by civil authorities.

Court Memorandum: This is a record of court-martial action when a guilty finding is made by the court and approved by the convening authority (CA). It's also used to report nonjudicial punishment (NJP) that affects pay.

Enlisted Performance Record: This page records your performance of duty chronologically. Far more than any other part of your service record, it shows how you are doing in the Navy and how those you serve under judge your performance—the petty officer who acts as your immediate supervisor, the division chief petty officer, the division officer, the executive officer, and the commanding officer.

Your evaluations—also called marks—are used in determining performance factors (multiples) for advancement in rate, for selection to training that can lead to a commission, for selection to special programs and advanced schooling, for the awarding of the Good Conduct Medal, for your type of discharge (honorable or otherwise), and to decide whether you'll be recommended for reenlistment.

In general, there are four types of marks: a required evaluation, assigned annually; an entry for transfer or permanent change of station (PCS) orders; an entry when performance indicates special cognizance should be taken of particularly meritorious or poor performance; or a memorandum entry noting, for example, a meritorious mast, a recommendation for advancement, or a special performance of duty. The evaluation form is also used to report changes in ratings (in the same grade only) and for advancement or reduction in rate.

Regularly scheduled marks are completed on the following schedule: E-1 through E-3, 31 January; E-4, 30 June; E-5, 31

March; E-6, 30 November; E-7 and E-8, 30 September; and
E-9, 30 April.

Record of Personnel Actions: This is a record of changes in proficiency pay or citizenship and of other administrative information.

Record of Naval Reserve Service: This page is used to record reservist retirement points.

Transfers and Receipts: This gives details about your transfers from past duty stations and your reporting aboard new duty stations.

Administrative Remarks: This is a place for significant entries not provided for elsewhere; it is also used when more detailed information may be required to clarify entries on other pages.

Record of Discharge, Release from Active Duty, or Death: This is prepared when active duty is terminated because of discharge, release, change of status, or death.

Uniforms

3

Your Navy uniform marks you as a professional, a member of a military service over two hundred years old, and a person currently in the service of your country. Over the decades there have been many uniform changes; the oldest part of the enlisted person's uniform is the petty officer (PO) rating badge, which has been used since 1886. A major uniform change came in 1973, when enlisted men began wearing chief petty officer (CPO)-type double-breasted coats, shirts, ties, and caps.

However, this decision was changed in 1977 after an overwhelming majority of enlisted sailors expressed the desire to return to the traditional bell-bottom jumper. The first phase of the return to the bells began on 1 January 1978, when a yearlong test by 20,000 fleet unit personnel was begun. The traditional uniforms are now prescribed for all E-1 through E-6 men. The white hat, known affectionately as the dixie cup, is part of the uniform and authorized for wear by all male E-1 through E-6s with all uniforms.

There has been considerable modernization of Navy uniforms for both men and women recently. Some changes are effective immediately; others will be phased in over a period of months. Consult U.S. Navy Uniform Regulations (NAVPERS 15665) for up-to-date information on uniforms and how to wear them.

The uniform is the first big change in your appearance after you join the Navy. A man may still wear sideburns and a woman may still wear eye shadow, but once you're in Navy blue you represent the United States government; and when overseas, you're an unofficial American ambassador. Not only must you wear the uniforms correctly, you must also set a good example by your conduct.

The matter of ranks, rates, and insignia will seem confusing at first, but once you learn the system you'll find it fairly simple. Become familiar with all officers' ranks, line and corps

Figure 3–1   Enlisted sailors wear, *clockwise from left,* service dress blue jumper, service dress white jumper, lightweight blue coverall, and dungaree uniforms.

Figure 3–2 Chief petty officers model, *from left,* summer khaki, full-dress white, winter blue with skirt, and service dress blue uniforms.

Figure 3–3 Officers wear, *from left,* service dress blue, maternity winter blue with skirt and slacks, and summer white with skirt

Figure 3–4 Female uniforms are, *from left,* service dress white, summer white, winter working blue with slacks, and dinner dress blue.

insignia, as well as special identification marks. Also learn all enlisted rates, rating badges, and special-qualification devices.

There are many special uniforms worn by submariners, aviators, sailors on cold-weather operations, and others. There also are various uniforms for women, including a variety of maternity outfits.

Identification

The first thing to look for in identifying a person in the Navy is the hat—usually called the cover—which differs for flag officers, commissioned officers, warrant officers, CPOs, and enlisted personnel. They also differ for men and women. For officers, sleeve markings, shoulder boards, and collar insignia show rank, corps, and specialty. For enlisted personnel, rating badges show both rate and rating. Various breast insignia and ribbons indicate the special qualifications, awards, and service of officers and enlisted personnel.

Headgear

Male officers, warrant officers, and CPOs wear hats with bills on them. The white hat is worn by all E-1 through E-6 men with the jumper-style uniform, dungarees, and the summer white, winter blue, and winter working blue uniforms. Women, both officers and enlisted, wear hats with the sides turned up. At sea, and when specified ashore, all hands may wear command baseball-type working caps. Other types of headgear are authorized for optional wear: the garrison cap for women, male officers, and CPOs. However, the prescribing authority must authorize the wear of all optional items.

Cap or hat devices for commissioned officers consist of a shield, an eagle, and crossed anchors. CPOs wear one anchor mounted vertically, with the letters USN. The device for senior CPOs has one star above the anchor. There are two stars for master chief petty officers (MCPOs), and three stars for the master chief petty officer of the Navy (MCPON). The cap or hat device worn on enlisted women's berets is a silver eagle with wings spread and the letters USN mounted above the wings.

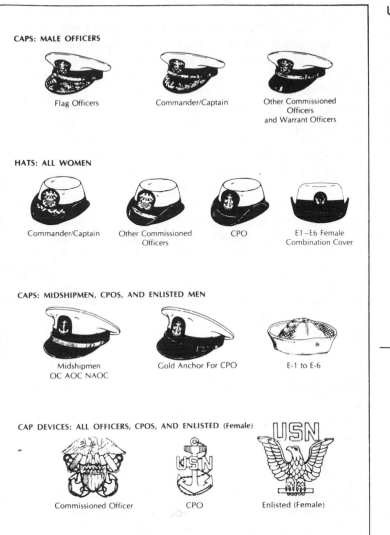

CAPS: MALE OFFICERS

Flag Officers   Commander/Captain   Other Commissioned
                                          Officers
                                          and Warrant Officers

HATS: ALL WOMEN

Commander/Captain   Other Commissioned   CPO   E1–E6 Female
                     Officers   Combination Cover

CAPS: MIDSHIPMEN, CPOS, AND ENLISTED MEN

Midshipmen   Gold Anchor For CPO   E-1 to E-6
OC AOC NAOC

CAP DEVICES: ALL OFFICERS, CPOS, AND ENLISTED (Female)

Commissioned Officer   CPO   Enlisted (Female)

51

Figure 3–5 Cap devices are identical for men and women in the same rank. The CPO device is a gold anchor with USN superimposed. Enlisted persons wear a silver eagle with USN above the wings. The midshipman's cap is also worn by all officer candidates.

Identifi-
cation

Insignia

Naval officers eligible to assume command of ships and stations are designated unrestricted line officers; other officers are with a staff corps or are specialists in various fields.

Staff corps include medical, supply, chaplain, civil engineer, judge advocate general's, dental, medical service, and nurse. (The Medical Corps consists entirely of physicians and surgeons; the Medical Service Corps is made up of pharmacists, medical administrative officers, medical technologists, etc.)

An officer's grade is indicated by gold sleeve stripes on blue coats; black sleeve stripes on aviation green coats; and shoulder boards on white coats, white shirts, blue overcoats, and reefers. Female officers wear sleeve stripes on white coats. They wear hard shoulder boards on summer white shirts and on the epaulets of reefers and overcoats. Above the stripes, line officers wear a five-pointed star; staff-corps officers wear the appropriate corps device as shown in figure 3-7. Officers also wear pin-on metal grade insignia on the shoulder straps of blue raincoats or aviation overcoats, and on the collars of khaki and blue shirts. Line officers wear the device on both collar tips; staff corps officers wear the grade device on the right collar tip, and the corps device on the left.

Corps devices for commissioned warrant officers appear in figure 3-8. Sleeve stripes and shoulder boards indicating grades are shown in figure 3-6.

Enlisted Personnel

The rates, ratings, and special qualifications of enlisted personnel are indicated by sleeve and breast insignia. These include group-rate marks, striker's identifications, apprentice-training graduate badges, rating badges, service stripes, specialty marks, and various breast insignia denoting special qualifications or designations.

Group-Rate Marks

These marks consist of short diagonal stripes indicating the paygrade (the color indicates the apprenticeship) of persons rated E-2 and E-3. The marks are worn on the left sleeve, not on the peacoat, dungaree shirt, working jacket, raincoat, or bluejacket (windbreaker) overcoat.

Seaman apprenticeship: Seamen and seaman apprentices wear white stripes on blue uniforms, blue stripes on white.

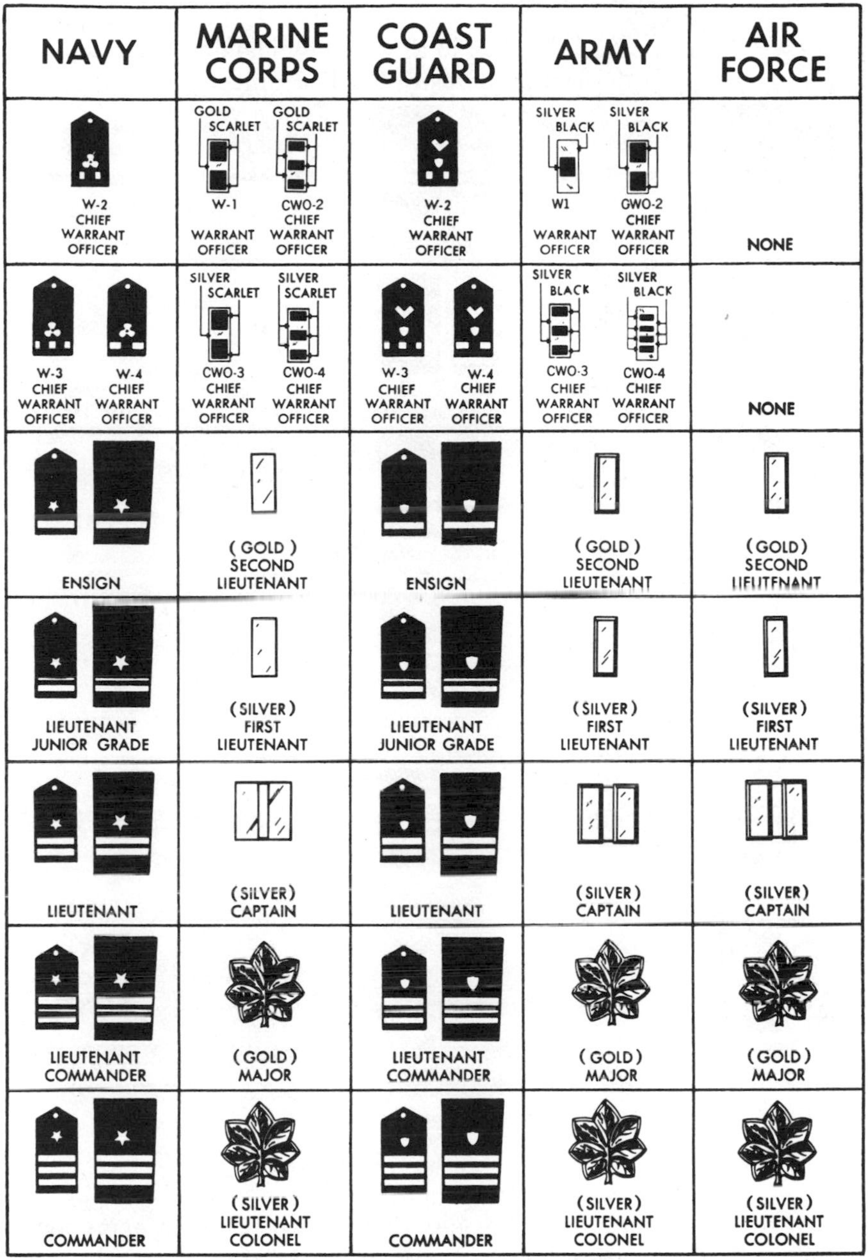

NAVY	MARINE CORPS	COAST GUARD	ARMY	AIR FORCE
W-2 CHIEF WARRANT OFFICER	GOLD SCARLET W-1 WARRANT OFFICER / GOLD SCARLET CWO-2 CHIEF WARRANT OFFICER	W-2 CHIEF WARRANT OFFICER	SILVER BLACK W1 WARRANT OFFICER / SILVER BLACK GWO-2 CHIEF WARRANT OFFICER	NONE
W-3 CHIEF WARRANT OFFICER / W-4 CHIEF WARRANT OFFICER	SILVER SCARLET CWO-3 CHIEF WARRANT OFFICER / SILVER SCARLET CWO-4 CHIEF WARRANT OFFICER	W-3 CHIEF WARRANT OFFICER / W-4 CHIEF WARRANT OFFICER	SILVER BLACK CWO-3 CHIEF WARRANT OFFICER / SILVER BLACK CWO-4 CHIEF WARRANT OFFICER	NONE
ENSIGN	(GOLD) SECOND LIEUTENANT	ENSIGN	(GOLD) SECOND LIEUTENANT	(GOLD) SECOND LIEUTENANT
LIEUTENANT JUNIOR GRADE	(SILVER) FIRST LIEUTENANT	LIEUTENANT JUNIOR GRADE	(SILVER) FIRST LIEUTENANT	(SILVER) FIRST LIEUTENANT
LIEUTENANT	(SILVER) CAPTAIN	LIEUTENANT	(SILVER) CAPTAIN	(SILVER) CAPTAIN
LIEUTENANT COMMANDER	(GOLD) MAJOR	LIEUTENANT COMMANDER	(GOLD) MAJOR	(GOLD) MAJOR
COMMANDER	(SILVER) LIEUTENANT COLONEL	COMMANDER	(SILVER) LIEUTENANT COLONEL	(SILVER) LIEUTENANT COLONEL

cont.

Figure 3–6   Rank insignia, worn as shoulder and sleeve markings in the Navy and Coast Guard, correspond to Marine Corps, Army, and Air Force collar devices.

NAVY	MARINE CORPS	COAST GUARD	ARMY	AIR FORCE
CAPTAIN	COLONEL	CAPTAIN	COLONEL	COLONEL
REAR ADMIRAL (Lower Half)	BRIGADIER GENERAL	REAR ADMIRAL (Lower Half)	BRIGADIER GENERAL	BRIGADIER GENERAL
REAR ADMIRAL (Upper Half)	MAJOR GENERAL	REAR ADMIRAL (Upper Half)	MAJOR GENERAL	MAJOR GENERAL
VICE ADMIRAL	LIEUTENANT GENERAL	VICE ADMIRAL	LIEUTENANT GENERAL	LIEUTENANT GENERAL
ADMIRAL	GENERAL	ADMIRAL	GENERAL	GENERAL
FLEET ADMIRAL	NONE	NONE	GENERAL OF THE ARMY	GENERAL OF THE AIR FORCE

Figure 3–6 *continued*

Fireman apprenticeship: Firemen and fireman apprentices wear red stripes on blue and white uniforms.

Construction apprenticeship: Constructionmen and construction apprentices wear light-blue stripes on blue and white uniforms.

Enlisted Personnel

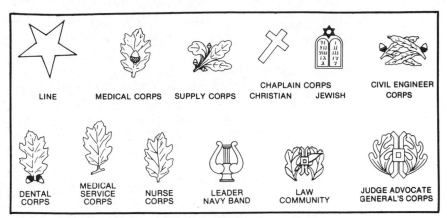

Figure 3–7   Line and staff corps insignia are worn on both sleeves, above the stripes, and on shoulderboards. Officers other than line officers also wear them on the collar tips of khaki and blue shirts.

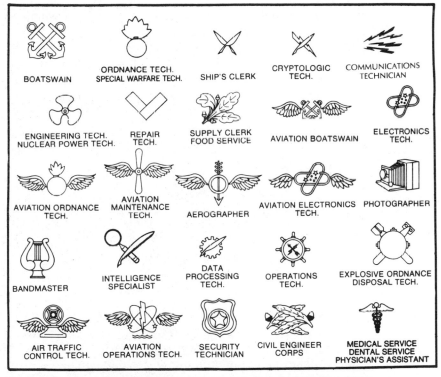

Figure 3–8   Warrant officer insignia are worn on sleeves, above the stripes, on shoulderboards, and as pin-on collar devices.

Airman apprenticeship: Airmen and airman apprentices wear emerald-green stripes on blue and white uniforms.

Hospital apprenticeship and dental apprenticeship: Hospitalmen and hospital apprentices, dentalmen and dental apprentices, all wear white stripes on blue uniforms and Navy-blue stripes on white uniforms. They also wear specialty marks that indicate their particular apprenticeship and distinguish them from seaman apprentices.

Rating Badges

Rating badges, worn on the left sleeve, consist of an eagle (called a crow), chevrons indicating the wearer's rate, and a specialty mark indicating rating.

Once you reach paygrade E-7 (CPO), a rocker, or arch, is added to the rating badge. The specialty mark is centered in the space between the eagle and the upper chevron. Senior chief petty officers (SCPOs) (E-8) also have a single silver star, centered above the eagle's head, while MCPOs (E-9) have two silver stars arranged horizontally above the eagle's wingtips. The rating badge for command MCPOs is the same as that for MCPOs except that an inverted five-point silver star takes the place of the specialty mark. The badge for fleet/force MCPOs is the same as that for command MCPOs except that all the stars are gold. The MCPON has three gold stars arranged in a horizontal line above the eagle's head.

| MCPON | FM/C CM/C | MCPO | SCPO | CPO |

Enlisted people in all services wear chevrons that indicate their paygrade. These are shown, along with the Navy paygrades, in figure 3-9. Personnel in the Coast Guard, for the most part, wear badges identical to those of the Navy.

Service Stripes

Service stripes, or "hashmarks," are worn on the left sleeve below the rating badge and indicate length of service. Each stripe signifies completion of four full years of active or reserve duty (or any combination thereof) in any of the armed forces. Scarlet stripes are worn on blue uniforms, Navy-blue stripes on forest-green uniforms (worn by aviation personnel).

NAVY	MARINES	ARMY	AIR FORCE	
MASTER CHIEF P.O.	SGT. MAJOR / MASTER GUNNERY SGT.	SERGEANT MAJOR / COMMAND SERGEANT MAJOR	CHIEF MASTER SGT.	E-9
SENIOR CHIEF P.O.	1ST SGT. / MASTER SGT.	FIRST SERGEANT / MASTER SERGEANT	SENIOR MASTER SGT.	E-8
CHIEF P.O.	GUNNERY SGT.	SGT. 1ST CLASS	MASTER SGT.	E-7
P.O. 1ST CLASS	STAFF SGT.	STAFF SGT. / SPEC. 6	TECHNICAL SGT.	E-6
P.O. 2ND CLASS	SGT.	SGT. / SPEC. 5	STAFF SGT.	E-5
P.O. 3RD CLASS	CORPORAL	CORPORAL / SPEC. 4	SENIOR AIRMAN	E-4
SEAMAN	LANCE CORPORAL	PRIVATE 1ST CLASS	AIRMAN 1ST CLASS	E-3
SEAMAN APPRENTICE	PRIVATE 1ST CLASS	PRIVATE	AIRMAN	E-2
SEAMAN RECRUIT	PRIVATE	PRIVATE	BASIC AIRMAN	E-1

Figure 3–9 Navy enlisted rates and paygrades are compared with those of the other services. The Coast Guard's badges are the same as the Navy's. Chevrons are red on blues with a white eagle, blue on whites with a blue eagle. CPO chevrons are red or gold as appropriate. Specialty marks are the same color as the eagle. Badges worn on dungaree shirts have dark blue chevrons but no specialty marks.

NAVAL ASTRONAUT

NAVAL AVIATOR

NAVAL AVIATION OBSERVER AND
FLIGHT METEOROLOGIST

NAVAL ASTRONAUT (NFO)

NAVAL FLIGHT OFFICER

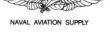

NAVAL AVIATION EXPERIMENTAL
PSYCHOLOGIST
NAVAL AVIATION PHYSIOLOGIST

NAVAL FLIGHT SURGEON
NAVAL FLIGHT NURSE
(Gold, Without Acorn)

AVIATION WARFARE SPECIALIST

NAVAL AVIATION SUPPLY

SURFACE WARFARE OFFICER
ENLISTED SURFACE WARFARE
(Cutlasses)

SUPPLY SURFACE WARFARE

AIRCREW

SUBMARINE

SUBMARINE MEDICAL

SUBMARINE COMBAT PATROL

NAVAL RESERVE
MERCHANT MARINE

SUBMARINE SUPPLY

SUBMARINE ENGINEER DUTY

SSBN DETERRENT PATROL

COMMAND AT SEA (Gold)

DEEP SUBMERGENCE (Gold)
ENLISTED (Silver)

SPECIAL OPERATIONS

SPECIAL WARFARE (SEAL) (UDT)

SMALL CRAFT

CRAFTMASTER

PARACHUTIST

BASIC PARACHUTIST

DIVING OFFICER (Gold)
MASTER DIVER (Silver)
DIVING MEDICAL
(With Caduceus)
DIVING MEDICAL TECHNICIAN
(Silver, with Caduceus)

COMMAND ASHORE
PROJECT MANAGER

EXPLOSIVE ORDNANCE DISPOSAL
SENIOR EOD (Star on drop bomb)
MASTER EOD (Additional star within
laurel wreath affixed to top of shield)

Gold Badges and Stripes
POs with a total of twelve years' broken or unbroken active-duty service in the Navy, Naval Reserve, Naval Ready Reserve, U.S. Marine Corps, or Marine Corps Ready Reserve who have fulfilled the requirements for successive awards of the Navy Good Conduct Medal, Reserve Meritorious Service Award, or Marine Corps Good Conduct Medal wear the gold rating badge and gold service stripes on their service-dress blue, dinner-dress blue, and dinner-dress white and blue jackets. Three service stripes are required to qualify; there is no required number of good-conduct awards.

Striker's Marks
Striker's marks are worn by enlisted men and women in paygrades E-1 through E-3 who have been designated as strikers by the Naval Military Personnel Command (NMPC). The specialty mark of the rating for which the sailor is qualified is centered immediately above the rectangular background of the group-rate marks for E-2 and E-3 on the left sleeve of blue and white uniforms.

Apprentice Training Graduate Badge
All enlisted personnel who graduate and complete apprentice training will wear this badge until authorized to wear a striker designation.

Breast Insignia

Metal or embroidered insignia are worn on the breast to indicate a special qualification or designation. Certain officers may wear insignia for aviation, submarine service, surface warfare, command, special warfare, parachuting, and underwater or explosive ordnance disposal. Only one warfare specialty device may be worn at a time.

All insignia are worn on the left breast, except those representing command at sea or ashore (incumbent); these are worn

---

Figure 3–10 Breast insignia. Not shown are first-class diver (silver helmet surrounded by sea serpents), second-class diver (silver helmet and breast plate), scuba diver (silver wet-suit hood, face mask with breathing apparatus).

on the right breast. Approved insignia are:

SEAMAN FIREMAN AIRMAN

Officer Insignia

Aviation: naval astronaut, naval astronaut (NFO), naval aviator, naval aviation observer and flight meteorologist, naval flight surgeon, naval flight nurse, naval flight officer, aviation experimental psychologist, aviation physiologist, aviation warfare specialist, and supply aviation warfare.

Submarine: submarine (dolphins), submarine medical, submarine engineer duty, submarine supply, submarine combat patrol, and SSBN deterrent patrol.

Surface warfare: special operations, surface warfare insignia, and supply surface warfare.

Command: command at sea, command ashore/project manager.

Special warfare: special warfare insignia.

Parachutists: naval parachutist and basic parachutist.

Underwater: diving, diving (medical), and deep submergence.

Explosive ordnance disposal: EOD insignia.

Enlisted Insignia

Aviation: aircrew, aviation warfare specialist.

Submarine: submarine (dolphins), submarine combat patrol, and SSBN deterrent patrol.

Surface warfare: surface warfare insignia.

Officer in charge/PO in charge: small craft and craftmaster.

Special warfare: special warfare insignia.

Parachutists: naval parachutist and basic parachutist.

Underwater: master diver; diver, first class; diver, second class; diver, scuba; diving medical technician; and deep submergence.

Explosive ordnance disposal: EOD insignia; senior, master.

Except when the command insignia is worn, a maximum of two insignia may be worn at any time. When two are worn they must be of different categories. When two are worn with ribbons or medals, one is centered above and the other below the ribbons or medals. The insignia of the current specialty should be the one worn above.

Command-at-sea or ashore insignia may be worn by officers and enlisted personnel even though they are not currently assigned to such duties. In such cases, the insignia are worn on the left breast. Details for wearing all insignia are contained in U.S. Navy Uniform Regulations.

Identification Badges

These badges publicly identify personnel on special assignments. The first four (figure 3-11) are worn by members of *all* military services.

Presidential Service: Worn by those on duty at the White House who have been awarded a Presidential Service Certificate. The badge is worn on the upper right pocket during and after the period of detail.

Vice Presidential Service: Worn by personnel assigned to the Office of the Vice President who have been awarded a Vice Presidential Service Certificate. The badge is also worn on the right pocket both during and after the period of detail.

Office of the Secretary of Defense: Worn by those who have received a certificate of eligibility from the Office of the Secretary of Defense authorizing them to wear the insignia. Worn on the upper left pocket during and after period of detail.

Joint Chiefs of Staff (JCS): The miniature may be worn during and after the period of detail by those assigned to the JCS organization. The regular size is worn on full-dress and service-dress uniforms. It goes on the upper left pocket.

Recruiting Command: Worn by all personnel assigned to duty with the Navy Recruiting Command. It is worn on the upper left pocket. Excellence of performance is acknowledged with the addition of a gold-colored metal wreath and gold or silver stars.

Navy/Fleet/Force/Command MCPOs: Worn by personnel in these billets, who must be designated to the positions in writing. The badge is worn centered on the left pocket during the period of detail only with uniforms requiring large medals or ribbons. A miniature size is worn on formal- and dinner-dress uniforms. When a tour is over, the miniature badge is worn on service uniforms only. A raised block in the center indicates the position held, i.e., Navy, fleet, force, or command.

Figure 3–11 Identification badges are worn by (*top row, from left*) persons performing presidential and vice presidential service, and those assigned to the Office of the Secretary of Defense; (*second row*) the Joint Chiefs of Staff, those in the recruiting service, and the Navy/Fleet/Force/Command master chief petty officers; and (*third row*) recruit company commander and career counselors. Badges not shown include CMAA (gold), MAA (silver), corrections (gold), police (gold and silver), guard (silver), and Merchant Marine service emblem.

Career Counselor: Worn by a designated person who is assigned to duty as a career counselor or a career information and counseling school instructor. It is worn on the upper left pocket.

Recruit Company Commander: Worn by personnel assigned as recruit company commanders. It is worn on the upper breast pocket only during the period of service.

Ceremonial Guard Patch: Enlisted persons below paygrade E-7 are authorized to wear an identifying sleeve patch while assigned to the U.S. Ceremonial Guard, Washington, D.C. The insignia is prescribed and worn at the discretion of the commandant of the Naval District, Washington (NDW).

Female personnel wear identification badges in a position centered above the left coat pocket flap or in a corresponding position on uniforms that do not have a pocket, with the exception of the Presidential and Vice Presidential Service badges, which are worn on the right side in the same relative position.

Uniform of the Day

This uniform is prescribed for all naval personnel within a command or geographical area. Usually the plan of the day (POD) for every ship or station lists the uniform for officers and enlisted personnel. A working uniform will be prescribed for "turn-to" hours, and a uniform of the day will be prescribed for after-working hours. The uniform for liberty, leave, special occasions, and ceremonies will also be prescribed in the POD. Changes in uniform appear in ship or station notices.

The regional coordinator is responsible for establishing and controlling uniform policies within his or her jurisdiction. He or she designates uniforms for the season, day, or special occasion. Uniform policies afloat and ashore outside his or her jurisdiction are the responsibility of the senior officer present.

Uniforms in General

As mentioned, a decision was reached in 1977 to return to the traditional uniform of white hat, rolled neckerchief, jumper, and bell-bottoms. This is the uniform now being issued to all male recruits entering the Navy It was required for all E-1 through E-6 men as of 1 October 1983.

Uniforms for women, officers and enlisted, are very much alike. The main difference is in the wearing of formal attire, which is generally authorized only for senior officers. Dinner dress blue jacket and dinner dress white jacket uniforms are authorized for CPOs; E6 and below wear dinner dress blue.

The CNO has approved service dress white jumpers with slacks/skirts for women (E6 and below). The jumpers will be issued to new recruits beginning 1 October 1991 and will be required by 1 October 1993.

Uniforms for Enlisted Men (E1–E6)

Service dress blue: blue jumper, blue broadfall trousers, neckerchief, white hat, ribbons, black shoes, and socks. **Service dress white:** substitute white jumper and trousers.

Winter blue: winter blue shirt, blue belted trousers, white hat, black necktie, and black shoes and socks.

Dinner dress: same as service dress, but with miniature medals.

Full dress: same as service dress, but with large medals.

Tropical white: tropical white shirt, white shorts and knee socks, black shoes, and white hat.

Tropical dungarees: dungaree shorts, short-sleeve dungaree shirt, black kneesocks, black shoes, and white hat.

Dungarees: dungaree trousers, blue chambray shirt, white hat (blue command ball cap when authorized), and black shoes and socks.

Winter working blue: winter working blue shirt, blue belted trousers, white hat, and black shoes and socks.

Uniforms for Enlisted Women (E1–E6)

Service dress blue: blue coat and unbelted skirt, with white short-sleeve shirt, black necktie, combination hat, dress shoes, and ribbons. For dinner dress blue, add miniature medals, black handbag, and white gloves. For full-dress blue, add large medals and white gloves. Service dress blue can be worn with belted slacks in lieu of skirt, and service shoes when authorized.

Winter blue: long-sleeve blue shirt and blue belted skirt, black tie, combination hat, dress shoes, and ribbons; service shoes and slacks in lieu of skirt can be worn when authorized. Winter working blue is worn without tie and ribbons.

Summer white: white short-sleeve, open-collar shirt, white belted skirt, combination hat, dress shoes, and ribbons. This can be worn with service shoes and belted slacks in lieu of skirt, without ribbons, when authorized.

Dungarees: blue chambray shirt, blue polyester-cotton slacks, blue command ball cap when authorized.

Women wear tropical uniforms like the men's.

Optional Uniform Items

Today's enlisted personnel also have several optional uniform items. For instance, they can wear a white scarf with an overcoat or raincoat; they can wear a blue sweater (at command discretion); an umbrella (plain black) may be used with any uniform. Blue working ball cap may be worn with dungarees when authorized. Medical personnel E-1 through E-6 wear black shoes. White shoes are authorized for CPOs and officers with summer white. Men's and women's uniforms are constantly undergoing modernization. Check Navy Uniform Regulations for the most recent changes.

Decorations and Awards

Awards include any decoration, medal, badge, ribbon, or attachment thereof bestowed on an individual or a unit. A decoration is awarded to an individual for an act of gallantry or meritorious service. A unit award is presented to an operating unit and can be worn only by members who participated in the action cited. A service award is made to those who have participated in designated wars, campaigns, and expeditions, or who have fulfilled a specified service requirement. The Navy Cross, Bronze Star Medal, and Purple Heart are examples of decorations; the Presidential Unit Citation (PUC) and Meritorious Unit Commendation (MUC) are examples of unit awards. Service awards, often called campaign or theater awards, include the Good Conduct Medal and the Vietnam Service Medal.

The Navy recognizes 19 military decorations, 5 unit awards, 23 nonmilitary decorations, 40 campaign and service awards, and a number of others by foreign governments. Many foreign awards may be accepted, but cannot be worn. There are more than 150 awards, including those bestowed by military societies and other organizations.

Military decorations and unit awards may be given at any time. They are listed below in order of precedence, with the four unit awards last. All other decorations are worn below these. Ribbons for decorations and awards are worn on the left breast. One, two, or three ribbons are worn in a single row, centered above the pocket. When more than three ribbons are authorized, they are worn in horizontal rows of three each. If not in multiples of three, the uppermost row contains the lesser number, with the ribbon(s) centered over the row beneath.

Medal of Honor	Meritorious Service Medal
Navy Cross	Air Medal
Defense Distinguished Service Medal*	Joint Service Commendation Medal*
Distinguished Service Medal	Navy Commendation Medal
Silver Star Medal	Joint Service Achievement Medal*

Defense Superior Service
 Medal*
Legion of Merit
Distinguished Flying Cross
Navy and Marine Corps Medal
Bronze Star Medal
Purple Heart
Defense Meritorious Service
 Medal*

Navy Achievement Medal
Combat Action Ribbon
Presidential Unit Citation Ribbon
Joint Meritorious Unit Award*
Navy Unit Commendation Ribbon
Meritorious Unit Commendation
 Ribbon
Navy "E"

*Not Navy decoration—listed for precedence only.

See U.S. Navy Uniform Regulations, chapter 10, for the order of precedence and proper wear of all awards.

Ownership Markings

Articles of clothing are legibly marked with the owner's name and the last four digits of the owner's Social Security number in black marking fluid for white clothes and chambray shirts. White marking fluid is used for blue clothes and dungaree trousers, or indelible ink when labels are provided for the purpose. All markings other than those on labels should be made with a half-inch stencil or stamp.

Detailed ownership marking instructions are furnished to recruits when clothing is issued to them. These instructions must be followed explicitly. As a general rule, instructions for marking clothes, as laid down in the uniform regulations, should be followed when additional uniform articles are obtained.

The word *right* or *left* means the owner's right or left when the article is worn. On towels, it means the owner's right or left when standing behind the article laid out for inspection. Markings on all articles, properly rolled or laid out for bag inspection, will appear right side up to the inspecting officer and upside down to the person standing behind them. Markings are placed as follows:

Enlisted Men E-1–E-6

Bag, Duffel: Along short strap on outer side, and on opposite side from carrying strap, centered, one foot from top.
Belts: Inside, near clip.

Caps:
> *Hat, white:* In back of brim. When brim is turned down, next to seam between brim and crown, so that marking will not show when brim is turned up.
> *Knit (watch):* Initials only, on inside label.

Gloves: Initials on inside only, near the top.

Jacket, Blue (Windbreaker): On inside of hem at right of center line on back.

Jacket, Utility: On inside of hem at right of center line of back, and last name only on left front, one inch above pocket.

Jumpers, Blue or White: Turn jumper inside out, front down, collar away from you, stencil three initials, 1/4 inch below collar seam to left of center, and last four digits of SSN 1/4 inch below collar seam to right of center; fill in manufacturer's tag, using indelible ink pen.

Neckerchief: Diagonally across center, initials only.

Necktie, Black, Four-in-Hand: Center back, inside, initials only.

Overcoat, Melton Wool (Peacoat): Last name, initials, and last four digits of SSN on left side of tail lining, three inches from and parallel to bottom edge.

Raincoat: Inside on lining, 3 inches below collar seam.

Shirts: Vertically, beginning 1 inch from bottom on inner side of right front fold on which buttons are sewn. Blue chambray is also stenciled, or embroidered, last name only, on left front (on right side for all shirts purchased after 1 February 1990), one inch above pocket.

Shoes: Initials only inside, near top.

Socks: Initials only on foot.

Sweater: On label on inside, below back of collar.

Towel: Right corner on hem, parallel to end.

Trousers:
> *Blue (Dress Type):* On designated nameplate.
> *Blue (13-Button, Broadfall):* Turn trousers inside out, fly down, waistband away from you. Stencil three initials and last four digits of SSN on rear pocket, 1/4 inch below horizontal seam using white ink; fill in manufacturer's tag using indelible ink.
> *Dungaree:* On front inside waistband, at right of center line; last name only, on outside, 1 inch above right hip pocket.
> *White:* Turn trousers inside out, fly down, waistband away from you, stencil three initials and last four digits of SSN on left rear pocket in between the two horizontal seams; fill in manufacturer's tag using ballpoint pen.

Trunks, swim: Inside on hem on right center of back.

Undershirt: On outside of front, 1 inch from the bottom of the shirt and at right of center.

Undershorts: On outside of right half of waistband, or immediately underneath waistband on undershorts with elastic waistbands.

Enlisted Women E-1–E-6

Anklets: On foot.

Bag, Duffel: Along short strap on outer side, and on opposite side from carrying strap, centered, one foot from top.

Belts: Inside.

Caps:
   Combination: On designated nameplate.
   Garrison: On designated nameplate.
   Knit, watch: On a label on inside, initials only.

Coat, Service Dress Blue: On designated nameplate.

Gloves: Initials only, inside cuff.

Handbag: On designated nameplate.

Hat Cover: Center back; inside band.

Jacket, Utility: On inside of hem at right of center line of back, and last name only on left front, 1 inch above the pocket.

Jacket, Blue (Windbreaker): On inside of hem at right on center line on back.

Necktie: Center back; inside.

Overcoat; raincoat: On designated nameplate, and inside left front panel.

Scarf: Inside along seam near end.

Shirts: Vertically, beginning 1 inch from bottom on inner side of right front fold on which buttons are sewn. The utility/blue chambray is also stenciled, last name only, on left front (on right side for all shirts purchased after 1 February 1990), 1 inch above pocket.

Shoes:
   Dress: Inside, initials only near top.
   Safety: On inside; initials near top.
   Service: On inside; initials only on inside of tongue.

Skirts: Center front, inside; on waistband.

Slacks:
   Blue: Center back, inside; on waistband.
   Dungarees: On inside waistband in front, at right of center line; last name only, on the outside, 1 inch above right hip pocket.

Stockings: Inside at top, initials only.

Sweater: On designated nameplate.

Towel: Right corner on hem parallel to end.

Undershirts: On outside of front, 1 inch from bottom of shirt and at right of center.

Optional articles of clothing are marked similarly to comparable items of required clothing.

No transfer or exchange of uniform clothing may be made without the authority of the commanding officer. When a transfer or exchange is authorized, or when clothing belonging to another is disposed of, the name of the former owner is stamped over with the mark "D.C." (discarded clothing) and the purchaser's name is placed above, below, or next to it.

Take care of your uniforms. They cost money to replace—your money.

Miscellaneous Uniform Items

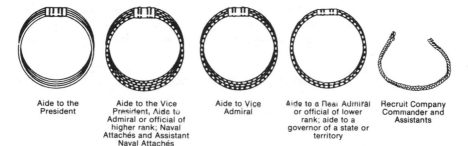

| Aide to the President | Aide to the Vice President, Aide to Admiral or official of higher rank; Naval Attachés and Assistant Naval Attachés | Aide to Vice Admiral | Aide to a Rear Admiral or official of lower rank; aide to a governor of a state or territory | Recruit Company Commander and Assistants |

Figure 3–12 Aiguillettes are worn by various aides to officials. Service aiguillettes are shown here. Dress aiguillettes, much more ornate, are fastened across the chest to the coat collar.

Aiguillettes are usually worn by officers performing specialized staff duty. They're worn by aides to the president, the vice president, the White House, the secretary of defense, the secretary and other officials of the Navy Department, the deputy or assistant secretaries of defense, and aides to flag officers. You probably already know of several enlisted people who wear them. The Integrated Training Brigade (ITB), battalion or regiment adjutants, company commanders, and assistant company commanders all wear one red-and-white-loop.

Brassards are bands of cloth, suitably marked with symbols, letters, or words, indicating a temporary duty to which the wearer is assigned. They are worn on the right arm, midway between shoulder and elbow, on outer garments. They are usually worn by officers of the day (OOD), junior officers of the day (JOOD), shore patrol (SP), masters-at-arms, armed forces police, personnel who are members of ambulance and first-aid parties (Geneva Cross), and by damage-control personnel of shore stations during drills and tests. The mourning badge, made of black crepe, is worn on the left sleeve of the outer garment, halfway between shoulder and elbow, for offi-

Officer of the Day (Deck)   Junior Officer of the Day (Deck)   Shore Patrol

Geneva Cross   Master-at-Arms

Figure 3–13   Brassards are worn on the right arm midway between the shoulder and elbow. The officer of the day (or deck) wears the OOD brassard, the junior officer of the day (or deck) wears JOOD, shore patrol wear the SP, corpsmen the Geneva Cross, and masters-at-arms the MAA.

cers; in the same position, on the right sleeve, for enlisted personnel.

A commanding officer may direct that officers and enlisted personnel wear name tags for easy identification during conferences, VIP cruises, open houses, or similar occasions, or in the performance of duties where some easy method of identification by name is desirable or beneficial. Name tags are rectangular, not exceeding dimensions of 1 inch by $3\frac{1}{2}$ inches, and may be any color as long as the same color is used throughout the command. Name tags are worn on the right breast, but are not worn when medals are prescribed.

Except for tie clasps, cuff links, and shirt studs, which may be worn as prescribed, no other personal items are permitted. Pencils, pens, watch chains, pins, combs, smoking material, and jewelry (except for one ring per hand in addition to a wedding ring, wristwatch, and identification bracelet) are not to be worn. Enlisted women may wear small silver ball ($\frac{1}{4}$ inch post or screw) earrings with a brushed matte finish while in uniform. Officers and CPOs wear gold with a brushed matte finish. Small, single-pearl earrings are authorized for wear with dinner and formal dress uniforms.

Uniforms of Other Services

Officers and enlisted personnel attached to a Marine Corps organization wear prescribed Marine Corps uniforms. Those

worn by enlisted personnel are furnished at no cost to the individual. Enlisted personnel wear their usual naval insignia on marine uniforms. Naval personnel on duty with the Army or Air Force normally wear their own uniforms. In some instances, they are authorized to wear Army or Air Force uniforms, provided these uniforms are furnished at no cost.

Wearing of Uniforms

There are rules and regulations for wearing uniforms, but some things are a matter of common sense. The hat or cap is part of the uniform, but if a particular duty or operation interferes, it may be removed. Persons riding in motor vehicles with insufficient headroom may remove their headgear. Those riding two- or three-wheeled motor vehicles should remove uniform headgear and wear safety helmets; they may also wear protective clothing over their uniforms. A cap no longer has to be worn at sea, except on specific watches and specific occasions. It is always worn squarely on the head, bottom edge horizontal.

Shoes are kept in good repair; those worn on watch and liberty and for inspections should be shined. White shoes should always be freshly cleaned.

71

Grooming Standards

Neatness, cleanliness, and safety are essential to your military image. Grooming standards are intended not to be restrictive or to isolate Navy men and women from society but rather to promote a favorable image for the Navy. The standards are not unreasonable, and they permit a degree of individuality.

Men

You should be neat, clean, and presentable at all times.

The hair should be tapered around the neck, $\frac{3}{4}$ inch up from the lower hairline. Don't let it hang over your ears. And don't let the hair on the back of the neck touch your collar. Don't let your hair grow longer than 4 inches. The hair on the top of your head, after you've groomed it, should not extend more than 2 inches from the scalp.

There's a reason for men having their hair shorter than shoulder length—safety. For instance, the headgear you wear—the helmet that could save your life—would not fit properly if you had long hair.

The $\frac{3}{4}$-inch rule is not ironclad. In the cases of curly, kinked, and wavy hair, a slightly greater length is acceptable, providing it doesn't interfere with headgear. Plaited or braided hair may not be worn in uniform or on duty.

Keep your sideburns neat and trimmed, no lower than the ear lobe. Flares, muttonchops, and other such styles are not permitted.

Beards are not permitted except when medically authorized, and then only until the problem clears up. If you wear a mustache, keep it trimmed and neat. Don't grow your mustache below the top line of your upper lip, nor more than a $\frac{1}{4}$ inch up from the corners.

If you're assigned to a Marine Corps unit and elect to wear the marine service uniforms, abide by Marine Corps standards for grooming.

You may wear a hairpiece or wig on active duty and in uniform only if it is used to cover up baldness or a deformity. Make sure the wig fits, looks natural, and doesn't interfere with your safety.

Women

Keep your hair clean, neatly arranged, and no longer than the lower edge of your collar. Your hair must not show under the front brim of the combination hat or garrison cap. Various hairstyles are permitted, including Afros, as long as they are not exaggerated and do not interfere with headgear.

Pigtails and pony tails are out. No more than two braids, neatly secured at all points to the head, are authorized.

Conspicuous rubberbands, combs, and pins are not authorized. Two barrettes, similar to hair color, may be used to pin up hair. Visible hairnets may be worn only if authorized for specific duties, such as in hospitals or galleys. The rule for wigs is the same as it is for men: it must look natural and must not interfere with your safety.

Keep cosmetics to a minimum.

Leadership, Discipline, and the UCMJ

4

There are two general types of Navy training: professional and military. You get professional training by attending service schools, qualifying for advancement, studying, and working at your job. You get military training by learning and understanding the qualities of leadership, discipline, standards of conduct, watchstanding, drills, and first aid. You learn most aspects of military training by following the example of the petty officers and officers senior to you.

Leadership

Before you can lead, you must have followers. Before you can be a *good* leader, you must have *willing* followers. Navy recruits are expected to be good followers, and they should learn the qualities of good leadership so they can assume important responsibilities in the future.

But what makes a good leader? A good leader must know his or her job, crew, and how to set a good example. The idea is to *inspire* subordinates to follow you, not to *order* them to.

Your first chance to demonstrate leadership will probably come when you're a leading seaman. You'll be part of the chain of command, with men and women you outrank and others who outrank you.

The chain of command exists to ensure that:

1. The Navy and its sailors do their jobs without confusion and without wasting time and effort.
2. Those in charge know what their responsibilities are.
3. Everyone is accountable to someone for his or her job and actions.
4. There is a sense of direction, so that everyone knows what they're supposed to do.

5. Clear communication exists, both up and down, so there will be no doubt where you or anyone else stands in the chain of command.

The Meaning of Leadership

Different leaders define the term in different ways. Eight chief petty officers (CPOs) who have served from fourteen to twenty-three years each have described what leadership means to them. Ask yourself the question. Do you see leadership as the ability to inspire others, or is it the ability to keep them in line? Here's what the eight CPOs said:

The first chief pointed out that, in the past, leaders were more educated than their followers. Since they knew more, they took charge. But today, the chief says, those expected to follow are educated and, in many cases, may be smarter than the people who outrank them. Today's educated followers need motivation. They want to know the reason for their work. If their boss can't give a reason and fails to motivate them, the job will suffer.

Chief no. 2 sees honesty as a key to leadership—honesty with yourself and those you work with. By listening to others' ideas before forming opinions and deciding what to do, a leader earns respect—more respect than one who decides immediately to do everything "my way." This chief says a leader should be flexible and willing to compromise when necessary. Leaders should be friendly, willing to help, and knowledgeable about the Navy and its professional fields.

A third chief, who has always led small, closely knit groups, likes the personal touch. By personal example, close direction, and a soft approach, chief no. 3 can get people to do their jobs well. And this makes his job easier. "We don't have to yell and scream at our people," he said. "We treat them as intelligent people, which they are."

Chief no. 4 stresses the ability to get along with her people. A leader doesn't have to be exceptionally smart, she feels, as long as she knows the capabilities of her people.

A fifth CPO feels the word *leadership* is worn out. "It's better to talk about management or directed effort," the chief says, but adds, "I've always looked at my job as a morale-type petty officer. Treat subordinates as human beings rather than coolies or slaves." Chief no. 5 denounces the old adage, "Do as I say, not as I do." The chief urges leaders to stand up for

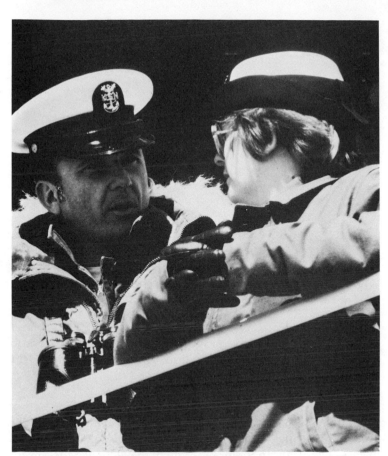

Figure 4–1 The chain of command is essential in establishing clear communications.

their people, back them up. The chain of command involves respect down as well as up.

Chief no. 6 feels a person's leadership is determined by his or her ability to get a job done promptly and efficiently, by making the best use of the workers available. A good leader will get the job done and still keep the respect of his or her crew. To accomplish this, a crew should work willingly, not out of fear.

The seventh CPO feels that followers must believe their leader knows how to get the job done. "I don't ask anyone to do anything that I can't do myself. In other words, personal example." This chief points out the need to be paternalistic

Leadership

Figure 4–2 Leadership calls for experienced personnel who know there is a fine line between being one of the gang and being their leader.

occasionally—father and child treatment. When you have to lay down your convictions, be firm, and be sure of them, the chief urges. "Praise in public, reprimand in private. Sarcasm and ridicule have no place in leadership."

The last chief says leadership is based on common sense: "Treat young sailors under your command as you'd want to be treated." Respect their problems. They may seem trivial, but they're important to them. Offer them the guidance they need. But, the chief warns, "avoid the trap of becoming one of the gang. If a discipline situation arises, your people shouldn't be sure of what your position will be. There is a fine line between being one of the gang and being their leader." Stay on the right side of that line.

The Quality of Leadership

When you look at a group, you can almost always tell who the leader is. It's the person who takes charge and directs others in getting the job done.

To some people, leadership is simply getting the job done. To others, it's *how* the job gets done. The how is important, for what good is a leader who gets a job done but loses the respect of his or her crew in the process? What good is a leader whose

Quality of
Leadership

efforts result in dissension, disorganization, and ineffectiveness, not to mention poor morale? Leaders who alienate their crews are only hurting themselves, because they'll have to count on those people in another job. And that job could be in combat.

Good leadership can be defined as the art of influencing people to win their obedience, confidence, respect, and willingness to cooperate. As a petty officer, you are given formal authority to lead. But to be a true leader, you must earn a different kind of authority—the kind that comes from those you're leading. Without it, you lose.

Personal Relations

Getting along in the Navy means more than just learning new duties, obeying regulations, standing watches, and showing up for drills. It means working and living with all kinds of people—enough to populate a small town—crowded into a space no larger than a big hotel. Going to sea means putting up not only with crowded living conditions but also with extreme operating conditions and long working hours, in intense heat or bitter cold, for perhaps weeks at a time. There are certain qualities a person should possess, or acquire, to endure these conditions.

Attitude Toward Others

Attitude involves respect, tolerance, and consideration. Perhaps for the first time you will be living with people from different social backgrounds and various levels of education. They will be of different races and have different religions. In fact, they will be just as different from you as you are from them. There is only one thing each of the half-million people in the Navy have in common—they're all in the Navy.

Because of all the differences in race, creed, religion, or national origin, discrimination may crop up, but it is the goal of the Navy to eliminate every vestige of prejudice. In recent years, the Navy has been successful in fostering racial harmony. The Navy's Affirmative Action Plan (NAAP) has done much toward establishing and maintaining equal opportunity in the Navy, countering racism, fostering equal opportunity for minorities and women, and recognizing the dignity and worth of every individual.

Figure 4–3 Attitude toward others, respect, tolerance, and consideration underscore the one thing all sailors have in common—they're all in the Navy.

Personal
Relations

While many individuals are available in the naval establishment for counseling and assistance in dealing with discriminatory practices, the ultimate responsibility for equal opportunity rests with each commanding officer. Assistance to commanding officers is provided by equal-opportunity program specialists and organizational effectiveness specialists (who operate under the control of the commanders in chief, type commanders, or other appropriate second-echelon commanders) and by Organizational Effectiveness Centers (OECs). Their job is to help make the Navy a place open to all persons, where minority groups are represented in enlisted and commissioned ranks, where bias is eliminated, and where intercultural and interracial understanding and cooperation is promoted and practiced.

Relations with the Public

When you put on the Navy uniform, you represent the United States Navy. When you go ashore, civilians will base some of their ideas about the Navy on the way you look and act. So be careful to make a good impression. Remember that at all times, no matter where you may be or what position you hold in the Navy, you are performing a public-relations duty. In a foreign country, you represent the United States, and the people you meet will take your appearance and behavior as representative of all Americans.

Overseas Diplomacy

You, as a modern American sailor, will serve in foreign nations more than any of your predecessors. Overseas service has, of course, always been part of the sailor's expectations. In the past, there were small forces permanently stationed in places like China and the Caribbean; but most of our fleet remained close to home, save for occasional trips to "show the flag." Despite the slogan "Join the Navy and see the world," the average American sailor of the past was apt to be much more familiar with San Diego, Long Beach, Brooklyn, or Norfolk than with Hong Kong, Bangkok, Naples, or Marseilles.

But the international situation since the end of World War II has demanded a new policy, often called foreign strategy. Put simply, it means the U.S. Navy must have ready combat units in places where combat may occur. For the individual sailor, this means more time overseas.

There are three basic kinds of overseas duty:

Regular Deployment: This is the most common type, involving service aboard a ship, with an aircraft squadron, or in a construction battalion. Deployed ships and aircraft engage in operational and training missions and regularly call on foreign ports for maintenance and crew R&R (rest and recreation). Some of these are regular ports of call for Navy ships: Subic Bay, Hong Kong, Kaohsiung, Yokosuka, Naples, and Rota. Other ports, such as Mombasa (in Kenya), Bangkok, Inchon, and Abidjan, are visited only occasionally.

Depending on the needs of the Navy, each command is rotated to duty in a forward area for six to nine months and then returns to CONUS (the continental United States) for repair, reassignment of personnel, and training.

Overseas Homeporting: Some ships are permanently assigned to foreign ports for periods of two years or longer. This type of duty permits crewmembers to have their dependents in the country and thus reduces long periods of family separation. Homeported units operate at sea and visit other foreign ports in the area.

Overseas Shore: To support fleet operations and carry out additional missions, the Navy needs foreign naval stations and other facilities. Overseas shore duty may be on a large naval base not too different from bases in CONUS, or the sailor can be part of a small unit in a remote location such as Diego Garcia, Iceland, and Kuwait.

For the Navy man or woman, overseas duty presents an unparalleled opportunity to learn about the world, to see strange and famous places, and to become acquainted with people of other cultures and points of view. But, as with all privileges, overseas service also carries with it a responsibility—to act as a positive representative of the Navy and the nation.

This duty is best fulfilled by enjoying things to the fullest and taking advantage of opportunities offered. Those sailors who spend all their overseas liberty in "sailor traps" or waterfront bars, will soon grow bored and dissatisfied with their duty. Similarly, Navy families that do not learn about a country and its people but only long for the familiar sights and sounds of home are not going to look forward to future overseas assignments. And in neither case is the Navy's mission being fully accomplished.

The Navy's Overseas Duty Support Program (ODSP) is designed to help Navy members and their families enjoy overseas tours and at the same time to foster good relations between Americans and host-country nationals. That is an important term, host country, because Navy personnel are guests and should act like it. Often people do not enjoy foreign service because of fear of the unknown and fear of a strange language. To help overcome these fears, ODSP provides—through local
command-overseas-duty support coordinators (ODSPCs)—accurate up-to-date information about host countries. Every

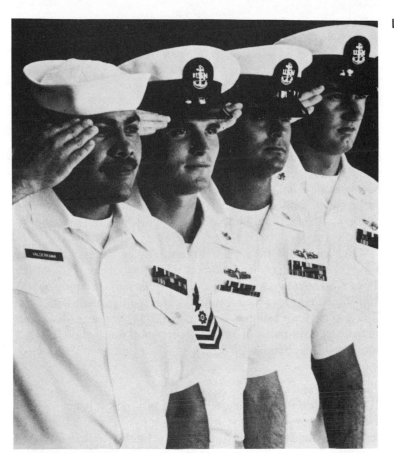

Figure 4–4 Strong leadership ensures good discipline.

effort is made to explain local transportation systems, alert personnel to recreational opportunities, and teach local customs. Above all, the program points out the benefits of learning and appreciating different ways of solving common human problems. Orientation lectures, publications, and other materials are provided.

As a U.S. citizen, you regard people from other countries as foreigners. But bear in mind that when you visit another country, *you* are the foreigner. Though the customs of other people may seem strange to you, don't make fun of anyone or anything in another country. At best it's impolite, and at worst such thoughtlessness can result in serious trouble. The United States came close to war with Mexico once because some

Personal
Relations

sailors at a bullfight cheered for the bull instead of the bull-
fighter.

Discipline

Discipline is sometimes understood to mean *punishment,*
but its real goal is to foster the best possible attitude, efficiency, and morale. A well-disciplined crew or team has the
right attitude, does its work efficiently, and exhibits high morale. Its members do the right thing because they *want* to, not
because they *have* to. Such men and women perform with
enthusiasm, individually or in groups, to carry out the mission
of their organization. They do their work without specific instructions.

When discipline fails, punishment may be necessary. In the
Navy, as in civilian life, there is a system of punishment for
those who fail to observe rules and regulations (see pp. 86–90).
Punishment is governed by U.S. Navy Regulations and the
Uniform Code of Military Justice (UCMJ). You must be familiar with certain parts of both. A brief outline of the UCMJ is
contained in appendix C.

Code of Conduct

Members of the military who are captured by enemy or unfriendly forces, in war or in peace, must be guided in their
actions by the six articles of this code. Each article is followed
here by a brief discussion of its meaning. You must be familiar
with the code and understand what you should do, or not do, if
captured.

I

*"I am an American, fighting in the forces which guard my
country and our way of life. I am prepared to give my life in
their defense."*

As a member of the armed forces it is always your duty to
oppose the enemies of the United States, regardless of the
circumstances in which you find yourself, whether in active
combat, or as a prisoner of war.

II

*"I will never surrender of my own free will. If in command, I
will never surrender the members of my command while they
still have the means to resist."*

As an individual, a member of the armed forces may never
voluntarily surrender. If you become isolated and can no

longer harm the enemy, it is your duty to evade capture and rejoin the nearest friendly forces.

The responsibility and authority of a commander never extends to the surrender of command while it still has power to resist or evade. When isolated, cut off, or surrounded, a unit must continue to fight until it is relieved or able to rejoin friendly forces.

III

"If I am captured I will continue to resist, by all means available. I will make every effort to escape and aid others to escape. I will accept neither parole nor special favors from the enemy."

The duty of a member of the armed forces to continue resistance by all means available is not lessened by the misfortune of capture. You should escape by any means possible and help others to escape. Parole agreements are promises given the captor by a prisoner of war, on faith and honor, to fulfill stated conditions (such as not to bear arms or not to escape) in consideration of special privileges—usually release from captivity or lessened restraint. No member of the armed forces will ever sign or enter into any parole agreement.

83

IV

"If I become a prisoner of war, I will keep faith with my fellow prisoners. I will give no information or take part in any actions which might be harmful to my comrades. If I am senior, I will take command. If not, I will obey the lawful orders of those appointed over me and will back them up in every way."

Informing, or any other action that harms a fellow prisoner, is shameful. Prisoners of war must not help the enemy identify fellow prisoners who may have knowledge of value to the enemy, and who may therefore be tortured.

Strong leadership is essential to discipline. Without discipline, camp organization, resistance, and even survival may be impossible. Personal hygiene, camp sanitation, and care of sick and wounded are imperative. Officers and noncommissioned officers of the United States will continue to carry out their responsibilities and exercise their authority after capture. The senior line officer or noncommissioned officer within the POW camp or group will assume command according to rank (or precedence), without regard to branch of service. Responsibility and accountability may not be evaded. If the senior officer or noncommissioned officer is incapacitated or unable to act for any reason, the next senior takes over.

V

*"When questioned, should I become a prisoner of war, I am
required to give name, rank, service number, and date of birth.
I will evade answering further questions to the utmost of my
ability. I will make no oral or written statements disloyal to my
country and its allies or harmful to their cause."*

When questioned, a prisoner of war is permitted to disclose
name, rank, service number, and date of birth. A prisoner of
war may tell the enemy about his or her individual health or
welfare and, when appropriate, about routine matters of camp
administration. The following are forbidden: oral or written
confessions (whether true or false), questionnaires, personal-
history statements, propaganda recordings and broadcasts,
appeals to other prisoners of war, signatures of peace or surrender appeals, criticisms, or any other oral or written communication on behalf of the enemy or critical or harmful to the
United States, its allies, its armed forces, or other prisoners.

It is a violation of the Geneva Convention to subject a prisoner of war to physical or mental torture or any other form of
coercion to secure information of any kind. If, however, a
prisoner is subjected to such treatment, he or she must strive
to avoid by every means the disclosure of any information, or
the making of any statement or the performance of any action,
harmful to the interests of the United States or its allies, or that
will provide aid or comfort to the enemy.

VI

*"I will never forget that I am an American, fighting for
freedom, responsible for my actions, and dedicated to the
principles which made my country free. I will trust in my God
and in the United States of America."*

The provisions of the UCMJ continue to apply to members
of the armed forces while prisoners of war. On release, the
conduct of prisoners will be examined based on the circumstances of capture and the time of detention, with due regard
for the rights of the individual and consideration for the conditions of captivity.

A member of the armed forces who becomes a prisoner of
war has a continuing obligation to remain loyal to country,
service, and unit.

The life of a prisoner of war is hard. Should you become a
prisoner, never give up hope and always resist enemy indoctrination. Prisoners of war who stand firm and united against the
enemy will help one another survive this ordeal.

Prisoners of War—Geneva Convention

Article 1123 of U.S. Navy Regulations defines the duties of an individual when captured by the enemy. A person in the Navy who is captured by the enemy must not disclose any information other than name, grade or rank, service number, and date of birth. A prisoner should try to communicate this same information, along with prison address and state of health, to the Central Prisoners of War Agency, normally the International Committee of the Red Cross in Geneva, Switzerland.

In turn, article 0741 makes the commanding officer of a POW camp responsible for assuring that prisoners are treated with humanity, that their personal property is preserved and protected, that they are allowed to use what they need to take care of their health, that they are supplied with proper rations, and that they are guarded properly and deprived of all means of escape and revolt.

Unauthorized Absence (UA)

This includes absence from duty station (quarters for muster, cleaning station, battle station), leaving your duty station, and overstaying leave or liberty.

Absence without leave (AWOL) is a serious offense. No matter what the reason for your absence, make every effort to return to duty and to notify your commanding officer of your whereabouts. If you cannot contact your ship, report to the nearest naval activity.

When on leave, allow plenty of time to get back. If, for reasons beyond your control, you are going to be late, notify your ship. There may be an excuse because of sickness, accident, or other emergency, but there is never any excuse for not notifying your commanding officer, the American Red Cross, or the nearest naval activity. If you are sick or in jail, a family member, a friend, or the shore patrol (SP) can send a message for you.

Furnish enough information so that the commanding officer can understand the situation and send instructions. Don't use the mail, use the telephone. You can always reach the duty officer of any station, or a shore patrol headquarters on any Navy base if your ship has gone to sea.

In most cities, naval activity is listed in the telephone directory under "U.S. Government"; otherwise the information operator can give you the number. Remember, the Navy has recruiting offices in nearly every major U.S. city. The officer or petty officer will advise you of the best course to follow.

Masters-at-Arms and Police Petty Officers

Masters-at-arms (MAA) and police petty officers have the task of maintaining order on a ship or station. They are assistants of the executive officer. Large ships will have a chief master-at-arms (CMAA) with several assistants. Personnel are assigned to the MAA force for several months or longer. While acting as MAAs, they are relieved of most of their normal watches and duties. Police petty officers usually remain with their divisions for work and watches. Their duties also include maintaining order, making reveille and taps, directing traffic, and turning lights on and off.

Shore Patrol and Armed Forces Police

The shore patrol is the military police unit in the Navy. It consists of officers and petty officers assigned to maintain order among naval personnel off ship or station. They are identified by brassards (armbands) with the letters SP.

The Army and Marine Corps have their military police (MP) and the Air Force has its air police (AP). You must obey the MPs and APs as well as SPs. In some areas, a combined or unified armed-forces police detachment (AFPD) is organized, with military police from all the services under one command.

Military police from the various services assist military personnel and investigate accidents and offenses involving military personnel.

SPs and the MPs have the authority to stop, question, apprehend, or take into custody any member of the armed forces. If stopped by the SP or AFPD, you must show your ID card, leave or other orders, and obey any directions.

If you need advice, directions, or help, you should call or visit the nearest SP petty officer or headquarters. It is the job of the SP to help and protect naval personnel.

Uniform Code of Military Justice

As a civilian, you were subject to the criminal laws of local, state, and federal governments. To a large extent you still are. But by enlisting, you have submitted yourself to the jurisdiction of the UCMJ as well. The basic criminal laws of the Navy are stated in the UCMJ. It is a "uniform" code of law because Congress made it apply equally to the Army, Navy, Air Force, Marine Corps, and Coast Guard—and it is under this code that the various services bring criminal charges against personnel who violate military law.

Under the UCMJ, service personnel are required to obey all laws established by Congress for the regulation of the military, and all lawful orders and regulations of the service and of its superior officers.

In the event of violations of the code, (refusal to obey lawful orders, insubordination, or disrespect of superior authority), a sailor receives punishment at the captain's (commanding officer's) mast, or if the offense is more serious, through Navy court-martial. UCMJ articles dealing with punishment for various crimes (articles 77 through 134) should be explained to all Navy personnel when they enter active duty, six months thereafter, and on reenlistment. Additionally, military law requires that the UCMJ be made available to all personnel. It is therefore posted in a conspicuous place in every ship and station.

The Navy has three masts: meritorious, request, and captain's mast. *Meritorious mast* is held for award presentations or commendations to personnel who have earned them. *Request masts* are simply audiences with the commanding officer (CO) requested by personnel who have matters to discuss with him. A *captain's mast* is a hearing at which minor charges against personnel are resolved. At this hearing an accused sailor is given a chance to rebut or explain charges brought against him. In the Navy, the accused has rights that must be fully explained, sometimes by a military lawyer, before the captain's mast. These rights are as follows: to be present before the officer conducting the mast; to be advised of the charges; not to be compelled to make any statement; to be present during testimony of witnesses or the receipt of written statements; to question witnesses or to have questions posed to witnesses; to have available for inspection all physical and documentary evidence; to present evidence in the accused's own behalf; to be accompanied by a personal representative who may or may not be a lawyer and whose presence is arranged for by the accused; to appeal the imposition of punishment to higher authority; and if assigned to a shore activity, to refuse captain's mast and demand trial by court-martial. It should be noted that an accused does not have the absolute right to be represented by a military lawyer at a captain's mast.

On hearing the evidence, both for and against, the CO (usually a lieutenant commander or higher rank) determines whether the person has committed the infraction he or she is charged with. If the findings are that the accused is guilty, the CO may order punishment, such as restriction of not more than sixty days, extra duties for not more than forty-five days, reduction in grade (for E-6 and below), correctional custody for not more than thirty days (for E-3 and below), forfeiture of not more than half a month's pay per month for two months, and if the guilty is attached to a ship, confinement on bread and water for not more than three days (for E-3 and below). Any punishment imposed is nonjudicial; this means there is no criminal record for the offender.

COs below the rank of lieutenant commander may also impose punishments at captain's masts, but the power of stiff punishment is reserved for officers of higher rank.

If an alleged offense is too severe to dispose of by captain's mast, the CO may recommend court-martial, of which there are three different levels: the lowest level is the summary court-martial, the next is the special court-martial, and the highest is the general court-martial.

If the offense is minor, and if nonjudicial action has been ruled out, the CO may refer the charges to trial by *summary court-martial*. This involves a summary or shortened procedure whose actions are judicial in nature. One officer serves as the judge, jury, prosecution, and defense counsel. The officer takes evidence on the charges and makes judgment according to judicial standards. The accused may be represented by an attorney if he or she desires, but this is not mandatory. The accused may also refuse trial by summary court-martial.

If an accused is convicted by summary court-martial, the court may impose confinement at hard labor of up to one month or hard labor without confinement for forty-five days. The court may also restrict the convicted to specified limits for a total of sixty days, or it may deny two-thirds of one month's pay. An E-5 and above may be reduced only one grade in pay, and may not be confined or ordered to perform hard labor. An E-4 and below may be confined for one month or assigned hard labor for forty-five days, and may be reduced to the lowest enlisted paygrade.

If a CO feels that an alleged offense against a service person is moderate to severe, the CO may refer the charges to trial by *special court-martial*. The special court-martial consists of three or more members who serve as the jury. A legally trained military judge is also assigned by the convening authority. An enlisted accused might, if he or she wishes, waive the right to trial before the court-martial jury and face the military judge alone. An enlisted accused standing trial before a special court-martial can also request that at least one-third the total membership of the jury be comprised of enlisted personnel. The maximum punishment a special court-martial may order is a bad-conduct discharge, six months' imprisonment, forfeiture of two-thirds pay per month for six months, and reduction to the lowest enlisted paygrade. Every accused person who stands trial by special court-martial is entitled to an attorney; either an attorney from the Navy is appointed for the accused, the accused may request an individual military counsel, or the accused secures the services of a civilian attorney at no expense to the government.

The *general court-martial* is reserved for more serious charges, such as common-law felonies (murder, rape, robbery, and arson) and more serious military charges (lengthy AWOL and desertion). The court is composed of a military judge, five or more members who serve as the jury, and military defense and prosecution attorneys. An accused may request trial before a military judge alone, or may be tried by the full court-martial. If an enlisted person so elects, at least one-third of the court members must be enlisted persons.

This is by far the most serious of all military courts. Its sentencing power extends to the death penalty and life imprisonment. This does not mean that a general court may sentence *anyone* convicted of an offense before that court to such extreme sentences. The court is limited by the sentences set forth for each offense in part IV of the Manual for Courts-Martial, which lists the maximum sentence that may be imposed for each offense by a court-martial under the UCMJ. This does not mean that military courts routinely impose maximum sentences under law. The court may sentence an accused to any sentence less than the maximum.

As mentioned, service personnel are also subject to civilian trial and punishment, though with certain reservations. Service personnel are not answerable to civil authorities for violations of a strictly military nature, such as AWOL, desertion, or misbehavior before the enemy. These offenses are subject to trial by military authorities only. Service personnel, however, may be subjected to joint jurisdiction (both civil and military) for offenses such as murder, robbery, or rape. In many situations involving crimes of this nature, both civil and military authorities can try an offender. Normally, the accused is subjected to trial before only one jurisdiction, but there are situations where he or she is tried in succession, by both civil and military jurisdiction, for the same offense.

Military law is a complex subject covered by thousands of books. The finer points of military law and court-martial procedure are not understood by most nonlegal personnel. But Navy lawyers are at your disposal, should the need arise, and will advise you at no cost on all matters of military justice matters.

UCMJ

Courtesies, Customs, and Ceremonies

5

The Salute

The hand salute is the military custom you will learn first and use most. It is centuries old, and probably originated when men in armor raised their helmet visors so they could be identified. Salutes are customarily given with the right hand, but there are exceptions. A sailor whose right arm or hand is encumbered may salute lefthanded, while people in the Army or Air Force never salute lefthanded. On the other hand, a soldier or airman may salute sitting down or uncovered (without cap on); in the Navy, a sailor does not salute when uncovered (unless failure to do so would mean embarrassment or misun derstanding) but may salute when seated in a vehicle.

Women in the Navy follow the same customs and rules as men in saluting, with one exception. A woman in uniform indoors, where men customarily remove their hats, does not remove her hat, nor does she salute. She does, of course, use the proper spoken greeting, just as she would outdoors.

How to Salute

Salute from a position of attention. If you're walking, salute from an erect position. Your upper arm should be parallel to the deck or ground, forearm inclined at a 45-degree angle, hand and wrist straight, palm slightly inward, thumb and fingers extended and joined, with the tip of the forefinger touching your cap beak, slightly to the right of the right eye. Face the person saluted, or if you're walking, turn your head and eyes toward the person. Hold the salute until the officer has returned or acknowledged it, then bring your hand smartly to your side.

Whom to Salute

Salute all officers, of all U.S. services and all allied foreign services. Officers in the U.S. Merchant Marine and Public Health Service wear uniforms that closely resemble Navy uniforms, and they too rate a salute.

When chief or senior petty officers perform duties normally assigned to an officer—such as standing JOOD (junior officer of the deck) watches or taking a division muster—they rate the same salute as an officer.

There is one simple rule for saluting: When in doubt, salute.

The Address

Addressing Officers

Officers are always addressed and referred to by their title or rank, such as Admiral, Captain, or Commander. If several officers of the same rank are together, it is proper to use both title and name, such as Admiral Taylor or Captain Smith, to avoid confusion. Officers of the rank of lieutenant commander and below, midshipmen, and aviation cadets are addressed as Mister or Miss.

By tradition, the commanding officer of any ship or station, no matter what his or her rank, is addressed and referred to as Captain. The executive officer, likewise, is Commander. Other captains or commanders in the same command should be addressed by rank and name.

An officer in the Medical Corps or Dental Corps is addressed and referred to by title, or as Doctor. A chaplain may be called Chaplain no matter what the rank.

Army, Air Force, and Marine Corps officers are addressed and referred to by their ranks.

Addressing Enlisted Personnel

A chief petty officer is addressed as Chief Petty Officer Smith, or more informally as Chief Smith, or as Chief if you do not know his or her name. But in recruit training, all chiefs acting as company commanders rate Mister/Miss and Sir/Ma'am. Master and senior chief petty officers are customarily addressed and referred to as Master Chief Smith, or Senior Chief Smith, or Master Chief or Senior Chief if you do not know their names.

Other petty officers are addressed and referred to by their specific rates. Nonrated personnel—those in paygrades E-1 through E-3—are addressed and referred to as Seaman Wells, or Fireman Clifton, regardless of their specific paygrade.

In the military, rank establishes the order of introduction: introduce the junior to the senior, regardless of either one's sex. Navy personnel, regardless of rank or sex, are introduced to a chaplain.

Flags and Flag Etiquette

Salutes to the American flag are prescribed in U.S. Navy Regulations, article 1007, as follows:

Each person in the naval service, coming on board a ship of the Navy, must salute the national ensign. He or she stops on reaching the upper platform of the accommodation ladder, or the shipboard end of the brow, faces the national ensign, renders the salute, and then salutes the officer of the deck. On leaving the ship, each person renders the salutes in inverse order. The officer of the deck returns both salutes in each case.

When passed by or passing the national ensign being carried in a military formation, all persons in the naval service must salute. Those in vehicles or boats follow the procedure prescribed for morning and evening colors.

The salutes prescribed in this article must also be rendered to foreign national ensigns and aboard foreign men-of-war.

Colors

The ceremony of hoisting the national ensign and union jack at 0800 and lowering them at sunset on ships in port is referred to as morning colors and evening colors. Shore stations make colors but do not fly the jack. All ships follow the motions of the senior officer present afloat (SOPA) in making colors. At 0755, "first call" is sounded on the bugle. (Ships without a bugle may play a recording, or the boatswain's mate of the watch may pipe and pass the word, "First call to colors.")

At 0800, the bugle sounds "Attention," then "To the colors," and the ensign and jack, respectively, are hoisted to the top of the flagstaff. If the ship has a band, the national anthem is played. Aboard ships with no bands or bugle, a whistle signal and the words "Attention to colors" are passed. At the end of the music, "Carry on" is passed or whistle signals are made.

The procedure for evening colors is the same, with first call sounded at five minutes to sunset. This can vary from about 1700 to 2100, according to time of year and latitude.

During colors everyone within sight or hearing renders honors. Personnel outside cease work, face the colors, and salute until the last note of the anthem. Passengers in a boat, seated or standing, remain at attention. The boat officer or coxswain salutes. Persons wearing civilian clothes or athletic gear stop and face the colors at attention. If a hat is worn, it should be held in the right hand, over the heart. If no hat is worn, salute by holding the right hand over the heart. A woman in civilian clothes, with or without a hat, stands at attention and places her right hand over her heart. Drivers of motor vehicles pull over and stop if traffic safety permits.

Shifting Colors

On unmooring, the instant the last mooring line leaves the pier or the anchor is aweigh, the boatswain's mate of the watch (BMOW) will blow a long whistle blast and pass the word to shift colors. The jack and ensign, if flying, will be hauled down smartly. At the same instant, the "steaming" ensign will be hoisted on the gaff and the ship's call sign and other signal flags will be hoisted or broken. On mooring, the moment the anchor is let go or the first mooring line is made fast on the pier, the BMOW passes the word to shift colors, the ship's call sign and the steaming ensign are hauled down, and the jack and ensign are raised.

Ships under way do not make morning or evening colors, but they do fly a steaming ensign at the gaff from sunrise to sunset. The jack is not flown at sea.

The ensign is sometimes flown at half-mast as a tribute to the dead. Whenever the ensign is to be half-masted, it is first closed up and then lowered to the half-mast position. The same procedure is used when lowering the ensign; it first must be closed up and then lowered.

On Memorial Day, the ensign is half-masted from 0800 until completion of the 21-gun salute fired at 1200, or until 1220 if no salute is fired.

During burial at sea, the ensign is at half-mast from the beginning of the funeral service until the body is committed to the deep.

Dipping

Merchant ships "salute" Navy ships by dipping their ensigns. When a merchant ship of any nation formally recognized by the United States salutes a ship of the U.S. Navy, she

Figure 5–1   Crewmen honor colors on board a guided-missile cruiser.

lowers her national colors to half-mast. The Navy ship, at her closest point of approach, lowers the ensign to half-mast for a few seconds, then closes it up, after which the merchant ship raises her own flag. If the salute is made when the ensign is not displayed, the Navy ship will hoist her colors, dip for the salute, close them up again, and then haul them down after a suitable interval. Naval vessels dip the ensign only to answer a salute; they never salute first.

Flags

Union Jack

The union jack is a replica of the blue, star-studded field of the national ensign; it is flown by ships at anchor from 0800 to sunset. The jack is hoisted at a yardarm when a general court-martial or a court of inquiry is in session. It is half-masted if the ensign is half-masted, but it is not dipped when the ensign is dipped.

Commission Pennant

The commission pennant is long and narrow, with seven white stars on a patch of blue field nearest the hoist. The rest of the pennant is divided lengthwise, red on top and white below. It flies from the time a ship is commissioned until she is decommissioned (except as noted below); it is hoisted at the after truck or, aboard a mastless ship, at the highest and most conspicuous point of hoist. A commission pennant is also flown from the bow of the boat in which the commanding officer makes an official visit. The commission pennant is not flown when a ship flies a personal flag or command pennant.

The commission pennant is not a personal flag, but sometimes it is regarded as the personal symbol of the commanding officer. Along with the ensign and the union jack, it is half-masted on the death of the ship's commanding officer. When a ship is decommissioned, the commanding officer keeps the commission pennant.

A ship carrying the officer who commands a fleet or unit of a fleet flies the personal flag of that officer from the main truck at all times, unless the officer is absent for more than seventy-two hours. This is a blue flag with four white stars for an admiral, three for a vice admiral, two for a rear admiral (upper half), and one for a rear admiral (lower half).

Command Pennants

An officer below flag rank, when in command of a force, flotilla, squadron, carrier or cruiser-destroyer group, aircraft wing or carrier air wing, flies a broad command pennant, white with blue stripes top and bottom. An officer in command of any other unit, such as an aircraft squadron, flies a burgee command pennant, which is white with red stripes top and bottom.

Absence Indicators

When a commanding officer or any flag officer is absent, an absentee pennant is flown. The absence of an admiral or unit commander whose personal flag or pennant is flying is indicated by the "first substitute indicator," flown from the starboard yardarm. The second substitute, flown from the port yardarm, indicates that the chief of staff is absent. The third substitute, also flown from the port yardarm, indicates the absence of the commanding officer. (If the commanding officer is to be gone more than seventy-two hours, the pennant shows the absence of the executive officer.) The fourth substitute means that the civil or military official whose flag is flying (such as the secretary of defense) is absent. It is flown from the starboard yardarm.

Church Pennant

The church pennant is the only flag ever flown over the national ensign at the same point of hoist. It is displayed during church services conducted by a chaplain, both ashore and afloat.

Other Flags and Pennants

Both in port and at sea, ships fly many single flags or pennants with special meanings. The SOPA may prescribe certain flag hoists for local use, such as a request for a garbage lighter or a water barge. At anchor, ships awarded the Presidential Unit Citation (PUC), Navy Unit Commendation (NUC), or Meritorious Unit Commendation (MUC) fly the pennant at the foretruck from sunrise to sunset.

Honors

Gun Salute

In the old days it took as long as twenty minutes to load and fire a gun, so that when a ship fired her guns in salute, rendering herself powerless for the duration, it was a friendly gesture.

The gun salutes prescribed by Navy regulations are fired only by ships and stations designated by the secretary of the Navy. A national salute of twenty-one guns is fired on Washington's Birthday, Memorial Day, and Independence Day, and to honor the president of the United States and heads of foreign states. Salutes for naval officers are as follows: admiral, seventeen guns; vice admiral, fifteen guns; rear admiral (upper half), thirteen guns; rear admiral (lower half), eleven guns. Salutes are fired at intervals of five seconds, and always in odd numbers.

Figure 5–2 Crewmembers man the rails before their ship renders honors.

Manning the Rail

This custom evolved from the centuries-old practice of "manning the yards." Men aboard sailing ships stood evenly spaced on all the yards and gave three cheers to honor a distinguished person. Now men and women are stationed along the rails and superstructure of a ship when honors are rendered to the president, the head of a foreign state, or the member of a reigning royal family. Men and women so stationed do not salute.

Dressing and Full-Dressing Ship

Commissioned ships are "full-dressed" on Washington's Birthday and Independence Day, and "dressed" on other national holidays.

When a ship is dressed, the national ensign is flown from the flagstaff and usually from each masthead. When a ship is full-dressed, in addition to the ensigns a "rainbow" of signal flags is displayed from bow to stern over the mastheads, or as nearly so as the construction of the ship permits. Ships not under way are dressed from 0800 to sunset; ships under way do not dress until they come to anchor during that period.

Passing Honors

Passing honors are ordered by ships and boats when vessels, embarked officials, or embarked officers pass (or are passed) close aboard—600 yards for ships, 400 yards for boats.

Such honors are exchanged between ships of the U.S. Navy, between ships of the Navy and the Coast Guard, and between U.S. and most foreign navy ships passing close aboard. "Attention" is sounded, and the hand salute is rendered by all

persons in view on deck (not in ranks).

Smaller ships use whistle signals when rendering honors. One blast indicates attention to starboard; two blasts indicate attention to port. Subsequent commands are one blast for hand salute, two blasts for ending the salute, and three blasts for carrying on.

The National Anthem

When the national anthem is played, sailors stand at attention and face the direction of the music. If the anthem is played at colors, those present face the ensign. When covered, they salute from the sounding of the first note to the last. Those in ranks salute together, on command. Persons in vehicles or in boats remain seated or standing; only the boat officer or the coxswain stands and salutes.

The same marks of respect prescribed during the playing of the national anthem are shown during the playing of a foreign national anthem. If you are uncovered, in uniform, it is customary to stand at attention during the playing of U.S. or foreign anthems.

If you are in civilian clothes and covered, remove your hat with your right hand and place it over your heart.

There are many occasions besides colors when honors are rendered to the ensign or national anthem. The usual rule is if the flag is displayed, face it. If the flag is not displayed, face the music. Hold the salute until the music has stopped or the flag has been hoisted or lowered, or has passed.

The Quarterdeck

The quarterdeck is that part of the ship designated by the commanding officer for official and ceremonial functions. It is normally on the main deck, but this may vary according to the type of ship. It is marked off by appropriate lines, deck markings, decorative cartridge cases, or fancy work, and is always kept particularly clean and shipshape. Observe these rules concerning the quarterdeck:

Watchstanders on the quarterdeck must be in the uniform of the day and present a smart and military appearance at all times.

Personnel not in the uniform of the day may appear on or cross the quarterdeck only as their work requires.

Aboard large ships with well-defined quarterdeck limits, salute every time you enter the quarterdeck.

Figure 5–3 Side boys render honors as a flag officer disembarks a nuclear-powered ballistic-missile submarine.

Do not smoke or engage in any recreational athletics on the quarterdeck except by permission of the captain, and then only after working hours.

Never walk on the starboard side of the quarterdeck except in the performance of quarterdeck-watch duty.

The starboard gangway to the quarterdeck is used by all commissioned officers, warrant officers, and their visitors; the port gangway is used by enlisted personnel, their visitors, workers, and other civilians. Changes in this rule are made at the discretion of the commanding officer. In heavy weather, the lee gangway is used by everyone. Flagships are sometimes equipped with an additional starboard gangway used by the embarked flag officer (admiral) and senior officers of the flag officer's staff. Aboard small ships with only one gangway, it may be rigged to either side and is used by all hands.

Side Boys

Side boys are a part of the quarterdeck ceremonies when an important person or officer comes on board or leaves a ship. Large ships have side boys detailed to the quarterdeck from 0800 to sunset. When the side is piped by the BMOW, from two to eight side boys, depending on the rank of the officer, will form a passageway at the gangway. They salute on the first note of the pipe and finish together on the last note.

Side boys must be particularly smart in appearance and well groomed, with polished shoes and immaculate uniforms. There is nothing in Navy regulations stating that side boys must be male. When side boys are required in ceremonies ashore, enlisted women may be, and have been, detailed. (Yes, they're still called side boys!)

Shipboard Customs

The quarterdeck is the most important place on a ship in port, but when the ship gets under way, the bridge becomes the center of operations. Like the quarterdeck, the bridge is a place where only those on watch are permitted.

Many ships require all nonwatch personnel to request permission from the officer of the deck (OOD) to come on the bridge, accompanying their request with a salute. If the captain

Figure 5–4 With a huge Spanish sombrero applied to her sail, the USS *Mariano G. Vallejo* (SSBN 658) goes down the ways at Mare Island, California.

is on the bridge, officers and civilians—and on some ships, senior enlisted personnel—will make a point of greeting him at this time.

Boarding or Leaving Ship

The OOD or the JOOD, who may be either an officer or senior petty officer, will meet all persons leaving or boarding the ship. Usually the OOD will attend the starboard side, the JOOD the port side. There are definite procedures to be used at all times on boarding or leaving a ship; learn them.

Boarding Your Own Ship: At the gangway, if the ensign is flying, salute in its direction, then turn to the OOD or the OOD's representative, salute, and say, "I request permission to come aboard, sir/ma'am." The OOD will return both salutes and say, "Very well."

Leaving Your Own Ship: Salute the OOD and say, "I request permission to leave the ship, sir/ma'am." If you are going to the pier to work and do not need the permission of your division officer and the executive officer, you salute and say, "I request permission to go on the pier to (state your task), sir/ma'am." When the OOD says "Permission granted" and returns your salute, drop your salute and step to the gangway. If the ensign is flying, salute in its direction and leave.

Boarding a Ship Other Than Your Own: Stop at the top of the gangway, salute the ensign if it is flying, then turn to the OOD or representative, salute, and say, "I request permission to come aboard, sir/ma'am." You may be asked to identify yourself or state your business before the OOD salutes and says, "Permission granted (denied)."

Leaving a Ship Other Than Your Own: Salute the OOD or representative and say, "With your permission, sir/ma'am, I shall leave the ship." After the OOD has said, "Permission granted," and returned your salute, step to the gangway and, if the ensign is flying, salute in its direction before leaving.

In a Party of People: Only the person in charge makes the request to the OOD to board and leave ship. All salute the ensign, if it is flying, and the OOD, both coming and going.

Crossing Nests: Destroyers and smaller ships sometimes tie up in nests (clusters) alongside a tender or pier, and you may have to cross several ships to get to your own. The usual quarterdeck procedure described for boarding and leaving a ship does not apply when crossing a ship, but there is still a

procedure to be followed. When you board the inboard ship,

salute the colors and the quarterdeck and, addressing the quarterdeck watch, say, "Permission to cross." Do not salute the quarterdeck or colors on leaving. Repeat this procedure on each ship until you reach your own. If you are going from your ship in a nest to the pier or tender, this procedure is reversed; after you leave your own ship, request permission to cross from the quarterdeck watch on each inboard ship.

Divine Services

When divine services are held on board, the church pennant is flown, and word is passed that services are being held in a certain space of the ship and to maintain quiet about the decks. A person entering the area where services are held uncovers, even if the person is on watch and wearing a duty belt and sidearm. There is one exception: remain covered for a Jewish ceremony.

Sick Bay

In the days of sailing ships, it was customary to uncover when entering sick bay, out of respect to the dying and dead. Though modern medicine has transformed the sickbay into a place where people are usually healed and cured, the custom remains. As in any hospital, silence is maintained. Smoking is usually not permitted in sick bay, partly because the oxygen used for medical purposes is a fire hazard.

103

Officers' and CPO Country

Officers' country includes all staterooms and the wardroom. CPO (chief petty officer) country includes CPOs' living spaces and mess. Do not enter these areas except on business, and do not use their passageways as thoroughfares or shortcuts. When entering the wardroom, or any compartment or office in officer or CPO country, uncover. Watchstanders wearing a duty belt or sidearm remain covered, unless a meal is in progress. Always knock before entering any officer's or CPO's room.

Enlisted Mess Deck

The mess deck for enlisted personnel is treated with the same courtesy as the wardroom. Always uncover when on or crossing mess decks, even if you are on watch and wearing the duty belt.

Boat Etiquette

Boat Vehicle and Passageway Manners

The basic rule in Navy manners, as in civilian life, is to make way for a senior quickly, quietly, and without confusion.

The procedure for entering boats and vehicles is seniors in last and out first. The idea is that the captain should not have to wait in a boat for anyone. Seniors get out first because normally their business is more important and pressing than that of the men and women under them.

A ship is judged by her boats and their crews. Whether in dungarees or dress blues, crews should observe the courtesies and procedures that build and maintain their ship's reputation. Boats play an important part in naval ceremonies, and each crewmember ought to know what is expected of the boat and of him or her. In general, boats exchange salutes when passing, as enlisted personnel and officers do when passing on shore.

It is not the size or type of boat that determines seniority, but who is embarked; a whaleboat carrying a commander is senior to a large boat with only an ensign aboard.

When one boat passes another carrying an officer, the coxswain and the boat officer, if embarked, render the hand salute. Others in the boat stand or sit at attention. If standing, they face the boat being saluted; if seated, they sit at attention but do not turn toward the passing boat. It is usually possible to tell by the uniform of the passenger officer or the flag flown which boat is senior. If in doubt, salute.

The senior officer in the boat salutes if he or she is visible outboard. Officers do not rise when saluting.

Boats passing U.S. or foreign men-of-war during colors on board must lay to.

Only the boat officer—or, if the boat officer is absent, the coxswain—stands at attention and salutes if safety permits. All others remain seated at attention.

If the boat is carrying an officer or official for whom a salute is being fired, the engine is slowed and the clutch disengaged after the first gun is fired, and the person honored rises.

Salutes While Not Under Way

A boat is not under way when it is anchored, moored, or lying at a boom, gangway, or landing. It is considered under way if it is merely stopped dead in the water, as when standing off from a ship or dock waiting to be called.

The rules of saluting while not under way are as follows:

Figure 5–5   Senior Navy officers salute the colors during an official full-dress
gathering.

Only the person in charge of the boat salutes.

Coxswains in charge of boats salute when officers enter or
leave their boats, unless there is an emergency. The coxswain
also salutes when the officer in his or her boat salutes or returns a salute. The coxswain salutes at the same time the officer salutes, and not before.

Personnel working aboard a boat do not salute unless attention is sounded.

Personnel seated in boats in which there is no officer, petty
officer, or acting petty officer in charge, rise and salute the
officers passing near. When an officer, petty officer, or acting
petty officer is in charge of a boat, he or she alone renders the
salute.

Enlisted personnel seated well forward in a large boat do not
rise and salute when officers enter or leave the stern sheets.
Enlisted personnel in the after section of a boat always rise and
salute when a commissioned officer enters or leaves.

Other Courtesies

The command "Gangway!" should be given by anyone who
observes an officer approaching where passage is blocked. The
courtesy is also extended to important civilians. The senior
petty officer present must be responsible for clearing the gangway properly and promptly. Enlisted personnel do not clear a

passage for themselves or other enlisted crewmembers in this way, but they should say, "Coming through."

The command "Attention" should be given, if possible, when officers are escorting visitors through their own ship. Attention and gangway commands must be strictly obeyed, whether the visitors are officers or civilians. If the party does not intend to move on promptly, the passing dignitary should give the order to carry on.

Do not overtake and pass an officer without permission. When it is necessary to walk past an officer, overtake him or her on his or her left side, salute when you are abreast, and ask, "By your leave, sir/ma'am?" When the officer returns the salute and says, "Very well," or "Permission granted," you drop your salute and continue past.

When walking with a senior, always walk on that person's left; that is, with the senior on your right. When walking with a woman, it is customary to have her on your right side, which is the position of honor. When a man and woman, both in uniform, are walking together, the man may insist that the woman walk on the right side even though she is junior. If so, she should defer to her senior's preference and accept the honor.

Sentry Duties and Recruit Drills

6

One of the first military duties a recruit will perform is a sentry or security watch. Security means protecting a ship or station against damage by storm or fire, and guarding against theft, sabotage, and other subversive activities. Chapter 7 discusses security in greater detail.

Security involves sentry duty, guard duty, fire watches, and barracks watches. *Sentry duty* is formal military duty governed by specific orders. *Guard duty* may be the same as sentry duty, or a guard may be permitted to relax military bearing, so long as he or she is on the job and ready to act. A *fire watch* may mean covering an assigned area on foot or in a vehicle, or it may mean assignment to a certain place for a specified period. A *barracks watch* may mean standing sentry duty, or merely being available to answer a phone, check people in and out, turn lights off and on, and preserve order and cleanliness.

Requirements for standing sentry duty are the same as those for all watches: keep alert, attend to duty, report all violations, preserve order, and remain on watch until properly relieved. The basic rules or orders for sentries are the same for all security watches.

Being detailed to a sentry watch involves two sets of orders: special orders and general orders. *Special orders* apply to a specific type of watch. They will be passed on and explained to you by the petty officer of the watch or the petty officer of the guard. *General orders* never change. You will—on any watch or duty, now and in the future—be responsible for carrying them out, even if no one has explained them to you or reminded you of them. The eleven general orders, with a brief explanation of each, follow. Memorize them and be ready to recite them whenever called on to do so.

The General Orders

1. To take charge of this post and all government property in view.

2. To walk my post in a military manner, keeping always on the alert and observing everything that takes place within sight or hearing.

3. To report all violations of orders I am instructed to enforce.

4. To repeat all calls from posts more distant from the guardhouse than my own.

5. To quit my post only when properly relieved.

6. To receive, obey, and pass on to the sentry who relieves me all orders from the commanding officer, command duty officer, officer of the deck, and officers and petty officers of the watch.

7. To talk to no one except in the line of duty.

8. To give the alarm in case of fire or disorder.

9. To call the officer of the deck in any case not covered by instructions.

10. To salute all officers, and all colors and standards not cased.

11. To be especially watchful at night, and during the time for challenging, to challenge all persons on or near my post, and to allow no one to pass without proper authority.

Orders 1, 2, and 3 mean that all persons in the service, whatever their ranks, are required to respect you in the performance of your duties as a sentinel and a member of the guard.

Report immediately, by telephone or other means, every unusual or suspicious event.

Apprehend and turn over to proper authority all suspicious persons involved in a disorder on or near your post, and anyone who tries to enter your post without authority.

Report violations of orders when you are inspected or relieved. If it is urgent and necessary, apprehend the offender and call the petty officer of the guard.

Order 4 means that you "pass the word" by calling "Petty officer of the guard, no. —," giving him or her the number of your post, when you need that person for any purpose other than relief, fire, or disorder.

Order 5 means that if you become sick or for any reason must leave your post, you call "Petty officer of the guard, no. —, relief." Do not leave your post for meals or other reasons unless properly relieved. If your relief is late, telephone or call the petty officer, but do not leave your post.

Order 6 names the officers whose orders you must obey. However, any officer can investigate apparent violations of regulations when he or she observes them.

Give up possession of your rifle only on receiving a direct order to do so from a person authorized to give you orders while you are on your post. No other person may require a sentinel to hand over his or her rifle or even require it to be inspected.

Order 7 is self-explanatory. When challenging or holding conversations with any person, take the position of "port arms" if you are armed with a rifle, the position of "raise pistol" if you are armed with a pistol.

Order 8 means that if fire is discovered, you must immediately call, "Fire, no. —," then turn in the alarm or make sure it has been turned in. If possible, put out the fire.

Order 10 covers saluting. (For more details on saluting, see p. 91.) A sentry salutes as follows: If walking post, he or she halts. If armed with a rifle, he or she salutes by presenting arms. If otherwise armed, he or she renders the hand salute. On patrol duty, he or she does not halt, unless spoken to, but renders the hand salute. In a sentry box, he or she stands at attention in the doorway upon the approach of the person or party involved and renders the hand salute (or, if armed with a rifle, presents arms).

When required to challenge, a sentry salutes an officer as soon as the officer is recognized.

A sentry salutes an officer as he or she comes on the post. When an officer stops to talk, the sentry assumes the position of port arms if armed with a rifle, or the position of attention throughout the conversation, and salutes again when the officer leaves.

When talking to an officer, the sentry does not interrupt to salute another officer unless the officer being addressed salutes. Then the sentry follows his or her example.

When the flag is raised at morning colors or lowered at evening colors, the sentry stands at attention at the first note of the national anthem or the call to colors and salutes. A sentry engaged in a duty that would be hampered doesn't have to salute. The sentry should face the flag while saluting, but if duty requires he or she may face in another direction.

Order 11 means when a person or party approaches a post during challenging hours, the sentry should advance rapidly toward them and at thirty paces challenge sharply, "Halt! Who is there?" Unless circumstances prevent it, the sentry should continue to advance while challenging. The sentry then assumes the best position to pass or apprehend the person and requires the person to advance, remain stationary, or face the light to determine whether he or she should be allowed to pass or turned over to the guard.

If a person is in a vehicle, the same procedure holds. If necessary, the sentry may require the person to get out of the vehicle.

A sentry permits only one member of a group to approach. If the sentry is not satisfied with that person's identification, he or she detains the person and calls the petty officer of the guard.

When two or more individuals approach from different directions at the same time, the sentry challenges each in turn and requires each to halt until told to proceed.

A sentry must never let himself or herself be surprised, nor should he or she permit two persons to advance at the same time.

A sentry should always say, "Advance one to be recognized." If the party has replied properly, the sentry says, "Advance, friend (or officer of the day, etc.)." As soon as recognition is certain, the sentry salutes and permits the person to pass.

Guard duties aboard ship will differ somewhat from those ashore. Some of the variations follow:

Where there are no marines, guard duty, if required, is performed by details from the ship's divisions and is known as the security watch.

The guard of the day is mustered only at morning and evening colors and in the daylight hours between the times honors are to be rendered.

Sentries do not challenge.

The guard does not raise nor lower the colors.

The guard, except the sentry on the brig post, is not responsible for any prisoners aboard ship.

The chief master-at-arms or his or her assistants always have access to prisoners.

The relief does not make the rounds of all posts as a unit when going on watch.

The petty officer of the guard visits sentinels when required by the commanding officer and as directed by the officer of the deck.

Use Of Weapons

Besides sentry and guard duties, others who may be armed are the guard mail officer, brig or prisoner guards, pay-line guards, gangway watches, and in some cases, shore patrols. Armed personnel are authorized to fire their weapons only under the following conditions:

To protect their own lives or the life of another person where no other means of defense will work.
To prevent the escape of a prisoner likely to cause death or serious bodily harm to another.
To prevent sabotage, arson, or other crimes against the government after all other means have failed.

No one is to be assigned to any duty requiring the use of a weapon until he or she has been properly trained and instructed in it, including all safety precautions.

111

Drill Commands

Preparatory commands are indicated in this section by *italic letters*, commands of execution by all CAPITAL LETTERS.
There are two parts to a military drill command:

1. The preparatory command, such as *Hand*, indicates the movement that is to be executed.
2. The command of execution, such as SALUTE, brings about the desired movement.

When appropriate, the preparatory command includes the name or title of the group concerned, as *First Division, hand* SALUTE.''
In certain commands, the preparatory command and the command of execution are combined, for example, FALL IN, AT EASE, and REST.
To call back or revoke a command or to begin again a movement that was not intended, give the command AS YOU WERE. The movement is supposed to stop and the former position is taken.

Figure 6–1 Navy recruits pass in review bearing M-1 rifles at the Recruit Training Command, San Diego.

The Positions

Position of Attention: A-*ten*-HUT or FALL IN. Heels close together, feet turned out to form an angle of 45 degrees, knees straight, hips level, body erect, with the weight resting equally on the heels and balls of the feet. Shoulders squared, chest arched, arms hanging down without stiffness so that the thumbs are along the seams of the trousers, palms and fingers relaxed. Head erect, chin drawn in, and eyes to the front. In coming to attention, the heels are brought together smartly and audibly.

The Rests: FALL OUT, REST, AT EASE, and (1) *Parade,* (2) REST.

FALL OUT. All hands break rank but remain nearby. All hands return to places and come to attention at the command FALL IN.

REST. Right foot is kept in place. Sailors are silent but may move about.

(1) *Parade,* (2) REST. Move the left foot smartly 12 inches to the left from the right foot. At the same time, clasp the hands behind the back, palms to the rear, the right hand clasping the left thumb, arms hanging naturally. Be silent and be still.

To resume attention from any rest other than FALL OUT the command is, for example, (1) *Detail,* (2) *A-ten-*HUT.

Eyes Right or Left: The commands are (1) *Eyes,* (2) RIGHT (or LEFT), (3) *Ready,* (4) FRONT. At the command RIGHT, each man or woman turns his or her head and eyes smartly to the right. Those on the extreme right file keep head and eyes to the front. At the command FRONT, head and eyes turn smartly to the front. The opposite is carried out for *eyes* LEFT.

Hand Salute: (1) *Hand,* (2) SALUTE, (3) TWO. The command TWO is used only when saluting by command. At the command SALUTE, raise the right hand smartly in the hand salute, then turn the head and eyes toward the person saluted. At the command TWO, drop the arm to its normal position by the side in one movement and turn the head and eyes to the front. While passing in review, execute the hand salute in the same way. Hold the salute until you are six paces beyond the person saluted.

Facings

Right or Left Face: (1) *Right* (*Left*), (2) FACE. At the command FACE, slightly raise the left heel and right toe. Face right, turning on the right heel, putting pressure on the ball of the left foot and holding the left leg straight. Then place the left foot smartly beside the right one.

Half Right or Left: (1) *Right* (or *Left, Half*), (2) FACE. Execute half face as prescribed above, turning only 45 degrees.

About Face: (1) *About,* (2) FACE. At the command, place the toe of the right foot about half a foot to the rear and slightly to the left of the left heel without moving the left foot. Put the weight of the body mainly on the heel of the left foot, right leg straight. Then turn to the rear, moving to the right on the left heel and on the ball of the right foot. Place the right heel beside the left to complete the movement.

Steps and March Commands

All movements executed from the halt, except right step, begin with the left foot. Forward, half step, halt, and mark time may be executed one from the other in quick or double time.

The following table prescribes the length in inches and the cadence in steps per minute of steps in marching.

Step	Time	Length	Cadence
Full	Quick	30	120
Full	Double	36	180
Full	Slow	30	—
Half	Quick	15	120
Half	Double	18	180
Side	Quick	12	120
Back	Quick	15	120

The full/slow step is executed only as a funeral escort approaches the place of internment. The cadence, in accordance with that set by the band, varies with different airs that may be played.

All commands of execution are given on the foot, right or left, in the direction of the movement. For example, if the march is to be to the right—as (1) *By the right flank,* (2) MARCH—the command MARCH is given on the right foot.

Quick Time: All steps and movements are executed in quick time, which is what most people understand as normal marching pace, unless the unit is marching double time, or unless double time is added to the command. Example: (1) *Squad right, double time,* (2) *March.*

Marching: At halt, to march forward in quick time, the commands are (1) *Forward,* (2) MARCH. At the command *Forward,* shift the weight of your body to the right leg. At the command MARCH, step off smartly with the left foot and continue marching with 30-inch steps taken straight forward without stiffness or exaggeration. Swing the arms easily in their natural arcs about 6 inches straight to the front and 3 inches to the rear of the body.

Figure 6–2 A woman recruit acts as flag bearer during graduation ceremonies at the Naval Training Center, Orlando.

Double Time: To march in double time, the commands are (1) *Double time*, (2) MARCH.

If at halt, at the command *Double time,* shift the weight of the body to the right leg. At the command MARCH, raise the forearms, fingers closed, knuckles out, to a horizontal position along the waistline, and take up an easy run with the step and cadence of double time, allowing the arms to take a natural swinging motion across the front of the body. Be sure to keep the forearms horizontal.

If marching in quick time, at the command (1) *Double time,* (2) MARCH, given as either foot strikes the ground, take one more step in quick time and then step off in double time.

To resume the quick time from double time, the commands are (1) *Quick time* and (2) MARCH. At the command MARCH, given as either foot strikes the ground, advance and plant the other foot in double time, then resume the quick time, dropping the hands by the sides.

Halt: The commands are (1) *Squad (Platoon, Company),* (2) HALT.

When marching in quick time, at the command HALT, given as either foot strikes the ground, execute the halt in two counts by advancing and planting the other foot and then bringing up the rear foot.

When marching in double time, at the command HALT, given as either foot strikes the ground, advance and plant the other foot as in double time, then halt in two counts as in quick time.

When executing right step or left step, at the command HALT, given as the heels are together, plant the foot next in cadence and come to a halt when the heels are next brought together.

Mark Time: The commands are (1) *Mark time,* (2) MARCH.

Being in march, at the command MARCH, given as either foot strikes the ground, advance and plant the other foot. Then bring up the rear foot, placing it so that both heels are in line, and continue the cadence by alternately raising and planting each foot.

Being at a halt, at the command MARCH, raise and plant first the left foot, then the right as described before.

Mark time may be executed in either quick-time cadence or double-time cadence. While marking time, any errors in alignment should be corrected.

The halt is executed from mark time, as from quick time or double time. Forward march, halt, and mark time may be executed one from the other in quick time or double time.

Half Step: The commands are (1) *Half step,* (2) MARCH.

Being in march at the command MARCH, take steps of 15 inches in quick time instead of the normal 30 inches. The half step is executed in quick time only.

To resume the full step from half step, the commands are (1) *Forward* (2) MARCH.

Right Step: The commands are (1) *Right step,* (2) MARCH. At the command MARCH, carry the right foot 12 inches to the right. Then place the left foot beside the right, left knee straight. Continue in the cadence of quick time. The right step is executed in quick time from a halt for short distances only.

Left Step: The commands are (1) *Left step,* (2) MARCH. At the command MARCH, carry the left foot 12 inches to the left. Then place the right foot beside the left, right knee straight. Continue in the cadence of quick time. The left step is executed in quick time from a halt for short distances only.

Back Step: The commands are (1) *Backward,* (2) MARCH. At the command MARCH, take steps of 15 inches straight to the rear. The back step is executed in quick time for short distances only.

To Face to the Right (or Left) in Marching: The commands are (1) *By the right* (or left) *flank,* (2) MARCH.

To face to the right in marching and advance from a halt, at the command MARCH, turn to the right on the ball of the right foot. At the same time, step off with the left foot in the new direction with a half or full step in quick time or double time as the case may be.

To face to the right in marching and advance, at the command MARCH, which is given as the right foot strikes the ground, advance and plant the left foot. Then face to the right in marching and step off with the right foot in the new direction with a half or full step in quick or double time as the case may be.

To face to the left, reverse directions for the above instructions.

To Face to the Rear in Marching: The commands are (1) *To the rear,* (2) MARCH.

In march at quick time, at the command MARCH, given as the right foot strikes the ground, advance and plant the left foot. Then turn to the right all the way about on the balls of both feet and immediately step off with the left foot.

In march at double time, at the command MARCH, given as the right foot strikes the ground, advance two steps in the original direction. Then turn to the right all the way about while taking four steps in place, keeping cadence; then step off.

To Change Step: The commands are (1) *Change step,* (2) MARCH.

Being in march in quick time, at the command MARCH, given as the right foot strikes the ground, advance and plant the left foot. Then plant the toe of the right foot near the heel of the left and step off with the left foot.

The same movement may be executed on the right foot by giving the command of execution as the left foot strikes the

118

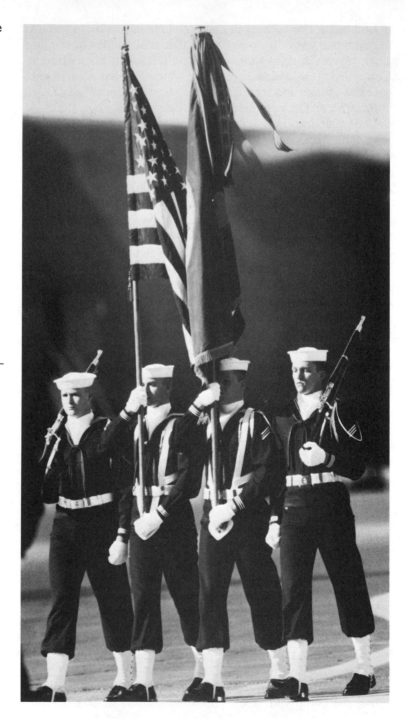

ground and planting the right foot. Then plant the toe of the left foot near the heel of the right and step off with the right foot.

To March at Ease: The commands are (1) *At ease,* (2) MARCH. At the command MARCH, all hands adopt an easy natural stride, without having to keep in step or a regular cadence. But they are still required to maintain silence.

To March at Route Step: The commands are (1) *Route step,* (2) MARCH. At the command MARCH, all hands adopt an easy natural stride; there is no requirement to keep step or a regular cadence, or to maintain silence.

Figure 6–3 Members of the Navy color guard perform at parades, funerals, and other official military functions. Members must be able to march precisely and present a spit-and-polish appearance at all times.

Security of Information **7**

The word *security*, as it is used in the Navy, can mean many things, but its most common usage refers to the safeguarding of classified information. Security can also mean the protection of ships and stations or property, which will be discussed later in relation to external security (pp. 129–30).

Because the safety of the United States in general, and of naval operations in particular, depends greatly on the protection of classified information, it is important that you understand what classified information is, who may have access to it, some rules for safeguarding it, and the penalties for security violations.

Security Classification

Information is classified when the interests of national security are at risk. It is assigned a classification designation, which tells you how much protection it requires. There are three classification designations—top secret, secret, and confidential—to indicate the anticipated degree of damage to national security that could result from unauthorized disclosure. The expected impact for each designation is as follows: top secret—exceptionally grave damage; secret—serious damage; and confidential—damage. Regardless of the level, all classified information must be protected against unauthorized disclosure. Unauthorized disclosure, or "compromise," means that classified information becomes available to a person not authorized to have it.

There is another category of information, for official use only (FOUO). This is not classified information (it does not involve national security), but it cannot be divulged to everyone. Results of investigations, examination questions, bids on contracts, etc., are "privileged information," kept from general knowledge under the designation FOUO.

Classification

Marking of Material

All classified material—publications, equipment, films, etc.—is plainly marked or stamped with its classification designation. Following the classification, some material may have additional markings that signal extra precautions in handling. For example, "restricted data" means that the material pertains to nuclear weapons or power and cannot be released to anyone who is not a U.S. citizen.

Security Clearance

Before a person is allowed to have access to classified information, he or she must have a security clearance. A security clearance is a determination that you are eligible for access to classified information up to the specified level—top secret, secret, or confidential. The standards for clearance are listed in the Information and Personnel Security Program Regulation (OPNAVINST 5510.1) or Security Manual, as it is commonly called. In general you must be trustworthy, of excellent character, and able to show discretion and good judgment. A person may be loyal to his or her country but unable to meet the standards for a position of trust and confidence. Conduct such as excessive drinking, gambling, promiscuity, and poor credit can lead to denial of clearance. This could cost a promotion. A clearance may be denied or revoked because of emotional disturbance, general ineptitude, drug abuse, general disciplinary causes, AWOL (absent without leave), or larceny.

An investigation is conducted to acquire information on which to base the security determination. A final top-secret clearance requires a satisfactory background investigation (BI). As a BI may take several months to complete, an interim clearance may be issued on the basis of a satisfactory national agency check (NAC) or the entrance NAC (ENTNAC), which is conducted on all first-term enlistees.

A final secret clearance is based on a NAC or ENTNAC. An interim clearance may be granted based on a check of the Defense Central Index of Investigations (DCII) by the Naval Security and Investigative Command, and a favorable review of the records available to the issuing command after the NAC or ENTNAC has been requested. The Navy currently plans to reinvestigate every 10 years everyone holding a secret clearance, beginning with those sailors who have held a secret

clearance the longest.

The investigative basis for a final, confidential clearance is also a NAC or ENTNAC. An interim confidential clearance may also be issued after a favorable local records review, while awaiting the results of a NAC or ENTNAC.

A favorable determination of your eligibility for access is recorded in your service record. If ever you lose your trustworthy status, your clearance eligibility will be revoked.

Access and Need to Know

Security clearances are granted only when access is necessary to perform official duties and only at the level of identified need-to-know. A security clearance at a particular level does not entitle you to information classified at that level in other locations or departments not related to your billet. When your duties no longer require access, or require a lower level of access, your security clearance is administratively withdrawn or lowered without prejudicing your future eligibility. Commanding officers may reinstate or adjust your security clearance as the need arises.

You are responsible for protecting any classified information you know. Before giving another person access to that information, it is *your* responsibility to determine that the person has the proper clearance and need to know, not the responsibility of the supplicant. Say, for example, that you have secret information on "The Flight of the Hummingbird." Two sailors, with secret clearances, ask you for the information. Proper authority has established that the first sailor needs the information to carry out his or her duties. The second sailor is only curious. Disclose the information only to the first sailor, who has a demonstrated need-to-know.

Safeguarding Information

Classified information or material is discussed, used, or stored only where adequate security measures are in effect. When removed from storage for use, it must be kept under the continuous observation of a cleared person. It is never left unattended.

Classified information may be communicated over secure circuits only; never discuss classified information on the telephone.

Classified material may not be removed from the command without permission. Authorized protective measures must be used when classified material is being sent or carried from one place to another and when it is being destroyed.

If you accidently come across some classified material—a letter, booklet, or device—that has been left unguarded, misplaced, or not secured, do not read or examine it or try to decide what to do with it. Notify your security manager or your commanding officer, then stand by to keep unauthorized personnel away until a responsible person arrives to take charge.

Aboard ship, depending on the type of equipment installed, there are various security areas, such as:

An Exclusion Area: Access to this area means access to classified information, because the equipment cannot be covered.

A Limited Area: This area has classified information a visitor could gain access to, such as uncovered gauges, machinery, etc.

A Controlled Area: This is next to, or surrounds, an exclusion or limited area. All of these areas are clearly marked by signs reading Security Area—Keep Out.

A proper topside (quarterdeck or gangway) watch, where everyone coming aboard must give proper identification, is in itself a controlled area. A person on watch in such an area must not be afraid to ask for identification. No responsible person in the Navy will object to being stopped politely but firmly until identified.

Don't talk about classified information to unauthorized persons, including family, friends, shipmates, and especially strangers. Classified information can be revealed unintentionally to unauthorized persons in many ways.

Bragging can snowball into a dangerous situation. A person brags to impress friends or family. Don't talk too freely. It is natural to talk with shipmates, but classified subjects should be avoided. The fact that you may be entrusted with certain classified information gives you no right to divulge it to anyone else.

In an argument, arising, for example, from a discussion of a news item, enthusiasm may cause a person to blurt out classified facts and figures to prove a point. Never add to a news story that appears incomplete, no matter how much you know. By doing so, you may divulge exactly what the Navy has tried to keep secret.

Threats to Security

Unfriendly foreign nations are always interested in classified information on new developments, weapons, techniques, and materials, as well as movements and the operating capabilities of ships and aircraft.

The people who collect such information cannot be stereotyped or categorized. That's why they succeed in their work. A person who has access to classified material should never talk to any stranger about any classified subjects. A foreign intelligence agent collects many odd little bits of information, some of which might not even make sense to the agent; but when they are all put together in the agent's own country, they may tell experts much more than the Navy wants them to know. Don't make their work easier for them.

When security breaks down, the Navy becomes vulnerable to sabotage and espionage. Especially vulnerable are factories and large hard-to-protect shipyards, piers, ships, planes, and stations.

The FBI and other agencies say that thousands of people, many of them American citizens, are associated with espionage. Someone attending an event such as the replenishing of a ship could sabotage the operation, even if only in a small way. Worse yet, they could do it without being detected.

So who is vulnerable to espionage tactics? You are if you talk about security matters at a booze fest while an agent is eavesdropping. Service people with relatives in communist countries aren't immune. Members of minorities can be tempted to divulge information if they feel the system within which they live isn't fair to them; and people with personal problems can be intimidated into doing favors for the enemy. The problems can be financial, drug-related, or sexual. Some people may feel a need for attention. If you have one of these problems and a stranger offers to solve it, you could be placed in the awkward position of accepting, without even knowing that your new friend is indeed from an unfriendly foreign nation. All this may sound like a scene from a James Bond movie, but it happens in real life—and during wars.

Here's how not to be exploited:

1. Don't talk about a sensitive job to people who don't need to know—not even to your family or friends.
2. Know how to handle classified material.

3. Don't be careless with carbons and typewriter ribbons used in connection with classified material. They're as classified as the original material.

4. Secure your working area before leaving if it has classified material.

5. If you have personal problems you feel might be exploited, use the chain of command to solve them. No one in the Navy is going to hit you over the head because you have a problem that might be solved by a senior petty officer or officer. If one of them can't help, go to the chaplain. Chaplains are in the service for more than promoting religion; they're there to help, whatever your problem is.

Any contact with a citizen of a communist-controlled country must be reported immediately. That includes contacts between ham radio operators, "pen pals," neighbors, or any other kind of contact. The contact will be reported to the Naval Investigative Service Command (NISC), which will then advise you of any further action. Such contacts are not, in themselves, wrong or illegal. It is just that NISC agents are the experts who will be able to evaluate the contact and tell whether it is an attempt to target you for espionage purposes.

If you suspect someone of gathering intelligence for an enemy, or if you suspect someone of violating security, report it. If someone is compromising the security of the Navy or of the United States, that person is compromising you. Who would you be without the security of the United States and the military? Reporting a security problem is not like "telling" on someone. It's protecting yourself and the country you serve.

What if you're confronted by a spy? Don't try to catch him or her. Just report the spy. If a citizen of an unfriendly nation tries to turn you against the United States, report that person.

Make reports by way of your chain of command. Every member of the chain has a superior. If you suspect someone in the chain of not being trustworthy enough to receive what you have to report, request permission to see the next higher-up. And the next, if necessary.

If you feel you can't approach the people in your chain of command, go to the NISC office. If you can't find one, look in the white pages of the phone book under U.S. Government, Naval Activities.

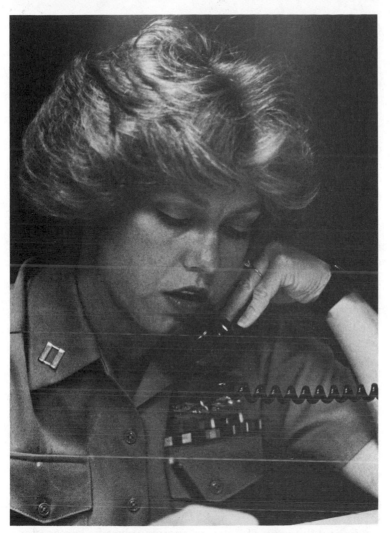

Figure 7–1   Classified information can be unintentionally revealed to unauthorized persons in many ways. Always be extremely cautious of everything you say when talking on an unsecure telephone line.

If you're going to make a report, make a note of the date, time, place, and nature of the encounter. Take names. Describe how you were approached and mention who else in the Navy was also approached. State your own name, grade, social security number, and anything else you feel is pertinent.

Clearance

Operational Security (OPSEC)

OPSEC's purpose is to keep the enemy from finding out about military operations before, while, and after they occur. Operations are military actions, missions, and maneuvers. They are destinations of ships and planes and their cargoes. They are your assignments and those of your shipmates.

The word *information* in connection with OPSEC means any detail that helps the enemy. With enough information, an enemy can determine what an operation is for and sabotage it.

Cargo loaded aboard a ship or plane may seem unimportant, but it can be vital information for an enemy wondering whether it's destined for the tropics or the arctic regions. The kind of ship carrying the cargo does not escape the enemy's attention. Is it a troop carrier or an icebreaker? Are the planes bombers or supply transports? What you take for granted as being unimportant, the enemy takes seriously. By piecing together bits of information from here and there, a spy can easily determine the general purpose of an operation before it even starts.

The OPSEC program has four parts:

Communications Security: This covers communications by telephone, telegraph, radio, teletype, documents, mail, and any other means.

Electronic Security: This includes radar, sonar, or any non-communicating signal. For example, if you're tracking a U.S. plane by radar, the echo of radio waves can tip off an enemy to that plane's whereabouts.

Operational Information Security: This refers to the protection of plans, maps, photographs, equipment (such as tanks, guns, and ships), attack and defense tactics, and unit movements and locations.

Physical Security: This means guarding classified areas, documents, equipment, buildings, and people from unauthorized access, sabotage, and other dangers.

Enemy Actions

During the war in Vietnam, the communists were able to find out about many U.S. operations before they took place. They found out not because there were security leaks, but because much of what they learned came from sources who didn't realize they were contributing information that would be valuable to the enemy. The slightest change in daily routine was noted and reported to an expert, who knew that any change, no matter how innocent or trivial, could be a piece in the puzzle of U.S. operations.

An example: Medical supplies are being loaded aboard a supply ship at the same time marines board an LPH. Then an air squadron makes an urgent request for maps of an area that would be ideal for an amphibious assault. Spies noting those three facts can quickly determine that something is up. Once they figure out what is likely to happen, they can take the steps necessary to ruin the operation—and kill a lot of American service people.

Unclassified news releases about American casualties and those of U.S. allies can be a big help to an enemy trying to determine the strength of U.S. forces. Enemies collect any and all publications released before an operation takes place. They read what they collect and try to figure out what will happen. If they guess right, the United States loses.

Enemies like to infiltrate social gatherings where U.S. service personnel dance, drink, and talk. The enemy is there for one reason only—to listen. Then he or she passes on whatever is heard to super spies. Some enemies even move into communities with service people so they can pump their neighbors for information.

So watch your mouth in the bars. Loose talk and a skilled listener can mean trouble.

External Security

Everyone aboard ship, whether on watch or not, must always be security-minded and on the alert for any sign of danger to the ship. A ship in port should be relatively safe, but it can be threatened in many ways—by hurricanes, tidal waves, flooding, fire, explosions, sabotage from within the ship, foreign saboteurs, sneak attacks, civil disorders, or riots.

Threats to security may originate outside the ship. Strangers approaching the ship should be regarded with suspicion, even though they appear to be ordinary visitors, salespersons, newspaper carriers, or delivery people. All individuals coming aboard must be identified by the officer of the deck (OOD) or his or her representative, and all items such as packages, parcels, briefcases, and toolboxes should be inspected. Persons standing gangway or quarterdeck watches assist the OOD in identifying approaching boats, screening visitors, and checking packages.

Sentries and guards posted for security purposes are guided by written instructions and must know how to challenge boats in order to identify occupants before they come alongside. All sentries may be armed when the situation demands. Armed guards should be reasonably proficient in the use of their weapons. An armed guard who does not know his or her weapon is useless at post and a danger to ship and shipmates.

Moored or anchored ships are vulnerable to sneak attacks and sabotage, particularly at night. Ships can be approached by swimmers, small boats, or submarines. Boarders may pose as gunboat crews. Saboteurs may mingle with a returning liberty party, pose as visitors, or sneak aboard when ships are moored to a pier. When such dangers of attack exist, the operations officer will organize special watches and issue instructions to them.

Signal-bridge watches report to the OOD any boats approaching the ship or operating in the vicinity of the ship in a suspicious or aimless manner, as well as any unusual disturbances or signs of distress in the harbor, aboard other ships, or ashore.

Internal Security

The safety of a ship may also be threatened from within. Sabotage is possible, especially during times of international tension. Abrasives in oil, nails driven into multiple-conductor cables, or foreign objects placed in turbines or reduction gears can cause great damage. Fire and flooding, accidental or otherwise, are always a danger.

All ships maintain the following two watches for internal security:

The Sounding and Security Watch: This is stood under way and in port by people from the R division, who make routine checks for watertight closures and security. The team also checks for fire hazards, takes soundings in shaft alleys and voids not in use, and makes draft readings.

The Cold-Iron Watch: Besides routine security and sounding patrols, a ship whose main machinery is inactive, or which does not have an auxiliary watch on duty below, stations a cold-iron watch. This watch consists of people from the B and M divisions, who check all machinery spaces for violations of watertight integrity.

During war, because modern science enables an enemy to detect almost any electronic emission, a condition known as EMCON—emission control—is set. When EMCON is set aboard ship, not even personal radios can be played if they have signal-emitting characteristics.

Internal security is also maintained by setting two other conditions: Darken ship and quiet ship. *Darken ship* must be observed by everyone going topside. The glow of a cigarette can be seen for miles on a dark night. The light from an improperly shielded hatchway will let a submarine make a successful periscope attack. *Quiet ship* is self-explanatory; banging or hammering can give away the position of an otherwise perfectly silent submarine, for instance.

Orders covering trash disposal and pumping bilges must be strictly obeyed. A ship littering the ocean with debris can be tracked down by an alert enemy.

Shipyard Security

In a shipyard, all workers coming aboard a ship must be identified. Compartments containing classified matter must be secured, either by locks or with sentries. Fire watches are normally assigned to each welder and burner who comes on board. Also, special precautions must be taken after each shift to inspect spaces for fire hazards.

The commanding officer has custody of all keys to the magazines, but others may be designated to have duplicate keys. Heads of departments are responsible for keys to locked spaces under their cognizance. Keys to other spaces are in the custody of designated officers and petty officers. Each department head maintains a locker containing all keys to spaces in his or her department. Keys to these lockers are always available to the OOD in case of emergencies.

Every sailor must provide a lock for his or her own locker and should always carry the keys. Any other keys with which he or she may be entrusted should never be carried off the ship.

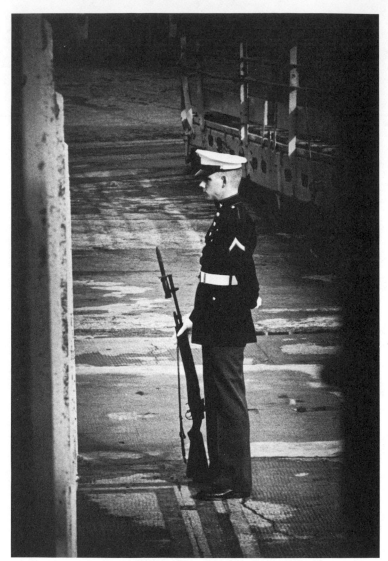

Figure 7–2 A marine guard on shipyard security watch.

Censorship

    In war or during certain peacetime emergency conditions,
censorship of personal mail may be imposed. The main intent
of censorship is to avoid security violations that might occur
Censorship through carelessness or lack of judgment in writing letters.

Under such emergency conditions, all letters written aboard a ship, or in a forward area, must be passed by a censor. When censorship is imposed, instructions will be issued detailing subjects not to be discussed in letters. These will include ships' movements, mention of combat actions, details of weapons, etc. Photographs may be censored too. Cameras may be barred and all pictures taken aboard ship may require clearance for release.

Hygiene, Health, and First Aid   **8**

The Navy will train you to perform your military and professional duties, but your ability to perform them quickly and efficiently will depend on your physical and mental condition. Good health and a cheerful attitude will make your job easier and improve your relations with others. However, no one can order you to stay healthy and keep cheerful. That's up to you.

In the days of "iron men and wooden ships," disease killed more men than cannonballs did. Sailors lived for months aboard damp and cold ships, ate salted or rancid meat and moldy or wormy bread, drank foul-smelling water, and bathed if at all in cold salt water. A man with a smashed leg received quick "kill or cure" treatment—the surgeon sawed it off. Good surgeons heated the saw so it wouldn't hurt so much, and sometimes the man got a shot of rum to take his mind off his troubles.

Sailors in the Navy today live better and are safer and healthier than most of the people in many nations of the world. Even the smallest ship has facilities to provide nourishing meals, well-ventilated and -heated berthing spaces, medical and dental attention, laundry services, hot and cold fresh water, and sanitary living conditions.

It's almost impossible not to be healthy. Still, there are those who contract such conditions as athlete's foot, ringworm, or "crabs."

Good Health Habits

Good health is no accident. You can achieve it through careful attention to personal and oral hygiene, a balanced diet, plenty of fresh air and exercise, good posture, and proper rest. Exercise invigorates and stimulates the whole body.

Mild exercise for 30 minutes every day is important to efficiency. If an exercise area is not available, or an exercise period is not provided in the daily routine, work out your own system of conditioning exercises and follow it. This should include warming-up exercises in various positions (standing, kneeling, sitting, and lying prone), limbering exercises (body stretching, twisting, bending, knee bending, and running in place), and deep-breathing exercises.

Remember that cleanliness and health go hand in hand. Most people with athlete's foot or ringworm have failed to practice good hygiene. It's not always easy to keep clean when washrooms are crowded, but the effort is worthwhile. Shower daily in warm weather or when you are sweating heavily. In cool weather, once every other day should be enough—but wash your face and hands well with hot water and soap before every meal. Wash your hair at least once a week.

Care of Teeth

The three most common dental diseases are tooth decay (caries); inflammation of the gums (gingivitis); and an affliction of the gums and bone surrounding the teeth (pyorrhea). They all can lead to the loss of teeth—which is needless, since they can be prevented or controlled.

There is no way completely to prevent tooth decay, but it can be cut down by brushing the teeth correctly and by cutting down on sweets. Flossing, the only way to remove harmful deposits from between your teeth, should be done once a day. At the first sign of tooth decay, see a dentist.

Normal and healthy gums are pale pink and firm in texture. If they are swollen or puffy, hang loosely about the teeth, and bleed easily, then you have gingivitis.

If gingivitis goes untreated, you may notice pockets or crevices between the tooth and gum, an indication of pyorrhea (or periodontitis). Surprisingly, more teeth are lost from these two diseases than from tooth decay. Most dental diseases result from poor mouth hygiene combined with inadequate brushing and flossing.

The Navy is doing what it can to prevent dental disease by requiring all sailors to have their teeth checked at least every year. Every commanding officer must see that the checks are indeed made, and individuals are notified when their checks are due. Navy regulations also require all personnel to have stannous fluoride treatments before deployment to an area

without adequate dental facilities.

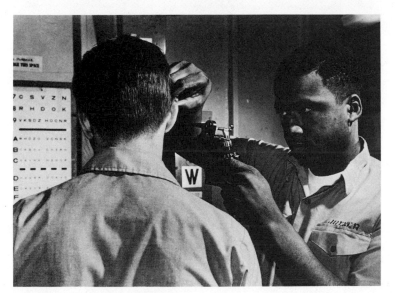

Figure 8–1 Sailors now live better and are healthier than ever. They receive regular medical and dental checkups.

Drug and Alcohol Abuse

Most drug abuse involves substances such as marijuana, LSD, heroine, and cocaine that have no legitimate medical use. However, some drugs that are abused, principally codeine and barbiturates, are invaluable tools for physicians in their efforts to cope with disease.

The important factor in drug abuse is the abuser, not the drug. Drug abuse has a particularly important consequence for the armed forces. For example, the lives of all hands on a ship may depend on the alertness of one sailor assigned to close a watertight door. No commander can trust the fate of his or her unit, ship, or plane to a person who may be under the influence of drugs or alcohol, or suffering from a serious hangover.

Since 1971, the Navy has had an alcohol and drug abuse control program. Objectives of the program are to identify all naval personnel abusing drugs, to restore to full duty all drug abusers who have potential for further useful service, and to ensure that every sailor has the facts necessary to make an intelligent decision concerning drug use. These objectives are pursued by three basic parts of the program: education, identification, and rehabilitation.

Figure 8–2 Navy drug-prevention poster.

Drug abusers are identified through self-referral, urinalysis, or normal investigative and law-enforcement procedures.

The Navy's control program encourages drug abusers concerned about their problem to come forward voluntarily and seek assistance, but only from qualified drug-screening, counseling, treatment, or rehabilitation personnel. Sailors seeking it are provided help with rehabilitation. If you are apprehended for a drug offense or make a disclosure to persons other than qualified drug-screening personnel, the information may be used against you for disciplinary action under the UCMJ. The SECNAVINST 5300.28 series outlines the alcohol and drug abuse control program.

All military personnel, regardless of rank or age, are subject to participation in the urinalysis program. Urinalysis may be conducted as an inspection (random sampling, unit sweeps, and service-directed testing), as a search and seizure (probable cause and consensual testing), or to determine fitness for duty (command- or physician-directed testing to identify personnel who may be physically or mentally unfit to perform military duties). The OPNAVINST 5350.4 series outlines the urinalysis program.

Investigative and law-enforcement assistance is provided to commanding officers by the Naval Investigative Service Command (NISC) base police, masters-at-arms, and various civilian law-enforcement authorities. The Navy also has drug-detection dog teams in many areas that have a heavy concentration of Navy personnel. An "alert" by a drug detection dog constitutes probable cause to conduct a search and seizure (including urinalysis) to produce evidence.

When alcohol/drug abusers are identified, they are detoxified, if necessary. Their commanding officer evaluates the extent of their abuse and their potential for further useful service. Those determined to have no potential for further useful service (and those apprehended a second time for drug abuse) are disciplined, if appropriate, and processed for separation. Those with potential for further useful service go for rehabilitation following any disciplinary action. Rehabilitation is available locally, within the command; at a Counseling and Assistance Center (CAAC) ashore or afloat; or at an Alcohol Rehabilitation Center (ARC) or an Alcohol Rehabilitation Department (ARD) in a naval hospital.

In military law, wrongful acts in connection with narcotics and marijuana ("controlled substances") are covered under UCMJ article 112A.

For the possession or use of a controlled substance, the Manual for Courts-Martial (MCM) calls for a maximum punishment of dishonorable discharge (DD), forfeiture of all pay and allowances, and confinement up to five years. Add ten more years' confinement for sale or possession with intent to distribute. If the offense takes place on board a military vessel or aircraft, on duty as a sentinel or lookout, in a hostile fire zone, or in time of war, the confinement is increased by five years.

UCMJ article 111 deals with drunken driving, article 112 with drunkenness on duty. Any intoxication that is sufficient to impair "the rational and full exercise of the mental and physical facilities" is drunkenness for the purposes of a military court. Violations of specific service regulations dealing with drugs or alcohol may be prosecuted as violations of article 92 of the UCMJ, "Failure to Obey Order or Regulation."

The Navy, recognizing that alcoholism is a disease that can be treated, is determined to aid sailors who desire such assistance. In recent years, there has been an increasing incidence of alcoholism among Navy personnel in their teens and early twenties. The Navy has instituted an intense program to educate, assist, and rehabilitate personnel afflicted with this disease. Today, experts on alcoholism from within the Navy—including a great many rehabilitated alcoholics—are offering their experience and assistance to other Navy men and women.

Treatment for habitual abusers and early-stage alcoholics is offered locally at a CAAC. More serious cases are treated at an ARC or ARD.

Serious drinking problems, which impair performance of duty and disrupt personal life, afflict 35 percent of all active-duty sailors. It is estimated that 10 percent of the total Navy force are chronic drinkers in need of help. Post-treatment studies show that about 80 percent of patients who attend Navy rehabilitation facilities return to duty and complete their service obligations. In purely financial terms—measured by the cost necessary to replace highly trained personnel who would otherwise have been lost to the Navy through alcoholism—the Navy saves many millions of dollars annually through its rehabilitation programs.

Diarrhea

Diarrhea, common in the tropics, is not unknown in the United States. The major symptom is loose stools, which can be accompanied by nausea, stomach cramps, and vomiting. Dirty water and flies can carry the bacteria that cause diarrhea, but it is more likely to be spread by food-handlers or through vegetables fertilized with human waste. Wherever diarrhea is known to be a problem, it is best to avoid uncooked foods. If you must eat ashore, eat in reputable restaurants and avoid "dives." In areas where diarrhea is easily contracted, water should be boiled for at least five minutes and then put into sterile containers. It's safer, though, to drink bottled water. Never buy food from small stands or pushcarts in a foreign country. Don't eat raw seafood (oysters, clams, shrimp) in a foreign country, particularly not in hot climates.

Homosexuality

There are a lot of mistaken ideas about homosexuality. Two examples: a homosexual can be detected by speech characteristics, manner, or dress (this is not true in most cases); and VD cannot be contracted through homosexual acts (it can and frequently is).

The Navy is concerned about homosexuals. They can be poor security risks and can be susceptible to blackmail. Persons who commit or attempt to commit homosexual acts run the risk of dismissal from the service through court-martial or administrative discharge. However, under certain circumstances a sailor recommended for discharge may have the case reviewed by the secretary of the Navy.

According to NAVMILPERSCOMINST 1910.1C, issued 26 February 1985, anyone who engages or attempts to engage in a homosexual act that is a departure from his or her usual and customary behavior, and who does not profess or demonstrate a desire to repeat the act, may be considered for retention. But a person will be allowed to stay in the service only if his or her conduct is not likely to have an adverse impact on the continued performance of duty, or on the readiness, efficiency, or morale of that sailor's unit. Persons processed for homosexuality are evaluated on a case-by-case basis.

Venereal Diseases (VD)

Venereal diseases, like alcoholism, were for many years swept under the rug and not mentioned in polite society. "Nice people" didn't know what to call the various types of infection, although that didn't prevent both royalty and riffraff from getting them. VD is no longer a hush-hush subject. It is discussed in newspapers and magazines, and it should be a matter of concern for everyone.

VD is any infectious disease that can be transmitted by sexual contact between one person and another. The contact is not always from prostitutes. More and more, VD is infecting young people. Its prevention depends almost completely on the individual—no contact, no VD.

There are several diseases categorized as VD: syphilis ("syph," "pox"), gonorrhea ("clap," "dose," "the drip," "GC"), chancroid (bubo), granuloma inguinale, lymphogranuloma venereum, and chlamydia (NSU). All are transmitted from an infected person to an uninfected person through sexual intercourse. Syphilis can also be transmitted by a kiss if an infected person has an open sore on the lips or in the mouth. A woman can transmit syphilis to her unborn child or gonorrhea to her newly born child.

The incubation period, or time from contact until first symptoms appear, varies—ten to ninety days for syphilis, two to fourteen days for gonorrhea and chancroid, and longer for the others. An infected person can transmit VD to another before signs of infection appear. During incubation, there is no way to tell if a person is infected.

The results of VD may appear years later. Latent syphilis, the state in which clinical symptoms of infection are absent, may appear "early"—four years after infection—or "late," as much as twenty years afterward. Among the infinite variety of results to be expected from untreated syphilis are destructive ulcers, disease of the heart or blood vessels, blindness, and insanity. Other kinds of VD have other effects, none of them pleasant.

Herpes Genitalis

Herpes genitalis is a viral infection that usually occurs within three weeks of sexual contact with a contagious person. The initial infection (characteristically more severe than recurrent infections) may start with fever, malaise, headache, and swollen glands. Painful or itchy blisters may appear in the genital area within a few days. At this stage, urination and intercourse may be painful. Symptoms usually resolve within two to three weeks. Medication is available to relieve the symptoms; however, it is not curative. The incubation period is from four to seven days. Lesions will heal in about ten days, and the infection may recur. A person who has contracted VD must refrain from sexual activity until the infection has cleared up—in the case of genital herpes, until the lesions have healed. Failure to do so may result in the spread of the disease.

AIDS

AIDS, or acquired immune deficiency syndrome, is an invariably fatal viral disease that destroys the body's ability to defend itself against disease. AIDS-related deaths are frequently attributable to diseases or organisms that would not ordinarily pose a serious threat to one's health. Persons at high risk for contracting AIDS are hemophiliacs, intravenous drug users, and homosexuals; however, the disease *can* be spread through heterosexual relationships. The Navy has begun a vigorous testing program to identify and treat those individuals who have contracted AIDS as well as those who may have been exposed to it. Presently there is no cure for AIDS, although intensive research continues. Your best defense is to exercise extreme caution in engaging in sexual relationships. Condoms are very strongly recommended for all sexual encounters.

First Aid

First aid is emergency treatment for sick or injured people. It consists *only* of immediate, temporary assistance necessary to save life, prevent further injury, or preserve the victim's vitality and resistance to infection. In administering first aid, remember your ABCs: ensure that the victim has an adequate *Airway*, is *Breathing*, and has blood *Circulating*. Administer CPR (artificial respiration) if necessary. After the ABCs come control of bleeding, applying dressings and splints, and treatment for shock.

Don't move a patient unless it is absolutely necessary to save him or her from fire, gas, drowning, or gunfire. A fractured bone may cut an artery or nerve. A broken neck or back may result in a spinal-cord injury, paralysis, or death. Make an injured person comfortable. Cover the victim to keep him or her warm. If a victim must be moved, make sure you know how to do it (see Transportation of the Injured, p. 167).

Know what to do, then do it. Serious bleeding must be stopped. If someone is bleeding from the mouth (or vomiting), roll the victim on his or her side with the head turned to the side and lower than the feet. Clear the mouth or throat, start artificial respiration if needed, then treat for shock.

Control the Situation

Ask for medical assistance by telephone, radio, or messenger. Have someone keep bystanders clear. Loosen clothing around the patient's neck, chest, and abdomen.

Determine the extent of injuries. Look for bleeding, wounds, fractures, or burns. Notice the color of the victim's face. Ask questions to determine if he or she is conscious. Bleeding from the nose and ears is often a symptom of a fractured skull. Bloody froth coming from the mouth can indicate damaged lungs. Check the pulse rate and strength. Check dog tags for blood type. See if the victim carries anything (bracelet, tag, or card) about drugs or medicines he or she must or cannot take.

CPR (Artificial Respiration)

The standard methods of CPR are mouth-to-mouth and manual (back pressure, arm lift). Mouth-to-mouth (or mouth-to-nose) is considered best and should be used in all cases in which it is possible to do so (figure 8-3).

Mouth-to-Mouth Method: Place the victim on his or her back immediately. Don't waste time moving the victim to a better place, loosening clothing, or draining water from the lungs.

Quickly clear the victim's mouth and throat. Remove any dentures, mucus, food, and other obstructions.

Tilt the victim's head as far back as possible (step A), until the head is in a chin-up position. Use the jaw-chin lift method, with neck extended to ensure an open airway (step B).

Pull the victim's lower jaw forward. Grasp the jaw by placing your thumb into the corner of the mouth (step C). Do not hold or depress the tongue.

Pinch the nose shut (or seal the victim's mouth). Prevent any air leakage. Open your mouth wide and blow in. Take a deep breath and blow forcefully (except with babies) into the victim's mouth or nose until you see the chest rise (step D). A one-person CPR is two breaths per fifteen compressions.

Quickly remove your mouth when the victim's chest rises. Listen for exhalation. If the victim makes snoring or gurgling sounds, the jaw is not high enough (step E).

Repeat these two steps fifteen to twenty times per minute. Continue until the victim begins to breathe normally.

Remove air blown into the victim's stomach. Periodically, between breaths, if the stomach is distended, place your hand on his or her upper abdomen and gently but firmly press the air out of the stomach (step F). Victims who require air to be expelled from the abdomen may vomit when this is done. If this happens, turn the victim's head to the side until vomiting has stopped. Clear the mouth of any material and proceed with mouth-to-mouth respiration.

For an infant, seal both the mouth and nose with your mouth. Blow with small puffs of air from your cheeks.

Sometimes the mouth-to-mouth method cannot be used, as when there are injuries to the face with bleeding around the mouth, or when gas masks must be worn in contaminated ar-

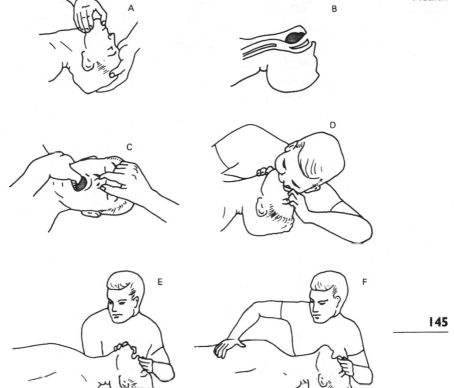

Figure 8–3 The above steps illustrate the proper method of administering mouth-to-mouth artificial respiration.

eas. In this case, a manual method must be used. Manual methods, which may fail to maintain a free and unobstructed airway, are not always effective. In all manual methods, the first consideration must be proper positioning of the head to avoid such obstruction. Two methods—the chest-pressure arm-lift method (figure 8-4) and the back-pressure arm-lift method (figure 8-5)—are discussed below.

Chest-Pressure–Arm-Lift Method: Place the victim in a face-up position and put something under his or her shoulders to raise them. Allow the head to drop backward (step A).

Kneel at the victim's head. Grasp his or her arms at the wrists. Cross them, then press them over the lower chest (step B). This should cause air to flow out.

Figure 8–4 Artificial respiration can also be administered manually by the chest-pressure–arm-lift method.

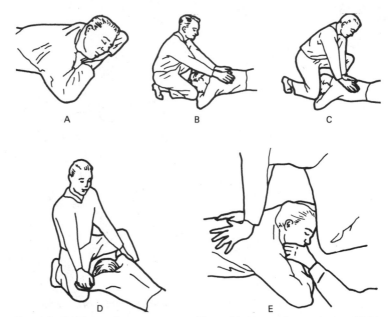

Figure 8–5 The back-pressure–arm-lift method is another manual artificial-respiration technique.

Immediately release this pressure, and pull the arms out and over the victim's head, and back as far as possible (step C). This should cause the air to rush in.

Repeat this cycle about twenty times a minute, checking the mouth frequently for obstruction. A victim in a face-up position may take vomit or blood into his or her lungs, so keep the head extended and turned to one side. If possible, the head should be a little lower than the trunk. If a second rescuer is on hand, have the person continuously check the victim's head so that the jaw juts out and the mouth is kept as clean as possible.

Back-Pressure–Arm-Lift Method: Place the victim face down. Bend the victim's elbows and place his or her hands, one upon the other, under the chin. Turn the head slightly and extend it as far as possible, making sure that the chin juts out (step A).

Kneel at the head of the victim. Place your hands on the flat of his or her back so that the palms lie just below an imaginary line running between the armpits (step B).

Rock forward until your arms are approximately vertical, and allow the weight on the upper part of your body to exert steady, even pressure downward on your hands (step C).

Immediately draw the victim's arms up and toward you, applying enough lift to feel resistance and tension at the shoulders (step D). Then lower the victim's arms to the ground. Repeat this cycle about twenty times a minute. If a second rescuer is available, have him or her hold the victim's head so the jaw juts out (step E). Check the mouth for any stomach contents and keep it as clean as possible.

Time your application of pressure to coincide with the victim's first attempt to breath alone. If the victim vomits, turn him or her on one side, wipe out the mouth, then reposition the victim.

Once begun, it is important to continue artificial respiration until medical assistance arrives or until the victim revives. Recovery from electrical shock, drug poisoning, or carbon-monoxide poisoning may be particularly slow.

When the victim revives, keep him or her quiet until breathing is regular. Keep the body covered and treat for shock until suitable transportation is available. Since respiratory and other disturbances may develop, a doctor's care is necessary during the recovery period.

Asphyxiation

This is loss of consciousness due to lack of oxygen. Drowning, electric shock, and gas poisoning are the most common causes, but suffocation, strangulation, and choking will produce the same results. Breathing stops, but the heart may continue to pump blood for some time. Even when the victim's heartbeat cannot be felt, artificial respiration should be administered and continued until assistance arrives.

Bandages

Bandages may consist of gauze, a gauze square, an adhesive compress, a bandage compress, or a plain strip of cloth. The compress, which directly covers the wound, should be sterile if possible. Bandages need not be sterile; they do not touch the wound. They should not be made of anything adhesive that will stick to the skin. The bandage may be applied in turns—circular, spiral, figure eight, or recurrent. Triangular bandages may be tied on the head or face, shoulder or hip, chest or back, foot or hand. Cravat bandages are used on head, neck, eye, temple, cheek, ear, elbow, knee, arm, forearm, or palm wounds. Roller bandages are wrapped on the hands and wrists, forearms or legs. The Standard First-Aid Training Course (NAVEDTRA 10081-C) and *First-Aid Textbook* prepared by the American Red Cross are invaluable for learning about the application of bandages, or any other first-aid problem.

Bleeding

An average human body contains five quarts of blood. One pint can be lost without harmful effect. A loss of two pints will usually produce shock. If half the blood is lost, death almost always results. Thus bleeding must be stopped quickly.

In arterial bleeding, bright red blood spurts out; this sort of bleeding is very serious. In venous bleeding, dark red blood flows steadily; this type of bleeding can also be serious. Capillary bleeding, usually not serious, comes from a prick or small abrasion.

Usually, bleeding can be stopped if pressure is applied directly to the wound. If direct pressure does not work, pressure should be applied at the correct pressure point. Where severe bleeding cannot be controlled by these methods, pressure by means of a tourniquet should be applied. (This, however, is dangerous, because if circulation is cut off entirely gangrene can set in.)

Direct Pressure: Use a sterile dressing or the cleanest cloth available—a freshly laundered handkerchief, towel, or article of clothing. Form a pad, place it directly over the wound, and fasten it in position with a bandage (figure 8-6).

If the bleeding does not stop, apply another snug bandage directly over the one you have already applied, then apply direct pressure by placing your hand, for five or six minutes, over the pad of cloth.

In cases of severe bleeding, don't worry about infection—stop the blood. If nothing else is available, jam a shirt into the wound. Remember, direct pressure is the *first* method to use in controlling bleeding.

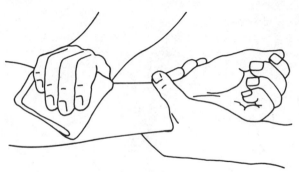

Figure 8–6 Control bleeding by applying direct pressure to the wound.

Pressure Points: Bleeding from a cut artery or vein can often be controlled by applying pressure to a pressure point (figure 8-7). A pressure point is a place where a main artery lies near the skin surface and over the bone. Pressure there compresses the artery against the bone and shuts off the flow of blood to the wound. The following lists pressure points for particular areas of the body:

A. Face, below the eyes: Pressure point is the lower jaw-bone, at a notch you can feel with your finger.

B. Temple or scalp: Pressure point is just in front of the ear. You can feel the pulse in the artery with your finger.

C. Neck: Apply pressure below the wound, just in front of the neck muscle. Press in and slightly backward. Apply pressure here only if absolutely necessary, since you may accidentally press the windpipe and choke the victim.

D. Shoulder or upper part of the arm: The pressure point is behind the collarbone. Press forward against the collarbone or down against the first rib.

E. Middle of the upper arm and elbow: Pressure point is on the inner side of the arm, about halfway between shoulder and elbow.

F. Lower arm: Pressure point is at the elbow.

G. Hand: Pressure point is at the wrist. If the arm can also be held up, the bleeding will stop sooner.

H, I, J. Upper part of thigh: Pressure point is in the middle of the groin (H). Sometimes it is better to apply pressure on the upper thigh (I). Heavy pressure is needed here, however. Use a closed fist and press at the side of the knee, or else push one

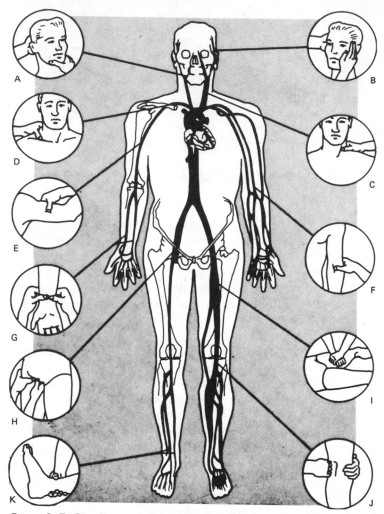

Figure 8–7 Bleeding can be controlled when pressure is applied at a point where the main artery lies near the surface and is over a bone.

fist against the back of the knee and hold one hand in front of the knee (J). As a last resort, fold a bandage behind the knee and bend the leg against it.

K. Foot: Pressure point is at the ankle. Elevating the leg will help control bleeding.

Remember to apply pressure at the point nearest the wound, between the wound and the heart.

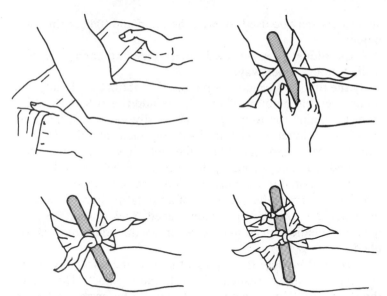

Figure 8–8 When applying a tourniquet, tie the bandage with an overhand knot, tie a square knot over the stick, and twist the stick to tighten the tourniquet.

It is very tiring to apply finger pressure, and it can seldom be maintained for more than fifteen minutes. As soon as possible, use a compress held securely over the wound by a bandage.

If the bleeding is still severe, you may have to apply a tourniquet. Remember—tourniquets are dangerous and may result in gangrene when left on too long.

A tourniquet (figure 8-8) consists of a pad (pressure object), a band, and a device for tightening the band as the blood vessels are compressed. The type found in many Navy first-aid kits consists of a web band, 2 inches wide and 5 feet long, with a buckle for fastening. The tourniquet is applied above the wound, that is, between the wound and the heart.

Wrap it once about the limb, then run the free end through the buckle. Draw the band tightly enough to stop the flow of blood. In an emergency, any round, smooth pressure object may be used—a compress, roller bandage, stone, rifle shell— and any long piece of cloth may be used as a band. At least $\frac{1}{4}$ inch from the top edge of the wound, place a thick compress of folded cloth 4 to 6 inches square. Do not use a rope, a wire, a string, or narrow pieces of cloth. They will cut into the flesh. A short stick may be used to twist the band and tighten the tourniquet.

A tourniquet is *never* used unless bleeding cannot be controlled in any other way.

By the time a tourniquet is put on, the victim has already lost a considerable amount of blood; the additional loss resulting from loosening the tourniquet may easily cause death. Thus, once a tourniquet is used, it should be released only by qualified medical personnel. Mark the patient's forehead with a "T" and the time, using a felt-tip pen, lipstick, or iodine, so that there is no doubt about how long the tourniquet has been in place. To avoid the necessity of amputating part of the limb on which a tourniquet has been placed, seek assistance from qualified medical personnel as soon as the tourniquet is applied.

Internal Bleeding: If the patient is bleeding internally, he or she may be thirsty, restless, fearful, and in shock. Don't give the victim anything to eat or drink, even if he or she is thirsty, for if anesthesia has to be administered the victim might vomit and take material into the lungs. Bleeding in the stomach may be determined from the location of the wound and bloody vomiting. The treatment for internal bleeding is the same as that for shock, except that stimulants must not be given. Seek medical care immediately, since internal bleeding can lead to death.

Blisters

The skin covering a blister is better protection than any bandage. If the blister is in a place where it can easily be broken, open it with a sharp knife or needle that has been heated in flame. Press out the fluid with a bit of sterile gauze and apply a sterile bandage.

Burns and Scalds

Burns and scalds are caused by exposure to intense heat (fire, bomb flash, sunlight, hot metal solids, hot gases, or hot liquids). An electrical current also can cause severe burns. The chief dangers from burns are shock and infection. First aid should be directed towards relieving pain, combating shock, and preventing infection.

Burns are usually classified according to the depth of tissue injury. A burn that reddens the skin is a *first-degree burn*. One that raises a blister is a *second-degree burn*. One in which the skin is destroyed and the tissue is charred is a *third-degree burn.* Severe third-degree burns extend to the muscles and bones. Third-degree burns, for many hours after an injury, frequently appear as white areas surrounded by reddened or blistered skin.

The size of the burn may be far more important than its depth. A first-degree burn that covers a large area of the body is almost always more serious than a small third-degree burn.

Rule of Nines: The "rule of nines" establishes the extent and percentage of burn in order to determine the amount of fluid the body will need during the first twenty-four hours after an injury. The front and back of the trunk and the lower legs are each rated 18 percent, totaling 72 percent. The arms and head are individually rated at 9 percent, the genital area 1 percent, totaling 28 percent. A first-degree burn over 72 percent of the body is more serious than a third-degree burn of the arm.

Minor Burns: Immediately cover the burn with a sterile bandage to prevent infection. Do not apply ointments or other medicines to the burn. The pain will be lessened greatly if the bandage is airtight and fairly firm.

Cold-water treatment is comforting and effective. Submerge the burn in water containing enough ice to chill (but not freeze). Continue until the burned part is painless when withdrawn from the water. Compresses wrung out of ice water are also comforting.

Serious Burns: Extreme pain increases the severity of shock. Relieve pain with morphine (see p. 163). Treat for shock immediately, before trying to treat the burns.

Keep the victim's head slightly lower than his or her feet, and see that he or she is warm. Do not remove clothing immediately. Remember that exposure to cold will increase shock. Cover with a blanket if he or she appears to be cold, but do not overheat the patient. Cover all burns with dry, sterile dressings.

A seriously burned person badly needs fluids. Give the victim water, sweet tea, fruit juices, or sugar water—*if* the patient is conscious, able to swallow, and has no internal injuries.

Burns of the Eyes: See Eye Injuries, p. 155.

Chemical Burns: Chemicals in contact with the skin or other membranes may cause burns by destruction of body tissue. This kind of injury can be caused by acids such as nitric, sulfuric, and hydrochloric acid, or by caustic alkalis such as potassium hydroxide (lye), sodium hydroxide (caustic soda, soda lye), and calcium oxide (quicklime). Phenol (carbolic acid) also causes chemical burns. Strong concentrations of various bleaches and disinfectants cause chemical injuries to the skin. Chlorine, ammonia, and other industrial chemicals—whether in liquid or vapor form—may cause serious chemical burns of the skin or eyes. Phosphorus burns are a combination of heat burns and chemical injury.

These are some guidelines for treating chemical burns:

Wash the chemical off immediately with large amounts of clean, fresh, cool water. If it is not possible to put the victim under running water, immerse the affected areas or pour plenty of water over the burns.

Neutralize any chemical that remains on the skin. For acid burns, apply a solution of sodium bicarbonate (baking soda) or other mild alkali. For alkali burns, apply vinegar, lemon juice, or a mild acid. For phenol burns, apply alcohol. Don't try to neutralize any chemical unless you know *for sure* what the chemical is and what substance will neutralize it!

Flooding the area with lots of cool water will suffice when in doubt. Wash the affected areas again with fresh water, then dry gently with sterile gauze. Do not break the skin or open any blisters. Cover the burns with dry, sterile dressings. If sterile dressings are not available, use the cleanest linens or other materials available.

Do what you can to relieve pain and treat for shock. See also Eye Injuries, below.

Choking

When something is lodged in the throat, a person will start choking and coughing. If the obstruction goes deep enough to block the air passage, the victim will die. Don't try to dislodge the object with your finger. Here's a quick and effective life-saving treatment:

Stand behind the victim and wrap both arms around his or her waist, clasping one hand around your other wrist.

Place your interlocked hands against the victim's abdomen just below the breast bone. Press into the victim's abdomen with quick upward thrusts until the object is forced out of the throat.

Your thrusts force air out of the victim's lungs. As the air moves up, its pressure will be enough to cause the object to fly out of the victim's mouth.

If the victim is lying down, turn him or her to the side and strike the back between the shoulders. The first method is better, if you can get the person to stand.

If breathing has stopped, you can try CPR. But it won't do much good if the air passage is completely blocked.

Eye Injuries

For eye wounds, apply thick, dry, sterile bandages. If the eyeball is injured, do not let the bandage press against it. If soft tissue around the eye is injured, apply a pressure bandage. Keep the victim lying down during transportation and until he or she receives medical aid.

To remove something from the eye, have the patient look up. Use the corner of a clean handkerchief, or a cotton swab moistened in clean water, and gently pull the lower lid down with your finger. You can also turn the upper lid back over a match stick or cotton swab by grasping the lashes of the upper lid between the fingers and the stick. If these methods fail, use a sterile syringe or medicine dropper to irrigate the eye with sterile water at body temperature, holding the lids apart with the fingers. If the object still cannot be removed, cover the eye by bandaging and obtain medical help. Never try to remove a foreign body from the eye with your fingers. Never try to remove any foreign body embedded in the eyeball; seek medical advice.

Heat Burns: Cover both the victim's eyes with moist pads and have him or her lie down. Do not let the victim rub his or her eyes. Get medical help.

Chemical Burns: Flush the eye immediately with large quantities of clean water. Hold the victim's head over a drinking fountain so that the water flows from the inside corner of the eye toward the outside corner, or have the victim lie down with his or her head turned slightly to one side. Then pour water into the inside corner of the eye and let it flow gently across the eyeball to the outside corner. If the victim is unable to open his or her eyes, hold the eyelids apart so that the water can flow across the eyeball. Do not use anything except water.

Another way to wash out chemical substances is to have the victim open and close his or her eyes several times while the face is immersed in a pan of fresh water.

Cover the eye with a small, thick compress. Fasten the compress in place with a bandage or an eye shield, and get medical care as soon as possible.

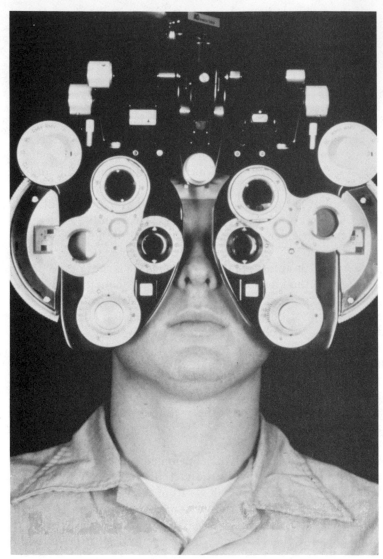

Figure 8–9 A crewmember has his eyes tested in the medical unit aboard an aircraft carrier.

Fainting

This is the nervous system's reaction to a slowdown in the flow of blood to the brain. To prevent fainting, a person should lie flat for 10 minutes with the feet slightly elevated. If a person who appears to have fainted does not recover consciousness almost immediately, he or she has not simply fainted. Uncon- sciousness may also be caused by asphyxia, deep shock, poisoning, head injury, heat stroke, heart attack, apoplexy, or epilepsy. Get medical help at once.

Fish Hooks

If a barb is buried in the flesh, clean the area, paint it with antiseptic, then push the hook through so the barb resurfaces through the skin. Then cut off the barb. The rest of the hook can be backed out. Watch out for infection. Check the patient's medical record to see if a tetanus shot is needed.

Fish Stings

Many sea creatures (Portuguese men-of-war, jellyfish, stingrays, scorpion fish) have a poisonous sting. The symptoms can be burning, stinging, reddening of the skin, hives, pus sores, abdominal cramps, numbness, dizziness, pain in the groin and armpits, nausea, muscular pain, difficulty in breathing, tightness of the chest, prostration, and shock.

For Portuguese man-of-war stings, remove the tentacles immediately and wash the skin with alcohol. Apply calamine lotion or ammonia water. The treatment for jellyfish is about the same. Apply ammonia water, vinegar, or a soothing lotion; then treat for shock.

A stingray wound should be washed immediately with cold salt water. Much of the toxin will wash out. The cold water causes blood vessels to constrict, slowing circulation and acting as a mild pain-killing agent. Then the wound should be immersed in hot water for 30 to 60 minutes, with the temperature as high as the victim can stand without injury. (Hot compresses can be applied for wounds in areas that cannot be immersed.) A sterile dressing should be applied after the soak.

Fractures

A simple fracture is a broken bone with no break in the skin. In a compound fracture, the broken bone protrudes through the skin. All fractures require careful handling—send for medical aid as soon as possible. Don't move a victim until the fracture has been splinted, unless it's necessary to save his or her life or prevent further injury. Do not try to set a broken bone.

Treat for shock if the victim shows signs of suffering from it.

Figure 8–10   Make sure splints are tied securely to prevent any movement of the limb.

Stop the bleeding in a compound fracture by using direct pressure or the pressure-point system.

Apply splints over clothing if the patient is to be moved a short distance or if a doctor will see him or her soon. Otherwise, apply well-padded splints after the clothing has been cut away. Be careful when you handle any fracture to avoid additional shock or injury. Splints vary according to the area and nature of the fracture. Generally, if the limb cannot be straightened, splint the fracture as it is. Follow these rules:

Forearm: Two well-padded splints, top and bottom, from elbow to wrist. Bandage in place. Hold the forearm across the chest with a sling.

Upper Arm: For a fracture near the shoulder, put a towel or pad in the armpit and bandage the arm to the body. Support the forearm in a sling. For a fracture of the middle upper arm, use one splint on the outside of the arm, shoulder to elbow. Fasten the arm to the body and support the forearm in a sling. For a fracture near the elbow, don't move the arm at all—splint it the way you find it.

Thigh: Use two splints, the outside one from armpit to foot, the inside one from crotch to foot. Fasten the splints around the ankle, over the knee, below the hip, around the pelvis, and below the armpit. Tie both legs together. Don't move the patient until all this has been done.

Lower Leg: Use three splints, one on each side and one underneath. They must be well padded, especially under the knee and at the ankle bones. Or use a pillow under the leg, with edges brought around in front and pinned, along with two side splints.

Kneecap: Carefully straighten the leg, and place a 4-inch-wide padded board under it, reaching from buttock to heel. Fasten it in place just below the knee, just above the knee, at the ankle, and at the thigh. Do not cover the knee.

Collarbone: On the injured side, place the forearm across the chest, palm turned in, thumb up, with the hand 4 inches above the elbow. Support the arm in this position with a sling. Fasten the arm to the body with several turns of bandage around the body and down over the hand.

Rib: A broken rib can be very painful, especially when deep breathing, sneezing, coughing, or laughing. It often takes many weeks to heal completely. A broken rib may puncture a lung, causing the victim to cough up frothy bright blood. In any case, seek medical assistance as soon as possible. *Never* wrap bandages around the victim's chest.

Jaw: If the injury interferes with breathing, pull the lower jaw and tongue forward and keep them there. Apply a four-tailed bandage under the jaw, with two ends tied on top of the front of the head and the other two on top at the back, so the bandage pulls the jaw forward. It must support and immobilize the jaw but not press on the throat.

Skull: It is not necessary to determine if the skull is fractured when a person has a head injury. The primary aim is to prevent brain damage. Do not let the patient move. Try not to move him or her any more than necessary. Do not let the victim get cold, do not give him or her anything to drink, and do not administer morphine. Stop any bleeding and get immediate medical assistance.

Spine: Pain, shock, and partial paralysis result from damage to the spine. Severe pain in the back or neck after injury should be treated as a fractured spine. Treat for shock. Keep the victim flat, and do not move his or her head.

If the victim cannot move legs or toes, the fracture is probably in the back; if the fingers can't be moved, it is probably in the neck. If the patient must be transported, carry face up on a rigid stretcher, a door, or a wide frame. Never try to lift someone with a spine injury with fewer than four people. Pick the patient up by the clothing and slide him or her onto the stretcher. To prevent further injury, it is crucial that the injured person be secured to the transportation device so that the head, neck, and back remain aligned. Use sandbags, rolled linen, tape, belts, or whatever materials are available. The patient must *not* be permitted to move.

Pelvis: Treat a person with a pelvis injury for shock, but do not move unless absolutely necessary. If the victim must be moved, handle him or her just as you would a victim of a fractured spine. Bandage legs together at ankles and knees.

Place a pillow at each hip and fasten the pillows in place. Secure the patient to the stretcher.

Frostbite

Exposure to dry cold causes frostbite, especially in the cheeks, nose, chin, ears, forehead, wrists, hands, and feet. The skin turns white or gray, then bright pink.

Frostbite may also be caused by contact with certain chemicals that cause rapid freezing, such as liquid oxygen, carbon dioxide, Freon, and other industrial gases. Such injuries are often called chemical burns, but the body tissue is actually frozen.

When the frostbitten area is warmed up, it immediately becomes red and swollen. Large blisters develop. Severe frostbite causes gangrene, which destroys soft body tissues and sometimes even bone. If deep tissue is destroyed, the injured part may have to be amputated.

First aid for frostbite is rapid thawing of the frozen tissues. Get the victim into the warmest available place as soon as possible and remove garments covering frostbitten areas. If the victim's feet or legs are frostbitten, do not let him or her walk. Do not handle the frostbitten area unnecessarily, and do not exert pressure against it. Do not thaw a frozen extremity until you can transport the patient to a place where the following steps can be taken:

Immerse the injured part in water kept at a temperature of 100–105 degrees F. If you have no thermometer, make sure that the water is just comfortably warm. Stir the water.

Dry the victim carefully. Place him or her in bed and keep the victim covered. Don't let anything touch the frostbitten parts. Keep a sterile gauze or cloth pads between toes and fingers, and keep frostbitten parts elevated. Get medical assistance as soon as possible.

Caution: Never rub or massage frostbite with ice or snow. Do not apply cold water, expose a frostbitten area to cold air, or open blisters.

Hypothermia

Hypothermia, or abnormally low body temperature, can result from exposure to cold weather or from total immersion in cold water. The victim will appear pale and unconscious, and may be taken for dead. Breathing is slow and shallow, the pulse faint or undetectable. Body tissues feel semirigid, and arms and legs may be stiff.

First aid consists mainly of bringing the body temperature back to normal. Wrap the patient in warm blankets in a warm room. Do not give him or her hot drinks or other stimulants until consciousness has been regained. Get medical attention as soon as possible.

Heat Exhaustion and Heat Cramps

In heat exhaustion, while the heat-regulating mechanism of the body is maintained, there is a serious disturbance of the blood flow similar to the circulatory disturbance of shock. Through prolonged sweating, the body loses large quantities of salt and water.

Heat exhaustion may begin with a headache, dizziness, nausea, weakness, and profuse sweating. The victim may collapse and lose consciousness but can usually be aroused rather easily. The temperature is usually normal or even below normal. Sometimes it may drop to as low as 97 degrees F. The pupils of the eyes are usually dilated. The pulse is weak and rapid. And the skin is pale, cool, and sweaty. Sometimes there may be severe cramps in the abdomen, legs, and arms.

Follow these first-aid measures:

Move the victim to a cool place, but not one where he or she will be exposed to strong drafts or become chilled.

Loosen the victim's clothing and make him or her as comfortable as possible. Keep the patient quiet and lying down, with feet and legs somewhat elevated. Be sure that the victim is neither too hot nor too cold. You may have to cover the body with blankets, even if the surrounding air is warm. If the victim is conscious and able to swallow, give him or her plenty of warm water to drink, along with one-fourth to one-half teaspoonful of salt in each glass. This is probably the most important part of the treatment; replacement of the salt and water lost by sweating often brings rapid recovery.

Prepare hot coffee or tea when the patient is able to drink it. If recovery is not prompt, get medical attention quickly.

Heatstroke (Sunstroke)

Both heatstroke and heat exhaustion are caused by excessive exposure to desert or jungle heat, the direct rays of the sun, and heat in machinery spaces, foundries, or bakeries. In the same environment, one person may develop heatstroke and another heat exhaustion. There are important differences, however, between the two conditions. Each represents a different bodily reaction to excessive heat. Thus symptoms and treatment also differ.

Heatstroke results from failure of the heat-regulating mechanism of the body. The body becomes overheated, the temperature rises to 105 to 110 degrees F, but there is no sweating or cooling of the body—the victim's skin is hot, dry, and red. He or she may have preliminary symptoms such as headache, nausea, dizziness, or weakness. But often the first signs are sudden collapse and loss of consciousness. Breathing is likely to be deep and rapid, and the pulse is strong and fast. Convulsions also may occur. Heatstroke may cause death or permanent disability; at best, recovery is slow and complicated by relapses.

The longer the victim remains overheated, the more likely he or she is to die. These first-aid measures are designed to lower the body temperature immediately:

Move the victim to a cool place, remove clothing, and place the victim on his or her back with head and shoulders slightly raised.

Sponge or spray the body with cold water, then fan it so the water will evaporate rapidly.

When the victim regains consciousness, give him or her cool, not cold, water to drink. Don't give stimulants or hot drinks.

Get the patient to a medical facility as soon as possible. Keep the victim cool during transportation.

Proper positioning of heat casualties is essential. The rule of thumb is, if the face is red, raise the head; if the face is pale, raise the tail.

Immersion Foot (or Trench Foot)

This is caused by prolonged exposure to a combination of moisture and cold. People on life rafts or in unprotected lifeboats are most likely to suffer immersion foot from exposure to near freezing sea waters. Cases have also occurred as a result of lengthy immersion in warmer waters. This condition can affect other parts of the body besides the feet, such as knees, hands, or buttocks. A person remaining for a long time in a cold, wet place, standing or crouching in one position, is likely to develop this condition.

Immersion foot brings with it a feeling of heaviness or numbness. All sensitivity may be lost, and the affected areas become swollen. The skin is first red, then waxy white, then a yellowish color, and finally a mottled blue or black. The injured parts usually remain cold, swollen, discolored, and numb. If they do thaw, the swelling increases and the skin becomes hot, dry, red, and blistered. In severe cases, gangrene may set in. Get the victim off his or her feet quickly, keep as warm as possible, and expose the injured part to warm, dry air.

If the skin is not broken or loose, the injured part may be left exposed. However, if it is necessary to move the victim, cover the injured part with loosely wrapped fluff bandages of sterile gauze. Do not apply salves or ointments. Be careful not to rupture blisters.

Insect Bites

Wash insect bites with soap and water and apply a paste of baking soda and water. Ice or ammonia applied to bee stings will prevent pain and swelling. Ticks can be dislodged by holding a lighted cigarette close to their behinds. Be careful not to crush the insect or leave its jaws embedded in flesh. Certain types of ticks can transmit Rocky Mountain spotted fever, which can be fatal. Inflamed bites require medical assistance.

Morphine

Morphine relieves severe pain. It should *not* be given if there is a head injury, chest injury, any injuries or burns that impair breathing, evidence of severe or deepening shock, or massive bleeding. Morphine should never be given to an unconscious person. Morphine should not be given if a doctor can be summoned in less than four hours. If morphine is given, the dosage must not be repeated for four hours.

Ordinarily, there is no need to administer morphine. If it must be used, follow these steps:

Inject morphine on the outer surface of the upper arm or into the thigh if the arms are injured. In very cold climates, morphine is sometimes injected into the back of the neck to avoid undressing the victim. If a tourniquet has been applied, the morphine must be injected above it (that is, between the tourniquet and the heart).

Sterilize the skin with antiseptic, alcohol, soap and water, or plain tap water. Pick up the tube with the Syrette at its shoulder, using your fingertips. Remove the shield, grasp the wire loop, and push the wire into the tube to break the seal. Pull out the wire and discard. Push the needle through the skin to its full length, then slowly squeeze out the contents of the Syrette. Withdraw the Syrette. Remove and discard the needle. Pin the empty Syrette tube to the person's shirt collar to show that morphine has been given. Also, with a skin pencil, colored antiseptic, ballpoint pen, etc., write the letter *M* and the time of the injection on the patient's forehead.

Poisoning

First-aid treatment here depends partly on how the poison enters the body—whether by swallowing, inhalation, skin contact, or injection. Here is a brief discussion of the symptoms and proper first aid for common types of poisoning.

Symptoms: Intense pain frequently follows poisoning. Nausea and vomiting may occur. The victim may become delirious or collapse and fall unconscious. He or she is almost always likely to have trouble breathing. Some poisons cause paralysis; others produce convulsions. Shock always follows acute poisoning.

Ingested Poisons: Many substances are poisonous if swallowed. *Corrosives* (substances that rapidly destroy or decompose body tissues on contact) may be *acids* (hydrochloric, nitric, sulfuric), *phenols* (carbolic acid, creosol [Lysol], creosote), or *alkalies* (lye, lime, ammonia). Iodine is also a corrosive.

Corrosives cause a burning pain in the mouth, a severe burning pain in the esophagus and stomach, retching, and vomiting. The inside of the mouth is eaten away. Swallowing and breathing become difficult. The abdomen is tender and distended with gas, and body temperature soars.

Irritants (substances that do not directly destroy body tissues but inflame the area they touch) are potassium nitrate, zinc chloride, zinc sulfate, arsenic, iodine, and phosphorus. Irritants cause faintness, nausea, vomiting, diarrhea, and cramps in the abdomen.

Depressants (substances that depress the nervous system) include atropine, morphine and its derivatives, bromides, barbiturates, alcohol, and most local anesthetics. They usually have a stimulating effect at first, then cause drowsiness, slow breathing, snoring, cold moist skin (with the face and fingers a bluish color), relaxed muscles, and dilated or contracted pupils.

Excitants (substances that stimulate the nervous system) are strychnine, camphor, and the fluorides. They cause delirium (mental disturbances, physical restlessness, and incoherence), a feeling of suffocation, hot dry skin, rapid and weak pulse, convulsions or jerking muscles, and dilated or contracted pupils.

Treatment: If possible, contact the poison-control center in your area for advice. Most likely you will be directed first to make sure that the patient is breathing, then to dilute the poison by having the patient drink one to two glasses of milk or water. Do not induce vomiting unless instructed to do so by the poison center.

One to three teaspoons of powdered mustard in a glass of warm water is an effective emetic (causes vomiting). Collect all vomitus in a container for further evaluation by authorities. Stabilize the patient and always seek medical assistance as soon as possible.

Inhaled Poisons: These can come from refrigeration machinery, firefighting equipment, paints and solvents, photographic materials, and other types of shipboard equipment that contain volatile and sometimes poisonous chemicals. Fuel oil and gasoline vapors are special hazards. Other poisonous gases are found in voids, double bottoms, empty fuel tanks, and similar places.

Carbon monoxide, the most frequent cause of gas poisoning, is colorless, odorless, and tasteless. It gives no warning. Carbon monoxide is present in the exhaust gases of internal-combustion engines.

First aid for carbon monoxide and other gases consists of the following:

1. Get the victim out of the toxic atmosphere into a well-ventilated space.
2. Remove his or her contaminated clothing.
3. Watch his or her breathing. Give artificial respiration if necessary.
4. Give oxygen if it is available and you know how to use it.
5. Keep the victim lying down. Keep him or her quiet. Treat the victim for shock.
6. Call a medical officer as soon as possible.

Gasoline, benzene, naphtha, and other petroleum products are poisonous if they are ingested, inhaled, or come into prolonged contact with the skin. The inhalation of gasoline fumes causes a kind of intoxication similar to drunkenness. The victim may become violent and self-destructive, or may injure others unless he or she is very carefully guarded. Caution: do not give morphine.

Carbon tetrachloride and other chlorinated hydrocarbons, such as methylene chloride, chloroform, dichloromethane, and tetrachlorethane, are used for dry cleaning, for removing grease from metal articles, for cleaning electrical and electronic equipment in various manufacturing processes, and in some fire extinguishers. They are extremely dangerous as fire-extinguishing agents because heat causes them to decompose, forming phosgene gas.

Someone exposed to these vapors may not realize the danger until he or she becomes dangerously ill with nausea, mental confusion, and in some instances, a kind of drunken behavior. Those required to work with chlorinated solvents must not drink liquor. Alcohol greatly increases susceptibility to this poisoning.

No antidote is known for poisoning by carbon tetrachloride and the other chlorinated hydrocarbons. Standard first-aid instructions should be followed.

Freon, a colorless, odorless gas used as a refrigerant, is toxic in high concentrations. First aid is the same as for other gases. Because even a very small amount of Freon can freeze the delicate tissue of the eye, medical attention must be obtained as soon as possible in order to avoid permanent damage. Meanwhile, cover each eye with a moist pad and have the patient lie down. Make sure the victim does not rub the eyes.

Hydrogen sulfide smells like rotten eggs. Its presence cannot always be detected because the gas paralyzes the sense of smell. It is flammable and poisonous.

The general signs of hydrogen-sulfide poisoning are eye, nose, and throat irritation and an abundant flow of tears. At first, breathing is deep, noisy, and grasping. Later it becomes feeble and irregular. Death is caused by paralysis of the brain.

Ammonia, an industrial gas used in many ways, is pungent, biting, and extremely irritating. No one can breathe a concentration of even $\frac{1}{10}$ of 1 percent ammonia; the irritation causes coughing and a spasm of the air passages. Death may occur from asphyxiation.

Administer standard first aid. In addition, hold vinegar or a weak solution of acetic acid close enough to the victim's face so that he or she can inhale the fumes. Stop if this does not give the patient relief.

Poisoning by Skin Contact: Poisoning by skin contact is not usually a first-aid problem. Such poisoning is frequently fatal, but it builds over a long period of time. There is no real cure, except to know the substances that cause it and to be careful in handling them. These include gasoline, benzene, naphtha, lead compounds, mercury, arsenic, carbon tetrachloride, and TNT.

Shock

When the nervous system is subjected to excessive shock, the nerves lose control of the blood vessels, allowing them to relax and thus reducing the supply of blood to the brain. Unconsciousness or "fuzzy-headiness" may result. The heart quickens its pace but the pulse is weak. All injury is attended by shock, which may be slight, lasting only a few seconds, or serious enough to kill. Shock may begin immediately, or it may be delayed as long as several hours.

How to Recognize Shock: The pulse is weak and rapid. Breathing may be shallow, rapid, and irregular. The skin feels cold to the touch and may be covered with sweat. The skin will be pale. In dark-complexioned people, the gums and fingernail beds turn ash gray. The pupils are usually dilated. A shock victim may complain of thirst. The victim may feel weak, faint or dizzy, and nauseated. He or she may be restless, frightened, and anxious. As shock deepens, these signs gradually disappear and the victim becomes less and less responsive, even to pain. A person in shock may insist that he or she feels fine, and then pass out.

Treatment: It is important to keep the patient flat on his or her back, feet higher than the body. Keep the patient warm with blankets, not artificial heat. Do all you can to relieve pain, but do not try to give any drugs. A person in shock is often thirsty. Moisten the mouth with cool water, but don't give the patient anything to drink.

Never give alcohol to a person who is in shock or may go into shock. Alcohol increases the blood supply to surface vessels, cutting the blood supply to the brain and other vital organs.

Transportation of the Injured

Take these precautions before transporting an injured person:

Locate all injuries to the best of your ability. Treat serious bleeding, breathing trouble, shock, fractures, sprains, and dislocations. Relieve the victim's pain if possible and make him or her as comfortable as possible.

Use a regular stretcher. If you must improvise, be sure that the stretcher is strong enough to hold the victim. Have several people carry the stretcher. Don't drop the victim; fasten the victim in the stretcher so that he or she cannot slip, slide, or fall off. Tie the victim's feet together unless injuries make this impracticable. Use blankets, garments, or other materials to pad the stretcher and to protect the victim from exposure.

An injured person should usually lie on his or her back while being moved, but someone having difficulty breathing because of a chest wound may be more comfortable with the head and shoulders slightly raised. Fracture cases should be moved very carefully, so the injury will not be made worse. A person with a severe injury to the back of the head should be kept on his or her side. A patient should always be carried feet first, unless there is some special reason for carrying the patient head first.

The three-man lift (figure 8-11) and the fireman's lift (figure 8-12) are recommended for carrying an injured person. The tied-hands crawl (figure 8-13) is used to transport a patient under special circumstances.

Three-Man Lift: No. 1 man takes head and shoulders of victim; no. 2, back and buttocks; no. 3, legs and feet. No. 1 says, "Ready, lift," and all lift together and keep the body straight. If the person has a chest wound, he or she is placed on the stomach. If a stomach wound, keep the victim on his or her back with knees bent.

Fireman's Lift: Turn the patient face down. Kneel over his or her head, facing the shoulders (A). Pass both your hands under the armpits and lift the victim to his or her knees. Then slide your hands down lower and clasp them around the back (B). Raise the victim to a standing position, stick your right leg between his or her legs (C), take the victim's right wrist in your left hand and swing his or her arm around the back of your neck, holding the victim close to you. Put your right arm between the victim's thighs (D), stoop quickly, pull his or her trunk across your shoulders, and straighten up (E).

To lower the patient, kneel on your left knee. Grasp his or her left knee with your right hand. Slide the victim around in front of you and down your right thigh into a sitting position. Shift your hands to his or her head and place the victim gently on the back.

169

Figure 8–11 The three-man lift is a recommended method of transporting an injured person.

Tied-Hands Crawl: Use this method when you must remain close to the deck, or when you must have both hands free for climbing a ladder.

Lay the patient on his or her back. Lie on your back alongside the victim and to his or her left. Grasp the victim's right arm above the elbow with your right hand. With your left hand, grasp the same arm below the elbow. Entwine your legs with the victim's and roll over on your chest, pulling him or her over onto your back. Now pull the victim's free hand (the left one) under your armpit. Tie his or her wrists together with a handkerchief or any other available material, then crawl forward.

Strokes Stretcher: This is a wire basket adaptable to a variety of uses. It will hold a person securely in place even when tipped. The Strokes stretcher is generally used for transferring the injured to and from boats or ships. It can be used to rescue people from the water. The stretcher should be padded with two blankets placed lengthwise so that one will be under each of the victim's legs, and a third folded in half and placed in the

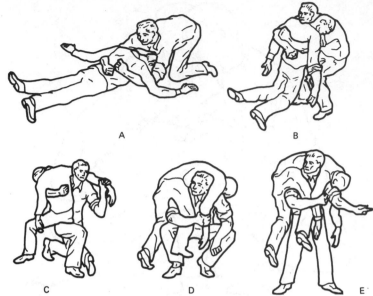

Figure 8–12   One person can transport an injury victim by using the fire-man's lift.

Figure 8–13   Transport an injured person with a tied-hands crawl when you must remain close to the deck or when you must have both hands free for climbing a ladder.

upper part of the stretcher to protect the head and shoulders.
The victim should be lowered gently onto the stretcher and made as comfortable as possible. The feet must be fastened to the end of the stretcher so that the victim will not slide up and down, and the body must be fastened into the stretcher by straps over the chest, hips, and knees. The straps go over the blanket or over the covering.

Neill-Robertson Stretcher: This stretcher is specifically designed for vertically removing victims in close spaces. It is all wood and canvas construction, and completely encloses the victim.

Army Litter: This consists of two wooden poles, $6\frac{1}{2}$ to 7 feet long, with canvas stretched across the poles. It is used for evacuation of the injured at land-based facilities. Check it for deterioration before using.

II. The Navy Career

Duty Assignments and Advancements

9

While you are in training or at school, everything will be organized for you, and after you report to your new ship or station, everything there will be organized too. But between the time you pick up your orders at your old station and turn them in at your new station, you may feel like a lost person. If you don't keep yourself organized, you might end up being just that.

Some transfers are simple; others are extremely complicated. You may be lucky and receive orders to a ship in port nearby. Or you may end up flying halfway around the world, check in at a base for a few days, ride a cargo ship somewhere else, and find out that your ship has just sailed back to where you came from. Suddenly you belong to no one. What do you do?

Remember, it's all one Navy, and no matter where you are, you can find someone to help. Always keep your orders in hand and not in your baggage, which may be lost. If you are given your records and pay accounts, keep them with your orders. You can obtain further transportation with your orders, and with your pay accounts you can draw pay—even from an Army or Air Force activity—if needed.

Make certain when you're checking out from your old duty station that you understand your orders. If they authorize DELREP (delay in reporting) to count as leave, check the date on which you must report to the new station. If commercial transportation is authorized at government expense, pick up the tickets or travel vouchers. If you have any questions at all, ask the transfer yeoman or personnelman before you leave; this may save you a lot of trouble later.

If you are ordered to a service school or other shore activity, any taxi driver at the airport, bus, or railroad terminal will know how to take you there. But finding a particular ship in a port city such as Norfolk or San Diego can be difficult—the ship could be anywhere within 30 or so miles. First check in with the Navy Shore Patrol (SP). If you can't find the SP, look in the telephone directory under U.S. Government to find some naval activity where you can obtain help. The Navy Recruiting Command, with recruiters in most major cities across the country, can be contacted if you're unable to contact a naval installation.

No matter what you wore on leave, be in complete and proper uniform when you report for duty. Be sure that you have all your gear with you; the ship may sail the same day, and what you checked at the airport or station will do you no good at sea. Hand your orders to the watch, either at the main gate or the quarterdeck, so that they can be endorsed and stamped with the time and date of reporting, and you can be logged in.

Centralized Detailing

At any one time, about two-thirds of the enlisted personnel in the Navy are in seagoing billets and the other third in shore billets. To make certain that everyone gets a fair share of each kind of duty assignment, a system of centralized detailing has been set up by the Naval Military Personnel Command (NMPC). Because it is a complicated system, full details are contained in the Enlisted Transfer Manual (TRANSMAN, NAVPERS 15909). Always check with a career counselor before making any requests under this system.

All personnel, except nondesignated seamen (SN), firemen (FN), and airmen (AN) who are under the control of the Enlisted Personnel Management Center (EPMAC) in New Orleans, are assigned by NMPC.

Duty-Type Codes

Eight duty-type designations are used to establish an equitable rotation of sea and shore assignments. Each of these duty types is credited as sea, shore, or neutral duty for rotational purposes. The codes are assigned (and, when necessary, changed) exclusively by NMPC.

The eight types are as follows:

Type 1 Shore Duty: Duty performed in CONUS (The continental United States) at land-based activities and other CONUS activities designated as "long-term" schooling programs. (Long-term means eighteen or more months; school assignments of less than eighteen months are considered neutral duty.)

Type 2 Sea Duty: Also known as arduous sea duty, this is performed in commissioned active-status vessels, homeported or homebased in CONUS, which operate away from their permanent homes for extended periods.

Type 3 Overseas Shore Duty: Duty performed at overseas land bases, including Alaska and Hawaii, at locations where the prescribed tour length is less than thirty-six months.

Type 4 Nonrotated Sea Duty: Duty performed in commissioned active-status vessels homeported overseas (outside CONUS), or performed with activities that operate away from overseas homeports or bases for extended periods.

Type 5 Neutral Duty: Duty in activities normally designated as shore duty for rotational purposes, but where the personnel are absent, for a significant length of time, from the corporate limits of their duty station while performing their assignments. It also includes school assignments of less than eighteen months.

Type 6 Preferred Overseas Shore Duty: Duty performed in specified overseas land-based activities, including Alaska and Hawaii, at locations having suitable dependent accommodations and support facilities. The tours normally last at least thirty-six months.

177

Type 7 Overseas Sea Duty: Duty performed in overseas land-based activities and considered full sea duty for rotational purposes.

Type 8 Double Sea Duty: This duty is performed in commissioned active-status vessels that operate away from their homeports or bases for extended periods. Owing to the nature of their missions, personnel assigned are awarded double-sea-duty credit.

For rotational purposes, types 1, 6, and 7 count as shore-duty credit; types 2, 3, 4, and 8 for sea-duty credit; and type 5 for neutral duty credit.

The length of tours at sea and ashore for each rating depends primarily on the ratio of shore billets to sea billets. For both personal and command stability, every effort is made to maintain a three-year sea/shore rotation pattern. Tour lengths for all rates and certain NEC (navy enlisted classification) codes are contained in the TRANSMAN.

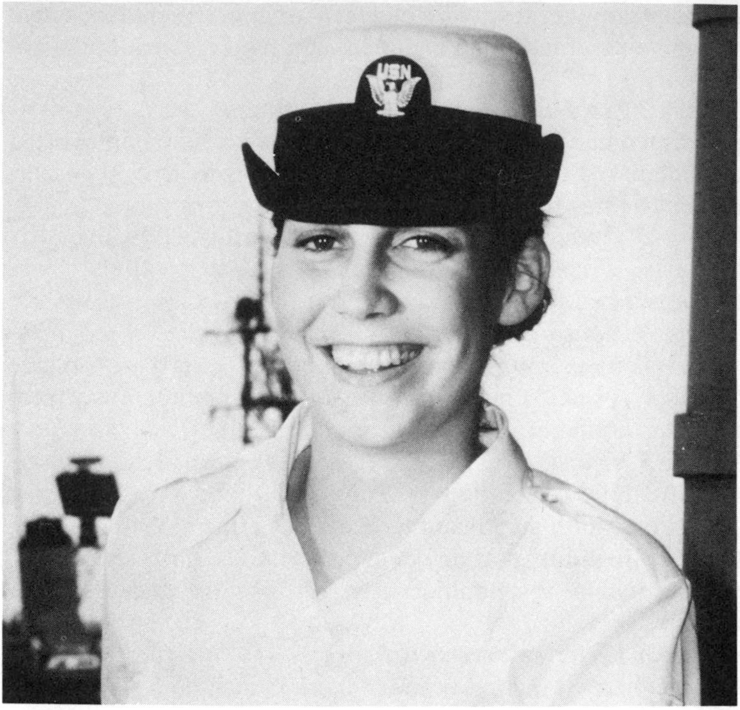

Figure 9–1 Rotation for enlisted women is categorized as in the United States (CONUS) or out of the United States (OUTUS), and for some ratings as sea or shore duty.

Rotation for Enlisted Women

The rotation for enlisted women is identified as SEA/SHORE and normally parallels that of their male counterparts. However, sea-duty opportunities as not as great for women because of the limited availability of shipboard billets. The rotation for enlisted women has been changed to allow more women to serve at sea, enter sea-intensive ratings, and be assigned on a rotation pattern more consistent with their rating. This provides all personnel the opportunity to develop their skills and fully use them.

Enlisted-Duty Preferences

For planning purposes, each person in the Navy is provided with a projected rotation date (PRD) that estimates the tentative month and year of the next assignment. Although the Navy will try to transfer you at a PRD, this date, established

Central-
ized
Detailing

for planning purposes, will not always reflect the precise time of your reassignment. PRDs are established and modified by NMPC.

There are two important forms used in this system: enlisted-duty preferences (NAVPERS 1306/63), and enlisted personnel action requests (NAVPERS 1306/7).

Duty-Preferences Form: If you want to be considered for the type of duty you prefer, you should complete a 1306/63. This allows you to state preferences as to type of ship; homeport for sea duty, overseas duty, and shore duty; and localities for overseas or shore duty. Concisely stated, detailing is the process whereby available personnel assets are matched with existing Navy-wide requirements in such a manner as best to satisfy the individual's duty preferences. If you have no duty preference on file, you will be assigned to fill any valid requirement.

Submission of the duty-preferences form is an individual responsibility. The initial 1306/63 is submitted upon arrival at your first permanent duty station. Subsequent forms may be submitted anytime your duty preferences change, and must be submitted when significant personal changes occur, for instance, a change in dependency status or in the physical location of household goods.

Although the 1306/63 was designed to reflect the information most pertinent to an individual's assignability, it is recognized that no form of this type can be all-encompassing. Accordingly, a remarks section has been incorporated for you to add useful information. Examples of such information are any skill you have not identified by NEC; the community-support skills of one of your dependents (teacher, nurse, dental technician, secretary, hairdresser, etc.); handicapped dependents and areas where appropriate treatment facilities are located; and expected delivery date if you have a wife who is pregnant.

Enlisted Personnel Action Request: This request form, NAVPERS 1306/7, gives you an opportunity to request participation in programs of a more immediate nature. In general, use the form only to request a program, school, reassignment, or special duty for which a particular requesting format has not been specified. These unspecified formats could include humanitarian assignments, reenlistment incentive, and the SCORE program. There is one important consideration for all such requests: You must be eligible for the type of duty requested.

Assignment to Programs

To answer the increasing complexity of the Navy's mission, special programs are established for tasks requiring skills not identified by existing ratings. Once a long-term requirement for a particular skill is identified, a program is integrated into the regular naval organization and, if necessary, a new rating is established for that skill.

One illustration is the establishment of the NC (Navy counselor) rating. It has been evident for some time that the existing Navy rating structure didn't provide a rating for personnel skilled in the fields of recruiting and retention. While most billets in recruiting are still filled by persons from a variety of ratings, NCs are now beginning to take over more and more of these specialized responsibilities. (The NC rating is more fully discussed on p. 38.)

Some of the programs discussed below have specific rating requirements, others do not. Since all of them are subject to change, you'll do well to check with your career counselor for the exact details.

Navy Food-Management Teams

Navy food-management teams provide technical and management assistance to mess-management specialists (MS) in the operation of enlisted dining facilities and afloat wardrooms. Members get on-the-job training in areas of food preparation and service, mess management, and sanitation. They assist both fleet units and shore activities. Teams are located at Norfolk, Charleston, San Diego, and Pearl Harbor.

Mobile Technical Unit Program

Mobile technical units (MOTUs) provide specialized electronic- and weapons-training service to the fleets. They also play an important part in maintaining readiness of fleet electronic and weapons equipment. MOTU headquarters are at Commander, Naval Logistics Command, Pearl Harbor, and Commander, Naval Surface Force, Norfolk. There are presently twelve MOTUs located at Pearl Harbor, Norfolk, New London, San Diego, San Francisco, Charleston, Mayport, Newport, and Kings Bay, Georgia. Three MOTUs are at overseas locations: Naples, Italy; Subic Bay, the Philippines; and Yokosuka, Japan.

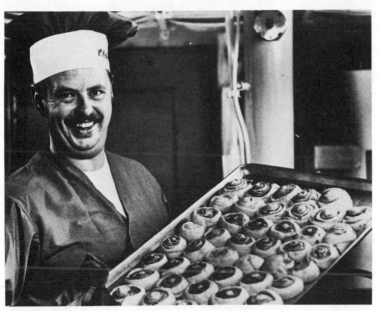

Figure 9–2 Navy mess-management specialists serve menus that have been planned to give you a proper diet and set good eating habits. Food-management teams provide technical and management assistance to MSs ashore and afloat.

Brig and Correctional Custody Unit Staffs

Brigs and correctional custody units, located in areas of fleet concentration, training commands, and overseas activities, serve a geographic region. They provide an exceptional opportunity for personnel to enhance their leadership qualities and counseling abilities, regardless of military specialty.

Career-Counseling Program

The NMPC-controlled counseling program assigns full-time career counselors to billets other than NC. These personnel assist commanding officers and unit commanders in maintaining an effective career-motivation program.

Naval Intelligence Support Center

The requirement exists for a small but growing number of submarine-qualified sonar technicians (STs) at the Naval Intelligence Support Center in Washington, D.C.

Special Staff Assignments

These assignments include duty in military assistance advisory groups (MAAGs), naval missions, military groups (and similar activities), NATO commands, and joint staff and Navy staffs. While the largest percentage of these billets is for yeoman (YN), radioman (RM), and storekeeper (SK) ratings—paygrades E-3 through E-9—some requirements also exist for a variety of other ratings and NECs. Those interested should contact the MAAGs mission desk in NMPC to see if a requirement exists for a particular rating and paygrade.

Pride, Professionalism, and Personal Excellence Programs

These programs provide for the assignment of full-time human-resource-management specialists, instructors, and consultants, in billets under the assignment control of NMPC. Personnel assist commands in establishing and maintaining an effective human-resource-management plan. Specialists assigned to the program are occupational-effectiveness specialists (OESs), human-resource-management specialists, collateral-duty alcoholism counselors (CODACs), race-relations education specialists (RRESs), drug and alcohol education specialists (DAESs), and alcoholism-treatment specialists (ATSs).

Naval Support Unit, State Department

The Navy has established the Naval Support Unit of the State Department to provide continuing Seabee support to the State Department security program. This duty involves security surveillance of foreign contract construction, and minor construction repairs and maintenance within the foreign service establishment. Personnel are desired on a volunteer basis. Nonvolunteers can also be used. Tours, normally three years, consist of a one-year unaccompanied tour followed by a two-year accompanied tour in the same general area.

Operation Deep Freeze

Each year the Naval Support Force, Antarctica, and Air Development Squadron 6 (VXE 6) participate in the Antarctic expedition. Personnel requirements for the summer support group are open to most rates and ratings on a continuing basis. An NMPC notice, published annually, outlines the specific qualifications for participants in the wintering-over party, known as Detachment Alfa.

Figure 9–3 An aviation boatswain's mate wears a face mask for protection against the cold Antarctica weather during a tour of duty with Operation Deep Freeze.

Blue Angels

The U.S. Navy Flight Demonstration Team—known as the Blue Angels, or The Blues—is based at the Naval Air Station in Pensacola. A number of enlisted support billets are available with the team. Because of the extensive time away from permanent duty stations, this duty is neutral duty for rotation and lasts for a period of three years. Requests may be made to NMPC through your chain of command and via the officer in charge of the team.

The USS *Constitution*

The USS *Constitution*, affectionately known as Old Ironsides, is an important part of the U.S. Navy's history. The *Constitution,* berthed in Boston, represents the Navy as it was in the 1800s. Because the *Constitution*'s crew is in constant contact with the public, they must be immaculately groomed and exhibit exemplary military bearing. Enlisted crewmembers are assigned directly from recruit training. Petty officers are selected from those eligible for shore duty.

Other Programs

Special programs are also provided so that personnel can qualify for assignment to the Aircrew Program; for the UDT (underwater-demolition team), SEAL (sea-air-land), and EOD (explosive-ordinance-disposal) programs; for the Deep-Sea Diver Program; and for the Service Craft Program. The latter includes persons designated as tugmasters (NEC 0161) and yard-craft boat captains (NEC 0162).

Instructor Duty

Owing to the level of expertise required, applicants for instructor duty must be petty officers. Request should be indicated on the NAVPERS 1306/63 form. Personnel selected as instructors are ordered to instructor school on a temporary-duty basis, en route to their final duty station. Instructor schools are located at Great Lakes, San Diego, Norfolk, and Millington, Tennessee. The four-week course covers the methods and techniques of training.

Those accepted for instructor duty are on probation for a period of at least ninety days, under the direct supervision of a seasoned instructor. After this period, the probation is usually terminated and a recommendation is made for the assignment of an appropriate NEC instructor designation.

In addition to the many instructor assignments to fill the Navy's large schooling system, there are also a number of specialized instructor assignments. These include recruit company commander and instructor at activities concerned with survival training, Naval Reserve, aviation, and nuclear propulsion.

Figure 9–4 A sailor in a special unit emerges from a mud swim while others strain under the weight of a telephone pole. This is part of their underwater demolition team and sea-air-land training at a Navy amphibious base.

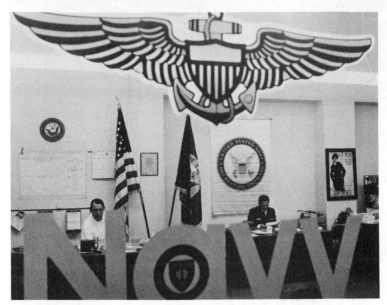

Figure 9–5 Personnel in all ratings may apply for recruiting duty.

Recruiting Duty

It is especially important that personnel assigned to the Navy Recruiting Command exemplify the highest standards of personal conduct. A recruiter is constantly under the scrutiny of civilians in the surrounding community. Enlisted personnel in paygrades E-5 and above are assigned mainly to recruiting districts located within CONUS. There are also a limited number of assignments available in Alaska, Hawaii, Guam, Puerto Rico, the Philippines, and Europe.

Personnel in all ratings may apply for assignment to recruiting duty. If selected, those in YN, SK, PN, DK, and JO ratings are normally assigned to recruiter support billets only. Female personnel of all ratings can apply for recruiter/canvasser duty.

On your way to recruiting duty, you'll stop off at the Navy Recruiting Orientation Unit in Orlando for five weeks of intensive training and instruction. The orientation course covers approximately 200 hours of instruction. At the completion of this course, prospective field recruiters should be thoroughly familiar with the many career programs available for volunteers, the proper method of explaining and presenting this information, and the necessary paperwork involved.

Exchange of Duty

There are occasions when the assignment of an individual to a specific area would be highly beneficial to the individual's morale, but not justifiable in view of the expenditure of government funds required. The Navy may effect such transfers, provided the individual agrees to bear all expenses involved. There are two types of duty exchange, usually called swaps. One is negotiated by NMPC and is based on a letter of request from you. The other is self-negotiated and requested on the NAVPERS 1306/7 form, the enlisted transfer and special-duty request. The specific requirements are contained in the TRANSMAN.

Humanitarian Reassignments

Detailing authorities are aware of the hardships confronting Navy families and of the additional aggravation imposed by long absences of service members from their families. Emergency leave frequently provides sufficient time to alleviate hardship; however, when an individual requires more time than leave can provide and has a reasonable chance of resolving the hardship within a specified time frame, reassignment for humanitarian reasons (HUMS) may be required.

Your personnel office can give you additional information regarding HUMS assignments and help you determine your eligibility for one.

The Navy also will make provision for the assignment or reassignment of members of the same family. According to the rules, family members include spouse, father, mother, sons, daughters, brothers, sisters, step-brothers, step-sisters, and adopted brothers and sisters. Specific requirements are contained in the TRANSMAN.

Enlisted Advancement System

Many of the above special-duty assignments require that applicants be senior petty officers. The following is a detailed examination of the enlisted advancement system you must go through to get to the rank of senior petty officer.

All advancements in the Navy (except for a few meritorious advancements under the Sailor of the Year and Command Advancement programs [BUPERSINST 1430.17]) are made

Figure 9–6 Uniform appearance and proper military bearing are factors considered in advancement in rate.

through centralized competition. Because the requirements sometimes change, it is always best to consult with your personnel office or educational-services office for the latest information.

General Requirements

In general, there are certain qualifications each person must meet to be eligible to compete in the semiannual or annual Navy-wide examinations for advancement in rate. These include the following:

Having the required time in rate (TIR). The specific TIR requirement for advancement from E-1 to E-2 is nine months; for E-3, nine months; E-4 nine months; E-5 twelve months; E-6 thirty-six months; and E-7, E-8, and E-9, are thirty-six months each. Time in service (TIS) is no longer a factor in establishing requirements for advancement. The elimination of TIS enables superior performers to advance commensurate with their ability and performance. It is possible, with hard work and diligent study, to become a chief petty officer within nine years.

Completing established personnel advancement requirements (PARs) for the projected paygrade. Each PAR contains descriptive information, instructions for administration, special rating requirements (such as physical, citizenship, or secu-

Advancement System

rity clearance), and advancement requirements of the following types: administrative; formal school and training; and occupational and military ability.

Successfully passing the military-leadership examination. This is a prerequisite for competing for advancement to paygrades E-4, E-5, E-6, and E-7. There is an examination for each grade. Personnel in paygrades E-2 and E-3 who are not eligible to take the professional exam (the semiannual or annual Navy-wide tests) may take the military-leadership examination. You need only pass once in each grade to establish eligibility.

If required, passing a performance test such as a typing test for YNs, PNs , RMs, and JOs; a semaphore test for SMs; and a flashing-light test for QMs.

Completing any required Navy training or correspondence courses and service schools.

Meeting requirements for proficiency marks.

And the most important requirement in the advancement system—being recommended by your commanding officer.

Final Multiple Score (FMS)

The competitive system uses a combination of factors to determine the final multiple for each person. For E-4s and E-5s, the maximum percentage you can earn is 35 percent from the examination, 30 percent for performance, 13 percent for length of service, 13 percent for service in paygrade, 4.5 percent for awards, and 4.5 percent for high-quality or passed-but-not-advanced points. The percentages for E-6s are the same, except they receive 30 percent for the examination and 35 percent for performance.

Because of selection-board screening for E-7s, the FMS advancement system is somewhat different. The E-7 FMS is calculated by taking 60 percent for the examination and 40 percent for the leadership evaluation (directing/counseling).

These are the only factors used in determining E-7 FMS. The system is designed to give more advancement consideration to members who, through outstanding performance and leadership ability, have exhibited the potential to assume increased levels of responsibility. Based on the final multiple score, each candidate's examination results fall within one of three categories: (1) SBE (selection board eligible), (2) SBI (selection board ineligible), or (3) fail. SBE candidates comprise 50 percent of the test-takers for E-7.

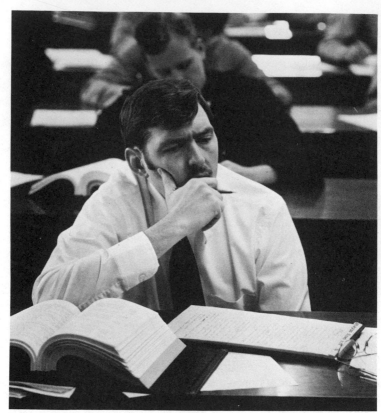

Figure 9–7 Formal classroom study is an important part of the Navy's system for advancement and produces a more proficient sailor for the fleet.

Promotion examinations for the top two enlisted grades, E-8 and E-9, are no longer given. Those who have three years in rate, have satisfactorily completed military requirements for senior and master chief petty officer (NAVTRA 91209), and are recommended will automatically be eligible for selection-board consideration.

In addition to the above advancement point credits, two additional FMS points may be added for each enlisted warfare specialty earned.

Senior Enlisted Grades

Until 1958, a person who had advanced to chief petty officer (CPO, E-7) had gone as high as possible in the enlisted rating structure. Then the grades of senior chief petty officer (SCPO, E-8), and master chief petty officer (MCPO, E-9), were established to give additional recognition to people with outstanding technical, leadership, and supervisory abilities.

While advancement to E-7 is considered normal for a 20-year career, the E-8 and E-9 paygrades are regarded as 30-year career plans. Candidates for E-8 and E-9, having met all the requirements, have their service records closely screened by a selection board at NMPC. This is where a good record becomes extremely important—those with the best records are selected over those with records that may be good, but not good enough.

Master Chief Petty Officer Of The Navy

The master chief petty officer of the Navy (MCPON) is the Navy's senior enlisted member. Assigned to the Office of the Chief of Naval Operations for a 3-year-tour of duty, the MCPON serves as senior enlisted representative of the Navy and as senior enlisted adviser to the chief of naval operations and the chief of naval personnel in all matters pertaining to enlisted personnel.

The MCPON also serves as an advisor to many boards dealing with enlisted personnel; accompanies the chief of naval operations on some trips; serves as the enlisted representative of the Department of the Navy at special events, celebrations, and ceremonies; and maintains a liaison with the Navy Wives' Club of America.

Fleet, Force, and Command Master Chief Petty Officers

The fleet and force master chief petty officers (F M/Cs) and the command master chief petty officers (C M/Cs) function as principal enlisted advisers to unit commanders and commanding officers. They have made better communications possible at all levels of command throughout the Navy and have fostered sensitivity to the needs and viewpoints of enlisted men and women, as well as their families.

They have the responsibility of keeping their commanders or commanding officers up to date on situations, procedures, and practices that affect the welfare, morale, and well-being of the enlisted crew. F M/Cs and C M/Cs have direct access to their commanders or commanding officers.

Presently there are four fleet and twenty-three force master chief billets in the Navy, and new command master chief billets are continuously being added to the existing list. Command master chief billets carry the secondary NEC of 9580. These billets are filled through NMPC by a C M/C detailer. The establishment of such a billet is determined by the number of personnel assigned to a command. Navy commands with 250 or more personnel are eligible to have a C M/C (SNEC 9580) billet. Commands that don't meet this criterion may designate an MCPO from within the command to serve as a collateral-duty C M/C. In commands with no MCPOs, a command senior chief (C S/C) may be designated, and where there are no MCPOs or SCPOs, a command chief (C Ch) may be designated.

To be assigned the secondary NEC of 9580 (C M/C), an MCPO is screened by NMPC. The process for this screen is much the same as for the E-7/8/9 selection board. Leadership and management ability is the primary consideration. The C M/C assists the commanding officer and executive officer in formulating policy that concerns the enlisted personnel of the command. The C M/C's advice is particularly helpful to the command on matters concerning the morale, personal problems, and quality of life for enlisted personnel and their dependents. Through the C M/C every sailor, regardless of rank or station, has a secure line of communication.

FLEET AND FORCE MASTER CHIEF BILLETS

Fleet Master Chief, U.S. Pacific Fleet*
Fleet Master Chief, U.S. Atlantic Fleet*
Fleet Master Chief, Naval Forces Europe*
Fleet Master Chief, Naval Education and Training*
Force Master Chief, Naval Security Group Command
Force Master Chief, Military Sealift Command
Force Master Chief, Naval Air Systems Command
Force Master Chief, Naval Medical Command*
Force Master Chief, Fleet Air Mediterranean
Force Master Chief, Naval Supply Systems Command
Force Master Chief, Naval Logistics Command, Pacific Fleet
Force Master Chief, Commander Naval Reserve Force*
Force Master Chief, Naval Air Training
Force Master Chief, Submarine Force, Pacific Fleet*
Force Master Chief, Naval Facilities Engineering Command
Force Master Chief, Naval Air Force, Pacific Fleet*
Force Master Chief, Naval Surface Force, Atlantic Fleet*

Force Master Chief, Naval Sea Systems Command
Force Master Chief, Training Command, Atlantic Fleet
Force Master Chief, Naval Technical Training
Force Master Chief, Naval Telecommunications Command
Force Master Chief, Naval Surface Force, Pacific Fleet*
Force Master Chief, Navy Recruiting Command
Force Master Chief, Mine Warfare Command
Force Master Chief, Naval Air Force, Atlantic Fleet*
Force Master Chief, Submarine Force, Atlantic Fleet*
Force Master Chief, Training Command, Pacific Fleet

* Members of the chief of naval operation's MCPO Advisory Panel, which meets annually for one week in Washington, D.C.

Chief of the Boat

The Navy's submarine service has assignments similar to those of C M/Cs; these assignments go to chiefs of the boat (COBs). But there are subtle differences. COBs are a little bit like the C Chs, the CMAAs (chief masters-at-arms), and the LCPOs (leading chief petty officers) of the surface and shore Navy. While their duties include many of the administrative functions associated with C Chs, many of the law-and-order functions associated with CMAAs, and much of the extensive hands-on work that LCPOs perform, there are still a number of differences.

An individual first becomes available for a COB assignment by volunteering. COBs are E-8s or E-9s. A special NEC is awarded to a person selected for COB duty. As you'll see, COB responsibilities are varied.

The COB assigns bunks and lockers; details personnel to compartment cleaning, mess cooking, and special details; and assists the executive officer in maintaining the watch, quarter, and station (WQ&S) bill. The COB is responsible for ship cleanliness and proper stowage of all special clothing and safety equipment (life jackets, escape hoods, breathing equipment, lines, and cables). In addition, the COB is responsible, under direction of the commanding officer, for ensuring strict compliance with all safety regulations.

One of the most important functions of the COB is serving as qualification officer for the on-board enlisted submarine-qualification program. The COB coordinates and supervises— through division leading petty officers (LPOs)—the conduct, performance, and administration of all enlisted personnel. Another responsibility is monitoring leave and special liberty.

The COB, considered an executive petty officer in all matters affecting enlisted personnel, is charged with departmental coordination at the level of LPO. As such, this person reports directly to the commanding officer and is the senior petty officer on board. By virtue of the position, the COB works closely with the executive officer and all officers on board.

Division Chief/Leading Petty Officer

Every command, whether afloat or ashore, is divided into departments and divisions, and in every division the senior enlisted person is the division chief or the LPO. In one respect, the function of the division chief or LPO is similar to that of the C M/C, only on a smaller scale. The division chief or LPO is responsible for the morale and welfare of his or her subordinates, but also functions as the technical expert for the division. In a larger division, there may be several work centers to which supervisors are assigned. The primary duty of the division chief/LPO is then in the area of personnel management, with the work-center supervisors responsible for the more technical aspects of the division's assignments. The division chief/LPO is responsible for all work performed by his or her division, and he or she reports directly to the division officer. The division chief/LPO also maintains liaison with the C M/C on all matters that concern the morale, welfare, and proper employment of enlisted members of the division.

Educational and Commission Opportunities

10

Education in the Navy begins with recruit training and continues throughout your naval career, whether it lasts for four years or thirty. Navy vocational/technical schools are only one phase of Navy education. Those not attending school can take Navy training courses (self-study). And every sailor at one time or another is involved in a formal or informal on-the-job training (OJT) program.

Every enlisted person must complete a training course or attend the equivalent school to become eligible for promotion. He or she also must demonstrate a mastery of the requirements for the next higher paygrade—measured by the personnel advancement requirement (PAR) system—before becoming eligible to compete for advancement.

Promotion in the Navy is determined by time in rate (TIR), quality of work, examination marks, and demonstrated ability. The Navy's promotion system is unique; no one fails to advance simply because he or she is assigned to a unit that doesn't need another person in the next higher paygrade. Competition for advancement is Navy-wide. Anyone who is qualified and recommended may take the exam. Typically, it takes twelve years or more to become a chief petty officer (CPO); it is possible, however, to advance from recruit to CPO in nine years.

While no specific amount of education is required for joining the Navy, it is obvious that a good education will contribute to the effectiveness of those who work in a vast technical organization. Most people joining the Navy today are at least high-school graduates.

Young men and women who want to learn and improve themselves have unlimited opportunities in the Navy today. They can take simple correspondence courses and attend a wide range of schools, both within the Navy and at civilian educational institutions. Those who have not completed high

Figure 10–1   A good education is the key to advancement and to getting the job done right in today's technological Navy. Knowing where and how to look up information to perform your daily mission effectively is part of your Navy education and what makes you a vital part of the Navy team. Here, flight-deck crewmen verify weight and steam pressure to adjust the catapult for the next aircraft launch.

school can earn an equivalency certificate, and those who qualify can take a full 4-year college course for a bachelor's degree or, through selection for officer training programs, earn a commission in the Navy.

Personnel Qualification Standards (PQS)

Every step of the way from E-2 to E-9 is governed by the Personnel Qualification Standards (PQS) Manual, often called the Quals Manual.

The manual sets up standards for the training courses and publications you will use, curricula for the schools you will attend, and specific programs for OJT you will enter. The PQS Manual also sets the standards for Navy-wide advancement exams and, in general, governs all preparations for advancement in the Navy. Your career counselor, the master chief petty officer of your command, or someone in the personnel or educational-services office is best qualified to explain the fine points to you.

Minimum requirements for advancement to specific pay-grades, including professional knowledge and practical work, are part of the military standards listed in the PQS. Occupational standards—specific practical skills and knowledge you'll need for advancement in a general rate or rating—are also listed. The career-pattern section of the manual outlines the path of advancement you will normally take. It also tells you some of the schools you must attend.

Service Schools

Navy service schools are located at the three training centers and at Memphis, Tennessee; Gulfport and Meridian, Mississippi; Norfolk, Virginia; and Port Hueneme (pronounced *Y-neemee*), California, among other places. For some ratings, graduation from a particular service school is necessary for advancement; the PQS Manual will tell you which ones. Selection for a service school depends on your rate, time in service, current duty assignment, school quotas, and the operational schedule of your unit. Although you can attend a service school on a temporary additional duty (TAD) basis from your current duty station, most school assignments are made with a permanent change of station (PCS).

The five types of enlisted service schools are:

Class A: Provides the basic technical knowledge required for job performance and, later, specialized training. A Navy enlisted classification (NEC) code may be awarded to identify the skill.

Class C: Advanced skills and techniques needed to perform a particular job are taught. This category includes schools and courses previously identified as Class B. An NEC code may also be awarded to identify the level of skill.

Class E: Designed for professional education leading to an academic degree.

Class F: Trains fleet personnel who are en route to, or are members of, ships' companies. Also provides individual training such as refresher, operator, maintenance, or technical training of less than thirteen calendar days. An NEC code is not awarded.

Class R: This is the basic school that provides initial training after enlistment. It prepares the recruit for early adjustment to military life by inculcating basic skills and knowledge about military subjects. Class R schooling does not include apprenticeships. However, apprenticeship schools are conducted at

Figure 10–2 To advance your Navy career, you've got to study and stay abreast of the latest developments in your field.

the three recruit training centers. Everyone attends one of three Class R schools in San Diego, Great Lakes, or Orlando.

The two remaining types of schools, Class P and Class V, are designed for officers. Class P, for officer-acquisition programs, is designed to provide undergraduate education and training for midshipmen, officer candidates, and all other newly commissioned officers, except those acquired through Class V programs. Class V schools provide the training that leads to designation as a naval aviator or naval flight officer.

Since the eligibility requirements for schools vary, and change frequently, you should check the Catalog of Navy Training Courses (CANTRAC), NAVEDTRA 10500. CAN-

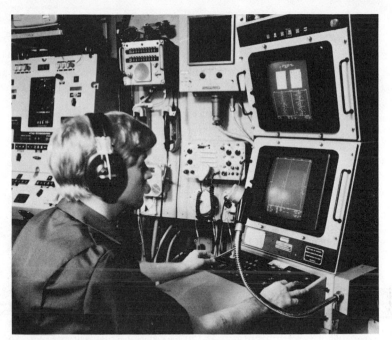

Figure 10–3   Basic and advanced schools provide the technical knowledge sailors need to perform their jobs.

TRAC has information on schools and courses under the direction of the chief of naval education and training (CNET). Be sides CANTRAC, you have three other sources of information on schools—your educational services office, your career counselor, and your personnel office. They can provide you with full information on how to apply for any of the following programs.

Selective Training and Reenlistment (STAR) Program

This program can guarantee early reenlistment, career designation, a variety of school programs, automatic advancement, and payment of a selective reenlistment bonus (SRB). Applicants must be E-5s, E-4s, or qualified E-3s. They also must have at least twenty-one months, but not more than five years, of continuous naval service (and not more than eight years of total military service). Applicants also should be recommended by their commanding officers, be serving in their first enlistment, meet the minimum test-score requirements for entrance into the appropriate Class A school, and agree to reenlist for or extend their enlistment to a period of six years.

Nuclear-power-trained personnel normally serve a tour of three years in an operational nuclear billet before attending the guaranteed school.

Although all ratings are eligible, the emphasis is on those serving in critical ratings or those with critical NECs.

Selective Conversion and Reenlistment (SCORE) Program

SCORE is for people in ratings that are overmanned or have limited advancement opportunities. It encourages them to shift into a critical rating. The program offers a variety of schooling guarantees, automatic advancement, early reenlistment, and payment of the SRB—although SRB is not considered a SCORE guarantee. Applicants in paygrades E-6, E-5, and E-4 and identified E-3 strikers who have more than twenty-one months of continuous active naval service (but not more than fifteen years of total active military service) are eligible.

Applicants must be recommended by their commanding officers, be within one year of expiration of obligated service (EAOS) as extended, and meet the obligatory service and test-score requirements to enter the appropriate Class A school. One of SCORE's chief benefits is that candidates have an opportunity to work in the rating to which they are converting before being assigned to school. SCORE is a six-year obligation.

Guaranteed Assignment Retention Detailing (GUARD III) Program

The purpose of the GUARD III program is to guarantee assignment as a reenlistment incentive to all petty officers and eligible E-3s with less than twenty-five years of service. GUARD III is also designed to encourage direct contact between reenlistment-eligible persons who are approaching their EAOS and their detailers in NMPC. Contact should be made after counseling by the command career counselor, informally (by telephone or personal letter) any time within six months prior to EAOS.

GUARD III guarantees two assignments; one must be used at first reenlistment, while the second may be used anytime before beginning the twenty-fifth year of service.

To be eligible for GUARD III, you must be without PCS orders; not more than six months away from your EAOS; qualified under current NMPC instructions; and eligible for the duty requested in accordance with the sea/shore or OUT-CONUS/CONUS rotation pattern. Candidates must also be recommended by their commanding officer, be willing to reenlist for four or more years, and have a consistent record of above-average or steadily improving performance.

Assignments are normally made for the appropriate sea, shore, or area tour.

The above GUARD III program does not apply to nuclear-trained personnel. A separate program, known as the Nuclear GUARD, guarantees assignment of top-quality nuclear-trained personnel who are qualified for operational reactor-plant duty.

The Nuclear GUARD program also encourages direct contact between those qualified for the program and their NMPC detailers. The program applies only to persons in the ET, EM, and MM ratings who have certain NECs. Specific options are detailed in a Nuclear GUARD letter sent to qualified individuals. Here are the general options:

1. Persons serving in an operational nuclear billet at sea may request a guaranteed assignment to shore duty; they may also request sea or neutral duty in a nuclear ship or at the homeport of their choice.

2. Persons serving in a nonoperational nuclear billet, or nonnuclear billet classified as sea or neutral duty, may request guaranteed assignment to a nuclear ship or to the coast of their choice.

3. Persons serving on shore duty may request a guaranteed assignment to a nuclear ship or the coast of their choice.

Assignment to School Incentive

The Navy also has provisions to guarantee reenlistees a specific school. Generally, a sailor must meet the service and entrance requirements for the appropriate school. Consideration of requests is based on composite training, sea/shore rotation, paygrade-versus-skill requirement, and fleet reserve eligibility. Assignments to schools normally occur at the member's projected rotation date (PRD).

Figure 10–4 Among the Navy's modern schools is a self-paced, computerized instruction center.

Changes in Rate or Rating

Since the Navy wants each sailor to serve in the rate or rating for which he or she has the greatest aptitude and interest, regulations provide for lateral changes in rate and rating. *Lateral change* means that you can change your apprenticeship field or occupational specialty without changing your paygrade. The program is rather complex, so if you're contemplating a change in rate or rating, you would do well to check current directives or consult with your career counselor, personnel office, or educational services office.

You can change your apprenticeship field through your commanding officer. Normally it will be approved if a greater need exists in the apprenticeship you want to switch to. Changes in rate or rating may also be accomplished via formal school training or "in-service training," through direct conversion, through successful competition in a Navy rating exam, and in rare cases, through forced conversion.

Nuclear Field (NF)

The supervision, operation, and maintenance of naval nuclear-power plants require a high level of competence. Consequently, all personnel assigned to operate the engineering plants of nuclear-powered ships are carefully screened and rigorously trained in nuclear-power-plant theory and operation. Although it is expected that the majority of NF personnel will volunteer for submarine duty, the nuclear surface-ship requirement must also be met. Therefore, not all NF persons who volunteer for submarine duty will be assigned to it.

NF training leads to qualification as a mechanical operator, electrical operator, or reactor operator. Mechanical operators are drawn from the MM rating, electrical operators from the EM rating, and reactor operators from the ET rating. All nuclear operators, regardless of rating, should expect to qualify as engineering watch supervisors.

Training, which requires more than a year of study, normally begins in boot camp, where the NF candidate is screened and classified into one of the program ratings (MM, EM, or ET) according to his or her capabilities and the needs of the service. The NF trainee attends Class A rating training, which is from two to five months in length. On completion of Class A school, trainees are ordered directly to Nuclear Power School in Orlando for a six-week fundamentals course. It is designed to provide instruction in general mathematics, physics, problem-solving techniques, and power plants (a simple introduction).

The basic nuclear-power course follows the fundamentals course. It is twenty-four weeks long and covers all academic subjects required for an understanding of the theory and operation of a nuclear-propulsion plant. Subjects include mathematics, physics, reactor principles, thermodynamics, radiological fundamentals, water chemistry, and the study of typical reactor-plant systems.

From Nuclear Power School, an NF trainee proceeds to one of the nuclear-power training units located near Idaho Falls, Idaho; Ballston Spa, New York; or Windsor, Connecticut. There the trainee is enrolled in a 24-week course of instruction, qualifying as a nuclear-propulsion-plant operator on one of several land-based nuclear-reactor plants located at these places.

Two additional courses are available for graduates from the above training: the 13-week engineering laboratory technician (ELT) course at the nuclear-power training sites; or the 13-week welding course for nuclear-propulsion-plant operators (MMs only) at the Naval Submarine School, Groton, Connecticut, or at the Naval Training Center, San Diego.

To enter the NF program, you must meet the listed ASVAB requirements; score at least the minimum on the NF qualification test (NFQT); be at least seventeen but less than twenty-four years old; be a U.S. citizen and meet the eligibility re-

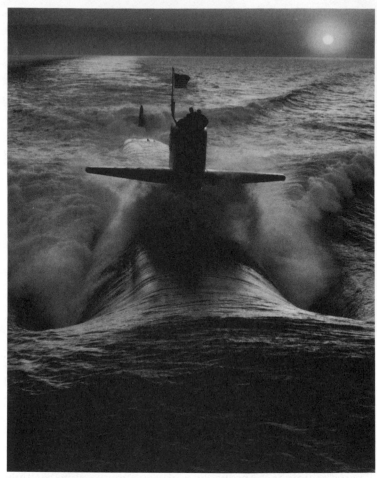

Figure 10–5 Volunteers for submarine duty must be under age thirty before training begins. Sailors in more than fourteen ratings (E-4 and E-5) and strikers are eligible.

quirements for a security check (you should at least pass an Entrance National Agency Check [ENTNAC]); be a high-school graduate; meet certain physical qualifications; and accept a commitment of six years' active service.

Submarine Training

Submarine
Training

Only volunteers are assigned submarine duty. More than fourteen ratings (E-4 and E-5) and identified strikers are eligi-

ble for submarine training. All must be under thirty years of
age before beginning training. They must meet certain test-score minimums and eligibility requirements for a secret clearance (although all applicants must first obtain a security clearance through ENTNAC).

Enlisted Basic Submarine School lasts eight weeks and is located at Groton, Connecticut. On completion of the course, 60 percent of the students are assigned additional training at Groton. Graduates will be assigned at least twelve months of duty aboard a submarine in commission or under construction.

Other Educational Opportunities

Navy Campus

Navy Campus is the Navy-wide system to coordinate voluntary, off-duty education and training programs and integrate them with on-duty education and training. It maintains a worldwide network of professional education specialists who assist Navy personnel in formulating their educational plans. Navy Campus also helps eligible persons take advantage of the in-service educational benefits of the GI Bill of 1966 and the Veteran's Educational Assistance Program (VEAP).

Key educational programs under Navy Campus are as follows:

College Degree and Certificate Program: Under this program, Navy students obtain academic degrees or vocational/technical certificates by combining education, training, and work experience received in both civilian life and the military. About fourteen institutions of higher learning are part of this program. Participating schools have agreed to waive residency requirements (the student does not have to take on-campus courses), accept up to 75 percent of the degree requirements from nontraditional sources, and grant credit for military education and training as recommended by the American Council on Education. At least two of the schools will allow 100 percent of the degree requirements to be earned through nontraditional sources. The individual policies of the participating institutions apply and may vary from school to school.

Tuition Assistance Program: This program provides financial assistance to eligible personnel who attend high school and postsecondary institutions on a voluntary, off-duty basis. Tuition assistance may be provided to regular Navy personnel, naval reserves on continuous active duty, and naval reserves ordered to active duty for 120 days or more. Tuition assistance cannot exceed more than 75 percent of the cost of tuition. Other expenses—including books, fees, and the individual's share of tuition—must be paid by the student.

Program for Afloat College Education (PACE): Under this program, even the sailor at sea has an opportunity to take college courses and, in some instances, vocational/technical courses. A number of fully accredited colleges and universities conduct tuition-free courses for seagoing students. These courses are taught by college teachers living aboard ship. When teachers are not on board, students can use study guides. Credits are assigned and transcripted just as if the courses had been offered on the college campus.

Instructor Hire Program: The purpose of this program is to enable commanding officers to hire qualified instructors to teach on- or off-duty noncredit courses on a wide variety of subjects. The objective of such instruction is to raise individual educational levels and to increase effectiveness on the job. Classes may be organized in academic, professional, technical, and vocational subjects at all educational levels. Instructors may be either military or civilian, but must be qualified in the subject or skill taught. Courses such as remedial mathematics, English, small-engine repair, American history, and speed reading have been taught under this program. The student pays no tuition.

High School Studies Program: The Navy would like all personnel to complete high-school before enlisting so they can be more effective in today's technical Navy. For those unable to do so, Navy Campus provides you with the opportunity to earn a diploma from your local high school, earn a certificate of high-school completion, or qualify for a high-school equivalency certificate. Navy Campus pays all tuition.

Enlisted Education Advancement Program (EEAP): EEAP allows career enlisted personnel to attend school full time and to obtain an associates degree in twenty-four months or less. Selectees receive full pay and allowances but must finance their own education. Applicants must have at least four years, or be an E-5 with a minimum of three years' but no more than fourteen years' active duty, and be willing to commit for six years.

Apprentice Program: The Department of Labor, in cooperation with the Navy, has made the National Apprenticeship

Program available to persons in selected ratings. (See your
Educational Services office for more details.)

VA Educational Benefits
The Veterans Administration (VA) has two programs for veterans seeking educational financial assistance. For those who served between 1 February 1955 and 31 December 1976, assistance is available under the GI Bill of 1966. For those who entered the Navy on or after 1 January 1977, assistance is available under the Veterans Educational Assistance Program (VEAP).

GI Bill: A new GI Bill went into effect on 1 July 1985. The new bill is a 3-year educational assistance program that gives service members a basic benefit of $300 a month for thirty-six months of schooling, totaling $10,800. The new bill affects the following service members: new recruits (with no prior service, entering active duty from 1 July 1985 to 30 June 1988); Vietnam-era personnel (on active duty prior to 1 January 1977); and VEAP member's (on active duty from 1 January 1977 to 30 June 1985).

To enter the program, eligible recruits have to contribute $100 a month for the first twelve months of their enlistment. Enrollment is automatic unless the recruit elects not to participate during the first two weeks of active duty. The $1,200 is not refundable. Benefits are $300 a month for thirty-six months for a 3-year enlistment, or $250 a month for thirty-six months for a 2-year enlistment. Members must receive a high-school diploma or equivalent prior to the completion of their first enlistment.

All persons covered under the new GI Bill will have to use their benefits within ten years of leaving the service.

Service members covered under the Vietnam-era GI Bill had until 31 December 1989, the termination date of that bill, to use their benefits. They became eligible, however, for the new GI Bill on 1 July 1988. Joining the program costs nothing, and members receive the full $300 a month for thirty-six months in addition to half of what the old GI Bill benefits would have amounted to. To be eligible for the new bill, you must have continuous active-duty service from 31 December 1976 to 1 July 1988. Members were automatically converted to the new GI Bill on 1 January 1990.

Service members covered under the VEAP are not eligible for the new bill if they enlisted after 31 December 1976 and before 1 July 1985. But they are still covered by VEAP if they elected to start contributing to VEAP before 1 July 1985.

Academic Credit for Military Experiences: The American Council on Education (ACE) Commission on Educational Credit and Credentials has evaluated formal Navy and Department of Defense schools and Navy rate/ratings and made academic credit recommendations. These recommendations appear in the ACE's Guide to the Evaluation of Educational Experiences in the Armed Services. Credit recommendations are for the vocational certificate, lower-division baccalaureate/associate degree, upper-division baccalaureate, and graduate-level categories. Many colleges and universities grant academic credit toward a degree based on these ACE recommendations. Schools may accept, modify, or reject recommendations based on their individual policies.

Commission Opportunities

If a commission is your goal, a number of programs can help you get one. The following officer programs lead to an appointment in the Naval Reserve for enlisted persons with bachelor's degrees or higher:

Officer Candidate School (OCS)
Aviation Officer Candidate School
Navy Judge Advocate General Corps Direct Appointment
Chaplain Corps Direct Appointment
Civil Engineer Corps Direct Appointment
Nuclear-Power Instructor and Naval-Reactor Engineer Direct
   Appointment

The requirements are generally the same for all programs: You must be a U.S. citizen, have a bachelor's degree from an accredited college or university, meet the age requirements for the desired program, be physically qualified, be serving on active duty in an enlisted status (in any rate and paygrade), be entitled to an honorable discharge, and be willing to meet the service requirements. Women applicants must meet the dependency requirements as outlined in the MILPERSMAN.

Enlisted Commissioning Program (ECP)

The ECP is an undergraduate education program for enlisted personnel on active duty who have previous college credit.

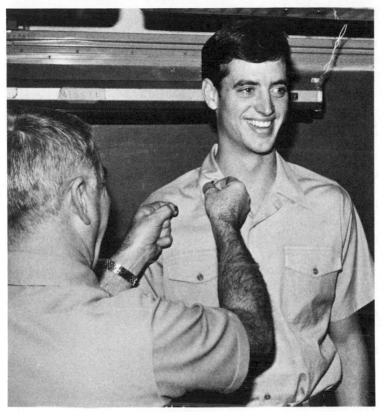

Figure 10–6 If a commission is your goal, a number of programs can help you get one.

Selectees will be ordered to the ECP on a permanent-change-of-station basis and enrolled as full-time students in a participating NROTC (Naval Reserve Officers Training Corps) host college or university to complete their degrees. Persons in technical degree programs have up to thirty-six months to complete their degrees. In nontechnical programs, persons may have up to twenty-four months to complete degrees. They will maintain their enlisted status during training, receiving all pay and allowances, but must pay any expenses incurred in the education program themselves. Upon completion of the program, ECP candidates will be ordered to OCS at Newport. Upon graduation they will be commissioned ensign, USN, in the unrestricted line. Enlisted applicants must be between twenty-two and thirty-one years of age at time of enrollment, have completed four but not more than eleven years of active service, and be willing to obligate for six years upon enrollment.

The Naval Academy

Most midshipmen are appointed from among high school or prep school graduates, but about eighty-five enlisted men and women who have passed the entrance exams are appointed by the secretary of the Navy. Enlisted candidates for Naval Academy appointments must be U.S. citizens, at least seventeen but not more than twenty-two years of age in the entering year, unmarried with no children, with at least one full year of enlisted naval service and a minimum of twenty-four months of active obligated service. They must also meet certain physical requirements and be recommended by their commanding officer.

Midshipmen receive one-half of an ensign's base monthly pay plus tuition, room, and board. Upon graduation, they receive a bachelor-of-science degree in one of eighteen majors and a commission in the regular Navy or Marine Corps.

Broadened Opportunity for Officer Selection and Training (BOOST)

This educational opportunity is designed for men and women who have leadership potential but haven't had enough education to compete successfully for commissioning programs. Participants spend six months to two years at the Service School Command in San Diego, where they study algebra, geometry, physical science, chemistry, and communications skills. Through a program of individually tailored academic and military instruction, participants can acquire the knowledge they need to compete for admission to one of the other officer programs.

For admission to the program, a BOOST applicant must be an enlisted member on active duty in the Navy or Naval Reserve, have two years of active service as of 1 January of the year in which BOOST training is to begin, agree to accept the minimum service requirements if selected for a specific program, meet certain physical requirements, and be recommended by the commanding officer.

Warrant Officer (WO) Program

Chief petty officers (paygrades E-7 to E-9) may apply for the WO program. There is no age requirement. Applicants must have completed at least twelve but not more than twenty-four years of naval service as of 16 January of the year in which they applied. Appointments are made to the grade of chief warrant officer (W-2). E-9s with two years in grade may apply for appointment to chief warrant officer (W-3).

Other specific requirements are that a candidate must be a U.S. citizen, physically qualified, a high-school graduate or equivalent, have a "clean" record for at least two years, and be recommended by the commanding officer. Applications must be submitted before 1 April. They are considered by a board convened by the secretary of the Navy in August or September. Names of selectees are released by an NMPC notice or an ALNAV (all-Navy commands) message. Those rejected are not notified.

Limited Duty Officer (LDO) Program

The LDO program is open to WOs with more than two years of service as warrants and to enlisted personnel in paygrades E-6 through E-8. Enlisted applicants must have completed at least eight but not more than sixteen years of active naval service. E-6s must compete in the E-7 examination and be designated LDO-selection-board-eligible.

The LDO program has the same basic requirements as the WO program. Deadline for application by WOs, E-7s, and E-8s is 1 April; the E-6 deadline is 16 May. Warrant applicants are appointed to the temporary grade of lieutenant (junior grade); all enlisted applicants are appointed temporary ensigns. If you accept the appointment, you must agree to remain on active duty for three years.

Naval Reserve Officers Training Corps (NROTC)

Enlisted persons may also enter the NROTC scholarship program, which can lead to a commission in the regular Navy or Marine Corps. You must be a U.S. citizen, under $27\frac{1}{2}$ years of age on 30 June of the year you become eligible for commissioned status, a high-school graduate or equivalent, and physically qualified, and you must have a clean record. Tuition, fees, books, uniforms, and a monthly subsistence allowance are paid for by the scholarship program. The program is available at more than fifty civilian colleges and universities. A NROTC student can get a bachelor's degree in various academic fields, although at least 80 percent of the program's participants must be majoring in engineering, mathematics, physics, or chemistry.

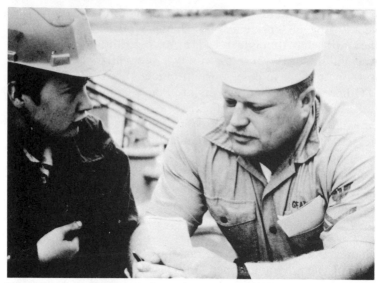

Figure 10–7 The dive and salvage departmental career counselor aboard a salvage ship discusses career opportunities with a boatswain's mate third class and the proper procedures for her to follow in applying for a commission.

Medical and Dental Programs

The Medical Service Corps (MSC) of the Naval Reserve: This program is open to qualified enlisted members on active or inactive duty. The program leads to a reserve commission. Applicants must be U.S. citizens, be physically qualified, and meet the requirements for an appointment outlined in the MILPERS Manual. Maximum age requirements are thirty-nine years for lieutenant, thirty-eight for lieutenant (junior grade), and thirty-five for ensign.

Health Care Administration: The MSC In-Service Procurement Program is a continuing program that enables senior regular-Navy HM and DT personnel, in paygrades E-6 through E-9, to obtain a commission.

Armed Forces Health Professions Scholarship Programs: The Navy, along with the Army and Air Force, offers scholarships to qualified students in the health professions. To be eligible, students must be enrolled or accepted for admission to study medicine/osteopathy, dentistry, clinical psychology, or optometry. This scholarship provides up to four years' full tuition, including books, fees, and necessary equipment, plus monthly pay. Selectees are commissioned as ensigns in the

Naval Reserve. In return for the scholarship, students serve one year on active duty for each year in the program, with a 3-year minimum, exclusive of periods of postgraduate professional education.

General Military Training (GMT)

This servicewide program provides the nontechnical orientation and follow-up training needed by everyone in the Navy. The training is designed to help Navy personnel fulfill their oath of service and to inform them on matters affecting their morale, both as citizens and as members of the Navy.

Presentation methods include the use of closed-circuit television, lectures, plan-of-the-day notes, spots on internal radio programs, and general-interest films. There has been nearly an 80 percent reduction in the number of formal GMT sessions. The American Forces Radio and Television Service (AFRTS) outlets, which provide information and entertainment to forces overseas, are also used as GMT forums.

The following subjects are covered: blood-donorship program, career counseling, character education, code of conduct, democracy and communism, dependents' assistance, educational advice, financial responsibility, health and fitness, human-resource management, information security, legal assistance, naval safety, savings-bond program, sea power, Uniformed Services Health Benefits Program (USHBP), and voting.

An education and training program (ETP) is also administered by the Defense Department. This program deals chiefly with informational materials such as pamphlets, movies, and booklets. It also produces various overseas pocket guides.

Leadership Training

It is a well-known fact that leaders are made, not born. Although leadership comes more easily to some than to others, acquiring leadership skills is difficult, requiring years of training and a lot of practice. To assist you in understanding and accepting your responsibilities as a leader, the Navy will provide extensive leadership training at various times throughout your career. These courses are taught at all major training centers throughout the fleet and vary in length from five to twelve days.

When you are selected for third-class petty officer, you will be required to attend the petty-officer indoctrination course. This course is designed to ease the transition into the petty-officer ranks. It covers subjects designed to make you a better leader.

As you advance to higher paygrades, you will have an opportunity to receive institutionalized leadership training under the Career Leadership Development Program (CLDP). It is taught at six levels: command excellence seminars (CESs) for lieutenant commanders and above, department heads, commanding officers, and executive officers; the division officer basic course (DOBC) for newly commissioned officers; the division officer advanced course (DOAC) for experienced second-tour lieutenants and newly commissioned limited duty officers and chief warrant officers; and courses for leading chief petty officers and leading petty officers. Courses are conducted at twenty-one existing training sites by certified Navy instructors.

The program teaches leadership skills and distinguishes superior from average performance. It is designed to enhance students' confidence and ability to be effective Navy managers and leaders.

CLDP's goal is to increase the effectiveness of Navy leadership across all levels of the chain of command.

As of 1 March 1990, all E-6 and E-7 personnel must have completed either the Leadership and Management Education and Training (LMET) or the CLDP program prior to their terminal eligibility dates for advancement purposes (January 1992 for E-6s, October 1991 for E-7s). When you advance to chief petty officer, you will attend an indoctrination course that addresses your change in rate as a leader. This is a milestone in your career.

As an E-8 or E-9, you may be selected to attend the Senior Enlisted Academy at the Navy Education and Training Center at Newport, Rhode Island. This course provides in-depth study in the following areas: communications skills, leadership and management technique, national security affairs, management of Navy resources, and other selected Navy topics.

Along with the promotions you receive in your Navy career come increased responsibilities as a leader and manager. These courses are designed to help you attain the level of skill required to accept such responsibilities and perform effectively.

Navy Pay, Benefits, and Retirement

All Navy pay accounts are handled by the Navy Finance Center in Cleveland, Ohio, through a computerized pay and leave accounting system called JUMPS (joint uniform military pay system).

JUMPS sends you a monthly leave and earning statement (LES) showing your pay for that month, the amount you can expect to receive on your next two paydays, your current allotments, the deductions taken from your pay, and the status of your leave account. This information is also sent—in the LES form—to your disbursing office. The LES helps you check the accuracy of your entitlements and manage your own earnings more effectively.

JUMPS: The Personalized System

Since your monthly JUMPS leave and earning statement contains a great deal of information on you and your progress in the Navy, you should know how to read the form. Because the system is personalized, no two forms are exactly the same.

A new and simpler LES form was introduced in March 1988. Its plain language and logical arrangement make it nearly self-explanatory. The following is a basic guide to orient you.

The first line of data, in the top right corner, is the period covered by that LES. Next is the unit identification code (UIC) of the disbursing office that maintains your record. (This may be different from the UIC of your command, since one disbursing office sometimes serves more than one unit.)

The next line identifies you by name, Social Security number, paygrade, and years of service. It also includes the leave you brought forward from the last fiscal year (BEG LV BAL), the leave you earned since the beginning of the last fiscal year (LV EARNED), the leave you have used (LV USED), and your leave balance at the end of the pay period.

U S NAVY
LEAVE AND EARNINGS STATEMENT

PERIOD COVERED	PAY UIC
	42555

NAME (LAST, FIRST, I.S.	SSN	PAY GRADE	YRS	LEAVE ACCOUNT						
				BEG LV BAL	LV EARNED	LV USED	END LV BAL	BAL TO EAOS	PAID LV	
		E6	13	0095	250	180	016	5087	5031	5

EARNINGS		DEDUCTIONS	
BASIC PAY	1407.00	SEPARATE RATIONS	
BAQ WITH DEPENDENTS	365.70	RETRO ENTRY	97.46
SEPARATE RATIONS	267.34	DEPENDENT DENTAL	3.93
VHA WITH DEPENDENTS	263.19	ADV PAY	
VHA WITH DEPENDENTS		STOP DATE 31JUL88	125.00
RETRO ENTRY	.03	INDEBTEDNESS	27.52
		SGLI FOR 50,000	4.00
		FEDERAL TAX	124.20
		FICA TAX	105.67
		CHARITY ALLOTMENT	2.00
		SAVINGS ALLOTMENT	85.00
TOTAL EARNINGS	2303.26	TOTAL DEDUCTIONS	574.78

NET PAY (2303.26-574.78)   1728.48

PAYMENTS POSTED SINCE LAST LES:
  15JUL88   861.45, DDS, DSSN 8522, NPR 00804
  01AUG88   867.03, DDS, DSSN 8522, NPR 00880

BASED ON CURRENT INFORMATION AT THE NAVY FINANCE CENTER YOUR
PAY IS EXPECTED TO BE:
  AUG88   MID-MONTH PAYMENT AMOUNT   923.00
  AUG88   END-OF-MONTH PAYMENT AMOUNT   928.00

REMARKS:
TOTAL ADVANCE OF PAY 3000.00 - BALANCE OUTSTANDING   .00
TOTAL INDEBTEDNESS   660.47 REMAINING BALANCE DUE   220.15
DETACHED PCS ON 13JUN88 FROM UIC 62980
REPORTED PCS ON 13JUN88 TO UIC 66760
CHARITY   ALLOTMENT WILL START AUG88   1.00
DAILY NORM EFFECTIVE 01AUG88 IS   61.56
"HAVE A SAY, VOTE YOUR WAY."

PERSONNEL AND PAY INFORMATION

	AMT DUE END OF LAST MO BROT FWD	TOTAL EARNINGS (+)	TOTAL DEDUCTIONS (-)	PAYMENT SINCE LAST LES (-)	AMT DUE END OF CURRENT MO/CF (=)	M S C	PAY DEL METHOD	DEBT TO U.S. GOVERNMENT		MEMBER UIC	DATE PREPARED
B A L	00	230326	57478	172848	00		DDS			0066760	23JUL88

	EXEM	FEDERAL TAX WAGE THIS PERIOD	FEDERAL TAX WAGE YEAR TO DATE	FEDERAL TAX YEAR TO DATE	FICA TAX WAGE THIS PERIOD	FICA TAX WAGE YEAR TO DATE	FICA TAX YEAR TO DATE	STATE WAGE YTD (CURRENT STATE)	STATE TAX YTD (CURRENT STATE)	SC
T A X	M02	140700	984900	86940	140700	984900	73966	00	00	TX

	PAY ENTRY BASE DATE	END ACTIVE OBLG SERVICE	OTHER PAY ENTRY DATE (OPED)	OPED	OPED		SEA SERVICE COUNTER			
							YRS	MOS	DAYS	
S V C	24MAR79	11DEC90	22MAY75CM				00	00	00	1105

	ENTITLEMENTS	DATE	AMOUNT	DEDUCTIONS	DATE	AMOUNT
F I E L D						

		PAYMENTS		
U S E	PR NO.	DSSN	DATE	AMOUNT

O N L Y NOTATION OF AMOUNT DUE

Your earnings block is next. This column contains the amounts of each type of pay or allowance accrued during the period covered by the LES. (If an entitlement started, stopped, or changed during this period, an explanation will appear under Remarks near the bottom of the box.)

The first figure is your basic pay. Basic allowance for quarters (BAQ) will be included if you are entitled. Basic allowance for subsistence (BAS) will be listed if you are entitled to compensation for subsistence (food). Variable housing allowance (VHA) is paid in addition to BAQ and varies by location and paygrade. An explanation of some of the other types of pay begins on p. 218.

On the right is the deductions block. Types of deductions are listed in plain language and include such things as state and federal taxes, charitable donations, and allotments. Other deductions that may appear include forfeitures, fines, and recoupment of advance pay.

Directly beneath the earnings and deductions columns is your net pay for the month. This is simply your total monthly earnings minus deductions.

Next is Payments Posted Since Last LES. These are usually two amounts, equal to your last two paychecks. DDS means that you are on the direct-deposit system, which deposits funds electronically into your savings or checking account. The DSSN (disbursing-station symbol number) identifies which disbursing office paid you.

Next comes the forecast of amount due on your next two paydays. If you feel the forecast is incorrect, see your disbursing officer or clerk immediately.

Under Remarks you will find such things as allotment starts and stops, reports of the dates you took leave, or dates you started or stopped receiving any special payments. Basically, the remarks section is for anything that doesn't fit anywhere else.

The first line under Personnel and Pay Information shows how your pay balances out. It is basically an abbreviated version of the Pay Computations block. The first block shows any amount due to you that was not paid the previous month. Next is your total earnings, followed by total deductions.

Figure 11-1 Your leave and earnings statement is a vital record of your pay, allowances, allotments, and deductions.

Payment since the last LES is the same as Net Pay in the top part of the form. Amount Due End of Month CF (carried forward) is any money not paid to you this month that will be posted on next month's LES.

Pay Delivery Methods tells how you get your money—usually by check or direct deposit. The UIC in the next block identifies your command and is used to send your LES, and therefore your pay, to the proper place. Date Prepared is simply the date on which the computer at the Navy Finance Center processed your form.

The entire next line is tax information. EXEM tells how many dependents you claim in figuring deductions of state and federal income tax.

Next is your total taxable pay for the period covered by this LES, followed by your total taxable pay to date for the calendar year. Federal Tax Year to Date tells how much has been deducted so far this year in federal taxes.

FICA Tax Wage This Period tells how much of your income in the current period is subject to Social Security (FICA) taxation. The next figure also pertains to FICA and shows how much of your wage so far in a calendar year is subject to FICA taxation. FICA Tax Year to Date tells how much Social Security tax you have paid during the year.

State Wage Year to Date (current state) is how much of your pay is reported to the state where you pay taxes. State Tax Year to Date (current state) shows how much has been deducted from your pay in state taxes. The last block is your state of record for tax purposes.

The line titled SVC (service) holds some of your service history. Pay Entry Base Date is the date you contracted for military service. End Active Oblig(ated) Service (EAOS) is the date your enlistment expires. Your years/months of sea duty appear on this line also.

Remember, every notation on your LES pertains only to you. If you have questions or suspect the LES is wrong, see your disbursing officer or clerk.

Pay

Basic Pay

Basic pay depends on your paygrade and years of service. It's the largest single item in your pay.

You will be paid twice a month, usually on the first and the fifteenth. Payment is by check, whether you're aboard ship or on shore or overseas stations. Aboard ship, you may cash your paycheck when you present it, with the proper identification, to a representative of the disbursing office. In almost every duty station, you may opt to participate in the direct deposit of your pay to the banking institution of your choice.

While on regular leave, you should make arrangements with your disbursing officer to mail your payday check to your leave address. While on leave from an overseas station or en route between duty stations, you can be paid at any military disbursing office—Navy, Marine Corps, Army, or Air Force. But you must have your personal financial record (PFR) with the disbursing office copies of your LES. Without it, you cannot be paid. You cannot be paid from a copy of your LES.

Basic Allowances

Allowances are extra payments designed to help you meet certain expenses of Navy life. Some are paid automatically;

ENLISTED MEMBERS MONTHLY BASIC PAY*

YEARS OF SERVICE

Pay Grade	2 Years or Less	Over 2 Years	Over 3 Years	Over 4 Years	Over 6 Years	Over 8 Years	Over 10 Years	Over 12 Years	Over 14 Years	Over 16 Years	Over 18 Years	Over 20 Years	Over 22 Years	Over 26 Years
E-9	—	—	—	—	—	—	2172	2221	2271	2323	2375	2421	2548	2796
E-8	—	—	—	—	—	1821	1873	1923	1973	2025	2071	2122	2247	2497
E-7	1271	1373	1424	1473	1523	1572	1622	1673	1749	1798	1848	1872	1998	2247
E-6	1094	1192	1242	1295	1343	1392	1443	1517	1565	1616	1640	1640	1640	1640
E-5	960	1045	1096	1143	1218	1268	1319	1367	1392	1392	1392	1392	1392	1392
E-4	896	946	1001	1079	1121	1121								
E-3	844	890	926	962	962	962								
E-2	812	812	812	812	812	812								
E-1	724	724	724	724	724	724								

* Effective 1 January 1990.

Quarters and Subsistence Allowances*

PAY GRADE	QUARTERS		SUB-SIST. ALLOW.
	With Dep.	Without Dep.	
E-9	508	386	179
E-8	468	354	179
E-7	435	302	179
E-6	402	274	179
E-5	362	252	179
E-4	314	220	179
E-3	293	216	179
E-2	278	175	179
E-1	278	156	179

* Figures rounded to the nearest dollar.

others you must apply for. Amounts and conditions under which they are paid are subject to change, so always check with your disbursing office for the latest information.

Basic Allowance for Quarters (BAQ): There are two kinds of BAQ. If you have dependents—wife, husband, children, or stepchildren (under twenty-one years old), parent or step-parent—who rely on you for more than half of their support, you can draw with-dependents BAQ. (It is not payable, however, when you are occupying public [government] quarters.) Single BAQ is available to a member without dependents. Persons entitled to BAQ (at the with-dependents rate) may also draw a family separation allowance (FSA) if (1) their ship is away for more than thirty days; (2) if transportation of dependents at government expense to a new duty station is not authorized; or (3) if they are on temporary additional duty (TAD) for a period of thirty days or more. High-cost CONUS areas, plus Alaska and Hawaii, now qualify you for increased BAQ in the form of variable housing allowance (VHA). The rates vary by area and paygrade.

Basic Allowance for Subsistence (BAS): This allowance is paid if you are not provided meals at government expense. The rates vary depending on whether (1) "rations in kind" (a government mess or government-provided mess) are available; (2) permission has been granted to mess separately (commuted rations or leave rations); or (3) you are assigned to duty under emergency conditions where no government messing facilities are available. Separate rations (SEPRATS) are usually limited to people living off base who have permission to eat away from their duty station. They are required to pay for each meal they eat in the mess hall.

Special Pay

This includes career sea pay, foreign-duty pay, proficiency pay, selective reenlistment bonuses, and numerous types of hazardous-duty pay.

Sea and Foreign Duty: The rates vary for each paygrade. In general, sea pay begins the day you report aboard ship for duty if you have more than three years' prior sea duty and are in paygrade E-4 or above. Foreign-duty pay begins the day you report aboard a designated foreign-duty station.

Selective Reenlistment Bonus (SRB): As the name implies, this retention incentive is paid to members serving in certain selected ratings or with certain NECs. SRB is computed by using applicable award levels, ranging from 0.5 to 6.0. The actual amount received depends on your award level, multiplied by your monthly basic pay and the term of your enlistment. Nuclear pay is available to certain qualified enlisted members. The SRB program is extremely complicated. You'll do well to check with your career counselor or personnel office for additional facts.

Incentive Pay for Hazardous Duty

Several types of incentive payments are made, the most common of which are aviation pay and submarine-duty pay. Rates for those two types are based on your paygrade and years in service. Additional monthly incentive payments are made for flight-deck hazardous duty (FDHD), parachute duty, demolition duty, and experimental stress duty (such as high-/low-pressure tests).

Diving pay, for members serving in an authorized diving billet, varies according to the skills involved. A scuba diver gets less per month than a master saturation diver.

Hostile-fire pay is given to members subject to the danger of enemy fire.

Miscellaneous Allowances

Clothing: The first clothing allowance is the initial clothing monetary allowance (ICMA), which differs for men and women. Second is the special initial clothing monetary allowance (SICMA) for those who must wear a uniform not worn by the majority of Navy personnel. It goes to those assigned to certain Navy bands, for example, and is also paid upon promotion to chief petty officer. The rates vary. Third is the yearly clothing maintenance allowance (CMA). This allowance is of two types: basic maintenance allowance (BMA) and standard maintenance allowance (SMA). The basic rate will be effective following the completion of six months of service through the thirty-sixth month; the first payment at the end of the twelfth month will be for an amount equal to one-half the annual payment; and thereafter the annual payment will be at the end of the anniversary month of entry into the service.

Travel and Transportation (T&T): The T&T allowances are paid to you when you receive orders to travel. You might be authorized to travel by privately owned vehicle (POV) or by government or commercial transportation. In addition, you may be paid a per diem (daily) allowance to cover the cost of lodging, meals, and other incidentals not included in the cost of transportation. An allowance for transportation of dependents at government expense is also provided for a permanent change of station (PCS). (If you are authorized transportation of dependents and own a mobile home that you're taking on a PCS move, you'll be reimbursed for the actual amount of the move, which will not exceed what it would have cost the government to move you.) Be sure you see your disbursing office for all the details before making the move. You can get an allowance for transportation of household goods (HHGs) or personal effects when you make a PCS move. A reduced weight allowance is sometimes allowed for temporary additional duty (TAD) orders. Partial reimbursement for incidental expenses incurred in a PCS move of HHGs is paid as a dislocation allowance (DLA). Single and married personnel may qualify for this entitlement.

There are several other allowances specifically designed to help you with excessive costs while you're on permanent duty outside CONUS. Some overseas stations will give you an overseas housing allowance (OHA) or cost-of-living allowance (COLA) and a temporary lodging allowance (TLA). The OHA is based on the average cost of local housing in the overseas area, compared with your BAQ. Items considered include rent, utilities, minor maintenance expenses, and initial occupancy expenses. COLA is derived by comparing the cost-of-living in your overseas area with the average cost-of-living in CONUS for a similar area. TLA provides partial reimbursement for the expenses incurred when you're moving to or from overseas areas. The amount is a graduated percentage, depending on the number of your dependents and the per diem allowances for travel to that specific area.

Other Pay Benefits

Allotments

Through allotments you may assign part of your pay regularly to a spouse, parents, bank, or insurance company. You may also take part in the Navy's Savings Bond Program. Disbursing officers make out allotment forms. Checks are mailed out monthly from the finance center in Cleveland.

Income Tax

Generally, all pay is taxable as income. Allowances are not taxable. For this reason a part of your pay is withheld, just as it would be in most civilian jobs. The amount depends on the amount of your pay and the number of dependents you have. When filling out your annual income-tax form, you will be able to credit the amount that's been withheld against the tax. Most ships and stations have an expert to assist you with tax matters.

FICA Social Security

While on active duty, you build up Social Security and Medicare coverage. You work toward Social Security benefits in addition to Navy retirement benefits.

Other Benefits

There's no doubt that the pay in today's Navy is one of the real benefits. There are others, such as commissary and exchange privileges, medical care in uniformed-services facilities or through CHAMPUS (Civilian Health and Medical Program of the Uniformed Services), a dental plan for dependents, and an extensive educational program. Other somewhat less tangible benefits also go to you (and in some cases to your family) because you're in the Navy.

Legal Assistance

The legal assistance officer (LAO) can draw up wills, powers of attorney, deeds, affidavits, contracts, and many other documents. The LAO also can advise you on transfer of property, marriage and divorce, adoption of children, taxation, personal injury, and other legal problems. The advice is free, and may help you avoid a lot of trouble. The Navy's legal-assistance program is specifically designed to advise and assist sailors and their dependents who have legal problems. All matters are treated confidentially.

All sailors are given the opportunity to review their personal legal affairs and obtain necessary advice and counseling from qualified LAOs. A handy legal questionnaire (NAVJAG form 5801/10) can, when filled out completely, tell you if you need legal counseling or assistance.

The Family Housing Program

The family housing program includes public quarters (government rental units), mobile-home parks, government-insured privately owned projects, and leasing of privately owned units. The Navy tries to make sure adequate housing facilities are available for sailors and their dependents at a reasonable cost and within reasonable commuting distance. Where Navy housing is not available, housing referral offices will assist you in locating private housing in the community.

Insurance Programs

Dependency and indemnity compensation (DIC) and dependents indemnity compensation (DICOMP) provide protection for your family if you die. Eligible survivors—including unmarried widows, unmarried children under twenty-three (with restrictions), and certain parents—are provided basic benefits when members die on active duty, or after separation as a result of service-connected disability. Social Security survivors benefits may also be payable if the member is survived by spouse and/or children of a minor age. A $3,000 death gratuity is payable immediately after death of the member.

You may also have a $50,000 life insurance policy while on active duty, through servicemen's group life insurance (SGLI). The cost is $4.00 per month. You may request that the amount be reduced to $40,000 or any lesser amount in increments of $10,000, with a reduction in your premium of 80 cents per $10,000 of coverage. This policy is optional. On separation, SGLI can be converted to a five-year nonrenewable term policy, veterans group life insurance (VGLI). The moderate cost of VGLI is based on age at the time of separation.

Uniformed Services Health Benefit Program (USHBP)

USHBP is a comprehensive health program that includes direct care provided in Uniformed Services Medical Treatment Facilities (USMTFs) and other care provided in civilian facilities at full or partial expense to the government. Active-duty members must be provided all *necessary* medical care. The primary source of care for all eligible beneficiaries is the USMTF. When care is not available from the USMTF for an active-duty member, it may be provided at government expense under the Non-Naval Medical Care Program. This care

must be preauthorized. Each USMTF can provide acute medical and surgical care to varying degrees. Since not all USMTFs
have the same medical capabilities, the health benefits advisor
(HBA) should be contacted to determine what services are
available. Dependent and retired personnel are provided care
at a USMTF if space, facilities, and proper medical staff are
available. As of 1 July 1985, dental care may also be provided
on a space-available basis. Active-duty members do not pay
for outpatient care but pay the subsistence rate for inpatient
care (hospital admission). There is no charge for USMTF outpatient care provided to a dependent or retired personnel;
however, there is a small charge for retired officers and dependent inpatient care. Retired enlisted do not pay for inpatient
care. A dependent will not be denied care on the basis of
service affiliation.

Civilian Health and Medical Program of the
Uniformed Services (CHAMPUS)

When USMTF cannot provide medical care for retired personnel or dependents, civilian care may be obtained at partial
government expense under CHAMPUS. CHAMPUS is not
free. Dependents of active-duty members, retired personnel
and their dependents, and dependents of personnel who died
on active duty or after retirement may receive health-care benefits under CHAMPUS. CHAMPUS does not cover active-
duty members, who use the Non-Naval Medical Care Program
discussed above. CHAMPUS is not an insurance program, but
the government does pay part of the cost for care that cannot
be obtained in a USMTF. CHAMPUS is made up of two parts:
(1) basic coverage, and (2) The Program for the Handicapped.
Since CHAMPUS will not cost-share all procedures, it is wise
to contact an HBA for assistance. The HBA's job is to help the
beneficiary obtain the medical care needed. As a general rule,
no prior authorization is required to obtain outpatient care
under CHAMPUS. However, if the beneficiary lives within the
catchment area—particular zip codes located around the
USMTF—a nonavailability statement (NAS) must be obtained
for any nonemergent inpatient care. The HBA can assist in
requesting an NAS form from the USMTF when it is unable to
provide inpatient care. If the beneficiary does not obtain the
NAS before getting nonemergent inpatient care from a civilian
hospital, CHAMPUS will not share the costs.

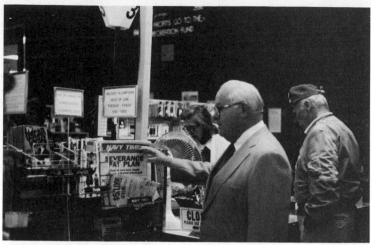

Figure 11–2 A retiree takes advantage of his exchange privileges, one of the Navy's many benefits.

Dependent Dental Plan

The Dependent Dental Plan (DDP) is a contracted insurance program that allows spouses and children of active-duty members to obtain basic dental care from the civilian sector. Dependents must reside in the United States, Puerto Rico, or the U.S. Virgin Islands to be eligible. There are two general categories of care: diagnostic/preventive/emergency care, which includes routine oral exams, fluoride treatment, teeth cleaning and polishing (limit, twice in twelve months), full mouth X-rays (once in thirty-six months), space maintainers, laboratory exams, and minor emergency treatments to relieve pain; and restorative care, which includes fillings, stainless steel or plastic crowns for "baby teeth," and repairs to existing dentures. The DDP is a voluntary plan with a 24-month enrollment. Participants pay a monthly payroll deduction plus a copayment for restorative care. The dental contractor pays allowable charges for diagnostic/preventive/emergency care, and 80 percent of allowable charges for restorative care when participating dentists are used. Members pay the remaining 20 percent for restorative care, plus any disallowed charges. First-term enlisted personnel must have at least twenty-four months until EAOS to enroll their dependents. There are no EAOS restrictions on officers or enlisted careerists.

Supplementation of Facilities

When a dependent/retired patient requires care beyond the capabilities of the USMTF, there are several options available. The USMTF is authorized to transfer the patient to the nearest USMTF unit if the patient desires. The USMTF may procure supplemental professional services or supplies from civilian sources, using operating funds. In the latter case, the USMTF retains "medical management" of the patient, who will return to the USMTF to complete the care. Another option is for the USMTF to release the patient to a civilian health-care professional of the patient's choice. When the USMTF gives up medical management of a case, it is known as patient disengagement. When disengaged, a patient may seek civilian medical care, in which case he or she assumes responsibility for payment. This sort of civilian care comes under CHAMPUS law and regulation. Active-duty members are never disengaged.

Counseling Assistance

The Navy has human relations experts ready to advise and help sailors with difficult personal and family affairs. A Navy chaplain, like a minister or priest at home, can perform marriage ceremonies or baptisms, conduct funerals, and offer family counseling.

Professionally trained specialists are also available through the human resources management system (HRMS) for counseling of problems relating to alcoholism, drug abuse, family and personal affairs, and the effects of discriminatory practices, in and out of the Navy. Chapter 8 contains information on how to cope with alcohol and drug abuse (pp. 137–40).

Overseas Schools for Dependents

The Department of Defense (DOD) operates many educational facilities for minor dependents of all U.S. active-duty military and DOD civilian personnel stationed overseas. Currently, there are a total of 270 DOD schools overseas; 26 of these are Navy sponsored. There are Navy schools from Spain to Japan, from Iceland to the West Indies. Army and Air Force schools in many countries are open to Navy dependents. From first grade through high school, Navy juniors can receive an education overseas at the government's expense.

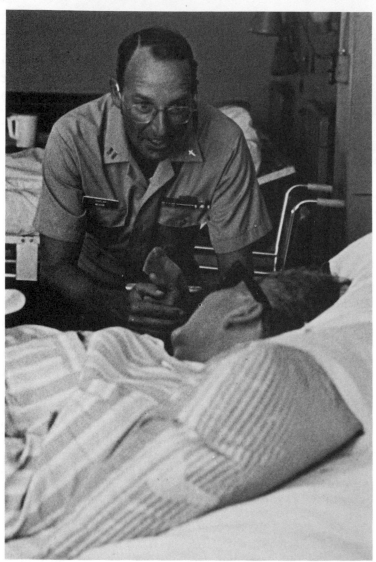

Figure 11–3 Navy chaplains not only provide family and individual counseling but also a warm smile and small talk when you're confined to sick bay. Just like your minister, priest, or rabbi back home, they're there when you need them.

Counseling

Federal Credit Unions

Most major Navy installations provide credit-union facilities for Navy personnel. In addition, the Navy Federal Credit Union (NFCU) in Washington, D.C., serves enlisted men and women stationed in the D.C. area, in foreign countries, or aboard ships homeported in foreign countries. NFCU has worldwide wire facilities plus an 800-number that allows members to call toll free anywhere in the continental United States. It offers signature loans, loans based on equal collateral, automobile loans, and personal loans for mobile homes and furniture. NFCU also has a policy of free life insurance that ensures loan protection for members. It pays interest on all savings accounts.

Leave

All personnel on active duty earn leave at the rate of $2\frac{1}{2}$ days each month, except for brig time or unauthorized absences of twenty-four hours or more. *Earned leave* is the amount credited to you "on the books" at any given date. If you take more leave than you are entitled to, this is *advance leave*. This means you have a minus leave balance on the books. *Excess leave* is the amount by which you exceed what you've earned, along with any advance leave you've been granted. Advance leave is taken out of the amount you would normally earn during the remainder of your enlistment.

As leave accumulates, it is carried over from one fiscal year to the next. No more than 60 days can be carried over; thus, if you have 67 days' leave on the books on 30 September (the end of the fiscal year), you lose seven days. Members entitled to hostile-fire or imminent-danger pay, or on extended deployment for more than 120 consecutive days, are authorized to carry forward more than 60 days at the end of the fiscal year.

Persons discharged with leave still on the books are paid a lump sum equal to their daily pay for each day. The most leave you can "sell back" in a military career is 60 days. Those discharged with minus leave will pay back approximately a day's pay for each day's leave owed.

Your commanding officer has the authority to grant all earned leave on a yearly basis, plus up to 45 days' advance leave. Personnel lacking enough earned leave during an emergency can be granted advance leave up to 60 days.

Convalescent leave is an authorized absence while you're under medical care and treatment. It must be authorized by your commanding officer on orders of a medical officer, or by the commanding officer of a military hospital. It is usually granted following a period of hospitalization and is not charged as leave.

In a personal emergency, such as a death in the family or a serious illness, you will normally be granted emergency leave to take care of personal matters that no one else can handle. Such emergencies must be verified by the Red Cross.

Figure 11–4   Golf courses at naval installations offer the off-duty sailor a chance to improve his or her skills.

Off-Duty Hours

Hobby shops, entertainment programs, and recreational facilities provide sailors on shore stations and many ships with plenty of leisure activities. More than thirty sports are offered in the Navy sports program, part of the special services organization of the Navy. There is also a program for high-caliber athletes in the Navy to be considered for selection to national and international-level sports.

The Navy sports program organizes formal and informal sports activities. Formal programs include intramural, intercommand, area, and All-Navy competitions. Informal sports are played in gymnasiums and on multipurpose courts, tennis courts, and football and softball fields.

Other offerings include marina facilities, golf, swimming, and so on. A variety of arts and crafts facilities for activities including woodworking, photography, ceramics, leatherworking, and boat building are also available.

Service Organizations

Many organizations provide assistance and services to sailors and their dependents. Three of the most important are listed below.

The Navy Relief Society (NRS)

Supported entirely by private funds, NRS assists sailors and their families in time of need. Though not an official part of the Navy, NRS is the Navy's own organization for taking care of its people. It is staffed and supported largely by naval personnel. NRS can give you financial aid in the form of an interest-free loan, a grant, or a combination of both.

The American Red Cross (ARC)

The Red Cross supplies financial aid to naval personnel, does medical and psychiatric casework, and provides recreational services for the hospitalized. It also performs services in connection with dependency discharge, humanitarian transfer, emergency leave, leave extensions, and family welfare reports.

The Navy Wives Club of America (NWCA)

This group is composed chiefly of wives of enlisted men serving at sea in the Navy, Coast Guard, and Marine Corps.

Figure 11–5 Off-duty crewmembers jog on the stern of a ship on convoy duty in the Persian Gulf. The guided-missile frigate *Hawes* (FFG 53) and the reflagged tanker *Gas King* are in the background.

Besides its many social activities, NWCA sponsors a special scholarship fund for the children of sailors. The club assists chaplains and participates in the blood-donor and NRS projects. Local chapters participate in community projects and hold dances, picnics, and similar affairs.

Reenlistment

A sailor who completes an enlistment or cruise in the Navy and then reenlists is said to ship over. If you reenlist on the expiration date of your current term of service, or within three calendar months after discharge, it's called a continuous-service reenlistment. Those who reenlist after more than three calendar months of being released from active duty make "broken service reenlistment." The first type is better; on the broken service reenlistment, you may have to come back in a lower rate. Also, if your rate is SRB eligible, you may lose a substantial portion of your reenlistment bonus.

Reenlistment is not a right, it's a privilege. To earn that privilege, you must be recommended by your commanding officer, be physically qualified, and meet certain standards of performance. If you reenlist with no break in service, you

Reenlist-
ment

reenlist "on board." Those with a break in service of more than twenty-four hours may reenlist only at recruiting stations.

Reenlistment Periods

Because of large reenlistment bonuses offered in a variety of specialties, many sailors choose to ship over for six years. But reenlistments for two to five years are also available.

Extensions of Enlistment

There are two types of enlistment extension. *Conditional extensions* may be made at any time during an enlistment if you wish to qualify for advancement, for a cruise or deployment, for entrance into a service school, for a special program, for any other duty requiring additional obligated service, or to obtain maternity benefits for a dependent wife. Extensions are executed in increments of one or more months, not to exceed an aggregate of forty-eight months on any single enlistment. *Unconditional extensions* may also be made at any time for a period of not less than twenty-four or more than forty-eight months.

Separation

This term includes discharge, release from active duty, transfer to the fleet reserve, or transfer to the retired list, including the temporary-disability retired list (TDRL). Separations from active duty because of death or desertion are not included.

Discharges

The type of discharge you receive will affect you after you leave the Navy. Certain discharges eliminate some veterans rights and benefits. And many employers will reject an exmilitary person who cannot produce an honorable-discharge certificate.

Honorable Discharge: An honorable discharge means separation with honor. It is given for one of the following reasons: expiration of enlistment, convenience of the government, dependency, or disability. To receive an honorable discharge, the final average of your performance marks must be at least 2.8, with an average of not less than 3.0 in military behavior. You can't have been convicted by a general court-martial, or more than once by a special court-martial. This rule won't apply if you held an average of at least 3.0 during the last 24 months of active duty.

General Discharge: A general discharge is given under honorable conditions for such reasons as minority enlistment, ineptitude, and unsuitability. In most cases, it goes to those whose conduct and performance, though technically satisfactory, has not been good enough to deserve an honorable discharge.

Other Discharges: These are the *undesirable discharge* (UD), *bad conduct discharge* (BCD), and *dishonorable discharge* (DD). The UD is given by administrative action for misconduct or breach of security, the BCD only by approved sentence of a general or special court-martial, and the DD only by approved sentence of a general court-martial.

Formal Reasons for Discharge

There are twelve formal reasons for discharge:

1. *Expiration of Enlistment:* An enlistment normally ends the day before the anniversary date of the enlistment. Depending on circumstances, it may be later. If you have lost days—because of injury, sickness, or disease caused by misconduct—you can be kept on active duty until the lost days are made up. Your expiration date may also be postponed if you are undergoing medical care or awaiting trial or official papers. All enlistments can be extended by the government during war or national emergency.

2. *Fulfillment of Service Obligation:* This discharge is given to regular Navy enlisted men and women on completion of their service obligation, or to reservists released to inactive duty after completing their active obligated service.

3. *Disability:* Given to sailors unable to carry out their duties because of a mental or physical disability.

4. *Convenience of the Government:* This term includes general demobilization after a war, acceptance of a permanent commission, and for women, parenthood or pregnancy.

5. *Dependency:* Discharges for reasons of dependency or hardship are authorized when it is shown that undue and general hardship exists at home. The hardship must be permanent and must have arisen or worsened since the person joined the Navy. Dependency discharges, commonly called hardship discharges, are not authorized for financial or business reasons,

or for personal convenience.

6. *Misconduct:* A misconduct discharge is given to deserters who have not returned to military jurisdiction, persons convicted by civil authorities, and those who have made fraudulent enlistments.

7. *In Absentia:* Deserters absent longer than eighteen months can be discharged *in absentia*. *In absentia* discharges cover those who flee to foreign countries, where the United States has no jurisdiction, or for whom the statute of limitations has run out. This applies only during peacetime. Deserters who have committed more serious offenses are given *in absentia* discharges. Authorities continue searching for them until they're apprehended and brought back for court-martial.

8. *Security:* Given to personnel considered security risks.

9. *Sentence of Court-Martial:* Self-explanatory.

10. *Unsuitability:* Given for such reasons as ineptitude, apathy, alcoholism, and financial irresponsibility, as well as "character" and "behavior disorders."

11. *Personal Abuse of Drugs:* Given to a drug abuser identified either by urinalysis or by the abuser's own admission.

12. *Good of the Service:* This type of discharge can be issued instead of taking action under the Uniform Code of Military Justice. Although a sailor may request an administrative discharge under other-than-honorable (OTH) conditions, he or she is still subject to the results of any disciplinary proceedings in the case.

Planning a Second Career

Planning for a second career or retirement is an important step that must be carefully considered. Your new life can offer fun, zest, or relaxation—or it can be one big headache.

The first step is getting to know yourself, especially if you want to find a new job. Often a sailor undersells his or her talents or, worse yet, his or her potential. If you've climbed the promotion ladder to senior petty officer or officer, you've shown not only talent but potential and leadership. In examining your career, look for areas that will support your job aims in civilian life. Don't think that because you've spent twenty years as a signalman, the only job you're qualified for on the outside is that of a construction flagman. In general, don't limit yourself to work that's directly related to your Navy occupation. Your experience as a supervisor or manager is probably even more important in the eyes of an employer.

You should also brace yourself for the social and psychological shock that comes from leaving military society, where rules and paths are well defined, and entering the civilian world. Don't expect this transition to happen overnight. It may take weeks, months, or even longer to make the adjustment.

A good way to begin is by listing potential occupations, then checking the list with people who know you to see what they say about your choices. If your list is not broad enough, prepare another covering categories, for example, such as federal, state, and local government; business, including the field of franchising; agriculture; public-service institutions like hospitals; and education and educational services.

Retirement

When enlisted men and women complete more than twenty years of active service, they are eligible for release to inactive duty and for transfer to the fleet reserve. After thirty years of combined active service and inactive duty in the fleet reserve, they are transferred to the Navy's retired list. Those with thirty or more years of active service may be transferred directly to the retired list. Technically, the pay received by a fleet reserve member is a retainer, while that received by those on the retired list is retired pay, though both are popularly called retired pay.

In either case, anyone on active duty prior to 1 October 1980 can figure their retired pay on this basis: 2.5 percent of basic (active-duty) pay times the number of years of active service. Anyone entering service between 1 October 1980 and 1 August 1986 can figure their retired pay using the average of the three highest annual earnings times the number of years of active service. Anyone entering service on or after 1 August 1986 comes under the Military Retirement Reform Act, P.L. 99-348. Under this new rule, the retired pay formula is the product of 2.5 percent times the years of creditable service, minus 1 percentage point for each year less than 30 years, times the average of the 3 highest annual earnings. To cite the example of a 25-year veteran: 25 years (2.5 times 25) minus 5 (5 years less than 30) equals 57.5 percent; 57.5 percent times the high-three average of base pay. These methods of computing retired pay are estimates; other factors are used in computing the precise amount. In any case, the longer the active service and the higher the paygrade, the greater the amount of retired pay.

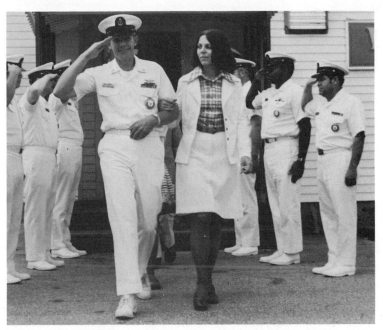

Figure 11–6 Colleagues pipe a retiring senior chief over the side as he walks away, accompanied by his wife, to start a new career in civilian life.

Survivor Benefit Plan

A family protection plan called the Survivor Benefit Plan (SBP) is available to provide for the continuation of up to 55 percent of retired pay to a deceased retiree's beneficiaries. Enrollment in SBP at maximum coverage is automatic unless the retiree or spouse wants less coverage or chooses not to participate in the program. There are six types of coverage: spouse only; spouse and children; children only; insurable interest; former spouse; and former spouse and children. The monthly amount deducted from retired pay varies with the coverage elected. Your career counselor should be consulted for up-to-date SBP information.

Retirement and Other Benefits

Appendix J of this manual has a separate listing of references that can assist you in planning your retirement and preparing for a second career. The following list may also prove helpful:

Navy Guide for Retired Personnel and Their Families (NAV-PERS 15891 series). Naval Military Personnel Command. Washington: Government Printing Office.

Provides comprehensive information on the rights, benefits, privileges, and responsibilities of members of the U.S. Navy and Naval Reserve entitled to retired or retainer pay.

Disability Separation (NAVEDTRA 46601 series [rev. 1987]). Armed Forces Information Service, Department of Defense.

Contains information about procedures leading to disability retirement or discharge and describes benefits accruing when physical disability ends an active military career.

Federal Benefits for Veterans and Dependents (VA fact sheet IS1). Washington: Government Printing Office.

Contains general information concerning most federal benefits enacted by the Congress for veterans, their dependents, and beneficiaries.

Once a Veteran (NAVEDTRA 46602 series). Armed Forces information sheet, Department of Defense.

Contains information on benefits available from the Department of Veterans Affairs and other federal agencies for service members who are to be released from active duty.

Reference Guide to Employment Activities of Retired Naval Personnel (NAVSO P-1778). Office of the Judge Advocate General, Department of the Navy, Washington, D.C. 20370.

Explains the Dual Compensation Act, conflict of interest, and other restrictions on civilian employment.

Your Social Security. Social Security Administration, Department of Health, Education, and Welfare.

Contains information concerning Social Security benefits as a result of military service.

Your Personal Affairs (NAVEDTRA 46600 series). Office of Information for the Armed Forces, Department of Defense.

Contains general information about matters affecting personal affairs, including insurance and benefits, of service members and their families.

Veteran's Preference in Federal Employment (EV2). Office of Personnel Management. Washington: Government Printing Office.

Explains the restrictions imposed on retired military personnel in federal employment.

Federal Job Information Centers Directory (BRE 9). Office of

Personnel Management, Washington, D.C. 20415.

Figure 11–7 A family welcomes their sailor home from the sea.

A listing of federal job-information centers where answers can be provided to questions about federal employment.

Your Retirement System (pamphlet 18). Office of Personnel Management. Washington: Government Printing Office.

Contains questions and answers concerning the Federal Civil Service Retirement Law.

Survivor Benefit Plan Made Easy (NAVEDTRA 46605 series). American Forces Information Service, Department of Defense.

Contains information about SBP, under which retired members of the armed forces can provide incomes for their widows and eligible surviving children after death.

III. Ships, Planes, and Weapons

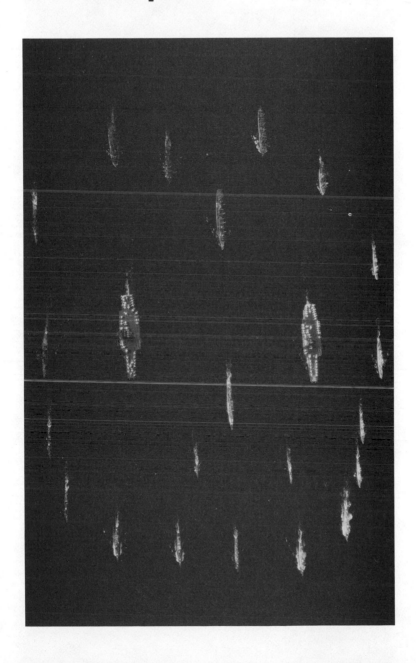

Ship Construction

12

Navy ships are highly complicated machines with their own propulsion plants, weapons, repair shops, supply spaces, and facilities for living, sleeping, and eating. Although there are great differences in types and missions of ships (see chapter 14), all ships have certain essential qualities.

Armament consists of all the weapons used to give battle to an enemy: missiles, guns, rockets, torpedoes, mines, depth charges, and aircraft.

Protection refers to those features that help a ship survive the effects of combat. Aside from weapons, a ship's sturdy steel construction is her best protection. Compartmentation, double bottoms, and other structural components all provide protection.

Seaworthiness means those features that enable a ship to operate in high winds and heavy seas. A ship's stability, or the way she recovers from a roll, is an essential part of her seaworthiness.

Maneuverability is the way a ship handles—in turns, backing down, moving alongside another ship, or evading enemy weapons.

Speed gets a ship to the scene of action quickly and helps her overtake an enemy or avoid being overtaken. Key factors are the power of her engines in relation to her size, and the shape of her underwater hull.

Endurance is the maximum time a ship can steam at a given speed. Most oil-powered ships can steam for one to two weeks without refueling. The Navy's nuclear-powered ships can cruise for years.

Habitability refers to whatever makes the ship comfortable for the crew. Adequate heads and washrooms, laundries, air-conditioning, and well-lighted and roomy berthing and messing spaces are some habitability features.

Terminology

Part of your first cruise will be spent aboard ship. No matter how specialized your professional training, you must still be thoroughly familiar with basic nautical terminology and ship construction. You need this knowledge to carry out routine orders and commands, and to act quickly during combat or emergency situations.

In some respects a ship is like a building. She has outer walls (forming the *hull*), floors (*decks*), inner walls (*partitions* and *bulkheads*), corridors (*passageways*), ceilings (*overheads*), and stairs (*ladders*). But unlike a building a ship moves, so you'll also have to learn new terms for directions and getting around. For example, when you go up a ship's ladder from the dock, you're using the brow to go *on board,* and what might be an entrance hall or foyer in a building is the *quarterdeck* on a ship.

The forward part of a ship is the *bow;* to go in that direction is to *go forward.* The after part is the *stern;* to go in that direction is to *go aft.* The uppermost deck that runs the entire length of the ship from bow to stern is the *main deck.* Anything below that is *below decks* and anything above is the *super-structure.* The forward part of the main deck is the *forecastle* (pronounced *focsle*), the after part is the *fantail.* To proceed from the main deck to a lower deck is to *go below.* Going back up again is *going topside.* As you face forward on a ship, the right side is *starboard,* the left side is *port.* An imaginary line running full length down the middle of the ship is the *centerline.* The direction from the centerline toward either side is *outboard,* and from either side toward the centerline is *inboard.* A line from one side of the ship to the other runs *athwartship.*

Basic Ship Structure

The hull is the main body of the ship. Structurally, it is a big box girder, similar to a bridge. *Shell plating* forms the sides and bottom, and the *weather deck* or *main deck* forms the top. The intersection of the weather deck with the shell or side plating is called the *deck edge* or *gunwale* (pronounced gunnel). The intersection of the side plating with the bottom plating is called the *bilge.*

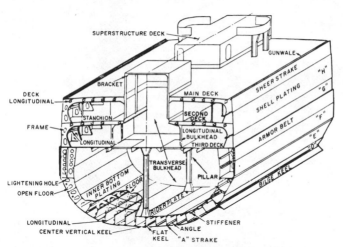

Figure 12–1   A ship's deck is strengthened by transverse beams and longitudinal girders. This is the hull structure of a cruiser.

The shape and construction of the hull depends on the type of ship. Ships designed for high-speed operations—destroyers and cruisers—have long, narrow hulls with fine lines and rounded bilges. Aircraft carriers and auxiliary ships have hulls with square center sections, vertical sides, and flat bottoms for greater carrying capacity. Submarines, designed to operate under water, have hulls that are rounded, like an egg, because that shape withstands great pressure.

Most ships have unarmored hulls. The hull consists only of the basic shell plating. Ships with armored hulls have a waterline armor belt of very thick steel running fore and aft to protect enginerooms and magazines from torpedoes or shellfire, and thinner armor steel plates on one or more decks to protect against bombs and shells.

The keel is the backbone of the hull. (Figure 12-1 shows the hull and other structural members discussed in this section.) The keel usually looks like an I-beam running the full length of the ship, with heavy castings fore and aft called *stem* and *stern posts. Frames,* fastened to the keel, run athwartships and support the watertight skin or shell plating. Most ships built for the Navy also have *longitudinal* frames running fore and aft. The longitudinal and athwartships frames form an egg-crate structure in the bottom of the ship called the *double bottom. Deck*

Figure 12–2 A starboard-side view of the carrier *America* (CV 66) illustrating the many deck levels.

beams, transverse bulkheads, and *stanchions* support the decks and help strengthen the sides against water pressure. The framework is assembled by electric-arc welding, which is lighter than riveting.

Compartments are the rooms of a ship. Some compartments are called rooms, such as *wardroom, stateroom,* and *engineroom,* but generally speaking, the word *room* isn't used. Don't refer to the space where you sleep as the bedroom, the place where you eat as the dining room. They are called the *berthing compartment* and the *mess deck,* respectively.

Decks divide a ship into tiers or layers of compartments, the way floors of a building divide it into stories. The deck normally consists of steel plates strengthened by transverse (athwartships) deck beams and longitudinal (fore and aft) girders. On some ships, the weather deck is covered by wood to provide better footing in wet weather and insulate below-deck space from heat and cold. Decks above the waterline are usually cambered, or arched, to provide greater strength and drain off water.

Decks are named according to their position in the ship and their function (figure 12-2). For purposes of compartment identification, decks are also numbered. The *main deck* is the uppermost of the decks that run continuously from bow to stern. The *second, third,* and *fourth decks,* continuous decks below the main deck, are numbered in sequence from topside down.

A partial deck above the main deck is named according to its position on the ship. At the bow it is called a *forecastle deck,* amidships it becomes an *upper deck,* and at the stern it is a *poop deck.* The term *weather deck* includes all parts of the main, forecastle, upper, and poop decks that are exposed to weather. A partial deck between two continuous decks is referred to as a *half deck.* A partial deck below the lowest continuous deck is a *platform deck.*

Armor-plated decks, or those constructed of armor steel, are referred to as *protective* or *splinter decks,* as well as being called by their regular (functional) names. If there is only one, it is a protective deck. If two, the heavier is the protective deck and the lighter the splinter deck.

Flats are platings or gratings installed as working or walking surfaces above bilges.

Any deck above the main, forecastle, or poop deck is called a *level.* The first is the 01 level, the second 02, etc. The top deck of an aircraft carrier is the *flight deck.* The deck below it, where aircraft are stored and serviced, is the *hangar deck.*

The *quarterdeck* is not a true deck or a structural part of the ship, but rather a location designated by the commanding officer as a place for ceremonies.

Compartmentation and Watertight Integrity

If a ship were built like a rowboat, one hole below the waterline could sink her. To prevent this from happening, naval ships are built with bulkheads that divide the hull into a series of watertight compartments. Cargo ships have widely spaced bulkheads serving as large hold areas. Ships designed to carry troops or passengers have smaller holds, and much of the inte-

Figure 12-3 Decks are named and numbered by their position and function on a ship.

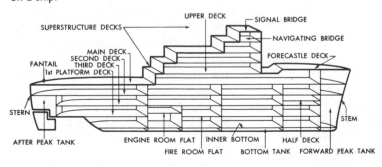

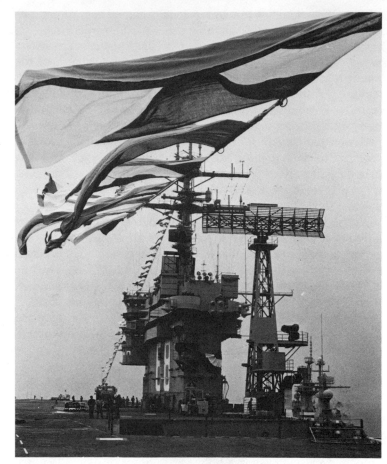

Figure 12–4   Aboard an aircraft carrier, the top deck is the flight deck, the main deck is the hangar deck, and the superstructure is the island.

rior is divided into smaller living compartments. Navy vessels are divided into many compartments, so that in case of damage flooding can be limited to as few compartments as possible.

Watertight doors and *watertight hatches* allow access through all bulkheads and decks. Any ship, divided into enough watertight compartments, could be made virtually unsinkable; but too much compartmentation would interfere with the arrangement of mechanical equipment and with her operation. A given number of compartments must be flooded before today's ships will sink.

Large ships have outer and inner *double bottoms*. These are divided athwartships and longitudinally into tanks, which are used for fuel oil, boiler feedwater, fresh water, or seawater ballast. In armored hulls, the double-bottom compartmentation may extend past the turn of the bilge (where the bottom meets the side of the hull) and all or partway up the side, as protection against torpedoes and other weapons.

Tanks at the extreme bow and stern, called the *forward peak* (or *forepeak*) tank and the *after peak* (or *aftpeak*) tank, are used for trimming the ship. Sometimes they carry potable (drinking) water.

A strong watertight bulkhead on the after side of the forepeak tank is called the *collision bulkhead*. If one ship rams another head on, the bow structure of the latter collapses at a point somewhere forward of the collision bulkhead, thus preventing flooding of compartments aft of it

All tanks are connected to a pumping and drainage system so that fuel, water, and ballast can be transferred from one part of the ship to another or pumped overboard.

Maintenance of *watertight integrity* is a function of damage control (see chapter 18). All doors and hatches through watertight bulkheads or decks must also be watertight. Wherever water, steam, oil, air piping, electric cables, or ventilation ducts go through a watertight bulkhead or deck, the hole is plugged by a stuffing tube, pipe, spool, or other device to prevent leakage. All watertight doors and hatches carry markings that state when they must not be opened.

Figure 12–5 Compartment and deck numbers are assigned starting with the main deck.

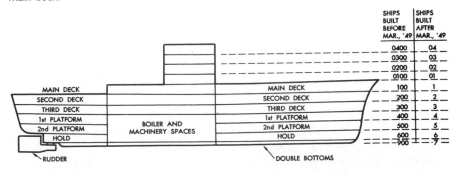

Compartment and Deck Numbering

Trying to find your way around a multideck ship that is several hundred feet long is like trying to get around a strange town where the street signs have been torn down. This is why the numbering system was devised. It gives each compartment an "address," enabling you to go directly to any designated space.

Every space aboard ship (except for minor spaces, such as peacoat, linen, and cleaning-gear lockers) is assigned an identifying letter-number symbol, which is marked on a label plate secured to the door, hatch, or bulkhead of the compartment. There are two numbering systems, one for ships built before March 1949, the other for ships built since then.

Ships Built Before March 1949

The letter part of a designation tells in which of three divisions a compartment is located. The letter is followed by three digits. The first digit indicates the deck, and the last two indicate the number of the compartment within the division. Even numbers indicate port side, odd numbers starboard side. A letter following the digits refers to the primary function of the compartment.

A ship has the following divisions: A (from the bow to the forward bulkhead of the engineering spaces), B (between forward and aft bulkheads of the engineering spaces), and C (everything aft of the engineering spaces). Decks are numbered from the main deck down (100, 200, etc.) and from the deck above the main deck up (0100, 0200, etc.). Double bottoms are always numbered in the 900 series, no matter how many decks the ship has.

The primary function of a compartment is indicated by the following letters:

A—Supply and storage   M—Ammunition
C—Control   T—Trunks and passages
E—Machinery   V—Voids
F—Fuel   W—Water
L—Living quarters

For example, C-217-A identifies a compartment in the C, or after part of the ship, on the second deck below the main deck, starboard side, which is used for supply and storage.

Compartment numbers contain the following information: deck number, frame number, relation to the centerline of the ship, and function of the compartment.

The *deck number* is the first part of the compartment number. If a compartment extends to the bottom of the ship, the deck number refers to the bottommost deck.

The *frame number,* the second part of the compartment designation, refers to the forwardmost bulkhead of a compartment. If the bulkhead is between frames, the number of the forwardmost frame in the compartment is used.

The third part of the compartment number refers to the compartment's relation to the centerline. Compartments located on the centerline carry the number 0. Those to starboard have odd numbers, while those to port have even numbers. If two or more compartments with the same deck and frame number are entirely to starboard or port of the centerline, they are numbered consecutively odd or even, from the centerline moving outboard. Thus, the first compartment outboard of the centerline to starboard is 1, the second is 3, and so on. The first compartment outboard of the centerline to port is 2, the second is 4, and so on.

When the centerline passes through more than one compartment, the compartment having that portion of the forward bulkhead through which the centerline passes carries the number 0, while the others carry the numbers 01, 02, 03, etc.

The fourth and last part of the compartment number is the letter that identifies the compartment's primary function. On dry- and liquid-cargo ships, a double-letter identification designates cargo-carrying compartments as follows:

A—Stowage spaces: store and issue rooms; refrigerated compartments

AA—Cargo holds: cargo holds and refrigerated compartments

C—Control centers for ship and fire-control operations (normally manned): the combat information center (CIC); internal communications (IC) rooms; plotting rooms; pilot house; electronic equipment–operating spaces

E—Engineering control centers (normally manned): main machinery spaces; evaporator rooms; steering-gear rooms; pump rooms; auxiliary machinery spaces; emergency generator rooms

F—Oil stowage compartments (for use by ship): fuel-, diesel-, and lubricating-oil compartments

FF—Oil stowage compartments (cargo): compartments carrying various types of oil as cargo

G—Gasoline stowage compartments (ship use): gasoline tanks, cofferdams, trunks, and pump rooms

GG—Gasoline stowage compartments (cargo): spaces for carrying gasoline as cargo

J—JP-5 fuel (ship use): jet-fuel stowage spaces

JJ—JP-5 fuel (cargo): spaces for carrying JP-5 fuel as cargo

K—Chemicals and dangerous materials (other than oil and gasoline): chemicals, semisafe materials, and dangerous materials carried as cargo or for ship's use

L—Living spaces: berthing and messing spaces; staterooms; washrooms; heads; brig; sick bay; and passageways

M—Ammunition spaces: magazines; handling rooms; turrets; gun mounts; shell rooms; ready service rooms

Q—Miscellaneous spaces not covered by other letters: laundry; galley; pantries; wiring trunks; unmanned engineering; electrical and electronic spaces; shops; offices

T—Vertical access trunks: escape trunks

V—Voids: cofferdam spaces (other than gasoline); void wing compartments

W—Water stowage spaces: drainage tanks; freshwater tanks; peak tanks; reserve feedwater tanks

Hull Reference Terms

Ballast: Weight added to a ship's inner bottom to balance her topside weight, or to keep her down in the water under light loads. Some ships carry permanent concrete ballast. Others pump salt water into tanks for the same purpose.

Bilge keels: Long, narrow fins fitted to both sides of the hull at the turn of the bilge to prevent the ship from rolling.

Bulwarks: Vertical extensions above the deck edge of the shell plating. Bulwarks are built high enough to keep personnel and equipment from going overboard.

Draft: The vertical distance from the waterline to the keel. Draft is measured in feet and inches, by scales marked on the hull at the stem and stern post. Draft numbers are 6 inches high and spaced 6 inches apart. The bottom of each number indicates foot marks, the top indicates half-foot marks.

Freeboard: Vertical distance from the waterline to the weather deck.

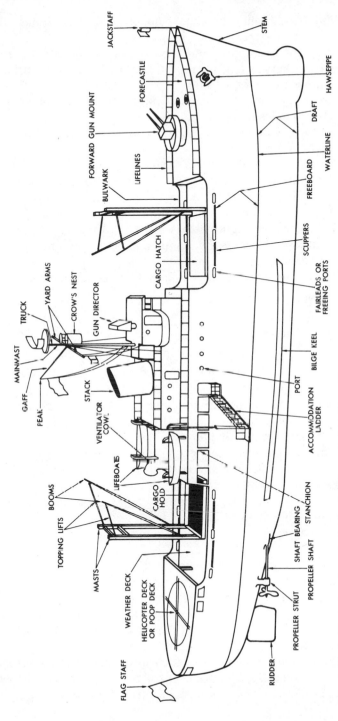

Figure 12–6 These are the principal parts of a typical auxiliary ship.

Lifelines: Light wire ropes supported on stanchions. They serve the same purpose as bulwarks.

Propeller guards: Steel braces at the stern, directly above the propellers. They prevent the propellers from striking a dock, pier, or another ship.

Stem: The point of the hull at the bow, where port and starboard sides meet.

Stern: The point of the hull at the after end, where both sides of the ship meet.

Trim and *List:* Trim refers to the relation between the fore and aft draft. A ship properly balanced fore and aft is "in trim," otherwise she is "down by the head" or "down by the stern." List refers to athwartships balance. A ship with one side higher than the other has a starboard or port list. List is measured in degrees by an inclinometer, mounted on the bridge exactly at the ship's centerline.

Waterline: The line where the hull meets the surface of the water.

Superstructure

The superstructure includes all structures above the main deck. The superstructure varies according to the type of ship, but all ships have a wheelhouse, bridge, signal bridge, chart room, combat information center, radio room, and probably sea cabin or emergency cabin for the captain. (These are discussed later in the chapter.)

The superstructure is topped off by the mast. At its simplest, a mast is a single pole fitted with a *yardarm* (*spar*) that extends above the ship and carries flag halyards and navigational and signal lights. Generally a mast consists of several structural members in tripod form. In addition to the usual yardarm, the mast may support various electronic devices, radar antennas, and radio aerials.

On older ships, and particularly on small escort and patrol craft, the mast is a distinct feature. If the ship has two masts, the forward one is called the *foremast,* the after one the *mainmast.* On single-masted ships, the mast, whether forward or amidships, is usually part of the superstructure and is simply called the mast.

The top of a mast is called the *truck.* The top of the foremast is the *foretruck,* while the top of the mainmast is the *main truck.* The *pigstick* is a slender vertical extension above the mast from which the ship's commission pennant or an admiral's personal flag flies. The *gaff* extends abaft the mainmast. It is from the gaff that the national ensign is flown when the ship is under way.

The small vertical spar at the bow and the slightly raked one at the stern are called the *jackstaff* and *flagstaff,* respectively. When a Navy ship is at anchor or moored, it flies the union jack on the jackstaff and the national ensign on the flagstaff from 0800 to sunset.

The *stack* of a ship serves the same purpose as the smokestack on a power plant ashore. It carries off smoke and hot gases from the boilers, and exhaust from the diesel engines. (Nuclear-powered ships do not need stacks, since their reactors produce no smoke or gas.) Some diesel-powered ships release their exhaust from the sides. On some new ships, the masts and stacks have been combined to form large towers called *macks.*

The Propulsion Plant

A typical steam propulsion plant consists of *boilers, main engines, reduction gears, propeller shafts,* and *propellers.* There are many variations, involving turboelectric drive, direct diesel drive, and diesel-electric drive. Nuclear-powered ships have steam propulsion, but the steam is produced in a reactor instead of in oil-fired boilers.

A *boiler* is a boxlike casing containing hundreds of water-filled steel tubes. These tubes are arranged so that heat from the fireboxes passes over them. Fuel oil, heated and sprayed into the fireboxes under high pressure, burns intensely, turning the water into steam. The steam then flows through pipes to the turbines. *Forced-draft blowers* increase the air pressure—either in the firerooms where the boilers are mounted, or in the boilers themselves—for better combustion. Fresh water used in the boilers is made from salt water by *evaporators* and *condensers.*

A *turbine* is a revolving rotor that has several rows of blades mounted in a steam-tight casing with additional rows of stationary blades. Rotor and casing blades are set in alternate rows. Thus, as steam passes through the turbine, each row deflects it to the next row. Most turbines have both high-pressure (HP) and low-pressure (LP) stages. After steam has passed through both stages, it is cooled, condensed into water, and then returned to the boilers.

Turbines cannot be reversed. To reverse the shaft, a *backing turbine* has to be installed, or else one section of the main turbine called an *astern element* is fitted inside a separate casing. Because backing turbines or astern elements have fewer rows of blades than the main turbine, they produce less power. A ship never has as much power for backing down as she has for going ahead.

Reduction gears connect turbines and shafts. They are required because turbines operate most efficiently at several thousand rpm, but propellers are not very effective above 400 rpm. With reduction gears, two turbines frequently drive one shaft.

In ships where the main drive is electric, a current is generated either by steam turbines (turboelectric) or diesel engines (diesel-electric). Submarines powered by diesel engines use electric drive when submerged, but on the surface their motors draw current from storage batteries charged by diesels. A new generation of electric propulsion systems is being studied for possible use in future surface warships.

Propeller shafts carry power to the propellers. Shafts run from the reduction gears through long watertight spaces, called *shaft alleys,* in the bottom of the ship. They take the water through *stern glands* and *stern bearings* and may be supported outside the hull by *struts*.

Propellers drive the ship. All aircraft carriers and most cruisers have four propellers. Most older destroyers have two, as do older submarines. Newer destroyer types and most nuclear submarines have one propeller. Ships are classed as four-screw, two-screw, or single-screw types. Newer single-screw ships have adjustable-pitch propellers. These propellers, instead of reversing the direction of rotation to back down, reverse the curvature of the blades.

Gas turbines, marine adaptations of aircraft jet engines, power newer destroyers and frigates as well as hydrofoil missile gunboats (PHM) and air-cushion landing craft (LCAC).

For relatively small ships that need no more than 5,000 to 6,000 horsepower, diesel engines are frequently used. Diesels are lighter, take up less space, and are more efficient than steam turbines. The diesel can be coupled directly to the shaft through reduction gears and perhaps a clutch; or it can drive a generator that produces current for the main drive.

Gasoline engines are dangerous for marine use, because

highly volatile gas fumes are heavier than air and tend to collect in such places as the bilge, where the slightest spark can cause an explosion. Diesel fuel, which does not vaporize as readily, is much safer.

Nuclear-Power Plant

A nuclear-power plant uses a reactor (instead of oil-fired boilers) to provide heat for the generation of steam. The primary system is a circulating water cycle consisting of a reactor, loops of piping, primary coolant pumps, and steam generators. Heat produced in the reactor by nuclear fission is transferred to circulating primary coolant water, which is pressurized to prevent it from boiling. This water is then pumped through the steam generator and back into the reactor by primary coolant pumps. It can then be reheated for the next cycle.

In a steam generator, the heat of pressurized water is transferred to a secondary system, where water is turned into steam. This system is isolated from the primary system.

Steam flows from the generator to the engineroom, where it drives the turbogenerators that supply the ship with electricity and the main propulsion turbines that turn the propeller. After passing through the turbines, the steam is condensed into water, which is fed back to the steam generators by feed pumps.

The generation of nuclear power does not require oxygen. Thus submarines can operate completely submerged for extended periods of time.

Nuclear-power plants give a ship the advantage of unlimited endurance at high speed. Instead of refueling every few thousand miles, like an oil-burning ship, a nuclear-powered ship can operate for years on one reactor core. This means she requires far less logistical support or maintenance. Such a ship can be better sealed against CBR (chemical, biological, radiological) attack, and she emits no corrosive stack gas. As of 31 January 1990, the Navy had a total of 146 nuclear-powered ships in service; of this number, 131 are submarines and the remaining 15 are surface ships—6 carriers and 9 cruisers. Thirty-one nuclear-powered warships are under construction.

Steering

Any ship or boat is steered by a rudder. The rudder is controlled by a tiller in an open boat (such as a motor whaleboat or motor launch), and by a wheel in the cockpit of a larger boat or on the bridge of a ship. In a boat, the motion of the wheel is transmitted to the rudder by a cable or shaft. In a ship, the rudder is turned by an electric or steam engine in the steering-engine room. This electrical or hydraulic engine is controlled by the wheel on the bridge.

A rudder acts by the force of water pushing against one side of it. There is no rudder action when the ship is motionless. The greater the speed, the greater the effect the rudders have. That's why they are usually mounted just astern of the screws, where the wash pushes directly against them. When the ship is backing down, the propeller wash goes forward and the rudder has little effect, especially at slow speeds.

To prevent loss of control in case of damage to the bridge (sometimes called the *main conn*), there is usually a second steering wheel mounted elsewhere (the *secondary conn*). If that wheel is disabled, the ship can be hand-steered by several sailors using special gear in the steering-engine room.

When a single-engine ship or boat moves at low speed, there is a tendency for the stern to swing to one side or the other. This is owing to a *side effect* set up by the propeller. The blades below the shaft get a better bite in the denser water and push the stern sideways. This effect is even more noticeable when the ship is backing down, because the propeller wash is moving forward and exerts no force on the rudder.

Ships or boats with two screws can be steered fairly well without a rudder by using the engines. If one screw turns faster than the other, the bow will swing toward the slower screw. If one screw goes ahead while the other goes astern, the bow of the ship will swing toward the backing screw. Boats, and even very large ships, can turn within the diameter of their own lengths using this method.

Ground Tackle

Ground tackle (pronounced *tay-kle*) refers to all the gear used to anchor a ship or moor her to a buoy. A ship is *anchored* when she is held in position by an anchor on the ocean bottom, and *moored* when she is made fast either to a buoy or a pier. A ship is moored to a buoy by anchor chain, but moored to a pier by mooring lines. Details on ground tackle are found on pp. 507–16.

All ground tackle is located on the forecastle. Some ships, particularly amphibious craft, may also carry a stern anchor used in retracting, or in hauling off from the beach.

Ladders and Booms

Although not permanent parts of the hull, ladders and booms are rigged for use when necessary.

Boat boom: A spar swung out from the ship's side when the ship is moored or anchored and to which boats are secured when not in use.

Accommodation ladder: A stairway suspended over the side of the ship, with a platform at the bottom that serves as a landing for boats. A *boat rope* or *sea painter* is provided to secure boats alongside while they load and unload.

Brow: A form of gangway used when the ship is moored alongside a pier or "nested" alongside other ships. The brow's size and construction depend on the size of the ship and her distance to the pier.

Chains: A small platform rigged over the side for use by the leadsman in taking soundings.

Ship's Equipment and Operations

Much of the hull space in ships is taken up by engines, engineering equipment, and related piping and electrical systems.

Firerooms contain the boilers that provide steam for the main engines. Enginerooms contain the main engine and reduction gears that drive the ship. Auxiliary enginerooms contain generators that produce electricity for the ship, as well as evaporators and condensers to make fresh water out of salt water. The steering-engine room houses the machine that powers the rudder. Fuel-oil tanks carry the oil burned in boilers.

Electrical System

A large ship has hundreds of electric motors driving everything from fans and tape decks to 50-ton elevators. Every other system in the ship depends on electric motors. The main power supply is produced in the engineering spaces by steam-driven generators. Emergency diesel-electric generators in other parts of the ship automatically cut in to supply power if the main generators are disabled for any reason.

Drainage System

This system includes the piping, valves, and pumps that discharge water from the ship. Its functions include the removal of sea water that has entered the hull because of damage, collision, or heavy weather.

The main drainage system is composed of large piping located in the main engineering spaces and used for pumping their bilges. The secondary drainage system is composed of smaller piping located in, and used for pumping the bilges of, spaces forward and aft of the main engineering spaces, such as pump rooms and shaft alleys. Installed eductors (jet pumps) are used in both systems and are situated to allow the pumping of one space's bilge from another space, in the event of extensive flooding, by using bulkhead stop valves, bilge sump valves, isolation valves, and the eductor's fire-main supply—suction and overboard discharge valves that can be operated locally and/or remotely.

The main and secondary drainage systems are often used as part of the deballast system so that voids, ballast tanks, peak tanks, and stern tanks can be pumped to control the list and trim of the ship when fuel cannot be transferred.

Spaces located below the waterline that may require periodic drainage, such as magazines, elevator/conveyor pits, refrigerator drain tanks, photochemical drain tanks, etc., often have their own eductor systems.

Weather-deck drains are piped directly overboard, but internal drains (from sinks, showers, galleys, decks, urinals, and commodes) are carefully controlled for environmental reasons. When a ship is moored pierside, waste is collected in specially designed ship's tanks and then pumped to a sewage-receiving connection on the pier through hard rubber hoses. When a ship is at anchor, the same procedure is used, except the waste is pumped into barges tied up alongside. When a ship is entering or leaving port, all waste is retained aboard. When the ship is approximately 50 miles from land, it is safe to deposit waste overboard. Drainage systems vary depending on the type of ship, but all are referred to as marine sanitation systems.

Ventilation Systems

These systems circulate air and exhaust. A ship has many separate ventilation systems that operate independently of each other. Each system is unique—it may provide ventilation to one space or many spaces—and each has its own electric fan motor, with one or two speed settings depending on the system's requirements.

Supply ventilation brings fresh (external) air into the ship and, in the event of cold weather, heats the air by means of a steam coil (preheater) installed in the ducting. *Exhaust* ventilation serves those spaces that generate heat and/or humidity (main engineering spaces, galley, head facilities, etc.) and maintains an air-pressure balance with the supply ventilation system. *Recirc* ventilation is provided to spaces containing electronic equipment (they require a cool environment for proper operation), as well as to berthing, messing, and office spaces. As its name implies, this system recirculates internal air to prevent stagnation and, when necessary, draws the air through cooling coils supplied by the ship's chilled-water system.

In the event of fire, flooding, or some other danger requiring the isolation of a space or spaces, ventilation systems can be secured by de-energizing the fan motor and/or segregated by closing valvelike closure devices in the ducting (often found where the ducting penetrates decks, overheads, and bulkheads).

Fresh (Potable) Water System

Water for drinking, showers, and cooking is provided by this piping system. Potable-water tanks are filled from the ship's evaporators, which convert it from salt water.

Feedwater System

The ship's evaporators also convert salt water into water for the boilers. Boiler water is much purer than potable water, since any trace of mineral or salt content might eventually cause damage to boiler tubing.

Saltwater/Fire-Main System

This piping system is supplied by steam and/or electric pumps. They draw salt water from the sea for firefighting protection, CBR washdown, and head facilities, to provide auxiliary cooling to engineering machinery and water pressure to eductor drain systems, and as a source of water for some ballast systems.

Fuel-Oil System

This system includes fuel-storage tanks, filling lines, and feed lines to the boilers. It also includes lines and connections for pumping oil from one tank to another to control trim or list when the ship is damaged.

Compressed-Air System

Compressors, storage tanks, and high-pressure lines to eject gases from guns after firing are part of this system. Compressed air is also used for testing and blowing out compartments, charging torpedoes, and operating pneumatic tools, dispatch tubes, automatic boiler controls, and other equipment.

Magazines

Ammunition for all guns is stored in magazines, which are placed well below the waterline whenever possible. Projectiles and powder may be stored in separate compartments. In case of fire, all magazines can be flooded by remote control (or automatically, with heat-sensitive sprinkler systems). Ammunition is passed to handling rooms, where hoists take it up to gun mounts or turrets.

Cargo Holds

Cargo holds are large spaces where auxiliaries carry material for other ships. Holds have hatches opening on the main deck.

Storerooms

Storerooms are spaces where ships carry supplies such as clothing, dry or refrigerated provisions, and various types of spare parts and supplies.

Crew Accommodations

The many compartments throughout a ship include the wardroom, officer's cabins (or state rooms), berthing compartments, pantrys, messes, heads, washrooms, and sick bay. Other spaces provided for the health and comfort of the crew include a barber and tailor shop, a cobbler shop, a laundry, galleys, bake shops, butcher shops, a library, a chapel, a ship's store, a soda fountain, a reception room, and hobby shops. Some larger ships such as aircraft carriers have several of each of these service compartments.

Shops and Offices

Besides offices for the captain and executive officer, a ship has office space, or a separate office, for every department and activity on board. Even a small ship has a carpenter's shop and

special repair shops handling everything from typewriters to
torpedoes.

Bridge

This is the primary control position for the ship when she is
under way, and the place where all orders and commands affecting the ship's movements and routine originate. The officer
of the deck (OOD) is always on the bridge when the ship is
under way. The captain is on the bridge during general quarters, during most special sea evolutions, and when the ship is
entering and leaving port. The ship can also be handled from
the *secondary conn* (secondary control station), the general
quarters (GQ) station for the executive officer. Thus if the
bridge is knocked out or the captain disabled in battle, the
executive officer can take over.

Bridge and Pilot-House Equipment

Sometimes called the wheelhouse, the pilot house contains
equipment and instruments used to control the movements of
the ship. Usually the bridge extends from both sides of the
pilot house. Some pilot-house equipment is duplicated on the
bridge.

263

Ship-Control Console: This consists of the engine and propeller order sections, which control the speed and direction
(ahead or astern) of the ship. The *engine order section* has a
dial for each engine, divided into sectors marked flank, full,
standard, 2/3, and 1/3 speed ahead; stop; and 1/3, 2/3, and full
speed astern. When a hand lever is moved to the speed sector
ordered by the OOD, the engineroom watch sets the engine
throttle for the same speed and notifies the bridge by moving
an answering pointer to the same sector. The ship control console is manned by the lee helmsman, who is sometimes also a
telephone talker. The *propeller order section* enables the OOD
to make minor changes in speed by ordering the enginerooms
to increase or decrease the rpm (revolutions per minute) of the
propellers.

Steering-Control Console: This contains the controls and indicators required to maintain the course of the ship. The steering wheel (helm) is operated by the helmsman. On the panel in
front of the helmsman are various indicators and switches. The
ship's course indicator is a gyrocompass repeater that shows

the ship's true course. Another indicator shows the course to be steered. Two more important indicators show the rudder angle (number of degrees) left or right of amidships, and the helm angle (number of degrees) left or right of amidships.

Tachometer: This is the same type of instrument used on a sports car; it shows shaft rpms. There's a tach for each propeller.

Lighting Panels: The two primary lighting panels in the pilot house are the signal and anchor light supply-and-control panel and the running lights supply-and-control panel.

Lights installed in combatant ships usually include aircraft warning lights, blinker lights, breakdown, man-overboard and underway-replenishment lights, steering lights, stern lights (blue), wake lights, and speed lights. Switches are located on the signal and anchor light supply-and-control panel.

The location of bridge equipment varies among ship types and may be different on ships of the same type. A bridge watchstander not only has to know where everything is located but must also be able to find it in the dark.

264

Chart House

The chart house is normally just aft of the pilot house and on the same deck, but it can also be on another deck and some distance away. On some ships the dead-reckoning tracer (DRT) is in the chart house. The chart house also contains navigational instruments such as sextants, stadimeter, bearing circles and stopwatches, parallel rulers, protractors, position plotters, and navigational books and tables.

Secondary Conn

This area contains steering equipment, engine-order telegraph, phone circuits, and other equipment necessary for ship control in the event primary control is unable to perform because of battle damage. The ship's magnetic compass may also be located here.

Signal Bridge

This is an open platform located near the navigational bridge and equipped with yardarm blinker controls, signal searchlights, and flag bags. From here signalmen communicate with other ships.

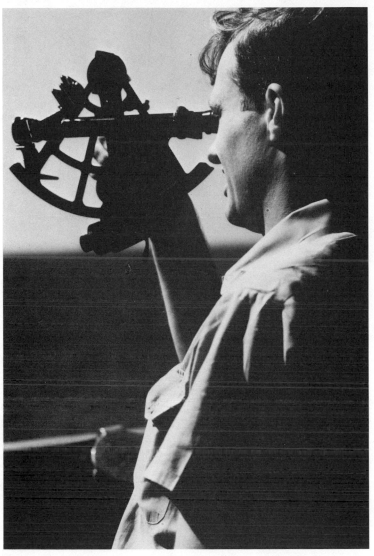

Figure 12–7 Even with all the electronic navigational equipment on board, the ship's navigator must be an expert at using the sextant.

Message Center

This is the station of the communication watch officer. Here outgoing traffic is prepared for transmission, and incoming messages are readied for local delivery. All messages, except

Figure 12–8 The combat information center is the nerve center of a ship.

tactical signals received and sent direct from shipboard control stations, go through the message center.

Cryptographic Center

The cryptographic center is the exclusive working area of the crypto board, which is responsible for encoding and decoding all cryptographic information. Access to the center is strictly controlled. It has a single entrance and an authorized entry list posted nearby.

Combat Information Center

The combat information center (CIC) is the nerve center of the ship. It has a fivefold function: to collect, process, display, evaluate, and disseminate information from sources both inside and outside the ship. A wide range of electronic equip-

Ship's
Equipment

Figure 12–9 Submarine maneuvering controls are more like those of an aircraft than those of a surface ship, since a sub moves up and down.

ment is installed in the CIC: radar, sonar, electronic-warfare intercept receivers, IFF (identification friend or foe), radio and visual communications, PPI (plan position indicator) repeaters, display screens, and computers. Installations include both air- and surface-search as well as fire-control radar.

Damage-Control Central

Damage-control central (DCC) maintains damage-control charts, machinery charts, and liquid-loading diagrams. DCC sees that the proper conditions of readiness are set and maintained. The conditions of stability and damage throughout the ship are known in DCC at all times and reported directly to the bridge. All repair parties report to DCC. (More details on actual DCC operation appear in chapter 18.)

Submarines

Because they are designed to operate under water, submarines have very few topside features and practically no superstructure. About all that projects above the hull is the *sail,* a streamlined tower on which diving planes are mounted and where a few people can stand a topside watch when the submarine operates on the surface. On some submarines being built today, these diving planes have been moved to the bow of the ship, leaving the sail even more streamlined.

Submarine hulls have nearly circular cross sections and are built to withstand tremendous pressure. The hull consists of the bow compartment, containing living accommodations; the operations compartment, containing the control room, sonar and radar rooms, the torpedo room, and some state rooms; the reactor compartment; the missile rooms (on fleet ballistic missile submarines); and the engineroom. Unlike surface ships, the sub has ballast tanks that can be quickly flooded when the boat is to submerge, or pumped out when she is to surface.

The controls by which a submarine is maneuvered are more like those of an aircraft than those of a surface ship (which merely steers left or right), because a sub also moves up and down. In fact, when operating submerged, she banks in her turns exactly like an aircraft.

Aside from these basic differences, a submarine contains all the systems and features found in a surface vessel.

Ships and Aircraft

13

Ships

The Navy operates nearly 600 ships. There are 515 active ships, oceangoing vessels operating under a commanding officer or, in the case of some replenishment ships operated by the Military Sealift Command (MSC), under a civilian master. Thirty-three fleet-support ships are manned by civilian crews, and there are 47 ships in the Naval Reserve. In addition to these, there are 854 active service craft. Some of these have part-time crews, but most are without crews. Many service craft are not self-propelled.

Most Navy ships have both a name and number. The number—called a designation—tells you two things about a ship: her type and her hull number. The USS *Texas*, for instance, is CGN 39. CGN is her classification symbol and 39 her hull number. The C means cruiser, the G means that she carries guided missiles, and the N means nuclear propulsion. Hull numbers also indicate the sequence in which ships of a type are ordered for construction. For example, the USS *Barry* (DD 2) was commissioned in 1902; another *Barry* (DD 248) was commissioned in 1920; and a third *Barry* (DD 933) went into commission in 1956. The Secretary of the Navy recently named a projected missile destroyer (DDG 52) as the fourth *Barry*.

Designations are used in correspondence, records, and plans and appear on ships' boats, ships' bows, and in other places. Referring to a ship by her designation can help avoid confusion. For instance, the Navy has a USS *George Washington Carver* and will soon have a USS *George Washington*. The former is designated SSN 656 and the latter will be CVN 73. As you can see, designations are often shorter than ships' names.

Sailors have traditionally given nicknames to their seagoing homes. Among aircraft carriers, for instance, the *John F. Kennedy* is the *JFK*, the *Enterprise* the *Big E*, the *Constellation* the *Connie*, and the *Dwight D. Eisenhower* the *Ike*.

Aircraft Carriers

The U.S. Navy currently has thirteen active aircraft carriers, plus one being modernized. Its carrier force has five nuclear-powered ships and eight oil-powered ones. The former are the *Enterprise* (CVN 65), the *Nimitz* (CVN 68), the *Dwight D. Eisenhower* (CVN 69), the *Carl Vinson* (CVN 70), the *Theodore Roosevelt* (CVN 71), and the *Abraham Lincoln* (CVN 72). The *George Washington* (CVN 73) and *John C. Stennis* (CVN 74) are under construction. The *United States* (CVN 75) has been authorized by Congress. These are the world's largest warships.

The non-nuclear carrier force has four ships of the *Kitty Hawk* (CV 63) class—the *Kitty Hawk, Constellation, America,* and *John F. Kennedy* (sometimes referred to as a single-ship class); four of the *Forrestal* (CV 59) class of the late 1950s and early 1960s—the *Forrestal, Saratoga, Independence,* and *Ranger;* and one of the 1945 *Midway* (CV 41) class—the *Midway.* Older carriers are progressively modernized over the years to enable them to accommodate newer types of aircraft and advanced ship technologies. The *Kitty Hawk* is receiving an extensive modernization designed to extend her service life through the end of this century.

The *Nimitz* is a good example of what, in many respects, is one of the world's most powerful warships. She is 1,092 feet in overall length, 252 feet in extreme beam, has a full-load displacement of 91,400 tons, and rides 38 feet deep. At the heart of her engineering plant are two nuclear reactors (compared with eight for the *Enterprise*) with a 280,000-horsepower drive turning four propellers. A nuclear-powered ship's reactors take the place of the oil furnaces in the boilers of an oil-fueled ship. The reactors generate heat to turn water into steam and power the turbines that drive the ship's propellers. Unlike oil-burners, nuclear ships can operate at high speeds for long periods of time without refueling. Weight and space taken by fuel tanks in conventional ships can be used for other purposes. As with all Navy warships, her precise top speed, listed as being "in excess of 30 knots," is classified.

When the *Nimitz* has an air wing embarked, she accommodates about 570 officers and 5,720 enlisted personnel. Nearly 100 aircraft—fighter, attack, electronic countermeasures (ECM), airborne early warning (AEW), and reconnaissance planes, and helicopters—operate from her flight deck. For defense she has, in addition to her own aircraft, three basic point-

Figure 13–1   The *Nimitz,* under way in the Atlantic, is one of the world's
most powerful warships, carrying nearly 100 aircraft and more than 6,000
men.

defense missile systems (BPDMSs). (See chapter 15 for details
on weapons.)

The four *Forrestal*-class carriers exemplify the oil-powered
types. They are 1,040 feet long, 252 feet in beam, displace
78,000 tons, have a crew of 5,000, and carry up to 90 aircraft.
Eight oil-burning boilers give these ships a steam-turbine drive
rated at 260,000 horsepower.

The oldest and smallest active CV is the *Midway.* Sizeable in
comparison with cruisers or destroyers, but small by comparison with later carriers, she displaces 64,000 tons and is 979 feet
long and 238 feet in beam.

Four *Essex*-class carriers, built during World War II and
modernized during the 1960s, remain in the "mothball fleet."
These have been earmarked for disposal.

Battleships

Since the 1880s, battleships have been large surface warships protected by heavy armor and armed with the biggest   Ships

guns. They reached the height of size, firepower, protection, and speed during World War II. The only surviving battleships in any navy are four ships of the *Iowa* (BB 61) class. Active in World War II and the Korean War, they went into reserve in the 1950s, although the USS *New Jersey* (BB 62) made one Vietnam deployment in 1968–69 as a bombardment and naval-gunfire support ship. Naval opinion for some years held that high-performance aircraft and missiles had made battleships obsolete. Later developments in electronics, including ECM, and ship-launched missiles have brought them back as powerful, versatile surface warships. The *New Jersey* and the *Missouri* have been recommissioned for duty with the Pacific Fleet; the *Iowa* and the *Wisconsin* are in Atlantic service. These ships are 887 feet long and displace 58,000 tons at full load. Geared turbines give them a top speed of 33-plus knots. Turret guns, command spaces, and vitals are shielded by heavy armor and comprehensive compartmentation. Now reactivated, their 16-inch/50 and 5-inch/38 guns are joined by Tomahawk and Harpoon missiles, improved radar, communications and control facilities, ECM, and the Phalanx CIWS (see chapter 15). New developments include ammunition to increase gun capabilities, improvements to the gun fire-control systems, and enhanced missile armament. Each battleship operates at the core of a surface-ship battle group or with a carrier battle group. Intensive work with the *Iowa's* 16-inch guns has demonstrated their capabilities as precise antiship weapons.

Cruisers

In a sense, cruisers may be regarded as large destroyers (DDs), since the two types have many similarities. But where DDs are primarily intended to operate with a task force, cruisers can operate independently as well. Larger than destroyers, cruisers also have more weapons, more elaborate electronic suits, larger crews, and greater steaming endurance.

The Navy has forty-two active cruisers, all missile ships. Like carriers, some cruisers are oil burning (CGs) and some have nuclear-power plants (CGNs). There are two CGNs of the *California* class: the *California* (CGN 36) and the *South Carolina* (CGN 37) of 1975 and 1976. These ships can travel around the world twenty-eight times before having their nuclear cores replaced. One of their principal roles is the screening and protection of fast carrier task forces. These ships are

The carrier *Theodore Roosevelt* (CVN 71)

The missile cruiser *South Carolina* (CGN 37)

The missile cruiser *Valley Forge* (CG 50)

The missile cruiser *Callaghan* (DDG 994)

The destroyer *Leftwich* (DD 984)

The missile frigate *Thach* (FFG 43)

Figure 13–2 Current Navy ship types

Figure 13-3 Current Navy ship types

The submarine tender *Dixon* (AS 37)

The amphibious assault ship *Tarawa* (LHA 1)

The strategic missile submarine *Mariano G. Vallejo* (SSBN 658)

The dock landing ship *Fort McHenry* (LSD 43)

The battleship *Iowa* (BB 61)

The amphibious assault ship *Guadalcanal* (LPH 7)

The amphibious command ship *Mount Whitney* (LCC 20)

The mine countermeasures ship *Avenger* (MCM 1)

The tank landing ship *Fairfax County* (LST 1193)

Amphibious cargo ship *St. Louis* (LKA 116)

The attack submarine *Chicago* (SSN 721)

The ammunition ship *Mount Baker* (AE 34)

Figure 13–4   Current Navy ship types

596 feet long, 63 feet in extreme beam, and they displace 11,000 tons. They have crews of about 540.

Closely following the *California* class is the *Virginia* (CGN 38) class of the mid- and late 1970s. The *Virginia, Texas, Mississippi,* and *Arkansas* are active. Though slightly smaller than their predecessors, they are equally well armed. Vital to their firepower is the Mark 86 weapon system, which can track up to 120 targets at a time, and which aims and controls the ship's guns and missiles. Each *Virginia*-class CGN has two multipurpose launchers that fire such missiles as Standard or Harpoon against air or surface targets, and ASROC against submarines. Antisubmarine torpedo tubes and two quick-firing 5-inch/54 lightweight guns are also fitted.

The *Bainbridge* (CGN 25) and *Truxtun* (CGN 35), completed in 1962 and 1967, respectively, were originally classed as missile frigates. They are the forerunners of the later *California*s and *Virginia*s. The larger *Long Beach* (CGN 9) was the Navy's first nuclear-propelled surface warship.

The *Ticonderoga* (CG 47)-class missile ships are armed with the Aegis fleet air-defense system (see chapter 15). Their basic design was derived from the *Spruance* (DD 963) class, which they generally resemble. Fifteen ships are in commission, with twelve building or authorized.

The nine CGs of the *Belknap* (CG 26) class (1964–67) form a large part of the Navy's cruiser force. Their displacement is 7,840 tons. They are 547 feet long and carry a 430-man crew. Weapon features are a Terrier/ASROC launcher, a 5-inch/54 gun, and torpedoes.

Nine *Leahy* (CG 16)-class cruisers are slightly smaller than the *Belknap*s and lack their 5-inch gun. Commissioned in 1962–64, they employ missiles, torpedoes, and ASROC.

Two *Des Moines* (CA 134)–class cruisers, completed in 1948–49, are in the inactive fleet. These ships are armed with rapid-firing 8-inch turret guns developed as a result of World War II battle experience. With the three *Iowa* (BB 61)-class battleships mounting 16-inch guns, these cruisers are the last ships in the Navy's inventory to have guns larger than 5 inches in caliber.

Destroyers

In today's Navy, destroyers perform a wide range of duties. For example, as part of a screen unit in a carrier task group,

they can detect and engage enemy submarines, aircraft, missiles, and surface ships. In an amphibious assault, a destroyer's weapons can help protect against enemy forces at sea and ashore.

The *Spruance* (DD 963) destroyers form the Navy's newest class, the *Spruance* having been commissioned in 1975. They are 563 feet long and 55 feet in beam, displace 7,800 tons, and have a crew of 250. Their 80,000-horsepower, gas-turbine-drive engineering plants can go from "cold iron" to full speed in 12 minutes. The *Spruance*s were the first major ships to be powered by gas turbines. Their weaponry consists of antisubmarine torpedoes, two rapid-fire 5-inch/54 guns, ASROC, and Sea Sparrow antiair missiles. Some *Spruance*s are beginning to receive the vertical launching system (VLS) to handle antiair and antiaircraft missiles. Thirty-one *Spruance*-class destroyers are now in commission.

Eleven ships of the *Forrest Sherman* (DD 931) class of the mid-1950s are in reserve. Armed with guns and antisubmarine weapons, they are 418 feet long, 45 feet in beam, and displace 4,050 tons.

Let's turn from conventionally armed destroyers to the DDGs—guided-missile destroyers—such as the sixteen ships of the *Charles F. Adams* (DDG 2) class of 1960–64. In size,

Figure 13–5 An artist's conception of the *Arleigh Burke*-class guided-missile destroyer (DDG 51).

engineering plant, and general appearance, they resemble the *Forrest Sherman* class. Their weaponry differs, however. Besides two 5-inch/54 gun mounts, the DDGs have launchers for firing Tartar or Standard surface-to-air missiles. Three former *Forrest Sherman*s have been converted to *Decatur*-class DDGs similar to the *Charles F. Adams* class in function. Like their conventionally armed former sisters, these have been placed in reserve. Eight *Farragut* (DDG 37)-class ships, enlarged versions of the *Charles F. Adams,* have a twin launcher for Standard ER missiles and one 5-inch/54. Some of the DDG 2 and DDG 37 classes are going out of commission in the near future; others are to follow. The *Kidd* (DDG 993)-class consists of four enhanced *Spruance*s with two twin Standard ER launchers. The projected *Arleigh Burke* (DDG 51) class will handle Standard as well as Tomahawk and Harpoon missiles for a multimission capability. Like the *Ticonderoga*-class CGs, they will have the new Aegis fleet-air-defense system. The first ship of this class, the *Arleigh Burke,* has been launched, and thirteen others are building or authorized; more are projected. They are intended to replace the aging *Charles F. Adams* and *Farragut* classes.

Frigates

The frigate first appeared during World War II (500 were built) as the destroyer escort (DE). It was later called an escort vessel, and in 1975 it received the designation frigate (FF).

The largest class is the *Knox* (FF 1052) with forty-six units. That class started with the *Knox* in 1969 and ended with the *Moinester* (FF 1097) in 1974. These ships carry crews of 230 and may be viewed as scaled-down destroyers specializing in antisubmarine work. With three ships of the earlier *Bronstein* (FF 1037) and *Clover* (FF 1098) classes, they protect amphibious forces, underway replenishment operations, and merchant-ship convoys.

The *Oliver Hazard Perry* (FFG 7) was commissioned in 1977 as the first of a new class of missile frigates, slightly larger than the *Knox* class, with gas turbines like those of the *Spruance*. Fifty-one *Oliver Hazard Perry*–class ships are in commission. Many frigates of the *Knox* and *Oliver Hazard Perry* classes have joined the Naval Reserve.

Sixteen units of the *Garcia* (FF 1040) and *Brooke* (FFG 1) classes have been decommissioned. Some have been transferred to other navies.

Submarines

The Navy has both attack and ballistic-missile submarines, depending on their primary mission. Submarines are also assigned secondary missions, which may include surveillance and reconnaissance, direct task-force support, landing-force support, minelaying, and rescue.

One active diesel-electric submarine is designated SS. It was built in the 1950s. All other submarines are nuclear powered. The last of the "diesel boats," *Blueback* (SS 580), is scheduled for decommissioning.

The Navy's ninety-six nuclear attack submarines (SSN) may be compared to the "fleet boats" of World War II, since their main job is to attack enemy ships and submarines. The SSN's principal weapon is the high-speed, wire-guided Mark 48 torpedo, whose target motion can be changed up to the point of impact. Some SSNs carry Harpoon and Tomahawk missiles for use against surface targets. The latest of the SSNs is the 6,900-ton *Los Angeles* (SSN 688) class. This class will continue building through the mid-1990s. They are the largest and most powerful of the SSNs, capable of operating more quickly, deeply, and quietly than any of their predecessors. Forty-two are in commission, with twenty more building or authorized. Newer *Los Angeles*–class boats have vertical launch tubes for Tomahawk cruise missiles. A new submarine design is called the SSN 21, since it will be the SSN class with which the Navy will enter the twenty-first century. The first of these submarines, to be named the *Seawolf*, started building late in 1989 under the 1989 building program.

The fleet ballistic-missile submarines (SSBN) have a strategic mission. They are on constant patrol in the world's oceans. Earlier SSBNs are armed with sixteen Poseidon missiles; the new *Ohio*-class ships carry twenty-four Trident I missiles. Newer *Ohio*-class ships, and eventually all of the class, will be armed with the more powerful Trident II. They also carry torpedoes, mainly as defense weapons. (Any weapon carried by attack submarines may also be used by the SSBNs.)

The earliest of the pre-Trident SSBNs were the five-unit *George Washington* (SSBN 598) class of 1959–61, carrying 16 Polaris missiles. All have been stricken from the Navy rolls. Two remaining ships of the *Ethan Allen* (SSBN 608) class of 1963–64 have been converted to SSNs. The 14-ship *Lafayette* (SSBN 616) class of 1963–64 and the 12-ship *Benjamin Franklin* (SSBN 640) class of 1965–67 can launch Poseidon missiles.

The largest of these four classes are the *Lafayettes*: 8,200 tons submerged displacement, 33-foot beam, 425-foot length, sixteen vertical missile tubes, and a crew of 168. Three *Lafayettes* will begin inactivation this year.

The *Ohio* (SSBN 726) class, with ten ships in commission and six more building or authorized, is the newest addition to the Navy's missile deterrent. This class will be the backbone of the strategic submarine force through the end of the century. Armed with the new Trident ballistic missile, the *Ohio*s are often referred to as Trident SSBNs. The *Ohio* displaces 18,000 tons, twice as much as earlier SSBNs, and is 560 feet long, 135 feet longer than the *Lafayette* and longer than a small World War II cruiser. This greater size permits the *Ohio* to carry twenty-four Tridents; earlier SSBNs could handle only sixteen missiles. Like battleships and some missile cruisers, the Trident SSBNs are named for states.

SSBNs are operated during alternate periods by two separate crews. One is called the blue crew and the other the gold crew. On return from an extended patrol, one crew relieves the other, and the ship returns to patrol following a brief period alongside her tender or in port. The relieved crew enters a month-long period of rest, recreation, and leave, followed by two months of training. This system allows each crew extended time ashore, while keeping the entire force of SSBNs cruising on deep patrol except for very brief periods.

Patrol Combatants

The principal vessels in this group are the six *Pegasus*-class hydrofoil missile craft (PHMs), armed with Harpoon missiles and a 76-mm rapid-fire gun. (Two *Asheville*-class patrol combatants, gas turbine–powered craft armed with Standard missiles, are in reserve.) Some smaller coastal and riverine craft are also in service. The Navy is doing experimental work with hydrofoils and surface-effect systems.

Mine Warfare Ships

This category includes the ocean minesweepers of the *Aggressive* (MSO 422) and *Acme* (MSO 508) classes. They are 172 feet long, displace 775 tons, and are designed to locate and sweep contact, magnetic, and acoustic mines. While two are assigned to the Atlantic Fleet, eighteen more serve with the Naval Reserve. MSOs have recently operated against Iranian mines in the Persian Gulf. The first four of a new class of mine

Figure 13-6   The hydrofoil missile gunboat *Hercules* (PHM 2).

countermeasures ship, the *Avenger* (MCM 1) class, are in commission, and ten more are building. Five new mine hunters of
the *Osprey* (MHC 51) class are under construction or authorized.

The *Avenger*s combine proven minesweeping gear with sophisticated modern systems for detecting and countering
mines. The *Osprey*s, based on the successful Italian *Lerici*
class, will specialize in locating and identifying all types of
mines. Recent experience in the Persian Gulf has underscored
the need for versatile mine-warfare ships manned by experienced crews.

Amphibious-Warfare Ships

Often referred to as the amphibs or gators, these ships work
mainly where sea and land meet, and where assault landings
are carried out by Navy–Marine Corps teams. Such operations
call for many different types of ships. The sixty-one active
amphibs are divided into seven types. Most are transports designed to sealift marines and their equipment from bases to
landing beaches. The differences lie in ship design and the way
troops and their gear are moved from ship to shore, which can
be done by means of landing craft, helicopters, or tracked
amphibious vehicles.

Figure 13–7 Some of the Navy's amphibious ships can carry up to 20,500 tons of cargo and combat troops.

Tank Landing Ships (LSTs): LSTs can run up to the beach, lower their extended bow ramp, and offload tanks, artillery, and logistic vehicles. Amphibious vehicles can be launched from a stern gate. All nineteen active "T"'s are in the *Newport* (LST 1179) class. They displace 8,400 tons and carry up to 430 troops. Two of these serve with the Naval Reserve.

Dock Landing Ships (LSDs): These ships have a well deck that can be flooded so that waterborne landing craft and vehicles can be floated out of the ship's stern gate. They can also carry troop helicopters. Five ships of the *Anchorage* (LSD 36) class are active. The new *Whidbey Island* (LSD 41) ships are improved *Anchorage*s, 609 feet long and displacing 15,726 tons. Five are in commission, with four more building. LSD 41 has a crew of 356 and carries 338 marines with vehicles and cargo. Her well deck handles landing craft, amphibious vehicles, and air-cushion landing craft (LCACs). The first ship of a cargo-carrying version of the LSD 41 class is in the 1990 program.

Amphibious Transports Dock (LPD): These ships deliver troops and equipment in landing craft or vehicles carried in a well deck and floated out through a stern gate, and in helicopters operating from a flight deck. Two ships of the *Raleigh*

(LPD 1) class displace 14,651 tons, are 521 feet long with a 104-foot beam, and carry a crew of 462 and 1,069 troops. Eleven units of the *Austin* (LPD 4) class displace 16,900 tons, are 569 feet long with a 105-foot beam, and carry a crew of 474 and 904 troops. They are similar in appearance and function to the LSD, but have more extensive helicopter facilities.

Amphibious Cargo Ships (LKAs): There are five of these ships, all of the *Charleston* (LKA 113) class of 1969–70. They usually land combat cargo rather than troops. Large ships of over 20,500 tons, with highly automated engineering plants, they have an elaborate array of masts and booms. This allows them to offload cargo over the side into landing craft.

Amphibious Assault Ships (LPHs): These are among the most advanced of the amphibs. The seven ships of the 18,000-ton *Iwo Jima* (LPH 2) class were the world's first helicopter carriers designed for that purpose. Twenty large Sea Knights are on board to do the job. LPHs are designed to carry and land the 2,000 men and equipment of a marine battalion landing team (BLT).

General-Purpose Assault Ships (LHA): Of all the ship types discussed so far, only aircraft carriers are larger than these. The five ships of the *Tarawa* (LHA 1) class, at over 39,000 tons' displacement, have nearly twice the displacement of the LPHs. They are capable of simultaneous helicopter and landing-craft operations, for they have both flight and well decks. LHAs and LPHs look much like aircraft carriers, with "island" superstructures set at the starboard edge of their large flight decks.

Multipurpose Assault Ships (LHDs): The first ship of the *Wasp* (LHD 1) class is in commission. Three more are under construction. The *Wasp* resembles the LHA but incorporates many changes as a result of experience with the *Tarawa* class. LHDs will operate air-cushion landing craft (LCACs) and heavy helicopters. They will also function when necessary as sea-control ships with AV-8B Harrier V/STOL airplanes and antisubmarine helicopters.

Amphibious Command Ships (LCCs): LCCs serve as floating command centers, providing control and communication facilities for embarked sea, air, and land commanders and their staffs. Two are active, the *Blue Ridge* (LCC 19) and the *Mount Whitney* (LCC 20). These measure 620 feet in length, displace over 18,000 tons, and have a crew of 1,514.

Auxiliary Ships

Underway Replenishment Ships

Warships must be able to remain at sea for weeks at a time with fuel, provisions, parts, and ammunition. The Navy has several underway replenishment (UNREP) techniques that use special cargo-handling gear to make transfers from one ship to another while the two are steaming abreast or, in some cases, astern. Vertical replenishment (VERTREP) is a form of UNREP in which cargo-carrying helicopters are used. The Navy has fifty-nine active UNREP ships.

Fleet Oilers (AOs): Currently there are five AOs in commission. AOs carry a variety of petroleum products needed by other ships and their embarked aircraft. A typical oiler has a number of stations from which fuel can be pumped to other ships. There are five of the highly automated *Cimarron* (AO 177) class. The *Cimarron*s are being jumboized to increase their payload. Six of the new *Henry J. Kaiser* (AO 187) class are operated by the MSC, with twelve more building or authorized. Eleven earlier AOs are also operated by MSC with civilian crews.

Fast Combat Support Ships (AOEs): At 52,480 tons, these are the largest and most powerful of the Navy's noncombatant seagoing units. All four AOEs are of the *Sacramento* (AOE 1) class. They are 793 feet long, 107 feet wide, and have a 100,000-horsepower drive. They can operate with the fast task forces. AOEs combine features of fleet oilers, ammunition ships, and store ships. Three units of the new *Supply* (AOE 6) class are building. Six more are projected.

Replenishment Oilers (AORs): These ships came on the scene in the early 1970s. All are of the seven-ship *Wichita* class and similar in size to the *Neosho*-class AOs, which are 655 feet long and displace 38,000 tons. Like the AOE, the AOR is a multipurpose replenishment ship. It transfers fuel, spare parts, provisions, freight, and ammunition.

Combat Store Ships (AFSs): AFSs carry general stores, dry stores, and refrigerated food. They can operate and maintain H-46 helicopters. There are seven commissioned ships of the *Mars* (AFS 1) class, as well as three of the British-built *Sirius* (AFS 8) class, operated by MSC.

Ammunition Ships (AEs): Of the thirteen AEs, all built within the last twenty years, two are of the *Suribachi* (AE 21) and three of the *Nitro* (AE 23) classes. Our newest AEs are the

Figure 13–8   The submarine tender *Dixon* (AS 37).

seven ships of the *Kilauea* (AE 26) class. They are 564 feet
long and displace more than 19,000 tons. Providing ammunition and missiles is their principal task. Besides equipment for
transferring materials to other ships, many UNREP ships have
their own VERTREP helicopters. One of the AEs is operated
by MSC. Five new ships of the AE 36 class are proposed for
construction in the 1990s to replace the *Suribachi*s and the
*Nitro*s.

Fleet Support Ships

The ship categories discussed so far have a degree of similar-
ity. This does not hold true for the Navy's more than seventy
active auxiliaries. It is difficult, for instance, to find similarities
between a 21,000-ton *Simon Lake*-class submarine tender and
a 1,640-ton *Cherokee*-class fleet ocean tug. The ships don't
look alike and have far different jobs.

"Auxiliaries" is not a catchall category. Rather, the wide
variety of auxiliary ships demonstrates the great variety of
functions needed to keep the fleet's other ships operating and
to support its many missions at home and overseas.

Destroyer Tenders (ADs) and Submarine Tenders (ASs):
These ships are the largest of the active auxiliaries. The newer
ones displace from 16,000 to 22,000 tons. Their crews are

formed largely of skilled technicians and repairmen. Eight submarine tenders specialize in supporting SSNs, while four others support SSBNs and are often based overseas for this purpose. Those of the *L.Y. Spear* (AS 36) class can take four submarines alongside and support another dozen.

Despite their designation, ADs service a variety of surface ships. Among these, two *Samuel Gompers–* (AD 37) and four *Yellowstone* (AD 41)-class ADs can accommodate ships up to and including the highly complex *Virginia*-class nuclear-powered missile cruisers. Three ships of the *Dixie* (AD 14) class have served since World War II. The *Prairie* (AD 15) went into commission in 1940; she has nearly fifty years of continuous active service, a record for today's fleet.

Repair Ships (ARs): Two *Vulcan* (AR 5)-class repair ships are 530 feet long and displace 17,000 tons. These versatile floating machine shops, like ADs and ASs, have the ability to perform a wide range of repair and service jobs for the fleet.

Salvage Ships (ARSs) and Salvage and Rescue Tugs (ATSs): Four ships of the *Bolster* (ARS 38) class, built during World War II, and three *Edenton* (ATS 1)-class ships, built in England and completed in 1971–72, are designed to salvage ships and support diving operations. Two more *Bolster*-class ships and one of the *Escape* (ARS 6) class train reservists. Four of a new *Safeguard* (ARS 50) class are active. Another is proposed for the 1990 program.

Submarine Rescue Ships (ASRs): Four World War II–built ships of the *Chanticleer* class generally resemble the *Bolster*-class ARSs. Two ships of the *Pigeon* (ASR 21) class, completed in 1973, have a twin-hull catamaran design with a 34-foot-wide well between their two hulls. They have a new system that can support divers at depths of up to 1,000 feet and operate deep-submergence rescue vehicles (DSRVs) for the rescue of submarine crews.

Other Auxiliaries: Two command ships (AGFs), modified from LPDs for a command-and-communications role, serve in the Middle East. They are painted white to help their air conditioners cope with intense heat. The auxiliary research submarine *Dolphin* (AGSS 555) is not a warship but an experimental ship. The *Lexington* (AVT 16) is a training carrier at Pensacola. Neophyte pilots learn carrier landings and takeoffs on the deck of this last active ship of the once numerous *Essex* (CV 9) class of World War II.

So far, only active Navy ships have been discussed. Another

Figure 13–9 Service craft, usually skippered by chief petty officers, are among the few vessels in the Navy with all-enlisted crews. They aid large ships in docking and undocking.

group of ships, forty-five in all, are in an inactive status, including twenty-five warships, eight landing ships, and twelve auxiliaries. Others include transports, cargo ships, and tankers. They could be placed back in service in an international crisis, as many already have been.

Whether large or small, most of the ships discussed earlier in this chapter are commissioned vessels with full-time crews under commanding officers. MSC ships, discussed on the following page, are civilian manned.

Service Craft

Also among the Navy's waterborne resources is a large and varied group of 854 active-service craft. Twenty-one more of these ships are on loan to Navy contractors. There are fifty-four different types. Some are huge vessels like the large auxiliary floating dry docks that can take aboard, and raise out of the water for repairs, vessels as large as battleships.

Barracks craft (non-self-propelled) accommodate crews when their ships are being overhauled or repaired. Open lighters and covered lighters—there are 391 of them—are barges used to store materials and to house pierside repair shops. Under tow, lighters haul freight or cargo.

Some gasoline barges, fuel-oil barges, and water barges are self-propelled; those that are not depend on tugs. These service craft moor at Navy bases or, like garbage lighters, anchor in harbors or roadsteads.

Floating cranes and wrecking derricks are towed from place to place as needed.

Diving tenders support diving operations and are essential to training in that area. Aircraft transportation lighters carry complete or dismantled aircraft and parts. Ferryboats or launches, which carry people, automobiles, and equipment, are usually located at Navy bases where facilities are spread out over large distances.

Best known of the service craft are the eighty-two harbor tugs, large and small. Commanded by a petty officer and with an all-enlisted crew, these essential craft can be found at Navy bases the world over. They aid ships in docking and undocking. Harborside and at sea, they tow non-self-propelled craft, act as people carriers, fight fires, and perform rescue duties.

The only nuclear-propelled service craft, the research submersible NR 1, has been used for experimental work since 1969.

Military Sealift Command Ships

Any summary of the Navy's ships must include those in the MSC, the Defense Department's water-transport service and an essential element of the seagoing forces. MSC ships are designated USNS (U.S. naval ship) rather than USS (U.S. ship), as commissioned ships are. They are "in service" rather than "in commission." One cargo ship (AK), nine "roll-on roll-off" vehicle cargo ships (AKRs), and eight transport oilers (AOTs), point-to-point fuel carriers, serve the Army and Air Force as well as the Navy.

Another twenty-three perform special-duty projects. Some of these are missile-range instrumentation ships. Others do ocean-bottom laying and repairing of cables used for detecting enemy submarines. Much of their work is done for other government agencies.

Surveying ships (AGSs) and oceanographic research ships (AGORs) explore the oceans. The *Point Loma* (AGDS 1) supports deep-submergence and submarine-rescue work.

Of special interest are twenty-three MSC fleet-support ships. As with other MSC ships, they have civilian officers and crews. They operate under Navy orders and have a military department of 1,015 Navy personnel aboard, performing visual and radio communications and otherwise assisting the ship's master and crew in operations with naval units.

These vessels include store ships, oilers, fleet ocean tugs, and cargo ships supporting our fleet ballistic-missile (FBM) submarines. Often referred to as AK-FBMs, the latter units carry supplies of all sorts from stateside ports to overseas-based tenders that support SSBNs. Ocean-surveillance ships (AGOSs) tow underwater sound arrays.

Type Classification

Since 1920, the Navy has used letter symbols to identify the types of ships and service craft. These shifted as the makeup of the fleet itself changed. Some of the types listed here are sea-going ships, others are smaller craft, while still others are experimental concepts.

Ship and Craft Classifications

AALC	Amphibious-assault landing craft		ARDM	Medium auxiliary repair dry dock (non-self-propelled)
AD	Destroyer tender		ARL	Repair ship, small
AE	Ammunition ship		ARS	Salvage ship
AF	Store ship		AS	Submarine tender
AFDB	Large auxiliary floating dry dock (non-self-propelled)		ASPB	Assault-support patrol boat
			ASR	Submarine rescue ship
AFDL	Small auxiliary floating dry dock (non-self-propelled)		ATA	Auxiliary ocean tug
			ATC	Mini-armored troop carrier
AFDM	Medium auxiliary floating dry dock (non-self-propelled)		ATF	Fleet ocean tug
			ATS	Salvage and rescue ship
AFS	Combat store ship		AVM	Guided-missile ship
AG	Miscellaneous		AVT	Training aircraft carrier
AGDS	Deep-submergence support ship		BB	Battleship
			CA	Gun cruiser (8-inch guns)
AGF	Miscellaneous command ship		CCB	Command and control boat
AGM	Missile-range instrumentation ship		CG	Guided-missile cruiser
			CGN	Guided-missile cruiser (nuclear propulsion)
AGMR	Major communications relay ship		CPC	Coastal patrol boat
AGOR	Oceanographic research ship		CPIC	Coastal patrol and interdiction craft
AGOS	Ocean surveillance ship			
AGP	Patrol craft tender		CV	Multipurpose aircraft carrier
AGS	Surveying ship		CVN	Multipurpose aircraft carrier (nuclear propulsion)
AGSS	Auxiliary research submarine			
AH	Hospital ship		CVS	ASW aircraft carrier
AK	Cargo ship		DD	Destroyer
AKR	Vehicle cargo ship		DDG	Guided-missile destroyer
AOE	Fast combat support ship		DSRV	Deep-submergence rescue vehicle
AOG	Gasoline tanker			
AOR	Replenishment oiler		FF	Frigate
AOT	Transport oiler		FFG	Guided-missile frigate
AP	Transport		IX	Unclassified miscellaneous
APB	Self-propelled barracks ship		LCA	Landing craft, assault
APL	Barracks craft (non-self-propelled)		LCAC	Landing craft, air cushion
			LCC	Amphibious command ship
AR	Repair ship		LCM	Landing craft, mechanized
ARC	Cable repair ship		LCPL	Landing craft, personnel, large
ARD	Auxiliary-repair dry dock (non-self-propelled)		LCSR	Landing craft, swimmer reconnaissance

LCU	Landing craft, utility	PB	Patrol boat
LCVP	Landing craft, vehicle personnel	PBR	River patrol boat
		PCF	Patrol craft (fast)
LHA	Amphibious assault ship (general purpose)	PCG	Patrol chaser (missile)
		PG	Patrol combatant (ex–patrol gunboat)
LKA	Amphibious cargo ship		
LPD	Amphibious transport dock	PGG	PGG patrol gunboat (missile)
LPH	Amphibious assault ship (helicopter)	PHM	Guided-missile patrol combatant (hydrofoil)
LSD	Dock-landing ship	PTF	Fast patrol craft
LSSC	Light SEAL support craft	SDV	Swimmer delivery vehicle
LST	Tank-landing ship	SES	Surface-effect ship
LWT	Amphibious warping tug	SS	Submarine (conventional)
MIUW	Mobile inshore underseas warfare craft	SSBN	Ballistic-missile submarine (nuclear propulsion)
MON	Monitor (small armored river gunboat)	SSG	Guided-missile submarine
		SSN	Submarine (nuclear propulsion)
MSD	Minesweeper, drone		
MSI	Minesweeper, inshore	SWAL	Shallow-water attack craft, light
MSI	Minesweeping launch		
MSM	Minesweeper, river (converted LCM 6)	SWAM	Shallow-water attack craft, medium
MSO	Minesweeper, ocean (nonmagnetic)	SWCL	Special warfare craft, light
		SWCM	Special warfare craft, medium
MSR	Minesweeper, patrol	SWOB	Ship waste offloading barge
MSSC	Medium SEAL support craft		
NR	Submersible research vehicle (nuclear propulsion)		

290   Aircraft

As of 30 September 1989, the Navy had an inventory of 6,353 operating aircraft. These include 542 fighter-attack, 815 fighter, 1,214 attack, 1,578 rotary-wing, 162 antisubmarine, 397 patrol, 162 early-warning, 107 transport, 64 aerial refuel, 86 observation, 125 utility, and 1,053 trainer (including jet and propeller) aircraft. Aircraft operate in squadrons and air wings. There are more than 225 squadrons in service.

Many types, designs, and modifications of aircraft—far more than for Navy ships—form the "naval air" arm of the Navy. A system of letters and numbers (aircraft designations) is used to distinguish these aircraft.

Aircraft Designations

Navy aircraft may be considered as fixed wing or rotary wing (helicopter). A designation is a simple letter/number combination. F-14, for example, indicates a Tomcat fighter plane. The F stands for fighter and the 14 for the design number.

Basic Mission and Type Symbols

A	Attack	P	Patrol
C	Cargo/transport	S	Antisubmarine

E	Warning	T	Trainer
F	Fighter	U	Utility
H	Helicopter	V	V/STOL
O	Observation	X	Research

Series Symbol: Future modifications to the F-14 would call for a series symbol indicating an improvement on, or a change to, the same design—F-14A or F-14C, for example.

Modified-Mission Symbol: When the basic mission of an airplane has been considerably modified, a modified-mission symbol is added. For example, an F-14C modified to act primarily as a reconnaissance plane would become RF-14C. These symbols are also used for the basic missions of helicopters and V/STOL (vertical/short takeoff and landing) aircraft, as well as for the modified missions of these types.

Modified mission symbols are:

A	Attack	O	Observation
C	Transport	Q	Drone
D	Director	R	Reconnaissance
E	Special electronics	S	Antisubmarine
H	Search/rescue	T	Trainer
K	Tanker	U	Utility
L	Cold weather	V	Staff
M	Mine countermeasures		

Status Symbol: Finally, there is the status symbol, a letter prefix indicating that the aircraft is being used for special work and experimentation, or that it is in planning or is a prototype.

Consider our imaginary RF-14C. If it were to be used for a permanent special test, it would have an N added to the designation and become an NRF-14C. Despite this, the basic airplane is still the F-14, and most Navy personnel would recognize it as such despite its changes.

Status prefix symbols are:

J	Special test, temporary	X	Experimental
N	Special test, permanent	Y	Prototype

Parts of a Fixed-Wing Aircraft

All fixed-wing aircraft have the same basic parts: fuselage, wings, tail assembly, landing gear, and power plant. These are defined as follows:

Fuselage: The main body of the plane.

Wings: Strong structural members attached to the fuselage. Their airfoil shape provides the lift that supports the plane in flight. Wings are fitted with flaps for increased lift and control surfaces—ailerons and spoilers—and may carry fuel tanks, guns, rockets, missiles and other weapons, engines, and landing gear.

Tail assembly: Consists of vertical and horizontal stabilizers, rudder, and elevators.

Landing gear: Usually means the wheels, but in certain aircraft these may be replaced by skis or floats.

Power plant: Develops the thrust or force that provides forward motion in flight. May consist of reciprocating (piston) engines that drive propellers, jet engines that develop thrust (turbojet and turbofan), or turbine engines and propellers or rotors in combination (turboprop or turboshaft).

The most common naval aircraft are listed below, categorized by mission. Each mission name is followed by a two-letter abbreviation that indicates the type of squadron in which the units usually serve. The V indicates fixed-wing aircraft.

Types of Aircraft Currently in the Navy Inventory

Attack (VA)

The attack aircraft's main job is to destroy enemy targets, at sea and ashore, with rockets, guided missiles, torpedoes, mines, and conventional or nuclear bombs.

A-6 Intruder: Medium-attack, carrier-based, all-weather day and night bomber. Has twin jet engines and carries a crew of two. The A-6E has an advanced electronics package and can carry external weapons loads of 18,000 pounds; it is configured for both Harm and Harpoon missiles. Constantly being improved, it is used for close air support, interdiction, and deep-strike missions. Weight: empty, 26,746 lbs; maximum catapult takeoff, 58,600 lbs. Length: 55 ft. Span: 53 ft. Speed: maximum at sea level, 647 mph; cruise at optimum altitude, 476 mph. Range: ferry, 2,380 nm (nautical miles); 878 nm with maximum military load.

A-7 Corsair II: Single-engine, single-seat, subsonic light-attack plane. The A-7E carries varying payloads of bombs and missiles as well as a 20mm gun pod; its maximum payload is more than 15,000 lbs. Weight: empty, 19,111 lbs; maximum

AV-8B Harrier

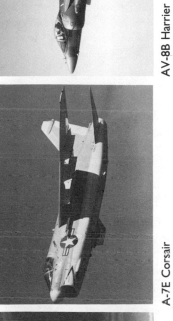

A-7E Corsair

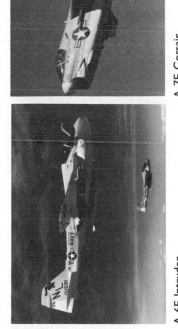

A-6E Intruder

P-3C Orion

F/A-18 Hornet

F-14A Tomcat

Figure 13–10 Operational Navy aircraft

Figure 13–11   Operational Navy aircraft

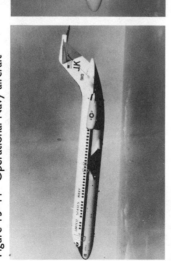

C-9B Skytrain

S-3A Viking

SH-60B Seahawk

UH-46D Sea Knight

SH-3H Sea King

E-2C Hawkeye

takeoff, 42,000 lbs. Length: 46 ft. Span: 39 ft. Speed: maximum
at 5,000 ft with twelve Mark 82 bombs, 646 mph; without
bombs, 684 mph. Range: maximum ferry with internal fuel,
1,981 nm; with internal and external fuel, 2,485 nm. The last
two A-7 squadrons are scheduled for transition to F/A-18s during FY 1992.

F/A-18 Hornet: See under Fighter.

AV-8B Harrier: A light-attack, single-engine, single-seat aircraft capable of V/STOL operations, the Marine Corps Harrier
is highly responsive to the needs of ground forces for close air
support. Its V/STOL capability enables it to operate from relatively unprepared sites close to the action, thus increasing its
sortie rate. It also operates from Navy amphibious assault
ships. The Harrier's armament includes cluster, general-purpose, and laser-guided bombs, rockets, Mavericks, Sidewinders, and 25mm cannon. Length: 46 ft, 3 in. Weight: empty,
12,800 lbs; maximum for short takeoff, 31,000 lbs; maximum
for vertical takeoff, 18,900 lbs. Height: 11 ft, 7 in. Span: 30 ft, 3
in. Speed: 630 mph. Range: ferry, 1,700 nm unrefueled.

Fighter (VF)

Like attack planes, fighters are both carrier based and land
based. They are faster and more maneuverable than attack
planes. They intercept and engage enemy aircraft, defend surface forces, escort attack and reconnaissance aircraft, and support ground troops. They can be equipped to carry nuclear
weapons, guided missiles, and a mix of other weapons.

F-14 Tomcat: Two-seater, twin-jet, variable-sweep-wing,
all-weather fighter-interceptor. Fires air-to-air missiles to destroy enemy aircraft. The aircraft's sophisticated radar/missile
combination enables it to track twenty-four targets simultaneously and attack six with Phoenix missiles while continuing
to scan the air space. It can select and destroy targets up to
100 miles away. The F-14D has improved computerization,
radar, communications and electronics, and weaponry. It
shares more than 80 percent of its avionics features with other
first-line aircraft, such as the F/A-18 and the A-6E. Weight:
empty, 40,104 lbs; maximum takeoff, 74,348 lbs. Length: 62.7
ft. Height: 16 ft. Span: 64 ft. Speed, maximum, 1,544 mph;
cruise, 576 mph. Range: combat, 500 nm; ferry, 2,000 nm.

F/A-18 Hornet: A supersonic, single-seat twin-engine jet designed as a multimission fighter-attack aircraft that will ultimately replace both the A-7 and the F-4. It can carry up to

17,000 lbs of armament, including Sparrow III and Sidewinder missiles, on nine stations. A reconnaissance version of the aircraft is being developed. Continued improvements will give it a night-attack, under-the-weather capability. It will be the key Navy/Marine Corps fighter-attack plane of the 1990s. Weight: fighter-mission takeoff, 36,710 lbs; attack-mission takeoff, 49,224 lbs. Length: 56 ft. Height: 15 ft, $3\frac{1}{2}$ in. Span: 37.5 ft. Speed: more than 1,360 mph. Range: fighter mission, 400 nm radius; attack mission, 575 nm radius; ferry, more than 2,000 nm.

Patrol (VP)

These large airplanes, with low speeds but very long flying range, have the primary mission of antisubmarine patrol. They also mine, bomb, and carry missiles. They have infrared, acoustic, and magnetic-detection devices for finding and tracking submarines.

P-3C Orion: Propeller-driven, land-based, long-range, overwater antisubmarine patrol plane. Since the prototype first flew in 1958, the P-3 has undergone many improvements and continues to play a major antisubmarine role for the Navy. The P-3 can carry a mixed payload: Mark 46 torpedoes, Bullpup air-to-ground missiles, Harpoon (AGM-84) cruise missiles, and sonobuoys. It carries a crew of ten. Weight: maximum takeoff, 142,000 lbs. Length: 117 ft. Span: 100 ft. Speed: maximum, 473 mph; cruise, 377 mph. Range: maximum-mission radius, 2,380 nm; 1,346 nm for 3 hours on station at 1,500 ft.

Transport (VR) (VRC)

Transport planes carry cargo and personnel. They are mostly land-based long-range types.

C-9B Skytrain: This Navy version of the commercial DC-9 series 32CF airliner can carry 32,444 lbs of cargo or passengers. It carries a crew of two, plus cabin attendants, and replaces three earlier transport types. Its mission is fleet logistic support, intratheater airlift, and airlifting reservists to and from training sites. The Navy's turboprop P-3 transport fleet aircraft are undergoing modernization to extend their operational use beyond the year 2000. Weight: maximum gross takeoff, 110,000 lbs. Length: 119 ft. Height: 28 ft. Span: 93 ft. Speed: maximum cruising, 576 mph; long-range cruising, 504 mph. Range: 2,538 nm at long-range cruising speed.

C-130 Hercules: Originally a transport aircraft for personnel, weapons, and supplies, the turboprop C-130 is also used by the Navy in a variety of roles. As an EC-130, it is an electronic surveillance aircraft. As a KC-130, it is used for aerial refueling of tactical aircraft from jets to helicopters. Probably the most versatile tactical-transport aircraft ever built, the Hercules is also used in search and rescue, space-capsule recovery, landing (with skis) on snow and ice, and special cargo delivery. It has even landed and taken off from a carrier deck without the benefit of arresting gear or catapults. Length: 98–106 ft. Span: 133 ft. Weight: empty, 75,331 lbs; maximum normal takeoff, 155,000 lbs. Speed: maximum cruise speed, 374 mph; economical cruise speed, 345 mph. Range: with maximum payload and allowance for 30 minutes at sea level, 2,045 nm; with maximum fuel and a 20,000-lb payload, 4,460 nm.

C-2A Greyhound: The C-2 Greyhound, a twin turboprop aircraft, has the primary mission of carrier on-board delivery (COD). The Greyhound provides critical support between shore facilities and aircraft carriers deployed throughout the world. Its cabin can be readily configured to accommodate cargo, passengers, or a combination of both. It is used for transporting personnel, mail, key logistics items, mission-essential cargo such as jet engines, and litter patients for Medevac. The C-2A is expected to carry the COD service for the Navy throughout the 1990s. Length: 57 ft. Weight: maximum takeoff, 54,354 lbs. Height: 16 ft. Span: 81 ft. Speed: maximum, 352 mph; cruise, 296 mph. Range: 1,440 nm.

Antisubmarine (VS)

Searching out submarines visually, by radar and magnetic detection, or by signals sent from floating sonobuoys, these airplanes attack with rockets, depth charges, or homing torpedoes.

S-3 Viking: This carrier-based, subsonic, all-weather, long-range, high-endurance turbofan-powered aircraft can locate and destroy enemy submarines, including newer high-speed, deep-submergence, quiet submarines. With a crew of four, the Viking operates primarily in the mid and outer carrier-battle-group antisubmarine zones, but it can also operate independently or in tandem with long-range, land-based antisubmarine units. Weapons carried by the S-3 include various combinations of torpedoes, depth charges, missiles, rockets, and special weapons. Modernization programs are aimed at enabling the Viking to counter the submarine threat of the 1990s. Length: 53 ft. Weight: empty, 26,650 lbs; maximum takeoff, 52,539 lbs. Height: 23 ft. Span: 69 ft. Speed: 518 mph. Range: more than 2,300 nm.

Reconnaissance (VQ) (VAQ)

Many aircraft have been modified for these complex missions.

EP-3, ES-3, and EC-130 are modified versions of the P-3, S-3, and C-130 used for reconnaissance.

EA-6B Prowler: The Prowler, the first Navy plane designed and built specifically for tactical electronic warfare, is an all-weather, four-seat, subsonic carrier-based plane. It is the most advanced airborne electronic-warfare aircraft in existence. Its missions are active and passive defense of a task force, and degradation and suppression of enemy defense systems by jamming. Length: 60 ft. Weight: empty, 32,162 lbs; maximum takeoff, 65,000 lbs. Height: 16 ft. Span: 53 ft. Speed: maximum at sea level, 651 mph; cruise, 481 mph. Range: combat, 2,083 nm with maximum external fuel.

Trainer (VT)

Trainers are generally two-seat airplanes (instructor and student). Most are turbine powered, designed with an emphasis on safety and versatility.

T-2 Buckeye: This trainer is used in basic training, instrument flying, combat maneuvers, and initial carrier work. Length: 38 ft, 4 in. Weight: empty, 8,115 lbs; maximum takeoff 13,179 lbs. Span: 38 ft, 4 in. Speed: maximum 512 mph at 25,000 ft.

TA-4J Skyhawk: This trainer model of the A-4 is used primarily in advanced jet training. It has a speed of 590 mph.

T-45A Goshawk: This trainer is used to provide training to prospective tactical Navy and Marine Corps jet pilots. The T-45A is to replace the T-2 and the TA-4 training aircraft. The Goshawk is the aircraft component of the T-45TS integrated jet-pilot training system. The complete system consists of the T-45A; an aircraft simulator suite; academic materials, training aids, and computer-aided instruction devices; a computer-based training integration system; and contractor logistic support.

Other prominent trainers are the propeller-driven, single-engine T-34C basic and primary trainer and the twin-engine

T-44A.

Airborne Early Warning (VAW)

Electronic-search and radar-countermeasures equipment is used by VAW airplanes to provide early warning of hostile aircraft, missiles, ships, submarines, and even bad weather.

E-2 Hawkeye: Recognized by the large revolving radar saucer above its fuselage, this carrier-based plane has two turboprop engines and a five-man crew. Hawkeyes perform all-weather airborne early warning and command and control functions for the carrier battle group. Additional missions include surface-surveillance coordination, strike and interceptor control, and search-and-rescue guidance and communications relay. The E-2C has a long-range, early-warning, and command-data link to the F-14. Length: 58 ft. Weight: empty, 37,678 lbs; maximum takeoff, 51,569 lbs. Height: 18 ft. Span: 81 ft. Speed: maximum, 374 mph; cruise, 311 mph. Range: 200 nm radius with 6 hours on station; ferry, 1,525 nm.

E-6 Hermes: The E-6A TACAMO (take charge and move out) is a modified Boeing 707/C-137/E-3 airframe that carries a crew of nine—four for flight and five for the mission. Its mission is to provide secure, survivable, jam-resistant strategic-communications relay for fleet ballistic-missile submarines. Very low frequency (VLF) radio signals are used because of their ability to penetrate seawater, making it unnecessary for submarines to surface and receive messages. Length: 153 ft. Weight: gross takeoff, 342,000 lbs. Height: 43 ft. Span: 148 ft. Speed: cruise, 523; maximum, 610 mph. Range: 1,000 nm with six hours loiter time on station.

Helicopter (Rotary Wing)

The other main type of aircraft, the helicopter—identified by an H designation—joined the fleet in the mid-1940s, 35 years after the Navy bought its first fixed-wing airplane. A score of different designs are in service, and they are as likely to be ship based as shore based.

Helicopters (variously called choppers, helos, and copters) get their lift from rotating airfoils (or blades) called rotors. The helo's flight characteristics are determined by the speed and pitch of the rotor blades. Helicopters have relatively low speeds and short ranges.

Helicopter Missions

Helicopter missions include antisubmarine activity, attack, minesweeping, general utility, vertical envelopment, and vertical replenishment (VERTREP).

Antisubmarine: An antisubmarine helo is equipped to detect a submarine and destroy it. When using sonar, the helo lowers a sonar "ball" into the water and attacks the target with torpedoes or depth charges.

Minesweeping: With minesweeping gear in tow, the helo flies a few feet above water along the route being swept.

General Utility: This may include transporting mail, light cargo, and men from one ship to another; searching for leads in the ice; searching for and rescuing downed flyers or shipwreck survivors; and helping ships check radar accuracy.

Vertical Envelopment: Assault landings of this nature are possible with helicopters. The copter pilots and the troops, usually marines, operate from amphibious-assault ships.

Vertical Replenishment (VERTREP): Helos help speed up cargo transfer between ships situated alongside one another. Underway replenishment ships have one or two helicopters assigned for such duties.

LAMPS: LAMPS (light airborne multipurpose system), built around the Seasprite helicopter, was installed in about a dozen destroyers in 1972. By 1982, about 200 ships had this system. The Navy now uses the SH-60B Seahawk, the airborne platform segment of the LAMPS Mark III integrated ship/air weapons system, aboard certain frigates and destroyers. The current LAMPS helicopter carries surface-search radar, a MAD (magnetic anomaly detector), sonobuoys, ESM (electronic support measures) equipment, a TACAN (tactical air navigation) system, and a UHF (ultra–high frequency) direction finder. A ship using LAMPS can station its helicopter 30 to 40 miles away in the direction of any expected enemy action. The helicopter can give the ship instant information on any radar contact within 15 miles.

Types of Helicopters in the Navy Inventory

SH-2F Seasprite: Since the first prototype flew in 1959, many versions of the Seasprite have been produced for the Navy under its LAMPS program. Avionics and equipment now installed include surveillance radar, MADs, passive radiation-detection receivers, active and passive sonobuoys, smoke markers, computerized TACAN systems, cargo hooks for external loads, and a rescue hoist. Armament includes homing torpedoes and the capability of carrying air-to-air missiles. The Seasprite carries a crew of three. Length: 53 ft. Weight:

Figure 13–12   A Seahawk hovers over the *McInerney's* flight deck, while
another performs a RAST (recovery assist secure and traverse system) landing. The helicopter will be secured to the flight deck upon touchdown.

empty, 7,040 lbs; normal takeoff, 13,300 lbs. Height: 15.6 ft.
Speed: maximum, 164 mph; cruise, 150 mph. Range: 367 nm
with maximum fuel.

SH-60B/F Seahawk: The SH-60B is the air subsystem of the
LAMPS Mark III weapon system, a computer-integrated ship/
helicopter system that increases the effectiveness of surface
combatants. It carries a crew of three—pilot, copilot, and sensor operator. (See LAMPS above.) The SH-60F is designed to
operate from carriers and to replace the SH-3H as the carrier
battle group's inner antisubmarine-zone helicopter. It employs
a new, longer-range active dipping sonar in addition to sonobuoys to track and to attack submarines. Length: 63 ft, 10 in.
Height: 17 ft. Weight: 20,508 lbs. Speed: 130 knots. Range: 100
nm with 2 hours on station.

SH-3H Sea King: A twin-engine, all-weather, ship-based antisubmarine helicopter equipped with variable-depth sonar,
sonobuoys, a data link, a chaff, and a TACAN system. The
Sea King is used to detect, classify, track, and destroy enemy
submarines. It has a crew of four, including two sonar operators. Length: 73 ft. Height: 17 ft. Weight: empty, 11,865 lbs;
maximum takeoff, 21,000 lbs. Speed: maximum, 166 mph;
cruise, 136 mph. Range: 542 nm.

UH-46 Sea Knight: Another example of a durable and versatile aircraft, the Sea Knight, first flown in 1962, is still providing valuable service in its vertical-replenishment role. It has a
crew of three and can carry approximately 6,000 lbs of cargo in

301

a sling beneath the fuselage. Length: 46 ft. Height: 17 ft. Weight: gross, 23,300 lbs. Speed: 165 mph. Range: 206 nm; ferry, 530 nm.

CH-53 A/D Sea Stallion: The Sea Stallion's primary mission is to transport supplies and equipment; its secondary mission is to transport personnel and conduct evacuations. It can carry thirty-seven fully equipped troops, twenty-four litter patients plus four attendants, or 8,000 lbs of cargo. The RH-53D performs airborne mine countermeasures (AMCM) and vertical on-board delivery (VOD). Length: 88 ft, 3 in. Height: 24 ft, 11 in. Weight: maximum gross, 42,000 lbs. Speed: 195 mph. Range: 578 nm; ferry, 886 nm.

MH-53E Sea Dragon: A multimission variant of the CH-53E, the Sea Dragon is used on CVs, LPDs, LPHs, and LHAs in its primary AMCM role. This includes minesweeping and ancillary tasks such as mine neutralization, mine spotting, floating mine destruction, and channel marking. This helicopter is replacing the RH-53D.

CH-53E Super Stallion: The largest and most powerful helicopter in production, the CH-53E is shipboard compatible and configured for the lift and movement of cargo, passengers, and heavy, oversized equipment. Assigned missions include VOD augmentation, transfer of damaged aircraft, mobile-construction support, high-priority container transportation, nuclear-weapons transportation, and AMCM. The Super Stallion has a crew of three. The combined nomenclature/designation of both this helicopter and the previous one is CH/MH-53E. Length: 99 ft. Height: 28 ft. Weight: empty, CH-53E, 33,226 lbs; MH-53E, 36,336; maximum loaded, 73,500 lbs. Speed: maximum at sea level, 196 mph; cruise, 173 mph. Range: 1,120 nm.

Aircraft Designations

Fighters

F-4	Phantom	F-5	Tiger		
F-4J		F-5E		F/A-18	Hornet
F-4N		F-5F		F/A-18A	
F-4S		F-86	Sabre	F/A-18B	
DF-4J		QF-86F		F/A-18C	
QF-4B		QF-86H		F/A-18D	
QF-4N		F-14	Tomcat	F-16N	Falcon
RF-4B		F-14A		F-21A	
YF-4J		F-14B			

Attack

A-3	Skywarrior
EA-3B	
ERA-3B	
EKA-3B	
KA-3B	
NA-3B	
RA-3B	
TA-3B	
NRA-3B	
NTA-3B	
A-4	Skyhawk
A-4E	
A-4F	
A-4M	
EA-4F	
NA-4F	
NA-4M	
OA-4M	
TA-4F	
NTA-4F	
NTA-4J	
TA-4J	
A-6	Intruder
A-6E	
EA-6A	Prowler
KA-6D	
EA-6B	
NEA-6B	
A-7	Corsair II
A-7B	
A-7C	
A-7E	
TA-7C	
NA-7C	
NA-7E	
YA-7E	
EA-7L	

Antisubmarine

S-3	Viking
S-3A	
S-3B	
US-3A	

Patrol

P-3	Orion
P-3A	
P-3B	
P-3C	
EP-3A	
EP-3B	
EP-3E	
NP-3A	
NP-3B	
RP-3A	
RP-3D	
TP-3A	
VP-3A	

Early Warning

E-2	Hawkeye
E-2B	
E-2C	
TE-2C	

V/STOL

OV-10	Bronco
OV-10A	
OV-10D	
YOV-10D	
AV-8	Harrier
AV-8B	Harrier II
AV-8C	
AV-8A	
TAV-8A	
TAV-8B	
YAV-8B	

Research

X-26A	

Helicopters

H-1	Iroquois
AH-1J	
AH-1S	
AH-1T	
AH-1W	
JAH-1W	
HH-1K	
TH-1L	
UH-1E	
NUH-1E	
UH-1N	
VH-1N	
H-2	Seasprite
HH-2D	
NHH-2D	
SH-2F	
YSH-2G	
H-3	Sea King
HH-3A	
SH-3D	
SH-3G	
SH-3H	
UH-3A	
VH-3A	
VH-3D	
H-46	Sea Knight
CH-46A	
NCH-46A	
CH-46D	
CH-46E	
HH-46A	
HH-46D	
UH-46A	
H-53	Sea Stallion
CH-53A	
NCH-53A	
CH-53D	
RH-53D	
MH-53E	
CH-53E	Super Stallion
TH-57A	Sea Ranger
TH-57B	
TH-57C	
SH-60B	Seahawk
UH-60A	
YSH-60B	
SH-60F	

Utility

NU-1B	
U-3A	
U-3B	
UA-3B	
U-6A	
U-8F	
U-8G	
U-11	Aztec
U-11A	
UC-8A	
UC-12B	
UC-12F	
UC-27	
UC-880	
UP-3A	
T-41B	

Cargo/Transport

C-1A	Trader
C-130	Hercules
C-130F	
DC-130A	
EC-130G	
TC-130G	
EC-130Q	
TC-130Q	
KC-130F	
KC-130R	
KC-130T	
LC-130F	
LC-130R	
C-131	Convair Liner
C-131H	
NKC-135A	Stratotanker
C-2	Greyhound
C-2A	
C-20D	Gulfstream IV
C-4	Gulfstream
TC-4C	
C-9B	Skytrain
DC-9	

Trainers

T-2	Buckeye
T-2B	
T-2C	

Ships,
Planes,
and
Weapons

T-34	Mentor	T-38A		CT-39E	
T-34B		T-38B		CT-39G	
NT-34B		QT-38A		T-44	King Air
T-34C		T-39	Sabreliner	T-44A	
T-38	Talon	T-39D		T45A	

304

Helicopters

Ship and Squadron Organization

14

Every Navy ship operates under the authority of a line officer assigned by the Naval Military Personnel Command. No matter what his or her rank, the commanding officer (CO) is called captain. In case of absence or death, the CO's duties are assumed by the line officer next in command, usually the executive officer (XO).

Though the absolute responsibility for the safety, well-being, and efficiency of command rests with the CO, in practice he or she delegates duties to the executive officer, department heads, and officer of the deck (OOD), and through them, to the crew.

The XO, often called the exec, is the line officer next in rank to the captain. The XO is responsible for all matters relating to personnel, ship routine, and discipline. All orders issued by the XO have the same force and effect as though issued by the CO. In case the captain is disabled, the XO takes charge. The XO is, by virtue of position, senior to all staff officers on board.

Executive's Assistants

Depending on the size of the ship, certain officers and enlisted personnel are detailed as executive assistants. Among them are the following:

The administrative assistant relieves the XO of as many administrative details as possible.

The chaplain has religious duties primarily, although the chaplain is involved in all matters pertaining to the mental, moral, and physical welfare of the ship's company.

The chief master-at-arms (CMAA) is responsible for the maintenance of order and discipline. The CMAA enforces Navy regulations, ship's regulations, and pertinent directives'

Figure 14–1   A high degree of organization and coordination is called for when ships steam in formation for underway replenishment of supplies and fuel. Here the *Sample* (FF 1048) and *Kitty Hawk* (CV 63) take on fuel from the *Sacramento* (AOE 1), while the *Goldsborough* (DDG 20), *Bainbridge* (CGN 25), and *Badger* (FF 1071) cruise behind.

and assists the OOD in seeing that the ship's routine is carried out.

The career counselor, working directly for the CO, runs the ship's career-counseling program and makes sure that current programs and opportunities are available to all crewmembers.

The drug abuse program adviser advises the CO and XO on drug and alcohol abuse aboard ship and on the approaches necessary to cope effectively with the problem. The adviser coordinates Navy policies and procedures on drug and alcohol education, rehabilitation, identification, and enforcement.

The educational services officer handles coordination and planning for officer and enlisted education programs.

Lay leaders may be appointed when a chaplain is not available to meet the need. For instance, if a unit has a Protestant chaplain but no priest or rabbi, the command may appoint Roman Catholic and Jewish lay leaders. The lay leader must be a volunteer, either officer or enlisted.

Executive's Assistants

The legal officer is an adviser and staff assistant to the CO and XO on the interpretation and application of the Uniform Code of Military Justice (UCMJ), the Manual for Courts-Martial (MCM), and other laws and regulations concerning discipline and the administration of justice within the command.

The personnel officer is responsible for the placement of enlisted personnel and for the administration and custody of enlisted personnel records.

The postal assistant looks after the administration of mail services to the command.

The public-affairs assistant prepares briefing material and information pamphlets, assists with press interviews, generates newsworthy material about the unit's operation, and publishes the command's newspaper.

The safety officer promotes maximum cooperation in safety matters at all levels.

The master chief petty officer of the command (C M/C)— who in some instances may be a designated senior chief petty officer of the command (C S/C) or chief petty officer of the command (C Ch)—assists the CO in matters of morale and crew welfare. (Details of the C M/C's job are contained in chapter 9.)

The senior watch officer, under the direction of the XO, is responsible to the CO for assigning and supervising all deck watchstanders, under way and in port.

The ship's secretary is responsible for administering and accounting for correspondence and directives, administering officers' personnel records, and establishing and maintaining a forms control point. The secretary acts as the captain's writer and supervises the preparation of his or her personal correspondence.

The special-services assistant administers the command's special-services program, which comprises all organized welfare, recreational, and athletic activities not assigned to other departments or officers.

The training officer handles the formulation and administration of the unit training program.

The 3-M coordinator directly supervises the unit's 3-M (maintenance and material management) program.

The security manager is responsible for classification management, personal security, information-systems security, the protection of classified material, and security education and training material.

Departments

All ships have these basic departments: operations, navigation, weapons (or deck), engineering, and supply. Aircraft carriers, LPHs, ships with VERTREP capabilities, and some tenders will have an air department. Most ships have a medical department.

Certain other departments may be established, depending on the type of vessel and her operational mission. These include repair departments on repair ships and communications-relay ships. Besides an air department, carriers have aircraft intermediate maintenance (AIMD) and safety departments. Ships assigned for special purposes may have other departments authorized by the chief of naval operations (CNO).

Departments, in turn, consist of divisions that are further subdivided into watches, sections, or both.

Each ship's department has a department head, an officer who is responsible for its organization, training, and performance. All departments fall into one of three categories: command, support, or special.

Command Departments

Command departments include air, aircraft intermediate maintenance, aviation, communications, deck, engineering, navigation, operations, reactor, and safety. When embarked, there also may be air-wing or -group departments.

Air: On ships that have air departments, the air officer (called the **air boss**) supervises and directs launchings, landings, and the handling of aircraft and aviation fuels.

The department consists of the V division. If additional divisions are assigned, they include V-1, plane handling on the flight deck; V-2, catapults and arresting gear; V-3 plane handling on the hangar deck; and V-4, aviation fuels.

The following, when assigned, report to the air officer: the flight-deck officer, catapult officer, arresting-gear officer, hangar-deck officer, aviation-fuels officer, aircraft-handling officer, and training assistant (air).

Aircraft Intermediate Maintenance: The head of AIMD is the aircraft intermediate maintenance officer, who supervises and directs intermediate maintenance for the embarked air wing or other aircraft, and for assigned ship aircraft. AIMD also keeps up ground-support equipment. When there's only one division aboard ship, it's called the IM division. Ships having more than one division include the IM-1 division, responsible for administration, quality assurance, production and maintenance/material control, and aviation 3-M analysis; the IM-2 division, for general aircraft and organizational maintenance of the ship's assigned aircraft; the IM-3 division, for maintenance of avionics, avionics support equipment, and armament systems, as well as precision measuring equipment; and the IM-4 division, for maintenance of aviation support equipment (nonavionics).

Communications: In units with a communications department, the head of the department is the communications officer. The communications officer is responsible for visual and electronic exterior communications and for internal communications systems. In units without a communications department, the communications officer reports to the operations officer. Assistants may include a radio officer, a signal officer, a communications security material system (CMS) custodian, a cryptosecurity officer, and a message center (traffic) officer.

Deck: On ships with a deck department, the first lieutenant is the head of that department. The first lieutenant is responsible for the supervision, direction, and use of equipment associated with deck seamanship and, aboard ships without a weapons department, of ordnance equipment. The following report to the first lieutenant: the gunnery officer (on ships whose chief jobs don't involve ordnance or aircraft), cargo officer, ship's boatswain, and boat-group commander. On ships with a deck department but without a weapons department, the weapons officer is an assistant.

Engineering: This department, headed by the engineering officer, is responsible for operating and maintaining the ship's machinery, damage and casualty control, repair of hull and machinery, power lighting, water maintenance, and underwater fittings. All repairs beyond the capability of other departments are handled by engineering. When the department consists of a single division, it's called the E division. Multiple-division ships have a B division, boilers; M division, main engines; A division, auxiliaries; E division, electrical; and R division, repair.

The engineer may have assistants for main propulsion, reactor control, damage control, and administration; an electrical officer; and specialists such as a fire marshal and a technical assistant for chemical, biological, and radiological (CBR) defense.

Figure 14–2 Members of the deck division haul in a line.

Executive: This department is headed by the XO and normally has a single X division, which includes personnel assigned to work in the CO's office, XO's office, chaplain's office, print shop, security office, training office, legal office, and Hospital Corps (when no medical officer is assigned). It may also include an I division for indoctrination of recruits and newly reported personnel. Embarked staff enlisted personnel are a part of a C division—normally called the flag division—in one-division ships. Ships with multiple divisions may have a C-1 division (administrative, operations, logistics, and other clerical personnel); a C-2 division (communications, radio and visual); a C-3 division (barge and boat crews, drivers, and orderlies); and a C-4 division (mess personnel).

Navigation: This department, headed by the navigator, is responsible for the ship's safe navigation and piloting and for the care and maintenance of navigational equipment. It consists of the N division.

Operations: Ops is headed by the operations officer, who is responsible for collecting, evaluating, and disseminating tactical and operational information. If the department consists of a

Departments

single division, it is called the O division. For ships with more than one division, the department could include OA, OI, OL, OR, OS, OE, OC, and OP divisions. OA includes intelligence, photography, drafting, printing and reproduction, and meteorology. OI includes the combat information center (CIC) and sometimes lookouts. OL is the lookouts division. OR (radio communications) and OS (visual communications) are normally combined in the OC division. (On carriers, OC is the carrier air-traffic-control-center [CATCC] division.) OE is the operations electronics/material division. OP is the photographic intelligence division.

The following officers, when assigned, report to the ops officer: air intelligence, CATCC officer, CIC officer, communications (COMM) officer, electronics material officer (EMO), electronic warfare (EW) officer, intelligence officer, meteorological officer, photographic officer, strike operations officer, and computer programmer (or computer-maintenance officer).

Reactor: The reactor officer, who heads this department, is responsible for the operation and maintenance of reactor plants and their associated auxiliaries aboard nuclear-powered ships. Assistants to the reactor officer may include a reactor-control assistant and a reactor mechanical assistant.

Figure 14–3 Assault transports have a department not found on most other ships—the boat group.

Because of the special responsibilities of running a reactor plant, the reactor and engineering officers must closely coordinate their activities in operation and maintenance.

Weapons: The weapons officer supervises and directs the use of ordnance and seamanship equipment, except for what is specifically assigned to other departments. The weapons department, of all shipboard departments, is the most complex and often the largest.

On ships with a weapons department but without a deck department, the first lieutenant is an assistant. On small ships, the duties of the weapons officer and the first lieutenant may be assigned to one officer.

On ships with antisubmarine warfare (ASW) arms and a weapons department, the ASW officer is an assistant.

On ships with missile arms and a weapons department, the missile officer is an assistant.

On ships with guns and a weapons department, the gunnery officer is an assistant.

On ships with nuclear weapons, the nuclear weapons officer is an assistant.

On ships requiring additional groups in the weapons department, the ordnance officer and the CO of the marine detachment may be assistants.

A fire-control officer may also be assigned to the weapons department.

The weapons department has a complex division organization. A single division is designated the first division. Ships with more than one division may have up to nine divisions responsible for gunnery and deck seamanship. Other divisions and divisional responsibilities include the W division (nuclear-weapons assembly and aviation ordnance); the F division (fire control); the F-1 division (missile fire control); the F-2 division (ASW); the V division (aviation, for ships without an air department but with an aviation detachment embarked); the G division (ordnance handling); and the GM division (guided missiles).

Support Departments

Support (also called staff) departments include dental, medical, and supply.

Dental: The dental officer is responsible for preventing and controlling dental disease and supervising dental hygiene. Assistant dental officers are sometimes assigned to larger ships. The D division is the only dental division.

Medical: The head of this department must be an officer of the Medical Corps (MC). This officer is designated the medical officer and is reponsibile for maintaining the health of personnel, making medical inspections, and advising the CO on hygiene and sanitation conditions. Assistant medical officers may be assigned. The H division is the only medical division. When no medical officer is assigned, Hospital Corps personnel run the department, but they are assigned to the operations department for military and administrative functions.

Supply: Headed by the supply officer, this department handles the procurement, stowage, and issue of all the command's stores and equipment. The supply officer pays the bills and the crew. Responsible for supervising and operating the general and wardroom messes, the supply officer is also responsible for the ship's laundry and store. A single-division ship has the S division only. Others have an S-1 division (general supply support); an S-2 division (general mess); an S-3 division (ship's stores and services); an S-4 division (disbursing); an S-5 division (officers' messes); an S-6 division (aviation stores); and an S-7 division (data processing).

On larger ships, the supply officer may have assistants for disbursing, food service, ship's store, or wardroom mess.

Special Departments

The eight special departments are aviation, boat group, deep submergence, ordnance repair, repair, research operations, safety, and transportation.

Aviation: On a nonaviation ship with a helicopter detachment embarked, an aviation department is organized and headed by the aviation officer. The aviation officer is responsible for the specific missions of the embarked aircraft. His principal assistant is the helicopter control officer, but often one officer performs both functions. The single divisional unit is known as the V division.

Boat Group: Assault transports (LPDs and LSDs) have a boat-group department. The division is the BG division.

Deep Submergence: Headed up by the deep-submergence officer, this department launches, recovers, and services deep-submergence vehicles (DSVs) or deep-submergence rescue vehicles (DSRVs).

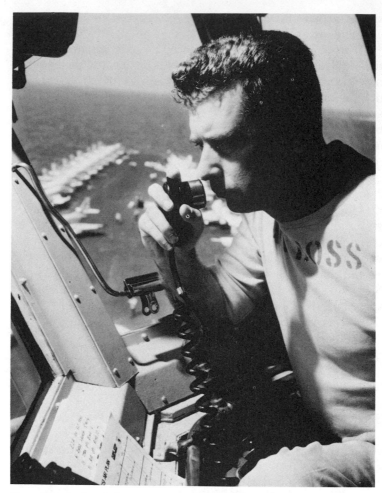

Figure 14–4 An air boss oversees carrier air operations.

Ordnance Repair: The ordnance-repair officer is in charge. This department, found only on submarine tenders, usually has a single division, designated SR. A large department may be subdivided into the SR-1 division (repair and service) and the SR-2 division (maintenance of repair machinery).

Repair: On ships with a repair department, the repair officer is in charge. On single-division ships, there is only the R division. Multiple-division ships have an R-1 division (hull repair); an R-2 division (machinery repair); an R-3 division (electrical

Depart-
ments

repair); an R-4 division (electronic repair); and an R-5 division (ordnance repair).

Research Operations: Units with this department are headed by the research officer, who is responsible for the operation, maintenance, and security of research, special-purpose communications, and associated equipment.

Safety: The safety officer heads this department, which is found only aboard aircraft carriers. The safety officer is responsible for ship and aviation safety. The AS division is the only designated safety-department division.

Transportation: Only Military Sealift Command (MSC) transports have this department, headed by the transportation officer. The department is responsible for loading and unloading, berthing and messing, and general direction of passengers. On ships without a combat cargo officer, the transportation officer is also the liaison with loading activities ashore. The single T division is used on small ships. Larger ones may have a T-1 division, which has the physical transportation responsibilities, and a T-2 division, which handles the administrative end of transportation.

Marine Department

The CO of the marine detachment, through not a department head, is in charge of matters pertaining strictly to the Marine Corps. The CO is generally assigned as a division officer of the weapons department. On a cruiser, the detachment could be made up of twenty-five or fourty personnel with larger detachments aboard carriers. Responsibilities include serving as the ship's landing party; ship security; serving as gun crews; operating the ship's brig; and serving as orderlies for the ranking officers.

Division Organization

The division is the basic working unit of the Navy. It may consist of twenty specialists on small ships or as many as several hundred persons in a division on an aircraft carrier. The boss is the division officer, who reports to the department head. Division officers are assigned by the CO.

The division officer is the one officer with whom division personnel come into contact every day. The junior officer (who also functions as the division's training officer), the division chief, and the leading petty officer are his or her principal

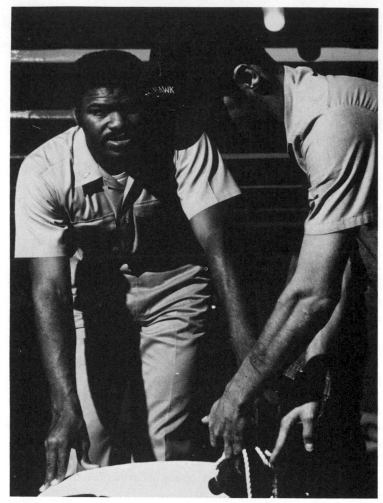

Figure 14–5 The division officer is the one officer with whom division personnel come into contact every day.

assistants. (Some divisions have a technical and material assistant, usually a warrant officer or limited-duty officer, to supervise the maintenance and repair of material or equipment.) Each division is organized into secions, the number depending on how many watch sections there are. A petty officer, who is a section leader, heads up each section.

Division Organization

The person to whom you are immediately responsible, your section leader, is enlisted. So are the next in the chain of command, the leading petty officer and then the division chief. Any requests you make, whether to the division officer, the CO, or the Navy Department in Washington, must first go through them. This is what is meant by going through the proper chain of command.

Quarters for Muster and Inspection

Depending on the type of ship and the ship's operating schedule, quarters for muster and inspection are held every work day before 0800. At this time, a muster of the entire crew is taken, every person on board is accounted for, including those on watch, on the sick (binnacle) list, late sleepers, prisoners, and those authorized to be absent. Unauthorized absentees are reported to the XO. Leading petty officers muster their divisions and report to the division officer, who inspects the division and gives the department head an accounting. Department heads report to the executive officer at "officer's call."

Each division is also assigned a parade—a space on deck for its formations. Fair-weather parades are on uncovered decks. Foul-weather parades are on covered decks and in designated living spaces.

Aircraft-Squadron Organization

Operating squadrons, like ships, have a CO, an XO, department heads, and division officers.

Commanding Officer

The CO, also known as the squadron commander, has the usual duties and responsibilities of any captain, insofar as they are applicable to an aircraft squadron. These include looking after morale, discipline, readiness, and efficiency, and issuing operational orders to the entire squadron.

Executive Officer

The XO, the second senior naval aviator in the squadron, is the direct representative of the CO. The XO sees that the squadron is administered properly and that the CO's orders are carried out.

Squadron Departments

The operational squadron is organized into five departments, each with its own department head responsible for or-

Figure 14–6   Steam drifts up from a catapult as an F/A-18 Hornet prepares to launch from the aircraft carrier USS *Constellation* (CV 64).

ganization and training, assignment of personnel, effectiveness of operation and planning, security, safety and cleanliness of assigned areas, and maintenance of records and reports within his or hear respective departments. Fleet replacement squadrons have two additional departments unique to their mission of training replacement pilots and aircrews.

Executive: This department includes the CO, XO, command master chief, and watchstanders.

Administrative: Duties include all department functions that are not assigned division functions. General responsibilities encompass records maintenance, squadron correspondence, legal matters, and public affairs. Divisions assigned under this department are personnel and the first lieutenant's office. The personnel division takes care of records, human-resources management, and equal-opportunity programs.

Operations: This department is responsible for aircraft schedules, communications, and navigation and squadron training.

Safety: The department head has direct access to the CO and is a member of the accident (investigation) board. As safety officer, the department head ensures compliance with all safety orders and directives.

Maintenance: This department oversees the planning, coordination, and execution of all maintenance work on aircraft; the inspection, adjustment, and replacement of aircraft engines and equipment; and the keeping of logs, records, and maintenance reports.

Training (only in fleet replacement squadrons): Responsible for flight crew and aircrew training in support of fleet operational squadrons.

FRAMP (Fleet Readiness Aviation Maintenance Personnel) (only in fleet replacement squadrons): Assigned to train enlisted maintenance personnel in support of fleet operational squadrons.

Weapons and Weapon Systems

15

To understand the weapons used by the Navy, one should first be familiar with these terms:

Ordnance: Everything that makes up a ship's or aircraft's firepower: guns, gun mounts, turrets, ammunition, guided missiles, rockets, and units that control and support these weapons.

Weapon system: An integrated system consisting of a weapon and the gear required to operate and control it.

Gun: Basically, a tube closed at one end from which a projectile is propelled by the burning of gunpowder.

Rocket: A weapon containing an explosive section and a propulsion section. A rocket is unable to change its direction of movement after it has been fired.

Missile: A vehicle containing an explosive section, a propulsion section, and a guidance section. A missile is able to change its direction of movement after it's fired (launched) in order to hit the target.

Torpedo: A self-propelled underwater missile used against surface and underwater targets.

Mine: An underwater explosive weapon put into position by surface ships, submarines, or aircraft. A mine explodes only when a target comes near or into contact with it.

Depth charge: Antisubmarine weapons fired or dropped by a ship or aircraft, and set to explode either at a certain depth or in proximity to a submarine.

Bomb: Any weapon, other than a torpedo, mine, rocket, or missile, dropped from an aircraft. Bombs are free-fall explosive weapons and may be either "dumb" (unguided) or "smart" (with a guidance system to steer them to their target).

Weapons are the mainstay of the military. Without them, the Navy could not carry out its combat missions or defend its ships, planes, bases, and personnel. This chapter deals with two kinds of weapons: small ones for individual use, and big ones—like missiles and rockets—that help the Navy's combatant ships fulfill their missions. The Navy's overall mission is to maintain sufficient military capability to deter the use of military power against the United States and its allies, or against other countries important to U.S. security and well-being. To this end, the Navy must be prepared to conduct prompt and sustained combat operations at sea.

Missiles and Rockets

Missiles are self-propelled, unmanned vehicles that carry conventional explosives or nuclear warheads. Each missile has a guidance system that controls its direction in flight. A rocket is a small missile—2.5 to 12.75 inches in diameter—that has no self-contained guidance system.

Missile Components

Each missile has four basic parts: airframe, power plant, warhead, and guidance system. If we compared the missile to an airplane, the missile's basic parts represent—in the same order—the aircraft, it engines, its bomb load, and its pilot.

The missile's airframe is a streamlined package that houses the power plant, guidance system, and warhead. It must be light, because the other parts are heavy. Airframes are made of aluminum alloys, magnesium, and high-tensile (high-stress) steel. These metals can withstand extreme heat and pressure.

The power plant must propel the missile at supersonic speeds to minimize its vulnerability and increase its chance of intercepting a target. The missile must be able to operate at altitudes where there is no atmosphere. Therefore, when liquid or solid propellants are used, the missile carries both the fuel and an oxidizer. Air-breathing plants carry only the fuel—gasoline, kerosene, or other petroleum products—but they cannot operate above about 70,000 feet.

Air-breathers are cheaper to use than rocket engines. The three types of air-breathing plants are as follows:

Pulse jet: This type of jet engine uses a flapper valve that alternately compresses and ejects air. It is also called an aerojet.

Turbojet: This plant uses a turbine to compress air and eject it at high pressure. It is powerful, but complex and expensive, and is capable of producing higher combustion temperatures than most metals can withstand.

Ramjet: A supersonic lightweight plant that is easy to build. It uses a lot of fuel, however, and develops no thrust until it reaches a supersonic speed. It has to be carried aloft by another vehicle, or else its takeoff must be rocket assisted.

The warhead is the part that does the damage. Its explosive may be conventional—TNT or another chemical—or nuclear.

Missile Guidance Systems

Missiles are either ballistic or guided. *Ballistic missiles* have a two-stage flight path. During the first stage, a preset guidance system sets the missile on the flight path to the target. In the second stage, the missile flies a free or unguided trajectory.

Guided missiles have a guidance system that constantly corrects the flight path until it intercepts the target. These missiles have one of four guidance systems: inertial, homing, command, or beam riding. Many missiles use a combination of two systems—one guiding in midcourse and the other at the terminal stage.

Inertial guidance uses a predetermined path programmed into an on-board missile computer before launch. Missile speed and direction are checked constantly, and the computer makes corrections to keep it on course.

Homing guidance means the missile picks up and tracks a target by radar, optical devices, or heat-seeking methods. An *active* homing system emits a signal that is reflected by the target and picked up by the missile's receiver. In *semiactive* homing, the signal comes from the launching ship or plane rather than from the missile itself. A *passive* homing system guides the missile to the target's radiation. The homing system will follow a target's evasive movements, and the missile is fast enough to overtake a target trying to escape.

Command guidance means the missile is controlled by signals from the launching ship or plane. After the missile is launched on an intercept course, a computer traces both it and the target and transmits to the missile orders to change its track so it can hit the target, even though the latter takes evasive action.

Beam-riding guidance requires the missile to follow a radar beam to the target. A computer in the missile keeps it centered within the radar beam. Several missiles may ride the beam simultaneously. If the missile wanders, it will automatically destroy itself.

Missile and Rocket Designations

All rockets and missiles carry three-letter designations, describing their launch environment, mission, types, and status:

Launch Environment		Mission		Type Vehicle		Status	
A	Air	D	Decoy	M	Guided missile	J	Special test, temporary
B	Multiple	E	Special	N	Probe		
C	Coffin		Electronic	R	Rocket	N	Special test, permanent
F	Individual	G	Surface attack				
M	Mobile	I	Intercept, aerial			X	Experimental
P	Soft pad	Q	Drone			Y	Prototype
R	Ship	T	Training			Z	Planning
U	Underwater	U	Underwater attack				
		W	Weather				

Missile Categories

Missiles may be air to air, air to surface, surface to air, or surface to surface. Some missiles can be used against air and surface targets alike. Missiles can be either air, surface, or submarine launched. Missiles are fired from surface ships, submarines, or aircraft; the marines use ground-launched weapons.

Air-to-air missiles include the Sidewinder (AIM-9) and the newer Phoenix (AIM-54). The Sidewinder is a supersonic homing weapon that uses passive infrared target detection, proportional navigation guidance, and torque balance control. The newest Sidewinder (AIM-9M), with infrared seekers, is flown on Tomcat (F-14) and Phantom (F-4) fighters and the F/A-18. Earlier Sidewinders are being converted to short-range antiradiation Sidearm missiles to arm Navy and Marine Corps helicopters for ground-attack missions. The Phoenix (AIM-54) was originally intended for the ill-fated F-111B aircraft. It, too, is flown on the Tomcat. The long-range Phoenix has a high-explosive warhead and proximity fuze, active-radar terminal homing, and an AWG-9 airborne missile-control system able to engage up to six targets at once. The Sparrow I became operational in 1956 and was replaced by the Sparrow III (AIM-7). An improved version of this all-weather radar-intercept missile, the AIM-7M, is designed to defeat electronic countermeasures. Sparrow will be replaced by the advanced medium-range air-to-air missile (AMRAAM) now entering production.

Air-to-surface missiles include the Shrike and the Harpoon. The Shrike (AGM-45) and the new HARM (high-speed ARM,

AGM-88) sense and home in on radiation targets. The Harpoon (AGM-84) is an antiship missile with active-radar terminal guidance. The wave-skimming Harpoon climbs rapidly in the last few seconds before hitting a ship to avoid its point defense. Laser-guided and infrared-homing versions of the Air Force's Maverick air-to-surface short-range missile are produced for Marine and Navy aircraft.

Other air-to-surface missiles include the Walleye (AGM-62), a TV-guided glide bomb (a larger version, the Walleye II, is nicknamed Fat Albert); the Standard ARM (AGM 78), a tactical antiradiation missile; the Bulldog (AGM-83A), a modified Bullpup with laser guidance used for more effective close air support; the Focus I (AGM-87), a modified Sidewinder that is under test and evaluation; and the HARM (AGM-88), a high-speed antiradition tactical missile evolved from the Strike and the Standard ARM for suppressing and destroying enemy-radar air defense.

Surface-to-air/surface missiles include the Tarter (RIM-24), developed as a medium-range air-defense missile for use in destroyers. The Terrier (RIM-2) is a supersonic, solid-fuel, radar-guided missile used for task force defense against surface and air attack. It can be armed with nuclear or conventional warheads.

The Sea Sparrow (RIM-7E), a surface-to-air version of the AIM-7E, has folding fins for use in a shipboard launcher. It can be used against ships. The improved NATO Sea Sparrow (RIM-7H) is a similar development. Both versions of the Sea Sparrow are designed for protection of individual ships against close-in attack by planes or missiles.

The Standard MR (RIM-66) is a medium-range surface-to-air weapon with surface-to-surface capability for shipboard use. It's roll stabilized and replaces the Tartar (RIM-24B).

The Standard ER (RIM-67) is an extended-range version of the RIM-66. It replaces the Terrier (RIM-2E). The difference between the ER and the MR is the propulsion system. The ER has a separable booster and a sustainer rocket motor. The MR has an integral dual-thrust-level rocket motor.

An improved Standard MR is being produced for use with the Aegis fleet air-defense system; newer versions of the ER have increased range and performance. The rolling airframe missile (RAM), developed with West Germany, is a high-performance point-defense missile in early production for shipboard evaluation.

Figure 15–1 A surface-to-surface Harpoon (RGM-84) missile is fired from a canister launcher aboard the *Spruance*-class destroyer *Fletcher* (DD 992).

The Harpoon is an antiship cruise missile fired from ships (RGM-84), subs (VGM-84), or planes (AGM-84). It can operate in any weather, with active target acquisition and terminal guidance.

The Tomahawk (BGM-109) cruise missile is nuclear armed and can make a highly accurate long-range attack against land targets. A conventionally armed version can be used against enemy surface ships as well as shore targets. The Tomahawk is an all-weather missile that can be launched from surface ships,

land vehicles, and aircraft. Some attack submarines (SSNs) are being built or modified to use it. The guidance system of the land-attack version is updated from time to time to match the contour of the terrain. A digital map is stored inside the missile. The antiship cruise missile has a modified Harpoon guidance system.

The principal *ground-launched missile* is the Redeye (MIM-43), a shoulder-fired air-defense weapon used by the Marine Corps. Two other ground launchers are the Hawk (MIM-23), a low-altitude air-defense weapon with an antimissile capability, also used by the marines, and the Stinger (XFIM-92), an improved Redeye. The Stinger has passive infrared homing and proportional navigation with a head-on launch capability. Stingers have been issued to ships operating in high-threat areas. The TOW (MGM-71) is an antitank weapon launched from helicopters or light vehicles. It is optically sighted and wire-guided.

Submarine-launched missiles include strategic and tactical types. The Polaris strategic ballistic missile was introduced during the 1960s in fleet ballistic-missile submarines (SSBNs). It has been replaced by the Poseidon C-3 (UGM-73), used in twenty-nine *Lafayette-* and *Benjamin Franklin*–class submarines. The *Ohio* (SSBN 726) class, now under construction, uses the longer-range Trident C-4 (UGM-96). This missile is designed to fit Poseidon tubes and will eventually replace the Poseidon in some of the older SSBNs. Each Trident strategic-deterrent missile is a three-stage solid-fuel weapon with improved guidance. Like the Poseidon, it carries multiple independently targeted (MIRV) warheads. An improved Trident D-5 is planned for complete, full-scale engineering development in FY 1991.

Tactical submarine weapons include the SUBROC (UUM-44), launched from a conventional torpedo tube. This is the submarine version of the ASROC (RUR-5) and consists of a rocket carrying a nuclear depth charge. When fired, the SUBROC surfaces, ignites its rocket motor, and flies to the vicinity of the detected target before landing and activating its payload. The submarine version of the Harpoon (UGM-84) is in a capsule for torpedo-tube launching. Like the SUBROC, it surfaces before taking off.

Antisubmarine weapons include the SUBROC, mentioned above, and its surface-ship equivalent, the ASROC, which joined the fleet in 1961. ASROC carries a homing torpedo. Another version, armed with a nuclear depth charge, is no

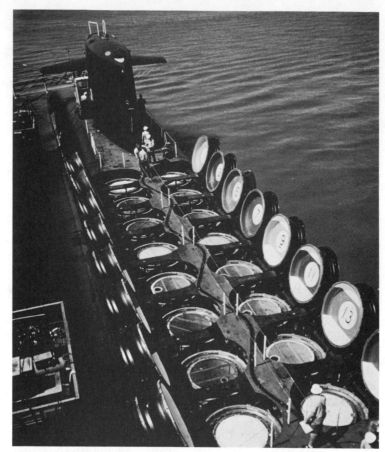

Figure 15–2 The Polaris submarine USS *Sam Rayburn* (SSBN 635) nears completion of its yard period.

longer in fleet use. A more capable, longer-range version (VLA) of the ASROC is being produced for the vertical launch systems (VLS) of cruisers and destroyers. The 12.75-inch Mark 46 homing torpedo is launched from ships, planes, and helicopters. The improved Mark 50 is being developed to replace it. The 21-inch Mark 48 torpedo is a long-range, wire-guided homing weapon fired from submarine tubes against other submarines. It can also be used against surface ships. The new antisubmarine standoff weapon Sea Lance was developed to replace the SUBROC and the ASROC. Like the ASROC, it will carry a depth charge or a homing torpedo. However, new budget cuts may cancel it.

Missiles

The principal *target missile (drone)* is the Firebee 1 (BQM- 34A), a jet-powered, swept-wing, subsonic aircraft-target system. It can be launched from the air or the ground and is recoverable. The Firebee II (BQM-34E) is a high-altitude supersonic version capable of simulating enemy aircraft. The BQM-34T is a modified BQM-34E with a transponder and autopilot. The Navy and Air Force have many versions of the Firebee.

Another target missile/drone is the Chukar (MQM-74), a recoverable gunnery aircraft weapon. This high-midwing monoplane can be launched from shore or ships. It can be used as a decoy aircraft.

Still other target missiles/drones include the Bomarc, HAST (high-altitude supersonic target drone), LAST (low altitude), the rocket-propelled Gunrunner, and several decoys and unnamed missiles. Pilotless aircraft, or remotely piloted vehicles (RPVs), are being used by battleships to spot gunfire at long ranges. A television camera transmits the fall of shot to shipboard spotters and also provides visual identification of over-the-horizon targets. Considerable interest is being shown in other uses, such as ground attack, for RPVs.

Fleet Operational Missiles

Name	Designation	Length (ft-in)	Weight (lbs)	Speed	Range (miles)
Tartar	RIM	14-10	1,425	Mach 2.5	10
Terrier	RIM	26-6	3,070	Mach 2.5	20
Sea Sparrow	RIM	12	450	Mach 2.5	12
ASROC	RUR	15	1,000		
SUBROC	UUM	20-6	4,000		
Poseidon	UGM	34	65,000	n/a	2,900
Sparrow III	AIM	12	350	Mach 3	5
Sidewinder	AIM	9-6	185	Mach 2	5
Phoenix	AIM	13	838	Mach 2	30
Harpoon	AGM/RGM	12-7	1,160		60
	UGM	15	1,450		
Standard MR	RIM	14-8	1,350		25
Standard ER	RIM	26-2	2,962		40
Trident	UGM	34	65,000		4,000
Tomahawk	BGM	18-3	3,200		250 (antiship) 1,350 (land attack)

Missile Launchers

Earlier missile systems had "dedicated" launchers—that is, a separate magazine-loaded launcher for each weapon. This took up valuable deck space and increased topside weight. Later launchers handled more than one type of missile, but still had to be individually loaded. The newest launcher is the Mark 41 VLS, going into current *Ticonderoga-* and *Arleigh Burke–* class ships and being retrofitted into the *Spruance* class. Missiles are carried in below-deck launching tubes; any needed mix of missiles can be fired in quick succession without the delays involved in reloading topside launchers.

Bombs

Bombs have four chief parts. The case or body is normally made of steel and contains the explosive. The fuze or fuzes explode the bomb on contact or after a predetermined time interval. A surface blast is produced by instantaneous fuzing, an explosion delayed after contact is produced by a delayed-action fuze, and an underwater explosion is produced by a delayed-action fuze triggered by water pressure. The fin or tail assembly stabilizes the bomb during flight. The arming-wire assembly keeps the fuze or fuzes from being armed until after the bomb is dropped. Bombs are classed as explosive, chemical, or practice. Smart bombs have remote-control movable-tail surfaces and can be steered to their target.

Explosive Bombs

General-purpose (GP) bombs, weighing 100 to 2,000 pounds, are generally used against unarmored ships or ground targets for blast or fragmentation.

Semi-armor-piercing (SAP) bombs, weighing 1,000 pounds, are used against carriers, cruisers, and "hardened" ground targets. They are designed to blow up after penetrating a ship.

Fragmentation bombs are very small explosives dropped in clusters against troops and ground targets.

Chemical Bombs

Gas bombs, containing mustard gas, phosgene, tear gas, or vomiting gas, are used to harass or kill troops.

Smoke bombs contain white phosphorus that ignites during the explosion and spreads over an area of 30 to 50 yards. They produce intense smoke for about 5 minutes and are used to conceal movements of ships or troops.

Incendiary bombs, containing a mixture of gasoline or jet fuel and a thickening agent, produce intense fire when ignited and are used against troops and ground targets. They are also called napalm bombs.

Figure 15–3 Aviation ordnancemen prepare missiles for loading onto an F-14 Tomcat on board the nuclear-powered aircraft carrier *Nimitz* (CVN 68).

Fuel-air explosive (FAE) bombs are used against airfields and other ground targets.

Practice and drill bombs used in training may be loaded with sand or water, but they are inert and will not explode.

Torpedoes

The torpedo is a self-propelled explosive-carrying underwater weapon with its own automatic guidance system. First developed more than a century ago, it was the first guided naval weapon.

A torpedo consists of tail, afterbody, midsection, and head. The tail section includes the screws, fins, and control surfaces. The propulsion system is contained in the afterbody. The midsection houses batteries, compressed air, or liquid fuel. The head contains the explosive charge, fuze, and any acoustic or magnetic sensing devices.

Guidance systems are either preset, wire guided, or homing. Preset torpedoes follow a set course and depth after they are launched. Wire-guided torpedoes have a thin wire connecting the torpedo and the firing ship. Through this wire, guidance signals can be transmitted to the torpedo to direct it to inter-cept the target. Homing torpedos are either active or passive. Active types depend on the sensing signals generated and re-turned to the torpedo through a sonar device inside the tor-pedo. Passive types listen for the noise generated by the target and home in on it.

Destroyer-type ships launch torpedoes from tubes mounted topside, or propel them to the target area with an ASROC. Submarines launch torpedoes from bow or midship tubes. Tor-pedos from helicopters and fixed-wing aircraft are parachuted from the craft. They activate once they're in the water.

Weapon-Control Systems

A weapon, however powerful, is only as a good as its accu-racy. The process by which a projectile, missile, bomb, or torpedo is guided to its target is called weapon control. A potential target is first *detected* by a sensor (radar, sonar, or lookout). It is then *evaluated;* if it proves to be hostile, a *decision* is made, according to prescribed weapons doctrine, whether or not to *engage*. If the target is to be engaged, the appropriate weapon is selected. All available information is assimilated by a computer to produce a weapon-control solu-tion that will guide the weapon to contact.

Ships, aircraft, and submarines all incorporate various types of weapon-control systems. Surface- and air-search radars have been continuously improved since World War II to detect high-performance targets at long ranges in any weather. The newer surface-ship control systems work with guns and mis-siles, and include radars and digital computers that can quickly acquire and track targets while directing shipboard weapons. The Mark 86 fire-control system is being installed in destroyers and large ships, while the lightweight Mark 92 system is going into missile frigates and smaller combatants. Perhaps the ulti-mate weapon-control system so far is the Aegis weapon-system Mark 7, a rapid-reaction, long-range fleet air-defense system developed for use against aircraft and missiles. It in-cludes the greatly improved AN/SPY-1 radar, a quick-reaction tactical computer for overall command control, a digital weapon-control system, and guided-missile launchers that use the improved Standard 2 missile. The Aegis system can also assist a force commander in controlling all the surface and aerial weapons of a battle group, particularly in a modern tacti-

cal environment in which electronic warfare (detection and

jamming) is heavily used. The first operational Aegis system joined the fleet in 1983 on the missile cruisers of the *Ticonderoga* (CG 47) class. It will also arm the *Arleigh Burke* (DDG 51) class. A new NATO AAW (antiair warfare) system is in initial development by the United States and five allied nations to meet the aircraft and missile threats of the next century.

Older electromechanical-analog director systems are still in use in the surface fleet, but their replacement by newer digital systems is planned. Submarines and aircraft have their own control systems, similar in general principle to those used in surface ships; submarines detect and track their targets by sonar rather than by radar. Surface ships similarly detect submarines and control weapons against them. The new SQQ 89 surface-ship ASW (antisubmarine warfare) combat system is an integrated system for detecting, identifying, tracking, and engaging modern submarines. Improvements are already being planned to cope with future submarines. Fleet ballistic missiles are controlled by a missile fire-control system, which is connected to the submarine's inertial navigation system. The navigation system keeps accurate track of the ship's position. When missiles are to be fired, the fire-control system takes current position data and quickly computes firing information to put missiles on the proper ballistic course. While in flight, the missile keeps itself on course with the aid of an inertial navigation system; the new Trident missile can supplement this with stellar navigation.

Mines

Most information on mines is classified, so this is only a general discussion. The several types of mines can be described according to the method of actuation (firing), the method of planting, and position in the water.

Method of Actuation

A contact mine fires when a ship strikes it. Usually it has lead horns containing glass tubes filled with an electrolyte. When the horn is struck, the glass breaks and the electrolyte generates enough current to fire the mine. Influence mines may be actuated by the underwater sound generated in a passing ship's current, by the ships' magnetic field, or by the mine's sensitivity to reduced water pressure caused by a passing ship.

Method of Planting

Mines may be planted by surface craft, submarines, and aircraft. Surface-planted mines are subject to enemy interception. Submarines can plant mines secretly but cannot return to plant more mines until those planted have been destroyed or become inactive. Aircraft plant mines in shallow waters where submarines and surface craft cannot operate.

Position in the Water

Moored contact mines are anchored in place and float near the surface of the water, where a ship might strike them. Bottom mines, which lie on the ocean floor, are used only in relatively shallow water. They are influence mines, set off by sound, magnetism, or pressure.

Guns

Caliber, applied to naval guns, has two meanings. In its first sense, it refers to bore diameter, expressed in inches or millimeters (mm). In its second sense, it expresses the ratio of the gun's length in inches divided by the bore diameter. Thus you can find the nominal barrel length of a gun if you multiply the bore diameter by the caliber of the gun. For example, a 5-inch/54 (54 refers to caliber) gun has a barrel 270 inches long. The higher a gun's caliber, the longer it is; for example, the 5-inch/54 gun is longer than a 5-inch/38 gun, though both have the same bore diameter.

Guns are categorized as *major* (8 inches and larger), *intermediate* (less than 8 inches but larger than 4 inches), and *minor* caliber (less than 4 inches). Guns may be described as follows:

Case Guns: All modern Navy guns are case types. The propelling charge of powder is contained in a metal cartridge or case. Ammunition for case guns is either fixed or semifixed. Fixed ammunition has a propellant powder case and projectile attached as one unit. Small arms and minor-caliber guns use fixed ammunition. Semifixed ammunition has two parts, powder case and projectile. All Navy 5-inch and 8-inch guns use semifixed ammunition.

Bag Guns: These are heavy-caliber guns using silk bags, rather than cases, to contain their powder charges. The only bag guns remaining in the fleet are the 16-inch guns in the battleships now in service.

Figure 15–4 Gun crews keep their hands away from the moving parts of a 3-inch/50 dual-purpose gun mount during exercises at sea. Attention to safety precautions can prevent deaths and injuries.

Automatic Guns: These use a recoil to eject the fired case and reload; 5-inch/54 and 3-inch/50 guns are automatic.

Semiautomatic Guns: These guns eject the fixed case and leave the breech open in a proper position for hand loading, as in the 5-inch/38 gun.

Dual-Purpose (DP) Guns: These can be used against both surface and air targets. The 5-inch/54 and 5-inch/38 guns are dual purpose.

Saluting Guns: These fire salutes using black-powder blanks.

Line-Throwing Guns: A line-throwing attachment is fixed to the muzzle of the M14 service rifle. This is used to shoot a light line across a distance too great for a heaving line to be thrown.

A *battery* is a group of guns of the same size, normally controlled from the same point. The main battery of a ship consists of the largest guns aboard. The secondary battery consists of dual-purpose guns or guns of the next size aboard. An antiaircraft (AA) battery consists of small-caliber guns and is usually called the machine-gun battery.

Parts of a Gun

The function and size of the mount determines a gun's major parts, but all guns have these components: stand, carriage, slide, housing, barrel, and breech assembly.

The *stand* is firmly attached to a ship's superstructure and contains the roller bearing on which the mount rotates.

The *carriage* usually has two parts, the base and gun carriage. The base is a platform that supports the gun carriage and rotates on a stand. The gun carriage supports the gun assembly in vertical pivot points, called trunnion bearings.

The *slide* does not move, but it contains the bearing surfaces that support and guide the moving (recoiling) barrel and housing. The slide also contains the trunnions, which enable the gun to be elevated.

The *housing* moves within the slide during firing. The housing contains the breech assembly, barrel (which is locked to the housing by a bayonet joint), and a locking key.

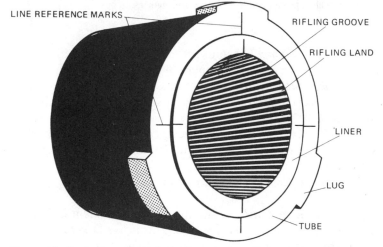

Figure 15–5 A view through the barrel of a rifled gun shows the lands, grooves, and righthand twist.

The *barrel* is a rifled tube closed at one end to contain the pressure of the rapidly burning powder. The rear end of the barrel is attached to the breech housing, which contains the breechblock, sometimes called a plug. Forward of the breech end is an enlarged chamber that holds the propelling charge. The forward end of the chamber is tapered down to guide the projectile into the rifling, where it is seated prior to firing. The bore of the barrel is rifled in a righthand twist of uniform diam-

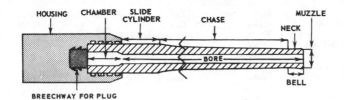

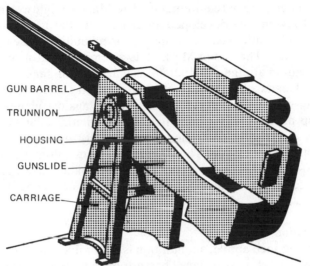

Figure 15–6   These are the main assemblies of a 5-inch/38 dual-purpose gun
and a cross section of the barrel and housing.

eter, end to end. Rifling in a barrel causes a projectile to spin.
This spinning motion keeps the projectile from tumbling once it
leaves the barrel and ensures greater accuracy. The slide-cylin-
der area is a bearing surface for the slide during recoil and
counter recoil. The chase area is the tapered part of the barrel.
Some guns have an enlarged area at the muzzle called the bell,
which prevents any tendency of the barrel to split.

The *breech assembly* is the plug or block, which closes off
the chamber end of the barrel. The breech assembly contains
the firing mechanism that ignites the powder primer in the
propellant case, and the extractors that remove the fired case
from the gun chamber.

Guns now in use in the fleet include the following:

Size (in/cal)	Range (yds)	Type	Projectile Weight (lbs)
16/50	42,300	Bag	1,900 and 2,700
8/55	30,400	Case–Semifixed	335
5/54 (Mk 45)	25,900	Case–Semifixed	75
(Mk 42)	25,900	Case–Semifixed	75
5/38	17,300	Case–Semifixed	55
3/50	14,000	Case–Fixed	13

Recent experience has shown a need for new gun systems to meet contemporary requirements. The Mark 45 lightweight 5-inch/54 system was developed for general use in surface ships. It is an automatic weapon designed for reliability and ease of maintenance. The 76mm Mark 75 is a remote-control, water-cooled automatic gun of Italian design, used in smaller warships. Phalanx, the Mark 15 close-in weapon system (CIWS), is an all-weather weapon for ship defense against planes and antiship missiles. It includes its own automatic radar system and an electrically controlled, hydraulically operated 20mm multibarrel Galting gun. The 20mm and 25mm automatic guns, with 50-caliber machine guns, are in use for defense against fast-attack craft. Other light automatic guns are being developed.

Ammunition

As mentioned above, ammunition is either fixed or semifixed and consists of a propellant charge (powder), the primer that sets off the propellant charge, and the projectile.

All naval guns use smokeless powder shaped into cylindrical grains. This shape, with holes through the powder grain, ensures that the powder will burn completely and predictably.

Ammunition Handling

Ammunition is perfectly safe to handle, as long as it is handled correctly. Safety precautions (see chapter 20) are posted in handling areas; learn them and follow them strictly. They

Figure 15–7 External features of a gun projectile.

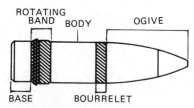

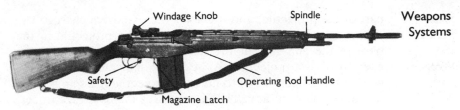

Figure 15–8   Right front view of a 7.62-mm M14 rifle.

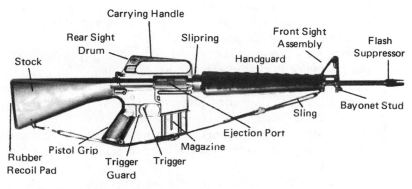

Figure 15–9   The 5.56-mm M16 rifle.

Figure 15–10   The 7.62-mm M60 machine gun.

have been instituted as a result of disasters that cost lives, ships, and port facilities. Strict adherence to proper procedures can avert accidents and save lives.

Projectiles

A projectile consists of five distinct parts. The *ogive* (pronounced *o-jive*) is the nose, the streamlined forward part. The *bourrelet* is the forward-bearing surface of the body, which steadies the projectile in the gun barrel. The *body* is the main part of the projectile, and it carries the explosive charge. The *rotating band,* normally of brass, seals the projectile in the bore of the gun so that the full force of propellant gases is exerted on the projectile. As its name indicates, it grips the gun's rifling (figure 15-5) to give the projectile the spin needed for range and accuracy. The *base* houses the base fuze tracer, or solid base plate. General types of projectiles include the following:

Thin-walled projectiles designed to damage by blast effect and fragmentation. The two subdivisions of this projectile type are high capacity (HC), for use against troops or surface targets, and AA, for use against aircraft.

Thick-walled projectiles are AP, designed to penetrate armor plating or thick concrete before exploding.

Common (COM) projectiles have a wall thickness midway between that of thin-walled projectiles and AP projectiles.

A rocket-assisted projectile (RAP) has a solid-fuel rocket motor in its base. This ignites after firing, considerably extending gun range. Five-inch/38 RAPs have seen service use; other calibers have been studied.

Terminal guidance for major-caliber projectiles, using laser illumination of the target, is under study. New types of 16-inch projectiles, intended to make the heavy gun more versatile or to increase its range, are in service or under development.

Special-purpose projectiles are not intended to inflict damage by explosion or fragmentation.

Illumination projectiles, called starshells, drop a flare attached to a parachute.

Smoke projectiles use white phosphorus to provide a smoke screen.

Window projectiles scatter metal foil strips to confuse radar.

Target projectiles, which do not contain explosives, are used for target practice. Projectiles may be fitted with any of the following fuzes or any combination of them:

The point-detonating fuze (PDF) explodes on impact.

The mechanical time fuze (MTF) contains a clock mechanism to explode the projectile at a preset time.

The proximity fuze (VT) contains a miniature radio transmitter that explodes the projectile when it senses a nearby target.

The auxiliary-detonating fuze (ADF) acts as a booster in conjunction with a nose fuze.

The base-detonating fuze (BDF) is set to explode a fraction of a second after impact so that the projectile can penetrate its target before it explodes.

All fuzes in naval guns begin to function, or arm themselves, after the projectile leaves the gun barrel and has traveled a safe distance.

Small Arms

Any weapon with a bore diameter of 0.6 inches or less is called a small arm. The military also classifies any hand-held or carried weapon as a small arm. The largest Navy small arm is the .50-caliber machine gun and the smallest is the .22-caliber pistol. The bore size of small arms is designated by caliber or gauge in the case of shotguns. Small arms have one of the following firing systems:

A semiautomatic weapon unlocks the bolt, extracts the fixed case from the chamber, ejects the fired case from the mechanism, cocks the hammer, and reloads automatically. The trigger must be released and pulled again to fire the weapon.

An automatic weapon follows the same chain of events as a semiautomatic weapon, except that as long as the trigger is held in the fire position, the weapon will continue to fire.

A double-action weapon, such as a revolver, operates off the trigger pull. When the trigger is pulled back, the cylinder rotates to align a chamber with the barrel, and the hammer is cocked and then released to fire the weapon. To fire again, the trigger must be released and pulled again.

The 45-caliber M1911A1 semiautomatic pistol, in use for more than seventy years, is one of the most dependable small arms ever made. It is a recoil-operated, air-cooled, magazine-fed semiautomatic hand weapon, and the only American service arm in use with a lefthand rifling. It contains four safety devices: two automatic safeties (disconnector and grip safety) and two manual safeties (thumb safety and a half-cock notch). A new pistol, using the 9mm NATO cartridge, has been ordered to replace the M1911A1. Anyone using a hand firearm must always remember that the only really effective safety system is responsible handling. Mechanical safeties are never foolproof and were never intended as a substitute for proper handling.

The .38-caliber revolver is a cylinder-loaded, exposed-hammer, single- or double-action, air-cooled hand weapon. For single-action firing, the hammer is pulled back to the full-cock position and the trigger is pulled to fire the weapon. In double-action firing, pulling back on the trigger both cocks the hammer and releases it to fire. Double-action firing requires two or three times the trigger-pull pressure of single-action firing. The revolver has two built-in safety mechanisms, the rebound slide and the hammer block.

The Berretta model 92 SB-F semiautomatic pistol, firing the 9mm NATO cartridge, was adopted to replace all other handguns in American service.

The M14 rifle is an air-cooled, gas-operated, 20-round, magazine-fed semiautomatic or automatic 7.62mm weapon. The rifle is normally issued with a selector-shaft lock preventing full automatic fire. The M14 is the rifle issued to all ships and shore stations. It has a manual safety in front of the trigger guard; to place the weapon on safe, press the lever back into the trigger guard.

The M16 rifle is a gas-operated, magazine-fed, air-cooled, lightweight 5.56mm shoulder weapon, capable of either semiautomatic or automatic fire through a selector lever on the left side of the receiver. Once the last round is fired from the magazine, the bolt is held open by a catch. The weapon is equipped with a manual safety, a three-position fire selector lever on the left side of the receiver (safe, semiautomatic, and fully automatic). The rifle is considered safe only when the magazine is out, the chamber is empty, the bolt carrier is to the rear, and the selector is on safe. This is the standard-issue rifle for all deployed and combatant forces.

The M60 machine gun is an air-cooled, belt-fed, gas-operated weapon firing the 7.62mm (NATO) cartridge. The M60 machine gun may have either a bipod or a tripod mount.

A 45-caliber line-throwing gun was used for many years to shoot a light line to another ship or to the beach when the distance was too great for a heaving line. This has been replaced by a line-throwing attachment to the M14 service rifle. The launching attachment is fixed to the muzzle of the rifle, and a special blank cartridge propels the small weight to which the messenger line is fastened.

Shotguns issued to the Navy are civilian models procured for training, skeet shooting, and certain guard duty. All shotguns are 12 gauge.

IV. The Sailor at Sea

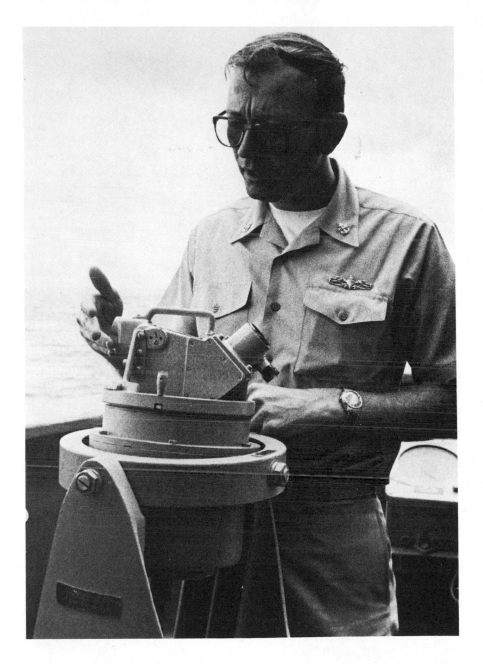

Living Aboard Ship

16

All ships have standard routines for in port and at sea. The routine varies on different ships; a submarine on extended patrol will run on a schedule different from that of an aircraft carrier on around-the-clock flight operations. Below is a sample standard routine. Departures from the normal routine are published in the plan of the day (POD).

Plan of the Day

This is "the word," the daily schedule of events, prepared and issued by the executive officer. It will name duty officers, assign various watches, and include any changes or additions to the normal routine and orders of the day—drills, training schedule, duty section, liberty section and hours, working parties, movies, examinations, or inspections.

The POD, distributed to the officer of the deck (OOD), all offices, officers, and division bulletin boards, is carried out by the OOD and all division officers.

Daily Routine at Sea

Note: When time is left blank, it is specified in the POD. Standard reports appear in quotation marks.

Weekdays	Sundays and Holidays	Routine
0030	0030	JOOW (junior officer of the watch) inspects the lower decks; hourly thereafter until sunrise.
0330	0330	Call the morning watch. Call galley force.

Weekdays	Sundays and Holidays	Routine
0400	0400	Reveille for duty cooks (cooks may specify time to be called by signing up in the wake-up log kept by the boatswain's mate of the watch).
Sunrise	Sunrise	Turn off running lights. If the ship is darkened, light ship. Hoist pennants and flags as necessary.
0530	0600	Call masters-at-arms (MAA), division police petty officers, and mess cooks. Early mess for designated persons.
0600	0630	"Up all idlers" (nonwatchstanders).
0605	0635	Announce weather.
0615	0645	"Turn to. Scrub down weather decks. Sweep down all compartments. Empty all trashcans." "Lay below to the MAA office for muster, all restricted persons." Pipe sweepers, MAA report to OOD, "Idlers turned out." Clean boats and fuel boats as necessary.
0655	0655	"Clear mess decks." Mess call.
0700	0700	Pipe to breakfast. "Testing general alarm." On completion: "Test of general alarm completed." "Uniform of the day——," or "Uniform for captain's inspection is——."
0720	0720	"Relieve the watch, on deck the—— section. Lifeboat crew of the watch to muster."
0755	0755	OOD reports "8 o'clock" to the admiral if embarked, and "8 o'clock; request permission to strike eight bells" to the captain.
0800		Officers' call.
0805		Assembly.
0815	0815	Sick call.
	0815	Rig for Church. "Knock off ship's work; shift into uniform for inspection." "Uniform for inspection is——."
	0915	Officers' call. "All hands to quarters for inspection."

Weekdays	Sundays and Holidays	Routine
	0930	"Knock off work. Shift into clean uniform of the day." Church call. "Maintain quiet about the decks during divine service." Hoist the church pennant. At the end of service, pennant is hauled down. Commence holiday routine.
1115	1115	Pipe sweepers. "Sweepers, man your brooms. Make a clean sweep down fore and aft. Empty all trashcans." Early mess for cooks, mess cooks, and MAA.
1145		"Knock off all ship's work."
1150	1150	Quartermaster reports "Chronometers wound and compared" to OOD. OOD reports "12 o'clock" to the admiral if embarked, and "12 o'clock, chronometers wound and compared; request permission to strike eight bells" to the captain.
1200	1200	Pipe to dinner.
1220	1220	"Relieve the watch, on deck the—— section. Lifeboat crew of the watch to muster."
1300		"Turn to." At this time, extra duty persons muster at MAA office.
1300	1300	Pipe sweepers. "Sweepers, man your brooms. Make a clean sweep down fore and aft. Empty all trashcans."
1300		Friday, or when ordered, inspections call, "Stand by for inspection on lower decks."
1545		"Relieve the watch, on deck the—— section. Lifeboat crew of the watch to muster."
1600	1600	Pipe sweepers. "Sweepers man your brooms. Make a clean sweep down fore and aft."
1600		"Knock off all ship's work."
1600	1600	Test running lights and emergency identification signals, report their read-

	Weekdays	Sundays and Holidays	Routine
			iness to the OOD (or at least one hour before sunset).
	1630	1630	Early mess for mess-deck MAA and mess cooks.
	1645		"Observe sunset." Set the prescribed material condition. Division damage-control petty officers report closures to damage-control central or sign the closure log maintained by the OOD on the bridge.
	1655	1655	Mess call. "Clear the mess decks."
	Sunset	Sunset	If the ship is to be darkened: "Darken ship. The smoking lamp is out on all weather decks." If ship is not to be darkened, turn on running lights and haul down colors following motion of senior officer present afloat (SOPA). Lookouts report running lights bright; lifebuoy watch on fantail reports stern light and lifebuoy light bright (and on the half hour thereafter until sunrise). Boatswains inspect weather decks and boats; when secured, report to the OOD.
	1700	1700	Pipe to supper. Close watertight doors, etc.: "Set material condition——throughout the ship."
	1720	1720	"Relieve the watch. On deck, the—— section. Lifeboat crew of the watch to muster."
	1730	1730	Security patrols make reports to the OOD, and hourly thereafter. Coxswain of lifeboat reports lifeboat crew mustered and boat ready for lowering (every half hour) and engine tested (once each watch). Corporal of the guard reports police conditions (every half hour thereafter).
	1745	1745	Sick call.
	1800	1800	Pipe sweepers. "Sweepers, man your brooms. Make a clean sweep down on

348

Routine
at Sea

Weekdays	Sundays and Holidays	Routine
		lower decks and ladders. Empty all trashcans." "Lay below to the MAA office for muster, all restricted persons."
		Rig for movies. Movie call. Time and place as designated in POD.
1930	1930	"Now lay before the mast all 8 o'clock reports."
1945	1945	"Relieve the watch. On deck, the—— section. Lifeboat crew of the watch to muster."
1955	1955	OOD reports "8 o'clock" to the admiral if embarked, and "8 o'clock, lights out and galley ranges secured; prisoners and lower decks secured; request permission to strike 8 bells," to the captain.
Dark	Dark	Dump trash and garbage. Pump bilges (Oil Pollution Act permitting). Blow tubes if wind favorable and plant requires it.
2000	2000	Hammocks. "Out lights, and silence in all berthing spaces."
2100	2100	MAA reports to the OOD "9 o'clock, lights out."
2155	2155	Tattoo.
2200	2200	MAA reports to the OOD "10 o'clock, lights out."
2330	2330	Call the watch.
2345	2345	Relieve the watch, on deck, the—— section. Lifeboat crew of the watch to muster.

349

Daily Routine in Port

Weekdays	Sundays and Holidays	Routine
0030	0030	JOOW inspects lower deck and boats in water (and hourly thereafter until reveille).

Weekdays	Sundays and Holidays	Routine
0330	0330	Call the watch.
0350	0350	Relieve the watch.
Daylight		Call galley force. Turn off all unnecessary lights.
Sunrise		Turn off anchor, boom, and gangway lights. Hoist guard flags, absentee pennants as necessary. If darkened, light ship; the smoking lamp is lighted on the top side.
0540	0600	Call MAA, division police petty officer, mess cooks, and boat crews. Early mess for designated personnel.
0600		Reveille. "Reveille, all hands, heave out and trice up."
0605		Announce weather to the crew.
0615		Pipe sweepers. "Turn to. Scrub down weather decks, sweep down compartments, empty all trashcans." Division police petty officers report to the duty MAA that persons of their divisions are turned out. MAA reports to OOD "Crew turned out." Fuel all boats and test engines.
0655	0715	Mess call. "Clear all mess decks."
0700	0720	Pipe for breakfast, "Uniform of the day is——," or "Uniform for inspection is——," Meal pennant is hoisted.
0705		Announce weather over officer's circuit.
0720	0740	Relieve the watch.
0750	0750	Guard of the day.
0755	0755	First call. Hoist PREP, signifying prepare for colors. OOD reports "8 o'clock" to the admiral if embarked, and "8 o'clock, request permission to strike 8 bells" to the captain.
0800	0800	Morning colors. Meal pennant hauled down.
0800		All hands to quarters for muster. Officers' call.
0805		Assembly.

350

Weekdays	Sundays and Holidays	Routine	
0815		Pipe retreat. "Turn to, commence ship's work."	
	0800	"Turn to, sweep and clamp down weather decks and living spaces."	
0815	0815	Sick call.	
	0815	Rig for church. "Knock off work. Shift into uniform for inspection. The uniform for inspection is——." Officers' call. "All hands to quarters for inspection."	
	0915	"Knock off work. Shift into clean uniform of the day."	
	0930	Church call. "Maintain quiet about the decks during divine service." Hoist the church pennant. At the end of divine service, haul down the church pennant. Commence holiday routine. Inspection of mess cooks.	**351**
1115	1115	Early mess for mess deck MAA and cooks.	
1115	1115	Pipe sweepers. "Sweepers, man your brooms. Make a clean sweep down fore and aft. Empty all trashcans."	
1145		"Knock off all ship's work."	
1150	1150	Quartermaster reports "Chronometers wound and compared" to the OOD.	
1155	1155	Mess call. "Clear the mess decks." OOD reports "12 o'clock" to the admiral if embarked, and "12 o'clock, chronometers wound and compared; request permission to strike 8 bells" to captain.	
1200	1200	Pipe to dinner. Hoist meal pennant.	
1220	1220	"Relieve the watch." "Commence holiday routine." Extra-duty persons muster at MAA office.	
1300		"Turn to."	
1300	1300	Pipe sweepers. "Sweepers, man your brooms. Make a clean sweep down fore and aft. Empty all trashcans."	Routine in Port

	Sundays and	
Weekdays	Holidays	Routine
1300		Haul down meal pennant. Friday, or when ordered, inspection call. "Stand by for inspection of lower decks."
1545	1545	"Relieve the watch."
1600	1600	Pipe sweepers. "Sweepers man your brooms. Make a clean sweep fore and aft."
1600		"Knock off all ship's work." All hands shift into the uniform of the day. Extra-duty persons muster at MAA office.
1600	1600	Test anchor and boom lights. Rig and test gangway lights and floodlights. Report their readiness to OOD (or at least one hour before sunset). Liberty call.
Half hour before sunset		Guard of the day.
5 minutes before sunset		First call. Hoist PREP.
Sunset		Evening colors. Turn on anchor, boom, accommodation ladder (brow), and flood lights. If ship is to be darkened, "Darken ship. The smoking lamp is out on the top side."
1645	1645	Early mess for mess-deck MAA and mess cooks.
1700	1700	Closure of watertight doors, etc. "Set material condition——throughout the ship."
1730	1730	Pipe to supper. Hoist meal pennant, if before sunset.
1750	1750	"Relieve the watch."
1800	1800	Haul down meal pennant at sunset or completion of supper. Rig for movies.
1815	1815	Pipe sweepers. "Sweepers man your brooms. Make a clean sweep down all lower decks and ladders. Empty all trashcans. Lay below to the MAA office for muster, all restricted persons."
		Movie call. Time and place as designated in POD.

Weekdays	Sundays and Holidays	Routine
1930	1930	"On deck, all the 8 o'clock reports."
1950	1950	"Relieve the watch."
1955	1955	OOD reports "8 o'clock" to the admiral if embarked, and "8 o'clock, lights out and galley ranges secured. Request permission to strike 8 bells" to the captain. XO (or command duty officer) reports to captain (if on board), "All departments secured for the night (or as appropriate)."
2000	2000	Hammocks. "Out all lights and silence in all berthing spaces."
2100	2100	MAA reports to OOD "9 o'clock, lights out." Tattoo. "Turn in, keep silence about the decks." Taps (5 minutes after tattoo).
2200	2200	MAA reports to OOD "10 o'clock, lights out."
2350	2350	"Relieve the watch."

Standard Organization and Regulations of the U.S. Navy

If you had to learn a new set of regulations and an entirely different organization every time you moved from one division, department, or ship to another, you would waste time. The Navy has standardized everything—routine, regulations, and organization—as much as possible on all ships.

This information is contained in the current edition of the Standard Organization and Regulations of the U.S. Navy (OPNAVINST 3120.32). You will be loaned a copy. Your daily and weekly routine aboard ship will be governed by it, as will the organization of your division and department. You must first know and become familiar with the general regulations, a list of which follows. You must read all of the regulations, and sign a statement to the effect that you have done so and that you understand them. Whether you are aboard a minesweeper or an aircraft carrier, the titles and numbers of the general regulations will be the same.

General Regulations

The Battle Bill

This bill assigns sailors to specific jobs at general quarters (GQ) stations and for all other conditions of readiness. Battle-station and duty assignments are made by billet number—a combination of number and letter indicating a person's division, section within the division, and seniority within that section.

Figure 16–1 Part of life aboard ship is swabbing decks—and getting your feet wet.

Figure 16–2 Watches are maintained for communication, security, and the safety of ship and crew.

Once you've reported aboard your ship and are assigned to a division, you will receive a billet slip containing your billet number and the duties for various bills. It's your responsibility to know your station and the duties required of you for each bill.

A new system of manning some classes of ships, called the *ship-manning document* (SMD), is now in effect. Rather than basing crew assignments on billets in the battle bill, it relates to man-hours already implemented in the Navy's 3-M maintenance system. Each ship included in this system receives an SMD outline from which assignments are made. All new ships joining the fleet are organized under the SMD system.

Watch, Quarter, and Station Bill

WQ & S
Bill

This bill displays in one place the duties of each person in each emergency and watch condition. It also shows your duty requirements in administrative and operational bills.

Watch Organization

A ship in commission always has sailors on watch. Even when the ship is tied up in port and is receiving steam and electricity from the pier or another ship, it is necessary to maintain a watch for communications, security, and safety. Those assigned to watches are called watchstanders. *Watch* may refer to the location of the person on watch, such as in forecastle watch or bridge watch, or it may refer to the section of the ship's crew on duty, as in "Relieve the watch, on deck the third section."

Traditionally, the 24-hour day is divided into seven watches.

0000–0400	Midwatch	1600–1800	First dog watch
0400–0800	Morning watch	1800–2000	Second dog
0800–1200	Forenoon watch		watch
1200–1600	Afternoon watch	2000–2400	Evening watch

The "dog watches"—from 1600 to 1800, and 1800 to 2000— alternate the daily watch routine so sailors with the midwatch one night will not have it again the next. They also give each watchstander an opportunity to eat the evening meal.

Conditions of Readiness

Officers and enlisted men and women assigned to watch-keeping duties are trusted with the safety of the ship, her machinery and equipment, and all the people on board. Watch officers are in charge of the various watches. The commanding officer may assign as watch officer any commissioned or warrant officer he or she considers qualified. When conditions require, the commanding officer may assign petty officers to such duty. The watch organization varies according to a ship's condition of readiness:

Condition I: GQ, all hands at battle stations.

Condition II: Modified GQ, used on large ships to let the crew relax.

Condition III: Wartime cruising. Usually only one of three sections on watch and only certain stations manned or partially manned.

Condition IV: Peacetime cruising. Only necessary persons on watch, rest of crew engages in work or training.

Condition V: Peacetime watch in port. Enough of the crew is on board to get the ship under way or handle emergencies.

Variations of these conditions include:

Condition IA: All hands on station to conduct amphibious operations and limited defense of the ship.

Condition IAA: All hands at battle stations to counter an air or surface threat.

Condition IAS: All hands at battle stations to counter a submarine threat.

Condition IE: Temporary relaxation from GQ for brief periods of rest and distribution of food at battle stations.

Condition IM: All hands at battle stations to take mine countermeasures.

Depending on the condition of readiness, which affects the disposition of the crew and the condition of armament, the ship establishes certain material conditions concerned with watertight doors and hatches and damage-control systems. (For details on markings of fittings and various material conditions, see pp. 394–95.)

The watch organization for condition IV, the normal peacetime cruising condition, is shown in figure 16-3. It includes an adequate number of qualified personnel for the safe and effective operation of the ship, yet allows for the most economical use of personnel in watch assignments. In condition IV, no weapon batteries are manned, the engineering plant is ready for speeds as ordered, material condition YOKE is modified for access in daylight, and aircraft are in the readiness condition required by the flight schedule. The combat information center (CIC) and the exterior and interior communication systems are manned for routine purposes. Complete surface lookout coverage is provided, and when flight operations are in progress, air lookouts are posted.

Watch Section

Each sailor is assigned to a numbered section of the watch. When the word is passed that a specific section has the watch, everyone in that section immediately reports to his or her watch station. A ship may have as many as five watch sections.

On some ships, especially for in-port watches, a division may consist of a port watch and a starboard watch. Each is divided into two sections. Odd-numbered sections, 1 and 3, are in the starboard watch. Even-numbered sections, 2 and 4, are in the port watch.

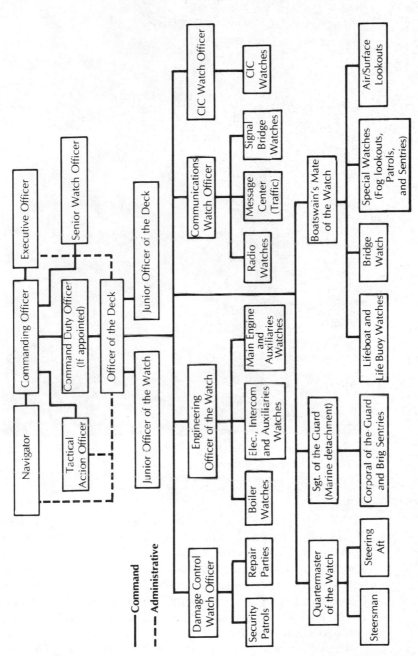

Figure 16–3 Watch organization under way.

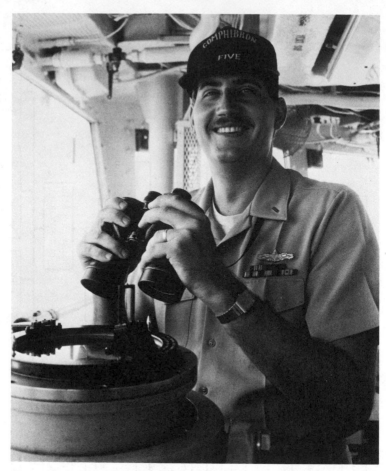

Figure 16–4 The OOD is in charge of the ship and is responsible to the CO for her safe and proper operation.

Relieving the Watch

The oncoming watch should be on station 15 minutes before the hour so the relief can receive information and instructions from the off-going watch. Some ships muster the oncoming watch to make sure each watchstander is ready ahead of time. Relieving the watch must be a controlled and precise function. Experience has shown that a ship's ability to handle casualties and tactical decisions is significantly reduced during the transition period between watches.

When reporting for watch, say "Ready to relieve." The person on watch then passes on pertinent instructions or information. When you understand all conditions and instructions say,

"I relieve you." Thereafter you assume complete responsibility for the watch.

Underway Watch

There are seven key watch assignments for the underway watch. All members of the watch section have important responsibilities in one or more of them.

Command Duty Officer (CDO): Although an official watchstander, the CDO may be on duty for a period of several watches. The CDO, who is eligible for command at sea, is designated and empowered by the captain to advise, supervise, and direct the OOD in matters concerning the general operation and safety of the ship.

Officer of the Deck (OOD): The OOD is in charge of the ship and is responsible to the CO for her safe and proper operation. This includes navigation, shiphandling, communications, routine tests and inspections, reports, supervision of the watch, and carrying out the POD.

Junior Officer of the Deck (JOOD): The JOOD is the principal assistant to the OOD. Anyone making routine reports to the OOD normally makes them through the JOOD or the JOOW.

Junior Officer of the Watch (JOOW): The JOOW, when assigned, is a line officer on watch, in training for qualification as OOD. The JOOW normally stands watch in the pilot house, but may be stationed on the open bridge during complex tactical operations or when directed by the OOD for indoctrination.

CIC Watch Officer: This officer supervises the operation of the CIC, which reports, tracks, and evaluates air, surface, and submarine contacts during the watch.

Engineering Officer of the Watch (EOOW): The EOOW is the officer or chief petty officer on watch who has been designated by the engineering officer to take charge of the engineering-department watches. The EOOW is responsible for the safe and proper performance of all engineering watches except damage control. The EOOW sees that the engineering log, the engineer's book, and other records are kept properly, and that all orders from the OOD are promptly and properly executed.

Damage-Control Watch Officer: The damage-control watch officer is responsible for maintaining any material condition of readiness in effect on the ship and for checking, repairing, and keeping in full operation the various hull systems. The damage-control watch officer reports directly to the OOD on all

Figure 16–6 A lookout stands watch at the M2 .50-caliber machine-gun station on board a ship on convoy duty in the Persian Gulf.

matters affecting watertight integrity, stability, and other conditions that affect the safety of the ship.

On certain occasions, a *tactical action officer* (TAO) may be assigned by the commanding officer, whose representative the TAO is in all matters concerning the tactical employment and defense of the unit. The TAO is responsible for the safe and proper operation of combat systems. The TAO normally stands watch in CIC and reports directly to the commanding officer.

The numbers and duties of enlisted watchstanders vary according to the type of ship and the operation being carried out. On the bridge, the minimum is helmsman, lee helmsman, quartermaster of the watch (QMOW), boatswain's mate of the watch (BMOW), lookouts, phone talker, and messenger. Depending on the construction of the ship, signalmen will stand their watches on the bridge deck or the signal bridge. Other underway watches—again depending on the ship and operation—include lifebuoy watches, lifeboat watches, and various watches in the CIC, main radio, brig, hangar deck, main engineroom, boiler room, and auxiliary engineroom. (See chapter 17 for the specific duties of these and other enlisted workers.)

WQ&S
Bill

A "bare-bones watch" is sometimes used in conditions III and IV. It consists of the OOD and a helmsman, lookout, quartermaster, and signalman. Ships using the bare-bones watch system are equipped with automatic bell loggers, fog signal timers, and steering devices.

In-Port Watch

The basic in-port peacetime watch (see figure 16-5) is based on condition V. In an emergency or war, additional watches may be required for security, antisabotage, and weapons-systems manning. As in the underway watch, the principal officers are the CDO and OOD. The OOD reports directly to the commanding officer for the safety and general duties of the ship, and to the CDO (the executive officer when a CDO is not assigned) for carrying out the ship's routine. The OOD also carries out the POD, handles honors and ceremonies, conducts routine inspections, observes safety precautions, inspects liberty parties, and prepares the deck log. A JOOD is also assigned in port. Assignment of a JOOW is optional; if assigned, he or she is an additional officer or petty officer on watch for qualification as an in-port OOD.

Other important people in the in-port watch organization include:

Boat Officer: When assigned, the boat officer is responsible to the OOD for the safe and proper operation of his or her boat and the proper conduct of all personnel embarked.

Department Duty Officer: This is the officer or petty officer responsible for the proper functioning of a department. He or she reports to the CDO.

Communications Watch Officer (CWO): The CWO, as a representative of the communications officer, is responsible to the OOD for the reliable, rapid, and secure operation of external, visual, and radio communications (other than tactical and air-control voice radio), and for the efficient administration of internal routing and related communications system.

Some of the enlisted bridge watchstanders—BMOW and messenger—move to the quarterdeck when in port. The signal watch continues on the signal bridge, and most of the engineering watches continue if the ship is providing her own steam, heat, and power. Other important watches include side boys, duty MAA, gangway watch (when required), sergeant of the

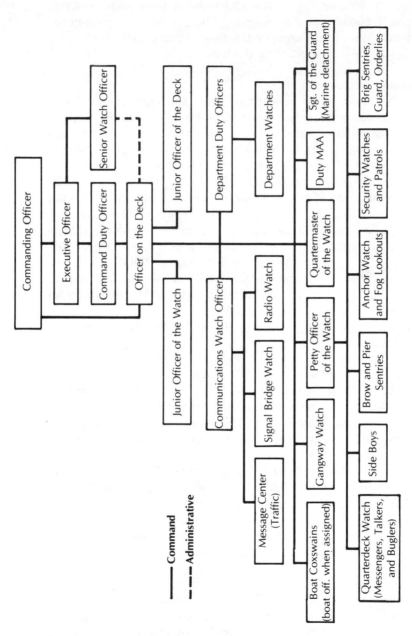

Figure 16–5 Watch organization in port.

—— Command

--- Administrative

guard (when marines are embarked), and various security watches and patrols. (See chapter 17 for details of these other watch assignments.)

Special Evolutions

The movement of a ship—in and out of restricted waters, getting under way, or returning to port—is complex and tedious. Navigation requires a concentrated effort by most of the crew. When a special detail is needed, the captain does what a professional football coach does—calls on the specialty team. In most cases, the special unit supplements the regular watch; in other instances, the special unit relieves the regular watch until the evolution is completed.

Special Sea Detail

Whenever a ship is leaving or returning to a pier or anchorage, the special sea detail is set. Getting a small ship under way or bringing her to anchor can be a fairly simple and quiet operation when the crew are on their toes. But the checklist for getting a big ship under way is like the countdown on a space launch. Each ship has its own list, and preparations may start up to 8 hours in advance of the actual event. There may be literally hundreds of things to do, and responsible sailors see that they are all done properly and promptly.

Those assigned to the special sea detail must be well trained and experienced, for moving a ship into or out of a crowded harbor can be difficult and dangerous. No mistakes are allowed.

Getting Under Way

As stated previously, each type of ship calls for a slightly different list of preparations representing the ideal routine for getting under way. The times listed are the hours prior to the actual event.

Eight Hours: Start gyros. Energize and calibrate all radar repeaters.

Six Hours: Verify schedule for lighting off boilers.

Three Hours: Verify arrangements for discontinuing services from the pier, such as shore power and crane service.

Two Hours: Ascertain from the executive officer (1) whether there is any variation in standard sequence of setting special sea and anchor detail, (2) the time of heaving short or "singling

Figure 16–7   The special sea and anchor detail moor the ship to the buoy.

up" lines, (3) the disposition of boats, (4) instructions concerning U.S. and guard mail, and (5) the number of passengers and expected time of arrival.

After obtaining permission from the executive officer, start hoisting boats and vehicles as soon as they are no longer required and rig in booms and accommodation ladders not in use. Secure for sea. Have the word passed as to when the ship will get under way. Energize all radars except those prohibited by local electromagnetic-emission restrictions.

One and a Half Hours: Muster the crew.

One Hour: Set condition YOKE. MAA inspects for stowaways. Tune and peak radars. Conduct radio checks on all required circuits. Ensure that pit sword is in a raised position.

Forty-five Minutes: Underway OOD, JOOD, and JOOW take stations on bridge. N, A, and E divisions man the after steering and pilot house and test steering engine, controls, communications, and emergency steering alarm. Ship is cleared of all visitors.

Thirty Minutes: Set the special sea and anchor detail. Prepare both anchors for letting go. OOD shifts watch to the bridge. Sound-powered phone circuits are tested. Departmental reports of readiness to get under way are received, as is the MAA report of inspection for stowaways. Draft of the ship, fore and aft, is recorded, and if required, deck-edge antennas are raised.

Fifteen Minutes: The commanding officer's permission is obtained to test main engines. After screws are checked for clearance, engineering control is directed to test engines. Report ready for getting under way to the executive officer. Test whistles. "Heave short" or "single up" lines when ordered. Standby to receive tugs and pilots, and if alongside a pier, ensure that all shore connections are broken and that the brows are ready to be removed. When required, sound "Quarters for leaving port."

Ten Minutes: The command "Maneuvering bells" is ordered by setting the engine-revolution indicator system on a certain repetitive number combination beyond the range of the engines. Warn engineering control to stand by to answer all bells. If a flag officer is embarked, request permission to get under way as scheduled.

Zero Time: Underway.

Entering Port

The schedule for entering port or restricted waters is as follows:

When Directed: Deballast as far in advance as possible and for as long as regulations permit. Pass the word "Go to your stations, all the special sea and anchor detail." Have both anchors ready for letting go prior to arrival at channel entrance. Determine and record fore and aft draft of the ship. Blow tubes. Dump all trash and garbage overboard. Pump bilges when conditions permit, and, subject to the concurrence of the navigator, raise the pit sword. Ensure smart appearance of the ship.

One Hour: Ascertain expected time of anchoring or mooring from the navigator and notify the engineering officer, weapons officer, first lieutenant, and engineering control. Pass the word "Make all preparations for entering port. Ship will anchor (moor——side to) at about——. All hands shift into the uniform of the day." Man depth-determining devices. Weather permitting, remove canvas covers that are normally off when in port. Obtain information concerning boating from executive officer and inform first lieutenant. Lay out mooring lines, if required, and set up and check all harbor and tug radio frequencies.

Thirty Minutes: Sound "Man all boats" as signal of execution for boat crews, winch crews, boathandlers, and boom and gangway rigging details to take their stations. Obtain information from navigator on depth of water at anchorage, and executive officer on the anchor and scope of chain to be used (and inform first lieutenant). When ship is mooring to a pier, inform first lieutenant on the tide and time of high water.

Twenty Minutes: When required, designated personnnel fall in at quarters for entering port. Direct CMAA to inspect upper decks to see that crew is in proper uniform.

Fifteen Minutes: Station in-port deck watches. Instruct to stand by on quarterdeck the guard-mail petty officer, mail clerk, movie operator, shore patrol, and any other details leaving ship in first boat. If ship is mooring to a buoy, lower a motor whaleboat with buoy detail as directed. Stand by to receive tugs and pilots.

On Anchoring or Mooring: Set the in-port watch. Secure main engines, gyros, and navigational radars as directed. Record draft of ship fore and aft.

When sea detail is set, the commanding officer (with an experienced telephone talker), the navigator (with quartermasters), and others are on the bridge, the first lieutenant and anchor detail on the forecastle, the line handlers at stations on the main deck and fantail. Other stations manned include CIC, main engine control, signal bridge, and sonar control.

Logs and Reports

A log is a permanent, written record. The ship's deck log, engineering log, compass record, and engineer's bell book are the official records of a ship. No erasures may be made in any of these logs. When a correction is necessary, a line can be drawn through the original entry so it remains legible and the correct entry inserted. Corrections, additions, or changes in any log are made only by the person required to sign it, and initialed by that person in the margin of the page.

Ship's Deck Log: This is the official chronological record of events occurring during a watch, which may concern the crew, operation, and safety of the ship, or may be of historical value.

The OOD supervises the keeping of the log, and the QMOW (or other designated watchstander) writes the log. Each event is recorded as directed by the OOD or in accordance with standing instructions. All log entries are made with a ballpoint pen, using black ink.

The navigator examines the log daily, and the commanding officer approves it at the end of each month. The original ship's deck log goes to the chief of naval operations every month. A duplicate copy is kept on board for six months, after which it may be destroyed.

Compass Record Book: This is a complete record of the reading of all compasses on board. It also records gyrocompass errors. When the ship is under way, comparisons between compasses are made on every course change and entered in the book.

Engineer's Bell Book: This is kept in the engineroom. It is the official record of the engine orders received from the bridge.

Logs may be consulted many years after they are written—even after the ship has been sunk or scrapped—in connection with claims for pensions by sailors who served in the Navy, or as evidence before courts and other legal bodies. For such reasons, log entries should be complete, accurate, and in standard naval language. Names should be printed, and figures must be recorded carefully. Sample deck-log entries are contained in the Watch Officer's Guide, which should always be available in the quarterdeck or bridge desk.

Daily routine reports are made to the commanding officer at 0800, 1200, and 2000. About 0750 the crew is mustered, the day's orders read, and a report of absentees made to the executive officer by department heads. The results are reported to the captain by the exec.

At 1200, the "12 o'clock reports," which consist of the fuel and water report, magazine temperature report, and 1200 position report, are made to the OOD by the engineer officer, weapons officer, and navigator, respectively. The OOD messenger makes the 12 o'clock report to the commanding officer in similar form:

"Good morning, Captain. The officer of the deck sends his or her respects and reports the hour of 12 o'clock. All chronometers have been wound and compared. Request permission to strike eight bells on time, sir/ma'am." (This procedure will vary from ship to ship, depending on the skipper's instructions.)

Under way, the 8 o'clock reports are made by all department heads at 1930 to the executive officer, who then takes them to the commanding officer. These usually consist of equipment status reports and 2000 position reports. In port, the 8 o'clock reports are made to the CDO by departmental duty officers.

Ship's Bell: Before timepieces were common, time aboard ship was marked by a so-called hourglass, which ran out every 30 minutes. The glass would be turned over to start measuring another 30 minutes, and the bell would be struck so all hands knew a half-hour had passed. At the end of each half-hour, the bell would be struck one more time. Thus it was struck once at the end of the first half-hour and eight times at the end of the fourth hour. This practice still continues despite the use of clocks and watches. After eight bells are struck, the sequence starts all over again. An odd number of bells marks a half-hour, an even number marks an hour. For the relation between Navy time, bells, and watches, see the table below.

Midwatch		Morning Watch		Forenoon Watch		Afternoon Watch		Evening Watch		Night Watch	
Time	Bells	Time	Bells	Time	Bells	Time	Bells	Time	Bells	Time	Bells
0030	1	0430	1	0830	1	1230	1	1630	1	2030	1
0100	2	0500	2	0900	2	1300	2	1700	2	2100	2
0130	3	0530	3	0930	3	1330	3	1730	3	2130	3
0200	4	0600	4	1000	4	1400	4	1800	4	2200	4
0230	5	0630	5	1030	5	1430	5	1830	5	2230	5
0300	6	0700	6	1100	6	1500	6	1900	6	2300	6
0330	7	0730	7	1130	7	1530	7	1930	7	2330	7
0400	8	0800	8	1200	8	1600	8	2000	8	2400	8

370

The bell is struck from reveille to taps, but not during divine services or in fog, when it is used as a fog signal. When the church call is sounded, the bell is struck once at the end of each phase of the call. When the bell is used as a fog signal at anchor, it is rung rapidly for 5 seconds at the end of each minute. On some ships, it is customary for the youngest member of the crew to strike eight bells on New Year's Eve.

Shipboard Duties and Watchstanding

17

There are literally hundreds of different jobs aboard a large ship, each important to her mission. Just as organization and routine are standardized as much as possible throughout the Navy, so are jobs—what you do—and your ship's routine employment. (Shipboard organization is covered in chapter 14, shipboard routine in chapter 16.)

Shipboard Operations

What your ship does depends on what type of ship she is. Most versatile are the warships—aircraft carriers, surface combatants, command ships, and submarines—all of which have many-faceted missions.

Carriers perform a variety of tasks, centered around their most unique feature, the ability to deliver aircraft within striking range of designated targets. Battleships conduct prompt and sustained combat operations worldwide in support of national interests. They operate as part of a carrier battle group or amphibious group; and in areas of lesser threat, they are capable of surface-action-group operations with appropriate antisubmarine warfare (ASW) and antiair escort ships. Destroyers also perform a wide range of duties: they screen carrier task groups, carry out antisubmarine warfare, and provide fire support for amphibious-assault operations. The principal function of cruisers is antiair and antimissile defense of fast-carrier task forces. Submarines are grouped in two general categories based on their primary mission: attack and ballistic missile. Submarines are also assigned secondary missions, which may include surveillance and reconnaissance, direct task-force support, landing-force support, minelaying, and rescue.

In most other cases, the name of the category suggests a ships' primary mission: amphibious warfare, mine warfare,

Shipboard Opera-
tions

Figure 17–1   Crewmen in the flight-deck control and launch operations room move the pieces that represent flight-deck activity aboard the carrier USS *Kitty Hawk* (CV 63).

combatant (which includes patrol, landing, mine-countermeasures, and riverine-warfare craft), auxiliary, and service.

Flight Operations

Flight ops are interesting, exciting, and often dangerous. They require the combined efforts of many people who prepare the planes, brief the pilots, plot the weather, fuel and arm the aircraft, evaluate the results of missions, and interpret photographic findings. Flight quarters for air-department and air-wing-squadron personnel are the general quarters (GQ) stations prescribed in the battle bill.

For a morning launch, aircraft are usually spotted (positioned) on the flight deck the night before. Jet aircraft, which must be catapulted, are spotted forward so they can taxi onto the catapults. The rescue helicopter is usually the first aircraft in the air and the last recovered (brought aboard).

At flight quarters, crewmembers swarm on the flight deck. When the order is given, pilots man their aircraft and start engines. The carrier turns into the wind to increase relative wind speed down the flight deck, and the air officer (also called the air boss) gives the catapult officer (the cat officer) a green light meaning aircraft may be launched. An entire deckload of carrier aircraft can be launched within a few minutes.

Landing aboard a carrier is the most dangerous part of flight
ops. All hands not directly involved must clear the flight deck
and catwalks. Arresting-gear crews raise the arresting-deck
pendants slightly above the deck to engage the aircraft's
tailhook. As the ship steams into the wind, the air boss orders
the optical landing system (made up of mirrors) to be turned
on, and gives the arresting-gear officer the okay to commence
landing operations. Aircraft fly a rectangular pattern on the
port side of the carrier and use the optical landing system in
their approach in order to maintain a constant angle of descent
and correct air speed.

The landing signal officer (LSO), located aft on the port side
of the flight deck, monitors all approaches. If the plane is not
on the glidepath or the deck is not prepared to receive aircraft,
the LSO flashes the pilot a waveoff, at which point the pilot
applies full power, goes around the traffic pattern, and makes
another approach. On a good approach with a clear deck, the
pilot stays on the glidepath until the aircraft touches the deck
and the arresting gear brings the plane to a stop. If it misses the
arresting gear, the pilot can fly off the angled deck and go
around again. (A plane that does this is known as a bolter.)

After all aircraft have landed, they are respotted for the next
launch. Tractors tow them to their final position. When refueling and rearming are complete, the carrier is again ready to
launch aircraft.

Flight-deck and hangar crews wear helmets and jerseys in
the following combinations for quick identification:

Blue and blue	Plane-handling crews, chockmen
Yellow and yellow	Plane-handling officers, directors
White and blue	Elevator operators
Green and green	Arresting-gear and catapult crews, hook runners, maintenance crews, photographers
Green and yellow	Arresting-gear and catapult officers
Red and red	Ordnance, crash and salvage, explosive ordnance disposal (EOD) crews
Purple and purple	Fueling crews
Brown and brown	Plane captains
Red and brown	Helicopter captains
White and white	Medical and transfer officer

| Green and white | Plane inspector |
| White and blue | Messengers and telephone talkers |

You will hear various flight-deck personnel referred to as yellow shirts or red shirts, a reference to their jobs.

Amphibious Operations

The goal of amphibious-warfare operations is the establishment of a military force on an enemy shore. Marines are normally included in landing operations, and very often units from all the armed forces take part.

A modern amphibious landing is a complicated operation that may involve hundreds of ships and small craft and thousands of men. Planning for such an operation may take months. After planning is completed, an operation order (OPORD) is issued. This covers organization, ships and units assigned, communications, minesweeping, naval gunfire and bombardment, air strikes, actual assault operations, and logistics. There will be training operations, perhaps even a full-scale rehearsal, before the actual amphibious operation takes place.

374

Antisubmarine-Warfare Operations

The basic ASW mission is to deny the enemy the effective use of his submarines. The U.S. Navy's destroyers and many helicopter and fixed-wing aircraft are specifically designed for ASW. In addition, most of our major American warships have an ASW capability. ASW operations entail protective and offensive phases. Protective ASW includes escorting merchant convoys and carrier task forces; offensive ASW includes strike operations, missions designed to search out and destroy submarines. The principal ASW weapons are torpedoes, antisubmarine rockets (ASROCs), submarine rockets (SUBROCs), and the light airborne multipurpose system (LAMPS).

Sonar is the principal instrument used to detect submarines. Active sonar signals, sent out by a transmitter unit, are reflected off the submarine and returned to their source. This type of sonar is called pinging, from the noise the transmitter makes. Another type, called passive sonar, keys into the signals or noises emitted by underwater vessels. Sonar is used by surface ships, submarines, and aircraft to detect and pinpoint enemy submarines. Helicopters hunt submarines by hovering

Shipboard
Opera-
tions

Figure 17–2 The Marine Corps's experimental vehicle LACH (lightweight amphibious container handler) removes an Army MilVan from an assault craft. In the background, a crane on the Navy's new elevated causeway removes a MilVan from another assault craft.

in one spot and lowering a cable holding a transducer (transmitter and receiving unit) into the water. Fixed-wing aircraft drop expendable sonobuoys equipped with radio hydrophones that pick up the broadcast underwater sounds. Patrol planes also use the magnetic anomaly detection device (MAD) to sweep a wide path.

Shipboard Duties

A compartment cleaner does the same job on a destroyer as on a nuclear-powered aircraft carrier. The Navy's various ships all go through the same cycle—repair, post-repair trials, underway training, deployment, upkeep, and material and military inspection—which requires similar if not identical work from Navy personnel.

A day's work aboard ship involves professional and military duties. "Turn to on ship's work" means that you carry out the professional duties of your rating. During general drills and on watch, you may perform both general military assignments and professional duties. (Duties of the various ratings are described in chapter 2. General bills and drills are detailed in chapter 19.

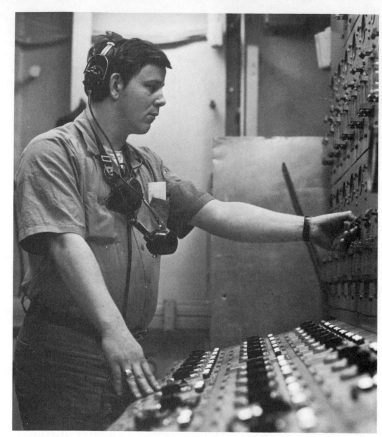

Figure 17–3 A USS *Coronado* crewman prepares to flood the ballast tanks, allowing amphibious craft to enter the ship's well deck.

The daily routine, at sea and in port, also requires people on duty at all times as watchstanders—see details in chapter 16.)

Enlisted Watchstanders

A ship in commission can never be left unattended. Boilers must be kept fired, except during overhaul and standdown periods, water and electricity systems maintained, and magazines and other vital equipment guarded. At sea, the various stations must be adequately manned. All these functions are carried out 24 hours a day, not just 0900 to 1700.

The watch system—divided into two parts, under way and inport—is detailed in chapter 16. Some key assignments for officers in the watch organization include the command duty officer (CDO), officer of the deck (OOD), junior officer of the deck (JOOD), and junior officer of the watch (JOOW). There are also a number of important assignments for enlisted watch-standers in the top echelon. (In fact, many senior petty officers qualify for officers' assignments.) While there are scores of other enlisted watch assignments, those described below are the most important and responsible jobs. The majority of other enlisted watchstanders report to, or through, these sailors.

Underway Watch Section

The two basic enlisted watches in the underway section are deck watches and navigational watches. The boatswain's mate of the watch (BMOW) is the petty officer of the watch (POOW). The BMOW's principal assistants include sky and surface lookouts, a messenger, bridge sound-powered-telephone talkers, a lifeboat watch, life-buoy and after lookouts, and fog lookouts. The navigational portion of the watch includes the quartermaster of the watch (QMOW), helmsman, lee helmsman, and aft steering watch.

Boatswain's Mate of the Watch: The BMOW is the OOD's most important assistant. His or her status is the same—regardless of the readiness condition in effect or the watch (sea or in port) that has been set. It is his or her responsibility that all deck watch stations are manned and that all hands in previous watch sections are relieved. Although it is the duty of the section leader and the division petty officer to instruct the people they send on watch, the BMOW must verify that every person on watch has been properly instructed and trained. A BMOW must be a qualified helmsman.

Sky and Surface Lookouts: Lookouts, who are trained in their duties by the combat information center (CIC) officer, perform their duties in accordance with the ship's lookout doctrine. Navy regulations require that night lookouts report on the navigational lights every half hour. By tradition, the starboard lookout reports, "Starboard side light, masthead light, bright lights, sir"; the port lookout reports, "Portside light, range light, bright lights, sir." (Details of specific lookout duties and techniques are covered in chapter 23.)

Messenger: The messenger stands watch on the bridge. The messenger delivers messages, answers telephones, and carries out other duties assigned by the OOD. The messenger normally comes from the weapons or deck department.

Figure 17–4 Sound-powered phones are an essential part of shipboard communications and control. Telephone talkers must speak clearly, be specific, and act businesslike.

Bridge Sound-Powered-Telephone Talkers: The JV talker mans the JV circuit on the bridge and must be familiar with other stations on the circuit. The JV relays all messages between the OOD and these stations; this includes forwarding all orders to the engine-order telegraph. The JV talker is normally a helmsman under instruction and is assigned from the weapons or deck department. The JL/JS talker mans the JL/JS bridge phones. The JL/JS has the same responsibilities for receiving and relaying information as the JV talker. The JL/JS talker is normally assigned from the operations department. (The use of sound-powered phones is described in chapter 24.)

Lifeboat Watches: Each ship must be capable of rapidly recovering personnel from the sea. Lifeboat watches are set as necessary to ensure this capability. The ship's maneuvering characteristics and the nature of her operations, sea conditions, and the availability of rescue helicopters are some of the factors that are considered when establishing the readiness required for lifeboat watches. Although lifeboat watches are not necessarily required for lifeboat stations, crews are always designated when at sea and are mustered as required.

Lifebuoy and After Lookout: This watch is stationed at a designated after station. The watchstander has a life ring and must be on the lookout for personnel overboard. In addition, he or she mans sound-powered phones and checks communications with the bridge every half hour. During periods of low visibility, this watchstander is augmented by the phone talker.

Fog Lookouts: Stationed during periods of low visibility, the watch is stood where approaching ships can best be seen or heard. The fog lookout must also be in communication with the OOD and is normally assisted by a phone talker.

Quartermaster of the Watch (QMOW): Assigned from the navigation department, the QMOW maintains the ship's log and assists the OOD in navigational matters, including changes of weather and the movement of shipping. This watchstander is a qualified helmsman.

Helmsman: The helmsman, also called the steersman, is normally assigned from the weapons or deck department. His or her qualifications must be recorded in the service record. The helmsman steers courses prescribed by the conning officer.

Lee Helmsman: This person stands watch at the engine-order telegraph on the bridge and rings up the conning officer's orders to the engines, ensuring that all bells are correctly answered. He or she must also be a qualified steersman. The lee helmsman is normally assigned from the weapons or deck department.

Aft Steering: This watch is stationed in after steering to line up and operate steering engines as directed by the OOD and to take over steering control in the event of a steering casualty. This watch, normally stood by a machinist's mate (MM) or electrician's mate (EM), must be qualified to shift steering units and handle emergencies in connection with this equipment.

In-Port Watch Section

Although the in-port watch is similar to the underway watch, there are some significant differences. Most importantly, the location of the in-port watch's primary station is shifted from the bridge to the quarterdeck. When the need arises, enlisted personnel may be designated as quarterdeck watch officers. The section is generally headed by the petty officer of the watch, although these duties are sometimes carried out by the BMOW. The remainder of the watch section consists of messenger, side boys, duty masters-at-arms (duty MAAs), the gangway watch, and various security watches and patrols.

Quarterdeck Watch Officer: This is one of the most responsible job an enlisted man or woman can have. It is provided for
by article 1003, U.S. Navy Regulations, as follows:

When the number of commissioned or warrant officers qualified for watchstanding is reduced to the extent that it might
interfere with the proper operation of the command or cause
undue hardship, the commanding officer may assign petty officers or noncommissioned officers to duty in charge of a watch
or to stand a day's duty, subject to any restrictions imposed by
a senior in the chain of command or by navy regulations. There
should be no confusion as to the official status of these petty
officers. They are officers of the deck, subject only to the
orders of the commanding officer, executive officer, and CDO.
The assignment of petty officers as OODs is made in writing
either in the ship's organization book, the senior watch officer's watch list, or in the plan of the day (POD).

Petty Officer of the Watch: The POOW is the OOD's primary
enlisted assistant in port. He or she supervises and instructs
sentries and messengers, and carries out the daily routine and
orders as the OOD directs. When neither the OOD nor the
JOOW is at the gangway, the POOW returns salutes, calls
away boats in sufficient time to ensure they are ready to leave
the ship at the time prescribed in the boat schedule, keeps a list
of persons who may be expected to be absent on duty from the
ship (and notifies the duty ship's cook of the approximate time
they will return for meals), and assembles liberty parties for
inspection by the OOD. If a QMOW is not assigned, the
POOW also notifies the OOD and JOOW of any changes in
weather or barometric pressure (readings are taken by the messenger), and requires the messenger to make calls listed in the
call book that is kept on the quarterdeck.

Messenger: The OOD messengers stand a 4-hour watch with
the OOD and JOOD. They should be familiar with various
departments of the ship and key ship's-company personnel.

Side Boys: Side boys are stationed for rendering formal honors. They are mustered, inspected, and instructed in their duties by the BMOW or POOW. (Their duties are described on
pp. 100–101.)

Gangway Watch: When required, the gangway watchstander is posted at the foot of the brow or gangway. This person
performs duties as directed by the OOD, which normally in-

clude maintaining security of the brow and ceremonial functions.

Security Watches and Patrols: Besides the watches described elsewhere in this chapter, other security watches and
patrols may be prescribed by the commanding officer to increase the physical security of the ship. Personnel assigned to
such watches are trained and qualified by the appropriate department heads. Duties include making hourly reports to the
OOD; checking classified stowage, being alert for evidence of
sabotage, theft, and fire hazard; checking the security of weapons magazines; obtaining periodic soundings of tanks and
spaces; and periodically inspecting damage-control closures.

Quartermaster of the Watch: When assigned, the QMOW
performs duties assigned by the OOD. These include maintaining the deck log, handling absentee pennants, checking anchor
and riding lights, hailing boats, and assisting in the rendering of
honors. The QMOW takes bearings (when at anchor) and temperature and barometer readings, keeping the OOD informed.
He or she also maintains a call book. (When a QMOW is not
assigned, the duties of this watch are carried out by the duty
quartermaster, the POOW, or a messenger of the watch.)

Anchor Watch: When the ship is at anchor, this watch is
stationed according to instructions from the captain. The
watchstander is posted in the immediate vicinity of the ground
tackle and maintains a continuous watch on the anchor chain
to observe the strain and how the chain is tending. Conditions
are reported to the OOD every half hour (or more often if
directed by the OOD). The anchor watch must communicate
rapidly and continuously with the OOD.

Deck and Engineering Logs

Although numerous records are kept by watch sections, four
sets of logs have significant official and historical purposes.
They are the deck log, the magnetic compass record, the engineering log, and the engineer's bell book.

The deck log is a daily record, made by watches, describing
every circumstance of interest concerning the crew and ship.
Information recorded includes operating orders, changes in
sea state or weather, courses and speeds, the ship's position,
the bearing and distance of objects and other ships, the tactical
formation of ships in company, the draft, soundings, the zone
description, and particulars of anchoring and mooring. The

deck log also records changes in the status of ship's personnel or passengers (except for transfers and receipts); damage or accident to ship, cargo, or equipment; death or injuries to personnel, passengers, visitors, longshoremen, harbor workers, or repairmen; and arrests, suspensions, and restorations to duty.

The log, written by the QMOW, is supervised by the OOD, who signs the log after the last entry made during his or her watch. The ship's navigator examines the log daily to see that it is properly kept, and he or she certifies it on a monthly basis. Then at the end of each month the commanding officer approves the log by signature.

The log is prepared according to a form prescribed by the chief of naval operations (CN). The log may not be filled out under two specific circumstances: (1) when designated ships are conducting special operations directed by the CNO, and (2) when a ship is undergoing a scheduled period of regular overhaul, conversion, or inactivation. In these cases, "noteworthy events" are recorded as they occur; daily entries are not made.

The magnetic compass record contains all readings of the magnetic compass. It also records errors of the ship's gyro compass. While the ship is under way, compass comparisons are made and entered every half hour (or whenever a new course is set). One magnetic compass is compared with the master gyrocompass or the ship's course indicator, used for steering. Compass comparisons are not required at half hour intervals when the ship is involved in emergency operations or when frequent changes occur, as in harbor maneuvering.

Signed and submitted to the commanding officer on the last day of every quarter, the magnetic compass record is the responsibility of the navigator.

The engineering log is a daily watch record of important events or data pertaining to the engineering department and to the operation of the ship's propulsion plant. It includes average hourly speed in revolutions and knots; total number of miles steamed for the day; draft and displacement; amounts of fuel, water, and lubricating oil on hand, received, or expended; disposition and changes of engines, boilers, and principal auxiliaries; and injuries to personnel and material casualties in the department.

Prepared according to COMNAVSEASYSCOM (commander, Naval Sea Systems Command) the engineering log is signed by the engineering officer.

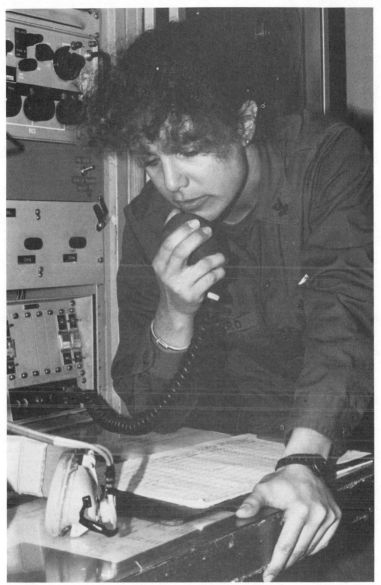

Figure 17–5 A duty air-traffic controller relays weather information to a pilot flying over McMurdo Station, Antarctica.

The engineer's bell book is a chronological record of engine-speed orders. It shows when an order for directing a propeller speed for each shaft is received, the meaning of the order, and the corresponding revolutions per minute. Ships and craft equipped with controllable-pitch propellers also record propeller pitch for each signaled change in speed. Shaft counter readings are recorded on getting under way, then hourly thereafter, and finally when the engine is shut down. All other entries are made at the time of receipt. The throttleman makes the entries in this book.

Departmental Watches

Many other watches may be introduced on your ship. The decision to initiate watches rests with the type commander and commanding officer. The following list contains some of the more common ones and, where necessary, a brief description of the duties involved:

Air Department: The air-department watch, air-department integrity watch, aviation-fuel security watch, conflagration-station watch, flight-deck security watch, and hangar-deck security watch are all carrier watches. They are stood by personnel from embarked squadrons or detachments and from the ship's V division company. In addition, the department may have a person from each of the rating specialty groups, for example, the duty AM (aviation structural mechanic) and the duty AD, sometimes called the duty mech (aviation machinist's mate).

Engineering Department: Watches include auxiliary engineering, damage control, electrical equipment, engineroom, fireroom, and sounding and security patrol.

Engineroom watches generally consist of lower level, upper level, evaporator, shaft alley and throttle watches. The pumpman is in charge of the lower-level watch and is responsible for maintaining a considerable number of pumps—main lube oil, lube-oil coolers, main condenser, main feed, main-feed booster and fire pipes—as well as other auxiliary machinery. Duties on the upper-level watch include recording periodic temperature and pressure readings, making valve adjustments to correct slight variations, and reporting unusual conditions. The shaft-alley watch inspects all equipment for proper lubrication and temperature and sees that the shaft-alley bilge is pumped. The evaporator watch must constantly check the pressure, temper-

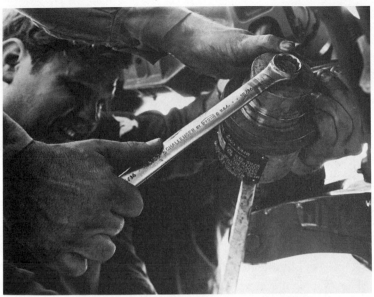

Figure 17–6 Duty aviation mechanics team up to change the flight-control bearing on a helicopter.

ature, vacuum, and salt content of sea water being distilled by evaporators. The throttleman must have knowledge of all gauges, instruments, and indicators on the throttle board. The throttleman also logs speed changes in the engineer's bell book.

Fireroom watches usually include a burnerman, blowerman, and checkman. The burnerman maintains steam pressure by cutting burners in or out or by regulating their fuel-oil pressure. The blowerman is responsible for operating the forced-draft blowers that supply combustion air to the boiler. It is important that the burnerman and blowerman cooperate with each other—both are concerned with the combustion of the fuel oil. The checkman is responsible for operating the feed-stop and feed-check valves. This is the checkman's only job, and it requires full attention. (In some ships equipped with automatic feedwater controls, a checkman is not needed.)

The sounding and security patrol—a continuous patrol of unmanned spaces below decks—is stood on most ships from the end of the working day until 0800 the next day. On larger ships, the watch is stood around the clock. Watchstanders are responsible for maintaining the proper condition of material readiness by checking all watertight air ports, doors, hatches, scuttles, and other damage-control fittings. Besides making hourly reports to the POOW or BMOW, watchstanders frequently relay the report of the cold-iron watch (discussed on p. 130).

The engineering department has boat engineers, although they do not necessarily constitute a watch. The department also has various rating specialties, such as duty HT (hull technician), duty IC (interior communications electrician), duty MM (machinist's mate), and duty EN (engineman).

Two other watches are unique to engineering: the "oil king" and the "freshwater king." The oil king is a petty officer assigned to keep records of fuel oil, make tank soundings, and assist when taking on fuel. The freshwater king is another name for the evaporator watchstander.

Executive Department: The duty master-at-arms (MAA) is one of the principal watches of this department. The duty MAA is a regular member of the MAA force who stands watch under the direction of the executive officer. On ships without Marines, he or she also performs the duties of the sergeant of the guard. This watchstander is responsible for posting and supervising the performance of brig sentries and orderlies.

In port, the executive department normally assigns several duty drivers. Other common departmental watches include a duty YN (yeoman) or duty PN (personnelman). On aircraft carriers there may also be a duty JO (journalist).

Navigation Department: Besides providing personnel for QMOW and bridge and signal watches, navigation also has many responsibilities in special evolutions—for example, the sea and anchor detail. The department also has a fog-signal watch and a gyrocompass watch. At other times the department assigns a duty QM and duty SM (signalman).

Operations/Communications Department: Besides supplying a variety of watchstanders serving under the CIC watch officer, this department has a guard-mail petty officer, a radio watch, a signal watch, and a telephone switchboard watch. Operations/communications also has personnel on duty representing their specialties, such as an RM (radioman), a PH (photographer's mate), or an AG (aerographer's mate).

Weapons/Deck Department: Besides duty-boat crews and deck, forecastle, and fantail sentries, the weapons/deck department is also responsible for providing and training the ship's helmsmen and lee helmsmen. This department also has an ordnance security patrol.

The ordnance security patrol watch is composed of the magazine and battery security patrols. Operating under the gunnery officer, the patrol inspects and reports every half hour to the OOD on the security of magazines, ready rooms, hoists, ordnance shops, radar-control rooms, guns, and directors.

Other Departments: The ship's medical/dental department has a duty HM (hospital corpsman) and a duty DT (dental technician); the supply department has a duty SK (storekeeper), a duty MS (mess management specialist), a duty SH (ship's serviceman), and on occasion, a duty DK (disbursing clerk). In the supply department, the person in charge of the provision issue room is traditionally known as the jack o' the dust.

Each division within a department has a division police petty officer (DPPO), who is an assistant to the ship's MAA. He or she performs duties in the part of the ship for which his or her division is responsible. The DPPO makes taps and reveille in the division's spaces, turns standing lights on at sunset and off at reveille, and during drills directs traffic and clears the compartments. When the commanding officer designates the posting of the antisneak/antiswimmer attack watch, a number of departments may be called upon to contribute personnel. This watch normally consists of topside sentries, a picket-boat crew, a sonar operator, and main-engine personnel.

Sometimes departments may be called on to furnish orderlies and sentries. On ships with marines, the marines stand orderly watches. Otherwise the executive officer assigns sailors to this duty. Orderlies may be assigned to flag officers or commanding officers of large ships. Their duties are much the same as those of messengers.

Personnel posted as sentries must know the general orders. (See pp. 108–10.) All sentries posted for security reasons are guided by written instructions that specify the limits of the post, steps to be taken in case of an alarm or breach of security, specific instructions on how and when to use assigned arms (rifle, nightstick, etc.), and requirements for periodic inspections and reports to the OOD. Some of the most common sentry assignments are fantail, forecastle, and pier sentry.

Another common assignment is brig sentry. The watch is maintained by personnel of the MAA force or by personnel assigned from departments with people in the brig.

When a ship moves alongside a repair ship or tender or into a naval shipyard and is receiving power from these activities, a security and fire watch is usually set by each department. The watch is commonly called the cold-iron watch. Each cold-iron watch makes frequent inspections to see that there are no fire hazards, that there are no unauthorized persons in the area, that all spaces are cleaned, and that no tools, rags, gear, and the like are left adrift. The watch reports hourly to the OOD.

Enlisted Detail

Although not a watch in the strictest sense, man overboard should be considered a permanent watch, to be stood by all hands at all times. It is everyone's responsibility to be constantly on the lookout for a shipmate overboard. If someone goes overboard, you must sound the alarm immediately.

Many jobs involve work and responsibilities not covered by a particular rating. Personnel may be assigned to these jobs by a division officer, a department head, or the executive officer.

Perhaps best known are the duty assignments of the messman (or more commonly, mess cook) and the compartment cleaner. Generally, personnel assigned these duties do not stand watches but take part in all drills. There are also assignments to the beach guard and shore patrol (SP). The beach guard are responsible for the in-port control of boat traffic and help maintain order at a fleet landing during liberty hours. The SP assist naval personnel ashore on leave or liberty and maintain order and discipline.

Other nonspecific enlisted rating assignments are master chief petty officer of the Navy (MCPON), master chief petty officer of the fleet or force (F M/C), and master chief petty officer of the command (C M/C)—or on submarines, chief of the boat (COB). Others, when qualified, may be assigned as career counselors, as Navy recruiter/canvassers, recruit company commanders, or to counseling and assistance jobs within the human-resource-management support system (HRMSS). These are discussed in chapter 9.

Damage Control and Firefighting

18

A ship's ability to do her job may someday depend on her crew's damage-control response. Damage control covers firefighting, lost watertight integrity resulting from battle damage, collision or grounding, and restoring damaged piping systems to enable the ship to carry out her assigned mission. The objectives of damage control are as follows:

Preventing damage by making the ship watertight and air tight, maintaining reserve buoyancy and stability, removing fire hazards, and ensuring that emergency equipment is ready.

Keeping the damage from spreading, while helping those who are hurt.

Repairing and restoring damaged equipment, which includes supplying emergency power.

389

Damage-Control Organization

The damage-control assistant (DCA) works under the engineering officer and is responsible for preventing and repairing damage, training the crew in damage control, and caring for equipment and piping systems assigned to the organization.

There are two damage-control organizations. One is a vital part of the engineering department. The other is the damage-control battle organization, which varies depending on the size, type, and mission of a ship. The latter organization includes damage-control central (DCC) and repair parties.

On large ships, the department damage-control chief petty officer (DDCCPO), a qualified chief petty officer, coordinates the relieving, qualifying, training, and duties of division damage-control petty officers (DDCPOs) as directed by the DCA and fire marshal. Section leaders are designated as duty DDCPOs outside normal working hours in port.

DDCPOs and their duty counterparts do the following:

DC Organization

Teach division sailors damage control, firefighting, and chemical-biological-radiological (CBR) warfare defense procedures.

Maintain compartment checkoff lists and the setting of specified material conditions of readiness within their division spaces.

Perform preventive maintenance on selected damage-control systems and equipment, portable firefighting equipment, and access closures (doors, hatches, scuttles) within their division spaces.

Inspect division spaces daily for fire hazards and cleanliness.

Battle Organization

Battle organization includes battle dressing stations (BDSs) and DCC repair parties for hull, propulsion, electronics, weapons, and air. DCC is the battle station for the DCA.

DCC uses a variety of administrative tools to keep track of casualties. These include the following:

Charts and diagrams that show the subdivisions of the ship and her systems.

A casualty board to visualize damage and any corrective action in progress (based on repair-party reports).

A stability board to show liquid loading, the location of flooding boundaries, the effect on list and trim, and the corrective action taken.

A list of access routes for ready shelter, deep shelter, electronic casualty control, and BDSs.

Graphic displays to record corrective damage control and electrical systems.

Deck plans to indicate areas contaminated by CBR agents, the location of BDSs and decontamination stations, and safe routes to them.

Repair Parties

Repair parties are the DCA's representatives at the scene of casualties or damage. They are the primary units in the damage-control organization. Parties may be subdivided to allow personnel to cover a greater area more rapidly, and to prevent loss of the entire party from a single hit.

The number and ratings of personnel assigned to a repair party as specified in the battle bill, are determined by the location of the station, the size of the area assigned to that station, and the total number of personnel available for all stations. Each repair party will usually have an officer or chief petty officer in charge, a scene leader to supervise all on-scene activities (who also functions as the assistant repair-party leader), a phone talker, an OBA (oxygen-breathing apparatus) person, and messengers. Additional personnel include petty officers and nonrated persons from various departments, such as electrician's mates (EMs), hull technicians (HTs), storekeepers (SKs), and hospital corpsmen (HMs).

Repair parties and teams are designated as follows:

Repair 1: Main-deck repair. Comprised of deck petty officers and nonrated persons, SKs, radiomen (RMs), EMs, HMs, and aviation details (except on aircraft carriers). Engineering petty officers may also be required.

Repair 2: Forward repair. Comprised of petty officers of the deck and engineering branches, EMs, SKs, HMs, and nonrated personnel.

Repair 3: After repair. Similar to repair 2.

Repair 4: Amidship repair. Similar to repair 2.

Repair 5: Propulsion repair. Comprised of an engineering officer or chief and a broad cross section of engineering ratings. Assignment to this unit is based more on fireroom/engineroom takeover qualifications than on damage-control qualifications.

Repair 6: Ordnance repair. Comprised of gunner's mates, fire-control technicians, and EMs. This party is sometimes divided into forward and after groups.

Repair 7: Gallery deck and island structure repair. This unit is used primarily on aircraft carriers and other ship types where it is needed. It consists of personnel from air, engineering, damage control, and other areas.

Repair 8: Electronics repair. Comprised of electronics, sonar, and fire-control technicians—ETs, STs, and FTs—as well as EMs. This party works under electronics casualty control.

Aviation-fuel repair teams and *crash and salvage teams* are peculiar to aircraft carriers and ships equipped for manned helicopter operations. On carriers, the teams consist of air department personnel. On ships equipped for helo operations the appropriate deck, engineering, and damage-control personnel are assigned.

The ordnance disposal team is made up of specially trained personnel, deployed aboard ships as required. The team is administered as a unit of the weapons department.

All ships except submarines, patrol and yard craft, minecraft, and small auxiliaries maintain at least one *at-sea fire-fighting team.* A smaller ship whose complement is not large enough to warrant formation of such a team may organize a fire party as appropriate.

Within each repair party there are hose teams; dewatering, plugging, and patching teams; investigation teams; shoring, pipe repair, structural repair, casualty power, interior-communications (IC) repair, and electrical repair teams; chemical detection, biological sampling, radiological monitoring, and CBR decontamination teams; and stretcher bearers.

Every man in the repair party should be able to perform effectively on any team.

Functions of Repair Parties

In general, repair parties must be capable of the following:

Maintaining watertight integrity.

Maintaining the ship's structural integrity.

Controlling and extinguishing all types of fires.

Giving first aid and transporting the injured to BDSs without seriously reducing the damage-control capabilities of the party.

Detecting, identifying, and measuring dosage and intensity of radiation, as well as carrying out decontamination procedures.

Evaluating and reporting correctly on the extent of damage in an area.

Besides general functions, certain repair parties are also responsible for the following:

Maintaining the ship's propulsion (repair 5).

Protecting ordnance and magazines (repair 6), and maintaining deck and hangar bays in aircraft carriers (repair 7, plus the crash and salvage team and the explosive ordnance disposal [EOD] team).

Maintaining electronics equipment on certain ships (repair 8).

Protecting exposed ordnance (EOD team).

Each repair party has an officer or senior petty officer in charge. The second in charge of a repair party is also a petty officer, qualified in damage control and capable of supervising the party. The DCA holds continuing drills in firefighting, flooding, collision, communications, and battle casualties.

Equipment and Facilities

Damage-control equipment is stowed in repair lockers. It includes patches for ruptured water and steam lines, broken seams, and the hull; plugs made of soft wood for stopping the flow of liquids in a damaged hull or in broken lines; soft-wood wedges for shoring; radiological defense equipment; an electrical repair kit for isolating damaged circuits and restoring power; and tools for forcible entry, such as axes, crowbars, wrecking bars, claw tools, hacksaws, bolt cutters, and oxyacetylene cutting torches. The equipment is reserved for damage control only and should never be removed for any other purpose.

Most ships have at least two BDSs equipped to handle personnel casualties. They're manned by medical personnel and are located so that stretcher cases may be brought directly to them by the repair party. Emergency supplies of medical equipment are also placed in first-aid boxes throughout the ship.

At least two *decontamination stations* are provided in widely separated parts of the ship, preferably near BDSs. Decontamination stations differ from ship to ship, but the basic requirements are the same. To prevent recontamination of personnel and ship locations, each station is divided into two areas: a clean section and a contaminated or unclean section with a washing area. Stations are manned by medical and repair-party personnel to ensure that proper decontamination procedures are followed.

Communication is vital to the damage-control organization. Without it the entire organization could fall apart. Normal communications include battle telephone (sound-powered) circuits, interstation two-way systems (the 4MC circuit), ship's service telephones, the ship's general announcing system (the 1MC circuit), and messengers. (See chapter 24.)

Compartmentation

The success of damage control depends partly on the proper use of watertight integrity equipment. Each ship is divided into compartments to control flooding, withstand CBR attacks, segregate activities, provide underwater protection with tanks and voids, strengthen the structure of the ship, and control buoyancy and stability.

Every Navy ship is divided by decks and bulkheads, both above and below the waterline, into as many watertight compartments as possible. In general, the more extensive a ship's compartmentation, the greater her resistance to sinking. Original watertight integrity, established when the ship is built, may be reduced or destroyed by enemy action, storms, collisions, or negligence.

Material Conditions of Readiness

These refer to the degree of access into an area and the system of closing hatches and other openings to limit damage. Maximum closure is not always maintained because it would interfere with the normal operation of the ship. For damage-control purposes, Navy ships have three material conditions of readiness, each representing a different degree of tightness and protection. They are X-RAY, YOKE, and ZEBRA. These titles are used in all spoken and written communications concerning material conditions.

Condition X-RAY provides the least protection. It is set when the ship is in no danger of attack, such as when she is at anchor in a well-protected harbor or secured at home base during regular working hours. During this condition, all closures marked with a black X or a circled X are secured; they remain closed when setting conditions YOKE and ZEBRA.

Condition YOKE provides somewhat more protection than condition X-RAY; YOKE is set and maintained at sea. In port, it is maintained at all times during war, and at times outside of regular working hours in peacetime. YOKE closures, marked with a black Y or a circled Y, are secured during conditions YOKE and ZEBRA.

Condition ZEBRA is set before going to sea or when entering port during war. It is set immediately, without further orders, when general quarters (GQ) stations are manned. Condition ZEBRA is also set to localize and control fire and flooding when GQ stations are unmanned. When condition ZEBRA is warranted, all closures marked with a red Z, a circled red Z, or a red Z within a black D, are secured.

Once the material condition is set, no fitting marked X-RAY, CIRCLE X-RAY, YOKE, CIRCLE YOKE, ZEBRA, CIRCLE ZEBRA or DOG ZEBRA may be opened without permission of the commanding officer (through the DCA or officer of the deck).

Special-purpose fitting markings allow modifications of the three basic conditions as follows:

CIRCLE X-RAY and CIRCLE YOKE fittings may be opened without special permission when going to or from GQ, when transferring ammunition, or when operating vital systems during GQ. The fittings must be secured when not in use.

CIRCLE ZEBRA fittings may be opened during prolonged periods of GQ, when the condition is modified. Opening these fittings enables personnel to prepare and distribute battle rations, open limited sanitary facilities, and ventilate battle stations, and it provides access from ready rooms to the flight deck. When open, the fittings must be guarded for immediate closure if necessary.

DOG ZEBRA fittings, secured during condition ZEBRA, are also secured separately during "darken ship" conditions. The DOG ZEBRA classification applies to weather accesses not equipped with light switches or light traps.

WILLIAM fittings, marked with a black W, are kept open during all material conditions. This classification applies to vital sea-suction valves supplying main and auxiliary condensers, fire pumps, and accesses to spaces that are manned during condition ZEBRA. It also applies to vital ship valves that, if secured, would impair the mobility and fire protection of the ship.

CIRCLE WILLIAM fittings, marked with a circled black W, are normally kept open but must be secured against CBR attack. Remember: It is the responsibility of all hands to maintain the material condition in effect. If it is necessary to break the condition, permission must be obtained (from the officer of the deck or DCC). A closure log is maintained in DCC at all times to show where the existing condition has been broken; the number, type, and classification of fittings involved; the name, rate, and division of the man or women requesting permission to open or close a fitting; and the date a fitting was opened or closed.

The number of times and circumstances in which DCC may give permission to break watertight integrity is determined by the commanding officer.

Watertight Integrity

The purpose of damage control is to keep the ship watertight. She may sustain a great deal of damage, but with proper watertight integrity, she will remain afloat.

All doors, hatches, scuttles, and manholes giving access to compartments must be securely "dogged," or closed down. Manhole covers to double bottoms should always be bolted except for inspection, cleaning, or painting. They must never be left open overnight or when crews are not actually working in them.

Watertight doors and hatches will work longer and require less maintenance if they are properly closed and opened. When closing a door, first set up a dog opposite the hinges,

Figure 18–1   An outside view of a quick-acting eight-dog watertight door.

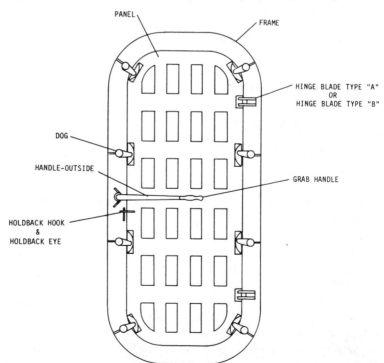

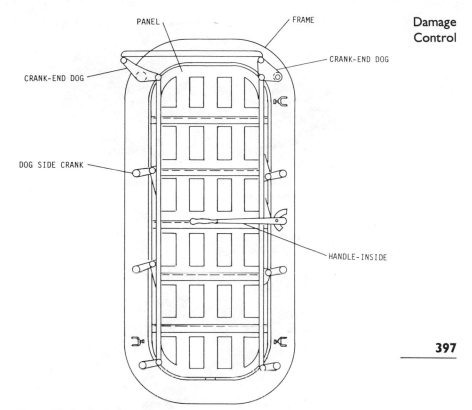

Figure 18–2 An inside view of a quick-acting eight-dog watertight door.

with just enough pressure to keep the door shut. Then set the other dogs evenly to obtain uniform pressure all around. When opening a door, start with the dogs nearest the hinges. This procedure will keep the door from springing and make it easier to operate the remaining dogs.

When the ship sustains damage, watertight doors, hatches, scuttles, and manholes should be opened only after making sure that the compartment is dry or has little flooding, so that there won't be more flooding when the closures are opened. They should never be opened without DCC permission. Extreme caution is always necessary in opening compartments below the waterline, near damage.

Types of Closures

The strongest doors are classified as *watertight (WT) doors*. They are used in watertight bulkheads or lower-deck compart-

Compart-
mentation

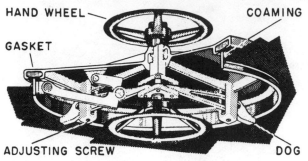

HAND WHEEL

COAMING

GASKET

ADJUSTING SCREW

DOG

Figure 18–3 This cutaway section of an escape shuttle shows quick-acting handwheels above and below.

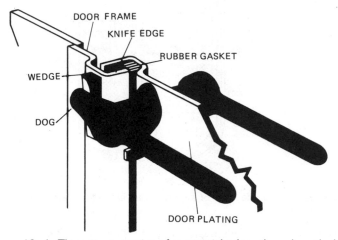

DOOR FRAME

KNIFE EDGE

RUBBER GASKET

WEDGE

DOG

DOOR PLATING

398

Figure 18–4 This cutaway section of a watertight door shows how the knife edge sits up against the rubber gasket for a tight seal.

ments and are designed to resist the same amount of pressure as the bulkheads. Some doors have dogs that must be individually closed and opened. Others, known as *quick-acting watertight doors*, have handles that operate all dogs simultaneously.

Nonwatertight (NWT) doors, used in nonwatertight bulkheads, usually do not have dogs.

Airtight doors (AT) are also flame-tight and fire retarding. When used in air locks, they usually have lever-type quick-acting closures. Others usually have individually operated dogs.

Passing scuttles may be placed in doors through which ammunition is passed. These are small tubelike openings, watertight and flashproof.

Joiner doors are ordinary shore-type metal doors to provide privacy for state rooms, wardrooms, etc.

Hatches are horizontal doors used for access through decks. A hatch is either set with its top surface flush with the deck or on a coaming raised above the deck. Hatches are usually not quick acting and must be secured with individually operated dogs.

An *escape scuttle* is a round opening with quick-acting closures that can be placed in a hatch, bulkhead, or deck to permit rapid escape from a compartment.

Manholes normally provide access to water, fuel tanks, and voids. They are sections of steel plate gasketed and fastened over openings where access is needed. They are seldom used by ship's personnel. Manholes are occasionally placed in bulkheads.

Most closure devices depend on a rubber gasket, usually mounted in the covering part to close against a fixed-position knife edge for tightness. Gaskets of this type are either pressed into a groove or secured with retaining strips held in place by screws or bolts. Never paint or "doctor" gaskets. If a new one is needed, install it.

Investigating and Reporting Damage

To investigate and report damage properly, you must know your ship and be familiar with certain basic principles.

Be cautious. Each investigating team should consist of two or more persons using safety equipment (oxygen-breathing apparatus [OBA], fire-resistant gloves, tapping tool, etc.).

Be thorough and determined. Find out the sort of damage, its location and extent, and how it can best be repaired or controlled.

Report the damage. A prompt, accurate report should be made to DCC by telephone or messenger.

Repeat the investigation until ordered to secure.

Damage Repairs

Battle-damage repair is emergency action taken to keep the ship afloat. Damage-control drills will teach everyone how to use damage-control equipment. Do your best with what you have in an emergency. If you are calm, alert, and work fast with the tools you have, you can do much to keep the ship afloat and make her ready for action again.

Any rupture, break, or hole in the ship's outer hull plating, particularly below the waterline, can let sea-water in. If flooding is not controlled, the ship will sink. When the underwater hull is pierced, there are only two possible courses of action. The first, obviously, is to plug the holes. The second is to establish and maintain flood boundaries within the ship and thus prevent more extensive flooding.

Plugging and patching materials include wooden plugs and wedges, wooden shoring, prefabricated wooden box patches, rags, pillows, mattresses, blankets, kapok life jackets, metal plate, folding metal-plate patches, flexible sheet-metal patches, prefabricated steel-box patches, bucket patches, and welded-steel patches.

Securing materials include assorted hook bolts, manila line, wire rope, chain, machine bolts, C clamps, and angle clips for welding and shoring.

Backup materials include mess tables, panel doors, buckets, plywood or lumber, and sheet metal.

Gasket materials include sheet and strip rubber, leather, canvas, rags, and oakum.

There are two general methods of temporarily repairing a hole in the hull: put something in it or over it. In either case, the effect is to reduce the area through which water can enter the ship, or through which water can pass from one compartment to another.

A riveted joint is not inherently watertight or oil-tight, because the surfaces or edges that are held together are not machined or ground. Therefore riveted joints or boundaries tend to loosen from shock of gunfire, collision, vibration, explosion, and racking from high-speed maneuvering. Repairs to this type of damage are usually made by caulking the loosened joint. The repairs must be made as soon as defects are discovered.

Shoring is often used aboard ship to support ruptured decks, strengthen weakened bulkheads and decks, build up temporary decks and bulkheads against the sea, support hatches and doors, and provide support for equipment that has broken loose.

Knowing the proper time to shore is a problem that cannot be solved by any one set of rules. Sometimes the need for shoring is obvious, as in the case of loose machinery or damaged hatches. But sometimes dangerously weakened supports under guns or machinery may not be noticeable. Although shoring is not always necessary, the best general rule is, When in doubt, shore!

The basic materials are shores, wedges, sholes, and strong-backs. A *shore* is a portable beam. A *wedge* is a block, triangular on the sides and rectangular on the butt end. A *shoe* is a flat block that may be placed under the end of a shore for the purpose of distributing pressure. A *strongback* is a bar or beam of wood or metal, often shorter than a shore, which is used to distribute pressure or to serve as an anchor for a patch. Many other pieces of equipment can also be used in connection with shoring.

Fire Protection

Fire is a constant threat aboard ship, and all measures must be taken to prevent it. Fires may start from spontaneous combustion, carelessness, hits by enemy shells, or collision. If a fire is not controlled quickly, it may cause more damage than the initial casualty and could mean loss of the ship.

Although firefighting is chiefly the responsibility of repair parties, you must learn all you can about it so that you can help if called upon.

For a fire to start, there must be a burnable material, the substance must be at its "firepoint" temperature, and there must be sufficient oxygen to sustain combustion. These requirements form what is called the *fire triangle*—fuel, heat, and oxygen. Removing any one will extinguish the fire. But that's not necessarily easy to do.

It is not always possible, for instance, nor even practical, to eliminate fuel. If, however, a flammable liquid fire is being fed by a pipeline, the flow of fuel can be stopped by closing valves in the pipe.

Removing heat is the most common method of extinguishing a fire. The usual cooling method is to use lots of water in the form of high- or low-velocity fog (spray).

Oxygen can be removed in two ways. In a closed space, carbon dioxide (CO_2) can be used to dilute the oxygen content of the air, thus starving the fire. The other method is to smother the fire with a blanket of foam or sand.

Classes of Fires

Fires have four classifications, indicating the type of material burning and the agents and methods required to extinguish them.

Class A fires involve solid substances—wood, cloth, paper—that usually leave an ash. Explosives are in this category.

Water is the usual means of extinguishing class A fires. In a large fire, the flame is usually knocked down (cooled) with fog, then a solid stream is applied to break up the material. Fog is then used for further cooling.

Class B fires involve flammable liquids—oil, gasoline, paint, etc. For small fires or in confined spaces, CO_2 and purple K powder (PKP) are effective. For large fires, other agents such as water and aqueous film-forming foam (AFFF) must be used. *Never* use a solid stream on class B fires. The water penetrates the fuel's surface, flashes to steam, scatters the fuel, and spreads the fire. Spaces subject to major fuel- or lube-oil spills (firerooms, enginerooms, fuel transfer and manifold rooms, etc.) are equipped with HALON 1301 (fluorocarbon gas) fixed flooding systems; these are manually activated only when other firefighting methods fail.

Class C fires ignite in electrical/electronic equipment. The primary extinguishing method is to de-energize the equipment, which reduces the fire to class A or B. The preferred extinguishing agent is CO_2, since it does not leave any residue. PKP may be used as a last resort, but its abrasiveness will further damage the equipment.

Class D fires involve combustible metals (magnesium, sodium, titanium, etc.) and any fires that require special handling. Special metals are used for building certain parts of aircraft, missiles, electronic components, and other equipment. An example is the magnesium aircraft parachute flare, which can burn at a temperature above 4,000°F with a brilliance of 2-million candle power. Water coming in contact with burning magnesium produces highly explosive hydrogen gas and toxic metal oxides; use high- or low-velocity fog at extreme range upwind of this type of fire. One important safety precaution: the intense light produced by this type of fire can easily cause permanent damage to the eyes, so never look directly at the fire, and wear protective welder's goggles with very dark lenses if they are available.

Fire-Prevention Rules

You can't win against a fire. You can fight it and hold down its damage. But some property will be destroyed, productive work is interrupted, and additional effort and materials are required to clean up the mess. The objective, therefore, is to prevent fires from starting.

Combustible	Class	Extinguishing Agent
Woodwork, bedding, clothes, combustible stores	A	Fixed-water sprinkling, high-velocity fog, solid-water stream, foam, dry chemical, CO_2
Explosives, propellants	A	Magazine sprinkling, solid-water stream or high-velocity fog, foam
Paints, spirits, flammable liquid stores	B	CO_2 (fixed system), foam (AFFF), installed sprinkling system, high-velocity fog, PKP, CO_2 (fixed)
Gasoline	B	Foam (AFFF), CO_2 (fixed), water-sprinkling system, PKP
Fuel oil, JP-5, diesel oil, kerosene	B	Foam (AFFF), PKP, water-sprinkling system, high-velocity fog, CO_2 (fixed system)
Electrical and radio apparatus	C	CO_2 (portable or hose reel), high-velocity and low-velocity fog, fog foam or dry chemical (only if CO_2 not available)
Magnesium alloys	D	Jettison overboard, low-velocity fog

Figure 18–5 The classes of fires and recommended extinguishing agents are listed in order of priority.

Keep things squared away—clean, shipshape, and in their proper places. Keep flammable products (gasoline, oily rags, paint, etc.) away from fire-starting articles such as torches, cigarettes, and sparking equipment. Don't take open flames near gasoline tanks, and don't bring flammable liquid near a welder's torch.

Make sure firefighting equipment is in the right place and in good condition. If a fire does start, you'll want to have the equipment on hand and ready to go. You may not be able to prevent a fire from starting, but you can prevent a little one from getting bigger.

There are some fire-prevention rules for each class of fire:

Class A fires: Don't throw lighted cigarettes or matches in trash cans. Don't smoke in bunks. Be careful of where and how you stow rags and oily paint-smeared cloth and paper. When welding or burning, protect Class A materials against flame and hot droppings. Inspect opposite bulkheads and maintain a fire watch.

Class B fires: Most low places, bilges, tanks, and bottoms have an accumulation of extremely flammable gasoline or oil vapors. Remember the danger of flashback where gasoline is concerned. Use only nonsparking tools in areas where class B substances have been or are stored. Don't carry matches, lighters, or keys, and don't wear metal buttons or nylon cloth-

Figure 18–6 Students spray foam on a replica of a bomb in a controlled-burn area during training at firefighting school.

ing near gasoline or oil vapors. Don't turn on lamps, flashlights, or electrical equipment that are not certified as sparkproof in an area where gasoline or oil fumes can accumulate.

Class C fires: Do not paint or splash paint, oil, grease, or solvents on electrical insulation or wires. Report all frayed or worn wires and all sparking contacts, switches, and motors. Report any electrical equipment that is hot, smokes, or makes an unusual noise. In case of fire, secure all electrical equipment in the space. Don't try to use unauthorized equipment, such as hotplates, shavers, extension lights, or radios, except in authorized spaces.

Class D fires: Protect class D fuels from welding and burning operations. Do not store class D fuels in areas that are susceptible to intense heat. Some of these fuels can ignite without flame.

Shipboard Firefighters

Despite the most careful precautions, fires can occur. If you discover one, report it immediately so that firefighting operations can begin. The efforts of one person may be enough to contain the fire until the fire party arrives. If you discover a fire, report it immediately to the officer of the deck. State the type of fire and its location (compartment name and designation), then do what you can to fight it. Always report the fire

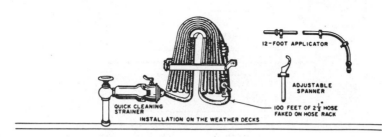

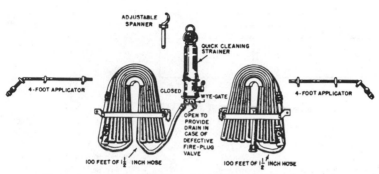

Figure 18–7 In a standard shipboard installation of fireplug, strainer, and
hose sections, note that the lower valve on the wye gate is open to provide
drainage in case of a defective fireplug valve.

before taking any action. A delay of even half a minute might
result in a minor fire becoming a major one.

To some extent, the procedures for fighting a fire depend on
the condition under which it occurs. Fires that break out during action, normal steaming, or when a full crew is aboard are
handled as battle casualties and the ship goes to GQ. These
fires, which may occur in port or at sea, are normally fought by
the firefighting party from the repair station in that section of
the ship. Aboard larger ships, it may not always be feasible to
go to GQ. Then a nucleus fire party is organized.

When a fire occurs in port and there is only a partial crew on
board, the duty repair party handles it. The regular firefighting
party is shown in figure 18-8.

Firefighting-Party Organization

Every firefighting party consists of two *hose teams* known as
the attack party. The no. 1 hose team is the attacking unit, and
the no. 2 team is the backup.

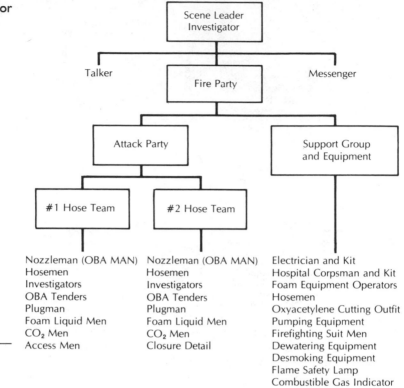

Figure 18–8 Organization of a firefighting party.

The *scene leader* is in charge of the firefighting party. The scene leader's first duty is to get to the fire quickly, investigate the situation, determine the nature of the fire, decide what type of equipment should be used, and inform DCC. Later developments may require different or additional equipment, but the scene leader must decide what equipment is to be used first.

Nozzlemen have their OBAs on and ready for immediate use. They help the scene leader investigate the fire when OBAs are needed to enter a compartment. Nozzlemen man an all-purpose nozzle and applicator and wear complete battle dress, with gloves and a miner's headlamp.

Hosemen lead out the hose from the fireplug, remove kinks and sharp bends' and tend it. When fighting the fire, they too wear OBAs.

Fire
Protection

Fire boundaries, designated by DCC, are set by fire-boundary personnel. They remove burnable materials from bulkheads and cool down bulkheads and decks if necessary. They make frequent status reports to the scene leader through investigators.

Investigators make continuous tours of inspection of those spaces adjoining the fire, looking for further damage, taking soundings, and leading personnel trapped in smoke-filled compartments to safety.

OBA tenders tend lines (when used) and keep spare OBA canisters available.

Plugmen stand by to operate fireplug valves when ordered. They rig and stand by jumper hoses, and clear fireplug strainers when necessary.

Access men open doors, hatches, scuttles, and other closures. They clear routes to gain access to the fire and carry equipment to open jammed fittings and locked doors.

AFFF supplymen prepare foam-generating equipment and obtain AFFF can spares from racks.

CO_2 supply men carry CO_2 and PKP extinguishers.

Figure 18–9 The all-purpose hose nozzle is used for high-velocity fog, low-velocity fog, and a straight stream.

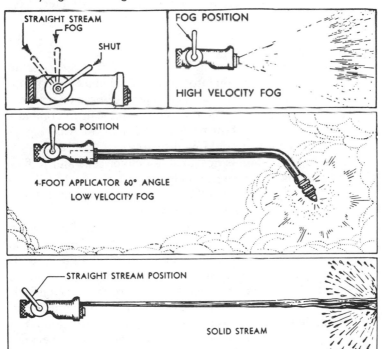

STRAIGHT STREAM
FOG
SHUT

FOG POSITION

HIGH VELOCITY FOG

FOG POSITION

4-FOOT APPLICATOR 60° ANGLE
LOW VELOCITY FOG

STRAIGHT STREAM POSITION

SOLID STREAM

The closure detail secures all doors, hatches, and openings around the area to isolate the fire. All ventilation closures and fans in the smoke and heat area are secured by this detail, which also establishes secondary fire boundaries by cooling down nearby areas.

The electrician deenergizes and reenergizes electrical circuits in the fire area and rigs power cables for portable lights, tools, and blowers.

The hospital corpsman provides on-scene first aid and is responsible for supervising the movement of seriously injured persons to sick bay for treatment.

The phone talker plugs into the nearest JZ circuit to establish and maintain communication with DCC, either directly or through the local repair party.

The messenger carries written communications from the scene leader to the repair party leader.

Other personnel and equipment assigned to a firefighting party may include foam-equipment operators, additional hosemen, proximity suitmen, a portable (oxyacetylene) cutting outfit (PCO) operator, the dewatering/desmoking equipment team, and an atmospheric test equipment (explosimeter, oxygen indicator, toxic-gas detector) operator.

Firefighting Equipment

All firefighting equipment is located in readily accessible locations and inspected frequently to ensure reliability and readiness. At any time, you may be called upon to serve on a repair/fire party, or you may be the only person present to combat a fire. If you don't know how to use equipment, or what equipment to use, the result could be disastrous.

The fire-main system is designed to deliver seawater to fireplugs and sprinkler systems and high-/low-capacity AFFF systems. It has a secondary function of supplying coolant water to flushing systems and auxiliary machinery.

Fire-main piping is configured as either a single line, horizontal loop, vertical loop, or composite system depending on the type of ship. On small combatant ships, single-line systems run fore and aft near the centerline. On large combatant ships, horizontal-loop systems circle around or through the engineering spaces. Vertical-loop systems wind through the superstructure on auxiliary ships. Composite systems (a combination of any of the other systems) are used on aircraft carriers because of their size and extensive compartmentation. In all systems, the main is located on or below the damage-control deck. There are many cross-connection points and cutout valves throughout the system to allow damaged sections of piping to be isolated or "jumped." Risers and branch lines lead from the main to fireplugs and AFFF systems throughout the ship.

Aboard larger ships most fireplug outlets are $2\frac{1}{2}$ inches in diameter. A wye gate provides two $1\frac{1}{2}$-inch outlets, or a reducing fitting can be used to provide a single $1\frac{1}{2}$-inch outlet. Fireplug outlets in engineering spaces are $1\frac{1}{2}$ inches.

The standard Navy firehose has an interior lining of rubber, covered with two cotton or synthetic jackets. It comes in 50-foot lengths with a female coupling at one end and a male coupling at the other. The female coupling is connected to the fireplug. The male coupling is connected to another length of hose or to a nozzle.

Destroyers and smaller ships use $1\frac{1}{2}$-inch hose throughout. Larger ships use $2\frac{1}{2}$-inch hose on weather decks and $1\frac{1}{2}$-inch hose below decks and in the superstructure.

One or more racks at each fireplug are used to stow the firehose. The hose must be faked on the rack so that it is free running, with the ends hanging down and the couplings ready for instant use. On large ships, each weather-deck fire station has 100 feet of $2\frac{1}{2}$-inch hose faked on a rack and connected to the plug. Below deck, 200 feet of $1\frac{1}{2}$-inch hose is stowed by each plug, but only two lengths (100 feet) are connected to the plug. On smaller ships, 100 feet of $1\frac{1}{2}$-inch hose is faked on the racks, with 50 feet connected to the plug. A spanner wrench (for disassembling the connections) and one or two applicators are also stowed at each fire station. Spare lengths of hose are rolled and stowed in repair lockers.

The all-purpose nozzle can produce a solid stream of water, high-velocity fog, and (with an applicator) low-velocity fog. It is available for use on both $1\frac{1}{2}$-inch and $2\frac{1}{2}$-inch hose. The nozzle can be controlled easily and quickly with a bale handle. Never pick up a charged hose by the handle of the all-purpose nozzle. If the handle moves to the fog or solid-stream position, the high water pressure (about 100 psi) could make the hose whiplash dangerously.

Sprinkler systems are installed in magazines, turrets, ammunition-handling rooms, spaces where flammable materials are stowed, and hanger bays aboard aircraft carriers (served by high-capacity AFFF stations). Water for these systems is piped from the fire-main. Some systems are automatically trig-

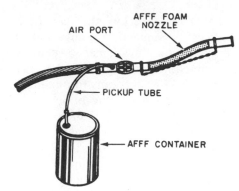

AIR PORT

AFFF FOAM
NOZZLE

PICKUP TUBE

AFFF CONTAINER

Figure 18–10   Navy pickup unit (NPU) nozzle assembly.

410

·gered when the protected compartment reaches a certain temperature, but most are opened manually by control valves.

AFFF, or "light water," a clear, slightly amber-colored liquid, is a concentrated mixture that was developed to combat class B fires. In solution with water, it floats on the surface of fuels and creates a film that prevents the escape of vapors and thereby causes a "vaporlock." The type used by the Navy is effective in no less than a 3.5 percent concentration, that is, 3.5 parts AFFF mixed with 96.5 parts of water.

AFFF is applied (as a foam) to the fuel surface. As the solution drains from the foam, if forms a vaportight film on top of the fuel. Although AFFF can be used separately, it is generally used in conjunction with purple PKP. PKP and AFFF when used together are highly effective.

AFFF concentrate and water may be mixed by using a water motor proportioner (FP-180 or FP-1000), Navy pickup unit (NPU) nozzle, in-line inductor, or injection pump system.

The portable FP-180 proportioner consists of a foam-liquid pump driven by a water motor. It has $2\frac{1}{2}$ inch connections at both the inlet and outlet sides, and uses two $\frac{1}{2}$-inch pickup tubes. When the valve is in either of the two foam positions, the pump injects AFFF concentrate into the water stream. With the valve in the off position, no AFFF is delivered, and the fire hose can be used for conventional firefighting. The FP-1000 proportioner is still found on some ships, where it is used in high-capacity AFFF systems that have not yet been modified for the new injection pump system. It functions the same way as the FP-180, except that the water inlet/outlet connections and the single AFFF connection are "hard-piped."

The Navy pickup unit (NPU) nozzle, originally designed for mechanical (protein) foam liquid, can be used in two different ways. When an FP-180 is not available, the NPU nozzle can draw AFFF concentrate directly from its container, using a water-jet syphon action, to its single pickup tube. The AFFF/ water solution passes through an aeration chamber, where outside air is drawn into the stream to increase the foaming action. The AFFF foam is then discharged through a flexible tube. Since the AFFF container must be kept with the nozzle handler, the handler's movements are hampered considerably. Used in conjunction with an FP-180, the NPU pickup tube is removed and replaced with a threaded plug. This allows the nozzleman complete freedom of movement.

The in-line inductor is a new addition to the Navy's firefighting inventory. It is replacing NPU nozzles and FP-180 portable and fixed units. Since AFFF solution does not require a special nozzle for firefighting applications, the simplicity and reliability of the in-line inductor is greatly improving shipboard firefighting capabilities. The unit consists of $1\frac{1}{2}$ inch female and male outlet hose connections on a "convergent/ divergent" nozzle; a pickup tube that includes a ball-check valve prevents water from flowing back through the tube to the container of AFFF concentrate. The unit is installed between two lengths

Figure 18–11   FP-180 water motor proportioner.

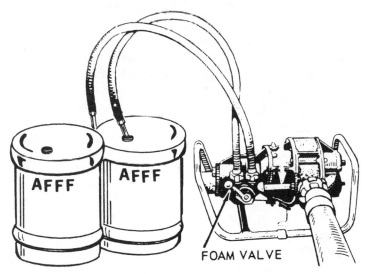

FOAM VALVE

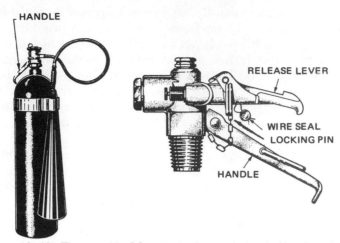

Figure 18–12   The portable CO_2 extinguisher, with detail of handle, release lever, and locking pin.

of hose behind the nozzle handler, which allows him or her freedom of movement.

Injection pumps are used on high-capacity AFFF systems. Individual "HICAP" stations are able to serve many different firefighting systems. Single-speed pumps serve the flight deck's "flush-deck" firefighting system, where each station serves its own area or zone. Two-speed pumps serve the hangar-bay sprinkler system, hose stations in the hangar bay and catwalk areas, and bilge flooding systems in the engineering spaces. When the station is activated, the pump injects AFFF concentrate into the piping downstream of the firemain-control valve after it opens. The agitation of the water in the piping mixes the AFFF solution. The HICAP system can be activated from numerous local and remote stations, but it must be secured at the HICAP itself. It is essential that the station be manned by qualified personnel once it is activated.

Two types of portable extinguishers are used. Both are effective in fighting class B and class C fires.

(CO₂) Extinguishers are used mainly for electrical fires, but they are effective on small fires, including burning oil, gasoline, paint, and trash cans. Because CO_2 is heavier than air, it forms a smothering blanket over the fire. The extinguisher's maximum range is 5 feet from the end of the horn.

To use the extinguisher, remove the locking pin from the valve, grasp the insulated handle of the horn with one hand,

and squeeze the grip with the other. If you are in the open, approach the fire from the windward side. This extinguisher is quick to use and leaves no residue but CO_2 "snow," which can be blown away by wind or a draft. While not poisonous, snow will not support life and can smother personnel as well as fires in confined spaces. When CO_2 is released from the bottle, it expands rapidly to 450 times its stored volume. This causes the gas temperature to drop to minus 110°F. Contact with snow can cause painful skin blisters.

Dry-Chemical Extinguishers are primarily for class B fires. The chemical used is potassium bicarbonate (similar to baking soda), also called purple K powder or PKP.

PKP is nontoxic and four times as powerful as CO_2. It is also effective on class C fires, but should not be used if CO_2 is available. PKP should not be used on internal fires in gas turbines or jet engines, since it leaves a residue that cannot be completely removed without disassembling the engine.

The dry-chemical extinguisher is available in two sizes. The K-20 contains 18 pounds of PKP, the K-30 contains 27 pounds of PKP, and both use CO_2 (from a cartridge) as a propellant. The extinguisher shell is not pressurized until it is to be used.

Handling the extinguisher is simple. Pull the locking pin from the seal-cutter assembly, and strike the puncture lever to cut the gas-cartridge seal. The extinguisher is then charged and ready for use. Discharge the chemical in short bursts by squeezing the grip on the nozzle and sweeping the fire from side to side. Advance on the fire only if safe, using a range of 10 to 20 foot. When you're finished, invert the cylinder, squeeze the discharge lever and tap the nozzle on the deck. This releases all pressure and clears the hose and nozzle of powder.

Dry chemical is an excellent firefighting agent, but its effects are temporary. It has no cooling effect and provides no protection against reflash. Therefore, it should always be backed up by AFFF. In confined spaces, PKP should be used sparingly. Prolonged discharge of the chemical reduces visibility and makes breathing difficult.

There are often two types of fixed fire-extinguisher installations in areas such as machinery spaces and hangar decks.

Fixed CO_2 extinguishers are a dependable, ready means of flooding spaces that are more-than-ordinary fire hazards. Cylinders have a 50-pound capacity and are mounted either singly or in banks of two or more. There are two types of installed

CO_2 extinguishers: the hose and reel for machinery spaces, or the flooding system for spaces such as paint lockers not continually occupied by personnel.

As mentioned before, PKP cannot prevent reflash. It is fully compatible, however, with AFFF.

An AFFF/PKP combination will extinguish a fire up to three times faster than the old mechanical foams. The dry chemical is used to knock down the fire, and the AFFF prevents a reflash.

Aircraft carriers have a portable AFFF/PKP system mounted either on its own carriage or on the back of an aircraft tractor, known as a twin-agent unit (TAU). Do not confuse this system with the twin agent system (TAS), which is a system installed in machinery spaces.

Pumps

There are two portable gasoline-powered pumps, the P-250 and the PE-250.

The P-250 is a self-priming centrifugal pump designed to pump 250 gpm (gallons per minute) with a suction lift of 16 to 20 feet. The pump has a 3-inch inlet, attached to one or more lengths of hard-rubber suction hose, on the end of which is a foot valve and strainer assembly. For suction lifts in excess of 20 feet, the suction hose must be manually primed through the priming bowl on top of the pump casing. The discharge is a $2\frac{1}{2}$-inch ball valve with hose threads that can be attached to either a standard tri-gate (three $1\frac{1}{2}$-inch hose connections), a special tri-gate (one $2\frac{1}{2}$-inch and two $1\frac{1}{2}$-inch hose connections), or a $2\frac{1}{2}$-inch hose, depending on whether the pump is being used for firefighting or dewatering.

Like any other gasoline engine, the P-250 produces carbon monoxide. When it is used below decks, the exhaust must be led outside the ship. Lengths of 2-inch hard-rubber hose are available for this purpose. The pump should never be run in a space containing explosive vapors.

The PE-250 pump is the same as the P-250, except that the PE-250 has an electric start feature whereas the P-250 uses a pull cord.

In fire fighting, a vast amount of water is discharged on the ship. For instance, a $2\frac{1}{2}$-inch hose with a pressure of 100 psi pumps nearly a ton of water per minute. Obviously, this water must be removed or the ship's stability will be greatly impaired.

Figure 18–13 Crash crewmen at a firefighting school test light water, which actually makes water float on gasoline or JP-5 fuel.

The P-250 pump can be used for dewatering by itself or with other equipment to increase the pumping rate dramatically. A pumping rate of 250 gpm is not always sufficient to dewater spaces. The dewatering rate of a single pump can be doubled with a jet pump called an eductor. The P-250 draws a suction from the space being dewatered and discharges it to an eductor in the same space. Since the eductor is virtually 100 percent efficient, the discharge from the eductor will be double the gpm of the P-250. Eductors are also used when the liquid to be pumped (gasoline or other flammables) cannot be handled by the pump itself. This practice eliminates the chance of damaging the pump or of igniting the liquid.

Eductors can be used when the required suction lift is greater than the P-250's capability. Using the special tri-gate, a $2\frac{1}{2}$-inch hose from the pump discharge is connected to the supply side of a standard (S type) eductor. The 3-inch suction hose of the P-250 is connected to the 4-inch discharge of the eductor using a reducer coupling. The two $1\frac{1}{2}$-inch outlets of the special tri-gate discharge the water. This arrangement allows a suction lift of up to 55 feet.

Eductors are often employed alone, using the ship's fire main as a source of water pressure. The standard eductor has a $2\frac{1}{2}$-inch supply coupling, a single $\frac{7}{8}$-inch diameter nozzle (jet), a foot valve and strainer assembly, and a 4-inch discharge connection. The perijet eductor has a $2\frac{1}{2}$-inch supply coupling, six $\frac{3}{8}$-inch diameter nozzles (jets), an inlet port that tapers from 3 inches to $2\frac{1}{2}$ inches with a 4-inch connection, and a 4-inch discharge connection. The perijet is 7 percent more efficient than the standard eductor and is able to pump debris that passes through the inlet port. A spring-loaded, lever-operated, quick-acting, gate-type back-flush valve comes with the perijet and should be attached to the end of the first length of discharge hose. Should a large piece of debris clog the inlet port, the back-flush valve is manually actuated, causing a temporary reverse flush of water that clears the inlet port.

A "basket" strainer should always be used to prevent debris from clogging pumping equipment.

The electric submersible pump is the most versatile and easiest to rig of all dewatering pumps. It is a 440-volt centrifugal pump with $2\frac{1}{2}$-inch suction and discharge connections. Three attachments are provided for the suction side. A bell-shaped foot valve and strainer, a shallow grill strainer, and a "fluted" strainer enclose the whole pump casing. The pumping capacity depends on the maximum height of the discharge hose (static head). With a static head of 50 feet, the pump discharges 200 gpm, but at a static head of 70 feet, it is capable of only 140 gpm.

When a large static head is unavoidable, it is possible to rig two pumps in tandem with a length of $2\frac{1}{2}$-inch hose between them. The lower pump is activated first and primes the upper pump, which is then activated. Since the water being pumped is also cooling the pumps, the upper one must be carefully monitored to prevent it from overheating. Overheating of the pump causes its internal seals to deteriorate and leak, resulting in an electrical short circuit that severely damages the pump.

Protective Clothing and Equipment

Any clothing that covers your skin will protect it from flash burns and other short-duration flames. In situations where there is a likelihood of fire or explosion, keep covered as much as possible, and protect your eyes with antiflash goggles.

If your clothes catch fire, don't run. This fans the flames. Lie down and roll up in a blanket, coat, or anything that will smother the flames. If nothing is available, roll over slowly, beating out the flames with your hands. If another person's clothes catch fire, throw the person down and cover him or her (except for the head) with a blanket or coat.

Figure 18–14 Since the danger of explosion, poisoning, or suffocation exists
in any closed compartment or poorly ventilated space, all hands are trained in
the use of the oxygen-breathing apparatus.

Aluminum-coated proximity suits are designed to protect
the wearer from the radiant heat of fire. The suits offer only
short-term protection. When worn by pilot-rescue personnel,
the suits are continuously sprayed down by the applicator-hose
team to prevent overheating and should never make contact
with actual flames. Proximity suits are used for open-air fires
only and should never be used to combat fires inside the ship.
An OBA worn beneath the suit protects breathing.

The Navy uses a type A-4 OBA. The self-contained unit is
designed to protect the wearer in an atmosphere lacking oxygen or containing harmful gases, vapors, smoke, or dust. The
wearer breathes in a closed-system canister; oxygen is supplied by chemicals that purify exhaled air. The wearer's breath
is circulated through the canister of chemicals, which react
with CO_2 and the moisture in the wearer's breath to produce
oxygen. The process continues until the oxygen-producing capacity of the chemicals is used up—in about 45 minutes, depending on the amount of physical labor involved.

All OBA equipment requires special instruction and practice. Don't try to use it until you have been properly instructed. Always observe these precautions:

When the face-piece needs cleaning, use only soap and water, never alcohol. Never grease or oil any part of the OBA.

Never enter a danger area until you are sure the apparatus is working correctly. Start the timer every time you start a new canister; when the timer goes off, or when it becomes difficult to exhale (meaning the canister needs to be changed), return to fresh air.

A used canister is very hot. Wear fire-resistant gloves or equivalent protection for your hands.

The chemical in canisters is very caustic to the skin. Open canisters with care. If the chemical is accidentally spilled on deck, clean it up immediately and dump it overboard, using a nonflammable metal implement for a scoop.

Oil, gasoline, or similar substances that come in contact with the chemicals will cause an explosion. Be sure you drop the used canister on a dry deck. Also be sure there is no chance for it to drop through or off a grating and into the bilges.

Do not throw a canister overboard without getting permission from the officer of the deck. Never throw a canister overboard if there is an oil slick on the water, or if the ship is in port. Always punch several holes in the bottom with a clean tool, so the canister will sink immediately. Never hold your face or any part of your body over a canister opening.

The air-line mask (figure 18-16) may be used for entering smoke-filled compartments or to rescue crewmembers. Since it produces no oxygen of its own, it should never be used when actually fighting a fire. The mask is a demand-flow air-line respirator with a speaking diaphragm, monocular lens with adjustable head harness, breathing tube, and belt-mounted demand regulator with quick-disconnect fittings. The mask comes with a 25-foot hose, also with quick-disconnect fittings.

When compressed air cylinders are not available, low-pressure ship's-service air may be used, if it is reduced to the proper operating pressure. Never use an oxygen bottle with this equipment. Oil, grease, or oily water in the apparatus might combine with the oxygen and explode.

Before entering a space filled with toxic gases or smoke, check the mask to be sure it is working properly. Take a breath to determine whether there is sufficient airflow.

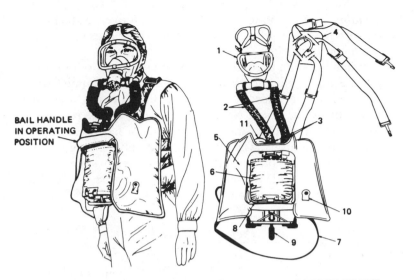

1. FACEPIECE
2. BREATHING TUBES
3. BREATHING TUBE
   COUPLINGS
4. BODY HARNESS
   AND PAD

5. BREATHING BAG
6. BREASTPLATE
7. WAIST STRAP
8. BAIL ASSEMBLY
   HANDLE
   (STANDBY POSITION)

9. CANISTER RELEASE
   STRAP
10. PRESSURE RELIEF
    VALVE AND PULL TAB
11. TIMER

419

Figure 18–15   Navy type A-4 oxygen-breathing apparatus.

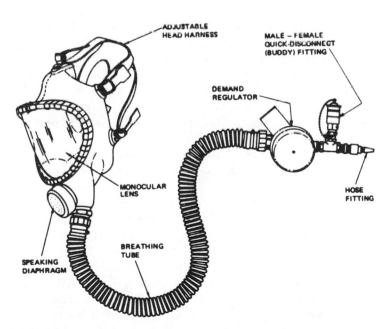

ADJUSTABLE
HEAD HARNESS

MALE – FEMALE
QUICK-DISCONNECT
(BUDDY) FITTING

DEMAND
REGULATOR

MONOCULAR
LENS

HOSE
FITTING

BREATHING
TUBE

SPEAKING
DIAPHRAGM

Figure 18–16   Air-line mask with buddy fitting.

Tending lines are 50-foot lengths of nylon-covered steel wire used with the OBA or the air-line mask. There are snap hooks at each end of the line.

Tending lines are used as a precautionary measure in rescuing a fire investigator or firefighter. Rescuers equipped with OBAs follow the lines to the victim; they do not drag the person out by the lines. Never attach a line to the rescuee's waist. If pulled, it might interfere with his or her breathing or cause internal injuries. The person should only be dragged out of a space when no other method of rescue is possible. OBAs are equipped with a D ring on the back of the harness assembly so that the life line can be more easily fastened.

Tending Line Signals	*Pulls*	*Meaning*
Tender to wearer	1	Are you OK?
	2	Do you want to advance?
	3	Should I take up slack?
	4	Do you need help?
Wearer to tender	1	I am OK.
	2	I am going to advance.
	3	I want you to take up slack.
	4	I need help.

The emergency-escape breathing device (EEBD), a fire-escape mask, consists of a head covering with a transparent face screen that can be donned quickly. Each EEBD carries a canister, which functions the same way as an OBA canister and provides the wearer with a minimum of 8 minutes' breathing time. This should enable the wearer to escape from any space to the ship's topside. It is especially designed to protect against smoke inhalation.

There are two types of atmosphere-testing indicators. All closed or poorly ventilated compartments (particularly those in which a fire has just occurred) are dangerous because the air in them may lack oxygen or contain toxic gases. Three steps should be taken as a matter of routine to test for combustible or toxic gases in confined spaces. Initial testing, performed from outside the space, is for oxygen content; the second, for combustible vapors or gases; and the third, for toxic substances.

Combustible-gas indicators (explosimeters) are used to detect the level of explosivity of various flammable gases and vapors. Several different types of indicators are available, but

Figure 18–17   Recruits receive instruction in the proper use of the ND
Mark V gas masks from a chief instructor during boot camp activities at the
San Diego Naval Training Center.

all operate on the same principles. The steps of procedure are
attached to the inside of the case cover. This type of indicator
can quickly, safely, and accurately detect all combustible
gases or vapors associated with fuel oil, gasoline, alcohol, ace-
tone vapors, illuminating gas, fuel gas, hydrogen, and acety-
lene in mixtures with air or oxygen.

The indicator is sensitive to small quantities. Although it
does not identify combustibles, it indicates what their explosive level (expressed on the gauge in % LEL) is. The instrument is equipped with a flame arrester to prevent flashbacks.

Intended solely for the detection of oxygen deficiency in the
atmosphere of a space, the oxygen indicator is designed to give
a continuous reading of oxygen concentration from 0 to 25
percent. The oxygen indicator should be calibrated before each
use.

The sensing head of the indicator should be introduced into
every part of the compartment, from top to bottom. If a deficiency of less than 20 percent oxygen exists, the compartment
should be fully ventilated and retested. Before using the oxygen indicator, you should become very familiar with the instructions for its operation.

The Draeger toxic-gas detector is a hand-operated, bellows-type aspirator pump into which the appropriate detector tube is inserted. The three gases that are commonly tested for are carbon monoxide, CO_2 and hydrogen sulfide.

Fires that seem to be out may start again from a smoldering fragment or through vapor ignition. The final step in firefighting is the establishment of a *reflash watch*. After a fire has been extinguished, it is usually necessary to desmoke the compartment(s). This is done with natural or forced ventilation. Several cautions should be noted:

Be sure the fire is really out.

Investigate the ventilation systems in the affected areas to make sure they are free of burning or smoldering materials.

Have fire parties and equipment standing by the blower and controller of the ventilation systems.

Obtain permission from DCC (or the engineer) to open ventilation-system closures and start the blowers.

It is best to use exhaust systems, rather than supply systems, for desmoking. Portable ventilating blowers—electric or pneumatic—can be employed for desmoking, although they are not as efficient or convenient as permanent ventilating systems. When explosive vapors or fumes are present, it may be dangerous to use the installed systems. Under these circumstances, use only portable blowers.

General Bills and Drills 19

Since the days of John Paul Jones, ships of the Navy have existed for one specific purpose—to fight. Everything a ship does in the way of training and maintenance is aimed at making her better able to fight when the time comes. As one of the Navy regulations says, "The requirements for battle shall be the basis for the organization of the ship."

If a ship is to perform her primary function well, she has to be organized in such a way that her crew can be effectively directed and controlled at all times. This means that every sailor aboard ship must know his or her station and duty—where he or she is to be and what he or she must do for every drill or emergency. It is the responsibility of the commanding officer to maintain such organization.

Since no one officer can assign hundreds of persons to their various duties, every ship is organized under a standard system that hands much of this detail to the departments and divisions.

The system involves the use of bills established by three official documents: the Standard Organization and Regulations of the U.S. Navy, the battle bill, and the watch, quarter, and station (WQ&S) bill. A bill is written to cover a certain emergency or job. It describes the duties involved and the stations to be manned, and lists the rates required to perform those duties and man the stations. The Standard Organization and Regulations of the U.S. Navy describes administrative bills, operational bills, emergency bills, and special bills.

Administrative Bills

These bills set procedures for the everyday administration of the ship's company, determine where specific assignments are required, and include the bills list.

Adminis-
trative
Bills

Berthing and Locker

The personnel officer is responsible for establishing and maintaining uniform policies for the assignment of berthing and locker facilities to personnel, both officers and enlisted. Division officers assign bunks and lockers for personnel within their divisions.

Cleaning, Preservation, and Maintenance

General procedures for cleaning and preservation are contained in the bill. Duties involve maintaining, preserving, and cleaning the exterior and interior of the hull, hull fittings, machinery, and equipment. Personnel manning cleaning stations are assigned by division officers and are supervised by either the division leading chief or leading petty officer—except for side cleaners, who are assigned by the first lieutenant to care for the ship's exterior.

Formation and Parade

Quarters and formations are held in accordance with the bill. Included are regular divisional quarters: fair- and foul-weather parades, personnel inspections, and mustering on station; officers' quarters; quarters for entering and leaving port; manning the rail; and general assembly. The executive officer (XO) is responsible for this bill.

Figure 19–1   Crewmembers stand in formation at parade rest during ceremonies aboard the nuclear-powered ballistic-missile submarine *Mariano G. Vallejo.*

General Visiting

Also the responsibility of the XO, this bill specifies procedures and restrictions necessary for the control of visitors to naval units, and ensures physical security, the integrity of classified information, and the reasonable privacy of the unit's company.

Official Correspondence and Classified-Material Control

This bill is designed to coordinate the receiving, sending, marking, accounting, inventory, control, and destruction of official correspondence and classified material. The XO, assisted by the command's designated security manager (SM), is responsible for the bill.

Orientation

This bill establishes procedures for the indoctrination of newly reported enlisted personnel within the unit, its departmental functions, and its routine. The I-division officer, under the XO, is responsible for the bill. It applies to personnel in paygrades E-1 through E-4 in small commands, and to all rates, including officers, in larger commands (aircraft carriers, battleships, etc.).

Personnel Assignment

This bill provides for the assignment and reassignment of officers and enlisted personnel to billets within the unit's organization, including collateral and special duties. The responsibility of the XO, it covers the assignment of a chief master-at-arms, a mess deck master-at-arms, and personnel as food servicemen and compartment cleaners.

Security

The security bill assigns responsibilities for the handling and safeguarding of classified material (except nuclear weapons) and information. The security manager is responsible for this bill.

Security from Unauthorized Visitors

The XO is responsible for this bill, which maintains a unit's security when "repel boarders" action is not appropriate. On larger commands or units with nuclear capabilities, the weapons officer/marine detachment captain is responsible for the bill and reports to the XO. This bill includes the handling of situations such as unauthorized persons (commercial agents, occupants of a pleasure boat, members of a nonmilitary organization, etc.) attempting to board the unit for various reasons, including mischief, revelry, or even politics.

Security Watch

For maximum security of the unit, certain security watches are established by this bill. The bill is the responsibility of the security officer.

Unit Security

The purpose of this bill is to establish the security measures peculiar to nuclear-capable ships, which also maintain the general shipboard security measures provided elsewhere, such as sounding and security patrols, bow and stern sentries, and the gangway watch. The security officer (or weapons officer, if none is assigned) is responsible for this bill.

Zone Inspection

Frequent zone inspections are necessary to keep machinery, spaces, and equipment operating and clean. The XO or the administration officer who reports to the XO is responsible for this bill.

Operational Bills

As the name implies, operational bills deal with specific evolutions by the ship's company. Most spell out duties and responsibilities for special operations.

Boat

The boat bill defines policies and methods for employing ship's boats. The first lieutenant, under the XO, is responsible for this bill, which also assigns specific responsibilities to the navigator, engineer, officer of the deck, boat officers, and coxswains.

Civil Disaster

Through this bill, the XO maintains an effective, organized force capable of participating in civil-disaster relief work. In providing disaster relief, units expect to deal with demoralized, hysterical, or apathetic survivors who are incapable, at least temporarily, of intelligent, cohesive action in their own behalf. Planning takes all of these factors into account.

Cold Weather

This bill is placed into effect prior to deployment in areas of extremely cold weather. Among many other things, it sees that a full allowance of cold-weather clothing is available; that a sufficient quantity of additional life and safety lines and de-icing equipment is on board; and that a shipboard "heating patrol" is established to monitor temperatures in living spaces. The ship's first lieutenant is responsible for this bill and reports to the XO.

Darken Ship

When ships steam at night with all lights out to avoid detection by enemy forces, it is called darken ship. When darken ship is set, all topside doors and hatches are closed, ports are blacked out, and smoking is prohibited on weather decks. To perform efficiently during darken ship, you must be able to find your way around the ship's topside in complete darkness and know how to open and close doors, plug in telephones, locate switches, and handle all other equipment at the underway or general-quarters station. During darken ship, only flashlights or hand lanterns with red lens covers can be used topside, and only when absolutely necessary. The damage-control assistant is responsible for maintaining this bill.

Diving

This bill, intended primarily for scuba diving, is designed to establish procedures and precautions for such operations. The guidelines may also be applied to dives made with lightweight diving equipment. The diving officer is responsible for the bill.

Dry-Docking

This bill, the responsibility of the engineering officer under the supervision of the XO, includes the responsibilities and duties of preparing the ship to enter dry dock and of servicing the ship while in dock. Navy regulations govern this bill. Docking and undocking are normally all-hands evolutions and require coordination with the docking facility. Thus adequate preparations, smart seamanship, and adherence to sound procedures are necessary. Provisions must be made on nuclear ships to shut down the reactor before the water level in the dock is permitted to fall below the ship's minimum draft.

EMCON

The procedures for setting EMCON (emission control) conditions, maintaining EMCON conditions, and designating an EMCON center (EMC) are contained in this bill. EMCON is the management of electromagnetic transmissions that supply a command with essential information. Modern science enables an enemy to detect almost any electronic emissions. When EMCON is set, personal radios with signal-emitting characteristics cannot be used. The operations officer is responsible for this bill.

Emergency Towing

Whenever the ship is towing or being towed, a watch is maintained for the purpose of observing towing conditions, keeping the officer of the deck informed, and casting off when ordered. This bill defines all of the relevant procedures and establishes policies for the assignment of personnel to duties and stations. The first lieutenant is responsible for this bill.

Equipment Tag-Out

428

Procedures for "tagging out"—that is, putting equipment out of commission—apply to all systems, steam, electrical,

Figure 19–2 Divers prepare for a swim under the ice in the Arctic during cold-weather operations.

Figure 19–3 An aquanaut trainee emerges during diving operations in California.

electronic, and fluids. Adhering to tag-out procedures improves safety and helps prevent costly accidents. This bill outlines procedures for preventing improper operation when a component, equipment, system, or portion of a system has been isolated, or tagged, because of malfunctioning. It is designed to standardize all tag-out procedures on ships and at repair activities. The engineering officer is responsible for this bill and reports to the commanding officer; it is administered through the engineering officer's department heads, who see that assigned personnel understand and comply with its procedures.

Flight Operations

All the assignments to flight-quarters stations for air department and air wing or detachment personnel are covered in this bill. Departmental responsibilities are also defined for engineering, communications, and medical wings. Responsibility for the bill rests with the air officer.

Heavy Weather

This bill provides for heavy-weather conditions both at sea or in port. The first lieutenant, under the XO, is responsible for it. In addition to the two officers already mentioned, the navigator, operations officer, engineer officer, gunnery officer, supply officer, medical department, and officer of the deck all have specific responsibilities and duties.

Helicopter Operations

The role of the helicopter has been extensively expanded in recent years, and this bill establishes standard, safe operating procedures. Helo missions now include search and rescue, vertical replenishment, antisubmarine warfare, amphibious as-

Figure 19–4 Helo operations offer a wide-range view of Norfolk Harbor.

sault, and minesweeping. Helicopters operate with virtually all fleet units. The XO assigns an officer to maintain this bill.

Helicopter Inflight Refueling

This bill ensures safe inflight-refueling operations for helicopters. Standard operating procedures are specified for each ship. The operations (or weapons) officer, as directed by the commanding officer, is responsible for this bill.

Intelligence Collection

This bill provides for the collection and reporting of intelligence information (secondary mission following after operations and training), as long as they don't interfere with the ship's principal mission. The intelligence officer, under the supervision of the operations officer, is responsible for maintaining the bill; the officer of the deck is responsible for its execution.

Landing Party

When required, units form a landing party to quell riots or disorders in the ship's vicinity, assist in disaster relief ashore, and participate in parades and ceremonies. The landing party is organized on the basis of the size of the ship's crew: one 10-man squad per 100 crew members, with a minimum of one squad. The size cannot exceed one company. Squads are commanded by petty officers, platoons and companies by junior officers. The weapons officer (or commanding officer of the marine detachment, if assigned) is responsible for this bill.

Navigation

This bill, the responsibility of the navigator, prescribes uniform responsibilities and procedures for the safe navigation of the ship, including navigation in restricted water under conditions of low visibility. It should be noted that the safe navigation of the ship ultimately rests with the commanding officer.

Replenishment

The assignment of personnel to duties and stations, as well as the establishment of certain procedures for replenishing the ship at sea, transferring passengers and light freight, fueling, defueling, and the internal transfer of fuel—all are spelled out in this bill. The first lieutenant, under the supervision of the

XO, is responsible for this bill. (Replenishment operations are also covered in chapter 21.)

Rescue and Assistance

Through this bill the damage-control assistant (the engineering officer under the XO) creates a special organization of qualified personnel within each duty section to render emergency assistance to persons or activities outside the unit, without lowering the unit's own security standards. This bill also prescribes the procedures for recovering persons from the water.

Rescue of Survivors

This bill, similar to the one above, establishes an organization capable of rescuing large numbers of survivors from the water. The weapons officer, under the supervision of the XO, is responsible for the bill. The organization is supplemented, as necessary, by personnel from all repair parties in order to meet the needs of a particular rescue operation.

Ship's Silencing

432

The engineer, working with and through the ship's silencing board, is responsible for reducing noise to enhance the performance of installed sonars and to decrease the ship's acoustic detectability. This bill is primarily concerned with tactical noise, not shipboard noise that may have an adverse physical or psychological effect on the crew.

Shore Fire-Control Party

This bill organizes and describes the responsibilities of the shore fire-control party, provides lists of equipment for them to use, and outlines the conditions under which they may be called into service. The operations officer, under the XO, is responsible for the bill. The primary mission of the shore fire-control party is fire control for the ship's guns (or other naval guns) in support of limited operations ashore. The party also has the secondary mission of tactical control of available aircraft support. The shore fire-control party is sent ashore under varying combat conditions.

Special Sea and Anchor Detail

Personnel assignments, and specific duties for periods when the ship is in restricted waters and preparing to get under way or return to port, are covered in this bill. The special sea and anchor detail supplements the regular steaming watch; in some instances, the detail personnel relieve the regular watch. The operations officer has responsibility for this bill. (The specific procedures for getting under way or returning to port are discussed in chapter 16.)

Visit and Search, Boarding and Salvage, and Prize Crew

Such operations were much more common in the days of square-riggers and muzzle-loaders, but they are still possible. The operations officer is responsible for maintaining the bill and for bringing to the XO's attention any matters that may have an effect on the bill. The purpose of visit and search is to determine the nationality of a ship, the character of her cargo, the nature of her employment, and other pertinent factors. The commanding officer dispatches the boarding and salvage party to take command of the ship, restrain the crew, and conduct necessary salvage operations. The prize master, although still responsible to his or her own commanding officer, exercises the full range of responsibilities of any commanding officer over the prize crew.

Emergency Bills

Emergency bills are probably the most important of all shipboard bills because they affect all hands. It is extremely important that you know what your responsibilities are for each situation, and that when the alarm is sounded, you go to your station on the double. You go forward and up the starboard side, aft and down the port side. It is essential that this route of travel be followed to prevent delay. Maintain silence; only key personnel in charge should speak.

General Emergency

The organization, procedures, and responsibilities during a major emergency or disaster are contained in this bill. It includes situations such as collision, grounding, internal and external explosion, CBR (chemical-biological-radiological) contamination, and earthquake, storm, or battle damage. This bill, the responsibility of the engineering officer, also provides for the orderly and controlled egress of personnel in case of abandon ship, and for salvage of the ship if feasible.

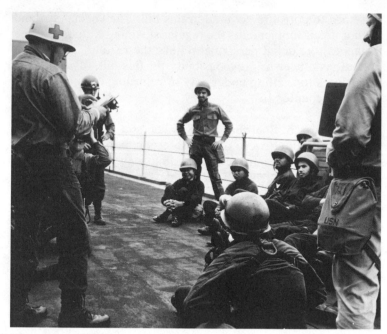

Figure 19–5 A damage-control repair party drills for emergency situations until their response to an alarm is second nature.

The training program for emergencies is a long-range one, encompassing the following:

Formal shore-based schools train personnel in firefighting, aircraft firefighting, repair-locker leader training, basic damage-control procedures, and CBR defense.

All officers and leading petty officers are responsible for indoctrinating and training their personnel in the fundamentals of emergency control.

In major catastrophes, the availability of personnel trained in first aid drastically reduces the number of serious casualties and fatalities. The medical officer (or senior hospital corpsman when no medical officer is assigned) is charged with conducting a training program for all hands in first-aid procedures, including measures in CBR defense.

Division officers are responsible for training their personnel in the use of individual protective equipment and in the performance of duties while they are wearing the Mark V gas mask and other protective clothing.

General emergency drills are held as ordered by the XO; there is generally at least one each month. During drills, the actions and duties prescribed in this and other supplemental bills must be fully carried out.

The general provisions of this bill are effective whether the ship is under way or in port. The bill goes into effect in the event of fire or other hazardous emergency. It also provides details for specific situations, for example, emergency with full crew on board, in-port general emergency with partial crew, CBR attack, or abandon ship.

Aircraft Crash and Rescue

Each ship must be prepared to implement this bill rapidly. Since the variances in ship's characteristics, organization, and

Figure 19–6 Crewmen undergo pickup training during at-sea aircraft crash, search, and rescue operations.

capabilities preclude the establishment of a general bill applicable to all units, each must establish its own guidelines. Type commanders distribute bills generally applicable to ships of their forces. Each ship, within the guidelines set by the type commander, prepares a bill to meet its specific requirements. The XO is responsible for appointing an officer to maintain this bill.

Emergency Steering

Since many of the detailed measures used to control a steering casualty are determined by a ship's installed equipment, supplemental instructions to this bill are necessary. It does, however, provide the general guidelines and define the responsibilities of the officer of the deck, steersman in the pilot house, quartermaster of the watch, boatswain's mate of the watch, duty electrician's mate, and auxiliary machinist's mate. The navigator, with the technical assistance of the engineering officer, is responsible for this bill.

Man Overboard

This bill is concerned with the recovery of one person or a small number of people from the water. Each sailor should be instructed in the action to take if he or she falls overboard, and what action to expect from a rescuing ship. Watch sections get frequent drill and instruction, and rescue details are conducted to ensure the successful execution of the provisions of this bill. The first lieutenant, subject to the approval of the XO, is responsible for updating it.

Nuclear Reactor Plant Casualty

The engineering/reactor officer, under the supervision of the XO, is responsible for this bill, conducting drills to test its adequacy, and evaluating the state of training. Although it is unlikely that reactor conditions will result in a power-plant breakdown and subsequent nuclear accident, the ship must be prepared to meet such an emergency. The bill also outlines procedures for the control, monitoring, and decontamination of affected areas and personnel.

Nuclear Weapons Accident/Incident

Potential or actual damage to a nuclear weapon or related system endangers personnel, the ship, and her vital equipment. This bill, which defines the specific hazards of and basic

Figure 19–7 A dummy called Oscar—named after the flag—is used in man-overboard drills.

considerations involved in such an accident, is the responsibility of the weapons officer, under the supervision of the XO. A nuclear-safety officer, if this duty is assigned to an officer other than the weapons officer, is the weapons officer's assistant in this area.

Toxic Gas

This bill outlines the procedures, duties, and responsibilities of controlling and minimizing the effects of toxic gases such as chlorine, smoke, tear gas, ammonia, carbon monoxide, and carbon dioxide. The damage-control assistant maintains this bill. It contains a complete listing of toxic gases aboard ship and includes information about how they are produced, how they are detected, and the effects of overexposure. Each ship has a designated gas-free engineer, usually the damage-control assistant or repair division officer.

Special Bills

The four bills in this category are employed in special situations. All but the first one are the responsibility of the XO. (The operations officer is in charge of the antisneak/antiswimmer attack bill.)

Antisneak/Antiswimmer Attack

When moored in foreign ports or anchored in foreign or hostile waters, ships are vulnerable to attack by swimmers and small boats. This bill ensures that the ship is capable of detecting and defeating sneak attack. The antisneak/antiswimmer watch is set at the discretion of the commanding officer.

Evacuating Civilians

The plans and procedures outlined in this bill are intended to serve as a guide for the execution of an evacuation mission involving civilian personnel. Each situation differs depending on the number and sex of passengers embarked and the length of time they are embarked; therefore, detailed plans must be formulated after assignment to a specific evacuation mission.

Prisoners of War

This bill applies to enemy combat forces, individuals traveling with an armed force (such as newspaper correspondents, contractors, technicians), and the officers and crews of enemy merchant ships. It also handles the particulars of custody, berthing, messing, and other needs of prisoners of war.

Troop Lift

Although the conditions under which troops are transported vary, the procedures and responsibilities prescribed in this bill are standard. In addition to the XO, who is responsible for the organization, supervision, and coordination of all phases of a troop lift, the weapons officer, first lieutenant, supply officer, operations officer, and personnel officer are also assigned responsibilities.

Drilling for Emergencies

During a major emergency, you will hear the continuous sounding of the general quarters alarm or on smaller ships, a siren, horn, or bell, plus the words "General quarters! General quarters! All hands man your battle stations!" over the 1MC system. Don't try to find out what has happened, just move—you'll know soon enough.

Man Overboard

When a person goes overboard, prompt action is essential. Anyone who sees someone go overboard immediately sounds the alarm "Man overboard, port (starboard) side," and drops a life ring or life jacket. If possible, keep the person in sight. If a smoke float and a dye marker are available, drop them in too.

Every underway watch is organized to handle this situation. The officer of the deck maneuvers the ship to a recovery position. At the same time, word is passed twice and six or more short blasts are sounded on the ship's whistle. The lifeboat crew stands by to lower away when directed. If available, a helo may be launched. The helo can quickly spot a person in the water and pick him or her up. If the identity of the person is not known, a muster of the crew may be held to find out who is missing.

The person overboard may be *you*. If this should happen, keep your head. Don't panic or despair. Hold your breath when you hit the water; the buoyancy of your lungs will bring you to the surface. Don't swim frantically away from the ship; the screws won't suck you under, because they are too deep in the water. Keep afloat and try to stay in one place. The ship will maneuver right back down her track toward you. (Note: The exact placement of a person overboard is pinpointed in the combat information center using a dead-reckoning tracer.)

Even if no one saw you go over, keep afloat. When a shipmate is missed, ships and aircraft begin an intensive search.

If a person goes overboard in port, the alarm is sounded as usual and the officer of the deck follows the best available rescue procedure. Boats in the water assist in the emergency.

CBR Defense

In the event of CBR attack, the crew can do a great deal to minimize casualties and damage. For those ships located at or near ground zero in a nuclear attack, or in an area of high concentration of biological or chemical agents, casualties and damage will, of course, be great. However, tests have shown that ships not receiving the direct effects of such attacks have a good chance of survival with relatively few casualties, and with weapons systems intact. Since formations are generally widely dispersed, it is probable that nearly all fleet units will escape the direct effects of a CBR attack.

Before the Attack: The preparatory measures when attack is declared imminent are as follows:

Go to general quarters to "button up" the ship. Before the attack wash down all topside areas using the water wash down system. The entire outer surface of the ship is kept wet so that CBR contaminants will wash overboard and not adhere to the external surfaces of the ship.

All nonvital openings of the ship are closed to maintain an envelope as gas-tight as possible. Personnel who are manning stations below decks, and must breathe air conducted directly into the ship during an attack, should have gas masks. These areas are generally firerooms, diesel-generator rooms, and other main-propulsion spaces that require large volumes of air to support combustion.

All topside personnel in exposed positions don protective clothing and masks. Personnel are also issued detectors that indicate what kind of CBR agent the wearer might be exposed to, and the degree of exposure.

The extreme effectiveness of some bacteriological agents, the toxicity of chemical agents, and the danger of radioactive fallout mean that protective clothing and gas masks must be carefully handled. It is mandatory that all personnel be periodically retrained in the use of protective clothing and masks.

Protective clothing worn in CBR defense is of four types:

Ordinary work clothing is initially effective in preventing droplets of chemicals or bacteriological agents from contacting the skin; however, this clothing quickly becomes contaminated and must be discarded.

Foul-weather clothing, including parkas, trousers, rubber boots, and gloves, protects the skin against penetration by

liquid chemical agents and low-energy alpha radioactive particles. It too retains contamination and must be discarded when
it can no longer be decontaminated by hosing down.

Permeable protective clothing has been treated with chemicals that neutralize blister-agent vapors and aerosols. It loses
its ability to neutralize these agents once soaked down. It is
thus not effective for long-term protection.

Impermeable protective clothing has a rubberized outer covering and hence will not permit air or water to pass through.
Needless to say, this clothing is hot and uncomfortable in
warm climates. It will provide, however, the best overall protection against biological- and chemical-warfare agents and alpha particles. Gamma and high-energy beta radiation will penetrate it.

There are several protective masks available for general use
in the Navy, and some can be used in CBR defense. Masks are
generally of two types. The first includes all masks that do not
provide oxygen to the user. This type of mask employs mechanical and chemical filters that remove solid or liquid particles and absorb or neutralize toxic and irritating vapors.

The Mark V gas mask is a good example of this type. It will
protect against the inhalation of some nerve, blister, choking,
vomiting, and tear agents. It will not protect against carbon
monoxide, carbon dioxide, ammonia, and many fuel gases or
vapors. This mask is not used in connection with firefighting or
smoke, or in an atmosphere containing less than 19.5 percent
oxygen, the amount necessary to support life.

The oxygen breathing apparatus (OBA) is an example of the
second type of mask. (see p. 417). The chemicals in the OBA
canister provide for about 45 minutes of light use or 30 minutes
of heavy use. Various other masks give some protection
against CBR agents, but only for short periods of time, and
only if air supplies to them are kept uncontaminated.

After the Attack: The detection of CBR agents—which
generally are invisible, odorless, tasteless, and give no hint to
the senses of their presence—requires special equipment and
training.

Radioactive particles betray their presence by giving off several kinds of radiation. Some kinds have no detectable mass or
charge and are classed as high-energy electromagnetic radiation, or gamma rays. Other types have charge or mass and are
further classed into neutrons, electrons, alpha particles, neu-
trinos, and additional subatomic particles too numerous to

mention. The ionizing radiations—alpha particles, beta electrons, and gamma waves—are the easiest to detect. The three primary types of radiation can be detected by instruments known as radiacs (radiation, detection, indication, and computation).

The use of radiacs depends on their specific internal configuration. They are used as intensity meters for measuring highly penetrating gamma radiation or less penetrating beta and alpha radiation. They are also used as survey meters to detect alpha particles, or as dosimeters for measuring the total amount of radiation an individual has received during an attack. The present individual dosimeter is the DT-60/PD; it is worn around the neck on a chain. It records accumulated whole-body gamma radiation from 10-660 roentgens and is read by a computer (CP-95). Film badges are also issued to measure whole-body beta and gamma radiation.

With early detection of radiation, prompt decontamination, and removal of hot spots from the ship, many lives can be saved and much radiation sickness avoided.

In biological-warfare detection, samples must be taken, cultured, and subjected to thorough laboratory testing before the agent can be identified. This is slow, exacting work; and if viruses are involved, they can greatly increase the difficulty of identification. Since identification is difficult, by the time the agent has been identified, many people could already be casualties.

Chemical agents are somewhat easier to detect, but no one procedure can detect all known chemical agents. Some of these are lethal in extremely small concentrations and hence could be deployed upwind over a great area with devastating results.

The monitoring and surveying of ships and stations is a vital part of CBR defense. Location of a hazard, isolation of contaminated areas, recording the results of a survey, and reporting findings up the chain of command are the functions of every military unit encountering contamination.

Two more types of surveys are required after an CBR attack. A gross survey, including weather decks, interior spaces, and machinery, is taken to locate any obvious contamination. Personnel decontamination starts as soon as the decontamination area itself is ready.

Specific instructions for monitoring surveys cannot be specified for all situations, but generally after a gross survey has been made, gross decontamination begins. This entails flushing the contaminated surfaces with large amounts of water. The water wash-down system is used for external surfaces. For internal contamination, firehoses and manual scrubbing are employed. Steam is a useful agent for decontamination, especially if biological-warfare agents are suspected or if the contamination is lodged in greasy or oily films.

Detailed decontamination is the next step, its purpose being to further reduce the contamination to such a level that no significant hazard remains. There are three general procedures: surface decontamination to reduce the agent without destroying the use of the equipment; aging and sealing to allow the contaminant to decay or lose its potency through evaporation or dissolution; and disposal or removal of contaminated materials to a place where they can do little harm.

Emergency Destruction

The commanding officer may order the destruction of classified documents and equipment to prevent their falling into enemy hands. Persons assigned duties under this bill are given specific and detailed instructions when the need arises. The emergency-destruction bill should be updated in each shipboard division and annotated on the WQ&S bill.

Abandon Ship

During an emergency of this sort, many senior officers and petty officers may be lost as battle casualties, in which case full responsibility falls on the shoulders of more junior personnel.

Abandon-ship stations and duties are noted on the WQ&S bill. Careful planning details who goes in which boat or raft, what emergency equipment is to be supplied, and who supplies it. Know your abandon-ship station and duties. Know all escape routes to the ship's topside from berthing spaces or working spaces below decks. Know how to inflate a life jacket. Know how to lower a boat or let go of a life raft. Know how to handle survival gear. And, if necessary, know how to do this all in the dark. New personnel reporting to shipboard commands should be thoroughly trained until they are able to exit from assigned working and living spaces blindfolded.

Only the commanding officer can order abandon ship. He or she will do so only after all efforts to save the ship prove futile. When the abandon-ship alarm sounds, act fast. It's your last chance. Survival at sea depends on knowledge, equipment, training, and self-control.

Disaster can strike suddenly at sea. A ship can go down within 3 minutes of a collision or explosion. If you don't know what to do before this happens, there won't be time to find out after it does.

Going over the Side: Make certain your life jacket is secured properly and that your knife, whistle, and flashlight are fastened to it. Go down a cargo net, boat falls, firehose, or line if you can, but don't slide down and burn your hands. If you have to jump, look out for wreckage or swimmers in the water. Don't try a fancy dive; go feet first, with legs crossed and arms over your face. If you have a pneumatic life jacket, don't inflate it until you are in the water—otherwise you will pop right out of it and possibly injure yourself because of the extreme buoyancy and force an inflated jacket exerts on your neck and body.

If possible, go over the windward side and swim upwind. If you go over the leeward side, the wind may blow the ship or burning oil down on you. Swim underwater to avoid burning oil; when you come up for air, splash the oil away as you break the surface. To protect yourself from underwater explosions, swim away for at least 150 yards, then climb aboard a raft, boat, or piece of wreckage, or float on your back. Stay calm. If you panic, you are more than halfway lost.

444

In the Water: Rafts, boats, nets, and floating wreckage should be tied together; this makes it easier for searchers to find you. Wounded persons should be put in boats or rafts first, others should hang on the sides. In cold water, everyone must get into a raft or boat as soon as possible. If you must remain in the water, stay as still as possible to prevent heat loss. Heat escapes most rapidly from the head, hands, and feet; use whatever clothing is available to protect these areas. Numbness occurs in waters below 35 degrees F. Breathe slowly and remain still. You may have to follow a rotation plan to get uninjured persons in and out of life rafts, thereby reducing hypothermia.

Frostbite and immersion foot can occur quickly in cold water. Don't rub; this will damage frozen tissues. Warm affected parts against your own body or a shipmate's.

In a hot climate, keep your shirt, trousers, and shoes on—you'll need them for protection against sun and salt water.

Boat Handling: In a power boat, the slowest possible speed
will give the best mileage. If the boat is fitted for sails, use them
and save the motor for an emergency. Otherwise, jury-rig a
mast and sails out of oars, boathooks, clothing, and tarpaulins.
If wind and sea are driving you away from the nearest land or
rescue area, rig a sea anchor to slow the drift.

Organization: The abandon-ship bill assigns an officer or
senior enlisted person to each boat or raft, but serious casualties may make you the senior person in a boat. If so, take
charge.

Make the wounded as comfortable as possible. Make a list of
all survivors, and try to list all known casualties. Inventory all
water and provisions and set up a ration system based on the
expected number of days to land. No one should eat or drink
for the first 24 hours.

Organize a watch. Lookouts must be alert and know how to
use available signal gear. Get under way for the nearest known
land or well-traveled shipping route. Time permitting, the
nearest landfall and coordinates by compass will be passed
over the 1MC. Each life raft is equipped with a compass.

Secure all gear so nothing will be lost. If you have fishing
gear aboard, use it; otherwise, make some. Rig a tarp for protection against the sun and to catch rainwater.

Try to keep all hands alert and cheerful. Save their energy;
unnecessary exertion uses up food and water.

Equipment: The vest-type life preserver is the most important item of abandon-ship equipment. Learn how to use it. The
vest preserver goes over other clothes. Tie the upper tape at
the waist fairly tight to keep it from sliding up in the water;
adjust the chest strap and fasten the snap hook into the ring; tie
collar tapes to keep them down under your chin; and pull
straps between the legs from behind, as tightly as possible
without becoming uncomfortable. Adjust the straps on an unconscious person before he or she is put overboard; the design
of this preserver will keep the person's head upright and prevent drowning.

The inflatable life preserver is carried in a pouch at your
back and fastens around your waist on a web belt. It can be
inflated with a carbon dioxide cartridge or by mouth. To inflate
the preserver, pull the pouch around in front, remove the preserver, slip it over your head, and jerk the lanyard down as far
as possible to release the gas into the chamber. For more buoy-

Figure 19–8 Front and back views of the kapok-type vest life preserver.

Figure 19–9 Front and back views of the CO_2-type jacket life preserver.

ancy, you can add air through the mouthpiece. To deflate, open the valve.

The 15-man Mark 5 inflatable lifeboat, the type carried aboard most ships, is a compact, relatively light, easily stowed, and easily launched boat. It is constructed of separate tubes. The upper, lower, and canopy support tubes are inflated by carbon dioxide cylinders; the thwart tubes are inflated with hand pumps. A fabric bottom is attached to the lower tube to support manually inflatable floors. The floors are equipped with hand lines and are removable for emergency use.

The boat has a carrying case with a release cable extending outside; pulling the cables will open and inflate the boat in about 30 seconds. Normally the boat should be inflated in the water. As soon as the boat is inflated, use the boarding net and grab ladders to board it. The first person to enter stays at the entrance to help others; the second in goes forward to open the opposite entrance, check the sea anchor, and help others board at that end.

Each boat is equipped with three waterproof containers of survival equipment. These are packed in the carrying case, not in the boat, so don't let the case get away—it is secured to the boat by a length of line. Two of the containers each hold two cartons of rations and one carton of water. The third container holds one carton of rations and the following items: a sea-marker dye, a flashlight, two C batteries, a jackknife, a signal mirror, two sponges, a whistle, a first-aid kit, and a distress-signal kit. The rations are sufficient to sustain fifteen sailors for five days.

Signaling equipment is extremely important because of the difficulty of spotting life rafts from the air, and from the surface in heavy weather. The signal mirror can be seen at a distance of 10 miles or more, if used properly. Hold the mirror to reflect sunlight onto a nearby object, then look through the hole in the center. You will see a bright spot that shows the direction of the reflected beam of sunlight. Keep your eye on the dot and move the mirror slowly until the dot is on the target.

The signal kit contains a dozen Mark 13 distress signals for day and night use, and to provide wind-drift information to helicopters picking up personnel. One end of the signal tube produces an orange smoke for day use; the other end produces a red flare for night use. The night flare can be identified in the dark by a series of small beadlike projections embossed around the edge. Each signal will burn for about 18 seconds.

Dye markers have a powder that produces a brilliant yellowish-green fluorescence when sprinkled on water. In decent conditions, the dye will be a good target for only about an hour, but it will retain some of its color for up to 4 hours. From an altitude of 3,000 feet, the detection range of the dye marker may be as great as 10 miles. The range decreases as the dye deteriorates. Unless the moonlight is very bright, the dye is not effective at night.

Never discard any article that will hold water. When it rains, every container that can hold water will be invaluable. To assist you in filling the containers, a rain-catcher tube is attached to the lifeboat canopy. The 15-man lifeboat carries no equipment for turning seawater into fresh water. Other types of rafts, however, such as those carried in aircraft, have solar stills.

In polar areas, fresh water can be obtained from old sea ice, which is bluish, splinters easily, and is nearly free from salt. Fresh water may also be obtained from icebergs, but be careful. As the berg's underwater portion melts, it gets topheavy and can capsize without warning.

Fire

An alarm for a real fire may be given at any time. For drill purposes, a fire may be assumed to be in a specific place—for example, in an ammunition space or berthing compartment.

The word for fire, passed twice over the general announcing system, gives the fire's compartment location; then the ship's bell is rung, followed by one stroke if forward, two if amidships, three if aft. Ships with nuclear weapons have a special FZ alarm, a rapidly ringing bell triggered automatically if temperature in a weapons space exceeds authorized temperatures, or if security there is violated.

The person who discovers an actual fire must give the alarm. The most important thing that person can do is notify at least one other person who can go for help. Too often a fire has gotten out of control because a person tried to put it out without calling for help.

Use any means at hand—telephone, messenger, or word of mouth—to notify the officer of the deck, or damage control central.

Once the alarm has sounded, personnel nearby should act promptly to check or extinguish the fire, using the means nearest at hand. All others respond to the alarm in accordance with the WQ&S bill. If you and several other people have begun to fight the fire, do not leave the scene until the fire or repair party arrives, unless you are caught in extremely heavy smoke or flames. Do not become a casualty yourself. Have all spaces adjacent to the affected areas evacuated promptly. (See chapter 18 for a comprehensive picture of shipboard firefighting operations and associated equipment.)

Safety and Maintenance

20

Safety

Safety is a job for all hands at all times. Every single operation aboard a naval vessel poses danger. Going to sea involves working with powerful machinery, high-speed equipment, steam of intensely high temperature and pressure, volatile and exotic fuels and propellants, heavy lifts, high explosives, stepped-up electrical voltages, and the unpredictable forces of weather. It is the responsibility of everyone aboard ship to observe all safety precautions.

Safety precautions for each piece of equipment used in the Navy are available and should be read and understood. The Navy Ships Technical Manual (NAVSHIPSTECHMAN), the Standard Organization and Regulations of the U.S. Navy, and numerous bureau and systems manuals contain written safety regulations.

451

Another important part of safety is the regular maintenance of equipment and systems. Maintenance involves much more than just cleaning and painting. For safety and efficiency, every item aboard ship—from the simplest valve to the most complicated electronic gear—must be clean and operable.

The following general instructions, listed alphabetically, serve as an introduction to the most important principles regarding shipboard safety.

Aircraft Operations

During aircraft operations, only those actually involved are allowed in the flight-deck area. All other personnel remain clear or below decks. Personnel engaged in flight ops wear appropriate safety equipment.

Passengers must be led to and from a helicopter or aircraft by a member of the transfer crew, handling crew, or flight crew. All loose gear in the flight-deck area is stowed elsewhere or secured to the deck. Personnel are taught about the shrapnel effect of rotor blades or propellers striking a solid object. Be careful around props and helo rotors. When turning, they are nearly invisible. Rotor tips cover a wide area and often dip close to the deck when the helo lands.

The engine noise of the plane you are watching will drown out the noise of planes you are not watching. Don't move without looking in all directions, and don't direct all your attention to a single aircraft.

Also beware of jet blast. Any place within 100 feet of a jet engine is dangerous. A jet blast can burn, knock down, or blow a person over the side.

Ammunition Handling

Everyone who handles ammunition must be instructed in safety regulations, methods of handling, and the storage and uses of ammunition and explosives. Only careful, reliable, mentally sound, and physically fit sailors are permitted to work with explosives or ammunition.

Anyone who knows of defective ammo or other explosive ordnance, defective containers or handling devices, the rough or improper handling of ordnance, or the willful or accidental violation of safety regulations must report the facts to his or her immediate superior.

Anyone supervising the inspection, care, preparation, handling, use, or disposal of ammunition or explosives must see that all regulations and instructions are observed, remain vigilant throughout the operation, and warn subordinates of the need for care and vigilance. Supervisors must also ensure that subordinates are familiar with the characteristics of explosive materials, equipment used to handle them, safety precautions, and the catastrophies safety regulations are designed to prevent. Supervisors must beware of hazardous procedures and be able to spot their subordinates' personal problems, so as to avert disaster.

Smoking is not permitted in magazines or near the handling or loading operations. Matches, lighters, and spark- or flame-producing devices are permitted in certain designated spaces, such as torpedo rooms, but only when specific written permission is received from command authority.

Crews working with explosives or ammunition are limited to the minimum number required to perform the operation properly. Unauthorized personnel are not permitted in magazines

or in the immediate vicinity of loading operations. All authorized visitors must be escorted.

The productivity of persons or units handling explosive ordnance is never evaluated on a competitive basis, except when
weapons are serviced in training or under prescribed conditions.

When fuzed or assembled with firing mechanisms, mines,
depth charges, rockets, projector charges, missiles, and bombs
are treated as if armed.

Live ammo, rockets, or missiles are loaded into guns or on
launchers only for firing, except where approved by the Naval
Sea Systems Command or as permitted below.

Nothing but inert ammo is used for drill purposes. But the
following may be used aboard aircraft carriers for loading drills
when specifically authorized by the commanding officer, and
when applicable radio-frequency hazard restrictions and other
safety regulations are adhered to: (1) aircraft gun ammunition,
(2) conventional, high-explosive bombs, (3) rockets and rocket
launchers with installed rockets, and (4) guided missiles and
torpedoes with exercise heads only.

Supervisors must require good housekeeping in explosive
spaces. Nothing is to be stored except explosives, containers,
and authorized handling equipment.

No warhead detonator should be assembled in or near a
magazine containing explosives. Fuzing is performed at a designated fuzing area.

Boats

In motor launches, only the coxswain and the boat officer or
senior line officer may ride on the coxswain's flat, although not
more than two persons may be on deck at once.

No boat may be loaded beyond the capacities established by
the commanding officer (published in the boat bill) without his
or her specific permission, and then only in emergencies.

No person may smoke in a boat under any circumstances.

No person is assigned to a boat crew unless he or she can
swim.

Boat crews must demonstrate a practical knowledge of seamanship, rules of the road, and safety regulations. Qualification is granted by the ship's first lieutenant.

No one not specifically designated by the engineering officer
is to operate or attempt to operate a boat engine; to test, remove, or charge the boat's battery, or tamper in any way with
the electrical system; or to fuel the boat.

No person may board a boat from a boat boom unless someone is standing by on deck or in a boat at the same boom.

All members of a boat's crew wear rubber-soled canvas shoes in the boat.

All boats leaving the ship must have local charts with courses to and from their destinations indicated. They must have an adjusted and lighted compass installed. Boats must also have enough life preservers to accommodate each person embarked. These should be readily available when rough seas, reduced visibility, or other hazards threaten.

No boat is dispatched or permitted to proceed unless released by the officer of the deck. Releases are not to be granted until it has been determined that the crew and passengers are wearing life preservers, and when advisable, that weather and sea conditions are suitable for small-boat operations.

Chemicals

Adequate precautions should be taken in the stowage, handling, and disposal of hazardous chemicals and materials. A review of potential hazards is not possible here, but substantial chemical-safety information is available in the following references:

The NAVSHIPSTECHMAN has requirements and safety guidelines on a wide variety of hazardous chemicals, including cleaning agents, solvents, paints and associated chemicals, chlorinated hydrocarbons, mercury, oxidizing materials, corrosive liquids, and materials in aerosol containers.

Safety Precautions for Shore Activities, OPNAV instruction 5100.23, includes information on the hazards of and precautions to be taken in using laboratory, photographic, and painting chemicals, as well as alkalies, acids, solvents, cleaning agents, cyanides, organic phosphates, toxic metals/dusts, halogenated hydrocarbons, etc.

Hazardous Material Information System, DOD instruction 6050.5, lists hazardous items in federal stock, classifies material according to the type of hazard, and recommends proper stowage. NAVSUP P-485, Afloat Supply Procedures, contains information on the receipt, custody, and proper stowage of hazardous materials.

Guidelines for procedures to follow when seeking information on the nature, hazards, and precautions of unknown chemicals and materials are outlined in the Navy Hazardous Material Control Program (NAVSUP instruction 5100.27).

Compressed Gas

Precautions must be taken when working on high-pressure air systems to prevent lines that are not completely isolated and bled down from opening.

No person should attempt repairs of any nature on an air flask or receiver under pressure. Bottles containing compressed gas must be kept capped and well secured when not in use.

Oxygen bottles and fittings must be stored away from oil and grease. Never substitute oxygen for compressed air.

Divers

Diving precautions and safety regulations are set out in the U.S. Navy Diving Manual.

Electrical and Electronic Equipment

Electrical equipment includes generators, electrically powered machinery and mechanisms, power cables, controllers, transformers, and associated equipment. Electronic equipment includes radars, sonars, power amplifiers, antennas, electronic-warfare equipment, computers, and associated controls. The most important precaution with all such equipment is never to work alone.

No one is to operate, repair, or adjust any electrical or electronic equipment unless he or she has been assigned that duty, except in definite emergencies, and then only when no qualified operator is present. (Electric light and bulkhead-electric-fan switches are exempted.)

No one is to operate, repair, or adjust electrical and electronic equipment unless he or she has demonstrated a practical knowledge of its operation and repair and applicable safety regulations, and then only when duly qualified by the head of the department.

No one is to remove, paint over, destroy, or mutilate any name plates, cable tags, or other identification marks on electrical or electronic equipment.

No one is to hang anything on, or secure a line to, any power cable, antenna, wave guide, or other piece of electrical or electronic equipment.

Only authorized portable electric equipment that has been tested and certified by the electric shop may be used. Portable electric equipment is tested weekly.

Figure 20–1 Extreme caution must be used when working with electrical power machines.

Electric equipment should be deenergized and checked with a voltage tester or voltmeter before being serviced or repaired. Circuit breakers and the switches of deenergized circuits must be locked or placed in the off position while work is in progress, and a suitable warning tag should be attached to them.

Work on live circuits or equipment is carried out only when specific permission has been received from the commanding officer. The person performing the work must be insulated from the ground and must follow all safety measures. Rubber gloves are worn. Another person stands by to cut the circuit and render first aid. Medical personnel are alerted before work begins.

Personal electrical or electronic equipment must be inspected by the electrical or electronic workshop to ensure that it conforms to NAVSHIPSTECHMAN regulations.

Always avoid electric shock of any voltage. Even 115 volts can kill.

Bare lamps or fixtures with exposed lamps should not be installed in machinery spaces. Only authorized fixtures are

Safety

installed in such spaces, to minimize hazards from flammable fuels.

No one is permitted aloft near energized antennas, unless it is determined that no danger exists. If there is any danger from rotating antennas, induced voltages in the rigging and superstructure, or high-power radiation, equipment must be secured and a suitable warning tag attached to the main supply switches. These precautions are also observed if any other antenna is in the vicinity, as on an adjacent ship.

Electrical- and electronic-safety precautions must be conspicuously posted. Personnel are to be instructed and drilled in their observance. All electrical and electronics personnel must be qualified to administer first aid for shock. Procedures for emergency resuscitation and use of airway breathing tubes are posted in spaces containing electronic equipment.

Rubber matting (except where vinyl sheet is specified) should be installed in front and in back of propulsion-control cubicles, power and lighting switchboards, interior communications (IC) switchboards, test switchboards, fire-control switchboards, and announcing-system amplifiers and control panels; in and around radio, radar, sonar, and countermeasures-equipment spaces that may be entered while servicing or tuning energized equipment; and around work benches in electrical and electronic shops where equipment is tested or repaired. A "shorting stick" should be available in every working space for electronic equipment.

Protective electrical enclosures must be closed and permanent electrical grounds maintained. Fuse boxes, lever-type boxes, and wiring accessories should be closed except during maintenance. Ground straps should not be painted, and care should be taken to maintain a positive ground to the ship's hull from all metal enclosures for electrical and electronic equipment.

Fire and Explosion Prevention

Reducing fire and explosion hazards is every sailor's responsibility. Whenever possible, hazards should be eliminated, including nonessential combustibles. Replace combustible materials with less flammable ones if you can. Limit the number of combustibles. Stow and protect essential combustibles to reduce the chance of fire.

Prevent the accumulation of oil and other flammables in bilges and inaccessible areas. Any accumulated material should be flushed out or removed immediately. Oily rags should be stowed in airtight metal containers. Stow paint, brushes, rags, thinners, and solvents in authorized locations only.

Do not use compressed air to accelerate the flow of liquid from containers of any type.

Keep damage-control equipment ready for any emergency.

Forklifts

Only authorized persons should operate forklifts. Before operating one, check its condition. Keep feet and hands inside the running line. No one other than the operator should ride a forklift, unless it has a second permanent seat.

Slow the forklift down on wet or slippery decks and corners.

No one should stand under loads being hoisted or lowered.

All cargo should be transported with the load-lifting rails tipped back. When you are moving, keep forks 4 to 6 inches above the deck, whether loaded or not. Do not exceed the specified load capacity. Lower and rest forks on deck when they are not in use.

Never bump or push stacks of cargo to straighten them. Forks should be worked all the way under their loads. Inspect each load before lifting. An unstable load should be repiled or banded before being lifted, at which point it's too late.

Come to a full stop before reversing the direction of travel.

Put on the parking brake when you complete your work, park the forklift in a fore and aft position near the centerline of the ship, and secure the lift with chains or cables. Use only special personnel pallets to lift personnel.

Hand Tools

Cold chisels should be held between the thumb and the other four fingers. On horizontal cuts, the palm should be up. Don't use a burred chisel, one with a mushroomed head, or one that is not properly tempered or sharpened. Wear goggles, and keep personnel away from flying chips.

Wood chisels should be free of cracks. Don't use one with a mushroomed head. Cup the chisel handle in the palm of your hand and exert pressure away from the body. Be sure no one is close enough to be hurt if the chisel slips.

Select the right hammer for the job. The head should be wedged securely and squarely on the handle, and neither the head nor handle should be chipped, cracked, or broken. Keep the hammer clean and free of oil or grease, otherwise it might slip from your hands, or the face of the hammer might glance off the object being struck. Grasp the handle firmly near the end, and keep your eye on the part to be struck. Strike so the hammer face hits the object squarely.

Hydraulic Machinery and Fluids

Hydraulically operated equipment must not be used until all personnel are clear of moving parts. This is particularly important in port, when masts, periscopes, rudders, and planes are operated only with the permission of the duty officer.

Because of the greater danger of auto-ignition explosions in systems exposed to high pressure, air, and petroleum fluids make sure that:

All hydraulic-system operating instructions are followed.

When operating a manual valve, especially one that isolates deadend piping, the valve is opened slowly until the pressure on both sides equalizes.

Machinery is secured and all equipment thoroughly checked when a hydraulic leak is detected.

Figure 20–2 Two Navy personnel work on an aircraft engine. Before any hydraulic equipment is turned on, hands must be clear of moving parts.

Integrity of Seawater Systems

To minimize the chance of flooding a ship when seawater systems fail, observe the following principles:

Systems not in use must be fully secured and proper log and status board entries made.

Supervisory and watch personnel must be aware of sea valves that are open.

No seawater system should be broken into for repairs, except as authorized by the appropriate department head. The duty officer or officer of the deck is kept fully informed, and adequate provisions are made to preclude the possibility of flooding. A hydrostatic test is made on reassembly. Before the system is restored to normal operation, a test must be conducted as specified in the system technical manual or NAVSHIPSTECHMAN.

Reach rods on all sea valves in the bilge must be kept in proper mechanical condition to permit operation from the platform deck.

460

Life Jackets, Life Rings, and Safety Harnesses

Life jackets and approved topside shoes are worn on weather decks when required.

A life ring with an attached distress marker is available topside near the quarterdeck, at each man-overboard station, and at each replenishment station. When on the surface for prolonged periods, submarines provide a life ring topside. Aircraft float lights, two at each man-overboard station, should be made available when the ship is under way. Ships with an antisubmarine capability have three available floats on both the port and starboard sides.

Submarines, when moored or anchored, have a Jacob's ladder rigged from the safety track to the waterline near the torpedo-loading hatch.

Life jackets worn in open-sea operations must be buoyant.

Life jackets are also worn when working over the side in port and at sea, on stages, on boatswain's chairs, or in boats and punts. They are worn during heavy weather, when handling lines or other deck equipment during transfers between ships, when fueling under way, during towing operations, in boats being raised or lowered, when entering boats from a boom or Jacob's ladder, in underway boats, and in rough water or low visibility.

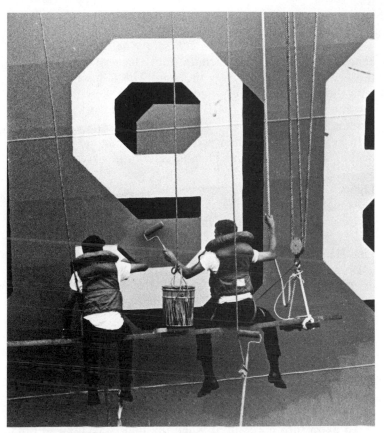

Figure 20–3 Sailors working over the side wear lifejackets and make use of life rings and safety harnesses.

Lifelines, Ladders, and Safety Nets

No one should lean, sit, stand, or climb on any lifeline in port or under way. People working over the side in port may climb over lifelines when necessary, but only if they are wearing life jackets and safety lines that are tended.

No lifeline should be dismantled or removed without specific permission from the first lieutenant, and then only if temporary lifelines are promptly rigged.

No person is to hang or secure any weight or line to any lifeline unless authorized by the commanding officer.

Ladders must not be removed without permission from the department head in charge. All accesses must be carefully and adequately roped off, or suitable railings installed. Work on ladders must, when possible, be performed when there is the least traffic.

No one may enter a flight-deck safety net or cargo net, except as authorized. A parachute safety harness is worn by all those working aloft or over the side. The following are used with the harness: a safety line with dynabrake shock absorbers, nylon working line (wire when doing hot work), and nylon tending line.

In heavy weather when personnel are required on weather decks, additional inboard life and safety lines are rigged.

Lights

At night, when the ship is in port, weather decks, accommodation ladders, gangways, and brows must be well lighted.

Line Handling

Do not under any circumstances stand in the bight of a line or on a taut fall.

Don't try to check a line that is running out rapidly by stepping on it.

When being handled, the standing part of a line is coiled or faked down to prevent fouling in case it runs out rapidly.

Nylon, dacron, and other synthetic lines are widely used for mooring and rigging. These lines are characterized by high elasticity and low friction. The following rules apply to them:

An extra turn is required when the line is secured to bitts, cleats, capstans, and other holding devices.

When easing a line out from holding devices, use extreme caution because of its high elasticity, rapid recovery, and low friction.

Nylon line, on parting, is stretched one and a half times its original length and snaps back. Do not stand in its direct line of pull when heavy loads are applied.

Put a strain gauge on all synthetic mooring lines.

Line-Throwing Gun

Bolo heavers and the line-throwing-gun crew must wear red helmets and highly visible red jackets for easy identification. Bolos and gun lines must be properly prepared for running. For the gun line, a loose coil in a bucket is better than a spindle.

When the receiving ship reaches the proper position, both ships pass the word: "Stand by for shot line. All hands take

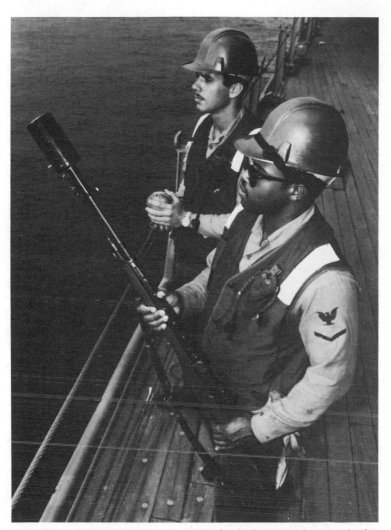

Figure 20–4 When a line-throwing gun is fired, all personnel not involved in the operation must stay clear.

cover." The officer in charge at each replenishment station in the firing ship sounds a one-blast signal on a mouth whistle or passes the word "Stand by" on electric megaphone. When everyone is ready to receive the shot line and the entire crew has taken cover, the officer in charge of the corresponding station on the receiving ship replies with a two-blast signal on a mouth whistle or passes the word "Ready" on an electric megaphone. After ascertaining that all hands in the target area are clear, the officer in charge of the firing ship gives the order to fire.

Only those designated by the officer in charge may leave cover to retrieve the bolo or shot line. All others must keep clear until all bolos or shot lines are on board and the word "Shot (bolo) lines secure" is passed.

The receiving ship (except in the case of an aircraft carrier) does not fire her line-throwing guns unless ordered or asked to do so by the delivering ship.

Luminous-Dial Devices

No luminous-dial devices using radioactive paints are permitted on board any time. Personal luminous-dial devices, such as wristwatches, are subject to the control of the engineering officer when atmosphere control is in effect.

Materials Handling

Safety shoes or toe guards must be worn when handling heavy stores or equipment.

Gloves are to be worn when carrying, lifting, or moving objects that have sharp edges or projecting points. Always remove rings when wearing gloves.

Material must not be thrown from platforms or trucks to the floor or ground. Use suitable lowering equipment.

Lifting or lowering operations performed by several persons should be done on a signal from one person only, and only after everyone is in the clear.

Don't overload hand trucks. On a ramp or incline, keep the load below you—pull it up and push it down.

To lift a load, stand close to it with your feet solidly placed and slightly apart. Bend your knees, grasp the object firmly, and lift by straightening your legs, keeping your back as straight as possible.

Working Aloft

No one is to climb the masts or stacks without first obtaining permission from the officer of the deck, and then only to perform necessary work or duty. Before authorizing anyone aloft, the officer of the deck must ensure that all power on radar and radio antennas in the vicinity is secure. Controls and related equipment are tagged "SECURED! WORKERS ALOFT." Main-engine control is notified so that it will refrain from lifting safety valves and, if parties are to work nearby, secure steam

to the whistle. The officer of the deck sees that everyone assigned to work near the stack gases wears protective breathing
masks and remains there for only a short time, and that everyone wears a parachute safety harness with lines attached to the
ship's superstructure at the same level. He or she also makes
sure that wind and sea conditions will not endanger anyone
aloft.

All tools, buckets, paint pots, and brushes must be secured
by a lanyard when used in work on masts, stacks, upper catwalks, weather decks, or sponsons that overhang areas where
other personnel may be.

Operation of Machinery

Machinery includes engines, motors, generators, hydraulic
systems, and other equipment supplying power or moving
force.

Except in emergencies, and then only when no qualified
operator is present, no one should operate, repair, adjust, or
otherwise tamper with any machinery or controls unless assigned by a department head to perform a specific function.

No one should operate, repair, or adjust machinery unless
he or she has demonstrated a practical knowledge of its operation and repair and of all applicable safety regulations, and
then only when qualified by the head of the department responsible for the machinery.

Machinery undergoing repair will have its power or activa-
tion source tagged out.

Personnel Protection

Do not wear clothing with loose ends or loops when working
on or near rotating machinery. Suitable leather, asbestos, or
other heavy gloves must be worn when working on steam
valves or other hot units. Keep the body well covered to reduce the danger of burns when working near steam equipment.

Goggles or a helmet and a protective welding jacket must be
worn when brazing, welding, or cutting. Personnel on fire
watches *must* wear protective goggles. Protective goggles
should also be worn whenever working with corrosive substances such as acid, alkali, monoethemolamine, and vinyl
paint. Water in plastic squeeze bottles or other containers
should be readily available.

When using an oxygen-breathing apparatus (OBA), you normally work with another person. An insulated line may be

attached to the two of you, but the line is used only to signal, not to pull. The OBA is not authorized aboard submarines.

Plastic face shields must be worn when handling primary coolant under pressure, and suitable eye protection—a shield, goggles, or safety glasses—must be worn when buffing, grinding, or performing other tasks hazardous to the eyes.

Fumes from burning teflon are very dangerous. There should be no smoking around teflon chips or dust. Precautions should be taken in the presence of asbestos dust, when you are doing jobs such as removing lagging.

Petroleum, Oil, and Lubricants

Because of the hazards of Navy standard fuel oil (NSFO), Navy distillate (ND) fuel, aviation fuel, and other petroleum products, everyone must be indoctrinated in their use and in the procedures for preventing fire and explosions. Portions of the NAVSHIPSTECHMAN and the Navy Precautions for Forces Afloat contain details.

Portable Electric and Pneumatic Tools

The rated speed of a grinding wheel cannot be less than that of the machine or tool on which it is mounted. Grinders are not operated without wheel guards. Face shields or safety goggles are required for all types of grinding, chipping, or scaling. Automatic securing devices, such as deadman switches, must be tested for satisfactory operation before they are used.

Radiation

Radioactive material is present in nuclear reactors and warheads, in the sources used for calibration of radiation-monitoring equipment, and in certain electronic tubes.

Radiation sources must be installed in the radiation-detection equipment, or stowed in their shipping containers in a locked storage area.

Spare radioactive electronic tubes and fission chambers are stored in clearly marked containers and locked stowage.

All hands are to scrupulously obey radiation warning signs and remain clear of radiation barriers.

Radiation Hazards

The power generated by electronic equipment can result in injury. This is called an r-f (radio frequency) radiation hazard, and where it exists, warnings must be posted.

No visual inspection of any opening, such as a wave guide, that emits r-f energy is allowed unless the equipment is secured for inspection.

All r-f hazard signs posted in an operating area must be inspected to ensure that the equipment is operating, and so that anyone near it is not subjected to hazardous radiation. Observe r-f warning signs.

When there may be exposure while the antenna is radiating, someone must be stationed topside, within view of the antenna (but well out of the beam), and in communication with the operator.

Radiation warning signs must be permanently posted and used to restrict access temporarily to certain parts of the ship where equipment is radiating.

Replenishment at Sea

Safety regulations are reviewed immediately before each replenishment operation. Only essential personnel are allowed near any transfer station. Lifelines should not be lowered unless absolutely necessary. If lowered, temporary lines are rigged. When line-throwing guns or bolos are used, all hands on the receiving ship take cover.

Topside personnel engaged in handling stores and lines must wear safety helmets and orange-colored, buoyant life-preserver vests. If helmets are not equipped with a quick-acting breakaway device, the chin strap is fastened behind the head or worn unbuckled. VERTREP (vertical replenishment) personnel may wear flight-deck vests and cranial impact helmets instead.

Cargo handlers must wear safety shoes. Those handling wirebound or banded cases wear work gloves.

Personnel are to keep clear of bights, handle lines from the inboard side, and be at least 6 feet from any block through which the lines pass. They must keep clear of suspended loads and rig attachment points until loads have been landed on deck.

Care should be taken to prevent the shifting of cargo, and no one should get between any load and the rail.

Deck space near transfer stations should be covered with something slip resistant.

A life-buoy watch must be stationed well aft on the engaged side. If a lifeguard ship is not available, a boat or rescue helicopter should be kept ready for anyone who falls overboard.

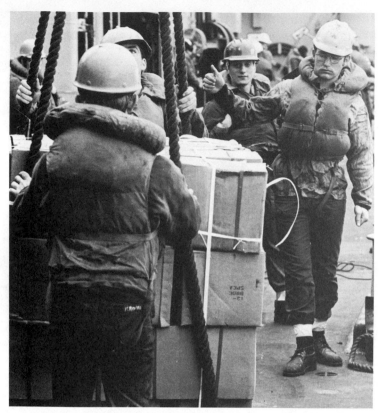

Figure 20–5 When replenishing at sea, sailors must observe a number of safety regulations. Note the helmets, life vests, and tucked-in pants legs.

Measures must be taken to avoid hazards associated with r-fs. This is important when handling ammunition and petroleum products.

Dangerous materials, such as acids, compressed gases, and hypochlorites, are transferred separately from one another and from other cargo.

When transferring personnel by highline, only manila line (hand tended by at least twenty-five people) is used. Persons being transferred wear orange-colored life preservers (except patients in litters equipped with flotation gear). When the water temperature is 59 degrees F or below or when outside air/water temperature is a total of 120 degrees F or below, immersion suits should be worn if possible.

When aviation fuel and fuel oil is received or transferred, no naked light or electrical or mechanical apparatus likely to

Safety

spark is permitted within 50 feet of an oil hose, an open fuel tank, the vent terminal from a fuel tank, or an area where fuel-oil vapors may be present. The term naked light includes all forms of oil lanterns, lighted candles, matches, cigars, cigarettes, cigarette lighters, and flame or arc welding and cutting apparatus. Portable electric lights used during fueling must have explosion-proof protected globes, and must be inspected for proper insulation and tested prior to use. Portholes in the ship's structure on the side from which fuel is being received are closed and secured during operations.

Safety Clothing

Personnel who may be exposed to mechanical, physical, or chemical dangers must have adequate protective clothing and devices. Specifics are covered in Safety Precautions Afloat (OPNAV instruction 5100.19), Safety Precautions for Shore Activities (OPNAV instruction 5100.23), Illustrated Shipboard Shopping Guide (NAVSUP P-4400), and applicable sections of the NAVSHIPSTECHMAN and Aircrew Systems Manual.

Safety Devices

Mechanical, electrical, and electronic safety devices are inspected at intervals specified by the preventive maintenance system (PMS), by type-commander instructions, or as usual circumstances or conditions warrant. When practical, these inspections are conducted when the equipment or unit is in operation. Machinery or equipment is not operated unless safety devices are working.

No one should tamper with or render ineffective any safety device, interlock, ground strap, or similar device without the commanding officer's approval.

Safety Tags

DANGER, CAUTION, OUT OF COMMISSION, and OUT OF CALIBRATION tags and labels must be posted for the safety of personnel and to prevent misuse of equipment. Safety tags are never removed without proper authorization.

Shore Power

All onboard shore-power equipment must be checked for safety. Shore-power cables should be thoroughly inspected and merged. Spliced portable cables are dangerous and should not be used except in an emergency.

Cables should be long enough to allow for the rise and fall of the tide, but not so long as to allow the cable to dip in the water or become wedged between the ship and the pier. Cables should not rest on sharp or ragged edges such as ship gunwales. Personnel should not step or walk on shore-power cables.

Smoking

There is no smoking in holds, storerooms, fuel-tank compartments; in fuel pump rooms, voids, or trunks; in any shop or space where flammable liquids are being used or handled; in the ship's boat; in bunks or berths; in magazines, handling rooms, ready-service rooms, gun mounts, or turrets; in fuel-control stations, oil-relay tank rooms, and battery and charging rooms; in the field projection room or in the vicinity of film stowage; in the photo lab; anywhere there is bleeding oxygen; in any area where vinyl or saran paint is being applied; on the flight deck, flight-deck catwalks, and gun platforms; or in hangar and gallery spaces open to the hangar.

No smoking is permitted in any area of the ship or alongside when ammunition is being handled, or in any part of the ship when she is receiving or transferring fuel oil, diesel oil, aviation gasoline, or other volatile fuel, except in spaces designated as smoking areas by the commanding officer.

There is no smoking during general quarters, general drills, or during emergencies except as authorized by the commanding officer. And there is no smoking when the word "The smoking lamp is out" is passed.

Tanks and Voids

No one is permitted to enter any closed compartment, tank, void, or poorly ventilated space aboard a naval or Navy-operated ship until the space has been ventilated and determined to be gas-free. In an emergency, if a space must be entered without gas freeing, a breathing apparatus such as an airline mask must be worn. In all cases, at least two persons must be present when such a space is occupied. One acts as tender or safety observer.

Additional precautions: the space entered should be continuously ventilated; a reliable person must be stationed at the entrance to keep count of the number of persons inside as well as to maintain communications; suitable fire-extinguishing equipment must be on hand; nonsparking tools are to be used;

and persons entering should not carry matches or lighters, or wear articles of clothing that could cause a spark.

Toxic Materials

The use of all hazardous materials is controlled by the medical officer or some other designated person.

Methyl alcohol—commonly used as duplicator fluid, "canned heat," paint thinner, cleaner, and antifreeze—is hazardous if inhaled, absorbed through the skin, or swallowed. Even small amounts can cause permanent blindness or death. Therefore, only the amount required to do a specific job is released. It is used only in well-ventilated spaces, and contact with the skin should be avoided.

Solvents, refrigerants, fumigants, insecticides, paint removers, dry-cleaning fluids, and propellants for pressurized containers are hazardous if inhaled, swallowed, or absorbed by the skin. They too are used only with adequate ventilation, by authorized personnel under supervision, and in such a way that contact with the eyes and skin is prevented. Use of carbon tetrachloride is prohibited aboard ship, except in laboratory and pharmacological work.

471

Welding and Burning

Welding and burning are performed only with the permission of the commanding officer or officer of the deck. The area where "hot work" is done must be cleared of flammable matter beforehand. Fire watches are posted until materials cool.

Various synthetic materials yield toxic gases when burned or heated. Use caution when burning or welding resin-coated vinyl surfaces. Vinyl coating must be chipped or scraped clear in the work area whenever possible; welders, fire watchstanders, and others required to be in the immediate area are equipped with line respirators. Exhaust ventilation in the work area has a minimum capacity of 200 cubic feet per minute for each 3-inch suction hose.

Although ship's personnel do not normally do welding work on the hull, if such work is required, proper precautions must be taken. The hull must be x-rayed at the first opportunity.

When they are cutting galvanized material, ship's personnel in the area wear air-line respirators. The area must be adequately ventilated to avoid illness caused by toxic fumes.

Fire Watch: A shipboard watch is assigned for the purpose of detecting and immediately extinguishing fires caused by welding or burning operations. The watch usually consists of at least two persons—one with the operator, the other in the space behind, below, or above the site of cutting, grinding, or welding. Remember, heat generated by welding or burning passes through bulkheads and decks and can ignite material on the other side. A fire watch must remain alert at all times, even though the assignment may grow boring. When the ship is undergoing an overhaul, for example, the ship's fire mains may be inoperative; if the watchstanders are ''goofing off'' or absent from their station, a fire could gain considerable headway before the arrival of the firefighting crew—resulting in extensive and unnecessary damage and possibly casualties.

Fire watchstanders should obtain safe and workable equipment and know how to operate it before going on duty. They inspect the work site with the hot-work operator. They should know where all firefighting equipment is in the work space and adjoining spaces and know how to use it. They must know where and how to sound the fire alarm, and know the assigned escape routes from the space.

When the hot-work operation is complete, fire watchstanders inspect both sides of the work area and remain on station for at least 30 minutes to be sure that there are no more smoldering fires or sparks and that the hot metal has cooled to the touch. They return all fire-watch equipment at the conclusion of their duty.

Working Over the Side

No work is done over the side without the permission of the officer of the deck, who must first notify the engineering officer to determine whether the screw will be turned over. If the screw is to be turned for any reason, people working over the side will be cleared. Crews working over the side on stages, boatswain's chairs, and work floats or boats wear buoyant life preservers and are equipped with parachute-type safety harnesses with lines tended from the deck above. When another ship comes alongside, all personnel working over the side should be cleared.

Division officers are responsibile for teaching personnel safety regulations and seeing that they are qualified before allowing them to work over the side. The division officer must also see that a competent petty officer is available for constant supervision.

All tools, buckets, paint pots, and brushes used over the side must be secured by lanyards to prevent loss overboard and injury to personnel below.

No person may work over the side while the ship is under way without permission of the commanding officer.

Maintenance

Because of the Navy's size and complexity, and the variety of equipment that must be maintained for ready use, a carefully planned program is required. The program must be the same for all equipment of the same type, regardless of the type of ship or location, so that a person transferred from one location to another can take on a new task easily. This program is called the 3-M (maintenance and material management) system.

Your shipboard duties include the maintenance of equipment associated with your rating. At first your responsibilities are minor, but as you gain knowledge through training and experience, you will be given more difficult tasks.

Broadly speaking, maintenance is preventive and corrective. Preventive maintenance forestalls equipment failure. It includes the inspection, cleaning, testing, and lubrication of equipment. Corrective maintenance is another name for repair.

Preventive maintenance is carried out according to procedures and schedules established by the 3-M system. Objectives of the system are to maintain equipment at maximum operating efficiency, reducing the cost of maintenance in both dollars and man hours, and to provide data on the cost of spare parts, failure rates, and man hours, as well as other information directly related to maintenance. More simply, the objective of 3-M is to improve the material readiness of the fleet.

The two main features of the system with which you will be concerned are PMS and the maintenance data system (MDS).

Planned Maintenance Subsystem (PMS)

PMS is designed to simplify maintenance. It defines types of maintenance, sets up maintenance schedules, prescribes the tools and methods used for a particular type of maintenance, and helps you detect and prevent impending casualties. PMS also provides a good foundation for training in equipment operation and maintenance.

This portion of 3-M also gives shipboard department heads the means to manage, schedule, and control the maintenance of their equipment. There are three components of PMS: the PMS manual, maintenance schedules (cycle, quarterly, and weekly), and maintenance requirement cards (MRCs).

You will use MRCs almost daily. Your work center will have a complete set of them. When the weekly schedule names you for a job, pull the appropriate MRC from its holder and take it with you for step-by-step guidance while performing your task. The MRC has a code that tells when or how often a job is done: D, daily; W, weekly; M, monthly; Q, quarterly; S, semiannually; A, annually; C, overhaul cycle; and R, situation requirement (for example, before the ship gets under way, or as a prefiring measure).

If the MRC indicates a "related maintenance," it means there are two jobs and that they are done together to save time.

Safety precautions are listed for each job. Make sure you read, understand, and observe all precautions. "Caution" means that a worker can damage the equipment; "warning" means that the equipment could damage the worker. The section labeled "Tools, parts, materials, and test equipment" tells you exactly what to use. Don't substitute. If a particular grease is called for but not available, don't use just any grease. Check with the leading petty officer to see if there is an approved substitute.

Maintenance Data System (MDS)

MDS is a management tool used by systems commands and fleet and type commanders to identify and correct maintenance and logistics support problems. This system has resulted in improvements in maintenance procedures, equipment design, the allocation of resources, and long-range-cost accounting. MDS is a means of recording planned and corrective maintenance actions. All planned maintenance actions, except daily and weekly preventive maintenance and routine preservation, are recorded in substantial detail. Recorded information concerns the number of man hours required to make a repair, materials used, delays encountered, reasons for delay, and the technical specialty or activity involved.

3-M Instruction

Many sailors are sent to a basic 3-M school for instruction on the entire system, but all the necessary manuals and instructions are on every ship, and expert work supervisors can teach you all about it. The best source of information is the 3-M manual; read it and ask questions of the work-center supervisor or 3-M coordinator, and you'll become a reliable part of the Navy's 3-M system. There are also several self-training courses available on the system.

Figure 20–6 Maintenance keeps equipment in operation, and the Navy's 3-M system provides the means to do this effectively.

Conservation

Every job in the Navy, whether it has to do with maintenance, cleanliness, or almost anything else, requires conservation. Conservation doesn't mean that you should set aside extra stores like a packrat because you think you might need them sometime. Nor does it mean that you should try to save a bit by using one coat of paint when two are required.

It *does* mean that you make effective use of material—and time—to do the most work at the least possible cost. The Navy is a business, just like a corporation, and everything used must be paid for. Just because all you do is sign a chit to draw something from supply doesn't mean it's free. Someone has to pay for it. You, as an American taxpayer, help pay.

General Preservation and Cleaning

You might think that a ship at sea does not get very dirty, but she does—and quickly. In the interest of sanitation and appearance, daily cleanups are necessary.

Sweepers

"Sweepers" is piped by the boatswain's mate of the watch shortly after reveille, at the end of the regular working day, and at other times as necessary. At these times, all men and women assigned as sweepers draw their gear, sweep and swab down their assigned areas, and empty trash receptacles. Trash and dirt should be picked up in a dustpan. If you sweep dirt over the side, the wind may blow it back on board or it may stick to the side, giving the ship an unsightly appearance. With repeated sweeping over the side, the ship will have to be scrubbed or chipped and painted sooner than normal.

Compartment Cleaners

If you are assigned duty as a berthing-compartment cleaner, you won't have to sweep down topside decks. Unless your division is shorthanded, you may not have any watches. But you will be expected to keep the compartment scrupulously clean. Neither you nor your shipmates want to live in a dirty compartment.

Periodically, a field day is held. Field day is cleaning day, when all hands turn to and clean the ship inside and out, usually in preparation for an inspection by the captain. Fixtures and areas (overhead cables, piping, corners, spaces behind and under equipment, etc.) sometimes neglected during regular sweepdown are cleaned; bulkheads, decks, ladders, and all other accessible areas are scrubbed; knife edges and door gaskets are checked, and any paint, oil, or other substances removed; brightwork is shined; and clean linen is placed on each bunk. Field days improve the ship's appearance and sanitary condition, preserve her by extending paint life, and reduce the dirt around equipment. Dirt must be minimized to keep electronic equipment from overheating, and to protect rotating machinery from abrasion.

If you arc in charge of a compartment, present the space to the inspecting officer by saluting and greeting him or her in the following manner: "Good afternoon (morning), sir/ma'am; Seaman Jones, compartment (name and number), —— Division, standing by for inspection."

Topside Areas and Deck Coverings

There will be many inclement days at sea when personnel cannot clean topside surfaces. At the first opportunity, these should be cleaned with fresh water and an inspection made for signs of rust and corrosion. If you see rust or corrosion, tend to the area immediately. A little work in the beginning will save a lot of work later.

Deck coverings receive more wear than any other material, and must be replaced early and at great cost unless proper care is given. Several types of material are used for deck coverings; the most common are resilient and nonslip.

Nonslip deck coverings do not require painting. They are kept up by sweeping loose dirt daily and wiping away spills as soon as possible. This type of deck covering is "clamped down" (cleaned with a wet swab) frequently, allowed to dry, then buffed with an electric buffing machine (for safety reasons this applies to indoor spaces only). For a more thorough cleaning when the deck is unusually dirty, apply a solution of warm water and detergent with a stiff bristle brush or circular scrubbing machine. Use water sparingly. Wet the deck with the cleaning solution, but do not flood it. Remove the soiled solution with a swab and rinse with clean water to remove residual detergent. Stubborn dirt and black marks left by shoes can be removed by rubbing lightly with a scouring pad, or fine steel wool, or a rag moistened with mineral spirits.

Waxing should not be done when the ship is going out to sea or when heavy weather is anticipated. This is an added precaution against slipping, even though approved emulsion floor waxes are designed to be slip resistant.

When rubber switchboard matting, ceramic tile, or painted decks need cleaning, they should be washed with a detergent solution, rinsed with a minimum amount of water, and dried.

Static conductive linoleum is ordinarily used as a deck covering in the medical operating room. You clean it in the same way as resilient deck covering, except that wax, oil, and polish should be avoided. They act as insulators and reduce the electrical conductivity of this type of deck covering. The deck's gloss may be increased by buffing lightly with fine steel wool and a floor-polishing machine.

Nonskid paint is cleaned with a solution of 1 pint detergent cleanser and 5 tablespoons dishwashing compound or 10 tablespoons metasilicate. This preparation is diluted with fresh water to make 20 gallons of solution. Apply with a handscrubber, let it soak for 5 minutes, then rinse with fresh water. Nonskid deck coverings should not be waxed or painted, otherwise their nonskid properties will be reduced.

Aluminum surfaces present a special problem, because if not treated properly, considerable corrosion can result. Corrosion is greatest when dissimilar metals such as aluminum and steel are in contact with each other and exposed to seawater.

Corrosion starts with a white, powdery residue on the aluminum surface, advances to pitting and scarring and culminates in complete deterioration. The best way to prevent corrosion is to insulate aluminum from other materials. Insulation is especially important when a joint is exposed to moisture.

When aluminum is to be joined to other metals, each surface is given one coat of pretreatment formula and two coats of zinc primer. Never use red lead as a primer on aluminum. If the joint is exposed to the weather, insulation tape must be placed between the two surfaces and the joint filled with caulking compound. If aluminum is joined to wood, the latter is given one coat of phenolic varnish.

When preparing aluminum surfaces for painting, handle power sanders with great care. It is best to use handscrapers, hand and power wire brushes, or sandpaper of a very fine grit. Avoid scaling hammers.

Painting

In the Navy, paint is used primarily for the preservation of surfaces. It seals the pores of wood and steel, arrests decay, and helps prevent rust. Paint serves several other purposes. It promotes cleanliness and sanitation because of its antiseptic properties and because it provides a smooth, washable surface. Paint is also used to reflect, absorb, or redistribute light.

Before painting, you must select suitable paints for the surfaces to be covered, prepare the surfaces, and learn the correct methods of applying paint.

Types of Paint

Most Navy paints are named according to color and use, such as exterior gray deck and pretreatment coating. The most common types are as follows:

Primers: Primers are base coats of paint that adhere firmly to wood and metal, providing a smooth surface for finishing coats. They also seal the pores, and those applied on steel are rust inhibitors as well. Two principal primers are used by the Navy: zinc chromate and red lead. Use only zinc chromate primers on galvanized and aluminum surfaces.

At least two coats of primer should be used after the surface is cleaned to a bright shine. A third coat should be added to outside corners and edges. At least eight hours' drying time should be allowed between primer coats.

Exterior Paints: Vertical surfaces above the upper limit of the boot topping (the waterline area, which is painted black) are given two coats of haze gray. Horizontal surfaces are painted with exterior deck gray (darker than haze gray), except the underside of deck overhangs, which is painted white.

A nonskid deck paint is used on main walkways. It contains a small amount of pumice, which helps to give a better footing.

The top of stacks and top hamper, subject to discoloration from smoke and stack gases, are painted black.

Interior Paints: Depending on the use to which individual compartments are put, several color schemes are authorized or prescribed for interior bulkheads, decks, and overheads.

The choice of colors for berthing, messing, and recreation spaces is usually left to the individual ship. All other spaces are painted the color prescribed by the Naval Sea Systems Command (NAVSEASYSCOM). Deck colors, for example, are dark green in the wardroom and in officers' quarters, dark red in machinery spaces, and light gray in enlisted living spaces.

Some common bulkhead colors are green for offices, radio rooms, the pilot house, and medical spaces; gray for the flag plot, combat information center, and sonar control; and white for storerooms and sanitary and commissary spaces.

Overhead colors are either the same as bulkhead colors or white.

Surface Preparation

For paint to adhere to a surface, all salt, dirt, oil, grease, rust, and loose paint must be removed completely, and the surface must be thoroughly dry.

Salt and most dirt can be removed with soap or detergent and fresh water. Firmly imbedded dirt may require scouring with powder or with sand and canvas. Do not use lye or other strong solutions, because they might burn or soften the paint. When oil and grease fail to yield to scrubbing, they must be removed with diesel oil or paint thinner, and extreme caution. If you use diesel oil, scrub the surface afterward to remove the oil. After scrubbing or scouring, rinse the surface with fresh water.

To remove rust, mill scale, and loose paint, you need hand tools or power tools, paint and varnish removers, or blowtorches. Hand tools are usually used for cleaning small areas; power tools are for larger areas and for cleaning decks, bulkheads, and overheads covered with too many coats of paint. (Normally, paint in interior spaces is not removed if it is in good condition, unless its thickness exceeds 0.005 inch or a total of four coats. Thickness on exterior surfaces may be determined by general appearance and is sometimes indicated by cracks.) Paint, varnish removers, and torches are used to remove paint from wood.

Hand Tools: The most commonly used hand tools are sandpaper, steel wire brushes, and handscrapers.

Sandpaper is used to clean corners and feather paint—that is, smooth the edges of chipped areas down to the cleaned surface.

A wire brush is useful for light work on rust or light coats of paint. It is also used for brushing weld spots and cleaning pitted surfaces.

Scrapers are made of tool steel, the most common type being L-shaped, with each end tapered to a cutting edge like a wood chisel. They are most useful for removing rust and paint from small areas and from plating less than 1/4 inch thick, when it is impractical or impossible to use power tools.

Occasionally, it is necessary to use a chipping or scaling hammer, but care must be taken to exert only enough force to remove the paint. Too much force dents the metal, resulting in the formation of high and low areas. In subsequent painting, the paint is naturally thinner on the high areas. Consequently, thin paint wears off quickly, leaving spots where rust will form and eventually spread under the good paint.

Power Tools: The most useful power tool is the portable grinder. It is usually equipped with a grinding wheel that may be replaced by either the rotary wire brush or the rotary cup wire brush. Light-duty brushes, made of crimped wire, will remove light rust. Heavy-duty brushes, fashioned by twisting several wires into tufts, remove deeply imbedded rust.

Scaling may be done with a chisel and pneumatic or hand-scaling hammer. With a pneumatic hammer and chisel, you must take care that the chisel strikes the surface at approximately a 45-degree angle. Use the same caution with the hand-scaling hammer to avoid denting the surface.

The rotary scaling and chipping tool—a "deck crawler"—has a bundle of cutters or chippers mounted on either side. As it is pushed along the surface, the rotary cutters do the work. This piece of equipment is particularly helpful on large deck areas.

The electric disc sander is another handy tool for preparing surfaces. However, great care must be exercised in its use. If too much pressure is applied, or if the sander is allowed to rest in one place too long, it will quickly cut into the surface, particularly a wood or aluminum one.

Paint and Varnish Removers: Paint and varnish removers are used mostly on wood surfaces but may be applied to metal surfaces that are too thin to be chipped or wire-brushed.

Three types of removers are in general use: flammable, non-flummable, and water-base alkali. All three are hazardous, and safety precautions must be observed. Removers should be used only in well-ventilated spaces. Alkali remover is not to be used on aluminum or zinc because of its caustic properties.

Procedures for using removers are the same, regardless of type. Wet the surface with a smooth coat of remover. Permit it to soak in until the paint or varnish is loosened, then lift the paint off with a handscraper. After the surface is cleaned, wet it again with the remover and wipe it off with a rag. Finally, wash the surface thoroughly with paint thinner or soap and water. This final rinse gets rid of any wax left by the remover and any acids that may have worked into the grain of the wood.

Fillers: Holes, dents, and cracks in surfaces and open-grained woods should be filled before finishing. Putty, wood fillers, and even sawdust mixed with glue can be applied to wood. Deep cracks and checks in wooden booms, spars, and the like should first be caulked with oakum or cotton caulking and then covered with putty. Epoxy cements are available for use on steel and aluminum surfaces. Methods of application vary with the type of cement, so carefully follow instructions. All fillers should be allowed to dry and then sanded smooth before you apply the first finishing coat.

Use of Brushes and Rollers

Smooth and even painting depends as much on good brushwork as on good paint. There is a brush for almost every purpose, so pick the proper brush and keep it in the best condition.

The two most useful brushes are the flat brush and the sash-tool brush. These and some other common ones are shown in figure 20-8.

With a flat brush, a skillful painter can paint almost any shipboard surface. Flat brushes are wide and thick, hold a lot of paint, and give maximum brushing action. Sash brushes are handy for painting small items, for cutting in at corners, and for less accessible spots. The fitch brush also is useful for small surfaces. The painter's dusting brush cleans surfaces.

Handling a Brush: The following are some general hints about using a paint brush.

Grip the brush firmly but lightly. Do not put your fingers on the bristles below the metal band. This grip permits easy wrist and arm motion. To hold the brush otherwise restricts your movement and causes fatigue.

When using a flat brush, don't paint with the narrow edge. This practice wears down corners and spoils the shape and efficiency of the brush. When using an oval brush, don't let it turn in your hands. An oval brush, if revolved too much, soon wears to a pointed shape and becomes useless. Don't poke oversized brushes into corners and around moldings. This bends the bristles, eventually ruining a good brush. Use a smaller brush that fits into such odd spots.

Dip the brush into the paint halfway up the bristles. Remove excess paint by patting the brush on the inside of the pot. (If you oversoak the brush, paint will drip and run down the handle.)

Hold the brush at right angles to the surface with the bristles just touching it. Lift the brush clear of the surface when starting the return stroke. If the brush is held obliquely and not lifted, the painted surface will have overlaps, spots, and a

Figure 20–7   Paint helps preserve surfaces that are exposed to weather.

daubed appearance. A brush held at any angle other than a right angle will soon wear away at the sides.

Paint Applications: For complete and even coverage, follow the Navy method and first lay on, then lay off. Laying on means applying the paint first in long strokes in one direction. Laying off means crossing your first strokes. This way the paint is distributed evenly over the surface, the surface is covered completely, and a minimum amount of paint is used.

Always paint overhead first, working from the corner that is farthest from compartment access. By painting the overhead first, you can wipe drippings off the bulkhead without smearing its paint.

Coats on overhead panels should normally be applied in a fore-and-aft direction, those on the beams, athwartships. But where panels contain many pipes running parallel with the beams, it is often difficult to lay off the panels fore and aft. In this case, lay off the panels parallel with the beams.

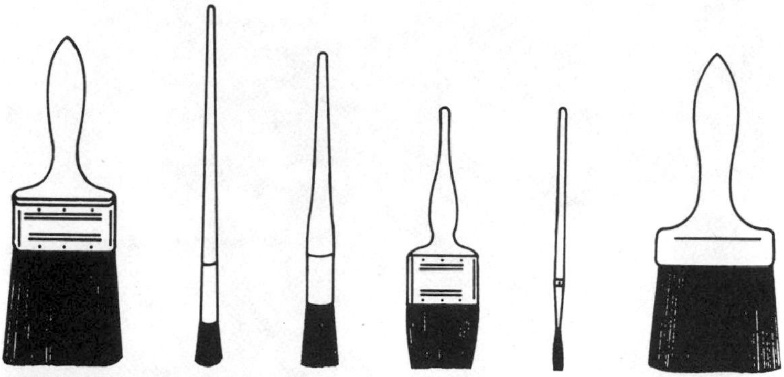

Flat   Fitch   Sash   Flat   Lettering   Painter's
                 Tool   Varnish   Dusting

Figure 20–8 Types of brushes.

To avoid brush marks when finishing up a square, use strokes directed toward the last square finished, gradually lifting the brush near the end of the stroke while the brush is still in motion. Every time the brush touches the painted surface at the start of a stroke, it leaves a mark. For this reason, never finish a square by brushing toward the unpainted area; instead, brush back toward the area already painted.

When painting pipes, stanchions, narrow straps, beams, and angles, lay the paint on diagonally. Lay off along the long dimension.

Always carry a rag to wipe up dripped or smeared paint. Carefully remove loose bristles sticking to the painted surface.

Cutting In: After you master the art of handling a brush, you should learn to cut in. Cutting in is a simple procedure, and anyone with a fairly steady hand can learn it quickly.

Film Thickness: Paint on interior surfaces must be applied in the lightest possible coat, only enough to cover the area. Heavy layers of paint are a fire hazard—the thicker they are, the faster they will burn; they are likely to entrap solvents and thinners that burn rapidly; they have a greater tendency to crack and peel; they are uneven, and may show marks and scratches more readily than thinner coats; and they do not penetrate as well as thinner coats, or dry as well. Moreover, heavy layers of paint, which add noticeably to the weight of the ship, may cut her speed.

Paint Rollers: The dip paint roller used in the Navy is equipped with a replaceable cylinder of knitted plush over a solvent-resistant paper core. It rotates on the shaft of a corro-sion-resistant steel frame.

Large areas, such as decks and ship's sides (free of rivets, bolts, cables, pipes, and so on), can be covered with paint quickly by the roller method. Paint should be laid on and laid off the same way as with brushes. A moderate amount of pressure must be applied to the roller so that the paint is worked into the surface. If pressure is not exerted, the paint will not adhere and soon it will peel off. With the proper amount of pressure, a roller applies a more even coat and uses less paint than a brush.

Care of Brushes and Rollers

Unfortunately, far too many good brushes are ruined simply because painters have little or no idea how to care for them. They should pay particular attention to the following advice. Treat brushes as though you paid for them yourself and must replace them when they are worn out.

Do not let a brush stand on its bristles in a pot of paint for more than a few minutes. The weight of the brush bends the bristles, making it almost impossible to do a good paint job. Never allow paint to dry on a brush. If you intend to leave a paint-filled brush for an hour or more, fold wax paper or some other heavy paper around the bristles to keep air out. Twist the paper around the handle and secure it with rope yarn or sail twine. Cover your pot of paint, and place both it and the brush in a safe place. Before resuming your job, stir the paint thoroughly with a paddle—not with the brush. At the end of the day, before turning in your paint and brush to the paint locker, clean as much paint from the brush as possible by wiping it across the edge of the paint pot or mixing paddle.

Ordinarily, those working in the paint locker will clean and stow any brushes turned in. Occasionally, though, they require help, and you may be detailed to the job. If so, follow instructions carefully, and thoroughly clean the brushes.

Paint lockers usually have containers with divided compartments for temporarily stowing different types of brushes (paint, varnish, shellac, etc.). Most of these containers have tight covers and suspend brushes so that the bristles and the lower part of the ferrule are covered by thinner or linseed oil.

Brushes to be used the following day should be cleaned in the proper thinner and placed in the proper compartment of the container. Those not to be used again soon should be cleaned in thinner, washed in soap or detergent and water, rinsed thoroughly in fresh water, and hung to dry. After drying, they should be wrapped in waxed paper and stowed flat. Do not leave a brush soaking in water. Water causes the bristles to separate into bunches, flare, and become bushy.

Paint rollers are cleaned differently. The fabric cylinder should be stripped from the core, cleaned in the solvent recommended for a particular type of paint, washed in soap and water, rinsed thoroughly in fresh water, and replaced on the core to dry. Combing the fabric's pile while it is damp prevents matting.

The following items must not be painted:

1. Start-stop mechanisms of electrical safety devices and control switchboards on machinery elevators.
2. Bell pulls, sheaves, annunciator chains, and other mechanical communication devices.
3. Composition-metal water ends of pumps.
4. Condenser heads and the outside surfaces of condensers made of composition metal.
5. Dry-sprinkling piping in magazines.
6. Exposed composition-metal parts of any machinery.
7. Glands, stems, yokes, toggle gear, and all machined external parts of valves.
8. Heat-exchange surfaces of heating or cooling equipment.
9. Identification plates.
10. Joint faces of gaskets and packing surfaces.
11. Lubricating gear, such as oil holes, oil or grease cups, zerkfittings, lubricators, and surfaces in contact with lubricating oil.
12. Lubricating oil reservoirs.
13. Machined-metal surfaces of reciprocating engines or pumps.
14. Metal lagging.
15. Rods, gears, universal joints, and couplings of valve-operating gear.
16. Rubber elements of isolation mounts.
17. Ground plates.
18. Springs.
19. Strainers.
20. Threaded parts.
21. Zincs.

22. Working surfaces.

23. Hose and applicator nozzles.

24. Knife edges, rubber gaskets, dogs, drop bolts, wedges, and the operating gear of watertight doors, hatches, and scuttles.

25. Electrical contact points and insulators.

26. The original enamel, lacquer, or crackle finish on all radio, electrical, and sound equipment, unless damage makes refinishing essential.

27. Decorative plastic such as tabletops.

V. Seamanship, Navigation, and Communication

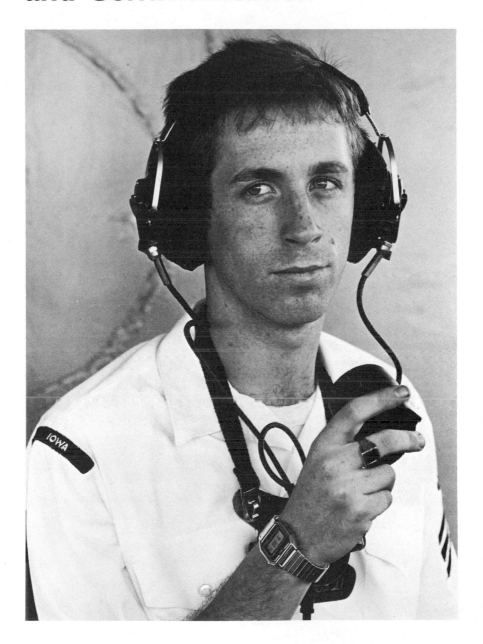

Marlinespiking and the Use of Ground Tackle

21

Marlinespike Seamanship

This is the art of working with line or rope. The marlinespike is an instrument used in handling rope.

Rope is manufactured from wire, fiber, or combinations of the two. Fiber rope—or line, as it is commonly called—is fashioned from natural or synthetic fiber. Lines made from a variety of natural fibers, such as cotton, agave, jute, hemp, sisal, and abaca, have seen service in the Navy for years. Some are still in use. Tarred hemp, known as marline and ratline, is one. Another, sisal, has been dropped from the supply system; manila—for lashings, frapping lines, steadying lines, etc.—serves in its place.

The Navy currently uses a three-strand line that has been twisted or braided. Fibers are twisted into yarns or threads, yarns are twisted in the opposite direction into strands, strands are twisted back in the first direction into ropes, and finally ropes are twisted into cable. Rope can be either three- or four-strand; the direction in which the strands are twisted determines the lay of the rope. That is, if the strands are twisted to the right, the rope is said to be right laid.

Braided lines have certain advantages over twisted ropes. They will not kink or cockle (these terms are explained later), nor will they flex open to admit dirt or abrasives. The construction of some, however, makes it impossible to inspect the inner yarns for damage. The more common braided lines are hollow braided, stuffer braided, solid braided, and double braided.

Synthetic-Fiber Lines

The synthetic fibers used in making line are nylon, polyester (dacron), polypropylene, and polyethylene (in descending order of strength). The characteristics of synthetic line differ from those of manila line.

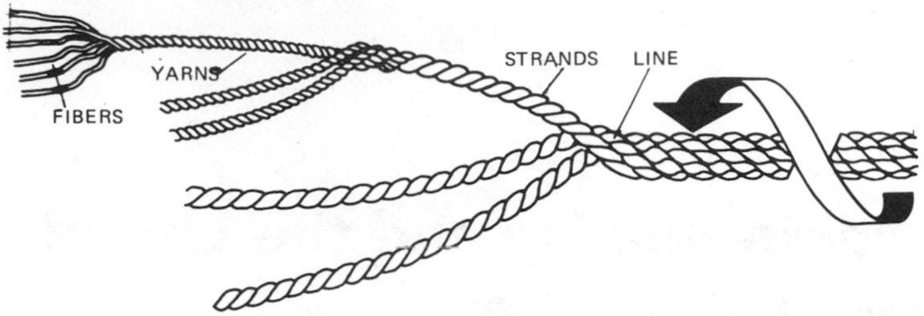

Figure 21–1   The method of twisting to form yarn, strands, and rope.

Synthetic line has nearly replaced natural-fiber line and is used in all sizes, ranging from 5/8 inch to 12 inches in circumference. Nylon is over twice as strong as manila, lasts five times as long, and will stand seven times the shock load. Its big disadvantage is that it will stretch. Dacron is even stronger when wet, and polypropylene is so light it floats.

Safety precautions are more exacting for synthetic line than for manila. You can find a complete list in the Navy Ships Technical Manual (NAVSHIPSTECHMAN), but the most important ones are cited below.

Because of the low friction of synthetic line, exercise extreme care when a line is being payed out or eased from securing devices—bitts, capstans, bollards, cleats, gipsy heads, etc. For control in easing out, fill bitt barrels with round turns and avoid more than two figure-eight bends.

There is the danger of pulling a line handler into a securing device when a line suddenly surges. To minimize it, safety observers should see that all line handlers stand as far as possible from the securing device.

Since a line that parts under tension inevitably snaps back, never stand in the direct line of pull. Instead, position yourself 90 degrees from the direction of the tension force.

Synthetic line has a higher breaking strength (BS) than manila. Blocks, padeyes, shackles, and line couplings can fail because of improper substitutions. Many fittings in common use in the fleet are designed for natural-fiber line. For this reason, identify and determine the capacity of all gear and fittings used with synthetic line to ensure that strength exceeds the minimum BS of the rope.

Synthetic line does not hold knots well. Some knots that are good for securing manila, such as the square knot, are not adequate for synthetic. The bowline is one knot known to offer reasonable security when bending together or securing synthetic line.

Normally, synthetic line comes on reels and is unreeled in the same fashion as wire rope (discussed on p. 496). Before you use new, three-strand synthetic, it should be faked down on deck and allowed to relax for 24 hours. The period can be shortened to about 2 hours by hosing down the line with fresh water.

When wet, synthetic line shrinks slightly but does not swell or stiffen. When tension is applied to the line, water squeezes out; under working loads, it appears as vapor.

Oil and grease do not cause synthetics to deteriorate, but they make them slippery. When this happens, the line should be scrubbed down. Spots may be removed by cleaning the line with light oils such as kerosene or diesel oil.

Line Characteristics

Every line is manufactured to certain specifications determined by the type of job for which it is employed. To ensure long life, a line should be used within its safe working load (SWL). The SWL of a line ranges from 1/15 to 1/5 of its BS, depending on its type, its condition, the blocks and other gear it is being used with, and the weather.

Sailors who work with natural-fiber line soon learn how to judge tension by the sound the line makes. Unfortunately, although synthetic line under heavy strain thins down considerably, it gives no audible indication of stress—even when it is about to part. For this reason, a tattletale cord should be attached to synthetic line when it is subjected to loads that may exceed its SWL. A tattletail cord is a bight of heavy cord or light "small stuff" hanging from two measure points on the working line. The line, when tensioned to its SWL, will stretch to a certain percentage of its length. When this point is reached, the small stuff becomes taut, warning that there is danger of exceeding the SWL.

Natural-Fiber Line

Although synthetic line is rapidly becoming the standard in today's Navy, natural line still has its uses. It requires special care and handling.

Coils of line should always be stowed on shelves or platforms clear of the deck. They should never be covered with

Figure 21–2   Line handlers fake down line on the deck of the nuclear-powered guided-missile cruiser *South Carolina* (CGN 37) as she leaves port.

junk, which may prevent the evaporation of moisture. Natural line is susceptible to mildew and rotting.

Coils of small stuff should be arranged along a shelf in order of size, and for ease of opening—that is, with the inside end at the bottom of the center tunnel. The burlap wrapper should be left on each coil. The stops that secure the coil are inside the wrapper. These should be cut and drawn up the inside end so that the line is started properly. It is custom, and a good idea, to set up a narrow, flat strip of wood horizontally over the shelf containing the small stuff, with a hole bored in the strip over each coil. The starting end of the line is drawn up through the hole and is prevented from dropping back by an overhand knot. Thus someone coming down for small stuff won't have to grope inside the tunnel for the end, and won't get hold of the wrong end when the coil is almost depleted.

Coils of large line should be stowed with the proper side up for opening. Line from 2 to 4 inches, needed in various lengths on deck, should be opened, and a few feet of the end led out. Mooring lines should not be opened until necessary. When a new coil of line is opened, give it your personal attention. Five minutes of your time here may save hours later trying to work kinks out of an improperly opened coil.

Whenever possible, a wet line should be dried before stowing. Sometimes this is impossible, as with mooring lines, which must be sent below before the onset of bad weather. If line must be stowed wet, it should be laid up on gratings in long fakes or suspended in some other way so that it will dry as quickly as possible. It should never be covered until dry.

Distortions, Kinks, and Twists

If a line doesn't lead easily to a winch drum (gipsy head), it will be badly distorted when heaved in. Frequently, therefore, you will need inside turns to obtain a fairlead. Because the outside end is attached to the load and unavailable, enough slack should be hauled up to make the necessary number of turns. The turns should be started from inboard.

Whenever possible, a right-laid line should be put on a winch drum or capstan righthanded, or in clockwise turns. Heaving on a right-laid line with lefthanded turns will eventually kink

Figure 21–3 Details on coiling, faking, and flemishing line.

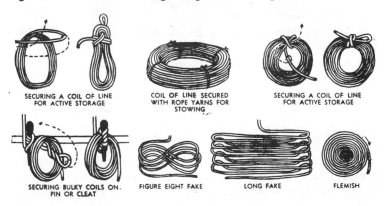

SECURING A COIL OF LINE FOR ACTIVE STORAGE

COIL OF LINE SECURED WITH ROPE YARNS FOR STOWING

SECURING A COIL OF LINE FOR ACTIVE STORAGE

SECURING BULKY COILS ON. PIN OR CLEAT

FIGURE EIGHT FAKE

LONG FAKE

FLEMISH

the line. About the only time lefthanded turns can't be avoided is when a winch is heaving on two lines at once, with one of them on either drum.

A line that has a kink in it, or tackle that is twisted from a dip, should never be heaved hard. Strain on a kinked or twisted line might permanently distort the line.

Deterioration

The following are some pointers on the use and care of natural-fiber line. Remember them.

Coil right-laid line righthanded or clockwise.

Keep line from touching stays, guys, or other standing rigging.

When surging a line around bitts or capstans, uncoil enough that it will not jerk but surge smoothly.

If the line becomes chafed or damaged, cut and splice it. A good splice is safer than a damaged section.

Do not lubricate the line.

Whip all line ends.

Inspect line frequently for deterioration. Open the lay and inspect the fibers. A white powdery residue indicates internal wear.

Do not drag a line over sharp or rough objects that can cut or break outer fibers. When line is dragged on the ground, dirt and other particles are picked up; eventually they work into the line, cutting the inner strands.

The strength of line exposed to the elements deteriorates about 30 percent in two years.

Line loaded in excess of 75 percent of its BS will be damaged permanently. Inspect the inside threads to see if all or a portion of their fibers are broken.

Keep bitts, chocks, and cleats in smooth condition to minimize abrasion.

Use chafing gear on rough, hard surfaces and sharp metal edges.

Apply loads slowly and carefully.

Wire Rope

Wire rope consists of individual wires made of steel or other metal, in various sizes, and laid together to form strands. The number of wires in a strand varies according to the purpose for

Figure 21–4   Caution must be used in handling wire rope to keep it from
bending, twisting, or kinking.

which the rope is intended. A number of strands are laid together to form the wire rope itself. Wire rope is designated by
the number of strands per rope and the number of wires per
strand. Thus, a 6 x 19 rope has six strands with a total of
nineteen wires per strand, but has the same outside diameter as
a 6 x 37 wire rope, which has six strands with a total of thirty-
seven wires of much smaller size per strand.

Wire rope made up of a large number of small wires is flexible, but small wires break so easily that the rope is not resistant
to external abrasion. Wire rope made up of a smaller number of
larger wires is more resistant to abrasion, but less flexible.

Wire rope is layed up in various ways as follows:

Right regular lay: Wires in the strands are twisted to the left;
strands in the rope are twisted to the right.

Left regular lay: Wires in the strands are twisted to the right;
strands are twisted to the left.

Right lang lay: Both wires in the strands and strands in the
rope are twisted to the right.

Left lang lay: Both wires in the strands and strands in the
rope are twisted to the left.

Reverse lay: Wires of alternate strands are twisted to the
right; those in the other strands are twisted to the left. Strands
are twisted to the right.

Uses of Wire Rope

The NAVSHIPSTECHMAN specifies the uses that may be
made of the various types of wire rope. A few of the common
ones and some of their uses follow:

6 x 7: Only the galvanized type is specified. It is not suitable
for general hoisting but is applicable for permanent standing
rigging.

6 x 19: Size for size, this is the strongest of wire ropes. When
made of galvanized wire, it is used principally for heavy hoisting and is particularly useful on derricks and dredges. Standing
rigging, guys, boat slings, and topping lifts for booms are often
made of 6 x 19 galvanized wire rope. When either noncorrosive
or nonmagnetic properties are needed, phosphor bronze 6 x 19
wire rope is used; for example, in lifelines, wheelropes, radio
antennas, antenna downleads, etc.

6 x 37: When made of ungalvanized steel wire, this type is
flexible, making it suitable for cranes and similar machinery; it

may also be used for heavy hoisting. When made of galvanized steel, it may be used for steering gear, boat-crane falls, towing hawsers, bridles, torpedo slings, and heavy-running rigging.

Care of Wire Rope

Never pull a kink out of a wire rope by putting strain on either end. As soon as you notice a kink, uncross the ends by pushing them apart; this reverses the process that started the kink. Then turn the bent portion over, place it on your knee or some firm object, and push down until the kink starts to straighten out somewhat. Then lay it on a flat surface and pound it smooth with a wooden mallet.

If heavy strain is put on a wire rope with a kink in it, the rope may be damaged. Cut out the kinked part and splice the ends together.

Frequently abrasions, reverse turns, or sharp turns cause individual wires to break and bend back. These wires are known as fishhooks. If several occur near each other or along the rope's length, the safe working load is reduced. When 4 percent of the wires in one rope lay have breaks, the rope is unsafe.

You should inspect wire rope frequently, checking for fishhooks, kinks, and worn spots. Worn spots show up as shiny flattened surfaces.

Wire rope should never be stored in places where acid is or has been kept. Prior to storage, wire rope should be cleaned and lubricated.

Wire-Rope Failure

Here are some common causes of wire-rope failure:

1. Using an incorrect size or construction, or using heavy-grade rope.
2. Dragging the wire over obstacles.
3. Lubricating the wire improperly.
4. Working with sheaves and drums of inadequate size.
5. Overriding or crosswinding on drums.
6. Working with misaligned sheaves and drums.
7. Working with sheaves and drums with improperly fitted grooves or broken flanges.
8. Jumping off sheaves.
9. Subjecting the wire to moisture or acid fumes.
10. Attaching fittings improperly.

11. Subjecting the wire to excessive heat.
12. Permitting the wire to untwist.
13. Allowing grit to penetrate the strands.
14. Subjecting the wire to severe or continuing overloads.
15. Kinking.

Making Ready Line and Splicing

Once a line has been removed from the coil, it may be prepared for storage or ready use, either by winding on a reel or in one of the following ways:

Coiling Down: Lay the line down in circles, roughly one on top of the other. Right-laid line is always coiled down right-handed, or clockwise. When a line has been coiled down, the end that went down last on top is ready to run off. If you try to walk away with the bottom end, the line will foul-up. If for some reason the bottom end must go out first, turn the entire coil upside down to free it for running.

Faking Down: The line is laid down as in coiling down, except that it is laid out in long, flat bights, one forward of the other, instead of in a round coil. This saves space a large coil might occupy. Faking down a heavy line is easier than coiling it down. A faked line runs more easily than a coiled line.

Flemishing Down: Coil the line down first, then wind it tight from the bottom end, counterclockwise, so that it forms a close mat. Slack ends of boat painters, boat falls, boat boom guys, or any other short lines not in constant use should be flemished down for neatness.

Securing Ends: Never leave the end of a line without a whipping. This prevents unlaying, which it will do on its own. Use tape to whip nylon line ends, then singe each strand.

A temporary plain whipping can be made with anything, even a rope yarn. Lay the whipping along the line and bind it down with a couple of turns. Then lay the other end on the opposite way, bind it with a couple of turns from the bight of the whipping, and pull the end tight.

A permanent whipping is put on with a palm and needle and threaded with sail twine, doubled. Shove the needle through the middle of a strand so that it comes out between two strands on the other side. Bind the end down with six to eight turns, wound on from inboard toward the end, and again push the needle through the middle of a strand near the end so that it

comes out between two strands. Then work it up and down
between strands, with a good, tight cross-seizing between each
pair. The needle comes out in the middle of a strand on the last
shove, and that strand will hold the end after you cut the sail
twine.

Seizings

Seizings (pronounced *seezings*) are used when two lines, or
two parts of a single line, are to be married permanently.
"Seizing stuff" is generally rope-laid, tarred American hemp
of six, nine, or twelve threads. To seize small stuff, however,
marline is adequate.

Many special types of seizings were used in old sailing ships;
the four described here should suffice for seamen in modern
ships.

Flat Seizing: This light seizing is used when strain is not too
great.

Round Seizing: Stronger than the flat type, it is used when
strain is greater.

Racking Seizing: Use this type when there is unequal strain
on the two parts of a line.

Throat Seizing: Throat seizing is actually a round seizing
employed whenever a permanent eye is needed in the middle
of a line. Sometimes this seizing is used to keep mooring spring
lines from chafing where they cross.

Splicing

Splicing means permanently joining the ends of two lines or
bending a line back on itself to form a permanent loop. If
properly done, it does not weaken the line. A splice between
two lines will run over a sheave or other object much more
easily than a knot.

Short Splice: For a short splice, both ends of line are unlaid
for a short distance and the strands interlaced. One strand is
tucked through the lay of the other line, which has been
opened by a marlinespike or wooden fid. The other strands are
similarly tucked. Threads are cut away from the ends of each
tucked strand until they are two-thirds their original size, then
they are tucked again. The strands are similarly cut away until
they are one-third their original size, at which point a third and
last tuck is taken. This produces a neat, tapered splice.

In splicing a four-strand line, the first strand is tucked under
two parts of the first tucking only.

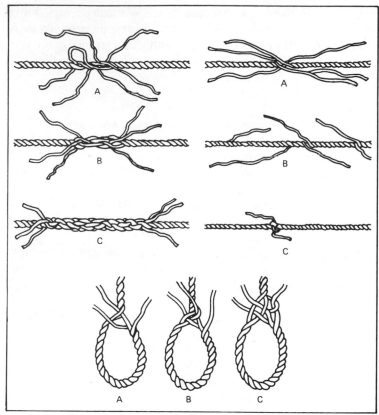

Figure 21–5   Three types of splice are the short splice, long splice, and eye splice.

Long Splice: The ends of a long splice are unlaid further than for a short splice and then similarly interlaced. A strand of one piece is unlaid for quite a distance, the corresponding strand being laid in the opening. The remaining ends of the two strands are twisted together for convenience, the line is turned end for end, and the first operation is repeated with two other corresponding strands.

The remaining strands of each part sit in their original positions. This leaves pairs of strands at three positions along the line. Each strand is halved. Two of these halves are tied together at each position with an overhand knot. The remaining two halves are tucked over one and under one of the full remaining strands of the line. After all strands have been tucked, the loose ends are trimmed off smooth. This splice will run over a sheave easily and is hardly noticeable. In splicing nylon line, make several extra tucks to be certain the splice holds.

Eye Splice: An eye splice is made the same way, except that the line is first brought back on itself enough to give the desired size of eye, and the strands are then tucked into the body of the line.

Worming, Parceling, and Serving: This is done to protect wire rope exposed to the weather or hard use.

In *worming*, the lay of the rope is followed between the strands with tarred small stuff. This keeps moisture from penetrating the interior of the rope and fills out the rope, giving it a smooth surface for parceling and serving.

Parceling means wrapping the rope spirally with long narrow strips of canvas, following the lay of the rope and overlapping turns to shed moisture.

Serving is wrapping small stuff snugly over the parceling, pulling each turn as taut as possible so that the whole forms a stiff protecting cover for the rope. A serving mallet is used for passing the turns in serving, and each turn is pulled taut by the leverage of the handle. Remember: Worm and parcel with the lay, turn and serve the other way.

503

Knots, Bends, and Hitches

To a seaman, a knot in line usually means the line is bent to itself. A knot forms an eye or knob, or secures a cord or line around something. A bend is ordinarily used to join two lines. A hitch secures a rope to another rope or object.

There are four classes of knots: (1) knots at the end of a line, used to fasten it to itself or around an object; (2) knots for bending two lines together; (3) knots that secure a line to a ring or spar (hitches or bends); (4) and knots used to give finish to the end of a line, to prevent unreeving, or for ornamentation. These last knots are called MacNamara lace. Some of the more common knots are described here and illustrated in figure 21-6.

Reeving Line Bend: This knot joins two small hawsers. It is the best knot for bending two lines together to reeve around a capstan or winch drum.

Double Matthew Walker: This knot has many uses in fancywork, but it also has practical applications, such as keeping the end of a line from coming unlaid. This is a temporary measure; a proper whipping should be put on the line at the earliest opportunity and the knot cut off.

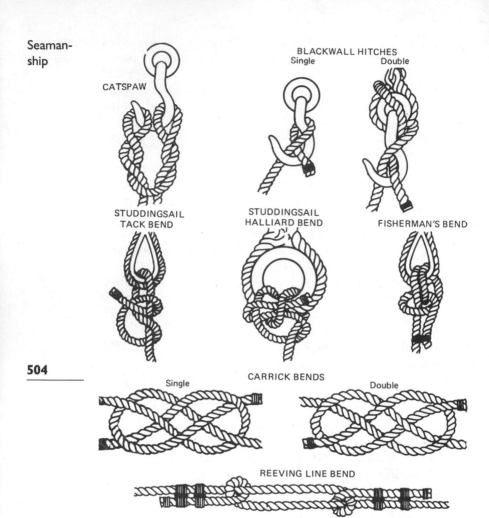

Figure 21–6 Completed knots, bends, and hitches.

Fisherman's Bend: This knot bends a line to a becket or eye (for example, a messenger to a mooring line). It can also secure a rope to a buoy, or a hawser to the ring of an anchor.

Bowline: This is a temporary eye in the end of a line. It will not slip or jam. A bowline on a bight is used to sling people over the side, since it will not slip and constrict them.

Masthead Knot: Although this knot is usually seen in fancy-work, it also has a practical purpose. In the days of sailing ships, these knots were set at the top of the masts, and the stays and shrouds were secured to the knots. It's a good knot to remember if you ever have to rig a jury mast.

Spanish Bowline: Whenever you want two eyes in a line, this is the knot to use. Primarily, however, it is used as a substitute for the boatswain's chair. Many prefer it to the French bowline because the bights are set and will not slip back and forth when weight is shifted.

Rolling Hitch: This is one of the most useful and important hitches on deck. It can pass a stopper on a boatfall or mooring line when you are shifting the fall or line from winch or capstan to cleat or bitt. It can also secure a reversed taut line. If properly tied, it will hold as long as there is strain on the hitch.

Timber Hitch: This is used on logs, spars, planks, and other comparatively rough-surfaced materials. It should not be used on pipes or other metal.

Marline Hitch: It is used on furled sails, awnings, and doubled mooring lines. When cinched up, it will hold itself tight.

Blackwall Hitch: The blackwall, single or double, secures ropes to hooks. It can be made quickly and, tied properly, is secure. It is used only when there is not enough rope end to make a bowline.

Round Turn with Two Half Hitches: This combination may be used in a ring or padeye, or on a spar. It is particularly good on a spar because it grips and holds its position.

Barrel Hitch: This is helpful in hoisting almost any bulky object, particularly barrels, drums, and boxes without tops.

Bale Sling: Closed barrels, drums, and boxes, as well as numerous other items, can be hoisted by means of the bale sling. A temporary sling may be fashioned simply by knotting the ends of a line together with a square knot or a becket bend.

Square Knot: Also called a reef knot. This knot is used for bending lines together. If not tied properly (both knots should be tied right- or lefthanded, instead of one right and one left), it becomes a granny knot, which will slip under strain. A square knot will jam with heavy strain.

Figure Eight: This knot prevents the end of a line from unreeving through a block or eyebolt.

Catspaw: This secures a sling to a cargo hook. It cannot slip or jam.

Carrick Bend: Used to bend two hawsers together, this knot will not slip or jam. No matter how long the hawsers are in the water, it can be easily untied.

Figure 21–7 A boatswain's mate applies the finishing touches to ornamental work on the captain's gig.

Ornamental Work

Ornamental work can be constructed with various materials. It promotes safety and habitability and enhances appearance. Only a few of the common types of work appear here; there are many encyclopedias on the subject that can be obtained through shipboard or local libraries.

Turk's Heads: Mistakenly thought of as strictly ornamental, they serve many purposes, such as keeping the leathers on lifelines and the looms of oars in position.

Coxcombing: Coxcombing covers boat tillers, bucket bails, handrails for ladders, etc. It looks smart and gives a more secure grip.

Cross-Pointing: This is generally for stanchions but can be employed wherever a round core is covered. It looks best on cores of fairly large diameter. Strips of canvas, leather, and small stuff are often used in multiples of four for cross-pointing.

Fox and Geese: This is a simple and fast way of covering a handrail or stanchion. It can be used any place coxcombing or cross-pointing can.

Sennit or Braid: Made of small cord, such as codline or Belfast cord, this work is used to form ornamental lines or lanyards. A well-known book of knots describes and illustrates close to 400 sennits; don't be misled into believing the examples in figure 21-7 are the only ones, or even the basic ones.

Ground Tackle

Ground tackle includes all the equipment used to anchor a ship: anchors, anchor cables or chains, connecting fittings, anchor windlasses, and miscellaneous items such as shackles, detachable links, mooring swivels, dip ropes, chain stoppers, chain-cable jacks, mooring hooks, and anchor bars.

Anchors

There are various types of anchors and different methods of anchoring. When a ship has one anchor down, she is anchored. When she has two anchors down and swings from a mooring swivel connected to both, she is moored. (A ship secured to a dock with lines or to a buoy with an anchor chain is also moored.) In a Mediterranean moor, a ship usually has the stern moored to a pier and an anchor out on each bow. A ship's biggest anchor is her sheet anchor. An anchor carried aft by amphibious ships to pull themselves off the beach (retract) is called a stern anchor. A stream anchor, now seldom used, is a small anchor dropped off the stern or quarter of a ship to prevent her from swinging to a current.

Stockless Anchors: Stockless anchors are easy to stow and were adopted by the Navy for this reason, despite the fact that they do not have the holding power of old-fashioned anchors. Three types of stockless anchors are in use on naval ships: commercial, Mark 2, and standard Navy stockless. Of the three, the Mark 2 with its long flukes has the greatest holding power; it is made only in the 60,000-pound size for use aboard aircraft carriers.

Mushroom Anchor: This anchors buoys and torpedo-testing barges.

Lightweight (LWT) Anchors: There are two types of LWT anchors used on Navy ships: The Mark 2 LWT and the wedge-block LWT. These, as well as the commercially made Danforth anchor, are shown in figure 21-8 for comparison. Both LWT types have holding power for their weights. For example, in a sand bottom, 10,000-pound LWT anchors are designed to have a holding power approximately equal to the

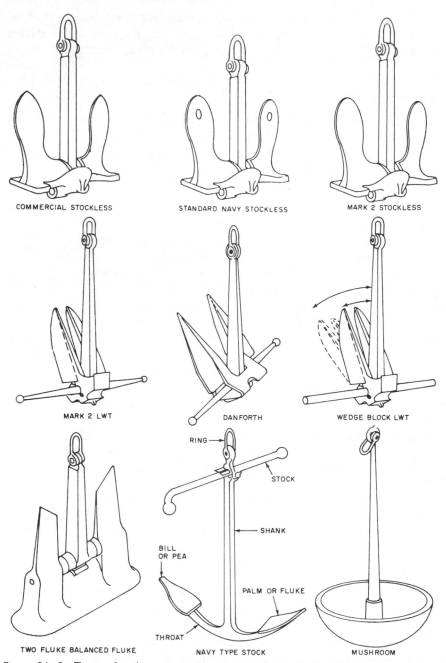

COMMERCIAL STOCKLESS   STANDARD NAVY STOCKLESS   MARK 2 STOCKLESS

MARK 2 LWT   DANFORTH   WEDGE BLOCK LWT

TWO FLUKE BALANCED FLUKE   NAVY TYPE STOCK   MUSHROOM

RING — STOCK

SHANK

BILL OR PEA

PALM OR FLUKE

THROAT

Figure 21–8 Types of anchors.

22,500-pound standard Navy stockless. Sizes below 150
pounds are used as boat anchors.

Two-Fluke/Balanced-Fluke Anchor: This anchors some surface ships and the newest submarines. It is normally housed in the bottom of the ship. In surface ships, it is used in place of a bow anchor, which would interfere with the bow sonar dome.

Old-Fashioned Anchors: These are no longer used. You will probably see them only on the lawns of some naval stations.

Chains and Related Equipment

Anchor Chains: These are made of steel. Their sizes vary according to the size of the ship and her anchors. Chain comes in 15-fathom lengths (90 feet) called shots. A destroyer will have one 8-shot chain and one 7-shot chain. Shots are connected by detachable links. These and their adjacent links are painted red, white, or blue to let the anchor detail know how much chain has run out. Each link of the next-to-last shot is painted yellow. The entire last shot is red. This is to warn that the bitter end of the chain is coming up. When an anchor is hoisted, the chain comes off the windlass and goes into the chain locker.

Shot Number	Color of Detachable Link	Number of Adjacent Links Painted White	Turns of Wire on Last White Links
1 (15 fathoms)	Red	1	1
2 (30 fathoms)	White	2	2
3 (45 fathoms)	Blue	3	3
4 (60 fathoms)	Red	4	4
5 (75 fathoms)	White	5	5
6 (90 fathoms)	Blue	6	6

Outboard Swivel Shots: On most ships, standard outboard swivel shots, also called bending shots, attach the anchor chain to the anchor. They make it possible to stop off the anchor and break the chain between the windlass and the anchor. Outboard swivel shots consist of detachable links, regular chain links, a swivel, an end link, and a bending shackle. They vary in length up to approximately 14 fathoms. Taper pins in the detachable links of an outboard swivel shot are secured with a wire locking clip, sometimes called a hairpin.

Bending Shackles: These attach the anchor to the chains.

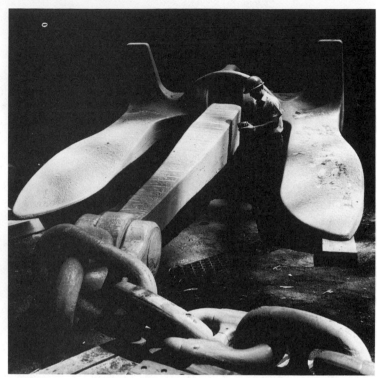

Figure 21–9   A 30-ton aircraft carrier anchor dwarfs the sailor painting it.

Riding and Housing Chain Stoppers: These consist of a turn-buckle inserted in a short section of chain, with a slip or pelican hook at one end of the chain and a shackle at the other. The housing stopper is the one nearest the hawsepipe. Any others are riding stoppers, used for holding the anchor taut in the hawsepipe, riding to an anchor, or holding an anchor when it is disconnected. When in use, a stopper is attached to the chain by straddling a link with the tongue and strongback of the pelican hook.

Mooring Shackles: These forged-steel shackles attach the anchor chain to mooring buoys. Forged-steel mooring swivels with two links at each end are inserted in the chain outboard of the hawsepipe to keep the chain from twisting as the ship swings.

Anchor Windlass: This machine is used to hoist the bow anchor. A ship with a stern anchor has a stern-anchor winch to hoist it. On combatant ships, the anchor windlass is a vertical type with controls, a friction-brake handwheel, a capstan and wildcat above deck, and an electric and hydraulic drive for the wildcat and capstan below deck. On auxiliary ships, the anchor windlass is a horizontal type above deck, with two wildcats, one for each anchor. The wildcat is fitted with ridges called whelps, which engage the links of the chain and prevent it from slipping. The wildcat may be disengaged from the shaft so that it turns freely when the anchors are dropped; it is fitted with a brake to stop the chain at the desired length or scope.

Anchor Detail: On most ships, the first lieutenant is in charge on the forecastle, with a boatswain's mate assisting and crews detailed to various duties. "Heave around" from the bridge is the order to the anchor-windlass watch to take a strain on the chain and start bringing it in. "Anchors aweigh" from the forecastle means that the anchor is clear of the bottom and the ship is under way, whether her propellers are turning or not.

Scope of Chain: Scope is the amount of chain in use from the ship to the anchor. In 10 to 15 fathoms of water, the length of chain is equal to six times the depth of water. In 15 to 20 fathoms, the length of chain is five times the depth. In 20 to 30 fathoms, the length is three times the depth.

Why the lesser scope in deeper water? Because if a ship puts heavy strain on her chain in bad weather, more of the length lifts off the bottom and the anchor will break out and drag. With too long a scope, the chain may part before its entire length lifts off the bottom.

Mooring

Unmooring, and mooring a ship to a pier, a buoy, or another ship, are the primary jobs of the deck department. These tasks involve mooring lines, winches, and fittings such as cleats, bitts, bollards, chocks, and towing pads. Quick, efficient line handling, when coming alongside or getting under way, is one of the marks of a smart ship.

Figure 21–10 Parts of a standard outboard swivel-shot assembly.

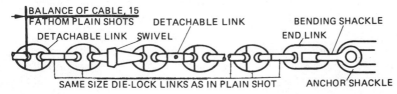

BALANCE OF CABLE, 15
FATHOM PLAIN SHOTS   DETACHABLE LINK   BENDING SHACKLE
  DETACHABLE LINK   SWIVEL   END LINK

SAME SIZE DIE-LOCK LINKS AS IN PLAIN SHOT   ANCHOR SHACKLE

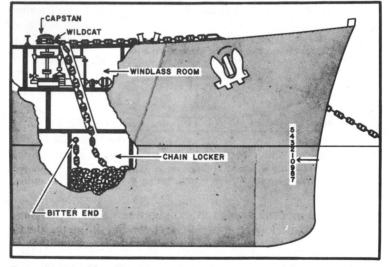

Figure 21–11   Ground-tackle installation on a typical ship is arranged on the forecastle and below decks.

Mooring Lines

Mooring lines are numbered from forward aft according to the order in which they run out from the ship, but their names describe their location, their use, and the direction in which they tend as they leave the ship. See figure 21-13.

The *bow line* (1) runs through the bull-nose or chock nearest the eyes of the ship and is led well up the pier to reduce the ship's after motion.

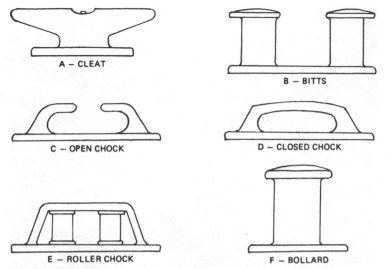

Figure 21–12 Deck fittings on a ship are the cleat, bitts, open chock, closed chock, and roller chock. The bollard is found on a pier or wharf.

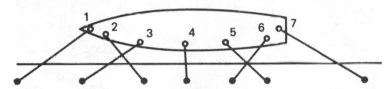

Figure 21–13 Mooring lines consist of (1) bow line, (2) after bow spring, (3) forward bow spring, (4) waist breast, (5) after quarter spring, (6) forward quarter spring, and (7) stern line.

The line used to reduce stern motion is the *stern line* (7). A *breast line* (4) leads nearly at right angles to the center line of the ship. Amidships, several breast lines may be used, in which case they are named from forward aft: *bow breast, waist breast,* and *quarter breast.* Spring lines lead out from the ship in pairs at sharp angles and cross each other. Those forward are called *after bow spring* (2) and *forward bow spring* (3) lines. Those aft are called *after quarter spring* (5) and *forward quarter spring* (6) lines. People who work with mooring lines are called line handlers.

Deck Fittings
A *cleat* consists of a pair of projecting horns for belaying a line. *Bitts* are cylindrical shapes of cast iron or steel arranged

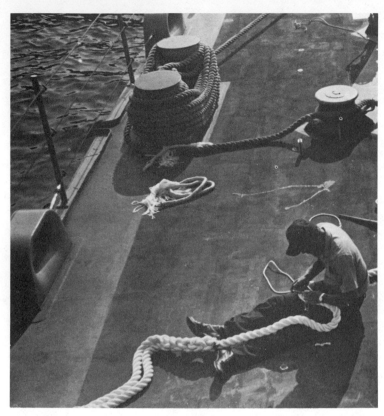

Figure 21–14 A boatswain's mate striker weaves a fender to protect the sides of his ship.

in pairs on deck, forward and aft of each chock. They are used to delay mooring lines. A *chock* is a heavy fitting through which mooring lines are led; the lines run from bitts on deck through chocks to bollards on the pier. The three types of chocks are open, closed, and roller. A *bollard*, which looks like half a bitt except it's larger, sits on the dock or pier where a bight of line is placed over it. A *towing pad* is a large padeye welded to the deck. It is used in towing operations.

Mooring may often involve putting out fenders, handling camels, and placing rat guards. Fenders are shock absorbers of various types placed between ships or between a ship and a pier. They are dropped over the side and tended from the deck. Camels are floats used to keep a ship, particularly an aircraft carrier, away from a pier or wharf so that elevators or other overhanging structures will not strike objects on the pier. Rat guards are circular metal discs lashed to mooring lines to keep rats from coming aboard.

In mooring, the messenger (a light line) is first sent over by heaving line, bolo, or line-throwing gun. Then it is hauled in with the attached mooring line. A heaving line is a light line with a weight, called a monkey fist, on one end; a bolo line is a nylon line with a padded lead weight or a monkey fist on it. A .45-caliber line-throwing gun looks like a small shotgun. It fires a projectile about the size of a pencil that carries a light nylon line. It will reach farther than a heaving line but is dangerous to use when many people are on deck. With practice, a good seaman can heave a bolo more than 100 yards.

When the ship is secured, her mooring lines are normally doubled up. A bight of line is passed to the pier or to another ship, giving three parts of line each taking an equal strain, instead of only one part. The size of mooring line depends on the type of line and ship. Destroyers generally have 6-inch manila or 5-inch nylon. Smaller ships have 5-inch manila or 4-inch nylon, while aircraft carriers have 10-inch manila or 8-inch nylon.

Commands to Line Handlers

Line handlng commands and explanation are listed below.

"Stand by your lines." Man the lines, ready to cast off or let go.

"Let go," or "Let go all lines." Slack off smartly to permit those tending lines on the pier or another ship to cast off.

"Send the lines over." Pass lines to the pier and place the eye over the appropriate bollard, but take no strain.

"Take 1 [name of line] to the capstan." Lead the end of the line to the capstan, take the slack out of the line, but take no strain.

"Heave around on [name of line]." Apply tension on line with the capstan.

"Avast heaving." Stop the capstan.

"Hold what you've got." Hold the line as it is.

"Hold." Do not allow any more line to go out (otherwise it could part).

"Check." Hold heavy tension on the line but render it (let it slip) as necessary to prevent parting.

"Surge." Hold moderate tension on the line, but render it enough to permit movement of the ship (used when she is moving along the pier to an adjacent position).

"Double up." Pass an additional bight on all mooring lines so that there are three parts of each line to the pier.

"Single up." Take in all bights and extra lines so that only a single part of each of the normal mooring lines remains.

"Take in all lines." When the ship is secured with your own lines, have the ends cast off from the pier and brought on board.

"Cast off all lines." When the ship is secured with another ship's lines in a nest, cast off the ends of the lines and allow the other ship to retrieve her lines.

"Shift." Move your line along a pier. This command is followed by a command telling you which line should be moved: "shift no. 3 from the bollard to the cleat."

"Take 1 [no. 1] to the winch [capstan]." This command is given when auxiliary deck machinery is used to haul in a line, It may be followed by "Heave around on 1" and then "Avast heaving on 1."

After a ship has completed mooring to another ship or a pier, rat guards are put out on all mooring lines. Putting out rat guards is a tiresome job, especially on a cold rainy night, but it is essential. Rats carry contagious diseases, and once they get aboard, it is almost impossible to get rid of them.

Towing

Most routine towing jobs in the Navy are handled by harbor tugs, fleet tugs, salvage vessels, and submarine-rescue vessels—all ships specially fitted for the work. Some ocean towing ships have automatic tension-towing machines, powerful electric-drive winches mounted in the stern that automatically heave in or pay out the towing hawsers and maintain proper tension at all times. Tugs working in harbors usually use the alongside method, because there is no room in crowded areas for a long stern tow, and with barges properly secured alongside, tugs have greatly increased maneuverability.

Combatant vessels—carriers, cruisers, and destroyers—can tow other vessels or can be towed, but such operations are usually done only in an emergency and involve what is called the fixed-towing method. The towing rig varies among classes and types of ships, but includes the following items in one form or another:

On the stern of the towing vessel, a *towing-pad eye,* usually on the centerline.

A *towing assembly,* chiefly a large pelican hook shackled to the towing pad and made fast to a towing hawser.

The *hawser* itself, a wire rope varying in length from 100 fathoms for a destroyer to 150 fathoms for a larger ship. The hawser is attached to one of the towed ship's anchor chains, which is disconnected from the outboard shot, let out through the bull-nose, and veered to 20 to 45 fathoms.

The length of the towline—hawser and chain—is adjusted to hang in a deep underwater curve called a *catenary,* which helps to relieve surges on the line caused by movements of the two ships. Whether towing is done with two motor launches or two cruisers, the towline should be of such a scope (or length) that the two craft are in "step." Both must reach the crest of a wave at the same time, otherwise the towline is whipped out of the water and may do great damage.

Once the towing hawser is rigged, the towing vessel gets under way very slowly, as the towed vessel commences to move. If the towing vessel does not move slowly, the line may part. Course changes must also be made slowly, for the towed vessel will flounder at the end of the line and may have difficulty steering a course.

Every naval ship is furnished with a plan (explained in the Standard Organization and Regulations of the U.S. Navy) showing the proper method of rigging for towing. Towing requires skillful seamanship, proficiency in shiphandling, and perfect communication between the towing craft and the craft being towed.

Cargo Handling

Cargo is loaded or offloaded by ship's gear or dockside or floating cranes when in port, by ship's gear in underway replenishment (UNREP), and by helicopters in vertical replenishment (VERTREP) operations. Combatant ships have limited cargo-handling equipment, except during UNREP operations. Amphibious-warfare ships and service ships are fitted with heavy-lift cargo systems. An LKA can lift a 70-ton boat, and the new AOEs can transfer cargo or pump fuel through fifteen replenishment stations at once.

Aboard such ships, deck seamanship is primarily concerned with heavy-cargo handling. A knowledge of the principal parts of cargo gear and of the various "rigs" or methods of handling cargo is essential for seamen in these ships. For a better under-

Figure 21–15 A deck hand rigs the vang line, which supports a boom.

standing of the terms mentioned in the following discussion,
see figure 21-16.

Rigging

Rigging is a general term for wires, ropes, and chains supporting masts or kingposts, as well as operating booms and
cargo hooks. *Standing rigging* includes all lines that support
but do not move, such as stays and shrouds. *Running rigging*

includes movable lines rove (run) through blocks, such as lifts, whips, and vangs.

Running Rigging

Booms are moved into position and cargo is moved into and out of holds with running rigging. Topping lifts working on lift blocks move the boom vertically and hold it at the required height. Inboard and outboard guys, or vangs, move the boom horizontally or hold it in working position over hatch or dock. The cargo hook is raised or lowered by whips, which run from

Figure 21–16 Rigging detail for single swinging boom.

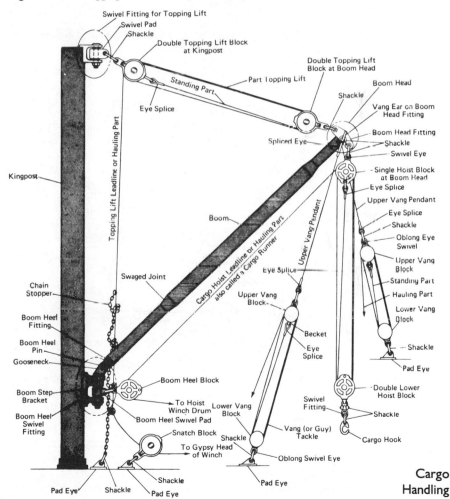

winches over heel blocks near the gooseneck and over head
blocks at the top of the boom.

Booms

A boom is a long pole built of steel. The lower end is fitted
with a gooseneck, which supports the boom in a step bracket.
The upper end is raised or lowered and held in position by a
topping lift. Booms range in capacity from 5 to 75 tons. When
booms are used in pairs, the one lifting cargo from a hold is
called the hatch boom. The boom that positions cargo over the
side to lower it to a dock or boat is called the yard boom.
Booms are used singly, or in combination as follows:

Figure 21–17 Details of burton or yard-and-stay rig, used for medium-
weight cargo of up to 3,500 pounds.

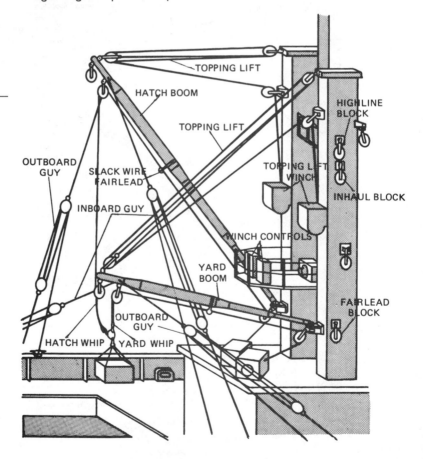

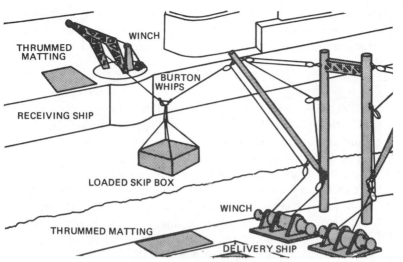

Figure 21–18 Burton rig for underway replenishment has a maximum load
of 3,500 pounds.

Single Swinging Boom: This arrangement is generally used
to hoist or lower landing craft on LPDs and LKAs. The topping lift is led to a winch that can raise or lower the boom with
a full load. The boom is swung over the side by vangs, and the
cargo hook is attached to the boat's lifting bridle. Another
winch takes up the cargo hoist leadline to raise the load. The
boom is swung over the side by the vangs, and the boat is
hooked on. Then the hoist winch raises the boat clear of the
railing, after which the vang on the side opposite the boat
swings it on deck. Cargo, in nets or pallets, can be handled the
same way.

Yard and Stay (or Burton): Two booms are used, a hatch
boom and a cargo boom (figure 21-17). The hatch boom is
centered over the working hatch. The yard boom is rigged out
with its head over the pier or receiving boat. There are two
cargo whips—a hatch whip and yard whip—rove through their
respective heel and head blocks on the hatch and yard booms,
and both shackled to the same cargo hook. Each whip has its
own winch. With the hatch boom secured above the center of
the open hatch and the yard boom rigged out over the side of
the ship, the cargo hook is dropped into the hold for a load.
The yard whip hangs slack while the hatch whip hoists the load
clear. The yard whip heaves around, the hatch whip is payed

out, and the load is racked (swung) across the deck and over the side. When the load is under the yard boom, the hatch whip is slackened off and the yard whip lowers away. In loading cargo, the procedure is reversed.

Inspecting Rigging

A weekly inspection of all booms and their rigging and associated fittings is conducted by the responsible officer of the weapons or deck department, in accordance with the requirements of the planned maintenance system (PMS).

Whenever a boom is to hoist or lower a load equal to its rated capacity as shown on the label plate, the first lieutenant or an officer designated by the officer of the deck makes a thorough inspection of the boom, fitting, and rigging before the lift is made. Details about the use, care, and testing of cranes, booms, and rigging are given in NAVSHIPSTECHMAN.

Underway Replenishment

UNREP refers to any method of transferring fuel, munitions, supplies, and personnel from one ship to another at sea. The term replenishment at sea, formerly used in this sense, now applies to all methods except fueling.

Before the techniques of UNREP were developed, a ship that ran low on fuel, supplies, or ammunition had to return to port, or the fleet had to lie to while she was replenished by small boats. The effectiveness of the fleet was reduced by the ships that had to leave; moreover, a fleet lying to for replenishment was more vulnerable to attack. With UNREP, an entire fleet can be resupplied, rearmed, and refueled within hours, while it is proceeding on its mission.

There are two general UNREP methods: connected and vertical. They may be employed separately or simultaneously. In connected replenishment (CONREP), two or more ships steam side by side, their hoses and lines connecting them. VERTREP is done by helicopters, with the ships close or miles apart, depending on the tactical situation and the amount of cargo to be transferred.

CONREP involves two processes, refueling and resupply. In refueling at sea (FAS), fuel is pumped from a delivery ship, which may be a replenishment tanker (AOR), oiler (AO), fast combat support ship (AOE), or large combat ship. Other replenishment ships, such as the combat store ship (AFS) and

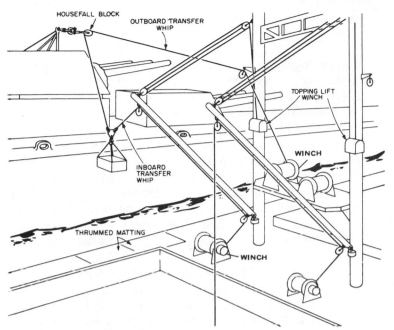

HOUSEFALL BLOCK
OUTBOARD TRANSFER WHIP
TOPPING LIFT WINCH
WINCH
INBOARD TRANSFER WHIP
THRUMMED MATTING
WINCH

Figure 21–19   The housefall rig has a maximum load of 2,500 pounds.

the ammunition ship (AE), can deliver lesser amounts of fuel. But their primary purpose is to deliver solid cargo—that is, supplies and ammunition—by methods now referred to as replenishment at sea (RAS).

The most common methods of refueling are the span wire and the close in. The span-wire method has several variations, single hose, double hose, and probe. The span wire may be either tensioned or untensioned. The tensioned span wire or highline, as it is called in RAS, also is used in the standard tensioned replenishment alongside method (STREAM) of transfer, described on p. 529.

Other common RAS methods include manila highline, wire highline, burton, housefall, modified housefall, and double housefall.

The illustrations in this chapter and the procedures described are meant to be representative only. For the sake of clarity, many of the variations have been omitted from illustrations. The latest revision of naval warfare publication Replenishment at Sea (NWP-14) should be consulted for more precise information about rigging, personnel, tools, etc.

Cargo Rigs

Here is a brief description of each rig or system:

Burton Rig: The cargo is moved from delivering ship to receiving ship by two burton whips, which correspond to the hatch whip and cargo whip. A winch on each ship handles one whip. The delivering ship hoists the load clear, then the receiving ship takes in her burton whip as the delivering ship slacks hers off. When the load is spotted over the deck of the receiving ship, her whip is slacked and the load is eased to the deck. The entire operation requires skillful coordination between the two winchmen. They must keep constant tension on both whips at all times, whether they are running in or out, and they must keep the load just clear of the water—if the load is too high, the strain on all rigging is greatly increased. The maximum load is 3,500 pounds.

Housefall Rig: In this method, both cargo whips are handled by the delivering ship. The whip that moves cargo to the receiving ship is called the outboard transfer whip (same as yard whip), and the whip that hauls the cargo hook back to the delivering ship is called the inboard transfer whip (same as cargo whip). Both winchmen are on the delivering ship. The maximum load is 2,500 pounds.

Modified Housefall Rig: This method is used when loads must be kept higher above the water than with a housefall rig. A trolley block carrying the cargo hook rides back and forth on the outboard transfer whip. Otherwise the rigging is the same as that for the housefall rig.

Double Housefall Rig: This is used to speed transfers to ships that cannot handle more than one housefall rig. It is slower than housefalling to two separate receiving stations, but faster than housefalling to one station. In this method, the delivering ship uses two adjacent housefall rigs attached to a single point on the receiving ship. In handling cargo with this method, the delivering ship sends over a loaded net with one rig at the same time the other brings back an empty net from the receiving ship. The two nets pass each other in opposite directions each time a load is transferred.

STAR Rig: The Surf, Traveling Actuated Remotely (STAR) rig is a star latch bolted to a surf. The latch assembly and probe fitting mate automatically when the rig is passed to the receiving ship. They are remotely unlatched when the rig is retrieved. The STAR rig eliminates the need to send sailors aloft for these purposes.

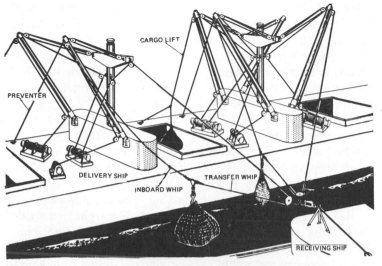

Figure 21–20   The double housefall rig's maximum load is 2,500 pounds.

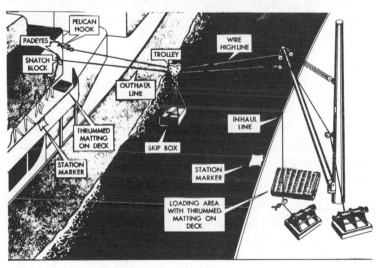

Figure 21–21   Wire highline rig.

Wire Highline Rig: This method involves a trolley moving
on a highline that extends from a winch on the delivering ship
through a block on a boom head and across to a pad eye on the
receiving ship. An outhaul line (same as a yard whip) is heaved
in by hand on the receiving ship to move the load over. A
winch-operated inhaul line (same as a hatch whip) on the deliv-

ering ship returns the trolley for another load. The wire high-line is the standard procedure in transferring cargo to destroyers and other small ships, and at times is the best means of transfer to large ships. In order to use this method, the receiving ship must have a place in her superstructure high enough to attach the line for good working conditions and strong enough to handle the load.

Manila Highline Rig: This is the same as the wire highline rig, except that manila is used instead of wire. Only light cargo can be handled. No boom is needed on the delivery ship. The receiving ship needs only a 12-inch snatch block attached to a padeye. The highline is kept taut during transfer either by twenty-five line handlers or a capstan. The capstan cannot be used if personnel are being transferred. The trolley that rides the highline is moved by in-haul and out-haul lines, both handled by personnel on deck. The rig is easily and quickly set up and is the safest method of transferring personnel from ship to ship. The maximum load is 600 pounds.

Personnel Transfer: Besides the manila highline rig, personnel can be transferred by the burton rig and by helicopter. With the burton rig, in particular used when many people must transfer quickly and time does not allow for a highline, a ship box sends over four or five people at a time. The danger of the burton system is having the transfer controlled by winchmen on two different ships. The only approved rig for transferring personnel ship to ship is the manila highline. This is because the line must be tended constantly to prevent parting if the ships roll away from each other, and manila can be tended by hand. Wire cannot, however. The maximum load is 600 pounds.

Fueling at Sea

The two basic systems are close-in and span-wire rigs. Which system is used depends on the ships involved, the kind of fuel being transferred, and weather and operating conditions. The two rigs differ mainly in the method by which the delivering ship sends the hose over to the receiving ship. For fuel, a 6-inch, 230-foot hose is used. Fleet oilers and many major combatant ships have equipment for the span wire method. Other ships use the close-in method.

Close-in Method: The hose is supported by saddle whips attached to the inboard and outboard saddles and running to booms or other high points on the delivery ship. If an outer

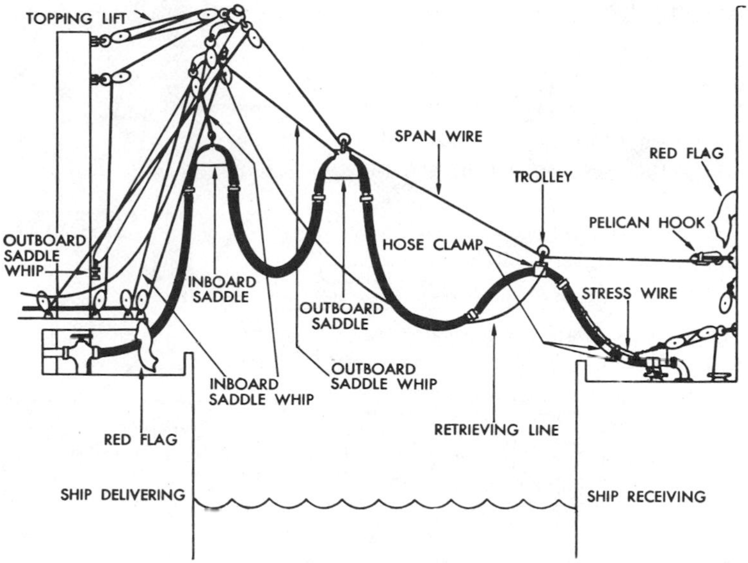

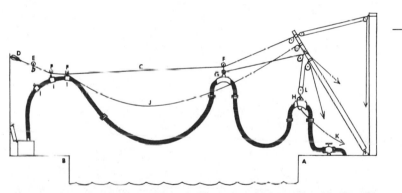

Figure 21–22   Fueling at sea by close-in method.

Figure 21–23   Fueling at sea by all-wire-span method: (A) delivering ship, (B) receiving ship, (C) wire span, (D) pelican hook, (E) free trolley, (F) trolley, (G) outboard saddle, (H) inboard saddle, (I) hose clamps, (J) retrieving wire, (K) wire pendant, (L) wire saddle whip.

bight line is used, it runs from the outboard saddle to the receiving ship. The ships steam about 60 feet apart.

Span Wire Method: A single span wire stretches a fuel hose between the two ships. The hose is suspended by a trolley that rides along the span wire. This method keeps the ships 140 to 180 feet apart, which makes shiphandling easier and allows the

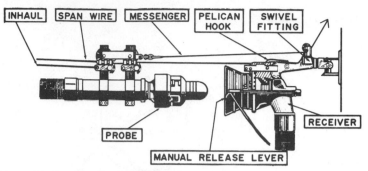

Figure 21–24 Details of fueling probe.

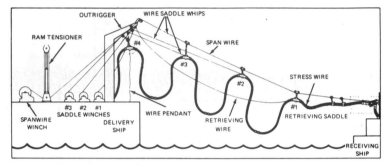

528

Figure 21–25 Fuel STREAM, single hose with probe.

use of antiaircraft batteries. The span wire, because it carries
the hose higher above the sea, gives it better protection in
rough weather. The hose may be rigged out by the all-wire or
the manila rig. The all-wire-span method involves a span wire
on which a trolley carries the outboard saddle and a retrieving
wire line. This method can be used only if there are enough
winches at the stations to be rigged. Generally, at least three
winches are required. Of the two span-wire methods, the
all-wire rig is most common.

Manila Rig: This rig is simpler than the all-wire one, but it
requires more people at each station to handle the inboard and
outboard saddle whips.

Probe Fueling System: This system has been developed to
reduce fueling time by eliminating the need for connecting and
disconnecting fuel lines. Its basic parts are a fueling probe at
the delivery end of a 7-inch fueling hose and a probe receiver

suspended between the bitter end of the span wire and the

padeye on the receiving ship. The receiver is mounted on a swivel fitting and so is always lined up with the span wire and the probe.

There is a single-probe and a double-probe fueling system. The difference between them is that the double-probe fueling coupling consists of a double probe and a double receiver.

Robb Coupling: This is a combined quick-release coupling and valve used by some ships. It consists of a male end attached to the fueling manifold on the receiving ship, and a female end on the hose sent over by the delivering ship. A spring-loaded valve in the female end is held closed until a lever on the male end moves a cam and opens the valve.

Standard Tensioned Replenishment Alongside Method (STREAM)

STREAM is actually a combination of replenishment methods and riggings. STREAM can be broadly divided into missile STREAM and cargo STREAM. Missile STREAM is a high-speed, automated, heavy-weather method of transferring uncrated missiles under precise, full-load control. With cargo STREAM, variously modified, almost any cargo that can be transferred by conventional methods can be moved more safely and quickly.

Vertical Replenishment (VERTREP)

VERTREP uses a helicopter to transport solid cargo from the deck of an underway replenishment ship to the deck of the receiving ship. Vertical replenishment augments or, in some cases, replaces CONREP. It can be conducted with the receiving ship alongside during CONREP, though it can also be done over the horizon, anywhere within range. Range depends on the helicopter, involved flying conditions, and the load.

Cargo can be carried internally, but the preferred method is to sling it from a hook installed in the rescue hatch at the bottom of the cabin. Internal cargo is restricted to what can be handled by an internal winch with a capacity of 600 pounds. External cargo, depending on the helicopter and flying conditions, can weigh up to 7,000 pounds.

Almost any ship can be replenished by helo if she has a small open area for landing cargo, a larger unobstructed area overhead in which the helo can hover, and unobstructed access to the hover area. Ships are specified by class according to their facilities for conducting VERTREP.

Fast Automatic Shuttle Transfer (FAST)

This is a completely mechanized system for transferring missiles from the hold of a delivery ship to the magazine of a receiving ship. FAST can also be used to transfer conventional cargo to frigates and aircraft carriers.

Common Features of Replenishment Techniques

Many features are common to all replenishment operations. First, it is the responsibility of the officer in tactical command (OTC) to select a suitable course and speed, taking into consideration the mission of the group and the condition of the sea. Generally, the delivering ship takes station, while the receiving ship maneuvers to come alongside and adjusts course and speed as necessary to maintain her position during the operation. When supplying large aircraft carriers, however, replenishment ships may complete the final phase of the approach, since the view from the carrier's bridge can be obstructed during this phase of the maneuver.

Except for gear rigged on the receiving ship, and the distance line and burton whips, the delivering ship furnishes all equipment. There is one major exception; when carriers and cruisers are alongside replenishment ships and personnel are to be transferred, the combatants must furnish and tend the manila highline. All stations involved in the evolution are in communication with one another via sound-powered telephone. This includes a communication link between the bridges of both ships.

Persons assigned to replenishment stations must be thoroughly schooled in and observant of safety precautions. Unfortunately, people tend to be careless, particularly when doing familiar tasks. For this reason, all personnel are rebriefed before each exercise. If you don't know what you're doing, or if you aren't sure where you're supposed to be, ask. It might save your life or the life of a shipmate.

Small Boats

22

The term boat refers to small craft limited in their use by size and usually not capable of making independent voyages of any length on the high seas. The Navy uses thousands of boats, ranging from 9-foot dinghies to 135-foot landing craft. They are powered by diesels, outboard motors, gas turbines, and underwater jets. Most boats are built of aluminum, plastic, or fiberglass. Landing craft are built of steel. A few boats are still made of wood.

Standard Boats

A standard boat is a small vessel carried aboard a ship to perform various tasks and evolutions.

Landing Craft

These boats, carried by various amphibious ships, are usually referred to by their designations rather than by full names. All landing craft are designed to carry troops, vehicles, or cargo from ship to shore under combat conditions, to unload, to retract from the beach, and to return to the ship. They are especially rugged, with powerful engines, and they are armed.

The principal types are the LCVP (landing craft, vehicle and personnel), LCP(L) (landing craft, personnel [large]), LCP(R) (landing craft, personnel [ramped]), LCM (landing craft, medium), and LCU (landing craft, utility). LCVPs and LCMs are common in today's fleet. A brief description of each follows.

The LCVP is a single-engine 36-foot boat with a hand-operated bow ramp. It is used for vehicles and personnel, although frequently it lands liberty parties, handles stores, and the like. When an LCVP is run up on the beach, the forward ramp is lowered and vehicles and personnel disembark across the lowered ramp. An LCVP can carry 36 men, 4 tons of cargo, or a combination of jeeps, trucks, or other equipment.

There are two types of LCMs, both larger versions of the LCVP. They have twin engines, power-operated bow ramps, and after structures with enginerooms, pilot houses, and storage compartments. The LCM-8, called Mike 8, is 73 feet long, has a 21-foot beam, and carries a heavy tank or 60 tons of cargo. The LCM-6, Mike 6, was produced in a variety of configurations for river warfare in Vietnam. One version, the monitor (MON), was fitted with heavy armor for shore bombardment and gunfire support. Another version, the command control boat (CCB), carried extensive communications equipment.

Motorboats (MBs)

MBs are fast, decked-over boats with closed compartments forward and aft, and open cockpits amidships where coxswains steer by wheel. The closed compartments are roofed over by rounded metal canopies. MBs are used mainly for carrying officers. Enlisted passengers, when aboard, occupy the forward cabin. Those designed for officers are painted haze gray. Those assigned for use by commanding officers, chiefs of staff, and squadron, patrol, or division commanders are called gigs. They are also painted haze gray. MBs assigned to flag officers (admirals) are called barges. They have black hulls and white canopies. MBs are either 35 or 40 feet long and diesel-powered.

Motor Launches (MLs)

These are heavy-duty, square-sterned boats. They are 40 or 50 feet long and diesel-powered, with removable seats (thwarts). MLs are used for hauling liberty parties and stores. The engine is aft, and the coxswain steers with a tiller bar from a platform called the coxswain's flat at the very stern of the boat.

Motor Whaleboats (MWBs)

These round-bottomed, double-ended, 26-foot, diesel-powered boats are used as lifeboats and shipboard utility boats. Many small ships use them as gigs and officers' MBs, in which case they have metal or canvas canopies. MWBs are divided into forward, engine, and after compartments. Not very seaworthy, the MWB is never overloaded because it swamps easily. It is steered by a tiller.

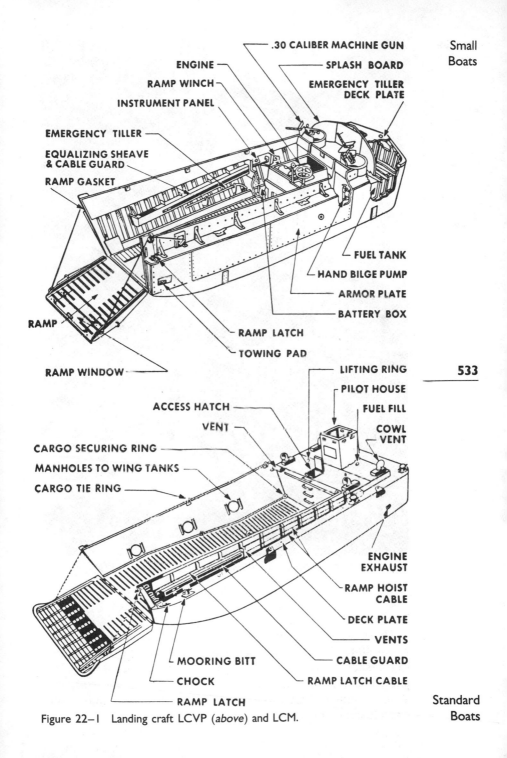

.30 CALIBER MACHINE GUN

ENGINE

SPLASH BOARD

RAMP WINCH

EMERGENCY TILLER
DECK PLATE

INSTRUMENT PANEL

EMERGENCY TILLER

EQUALIZING SHEAVE
& CABLE GUARD

RAMP GASKET

FUEL TANK

HAND BILGE PUMP

ARMOR PLATE

BATTERY BOX

RAMP

RAMP LATCH

TOWING PAD

RAMP WINDOW

LIFTING RING

PILOT HOUSE

ACCESS HATCH

FUEL FILL

VENT

COWL
VENT

CARGO SECURING RING

MANHOLES TO WING TANKS

CARGO TIE RING

ENGINE
EXHAUST

RAMP HOIST
CABLE

DECK PLATE

VENTS

MOORING BITT

CABLE GUARD

CHOCK

RAMP LATCH CABLE

RAMP LATCH

Figure 22–1   Landing craft LCVP (*above*) and LCM.

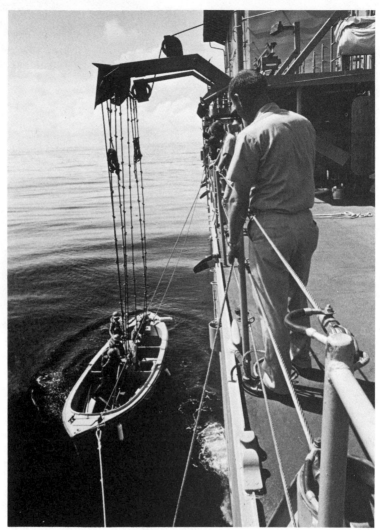

Figure 22–2 A whaleboat is lowered for a man-overboard drill.

Personnel Boats (PERS)
These are fast, V-bottomed, double-ended, diesel-powered,
28- or 40-foot boats with enclosed spaces specifically designed
to transport officers, although smaller types are used for shore-
party boats, lifeboats, and mail boats. A 40-foot boat will carry
a maximum of forty-three persons. Smaller types have only
one closed compartment.

Punts

These are open square-enders, 10 or 14 feet long. They are either rowed or sculled, and are generally used by side cleaners.

Utility Boats (UBs)

These boats, varying in length from 22 to 65 feet, are mainly cargo and personnel carriers or heavy-duty work boats. Many have been modified for survey work, tending divers, and minesweeping operations. In ideal weather, a 50-foot UB will carry 146 men plus crew. The largest UB, a general-purpose work boat with a 24,000-pound carrying capacity, is steered from a pilot house.

Wherries

These, also open, are 12, 14, and 16 feet long with square sterns. Wherries are either rowed or powered by outboard motor.

Special Boats

These boats, used by shore stations, are seldom seen in the fleet. They include line-handling boats, buoy boats, aircraft-rescue boats, torpedo retrievers, and various patrol and picket boats.

Landing-Craft Swimmer Reconnaissance (LCSR)

This 23-ton, 52-foot fiberglass boat, powered by two 1,000-horsepower gas turbines, has a top speed of 38 knots. It is designed to speed into enemy territory and drop sea-air-land teams (SEALs), underwater demolition teams (UDTs), and other special operations personnel.

Patrol Craft, Fast (PCF)

This twin-diesel, 25-knot, radar-equipped patrol boat, with only a $4\frac{1}{2}$-foot draft, was designed to operate, intercept, and search native craft in shallow rivers in Southeast Asia.

Patrol Boat, River (PBR)

This is a 31-foot, 25-knot twin-diesel boat with a fiberglass hull and water-jet-pump propulsion that permits it to operate in 15 inches of water. The PBR is highly maneuverable and can reverse course in its own length. It carries radar, communications equipment, and machine guns.

Figure 22-3   Current Navy fleet boats.

A 26-foot personnel boat

A 33-foot personnel boat

A 40-foot utility boat

A 26-foot whaleboat

A 50-foot utility boat

A 40-foot personnel boat

Patrol Air-Cushion Vehicle (PACV)

This boat is the Navy's smallest fast craft. It rides about a foot above the surface on a cushion of air, at a speed of 60 knots over water and 40 over land.

Fast Patrol Boat (PTF)

This is a modern version of the famous World War II PT boats. PTFs are 80 feet long, displace 82 tons, and can make 45 knots with twin-diesel engines. They are known as the Nasty class.

Miscellaneous Boats

These are experimental, commercial, and obsolete types used when other boats are in short supply. Landing craft no longer fit for amphibious use, and others not classified as standard boats, along with small landing craft or special boats, all belong in this category. Miscellaneous boats include the 9-foot dinghy; 12-foot punt; 22-foot MB; 26-, 30-, and 36-foot ML.

Boat Crews

Most boats have permanently assigned crews. Crew size varies depending on the type of boat, but there are always the coxswain, engineer, bowhook, and sternhook. All must be qualified swimmers.

Coxswain

The coxswain and coxswain's crew are in charge of the lives and property of passengers and equipment. Subject to the orders of the officer of the deck and the senior line officer embarked, a coxswain otherwise has full charge and is responsible for the boat's appearance, safety, and efficient operation. The crew and passengers are required to cooperate fully with the coxswain. In fulfilling his or her responsibilities, the coxswain must be familiar with all details relating to the boat's care and handling. Equally important, the coxswain must be able to instruct the crew in all aspects of the general service and drills. The coxswain is also responsible for the appearance and behavior of the crew.

Coxswains and boat crews represent their vessel and should for that reason take pride in their appearance and that of their boat. The efficiency and smartness of a ship's boats and boat crews reflect the standards of the ship. Clean white uniforms

Figure 22–4 The coxswain and boat crew must take pride in their appearance, which reflects on the ship they represent.

can be hard to maintain on some ships, but custom dictates
that every day the ship's laundry wash and press a uniform for
each member of the duty boats' crews. Ship regulations frequently require crewmembers to wear sneakers. This is a
safety factor, but it also keeps boats themselves looking good.

The coxswain must always obey the rules of the road. Tax-
ing planes and underway ships do not maneuver as readily as
small boats, so it is smart to keep clear of them. The coxswain
should avoid cutting close across the bow or stern of a moored
or anchored ship, and passing close around the corner of a
pier. The coxswain should also run dead slow when passing
other boats alongside ships or landings, when passing heavily
loaded boats, or in narrow or crowded waters.

The coxswain is responsible for recording courses to and
from all landings and the length of time spent on each course.
Entries are kept in the compass course book for use in low-
visibility conditions. In an LCVP or LCM, the coxswain sees
that the engineer and deck hands perform their duties promptly
and efficiently. The coxswain also has authority over troops
while they are in the craft. The coxswain directs and controls
the operation of the ramp. The coxswain is also responsible for
boat checks before getting under way and while securing.

In gigs, barges, and MBs, the coxswain controls engine
speed. In MLs and MWBs, he or she signals the engineer by
the standard bell codes:

| One bell | Ahead slow |
|
| Three bells | Back slow | |
| Four bells | Full speed in direction propeller is turning | |

Engineer

In an open boat, the engineer sits abaft the power plant facing forward. In a decked-over craft, the engineer is stationed in the engineroom. The engineer must see that the engine is in good condition and ready to run. Only the engineer should work on the engine. In the LCPV, the engineer's station is on the starboard side of the engine, and the engineer operates the hand winch to raise or lower the ramp. In the LCM, the engineer stands by the port engine, which powers the ramp.

Bowhook

The bowhook mans the bow boathook, painter, and bow line. The bowhook also tends fenders and forward weather cloths (canvases spread for protection against the wind). In an open boat, the bowhook usually sits on the starboard side, outboard, on the forward thwart. In storms, the bowhook may move to the lee side. The bowhook faces the bow and serves as a lookout. If the boat is decked over, the bowhook stands on the starboard after deck facing forward.

The LCVP bowhook serves as forward lookout, releases the ramp latch when the coxswain directs, and handles fenders, bow line, and other lines; in combat, the bowhook mans the starboard machine gun.

When the boat approaches the landing, the bowhook should be ready to spring ashore with the painter and take a turn on the nearest cleat. When the boat approaches a ship's gangway, the bowhook should be in the bow with the boathook, ready to snag the boat line and make it fast. The bowhook should always have a fender ready to drop over the side if a bump is unavoidable.

Sternhook

The sternhook, likewise, should be ready at once to jump ashore with the stern fast. Frequently, the stern is off the landing and the sternhook has to make quite a leap. In an open boat, the sternhook normally sits on the starboard side, outboard on the after thwart, facing aft. On decked-over craft, the sternhook usually stands on the port side of the after deck, facing forward. The LCVP sternhook serves as a signalman, besides tending the stern line, fenders, and other gear. The sternhook mans the portside machine gun and assists the engineer in handling the winch when the ramp is raised. Duties and stations for the LCM crew are similar to those for the LCVP crew. The third deck hand, however, remains at the ramp during the run to the beach, while the other two man the guns.

Boat Officer

During heavy weather and other times as deemed necessary, an officer (sometimes a chief petty officer) is assigned to each duty boat. A boat officer naturally has authority over the coxswain. The boat officer does not assume the coxswain's responsibilities nor relieve the coxswain of his or her normal duties. The situation is somewhat like the relationship between the officer of the deck and the commanding officer on the bridge. The coxswain and boat officer are responsible for the boat and for the safety and welfare of the crew and passengers.

Care of Boats and Equipment

A boat crew cares for the boat and its equipment. Proper maintenance greatly increases its service life and assures its operational readiness.

In wooden-hulled boats, every effort should be made to provide thorough ventilation and drainage and to prevent freshwater leakage. To this end, all ventilation terminals are to be kept open.

Deck seams, especially in the plank sheer area, must be carefully caulked and maintained. Decks are sanded carefully to retain the proper camber and to eliminate low areas where water might accumulate. Hatches and deck plates should be opened during fair weather to increase air circulation. Wet dunnage, rope, and life jackets in lockers and forepeak spaces should be removed and aired out.

Wooden boats should be washed down with salt water, not fresh water. Salt is removed from varnished surfaces, chrome and brass fittings, and windows with a sponge or chamois dipped in fresh water. On wooden boats, the stem, stern, and bilge areas are purposely left unpainted. Wood preservative solutions should be used there.

Figure 22–5 Proper stowage of a motor launch requires secure lashings of the canvas cover.

Great care must be taken to prevent corrosion of steel-hulled boats. Maintain paint and preservation coatings in good condition. Install the proper number of zincs in the stern area on steel (and some wooden) hulls to prevent electrolytic corrosion.

Maintenance and repair of plastic and fiberglass hulls involve the same materials and techniques used on sports cars. Do not use laminates, resins, or hardeners without fully reading instructions in the training manuals for hull-maintenance technicians.

Repair minor damage, tighten loose bolts, and fix or replace leaking gaskets as soon as possible to prevent more difficult repairs later. Secure all loose gear to avoid damage. Keep the boat and its equipment free of dirt, corrosion, and accumulated grease.

The propeller shaft should be checked for alignment monthly, and crankcase oil should be changed after every 100 hours of running. Gear housings, steering mechanisms, and other moving parts must be well lubricated. Fenders should be placed between boats when they are tied up. When a boat is hoisted out, the struts, propeller, sea suctions, and shaft bearings should be checked. Dog-eared propellers or worn shaft bearings cause heavy vibration, resulting in severe damage to hull and engine.

All rubber exhaust couplings should be checked for tightness and condition. Batteries being charged must be ventilated to avoid a hydrogen explosion.

Oil-soaked bottom planking on wooden boats can't be successfully painted or caulked. On steel or plastic hulls, oil-soaked bilges are a fire hazard. When draining or filling fuel tanks or engine crankcases, avoid spilling diesel fuel or engine oil.

Improper stowage of boats results in hogging of the keel, misalignment of shafts, and distortion of the hull. Boats must have a full-length keel rest for support while in stowage. Overhang at the stem and stern should be supported by wooden blocking and wedges. Chocks should be located opposite frames or bulkheads. Loads imposed by gripe pads on a hull are distributed over as wide an area as possible to prevent hull damage. Take-up devices on the gripes should be marked at the limit of tightening required, and that limit should not be exceeded.

Boat Markings, Indentification

The national ensign is displayed from Navy boats when:

They are under way during daylight in a foreign port.
Ships are dressed or full dressed.

They are alongside a foreign vessel.

An officer or official is embarked on an official occasion.

A uniformed flag or general officer, unit commander, commanding officer, or chief of staff is embarked in a boat of his or her command or in one assigned for his or her personal use.

Prescribed by the senior officer present. Since small boats are a part of a vessel, they follow the motions of the parent ship regarding the half-masting of colors.

Personal Flags, Pennants, and Bow Insignia

When embarked in a Navy boat on official occasions, an officer in command displays from the bow the officer's personal flag or command pennant—or, if not entitled to either, a commission pennant. An officer entitled to display a personal flag or command pennant may display a miniature of the flag or pennant near the coxswain's station when embarked on any unofficial occasion.

In a boat assigned to the personal use of a flag or general officer, unit commander, chief of staff, or commanding officer, on which a civil official is embarked, the following flagstaff insignia are fitted at the peak:

Spread Eagle: For an official whose authorized salute is nineteen or more guns (secretaries of the Navy, Army, Air Force, and above).

Halberd: For a flag or general officer whose official salute is fewer than nineteen guns and for a civil official whose salute is eleven or more, but fewer than nineteen guns (assistant secretaries of defense down to and including consul generals).

Ball: For an officer of the grade or relative grade of captain in the Navy and for a career minister, counselor, or first secretary of an embassy, legation, or consul.

Star: For an officer of the grade or relative grade of commander in the Navy.

Flat Truck: For an officer below the grade or relative grade of commander in the Navy, and for a civil official on an official visit for whom honors are prescribed.

The head of the spread eagle and the cutting edges of the halberd must face forward. The points of the star must face fore and aft.

Barges are marked with chrome stars on the bow, arranged as on the admiral's flag. The official abbreviated title of the flag officer's command appears on the stern in gold-leaf decal letters—CINCPACFLT, for example. On gigs assigned for the personal use of unit commanders not of flag rank, the insignia is a broad or burgee replica of the command pennant with squadron or division numbers superimposed. The official abbreviated title of the command, such as DESRON NINE, appears on the stern in gold-leaf letters.

The gig for a chief of staff not of flag rank is marked with the official abbreviated title of the command in chrome letters, with an arrow running through the letters. Other boats assigned for staff use have brass letters but no arrows. Boats assigned to commanding officers of ships are marked on the bow with the ship type or name, and with the ship's hull number in chrome letters and numerals; there is a chrome arrow running fore and aft through the markings. On officers' boats the arrow is omitted. Letters are brass. The ship's full name, abbreviated name, or initials may be used instead of the ship's type designation. An assigned boat number is sometimes used instead of the ship's hull number.

Amphibious ships' boats carry identification markings on their sterns and transoms, consisting of the ship-type abbreviation (KA, PD, LSD, etc), hull number, and boat's shipboard number. Landing craft assigned to amphibious ships, except for LSTs, also carry a two-letter abbreviation of their ship's name on the bow ramp. LCVPs assigned to LSTs carry the hull number of the parent ship on the bow ramp.

Other ships' boats are marked on the bow either with the ship's type and name or with her initials, followed by a dash and the boat number—for example, ENTERPRISE-1. These markings also appear on the sterns of all boats except whaleboats. Letters and numbers are brass, painted black. Numerals are painted on miscellaneous small boats such as line-handling boats, punts, and wherries.

Boat Equipment

Every Navy boat in active service must have a complete outfit of equipment for meeting any ordinary situation. Formerly, outfits were issued with the boat, but now it is necessary to requisition part of the outfit. The coordinated shipboard allowance list (COSAL) gives items allowed for each boat. Items for a 26-foot MWB, for instance, would consist of an anchor, a bucket, life rings, fenders, a grapnel hook, a boathook, an anchor line, a grapnel line, a bow painter, a stern fast, and a portable fire extinguisher.

When a boat is turned in, its outfit also must be turned in, unless the boat is to be replaced by another of the same type. In that event, the outfit is retained. If a boat is to be replaced by one of a different type, the only items retained are those allowed for the new boat.

Hoisting and Launching Boats

The process of hoisting and lowering boats with a crane is fairly simple. Slings are handled with the safety runner. The safety runner, a short wire pendant, is attached to the bill of the hook on a boat crane and connected to a tripping line. With a pull on the tripping line, the safety runner dumps the ring of the boat slings off the hook.

When a boat comes alongside an underway ship to be hoisted in, it first secures the end of the sea painter—a long, strong manila line that hangs over the side of the ship and is forward of the spot where the boat will be hoisted. The shipboard end of the line is bent securely to a cleat or a set of bitts. The boat end is lowered by a light line and tied to the inboard end of the forward thwart or on an inboard cleat.

The sea painter is never bent to the boat's stern or to the side of the bow away from the ship. If it is, the boat, when riding to the painter, will dive against the ship's side and perhaps capsize. It is also important that the boat be driven ahead and allowed to drop back on the sea painter to position itself exactly under the crane before lifting. Otherwise, it may broach to and capsize as it starts to leave the water.

Once the boat rides to the painter, its engine is secured and the slings are attached. Steadying lines are secured to the cleats on the outboard side of the boat and brought back on deck to hold it steady as it rises. The bowhooks and sternhooks must fend if off the side. When the boat is in the air, the plugs should be removed so the bilges will drain before the boat reaches the deck.

Hoisting boats with davits is somewhat more complicated than lifting them with a crane. The boat is attached to the sea painter in the same manner as with a crane—particularly if the ship has headway and must therefore take the same precautions against broaching to when the boat is lifted. The lower block of the forward fall is slacked down to the bowhook first, and is always attached before the after block. Before being hooked on, the bowhook must rotate the block until all the twists are out of the falls. Otherwise a dangerous jam will occur as the blocks draw together. Once the forward block is

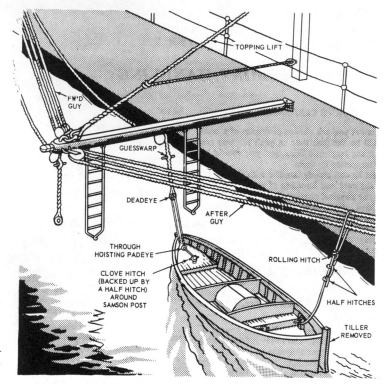

Figure 22–6 The proper way of securing a boat at a boom.

hooked on (hook pointing aft), and the slack in the falls is taken up, the sternhook removes the twists in the after fall and attaches the after block (hook pointing forward). Both then stand by to hold the releasing hooks by their lanyards.

Lifelines from the span are lowered to the boat, and each person aboard must keep one of them in hand as the boat rises. Frapping lines are passed around the falls. Then the order "Set taut" is given, at which point power is applied to the hauling part of the falls—either by manual hauling or winches. When the falls are taut and the boat is just about to rise, the boatswain's mate in charge sings out, "Vast heaving." Heaving is stopped while the boatswain's mate checks everything. When satisfied, the boatswain's mate calls out, "Hoist away," and the steady heave-up begins.

When the boat is high enough to swing in, the order "Vast heaving" is given again, and heaving stops. People in the boat now come aboard. The falls are held taut while the stoppers are passed. These short lines, usually braided, are called rattail stoppers; they are fastened to strong points on the davits, above the cleats where the falls are to be belayed (fastened).

A rolling hitch is passed around the fall, and a short distance above that, a half hitch. Spiral turns then are taken in the reverse direction, and the end of the stopper is joined securely to the fall by hand.

When all stoppers are passed, the order "Walk back" is given. If the falls are hoisted by hand, the people holding them walk back slowly and the stoppers gradually take up the strain. If the falls are catheads or capstans, they are slacked by slowly working the turns back. No turns are thrown off, because it is possible for a stopper to slip and drop the boat.

When satisfied that the stoppers have taken hold, the boatswain's mate orders "Up behind," which means to run back the slack. Until the falls are belayed on the cleats, only the stoppers are holding up the boat. People at catheads or capstans rapidly throw off their turns, grab up a handful of slack, and run with it toward the cleat.

The next order is "Belay!" which means the boat falls are secured on a cleat. Because the boat must be lowered from the cleat, the falls must be belayed in such a way as to make the lowering without dropping the boat. For belaying, two round turns and several figure eights are taken.

Before winging out a boat to be lowered, you must first make sure that the plugs are in. With quadrantal (quarter of a circle) davits, your falls must be good and taut; otherwise your boat won't lift off the chocks. With any type of davit, the falls must be belayed securely. Each person in the boat wears a life jacket

Figure 22–7 Types of davits include radial or round-bar.

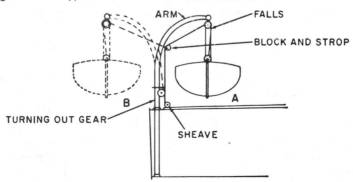

and has a lifeline in hand. Run your sea painter outboard of everything on the ship, to the ship side of the bow, and belay with a toggle, so you can let it go without difficulty. If there are any preventer wires on the falls, they must be released before you start to swing out. After swinging out over the water, pass the frapping lines. Gripes must be let go, and the hinged half of the chocks must be dropped on boats' quadrantal davits.

Only experienced sailors should be stationed at the cleats to slack the falls. Slowly and carefully, they take off all but the two round turns. At "Lower away!" they carefully start to slack, making sure they don't allow the hauling part to ride off the cleat. The boatswain's mate watches to keep the boat level, or slightly by the stern, and, if one end starts to get ahead of the other, orders, "Hold her forward (aft)!" Keep your eye on the boatswain's mate, and be sure you know which end of the boat you are lowering.

When the boat reaches the water and tows to the painter, the order "Up behind!" is given and the falls are thrown off the cleats. In releasing the boat, the after block is always unhooked first. The boat's engine is started while the boat is in the air, but the clutch is never engaged until the falls are unhooked and hauled clear. Before starting ahead, take care that there are no trailing lines astern that might foul the screw. When the boat runs ahead and the painter slackens, the boat is thrown off by pulling out the toggle. The sea painter is hauled back to the ship by the light line attached to it.

Types of Davits

Radial davits, sometimes called round-bar davits, are usually used for MWBs. When the boat is stowed, the davit arms point inboard. To get the boat out to the lowering position, hoist the boat high enough for the keel to clear the forward davit. Next, swing it out, forward, and then aft to the lowering position.

Quadrantal davits are used chiefly on merchant vessels. The boat rests in chocks under the davits. Outboard sections of the chocks are usually hinged so that, once the weight of the boat is off them, they can be laid flat on the deck, making it unnecessary to raise the boat high enough to clear them in their normal positions. Turning the crank that operates the worm gear raises the boat high enough to clear the flattened chocks.

Continued cranking racks the boat out to the lowering position. The boat is lowered away, as with the radial davit.

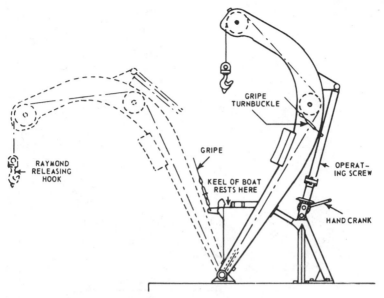

Figure 22–8 The crescent davit.

Crescent davits and other hinging-out davits (which have
largely superseded radial and quadrantal mechanical davits)
have been used in all classes of Navy vessels, including combatant ships. They generally handle boats that are 26 to 30 feet
long and weigh up to 13,500 pounds. In this type of davit, the
arms are generally crescent-shaped and racked in and out by
means of a sheath screw.

Gravity davits are found on newer ships. They are the trackway pivoted boom or the double-linked pivoted type. Gravity
davits that handle the larger boats, such as LCPLs and
LCVPs, are generally equipped with a strongback between the
davit arms. An electric-powered two-drum winch, located near
the davits, provides power to hoist the boats. Cranks can be
attached to the winch for manual hoisting. Power is not required to lower boats. The boat lowers by gravity as it is suspended from the falls, and the descent speed is controlled with
the boat's davit-winch manual brake.

Several types of gravity davits are used. Depending on the
design, a pair of modified davits may handle one to four boats;
they are designated as single-, double-, or quadruple-bank davits. These are used mainly with amphibious craft.

A single-arm gravity davit, introduced on DD, CGN, and
FFG ships, makes for superior boat-handling operations and

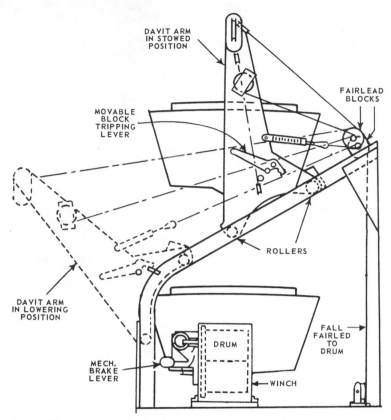

DAVIT ARM
IN STOWED
POSITION

FAIRLEAD
BLOCKS

MOVABLE
BLOCK
TRIPPING
LEVER

ROLLERS

DAVIT ARM
IN LOWERING
POSITION

FALL
FAIRLED
TO
DRUM

DRUM

MECH.
BRAKE
LEVER

WINCH

FALL FAIRLED TO DRUM

Figure 22–9   The Welin trackway gravity davit.

allows rescue-boat handling in higher sea states than are considered safe with conventional double-arm davits.

Ready Lifeboat

Regulations require that a ship at sea have at least one boat
rigged and ready to be lowered for use as a lifeboat. The ship's
boat bill states the exact specifications a lifeboat must meet,
and the equipment it must have.

At the start of each watch, the lifeboat coxswain musters the
crew, checks the boat and gear, has the engine tested, and
reports to the officer of the deck. On some ships, the crew
always remains near the boat. The boatswain's mate of the
watch (BMOW) is in charge of lowering the boat. Everyone
must know boat recovery procedures, because a person who

goes overboard can only survive a few minutes. Don't lose time trying to get the boat in the water.

The ready lifeboat, usually a MWB, is secured for sea in the davits and swung out, ready for lowering. As a safety measure, wire preventers connected to davit heads may be attached to the boat's hoisting eyes. Preventers must be removed before lowering. The lifeboat has its sea painter already rigged, and the lifelines from the span are coiled down clear for running. To keep the boat from swinging, it is held against a pair of soft paddings on a heavy spar called a strongback, securely lashed between davits.

The boat should have a full tank of fuel, and the lubricating oil reservoir should be full. Keep an extra can of oil on board. The bilge should be clean and dry and the boat plug in place. Life jackets are to be ready nearby or in the boat so the crew may don them before lowering away.

Navigation and Electronics

23

All navigational methods depend on exact measurement of distance, speed, direction, and time. Marine navigation also sometimes requires measurements of water depth, or soundings, to locate a position, usually called a fix.

Location

The location of any place on earth is determined by its latitude, the distance north or south of the equator, and longitude, the distance east or west of the prime meridian, which runs from the north pole to the south pole through Greenwich, England. Latitude is measured in degrees north or south of the equator, with 0 degrees at the equator and 90 degrees at each pole. Longitude is measured in degrees from Greenwich—180 degrees east and 180 degrees west. The place where 180 degrees east and 180 degrees west meet, halfway around the world from Greenwich, is called the international date line.

Charts

Charts, which show ocean areas and shorelines, and maps, which show land masses, are marked off in parallels of latitude (degrees north or south) and meridians of longitude (degrees east or west). Each degree (°) is divided into 60 minutes (') or nautical miles. A nautical mile measured along the equator is 6076 11549 feet, or roughly 2,000 yards. Any position at sea or place ashore is stated in degrees and minutes north or south and east or west. For example, Cleveland, Ohio, is 41°30'N and 81°45'W; the island of Funafuti in the South Pacific is 8°30'S and 178°30'E.

Distance

Distance at sea is measured in nautical miles. A nautical mile is one minute, or one sixtieth of a degree. Speed is measured in knots, a seaman's term meaning nautical miles per hour. A ship makes 27 knots, never 27 knots per hour. (In electronic navigation, distance measured by radar is called range.)

Direction

This is determined by a compass, either magnetic or gyro. The four cardinal directions are north, east, south, and west. All directions are measured from north on a system of 360 degrees, in which east is 090 degrees, south is 180 degrees, west is 270 degrees, and north is either 360 or 000 degrees, whichever designation is most convenient.

Time

Two kinds of time are used at sea: local apparent time, as determined by the passage of the sun across the sky, and Greenwich mean time (GMT), which is time based on the location of the sun at the prime meridian in Greenwich, England. Standard time is also measured from that meridian. GMT is used for observations in celestial navigation and is registered by chronometers, highly accurate clocks. (GMT is also used in communications, as described in chapter 24.)

Each standard time zone bears a number, a plus (+) or minus (−) sign, and a letter. The number refers to the difference in time between that zone and GMT. The sign tells whether the time is earlier (+) or later (−) than GMT, and shows how to find GMT from the standard time in any zone. If a ship is in zone +4, and her clock shows the time to be 1300, it would be 1300 +4, or 1700 in the Greenwich zone. In radio traffic, when the time of origin of a dispatch is expressed in GMT, that fact is indicated by inserting "ZULU" after the date-time group (for example, 1700 ZULU).

Soundings

Soundings are made with an electronic device, usually a fathometer. A ship is said to be "on soundings" when she is in water shallow enough that a lead line can be used to determine depth. Deep-sea soundings will indicate when a ship crosses a submarine canyon, sea mount, or other bottom feature. When a chart shows bottom contours, soundings may be used to establish an actual fix.

Location

Methods of Determining Position

Piloting

This is the oldest form of navigation, used before men ventured beyond sight of land and across the seas. It is a method of determining position and directing the movements of a ship by reference to landmarks, navigational aids, or soundings. Ordinarily, piloting is the primary means of navigation when entering or leaving port and in coastal navigation. It may be helpful at sea when the bottom contour allows you to establish a fix. In piloting, the navigator looks for signs of danger, fixes the ship's position frequently and accurately, and guides her on a proper course.

Piloting Aids: Navigational aids used in piloting include the compass, for determining ship's heading; the bearing circle and telescopic alidade, for determining the direction of objects on land, buoys, ships, etc.; the stadimeter, for figuring the distance to a building (when the height is known) by measuring the angle from the horizon to your eye back to the top of the building; charts, which show shorelines as well as land- and seamarks and water depth at many locations; and buoys and navigational lights. Also helpful is the echo sounder or fathometer, which determines water depth under the ship's keel by measuring the time it takes a sound signal to reach the bottom and return to the ship, and the lead line, which determines depth by actual physical measurement.

Special Publications: Coast Pilot and Sailing Directions contain detailed information on coastal waters, harbor facilities, etc., for use in conjunction with charts of the area. Tide tables, which predict the height of the tide at given times, and current tables, which predict the direction and velocity of the tide at given times, are also handy. The Defense Mapping Agency Hydrographic/Topographic Center's publication List of Lights contains information on the location and characteristics of every light in the world not located in the United States or its possessions. Brief descriptions of lighthouses and fog signals are also included. Published by the U.S. Coast Guard, *Light Lists* has information on lighthouses located on the continental coasts of the United States, its possessions, and its inland waterways.

Bearing, Range, and Fixes: In clear-weather piloting, the ship's position is usually determined by taking simultaneous

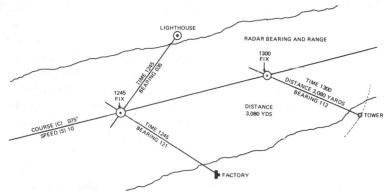

Figure 23–1   Fixes established by gyrocompass (1245 fix) and by radar
bearing and range (1300 fix).

gyrocompass bearings on two objects of fixed position. Radar
may be used for ranges and bearings. ⊙ is the symbol for a fix.

Figure 23-1 shows how the ship's position can be fixed by
simultaneous visual bearings of two known objects, and also
by a radar bearing and range on a single object, which is plotted or drawn on the chart. The lighthouse bears 035 degrees,
below the line.

The intersection of these two lines represents the actual position of the ship on the chart. A position that has been accurately established is called a fix, and is recorded together with
the time it was established.

A line drawn from the fix in the direction in which the ship is
steaming is called a course line. The direction or course is
labeled above the line; speed in knots is indicated below the
line.

The manner of obtaining a fix by radar bearing and range or
distance is also shown in figure 23-1. Radar gives a bearing of
112 degrees on a prominent tower and a range of 3,080 yards.
The navigator again plots a line from the tower, uses dividers
to measure 3,080 yards on the chart scale, then puts one leg of
the tower dividers on the chart and marks the bearing line with
the other end. This establishes the fix by bearing and range.

Dead Reckoning (DR)

This is a method of navigation in which position is determined by plotting the direction and distance traveled from a

known point of departure. A ship under way is moving through

water, which is a very unstable element. She might leave point
A, steer an exact course according to the true bearing between
point A and point B, and still wind up a long distance from B,
depending on how much leeway she makes. Estimating distance traveled seldom produces an exact result either. The DR
position is only an estimated position, calculated from values
that are rarely exact. A fix, on the other hand, is a relatively
exact location derived from the intersection of two or more
lines of position (LOPs). A DR position is not a fix but rather a
calculation from the last fix obtained. ⌒ is the DR symbol.

Figure 23-2 shows the DR plot on the chart. The 1200 fix is
plotted and labeled. A course line is drawn from the fix on the
ship's course of 073 degrees. Course is labeled above the line,

Figure 23–2 Dead-reckoning plot, showing 1200 fix, 1300, 1330, and 1400
DR position. At 1400 a new fix is taken, and the ship's position on the chart is
changed accordingly.

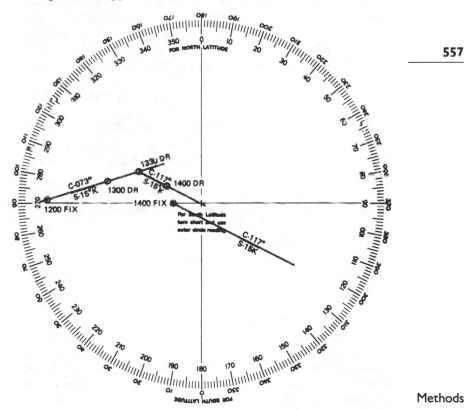

SYMBOL	DESCRIPTIVE LABEL	MEANING
⊙	FIX	AN ACCURATE POSITION DETERMINED WITHOUT REFERENCE TO ANY PREVIOUS POSITION. ESTABLISHED BY ELECTRONIC, VISUAL, OR CELESTIAL OBSERVATIONS.
⌂	DR	DEAD RECKON POSITION. ADVANCED FROM A PREVIOUS KNOWN POSITION OR FIX. COURSE AND SPEED ARE RECKONED WITHOUT ALLOWANCE FOR WIND OR CURRENT.
⊡	EP	ESTIMATED POSITION. IS THE MOST PROBABLE POSITION OF A VESSEL, DETERMINED FROM DATA OF QUESTIONABLE ACCURACY, SUCH AS APPLYING ESTIMATED CURRENT AND WIND CORRECTIONS TO A DR POSITION.

Figure 23–3   Fix symbology.

the speed of 15 knots below the line. In one hour, at 15 knots, the ship will cover $\frac{1}{4}$ degree, or 15 minutes on the chart. To determine the 1300 position, the navigator uses dividers to measure 15 minutes of latitude on the vertical latitude scale printed on either side of the chart. (One degree of latitude equals 60 nautical miles; 1 minute of latitude equals 1 mile.) This distance is marked off from the fix along the course line, and the resulting spot is labeled "1300 DR," as shown.

The captain orders the officer of the deck to put the ship on a new course, 117 degrees, at 1330. Using his dividers, the navigator marks a spot $7\frac{1}{2}$ miles from the 1300 DR position along the direction in which the ship is steaming, labels it "1300 DR," and draws in a new course line in the direction of 117 degrees.

When properly maintained, the DR plot permits the ship's approximate position to be quickly determined.

Electronic Navigation

In electronic navigation, a form of piloting, a ship's position is obtained by referring to visible objects on the earth whose locations are known. Usually, the bearing and distance on a single object, crossbearings on two or more objects, or two bearings on the same object with an interval between them are obtained. Position is determined in electronic navigation much as it is in piloting, but there is one important difference: the objects by which position is determined need not be visible from the ship. Instead, bearings (and sometimes ranges) are obtained by electronic means, normally in the form of radio waves.

Figure 23–4 One of the miniaturized components used in electronic navigation.

There are several different systems current throughout the Navy; many other electronic navigation systems are available but less widely employed.

Loran: The Loran (long-range navigation) system was originally developed by the United States in the 1940s. The first-generation system, Loran-A, consisted of paired master and slave stations transmitting sequential pulsed radio waves. LOPs were obtained based on differences in the times of receipt of master- and slave-station pulses. Crossing LOPs generated by two or more pairs yielded a fix.

More sophisticated electronics in the 1960s and 1970s made possible the deployment of a lower-frequency and longer-range system called Loran-C. This system uses both a time-difference measurement and phase-comparison of the pulses of the master and one or more of several secondary stations in each Loran-C chain to establish LOPs and the resulting fix. Ranges of 800 to 1,200 nautical miles for each chain are typical, depending on transmitter power, receiver sensitivity, and propagation losses over the signal paths. Some thirteen Loran-C chains are in operation today, covering the Mediterranean Sea

Figure 23–5   An electronics expert searches for a bad circuit in the wiring used for satellite navigation.

and most of the northern Atlantic and Pacific coastal regions. The Coast Guard operates all stations on U.S.-controlled soil. Loran-A was essentially phased out of existence in 1978.

Satellite Navigation: There are at present two principal all-weather-navigation satellite systems in use or under development. The first, called NAVSAT by the Navy and Transit by civilians, consists of a group of some seven satellites in 600-mile-high polar orbits that transmit sequential 2-minute messages to shipboard or aircraft NAVSAT receivers. By decoding position information in five to seven of these messages, and by determining the receiver's position relative to the transmitting satellite via Doppler-shift analysis of the signal, the NAVSAT receiver develops an accurate fix to within 50 yards. Although NAVSAT can be used worldwide, fix information is available only when a satellite passes over the horizon high enough to enable the receipt of the required minimal number of

Methods

messages. Periods between suitable passes vary from about 90 minutes at the equator to 35 minutes or less in higher latitudes.

The other, more recent navigation satellite system now being developed is called the global positioning system (GPS). When fully operational, it will consist of a constellation of some eighteen satellites in six 10,900-mile-high orbits. Each satellite will transmit a continuous signal. By receiving signals from at least three satellites and determining ranges to them, the GPS receiver can develop a fix accurate to within 10 yards. When a fourth satellite is receivable, as it will be once all satellites are in orbit, the system will determine altitude precisely. The GPS therefore represents a revolutionary development in navigation. With it, fixes of unprecedented accuracy will be determined worldwide, in any weather, on land, at sea, or in the air. In all probability, GPS will render all other long-

Figure 23–6 Plans are to place the last several GPS satellites into orbit on the space shuttle.

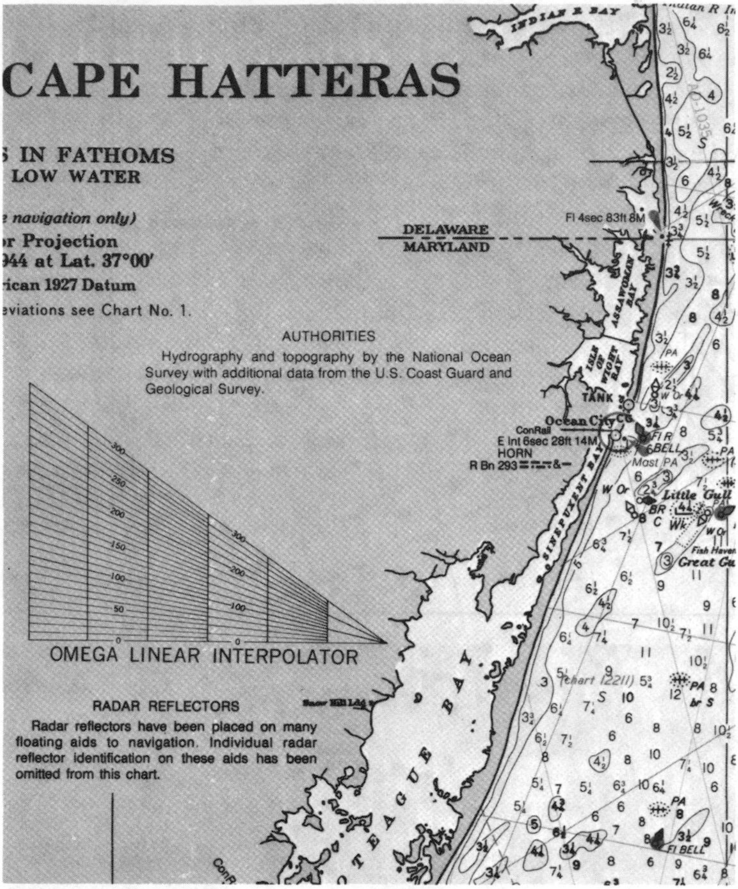

Figure 23–7 Extract from an Omega chart.

range electronic-navigation systems, including Loran-C and
Omega, described below, obsolete during the 1990s.

Omega: Omega is an expansion of Loran. It is a very low
frequency (VLF) navigation system that enables navigators to
obtain reliable positions, comparable in accuracy to those of
Loran-C, on a worldwide and nearly continuous basis. There
are eight stations, located in North Dakota, Liberia, Norway,
Argentina, Île de la Réunion (in the Indian Ocean), Hawaii,
Japan, and Australia. With these transmission stations, the
extremely long-range VLF signals ensure that the user can
receive at least three stations almost anywhere on earth. Depending on location, a navigator may be able to receive as
many as six stations.

The receiver's measurement is a comparison of the relative phase angles of VLF signals. The navigator can determine LOPs by using any convenient pair of transmitting stations, then crossing it with one or more lines derived from another pair of transmitting stations to plot a fix.

Radar: Radar, developed in World War II as a means for detecting and approaching targets in warfare, has since evolved into a valuable electronic navigational aid. Its great advantage over Loran is that it does not require shore transmitting stations. Its disadvantage is that its maximum range barely extends over the horizon. Despite its limitations, radar remains an important navigational aid. The Navy now uses several types of radar, designed especially for surface search, air search, fire control, missile guidance, and airborne early warning.

In radar transmission, a narrow beam of ultra high frequency (UHF) or super high frequency (SHF) radio waves (300 to 30,000 MHz) is sent out. Upon striking any object in their path, the waves are reflected and return to the transmitter as "echoes." Exact measurement of the time of return of each—based on the fact that radio waves travel at the speed of light, about 186,000 miles a second—gives the distance (or range) to the object or target. The bearing of a target can be determined by the position of the antenna, which is indicated by a bright line on an oscilloscope. Targets appear as bright spots of light called pips.

The scope may be marked with a scale of miles, yards, or degrees, or with a combination of miles and yards, so that from the position of a single echo on the scope an observer can tell the range, bearing, and, depending on the kind of equipment used, the altitude of the target.

The most common oscilloscope is the plan position indicator (PPI) (see figure 23-8), which provides a bird's-eye view of the area covered by the radar, with your ship in the center. The straight-line sweep originates in the center of the scope and moves to the outside edge. The sweep is synchronized with the radar antenna and rotates 360 degrees. This type of scope shows surface targets and navigational features such as islands, lighthouses, and buoys.

Radars designed to track aircraft record altitude on a range height indicator (RHI). The RHI scope cannot show range, so it has to be used with a PPI.

Sonar: Sonar uses the pulsed transmission of sound waves in water to detect and track a target, and to determine the range

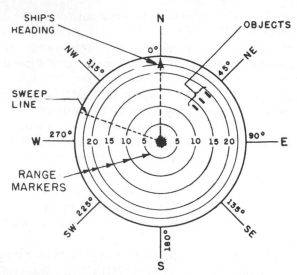

Figure 23–8   Drawing of a PPI presentation. The ship is at the center of the scope, and the sweep has just passed 045 degrees.

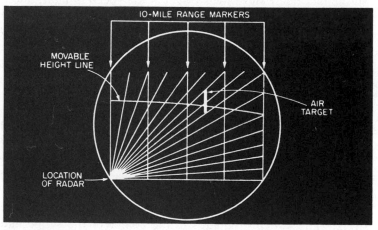

Figure 23–9   RHI presentation, showing an aircraft about 25 miles out from the tracking ship.

and bearing of underwater objects. Sonar is similar in principle to radar. Where radar employs electromagnetic waves traveling through air, sonar uses sound waves traveling through water. Sonar can detect submarines and surface ships, measure depth, and serve as an aid to navigation.

Sonar equipment is classed as active or passive. Active sonar involves transmission of sound energy into the water; the range and bearing of the target is determined by reflected sound waves. In passive sonar, the sound originates with the target, such as propeller or machinery noise. Active sonar, normally used on surface ships, is a transmitting ("pinging") and receiving system. The device used to transmit sound energy in an active system is a transducer; it contains a diaphragm that is made to vibrate at a frequency corresponding to an applied voltage from the system's transmitter. The vibration of the diaphragm produces a series of compression waves. Compression waves, propagated through water, are sound waves.

The wave generated by the transducer moves outward in a circle. When it strikes an object, a small portion is reflected back to the transducer, just as in radar. The transducer converts outgoing electrical signals from the transmitter into sound waves and converts the returning sound echoes to electrical signals for use by the receiver. The receiver amplifies the extremely small signals resulting from the sound echo and converts them to signals audible over a loudspeaker or headphone.

Passive sonar is used primarily by submarines that want to remain undetected. They transmit no sound, depending entirely on the target's noise as the sound source. The passive sonar designed for modern submarines is so efficient that a skilled operator can identify and track targets miles away.

In active sonar, the signals are presented by azimuth-range indicators, which show the target bearing, range, and audio response from targets.

Other Systems: Several other electronic-navigation systems that are available but less widely used are decca, consol, star tracker, SINS, and NAVDAC.

Decca is a British system which, like Loran, requires special receiving equipment. The receiving unit measures phase differences between a master and a group of three slave stations, all of which are transmitting at different frequencies. Fixes are obtained by plotting the phase differences directly on a chart printed with decca hyperbolic lines.

Consol is a long-range, short-baseline system whose signals may be received by ordinary radio equipment. The signals consist of a series of dots and dashes counted by the receiving operator.

Star tracker is an extremely sensitive optical telescope with radio or infrared components that calculate elevation (altitude) and azimuth date from celestial bodies, including the sun. The system may be used even during periods of poor visibility.

Ship's internal navigation system (SINS) is, at present, chiefly a navigational aid for submarines and aircraft carriers. Eventually it will be operational on most surface vessels. SINS provides ships with an accurate and continuous DR position. Because SINS is a self-contained system, it is a valuable wartime navigational aid. When the Loran and similar systems are knocked out, SINS remains operable. SINS relies on gyros and accelerometers.

NAVDAC is among the most advanced navigational systems. NAVDAC (navigation data assimilation computer) combines, evaluates, and stores data received from navigational systems such as Loran-C, SINS, and star tracker. In effect, it is a memory bank of highly reliable navigational data, capable of rejecting solutions of poor quality and accepting only those with a high degree of probable accuracy.

Celestial Navigation

Piloting (including its electronic phases) and DR make up that branch of navigation that determines position by reference to objects or localities on earth. Another branch, in which position is determined by reference to heavenly bodies—the sun, moon, stars, and planets—is called celestial navigation. A carefully measured and properly corrected altitude on any navigational body can give an accurate LOP.

This is the most widely used offshore navigation method. Observations are made with a sextant by measuring the altitude (above the horizon) of navigational stars or other bodies. The observations are called sights. When the navigator and quartermaster take a sight, they are said to be shooting a star.

Many of the navigational aids used in piloting are also used in celestial navigation. Some additional equipment is required, such as chronometers and sextants; these are discussed below. A DR plot is always maintained; on some ships this is done automatically by a dead-reckoning tracer (DRT).

Instruments and Equipment

The following sections list and explain the basic functioning of major navigational instruments and equipment.

Sextant
The sextant is a precision instrument that can measure angles in degrees, minutes, and seconds. Through a system of mirrors, the image of a star is brought down to the horizon; the scales allow the navigator to read the exact angle between the actual star and the horizon. This angle, called the altitude, is the basic measurement in celestial navigation.

In establishing a position by star, several observations are taken. Each one is reduced or worked out with the Nautical Almanac and reduction tables to produce a single LOP that passes through the ship's position. The ship's location is represented by the point at which various LOPs intersect on the chart. This is the location at the time of observation and is marked "2000 posit," "0530 posit," etc.

Stadimeter
The stadimeter measures the distance of an object of known height, such as a masthead light, between heights of 50 and 200 feet, at distances of 200 to 10,000 yards. Like a sextant, the stadimeter measures an angle. The height of an object is set on a scale, then the reflecting image is made to coincide with the actual direct image. The distance is read from another scale.

Azimuth Circle and Bearing Circle
An azimuth circle is a metal ring that fits over a compass bowl. It measures bearings of objects on the surface of the earth, and azimuths (or bearings) of celestial bodies.

Telescopic Alidade
A telescopic alidade is a telescope equipped with crosshair, level vial, polarizing light filter, and internal focusing. The telescope is mounted on a ring that fits on a gyro repeater or magnetic compass. The optical system simultaneously projects an image of approximately 25 degrees of the compass card, together with a view of the level vial, onto the optical axis of the telescope. By this means, both the object and its bearing can be viewed at the same time through the alidade eyepiece.

Plotting Equipment
Position plotting on a chart is usually done with a universal drafting machine, also called a parallel motion protractor (PMP), which is clamped to a chart table and allows both distance and bearing to be plotted at once. Sometimes a simple plastic protractor and straightedge are used.

Chronometer

This is a highly accurate clock, mounted in a brass case, which is in turn supported in gimbals in a wooden case to counteract the ship's motion. Chronometers are kept in a cabinet in the chart room, usually on the ship's centerline, where they are protected against shock and temperature changes. Chronometers are set to show GMT and are wound every day at exactly the same time. Once a chronometer is started, it is never allowed to stop, and it is not reset while aboard ship. A record is kept of its speed, fast or slow; a good chronometer never deviates more than a hundredth of a second from its average daily rate. Chronometers are checked against radio time signals, which are broadcast all over the world. To check, or "get a time tick," the quartermaster uses a comparing or hack watch. The exact GMT time, announced by radio, is never used to change the chronometer, only to show whether it is running fast or slow.

Celestial navigation requires an exact measure of time, since it is based on tables using GMT. The time of a celestial observation anywhere in the world must be converted to GMT before the navigator can work out his position.

Magnetic Compass

The magnetic compass's needles align themselves with the earth's magnetic field and are fastened to either a disc or a cylinder marked with the cardinal points of the compass: north, east, south, and west. North, on the magnetic compass, points to the magnetic north pole, which is several hundred miles from the geographic north pole.

The compass's card and needles are supported on a pivot. No matter how the ship, aircraft, or boat swings, the card is free to rotate until it has realigned itself with magnetic north.

The moving parts are contained in a bowl or compartment provided with a window through which the compass card may be seen. Ship's compasses usually have a flat glass top for all-around visibility and for taking bearings.

The lubber's line, a mark in the window of the compass or on the compass bowl, indicates the fore-and-aft line of the ship or boat (figure 23-10).

The compass direction under the lubber's line tells the ship's heading. Attached to the binnacle—the stand in which the compass is housed—or nearby, is a deviation card. It gives the
deviation for various headings, in this form:

Ship's Heading (magnetic)	Dev	Ship's Heading (magnetic)	Dev	Ship's Heading (magnetic)	Dev
000°(360°)	14°W	120°	15°E	240°	4°E
015°	10°W	135°	16°E	255°	1°W
030°	5°W	150°	12°E	270°	7°W
045°	1°E	165°	12°E	285°	12°W
060°	2°E	180°	13°E	300°	15°W
075°	5°E	195°	14°E	315°	19°W
090°	7°E	210°	12°E	330°	19°W
105°	9°W	225°	9°E	345°	17°W

Figure 23–10 The lubber's line on the Navy's standard magnetic compass shows the heading as 104½ degrees.

Variation: This is the difference between geographic north and magnetic north (figure 23-11). Variation for any given locality, together with the amount of yearly increase or decrease, is shown on the compass rose of the chart for that particular locality. Figure 23-12 shows a compass rose on a chart dated 1945, which indicates a 14°45′ westerly variation in that area, increasing 1′ yearly.

To find the amount of variation in that place, figure out how many years have passed since 1945 and multiply the number by the amount of yearly increase; then add the result to the variation in 1945. The number should be added in this case because it is a yearly increase; if the chart showed a decrease, the result would be subtracted from the variation for 1945. Variation remains the same for any heading of the ship at a given position.

Deviation: This error is caused by the magnetic effect of any metal near the compass. It changes depending on the heading of the ship. Periodically the navigator and quartermaster perform an operation called swinging ship. The ship steams in a complete circle from 0° to 360 degrees, and the amount of her compass deviation is noted at every 15 degrees. The results are compiled in a deviation table kept near the compass. There is a similar table near the magnetic compass in every aircraft. *Compass error* for any compass is the combination of locality variation and deviation of the ship's heading. In some cases, these must be added; in other cases, one is subtracted from the other, as explained above.

True Course: This is the heading of the ship in degrees measured clockwise from true north.

Magnetic Course: This course is the heading of the ship in degrees measured clockwise from magnetic north.

Compass Course: The reading of a particular magnetic compass, that is, the course that the compass actually indicates, is called the compass course.

Correcting for Compass Error: Combining variation and deviation gives what is known as *magnetic compass error.* The course the ship will ultimately follow is the true course, worked out from the chart, on which only true courses and bearings are given. However, the ship must steer the compass course to make good the true course. Figure compass course by applying variation and deviation to the true course. This is done with a simple rule that you can remember by repeating the question, Can Dead Men Vote Twice?

To change from true to compass course, or vice versa, set up
the columns as follows:

Can	Compass
Dead	Deviation
Men	Magnetic
Vote	Variation
Twice	True

Going up, or changing from true to compass, is called *uncorrecting*. Coming down, or changing from compass to true, is called *correcting*. Just remember this rule:

When correcting, add easterly error and subtract westerly error.
When uncorrecting, subtract easterly error and add westerly error.

All compass errors are either easterly or westerly; there are no northerly or southerly errors. To correct a compass course

Figure 23–11 The diagram shows how variation affects a compass. The magnetic needle points to the magnetic north pole (MN) instead of the geographic north pole (NP).

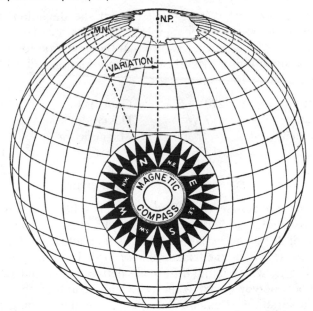

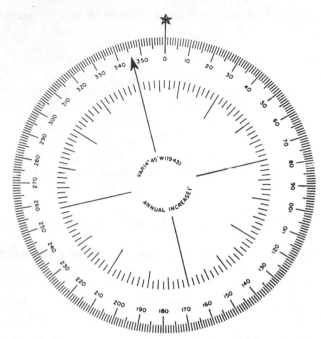

Figure 23–12 The compass rose shows a variation of 14 degrees, 45 minutes west, the year 1945, and an annual increase of 1.

of 270° to the true course, first correct the deviation, then correct for variation. An example is given below. The deviation table described earlier shows that the deviation for 270° is 7° W. Assume that the chart shows the variation to be 12° E. Make a table as follows:

Compass	270°	Compass	270°
Deviation	7°W	Deviation	7°W
Magnetic		Magnetic	263°
Variation	12°E	Variation	12°E
True		True	275°
Total error		Total error	5°E

To find true course, the 7°W deviation is subtracted from the compass course of 270° (column 2), which gives a magnetic course of 263°. The variation, 12°E, is then added to the magnetic course, giving the true course of 275°. The total compass error is 5°E, which is the difference between 7°W and 12°E.

But how do you decide whether to add or subtract the deviation or variation? Remember: when correcting—going from compass course to true course—add easterly errors and sub- tract westerly errors.

Note that true differs from magnetic by the amount of variation, and that magnetic differs from compass by the amount of deviation.

Uncorrecting: The process of finding the compass from the true course is called uncorrecting. Suppose that the given true course is 180° and variation is 10°W.

Compass		Compass	176°
Deviation		Deviation	14°E
Magnetic	190°	Magnetic	190°
Variation	10°W	Variation	10°W
True	180°	True	180°
Total error		Total error	4°E

This is uncorrecting, so reverse the rule and add westerly variation, giving a magnetic course of 190°.

Refer to the deviation table previously discussed. Take the deviation nearest the heading you are on. In this case, the nearest deviation is 14°E, or that shown for 195°. Remember: when uncorrecting—going from true to compass—add westerly errors and subtract easterly errors.

Gyrocompass (GYRO)

This instrument is essentially a heavy flywheel driven at high speed by an electric motor and mounted on gimbals so that it is free to move in all directions. It is usually located in a well-protected place below deck. Repeaters—compass cards electrically connected to the gyrocompass and placed on the bridge and in other parts of the ship—show the same readings as the master gyrocompass.

Gyro Error: The gyrocompass is not affected by variation or deviation. The motion of the earth causes the rotor to move so that its axis lies in a north-south direction. For mechanical reasons and because of the ship's vibrations, even the best gyrocompass will sometimes vary from true north. This gyro error is rarely more than a few degrees, and normally it is constant over a long period of time and on any heading of the ship.

Correcting for Gyro Error: Gyro error is determined by taking an azimuth, or bearing, on a celestial body where the exact bearing can be determined. This error is applied every time the compass is used, and the rule for magnetic compasses is fol-

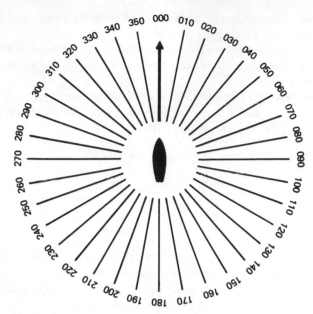

Figure 23–13 Relative bearings, measured clockwise from the ship's head, locate an object in relation to the ship. They have nothing to do with geographical directions.

lowed: when *correcting*, add easterly errors and subtract westerly errors.

Bearings

Bearings are lines drawn or sighted from one's own position to another. For accurate navigation, a system of true and relative bearings has been worked out so that all directions at sea are given in bearings measured in degrees.

True bearings are based on a circle of degrees with true north as 000 degrees (or 360 degrees), east as 090 degrees, south as 180 degrees, and west as 270 degrees.

Relative bearings are based on a circle drawn around the ship herself, with the bow as 000 degrees, the starboard beam as 090 degrees, the stern as 180 degrees, and the port beam as 270 degrees (figure 23-13). Thus, if a ship is on a course true north (000 degrees), another ship sighted dead ahead would bear 000 degrees true and 000 degrees relative. If, on the other hand, the ship were on a course true east and sighted a ship dead ahead, the sighted ship would bear 090 degrees true but would still be dead ahead or 000 degrees relative.

Relative Bearings

Relative bearings are taken whenever there is no compass. Lookouts cannot have accurate compasses on hand, nor can they be expected to know the course of the ship and the true directions around her. They need a way to point out where objects lie, and it must be fast and accurate. With the Navy system of relative bearings measured in degrees from the bow of the ship, a person can soon learn to report objects in such a way that anyone can locate them immediately.

True Bearings

True bearings can be obtained directly from a gyro repeater, from a magnetic compass situated to make bearings on outside objects (and with the appropriate corrections), or by calculation from a relative bearing.

Pelorus

This is a flat, nonmagnetic metal ring mounted on a vertical stand about 5 feet high. The inner edge of the ring is graduated in degrees from 0 at the ship's head, clockwise through 360. The ring encloses a gyro repeater. Upon the ring is mounted a pair of sighting vanes, which work much like the sights on a rifle.

Gyro Bearings

Since the gyrocompass, and therefore the gyro repeater in the pelorus, is already closely lined up with the true geographical directions, taking a true bearing over the gyro card is the easiest and most common method. Merely line the vane sights of the bearing circle on the object, steady the compass bowl in its gimbals until the leveler bubble shows that the vanes are level, then read off the bearing in degrees on the compass card.

Other Navigational Factors

Tides

Tides are very important in naval operations. Amphibious landings are scheduled for high tide so that troops and equipment can land well up on a beach. In some harbors, deep-draft ships may be able to enter only at high tide. Large ships are usually launched or dry-docked at high tide. Ships going along-

Figure 23–14 A pelorus.

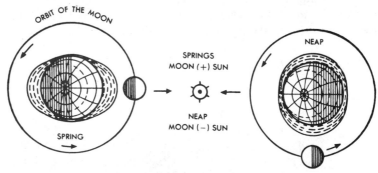

Figure 23–15 Relation of positions of the sun and moon to the tides.

side piers in channels subject to strong tides and currents nor- mally wait for slack water, when the tide is neither ebbing nor flooding. Every sailor whose responsibility is the handling of a vessel must understand the meaning and cause of various tidal conditions.

The term *tide* describes the regular rise and fall of the water level along a coast or in a port. The gravitational attraction of the moon is the primary cause of tides; it pulls water away from the earth. There is an almost equal bulge of water on the opposite side of the earth, as shown in figure 23-15, because the earth's centrifugal force keeps water from piling up except where the pull of the moon is strongest.

Since the moon orbits the earth every 24 hours and 50 minutes, there are two low and two high tides at any place during that period. The low and high tides are each 12 hours and 25 minutes apart. The sun also affects the tide, but it is so much farther away than the moon that its pull is not nearly as great. A tide rising or moving from low to high water is said to be flooding. When the tide is falling, after high tide, it is said to be ebbing.

The difference in depth between a high and the next low tide is considerable in many harbors; areas that are safe for a powerboat at high tide may be completely dry at low water.

Currents

In most harbors and inlets, tides are the chief causes of currents; however, if the port is situated on a large river, its flow may have a marked effect on tidal currents. The flow of a large river will prolong the duration of an ebbing current, and the velocity of that current will be considerably greater than that of the flooding current.

Where currents are chiefly caused by the rise and fall of the tide, their direction and speed are largely governed by the shape of the shoreline and the contour of the ocean bottom. Where there is a long beach, or a straight section of waterway, the current tends to flow most rapidly in the center and much more slowly in the shallower water near either shore. If a boat goes with the current, the coxswain generally wants to stay near the center of the waterway. If a boat goes against the current, the coxswain stays as close to shore as the prevailing water depth will allow.

In many wide inlets, near the time of slack water, the current may actually reverse itself in part of the inlet; while the ebb is still moving out of the main channel, a gentle flood may start near one shore. This condition, where it exists, can be helpful to a small-boat operator.

Where there is a bend in the channel, the current flows most strongly on the outside of the bend. This effect is very marked, particularly with a strong current.

In some areas, a strong current can create rough water called tide rips. These are usually shown on charts and should be avoided.

Every vessel, regardless of size, must make some allowance for the current's set and drift, which may affect the course to be steered.

One more thing to bear in mind about currents: only on the coast does the turn of the current occur at the time of high water. In many ports, owing to the effect of the land's shape on water flow, there may be a very considerable difference between the time of high (or low) water and the time that the current starts to ebb (or flood).

Winds

Modern naval vessels are not dependent on the wind for power, as sailing ships were, but at times the wind's effect must be considered. During flight operations, a carrier most often steams into the wind, because the increased *apparent wind* speed helps aircraft take off and land. A strong wind blowing across a ship from side to side makes steering more difficult, and ships with high superstructures may list, or lean away from the wind.

When a ship is under way, the wind usually seems to blow from straight ahead to straight astern. This is apparent wind, the combination of real wind and the wind created by the ship's motion. If there is no real wind and a ship is making 25 knots, the apparent wind is 25 knots from dead ahead. If the real wind is 25 knots and the ship makes 25 knots upwind (straight into it), the apparent wind is 50 knots. If the ship turns around and makes 25 knots downwind (with the wind), the apparent wind is 0.

A wind takes the name of the direction it blows from; a north wind comes from the north, a west wind comes from the west. *Windward* means toward the wind, *leeward* means away from the wind; the side of the ship toward the wind is the windward side, away from the wind is the leeward side. When the wind changes direction to the right, or clockwise, it veers; when it changes in the other direction, it backs. At sea, the true wind is indicated by streaks of foam down the back sides of waves, while the apparent wind is shown by the way the commission pennant or stack gas blows.

Lookouts

Radars and sonars may fail to detect such things as smoke, small navigational markers, objects close to the ship, flares, or people in the water. These must be reported by the lookouts— the eyes of the ship. Upon their alertness rests much of the safety of the ship and her crew.

A lookout must do much more than keep his or her eyes open. A lookout must learn how to search in a way that will cover every inch of the sector, and how to report the location of an object to the officer of the deck. A lookout must watch for ships, planes, land, rocks, shoals, periscopes, discolored water, buoys, beacons, lighthouses, distress signals, floating objects of all kinds, and anything else of interest to the officer of the deck. The lookout also reports sounds of objects heard but not sighted, such as fog horns, ships' bells, whistle buoys, airplanes, and surf.

The number of lookouts and how they are assigned depend on the ship's organization. Small ships will have only bridge (port and starboard) lookouts and one after lookout (life-buoy watch). Each is stationed where he or she can best cover the surface and sky within an assigned zone. In fog or bad weather, special lookouts are stationed immediately in the "eyes of the ship" and on the bridge wings.

Forward lookouts keep a sharp watch on either bow. Lookouts on the bridge wings watch from ahead to astern. The after lookout scans for anything that might overhaul the ship from astern.

Sound carries much farther in fog than on clear days, so a lookout must listen closely, especially if he or she is located in the bow, for whistles, bells, buoys, and even the wash of water against the ship's stem. For this reason, fog lookouts do not wear sound-powered phones. Another sailor is required to man the phones at each fog lookout station.

Night Vision

If you were to go on night watch directly from a lighted compartment, you would be almost blind for a few minutes. As your eyes become accustomed to the weak light, your vision gradually improves. After 10 minutes you can see fairly well, and after 30 minutes you have your best night vision. This improvement is called dark adaptation.

You will put on specially designed red goggles before going on night lookout duty. They prepare your eyes for darkness without affecting your ability to write letters or to get ready for your watch. You should wear them without interruption for at least a half hour before going on watch. Even then, it will take you at least 5 minutes more in darkness to develop your best night vision.

Next you must learn to use your "night eyes." In the daytime, you look directly at an object to see it best. In the dark, however, you may have to look to one side of an object.

At night, it is easier to locate a moving object than a stationary one. Because most objects in or on the water move relatively slowly, move your eyes instead—the effect is almost as good. At night, a lookout slowly scans the area in broad sweeps, instead of stopping to search a section at a time.

Binoculars

Contrary to widespread belief, it is not always better to search with binoculars. Several factors govern when and how they should be used. In fog, for instance, they should not be used at all. At night, however, they should be used often. The field of view is only about 7 degrees with binoculars, so narrow that it hampers proper scanning techniques for certain types of searching.

Scanning Procedure

In good weather, lookouts can easily spot planes at 15 miles with the naked eye. With binoculars and in unusually clear weather, lookouts have detected planes at 50 miles. At night, skilled lookouts will detect objects that the untrained lookout would never suspect were there.

The lookout's technique of searching is called scanning, which is a step-by-step method of looking. It is the only efficient and sure way of doing the job. Scanning does not come naturally—you must learn it. In the daytime, your eyes rest on an object to see it. Try moving your eyes around the room or across the water rapidly, and note that as long as your eyes are in motion, you see almost nothing. Allow your eyes to move in short steps from object to object. Now you can see what is

there.

Figure 23–16 Step-by-step method of scanning.

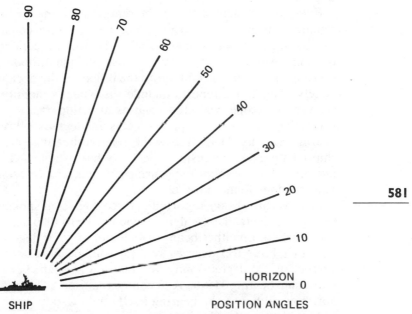

SHIP   POSITION ANGLES

Figure 23–17 Position angles locate an object in the sky. They measure up, not down.

Figure 23-16 shows how you should search the horizon. (You must also cover the surface between your ship and the horizon.) Search your sector in 5-degrees steps, pausing between steps for approximately 5 seconds to scan the field of view. At the end of your sector, lower the glasses and rest your eyes for a few seconds, then search the sector in the reverse direction with the naked eye.

A sky lookout searches from the horizon to the zenith (overhead), using binoculars only to identify a contact. Move your eyes in quick steps—also about 5 degrees—across your sector just above the horizon, shift your gaze up about 10 degrees, and search back to the starting point. Repeat this process until

the zenith is reached, then rest your eyes for a few seconds
before starting over.

When searching at night, keep your eyes moving. Try to
adhere to the sector scan (and upward shift) even though the
horizon may not be visible. If you spot a target or think you
have, don't stare at it. Instead, look about 10 degrees to either
side.

Reports

Every object sighted should be reported, no matter how in-
significant it may seem to you. The initial report consists of
two basic parts: what you see, and its bearing (direction) from
the ship. Aircraft sighting reports also include altitude (position angle). Report the contact to the officer of the deck immediately. Amplifying reports include the object's identity—destroyer, periscope, log, etc.—and its direction.

Bearings: Lookouts report objects in degrees of relative
bearing. (Figure 23-13 shows the relative bearings around a
ship.) To prevent confusion, the Navy has established a definite procedure for reporting bearings, ranges, etc. (A pronunciation guide is found on p. 609.)

Bearings are always reported in three digits and spoken digit
by digit. Objects that are dead ahead or astern (000 degrees or
180 degrees), on either beam (090 degrees or 270 degrees), or
on either bow (045 degrees or 315 degrees) or quarter (135
degrees or 225 degrees) may be indicated as such. For example, a ship bearing 315 degrees can be reported as being on the
port bow, although the bearing itself could also be used.

An object in the sky is located by its relative bearing and
position angle. The position angle of an aircraft is its height in
degrees above the horizon, as seen from the ship. The horizon
is 0 degrees and directly overhead is 90 degrees. The position
angle can never be more than 90 degrees (see figure 23-17).

Position angles are given in one or two digits and spoken as a
whole number, not digit by digit. The words *position angle* are
always spoken before the numerals.

Ranges: Range estimates take practice. A lookout has to
learn how a certain type of ship looks a mile away, two miles
away, etc. Knowing your height above water will help you in
estimating ranges. At a height of 50 feet, for example, the
distance to the horizon is about 16,000 yards (8 miles); at a
height of 100 feet, the distance is about 23,000 yards ($11\frac{1}{2}$

miles).

Communications

24

When you mention communications in the Navy, most sailors think of a radioman copying a radio message or a signalman handling flag hoists during fleet operations. But communications is much more than that—it involves everyone. The bow lookout using a sound-powered telephone to report to the bridge is communicating; so is the officer of the deck (OOD) using the talk-between-ships (TBS) link to advise another ship of a course change. The lookout is using internal communications; the OOD is using external communications. All naval communications can be classified as one or the other.

Internal Communications

Internal communications are relayed aboard a single ship using both sound and visual methods. Communication by messenger, probably the oldest of all means, is still the most reliable. Other means include everything from "passing the word" over the intercommunications voice (MC) circuits to using "squawk boxes," sound-powered telephones, dial phones, bell and buzzer systems, or boat gongs.

Internal communications also means printed or written material such as the plan of the day (POD), visual-display systems such as the rudder-angle indicator and engine-order telegraph on the bridge, the combat information center (CIC) plot, and even the "on-board/ashore board" for officers on the quarterdeck. Everyone aboard the ship must be aware of the internal communications system at all times.

Passing the Word

In the old Navy, before the days of loudspeaker systems, the boatswain's mate (BM) passed any orders for the crew by word of mouth. The BM of the watch (BMOW) sounded "Call mates" on his pipe to get the BMs together, and they answered repeatedly with the same call while converging on the bridge or quarterdeck. Upon hearing the word, they dispersed fore and aft to sing it out at every hatch.

While this procedure was colorful, it took a lot of time. Today a single BM can quickly pass the word over the MC network while the others stay where they are. The basic MC circuit is the 1MC, the general announcing system, over which the word can be passed to every space in the ship. The general alarm system is also tied into it. Transmitters are located on the bridge and quarterdeck; additional transmitters may be installed at other points.

An announcement is preceded by a boatswain's call or pipe. "All hands" is piped before any word concerning drills and emergencies. "Attention" is piped before the passing of routine messages.

Common shipboard events are listed below, with the appropriate orders following each one. The orders may differ slightly from ship to ship.

Air bedding: "All divisions, air bedding."

Arrivals and departures: Title of officer, preceded by proper number of boat gongs, for example, (chief of naval operations) arriving (departing)."

Boats: "Away, the motor whaleboat (gig, barge), away."

Church call: "Divine services are now being held in (space). Maintain silence about the decks during divine services."

Eight o'clock reports: "On deck all 8 o'clock reports."

Extra-duty personnel: "Lay up to the quarterdeck for muster, all extra-duty personnel (or other special groups)."

Fire: "Fire! Fire! Class (A, B, etc.), compartment A205-L (or other location, including deck, frame, or side). This is not a drill. Away the duty fire party."

Flight quarters: "Flight quarters. Flight quarters. Man all flight quarters stations to launch (recover) aircraft (helicopters)."

Hoist boats: "First division stand by to hoist in (out) no. (1, 2, etc.) motor launch (gig)."

Inspection (personnel): "All hands to quarters for captain's personnel inspection."

Inspection (material): "Stand by all lower deck and topside spaces for inspection."

Knock off work (before evening meal): "Knock off all ship's work." (First pipe "All hands.")

Late bunks: "Up all late bunks."

Figure 24–1   Signalman uses signal flags, one of several means of external
communications, to signal from ships. (See p. 596.)

Liberty: "Liberty to commence for the (first) and (third) sections at 1600; to expire on board at (hour, date, month)."

Mail: "Mail call."

Meals: "All hands, pipe to breakfast (noon meal or dinner, evening meal or supper)." (First pipe "Mess call.")

Mess gear (call): "Mess gear (call). Clear the (all) mess decks." (First pipe "Mess call.")

Mistake or error: "Belay my last."

Muster on stations: "All divisions muster on stations."

Pay: "The crew is now being paid (space is given)."

Preparations for getting under way: "Make all preparations for getting under way."

Quarters for muster: "All hands to quarters for muster, instruction, and inspection."

Quarters for muster (inclement weather): "All hands to quarters for muster. Foul-weather parade." (First pipe "All hands.")

Rain squall: "Haul over all hatch hoods and gun covers."

Readiness for getting underway reports: "All departments, make readiness for getting underway reports to the OOD on the bridge."

Relieving the watch: "Relieve the watch. On deck the (no.) section. Lifeboat crew on deck to muster. Relieve the wheel and lookouts." (First pipe "Attention.")

Rescue and assistance: "Away rescue and assistance party, (no.) section."

Reveille: "Reveille. Reveille, all hands heave out and trice (lash) up." Or, "Reveille. Up all hands, trice up all bunks." (First pipe "All hands.")

Shifting the watch: "The OOD is shifting his watch to the bridge (quarterdeck)."

Side boys: "Lay up on the quarterdeck, the side boys."

Smoking: "The smoking lamp is lighted (out)." (Unless the word applies to the whole ship, the space should be specified.)

Special sea detail: "Go to (man) your stations, all the special sea and anchor detail." Or, "Station the special sea and anchor detail."

Sweepers: "Sweepers, start (man) your brooms. Make a clean sweep down fore and aft." (First pipe "Sweepers.")

Taps: "Taps, lights out. All hands turn in to your bunks and keep silence about the decks. Smoking lamp is out in all living spaces." (First pipe "Pipe down.")

Turn to: "Turn to (scrub down all weather decks, scrub all canvas, sweep down compartments, dump trash)."

The OOD is in charge of the 1MC. No call can be passed over it unless it is authorized by him, the executive officer, or the captain, except for a possible emergency call by the damage-control officer.

Normally, the 1MC is equipped with switches that make it possible for certain spaces to be cut off from announcements of no concern to them. The captain, for instance, does not want his cabin blasted with calls for individuals to lay down to the spud locker. If the BMOW is absent, and you are required to pass the word yourself, be sure you know which circuits should be left open. Some parts of the ship have independent MC circuits, such as the engineers' announcing system (2MC) and the hangar-deck announcing system (3MC).

The bull horn (6MC) is the intership announcing system, but is is seldom used for communication between vessels. It is, however, a convenient means of passing orders to boats and tugs alongside or to line-handling parties beyond the range of the speaking trumpet. If the transmitter switch is located on the 1MC control panel, do not cut the bull horn when you are passing a routine word.

The 1MC, 2MC, 3MC, and 6MC are all one-way systems. A partial list of loudspeaker systems is given below:

Commu-
nications

*1MC	General	42MC	CIC coordinating
*2MC	Propulsion plant	43MC	Unassigned
*3MC	Aviators	44MC	Instrumentation
4MC	Damage control		space
*5MC	Flight deck	45MC	Research opera-
*6MC	Intership		tions
7MC	Submarine control	*46MC	Aviation ordnance
8MC	Troop administra-		and missile han-
	tion and control		dling
*9MC	Underwater troop	47MC	Torpedo control
	communication	49MC	Unassigned
18MC	Bridge	50MC	Integrated opera-
19MC	Aviation control		tional intelligence
21MC	Captain's command		center
22MC	Electronic control	51MC	Aircraft mainte-
23MC	Electrical control		nance and han-
24MC	Flag command		dling control
26MC	Machinery control	52MC	Unassigned
27MC	Sonar and radar	53MC	Ship administrative
	control	54MC	Repair officer's
*29MC	Sonar control and		control
	information	55MC	Sonar service
30MC	Special weapons	56MC	Unassigned
31MC	Escape trunk	57MC	Unassigned
32MC	Weapons control	58MC	Hangar-deck dam-
35MC	Launcher captains		age control
39MC	Cargo handling	59MC	SAMID alert
40MC	Flag administrative		

587

* Central amplifier systems

Squawk Boxes

MC circuits such as the 21MC, known as squawk boxes, differ from public-address systems in being two-way. Each unit has a number of selector switches. To talk to one or more stations, all you have to do is throw the proper switches and operate the press-to-talk button. A red signal light mounted above each selector switch shows whether the station called is busy. If it is busy the light flashes; if it burns with a steady light, you know that the station is ready to receive.

Internal

The following is an example of how to operate the intercom.
You're on the signal bridge, at the 24MC transmitter, and you
want to call conn. First you throw the selector switch marked
"Conn." We'll assume the line is clear for your message. (If
the called station is busy, you will see a busy light.) Now you
can operate the press-to-talk button and start your message.
Any other station attempting to cut in gets the busy signal. The
called station does not need to use the selector switch, only the
press-to-talk switch.

The chief disadvantage of the intercom is that it raises the
noise level in any space in which it is located. For this reason,
it is seldom used when telephone circuits are available.

Sound-Powered Telephones

You will probably stand some sort of watch aboard ship as a
telephone talker. A ship at sea requires many talkers, even
during a peacetime cruising watch. In addition to the lookouts,
there are talkers on the bridge, in firerooms, and in enginerooms, to mention only a few. To do your job properly, you
must learn proper telephone-talking procedures.

These phones are used on all ships, and some ships have
hundreds of them. They do not require outside electrical
power; the user's voice acts on a carbon-filled cell and diaphragm to generate enough current to power the circuit.

The headset phone consists of a headband that holds the
receivers over the ears, a breastplate supported by a cloth neck
strap, and a yoke that holds the transmitter in front of the
mouth. The phone has a lead, which may be up to 50 feet long,
with a jack on the end. The jack plugs into a box connected to
the circuit.

The headset is delicate and can be easily damaged. When
you pick it up, hold the entire unit in your left hand. You will
find the headpiece hung over the transmitter's supporting yoke
and the lead wires coiled.

To put the gear on, first unhook the right side of the neck
strap from the breastplate. Second, put on the earphones and
adjust the headband so that the center of the earpiece is directly over your ear. Last, insert the plug into the jackbox and
screw the collar on firmly.

Adjust the mouthpiece so that it is directly in front of your
mouth when you stand erect. When you speak into the transmitter, it should be about 1/2 to 1 inch from your mouth. In

making this adjustment, remember that the fine wire that goes to the transmitter can be broken easily. Be sure that there are no sharp bends in it, and do not allow it to get caught between the transmitter and the yoke.

When you are wearing the headset, always keep some slack in the lead cord, and be sure it is flat on deck. If you have the cord stretched taut, someone may trip over it and damage the wires, injure him- or herself, or injure you. Do not allow objects to roll over or rest on the cord.

After plugging in the phones, test them with someone on the circuit. If they are not in order, report the fact to the person in charge of your station and don a spare set; don't attempt to repair the set yourself.

If you're on lookout and should be listening as well as searching, cover only one ear with an earpiece so that you can also hear outside noises. Keep the unused earpiece flat against the side of your head to keep noises from being picked up by the transmitter.

Never secure the phones until you have permission to do so. When permission is given, make up the phones for stowage in accordance with the following instructions:

Remove the plug from the jack box by holding the plug in one hand and unscrewing the collar with the other. When the collar is loose, grasp the plug and pull it out, lay it carefully on the deck. Immediately screw the cover on the jack box—dust and dirt will cause a short circuit in a box that has been left uncovered. (If you see an uncovered jack box, cover it, even though you are not responsible for the carelessness.)

Remove the headpiece and hang it over the transmitter yoke.

Coil the lead cord, starting from the end at the phone. Coil the lead in a clockwise direction, holding the loops in one hand. The loops should be 8 to 10 inches across, depending on the size of the space where the phones are stowed. When you are coiling the lead, be careful not to bang the plug against anything.

When the lead is coiled, remove the headpiece from the transmitter yoke and put the headband in the same hand with the coil. Use this same hand to hold the transmitter while you unhook one end of the neck strap from the breastplate. Fold the transmitter yoke flat, being careful not to put a sharp bend in the transmitter cord.

Wrap the neck strap around the coil and headband two or three times and snap the end back on the breastplate, then fold the mouthpiece back up against the junction box. You then have a neat, compact package to be stowed.

Put the phones into the box, or hang them on the hook provided. Be careful not to crowd or jam the leads.

Headset phones should always be unplugged when not in use. If they are left plugged in, the earpieces will pick up noise and carry it into the circuit. Never place the phones on deck. Not only may someone step on them, but decks are good conductors of noise, which the phones can pick up.

The J Circuits

The circuits listed here may not all be installed in your ship, but you should learn them all.

JA	Captain's battle circuit	61JS	Sonar information
JC	Weapons control	1JV	Maneuvering and
JL	Lookouts		docking
21JS	Surface search and radar	2JZ	Damage control
22JS	Air search radar	X8J	Replenishment at sea

Every one of the circuits listed, if it is in the ship at all, has an outlet on the bridge. Some of them are manned at all times; most of them are manned during general quarters. You must know where the outlet for each circuit is, when the circuit should be manned, and the type of traffic it handles. Circuits fall into three categories: primary, auxiliary, and supplementary systems.

The primary system includes all circuits necessary for controlling armament, engineering, damage control, maneuvering, and surveillance functions during battle. These circuits are designated JA through JZ.

The auxiliary system duplicates many of the primary circuits. It maintains vital communications in the event of damage to the primary system. Auxiliary circuits are separated as much as possible from primary circuits. Circuit designations are the same as those for the primary system, preceded by the letter X, as in the XJA, X1JV, etc.

The supplementary system, S1J through S61J, consists of several short, direct circuits such as those from the bridge to the quarterdeck, the quarterdeck to the wardroom, etc. Circuits in primary and auxiliary systems can be tied together at various switchboards, or individual stations may be cut out of the circuits. The supplementary system, however, does not have these provisions. Because supplementary circuits are not manned, most circuits contain a buzzer system so that one station can alert another that communications between the two are desired.

The following explains the standard purpose of each J circuit.

The JA circuit is used by the commanding officer to communicate with his department heads and their assistants.

The JC is the weapons officer's command circuit on ships with a single-purpose main battery. The circuit is controlled by the weapons officer, but is has a bridge outlet for use by the commanding officer and the OOD.

The JL is the circuit over which lookouts report. It is a vital channel to the bridge, CIC, and gun control. In wartime, the JL circuit is manned under all cruising conditions. In peacetime, it is manned when circumstances require extra precautions, but then it may be combined with other circuits. The controlling JL station is on the bridge, and the bridge talker is often designated the lookout supervisor.

On a ship with a dual-purpose main battery, the 2JC circuit serves the same purpose as the JC on a ship with a single-purpose main battery and a separate secondary battery. Ships having both use the 2JC as the air-defense officer's circuit.

The 1JS is used as an antisubmarine warfare (ASW) command circuit and also as a CIC dissemination circuit. When the 1JS is used as an ASW command circuit, there are communication links to sonar control, CIC, underwater battery (UB) plot, and the bridge. This circuit enables stations on the communication link to exchange information without interrupting the flow of information on other circuits. On some ships, the 1JS is used to disseminate CIC information to the conning, gunnery, and aircraft control stations. The 1JS is usually controlled by the CIC evaluator.

The 1JV, called the primary maneuvering circuit, is the one with which the quartermasters are chiefly concerned. It connects the bridge and other conning stations with main-engine control, after steering, and other emergency steering stations. Also, it has outlets on the main deck for control of the anchor detail and line-handling parties fore and aft. This circuit is always manned in CIC; other control stations may do likewise when advisable. The conning officer controls the 1JV, and the circuit is always manned—or at least ready for instant use—whenever the ship is under way.

The JW is the navigator's circuit, by which quartermasters stationed at peloruses and navigational rangefinders may report directly to the navigator at the chart table. During piloting, the JW is especially useful.

The JX is the circuit by which the communications officer, at his battle station on the bridge, is connected with communications spaces.

The JZ circuit is a damage-control circuit.

Some of the foregoing circuits may vary slightly from ship to ship. As soon as you report aboard a new ship for duty, you should find out about any differences.

Telephone Technique

The way you ordinarily talk is not the way you should talk on a telephone. The person on the other end of the line cannot see you, he may not know you, and he may be unfamiliar with the things you are talking about. Telephone talkers must speak clearly, be specific, and act businesslike; they are not on the circuit for chitchat. When using the phones, follow these suggestions:

Use a strong, calm voice. Speak slowly, pronounce words carefully.

Don't mumble, run things together, or talk with gum or a cigarette in your mouth.

Use standard terms and phraseology. Avoid slang.

When transmitting numbers and letters, use approved communication procedures. The expression "item 5C" may sound like "Item 9D," but "fife Charlie" will not be mistaken for "Nin-er Delta."

Circuit Discipline: Circuits are like a party line—everyone can talk and listen at the same time. To prevent confusion, strict circuit discipline must be maintained.

Send only official messages.

Keep the button on the off position except when you're actually talking.

Do not leave your station or engage in other work or activities without permission.

Use only standard phraseology.
Never show anger, impatience, or excitement.
Each phone talker is a key link in the ship's interior communications chain. Unauthorized talking means that the chain is weakened. Don't engage in it, and don't permit others to.

Circuit Testing: To find out if stations on the circuit are manned and ready, the control station talker says, "All stations, control, testing." Each talker then acknowledges in the assigned order (or sequence). Here's how it would go on a gun circuit:

Gun no. 1: "One, aye, aye."
Gun no. 2: "Two, aye, aye."
Gun no. 3: "Three, aye, aye."

Normally each station answers in order, but does not wait more than a few seconds if the station ahead of it fails to acknowledge. If you are on gun no. 3, and gun no. 2 fails to answer, acknowledge for your gun. Gun no. 2 then can come in at the end.

The test is not complete until each station has answered and any equipment faults have been checked.

593

Message Form: Most messages have three parts: the name of the station called, the name of the station calling, and the information to be sent. This format must always be followed. Call the station the message is for, identify your station, then transmit the message. Remember the order: who to, who from, what about. If you are on the anchor detail and want to call the bridge, the message is "Bridge (who to), forecastle (who from); anchor secured (what about)."

Messages are acknowledged when the station identifying itself adds "Aye, aye." This lets the sender know the message has been received by the station it was intended for, and that it is understood. If you don't understand, ask for a repeat. If the sender wants to make certain an important message has been received correctly, he or she may ask you to repeat it.

Sending a Message: First name the station being called, next name the station doing the calling, then add the message, "Bridge, forecastle; anchor ready for letting go."

Receiving a Message: First identify your station, then acknowledge for the message. If your station is the forecastle and the bridge has just ordered the anchor "Let go," acknowledge with "Forecastle, aye, aye."

Sometimes there are three or four steps involved. For example: "Forecastle, bridge, how many lines are to the pier?" If you don't know, you say, "Forecastle, aye, aye, wait." After getting the information, call the bridge: "Bridge, forecastle, five lines to the pier." The bridge will acknowledge: "Bridge, aye, aye."

Requesting Repeats: If an incoming message is not clear, the receiving station says, "Repeat." When the message is repeated and understood, the receiving station acknowledges it by repeating the name of the sending station and adding, "Aye, aye."

Spelling Words: Difficult or little-known words are spelled out phonetically: "Stand by to receive officer from CHINFO. I spell Charlie, Hotel, India, November, Foxtrot, Oscar— CHINFO."

Securing the Phones: Never secure until you have permission from the control station.

Forecastle: "Bridge, forecastle, permission to secure?"

Bridge: "Bridge, aye, aye, wait."

After the bridge talker learns that the forecastle may secure, he or she says "Forecastle, bridge, you may secure."

"Forecastle, aye, aye, securing."

Remember to make the phones up properly and stow them before leaving your station.

Voice Tube

On most minecraft, patrol boats, and the like, the voice tube is still the primary means of internal communication, although some have sound-powered-telephone circuits. A voice tube requires neither electrical nor sound power; but its effectiveness decreases in direct ratio to the length of the tube. On large ships, the voice tube is for short-distance communication only, as between open conning stations and the pilot house.

External Communications

External communication involves two or more ships, stations, or commands. A ship's external communication is done by delivery, telecommunication, or any combination of the two. Delivery includes messengers and mail. Telecommunication, which means communication over a distance, includes any transmission or reception using visual, electrical, or sound systems.

Methods of visual signaling include the flag hoist, semaphore, and signal searchlight or blinker. Whistles, bells, foghorns, or even a gun (for distress signals) may be part of the sound system. Electrical and electronic communication is done by radiotelegraph (CW), radiotelephone (RT), radioteletype (RATT), facsimile (FAX), and voice radio.

In delivering each communication, transmitting stations must take into account the precedence (urgency), the security requirement, and the limitations of available equipment. From a security standpoint, the order of desirability is (1) messenger, (2) registered mail, (3) approved wire circuit, (4) ordinary mail, (5) nonapproved wire circuit, (6) visual, (7) sound system, and (8) radio.

With ships operating 24 hours a day around the world, the Navy must have rapid, accurate communications, not only for the tactical and strategic control of fleets in war but also for administration and logistics. No ship is ever out of touch with her base of operations or her tactical, type, or administrative commander.

Visual Signs

Despite this age of high technology, when satellites and radios transmit communications at incredible speed, the oldest form of communication continues to play a vital role in the Navy. Visual communication has a distinct advantage over other forms. For all its advances, science has yet to produce a silent form of communication, one that cannot be detected by advanced technological equipment. Visual communication fills the need for a reliable, silent, and relatively secure means of communication at ranges up to 15 miles.

The three main types of visual signals are flashing light, semaphore, and flag hoist.

Flashing-light Signaling: Letters and numbers are broken down into short and long flashes of light collectively known as the Morse code. A transmitting signalman sends messages one word at a time, letter by letter, with a slight pause between each letter. The receiving signalman flashes a light for each word received until the message is complete.

Flashing-light signaling is done by two methods, directional and nondirectional. With the directional method, the sender aims his light directly at the receiving ship or installation. Other types of directional gear are the blinker tube (or blinker gun) and the multipurpose lamp; both are battery operated, with trigger switches to control flashes.

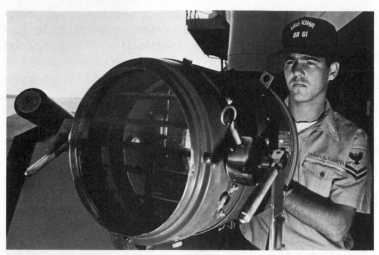

Figure 24–2 A flashing light enables a signalman to send a Morse code message when distance or darkness make flag messages impractical.

The nondirectional method is also called all-around signaling. Most of it is done by yardarm blinkers, lights mounted near the ends of the port and starboard yardarms on the mainmast and controlled by a signal key, similar to a telegraph, located on the signal bridge. This method is best for sending messages to several ships at once.

While the other two signal systems rely on "white" light, a system called Nancy uses invisible infrared light. Messages sent by this system can be seen only by those who have a special Nancy receiver, which gathers infrared rays and converts them to visible light. Nancy, with a range of from 10,000 to 15,000 yards, can be used only at night and is a very secure method of communication.

Semaphore Signaling: Semaphore is much faster than flashing light for short-distance transmissions in clear daylight or at night using special cone adapters for flashlights. Semaphore may be used to send messages to several ships at once if they are in suitable positions. Because of its speed, semaphore is better adapted than the other visual methods for long messages. When radio silence is imposed, semaphore is considered the best substitute for the handling of administrative traffic.

Although semaphore's usefulness is limited somewhat by its short range, it is more secure than flashing light or radio because there is less chance of interception by an enemy or unauthorized persons. Speed and security, therefore, are the two factors favoring the use of semaphore.

Semaphore requires little in the way of equipment. Two hand flags attached to staffs are all you need. The standard semaphore flags are usually 15 to 18 square inches, and each staff is long enough to grasp firmly. For night semaphore, flashlights are held in the same manner as semaphore flagstaffs. Most semaphore flags issued to the fleet today are fluorescent and made of sharkskin. (When sender and receiver are close, as when their ships are alongside one another for underway replenishment, no special equipment is necessary. The semaphore characters are made simply by moving the hands to the proper positions.)

When you're using fluorescent flags, your background is relatively unimportant. With cotton flags, however, you must have a good background to enable the receiving operator to see them clearly.

A good signalman can send or receive about twenty-five five-letter groups a minute. Only thirty positions need to be learned; they are shown in figure 24-3.

Flag-hoist Signaling: This is the most rapid system of visual signaling, but it can be used only in daytime. It is generally for tactical orders. The meanings of each signal must be looked up in a signal book. There is a signal flag for each letter of the alphabet, one for each numeral 0 through 9, and others with special meanings. A compete set of signal flags will have sixty-eight flags and pennants; with them, thousands of different signals can be sent. Most ships carry only two or three complete sets of flags, and substitutes must be employed when certain flags are already flying. The first substitute repeats the first flag or pennant in the same hoist, the second substitute repeats the second flag or pennant, and so on.

Other Important Flags: The following six flags should be familiar to every sailor:

BRAVO: Ship is handling explosives or fuel oil
CODE PENNANT ALFA: Divers in water.
FIVE FLAG: Breakdown.
OSCAR: Man overboard.
PAPA: All hands return to ship.
QUEBEC: All boats return to ship.

A

B

C
AND
ANSWERING
SIGN

D

E

F

G

H

I

J

K

L

M

N

Figure 24-3 The semaphore alphabet is fast but useful only for short-range visual transmission.

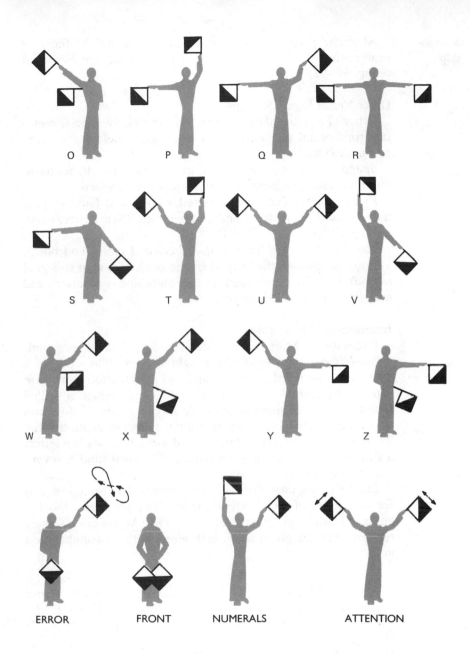

O   P   Q   R

S   T   U   V

W   X   Y   Z

ERROR   FRONT   NUMERALS   ATTENTION

Absentee pennants, flown when the commanding officer or senior officer is absent from his or her command, are described on pp. 96–97.

Other Visual Signal Systems

Other visual signaling systems give the Navy special methods for special and emergency occasions. Below are some common systems.

Speed indicators: These flags, or red and white lights flashing in various combinations, indicate a ship's speed.

Pyrotechnics: These are colored smoke and flare signals, usually used for distress and emergencies. (See Distress Signals, p. 610.)

Panels: These are large strips of colored cloth, laid out in various designs on the ground or the deck of a ship to signal aircraft; they are beach markers for amphibious operations and are also used in emergencies.

International Morse Code

International Morse code is standard for all naval communications transmitted by flashing light or CW. The code is a system in which letters, numerals, and punctuation marks are signified by various combinations of dots and dashes. A skilled radioman or signalman sends code in evenly timed dots and dashes, in which a dot is one unit long, a dash three units long. There is a one-unit interval between dots and dashes in a letter, a three-unit interval between letters of a word, and a seven-unit interval between words.

The following chart lists the international Morse code signal for each letter of the alphabet, along with a phonetic-alphabet equivalent and a pronunciation guide. (The Morse code signals for numbers are given on p. 609, along with a pronunciation guide.)

Letter	Phonetic Alphabet	Pronunciation Guide	International Morse Code
A	Alfa	**Al**-fah	.−
B	Bravo	**Brah**-voh	−...
C	Charlie	**Char**-lee	−.−.
D	Delta	**Dell**-tah	−..
E	Echo	**Eck**-oh	.
F	Foxtrot	**Foks**-trot	..−.

G	Golf	Gold	– –.	Commu-
H	Hotel	Hoh-**tell**	....	nications
I	India	**In**-dee-ah	..	
J	Juliett	**Jew**-lee-ett	.– – –	
K	Kilo	**Key**-loh	–.–	
L	Lima	**Lee**-mah	.–..	
M	Mike	Mike	– –	
N	November	No-**vem**-ber	–.	
O	Oscar	**Oss**-cah	– – –	
P	Papa	Pah-**pah**	.– –.	
Q	Quebec	Keh-**beck**	– –.–	
R	Romeo	**Row**-me-oh	.–.	
S	Sierra	See-**air**-rah	...	
T	Tango	**Tang**-go	–	
U	Uniform	**You**-nee-form	..–	
V	Victor	**Vik**-tah	...–	
W	Whiskey	**Wiss**-key	.– –	
X	X ray	**Ecks**-ray	–..–	
Y	Yankee	**Yang**-key	–.– –	
Z	Zulu	**Zoo**-loo	– –..	

Electronic Communications

Electronic communications are relayed by various means, including radio, wire, or telegraph. Wire communications go directly from sender to receiver. Radios send electromagnetic waves, which are broadcast through the atmosphere in all directions. CWs, RTs, RATTs, and FAXs are different types of radios.

Radiotelegraph (CW): CWs communicate by international Morse code. If a transmission is in plain language, anyone can intercept and read it. Important messages may be encrypted and sent in a code or cipher known only to the sender and receiver. *Codes* are word-for-word substitutions, and both sender and receiver must use the same codebook. *Ciphers* are letter-for-letter substitutions, which may require a machine for encoding and decoding. A coded message may be copied by anyone, but without the codebook it is difficult to read.

CW messages, called traffic, are sent to the fleet in two ways. The first is by broadcast, when one station transmits traffic for many ships, and every ship copies all traffic. Ships do not acknowledge the traffic, so an enemy cannot determine how many ships are listening or where they are positioned. The other is by receipt, when each station acknowledges its traffic. This way there is no doubt that it has been received. The disadvantage of this system is obvious: it allows the enemy, with radio direction-finding equipment, to locate stations acknowledging traffic.

Radiotelephone (RT): RT, commonly known as the voice radio, is an effective and convenient method of communication. It is used extensively for ship-to-ship tactical communication, convoy work, the control of airborne aircraft, and countless tasks requiring rapid, short-range communication. Small vessels such as district craft rely almost entirely on voice radio.

RT supplements both CW and visual methods of communication, but it does not replace either. It has the advantage of direct transmission of the spoken word and of simplicity of operation, though the latter may lead to abuse. Careless voice procedure, plus circuit overloading, has created confusion at times when good communication was imperative.

RT is considered the least secure means of electronic communication. Anyone who has the necessary receiving equipment and is within reception range can copy messages.

Radioteletype (RATT): This is an electrically operated typewriter which, by either radio or telegraph line, can operate another similar typewriter elsewhere. RATT is used extensively both at sea and ashore. A typewriter keyboard produces printed letters simultaneously at sending and receiving machines, no matter how many machines are on the circuit. Perforated tapes may be prepared in advance for use in later transmissions.

Facsimile (FAX): FAXs transmit pictorial and graphic information electronically by wire or radio. The information is reproduced in its original form at the receiving station. The image to be sent is scanned by a photoelectric cell; electrical variations, corresponding to the light and dark areas being scanned, are transmitted to the receiving unit. The process is similar to that of television, but is much slower and cannot produce a moving picture. FAX signals may be transmitted by wire or radio. FAXs are often used to transmit complete weather charts and data.

Transmitting Techniques

Because RT is used so widely in ships, aircraft, and motor vehicles, everyone should understand the basics of circuit discipline. Under most circumstances, the following practices are specifically forbidden:

Violation of radio silence.
Unofficial conversation between operators.
Transmitting in a directed net without permission.
Excessive tuning and testing.
Unauthorized use of plain language.
Transmission of an operator's name or personal sign.
Use of unauthorized procedure words.

Linkage or compromise of classified call signs and address groups by plain-language disclosures or association with unclassified call signs.

Unauthorized use of plain language in place of applicable procedure words.

Use of profane, indecent, or obscene language.

Listen before transmitting, for break-ins cause confusion. Speak clearly and distinctly; slurred syllables and clipped speech are difficult to understand. Speak slowly, so that the recorder has a chance to understand the entire message the first time. This way, you'll save time and avoid repititions. Avoid excessive voice modulation.

Be natural, and maintain a normal speaking rhythm. This is a form of essential communication, not "big-time" radio. Send your message phrase by phrase instead of word by word.

Use standard pronunciation, not regional accents. Keep the correct distance (about 2 inches) between your lips and the microphone. Speak in a moderately strong voice to override background noise. While transmitting, keep your head and body between sources of noise and the microphone.

Keep the volume of the headset earphone low. Also keep speaker volume at a moderate level. Give an accurate evaluation in response to a request for a radio check. Pause momentarily, when possible, during your transmission; pausing allows any other station with higher-precedence traffic to break in.

Follow closely prescribed procedures. Transact your business and get off the air. Preliminary calls are unnecessary when communications are good and the message is short. Do not hold the microphone button in the push-to-talk position until you're ready to transmit. Apply firm pressure to the microphone button to prevent an unintentional release, which may cause a signal interruption.

Procedure Words and Procedure Signs

Procedure words (prowords) and procedure signs (prosigns) are words and phrases used to speed up radio traffic. They shorten certain common orders, requests, and instructions. Prosigns may be sent by RATT, CW, semaphore, or flashing light. Signs with a line above them are sent without the usual pause between letters.

Proword	Explanation	Prosign
ADDRESS GROUP	The group that follows is an address group.	
ALL AFTER	The portion of the message to which I refer is all that follows ____.	AA
ALL BEFORE	The portion of the message to which I refer is all that precedes ____.	AB
AUTHENTICATE	The station called is to reply to challenge that follows.	
AUTHENTICA-TION IS BREAK	The transmission authentication of this message is ____. I hereby indicate the separation of the text from other portions of the message.	BT
CALL SIGN	The group that follows is a call sign.	
CORRECT	You are correct, or what you have transmitted is correct.	C
CORRECTION	An error has been made in this transmission. Transmission will continue with the last word correctly transmitted. An error has been made in this transmission (or message). The correct version is ____.	EEEEEEEE
DISREGARD THIS TRANS-MISSION—OUT	This transmission is in error. Disregard it. (This proword shall not be used to cancel any message that has been completely transmitted and for which	EEEEEEEE $\overline{\text{AR}}$

	receipt or acknowledge- ment has been received).	
DO NOT ANSWER	Stations called are not to answer this call, acknowl- edge receipt of this mes- sage, or otherwise trans- mit in connection with this transmission. (When pro- word is employed, the transmission is ended with the proword OUT.)	F
EXECUTE	Carry out the purport of the message or signal to which this applies. (To be used only with the execu- tive method.)	$\overline{\text{IX}}$ (5-sec dash)
EXECUTE TO FOLLOW	Action on the message or signal that follows is to be carried out upon receipt of the proword EXECUTE. (To be used only with the delayed executive method.)	$\overline{\text{IX}}$
EXEMPT	The addresses immedi- ately following are ex- empted from the collective call.	XMT
FIGURES	Numerals or numbers follow.	
FLASH	Precedence FLASH.	Z
FROM	The originator of this mes- sage is indicated by the address designator imme- diately following.	FM
GROUPS	This message contains the number of groups indi- cated by the numeral fol- lowing.	GR
GROUP NO COUNT	The groups in this mes- sage have not been counted.	GRNC
I AUTHENTI- CATE	The group that follows is the reply to your chal- lenge to authenticate.	

IMMEDIATE	Precedence IMMEDIATE.	O
IMMEDIATE EXECUTE	Action on the message or signal following is to be carried out on receipt of the word EXECUTE. (To be used with the immediate executive method.)	$\overline{IX}$
INFO	The addresses immediately following are for information.	INFO
I READ BACK	The following is my response to your instruction to read back.	
I SAY AGAIN	I am repeating transmission or portion indicated.	$\overline{IMI}$
I SPELL	I will spell the next word phonetically.	
I VERIFY	What follows has been verified at your request and is repeated. (To be used only as a reply to VERIFY.)	
MESSAGE	A message that requires recording is about to follow. (Transmitted immediately after the call.)	
NET NOW	All stations are to net their radios on the unmodulated carrier wave that I am about to transmit.	
NUMBER	Station serial number.	NR
OUT	This is the end of my transmission to you and no answer is required or expected.	
OVER	This is the end of my transmission to you and a response is necessary. Go ahead; transmit.	K
PRIORITY	Precedence PRIORITY.	P
READ BACK	Repeat this entire transmission back to me exactly as received.	G

REBROADCAST YOUR NET	Link the two nets under your control for automatic rebroadcast.	
RELAY (TO)	Transmit this message to all addressees immediately following.	T
ROGER	I have received your last transmission satisfactorily.	R
ROUTINE	Precedence ROUTINE.	R
SAY AGAIN	Repeat all of your last transmission. Followed by identification data, it means "Repeat ____ (portion indicated)."	
SERVICE	The message that follows is a service message.	SVC
SIGNALS	The group that follows is taken from a signal book. (This proword is not used on nets primarily employed for conveying signals; it is intended for use when tactical signals are passed on nontactical nets.)	
SILENCE (repeated three or more times)	Cease transmissions on this net immediately. Silence will be maintained until lifted.	H̅M̅ H̅M̅ H̅M̅
SILENCE LIFTED	Silence is lifted.	
SPEAK SLOWER	Your transmission is too fast. Reduce speed.	
STOP REBROADCASTING	Cut the automatic link between the two nets that are being rebroadcast, and revert to normal working.	
THIS IS	This transmission is from the station whose designator immediately follows.	DE
TIME	What immediately follows is the time or date-time group of the message.	

	TO	The addressees immediately following are addressed for action.	TO
	UNKNOWN STATION	The identity of the station with which I am attempting to establish communications is unknown.	$\overline{AA}$
	VERIFY	Verify the entire message (or portion indicated) with the originator and send correct version. To be used at the discretion of or by the addressee to which the question is directed.	
	WAIT	I must pause for a few seconds.	$\overline{AS}$
	WAIT OUT	I must pause for longer than a few seconds.	$\overline{AS}$ $\overline{AR}$
	WILCO	I have received your signal, understand it, and will comply. (To be used only by addressee. Since the meaning of ROGER is included in that of WILCO, the two prowords are never used together.)	
	WORD AFTER	The word of the message to which I refer is that which follows ___ .	WA
	WORD BEFORE	The word of the message to which I refer is that which precedes ___ .	WB
	WORDS TWICE	Communication is difficult. Transmit(ting) each phrase (or each code group) twice. (This proword may be used as an order, request, or information.)	
	WRONG	Your last transmission was incorrect. The correct version is ___ .	

Pronouncing Letters and Numbers

When necessary, identify letters of the alphabet with the standard phonetic alphabet (see p. 600). Take care to distinguish numbers from similarly pronounced words. Before numbers, you may use the proword *figures*. The numeral 0 is always referred to as "ze-ro," never as "oh." It is written as 0. Decimal points are referred to as "day-see-mal." For example, 123.4 is spoken, "Wun too thuree day-see-mal foo-wer." Numbers are transmitted digit by digit, except that exact multiples of thousands may be spoken as such.

Numbers	*Pronunciation*	*International Morse Code*
1	Wun	.– – – –
2	Too	. .– – –
3	Thuree	. . .– –
4	Fow-er	. . . .–
5	Fife	. . . . .
6	Six	–. . . .
7	Sev-en	– –. . .
8	Ait	– – –. .
9	Nin-er	– – – –.
0	Ze-ro	– – – – –
44	Fow-er fow-er	
90	Nin-er ze-ro	
136	Wun thuree six	
500	Fife ze-ro ze-ro	
1,478	Wun fow-er scv-en ait	
7,000	Sev-en tou-sand	
16,000	Wun six tou-sand	
812,681	Ait wun too six ait wun	

Some special instances require procedures other than those in normal digit-by-digit communication. Ranges and distances given in mile units and speed given in knots, for instance, are always transmitted as cardinal (whole) numbers. For example, 10 is spoken as "ten," 13 as "thur-teen," 25 as "twen-ty fife," 50 as "fif-ty," 110 as "wun hun-dred ten," 300 as "thuree hundred."

Bearings are always given in three digits and are transmitted digit by digit. For example, bearing 090 is spoken as "ze-ro niner ze-ro," 180 as " wun ait ze-ro," 295 as "too nin-er fife."

Sound Signaling

Owing to the nature of the device involved—a whistle, siren, or foghorn—sound signaling is necessarily slow. Moreover, the misuse of sound signaling can create serious confusion at sea. Sound signaling in fog should therefore be reduced to a minimum. Signals other than the single letters should be used only in extreme emergencies and never in heavily traveled waters.

The signals should be made slowly and clearly. They may, if necessary, be repeated, but at sufficiently long intervals to ensure that no confusion arises and that one-letter signals are not mistaken for two-letter groups.

Mail Systems

A vast amount of administrative detail concerning personnel, supplies, logistics, and operations is handled by official mail, which is carried through the U.S. postal system. Official mail between ships in the same port is carried by guard mail. Ships and stations have guard mail petty officers designated to log and receive this type of correspondence. Classified mail is carried by designated couriers.

Personal mail in the Navy is handled much as it is in the civilian community. Every ship has a post office and postal clerks (PCs) specially designated to handle U.S. mail. Every ship also has a fleet post office (FPO) number to enable the New York and San Francisco FPOs to better direct mail to ships at sea or overseas.

In time of war, all letters written by personnel on ships or at overseas bases must be examined by official Navy censors before they are sent.

When censorship is in effect, censors delete such information as the location, identity, and actual or prospective movements of ships and aircraft; the forces, weapons, military installations, or plans of the United States or its allies; the employment of any naval or military unit of the United States or its allies; effects of enemy operations, including U.S. and allied casualties; and criticism of the equipment or morale of U.S. or allied forces.

Distress Signals

Distress signals may be made either separately or together. Despite popular opinion, the national ensign, hoisted upside down, is not a recognized signal of distress. No man-of-war would ever subject the colors to this indignity. But if you see a private craft with her insignia hoisted upside down, she is probably in distress, and you should go to her assistance without delay.

Distress signals are as follows:

A gun or other explosive fired at intervals of about 1 minute.

A continuous sounding with any fog-signal apparatus.

Rockets or shells throwing red stars and fired one at a time at short intervals.

The signal group . . . – – – . . . (SOS) in Morse code.

The RT signal "Mayday."

The letters NC, the international signal of distress.

A square flag with a ball above or below it, or anything resembling a ball.

Flames on a vessel, as from a burning tar or oil barrel.

A rocket-parachute flare or a hand flare showing a red light.

A signal giving off a volume of orange-colored smoke.

Outstretched arms slowly and repeatedly being raised and lowered.

The signals below are prescribed for submerged submarines in emergency situations.

A yellow smoke flare fired into the air from a submarine indicates that the submarine is coming to periscope depth in preparation for surfacing. Ships should clear the immediate vicinity but not stop propellers.

A red smoke flare fired into the air from a submarine is a signal that she is in serious trouble and will surface immediately if possible. Smoke flares of any color, fired into the air at short intervals, mean that a submarine requires assistance. All ships in the vicinity should stand by to give aid.

Appendices

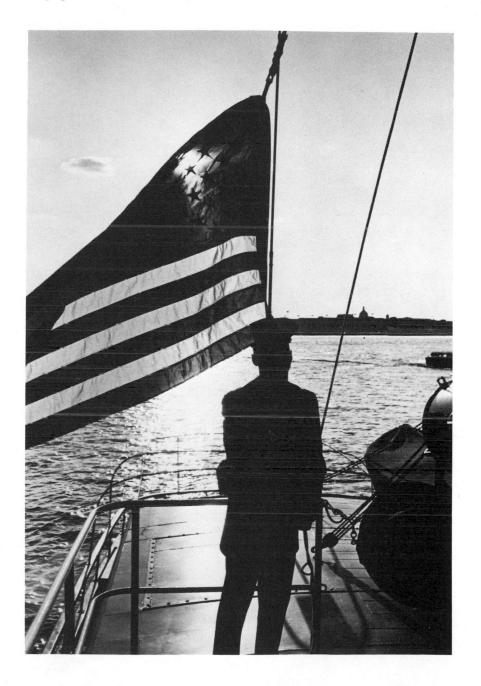

Navy Organization

The Navy, along with the Army and Air Force, is part of the Defense Department (DOD). Until 1947, the Navy was a separate department of the government, as was the Army. The National Security Act of 1947 created the National Military Establishment (NME), which in 1949 became DOD. DOD is headed by the secretary of defense (SECDEF), a cabinet officer and a civilian.

The Department of the Navy (DON) was created in 1798 when Benjamin Stoddert was appointed the first secretary of the navy (SECNAV). In 1815, a three-man board of naval commissioners was created to manage the Navy. In 1842, this was changed to a bureau system, which lasted with minor changes until 1966. The position and title of chief of naval operations (CNO) was created in 1915.

Department of Defense

DOD is the largest government agency in the United States. It spends approximately 23.9 percent of the national budget and employs approximately 3 million people directly (including 1 million civilians). Another million people serve in a reserve military status.

DOD is composed of the Office of the Secretary of Defense (OSD), defense agencies, the Joint Chiefs of Staff (JCS), unified and specified commands, and the Departments of the Army, Navy, and Air Force. It provides for military security and supports national policies and interests. The National Security Act of 1947, as amended, codifies the controlling military law of the United States.

The Defense Act of 1986 effected significant changes in the overall organization and functional responsibilities of DOD. Major changes were made in the assignment of responsibilities to civilian and military executives of OSD and the military

Figure A–I   DOD organization chart.

DEPARTMENT OF DEFENSE

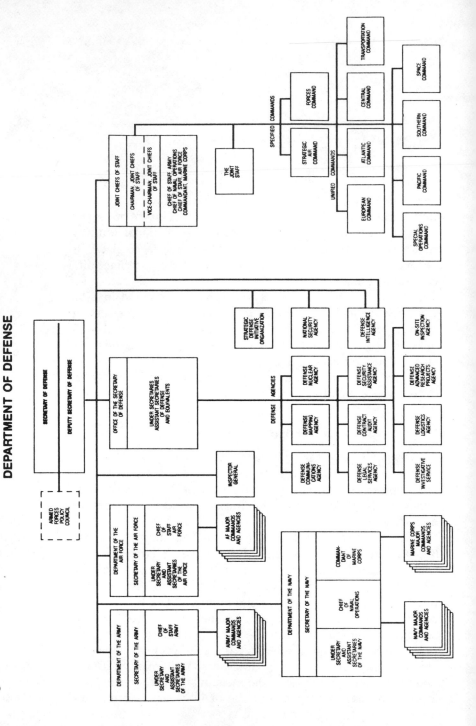

departments, in the structure and role of the JCS, and in the relationship of unified and specified command officials to other DOD officials and components.

The Office of the Secretary

The SECDEF is the principal assistant to the president in all matters relating to DOD. The SECDEF exercises direction, authority, and control over the department.

The deputy SECDEF supervises and coordinates the activities of the department and takes the place of the SECDEF when necessary.

The Joint Chiefs of Staff

The JCS consists of a chairman, the chiefs of staff of the Army and Air Force, the CNO, and the commandant of the Marine Corps (CMC). The JCS also has a vice chairman as a nonvoting member. The vice chairman acts as chairman in the latter's absence.

The chairman of the JCS, assisted by other JCS members and supported by the Joint Staff, is responsible for strategic direction of the armed forces; strategic planning; contingency planning and preparedness; advice on department and combatant command requirements, programs, and budgets; doctrine, training, and education for the joint employment of the armed forces; United Nations representational duties; and other duties prescribed by law, the president, or the SECDEF.

Unified and Specified Commands

Unified and specified commanders operate under the control and direction of the president and the SECDEF. Subject to the authority, direction, and control of the latter, the chairman of the JCS serves as spokesman for the commanders of the combatant (unified and specified) commands, especially on the operational requirements of their commands.

A unified command, composed of elements of two or more services, has a broad continuing mission and a single commander. The unified commands are Atlantic Command, Pacific Command, European Command, Southern Command, Central Command, Transportation Command, Space Command, and the Special Operations Command.

A specified command also has a broad continuing mission, but it is composed of forces from one service. There are two specified commands: the Strategic Air Command, Omaha, Nebraska, and Forces Command, Fort McPherson, Georgia.

Figure A–2 DON organization chart.

ORGANIZATION OF THE DEPARTMENT OF THE NAVY

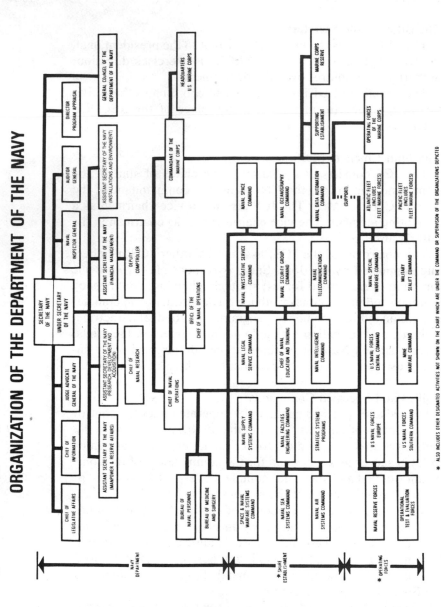

* ALSO INCLUDES OTHER DESIGNATED ACTIVITIES NOT SHOWN ON THE CHART WHICH ARE UNDER THE COMMAND OR SUPERVISION OF THE ORGANIZATIONS DEPICTED

The Department of the Navy (DON)

Since its formal beginning as a military department in 1798, DON has consisted of three distinctly separate bodies: the Navy Department, the shore establishment, and the operating forces.

Navy Department

The Navy Department (as opposed to DON) refers to the central executive offices of DON located at the seat of government. Organizationally, the Navy Department comprises the Office of the Secretary of the Navy; the Office of the Chief of Naval Operations; Headquarters, United States Marine Corps; and under the command of the CNO, the Bureau of Naval Personnel. Headquarters, United States Coast Guard, is also included when operating as a service in the Navy.

The Navy Department establishes policy, provides direction, and exerts control over the operations of the other two components of DON, the shore establishment and the operating forces of the Navy.

Secretary of the Navy (SECNAV)

The SECNAV, a civilian, is in charge of DON. Under the direction, authority, and control of the SECDEF, the SECNAV is responsible for the policies and control of DON, including its organization, administration, operation, and efficiency.

The Office of the Secretary of the Navy is composed of the undersecretary of the Navy (UNSECNAV), assistant secretaries of the Navy, general counsel of DON, judge advocate general of the Navy, naval inspector general, chief of naval research, and other offices and officials established by law or the SECNAV. The Office of the Secretary of the Navy exercises sole responsibility within DON for the following functions: acquisition, auditing, comptroller (including financial management), information management, inspector general, legislative affairs, and public affairs.

Undersecretary of the Navy (UNSECNAV)

The UNSECNAV is the deputy and principal assistant to the SECNAV. The UNSECNAV is responsible for internal audit (through the Office of the Auditor General), counterintelligence, security, law enforcement, and related investigative activities.

Assistant Secretary of the Navy (Manpower and Reserve Affairs)

This assistant SECNAV supervises manpower and reserve component affairs of DON, including policy and the administration of affairs related to military (active and inactive) and civilian personnel, and the supervision of offices and organization as assigned by the SECNAV (specifically the Naval Council of Personnel Board and the Board for Correction of Naval Records).

Assistant Secretary of the Navy (Installations and Environment) (ASN[I&E])

The ASN(I&E) is responsible to SECNAV to formulate policies and procedures for and oversee all DON functions and programs related to construction, management, maintenance, and repair of facilities; acquisition, utilization, and disposal of real property and facilities, including all planning connected therewith; environmental protection, planning, restoration, and natural resources conservation; safety (less survivability) and occupational health for both military and civilian personnel; and allocation of resources and requirements relating to the above.

Assistant Secretary of the Navy (Research, Development and Acquisition) (ASN[RD&A])

The ASN(RD&A) is responsible to serve as the DON Acquisition Executive (NAE) and represent the DON to the Under Secretary of Defense (Acquisition) and Congress on all matters related to DON acquisition policy and programs; perform as the Navy Senior Procurement Executive; establish acquisition policy and procedures and manage all DON research, development, production, shipbuilding and logistics support programs; perform as the DON Senior Information Resource Management (IRM) Policy Official and develop policy for and provide management oversight of the Navy's international RD&A efforts, competition, product integrity, logistics management, and Integrated Logistics Support (ILS), and acquisition workforce education and training.

Assistant Secretary of the Navy (Financial Management)

This is the comptroller of the Navy, responsible for all matters related to the financial management of DON, including budgeting, accounting, disbursing, financing, internal review, progress and statistical reporting, and automatic data-processing systems and equipment (except for ADPE integral to a weapons system). He or she also serves as an advisor and assistant to the CNO and CMC with respect to financial and budgetary matters.

Office of the General Counsel

The Office of the General Counsel, reporting directly to the SECNAV, provides legal advice, counsel, and guidance to that person and other civilian executive assistants. The office also provides services to the Navy and the Marine Corps relating to general legal issues, litigation, business and commercial law, real and personal property, civilian personnel law, patent law, the fiscal budget, accounting, etc.

SECNAV Staff Offices

Office of Information

This office provides services to the public such as answering inquiries, assuring a prompt and accurate flow of information to the news media, and coordinating Navy participation in community events.

Office of the Judge Advocate General (JAG)

JAG provides all legal services pertaining to functions of DON, except those areas of business and commercial law assigned to the general counsel of the Navy; supervises the administration of military justice throughout DON, and performs the functions authorized by the Uniform Code of Military Justice (UCMJ), including free legal counsel for any member of the naval service charged under the code with a serious offense; conducts investigations; provides legal assistance and advice; processes various claims for and against the Navy; reviews officer promotion and retirement proceedings for legality; and advises on admiralty matters not involving procurement.

Office of Legislative Affairs

This office arranges and coordinates the presentation of statements, testimony, briefings, and reports to members and committees of Congress by military and civilian personnel of DON; monitors and evaluates congressional actions affecting

DON; and arranges for congressional travel (an official responsibility of DON).

Office of Program Appraisal

This office reports directly to the SECNAV, giving independent appraisals of existing and proposed Navy and Marine
Corps programs. The office analyzes DON objectives, and the
validity, adequacy, feasibility, and balances of proposed programs to meet them, to help the SECNAV assess the overall
direction of DON's efforts.

Auditor General

The auditor general, under the UNSECNAV, is responsible
for internal DON audits and commands the Naval Audit Service Headquarters and field regions.

Office of the Comptroller

This office, under the assistant secretary (financial management), is responsible for the Navy's budgeting, accounting,
progress and statistical reporting, administrative organization,
and related managerial tasks. The deputy comptroller advises
the CNO and the CMC.

Office of the Chief of Naval Research (OCNR)

This office, under the assistant secretary of the Navy (resources), coordinates research programs for DON; advises on
worldwide findings and trends in research and development,
and disseminates such information to naval activities, government agencies, and private concerns; administers activities
within or on behalf of the Navy relating to patents, inventions,
royalty payments, and other matters relating to the patent and
copyright function; and executes contracts for the conduct of
research at educational and other nonprofit institutions.

Naval Inspector General (NAVINSGEN)

NAVINSGEN serves as principal advisor to the SECNAV,
CNO, and CMC on all matters relating to inspection and investigation of importance to DON, with particular emphasis on
readiness; identifies areas of inefficiency in DON and recommends improvement; and receives and investigates, or refers
for investigation, allegations of inefficiency, misconduct, im-
propriety, mismanagement, or violations of law.

Chief of Naval Operations (CNO)

In the performance of his duties within DON, the CNO takes precedence over all other officers of the naval service. As Navy representative on the JCS, the CNO keeps the SECNAV informed on JCS activities and is responsible to the president and the secretary of defense for duties external to DON as prescribed by law. The CNO commands OPNAV (Office of the Chief of Naval Operations) and other major Navy headquarters and shore commands and activities, the operating forces of the Navy, and shore activities as assigned by the SECNAV.

Office of the Chief of Naval Operations (OPNAV)

OPNAV is the headquarters of the CNO and is responsible for assisting in execution of CNO duties. OPNAV also assists the SECNAV, the UNSECNAV, and the assistant secretaries of the navy. Organizationally, OPNAV consists of the CNO, the vice chief of naval operations (VCNO), deputy chiefs of naval operations (DCNOs) and their offices, assistant chiefs of naval operations (ACNOs) and their offices, directors of staff offices (DSOs) and their offices, and special assistants. Together DCNOS, ACNOS, DSOs, and SAs comprise the principal officials of OPNAV. Principal officials execute assigned functions within their respective organizational sections. Orders issued by the principal officials in performing their duties are considered as coming from the CNO.

Vice Chief of Naval Operations (VCNO)

The VCNO is appointed by the president, by and with the advice and consent of the Senate. Orders issued by the VCNO have the same effect as those issued by the CNO, who has delegated to the VCNO complete authority to act for him or her in all matters not specifically reserved by law to the CNO alone. The principal duty of the VCNO is to act as executive for the CNO.

In the absence of the VCNO, the DCNO, navy program planning, carries out routine Navy administrative business except for administrative JCS matters, which are the responsibility of the DCNO, plans, policy, and operations.

Deputy Chiefs of Naval Operations (DCNOs)

There are five DCNOs: manpower, personnel, and training; logistics; plans, policy and operations; naval warfare; and navy program planning.

Assistant Chiefs of Naval Operations (ACNOs)

There are three ACNOs: undersea warfare, surface warfare, and air warfare.

Directors of Staff Offices (DSOs)

There are nine DSOs: assistant vice chief of naval operations; director of naval nuclear propulsion program; director of naval intelligence; director of naval medicine/surgeon general of the Navy; director of space, command, and control; director of naval reserve; oceanographer of the Navy; director of religious ministries/chief of chaplains of the Navy; and director of research and development requirements, test, and evaluation.

Special Assistants

There are seven special assistants for the following areas: public affairs support; safety matters; inspection support; legal services; legislative support; naval investigative matters and security; and material inspections and surveys.

Chief of Naval Personnel (CNP)

The CNP commands shore activities assigned by the CNO, including the Naval Military Personnel Command, the Naval Civilian Personnel Center, and the Navy Recruiting Command. The CNP directs the procurement, distribution, administration, and career development of Navy personnel and implements servicewide programs for improved human rights.

Bureau of Medicine and Surgery (BUMED)

This command directs health care services for Navy and Marine Corps personnel and other authorized persons.

Commandant of the Marine Corps

The CMC is responsible, under the SECNAV, for the administration, discipline, internal organization, training, efficiency, and readiness of the Marine Corps. As the Marine Corps representative on the JCS, the CMC keeps the SECNAV informed on JCS activities and is responsible to the president and the secretary of defense for external duties as prescribed by law. The CMC's command includes Marine Corps

headquarters, operating forces, support establishment, and reserve. The CMC is not a part of the command structure of the CNO; there is, however, close cooperation between the two.

Major Navy Commands of the Shore Establishment

The shore establishment consists of major shore commands and shore activities that have been established by the SECNAV.

A major shore command is generally charged with a Navy-wide or areawide mission and includes subordinate shore facilities to carry out its mission. For example, the Naval Telecommunications Command, a major shore command with headquarters in Washington, is responsible for the naval telecommunications system. Shore activities known as communications stations, located throughout the world, are included in this command.

Naval shore activities are formally organized installations with a prescribed mission for a specified local area. Naval shore activities include air stations, hospitals, submarine bases, amphibious bases, and shipyards and aircraft rework facilities—large, production-oriented activities employing thousands of employees. There are also many specified one-of-a-kind activities such as the Naval Academy and the Naval Observatory.

Chief of Naval Education and Training (CNET)

The CNET is in charge of the Navy's education and training programs. He or she manages the funds that pay for education, the facilities that house classrooms, and curricula. The CNET supervises all training except some aspects of fleet training and that which is BUMED's responsibility. Technical training at shore stations, at air stations, and at sea comes under the CNET's jurisdiction. Under CNET are the chief of naval air training and the chief of naval technical training.

Commander, Naval Telecommunications Command (COMNAVTELCOM)

The COMNAVTELCOM, under the CNO, commands NAVTELCOM, exercises configuration control of the naval telecommunications system, and serves as the operations and maintenance manager for the Defense Communications System.

Commander, Naval Intelligence Command (COMNAVINTCOM)

The COMNAVINTCOM, under the CNO, directs and manages the activities of NAVINTCOM to fulfill intelligence requirements and the responsibilities of DON.

Commander, Naval Space Command (COMNAVSPACECOM)

The COMNAVSPACECOM, under the CNO, is responsible for providing, operating, and maintaining naval space resources; coordinating naval use of existing space capabilities and resources; supporting space activities; coordinating approved space programs; and commanding and supporting naval space programs in support of national maritime strategy.

Commander, Naval Security Group Command (COMNAVSECGRU)

The COMNAVSECGRU, under the CNO, performs cryptologic and related activities; runs NAVSECGRU; approves requirements for the use of NAVSECGRU resources; and is responsible for the primary support of the shore activities of NAVSECGRU.

Commander, Naval Investigative Service Command (COMNISCOM)

The COMNISCOM, under the CNO, maintains, commands, and operates a worldwide organization that handles matters relating to counterintelligence, law enforcement, physical security, information and personnel security of DON (less those combat-related counterintelligence activities that are the responsibility of the Marine Corps).

Commander, Naval Oceanography Command (COMNAVOCEANCOM)

The COMNAVOCEANCOM manages oceanographic activities (oceanography, meteorology, mapping, charting, geodesy, astronomy, and chronometry) under the Naval Oceanographic Program. The COMNAVOCEANCOM provides technical guidance in such matters throughout the Department of the Navy.

Commander, Naval Legal Service Command (COMNAVLEGSVCCOM)

The COMNAVLEGSVCCOM, under the CNO, administers the Navy's legal services program and provides command direction for all legal-service activities and resources.

Commander, Naval Data Automation Command (COMNAVDAC)

The COMNAVDAC is responsible for administering and coordinating the Navy's nontactical automatic data processing (ADP) program. This responsibility includes coordinating ADP matters and ADP claimants; developing policy and procedures; approving systems development, acquisition/utilization of ADP equipment, and service contracts; sponsoring ADP technology; and training ADP personnel.

Commander, Naval Sea Systems Command (COMNAVSEASYSCOM)

The COMNAVSEASYSCOM provides material support to the Navy and Marine Corps for ships, submersibles, other sea platforms, shipboard combat systems and components, other surface and undersea warfare and weapons systems, and ordnance expendables not specifically assigned to other systems commands.

Commander, Naval Air Systems Command (COMNAVAIRSYSCOM)

627

The COMNAVAIRSYSCOM is responsible for providing for material support to the operating forces of the Navy in the areas of aeronautical weapon systems, their associated subsystems, and related systems and equipment. The COMNAVAIRSYSCOM provides similar material support to the Marine Corps, DON, DOD, Coast Guard, and other organizations as assigned. He or she also operates shore facilities and ranges for the support of these needs.

Commander, Space and Naval Warfare Systems Command (COMSPAWARSYSCOM)

The COMSPAWARSYSCOM is responsible for providing material and technical support to the Navy and Marine Corps for space systems, command, control, communications, intelligence, electronic warfare, and undersea surveillance. This person also integrates requirements among naval battle forces.

Commander, Naval Supply Systems Command (COMNAVSUPSYSCOM)

The COMNAVSUPSYSCOM is responsible for providing materials, supplies, and support services to the operating forces of the Navy and Marine Corps and for administering the security assistance program.

Commander, Naval Facilities Engineering Command
(COMNAVFACENGCOM)

The COMNAVFACENGCOM is responsible for providing
material and technical support to the Navy and Marine Corps
in the following areas: shore facilities, real property, utilities,
fixed ocean systems and structures, transportation equipment,
and energy. This person also handles the Naval Construction
Forces.

Operating Forces

The operating forces of the Navy consist of fleets, seagoing
forces, fleet marine forces, and other assigned Marine Corps
forces, the Military Sealift Command, and other forces and
activities assigned by the president or the SECNAV.

There is a dual chain of command in the operating forces—
an operational chain running from the president through the
secretary of defense, to a commander of a unified or specified
command and then to the assigned operational forces; and an
administrative chain running from the SECNAV and the CNO
to the operating forces. In some cases, as with the Military
Sealift Command, a portion of the operating forces may operate or be temporarily assigned directly under the CNO and
outside the unified chain of command.

It must be understood that the operating forces are permanently organized in the administrative chain of command,
while the operational chain of command is task oriented and
can be structured as necessary to meet operational requirements.

The CNO commands the operating forces of the Navy and is
responsible to the SECNAV for their administration and use,
including training and readiness.

The Pacific and Atlantic fleets include ships and craft classified and organized into commands by type. These commands
are training commands, surface forces, fleet marine forces,
naval air forces, and submarine forces.

The commander in chief, U.S. Pacific Fleet (CINC-
PACFLT), commands the Third and Seventh fleets; the com-
mander in chief, U.S. Atlantic Fleet (CINCLANTFLT), the
Second Fleet; and the commander-in-chief, U.S. Naval
Forces, Europe (CINCUSNAVEUR), the Sixth Fleet. The
CINCUSNAVEUR commands the naval component of the
unified command under the U.S. commander-in-chief, Europe

(CINCEUR). Ships that make up the operational (numbered) fleets are provided by type commanders. Thus, an aircraft carrier would be under the administrative command of commander, Naval Air Force, Pacific (COMNAVAIRPAC). Fleet marine forces are Navy type commands but are under the administrative control of the commandant of the Marine Corps. These forces operate under the respective commanders in chief, as do other type commands.

The Military Sealift Command (MSC), operated by the Navy for all armed services, consists of ships and commercial vessels manned by civil service personnel employed on a contract basis. These ships transport servicemen, their dependents, combat troops, and material throughout the world. MSC's prime mission is to provide immediate sealift capability in an emergency. MSC also operates the ships used for scientific projects and for various programs run by U.S. agencies.

The commander, Naval Reserve Force, commands all commissioned units of the Naval Reserve, both surface and air, and provides trained units and qualified individuals for active duty in time of war and whenever else national security requires them.

The commander, Naval Special Warfare Command, assists the commander in chief, U.S. Special Operations Command (USCINCSOC), in developing strategy, doctrine, and tactics and in preparing special-warfare forces for joint operations.

The commander, Mine Warfare Command, acts for the CNO in all matters affecting mine warfare readiness, training, tactics, and doctrine for active naval forces and corresponding Naval Reserve programs; coordinates with the fleet commander in chief, and within OPNAV, on matters affecting mine-warfare readiness; and performs the duties of technical advisor for mine warfare to CINCLANTFLT, CINCPACFLT, and CINCUSNAVEUR.

The commander, Operational Test and Evaluation Force, conducts operational tests and evaluations of specific weapon systems, ships, aircraft, and equipment, including procedures and tactics where required; and, when directed by the CNO, assists agencies in development, test, and evaluation.

The commander, U.S. Naval Forces Southern Command, supports the commander in chief, U.S. Southern Command, in naval matters.

The commander, U.S. Naval Forces Central Command, has overall command and operational control of naval forces assigned to commander in chief, U.S. Central Command; coordinates with naval forces operating in support of commander in chief, U.S. Central Command; and carries out responsibilities as commander of the naval component of the U.S. Central Command.

Task Force Organization
Developed during World War II, this divides fleets into forces, groups, units, and elements. Each subdivision has a numbered designation and an appropriate communication call sign.

Figure A–3 Task force organization chart.

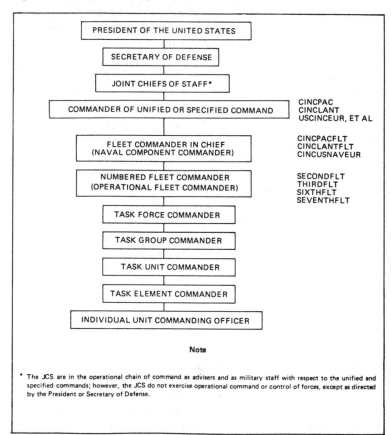

PRESIDENT OF THE UNITED STATES

SECRETARY OF DEFENSE

JOINT CHIEFS OF STAFF *

COMMANDER OF UNIFIED OR SPECIFIED COMMAND
— CINCPAC / CINCLANT / USCINCEUR, ET AL

FLEET COMMANDER IN CHIEF
(NAVAL COMPONENT COMMANDER)
— CINCPACFLT / CINCLANTFLT / CINCUSNAVEUR

NUMBERED FLEET COMMANDER
(OPERATIONAL FLEET COMMANDER)
— SECONDFLT / THIRDFLT / SIXTHFLT / SEVENTHFLT

TASK FORCE COMMANDER

TASK GROUP COMMANDER

TASK UNIT COMMANDER

TASK ELEMENT COMMANDER

INDIVIDUAL UNIT COMMANDING OFFICER

Note

* The JCS are in the operational chain of command as advisers and as military staff with respect to the unified and specified commands; however, the JCS do not exercise operational command or control of forces, except as directed by the President or Secretary of Defense.

Under the fleet numbering system, the commander Sixth
Fleet, for instance, would designate certain numbered task
forces. A task force (TF) breakdown could include a battle
force, TF 60; an amphibious force, TF 61; a service force, TF
63, etc. Within each force, there could be further subdivisions
called task groups (TGs). For example, within TF 60 there
might be a carrier group, TG 60.1, and a heavy support group,
TG 60.2.

Task groups may be further subdivided into task units
(TUs). For example, TG 60.1—the carrier group—may have a
carrier unit designated TU 60.1.1. A destroyer screen considered to be part of that unit would be a task element; its new
designation would be TE 60.1.11. Another element, perhaps an
advanced screen, would be designated TE 60.1.12. And so on.

With this system, the task force is adaptable to any change in
size.

Shore Activities

This section concerns those shore activities that have the
primary function of supplying, maintaining, and supporting operating forces with material, services, and personnel. Shore
activities are established by the SECNAV, who gives them a
prescribed mission.

A typical list of such activities might include naval bases, air
facilities and stations, reserve training units, ammunition depots, communication stations, fleet intelligence centers, fuel
depots, naval hospitals, laboratories, medical centers, recruiting stations, shipyards, supply centers, and schools.

Many shore activities are located at strategic points along
the American coasts and overseas where they can most directly serve the needs of the operating forces. Activities for
which such proximity is not essential or practical, however,
are distributed at various points within the United States.
These activities include finance offices, recruiting stations, research and development labs, and training centers.

Regional Coordination

Designated area coordinators and their subordinate regional
coordinators are responsible to the CNO for coordinating
shore activities. Although coordinators have no authority over
the internal affairs of specific field activities, they must see that
there is ready support for the fleet within their areas.

Regional coordinators may delegate some of their responsibilities to local coordinators (commands and activities within their jurisdiction).

Naval Bases

A naval base includes all shore activities located in a given locality. Its primary purpose is to coordinate support services provided to the fleet by naval activities close to one another. The base commander has jurisdiction over such activities (including, in some cases, naval stations and naval air stations) as directed by the CNO or the fleet commanders in chief. The base commander is generally under the command of the appropriate fleet commander in chief.

Regular Navy

The United States Navy consists of the Regular Navy and the Naval Reserve. Each has its own important function, and each must work closely with the other branches of the military. The Regular Navy consists of officers, either in the line or in a staff corps, and enlisted men and women. The Navy's FY 89 budget covered approximately 593,200 active officers and enlisted personnel.

Line and Staff Corps: The sleeve and shoulder insignia of various ranks are shown on pp. 53–54. All officers serve either in the regular line or in a special staff corps, according to their specialties. An officer wears the device of his or her specialty on the sleeve above the stripes, or on shoulderboards or collar, depending on the uniform worn. Line officers exercise military command; only line officers command at sea, and in general, only line officers exercise command on shore. Members of certain staff corps, such as the Medical, Supply, and Civil Engineer Corps, command shore activities and units and come under the control of their respective bureaus.

Medical Corps (MC): Commissioned doctors provide medical services and administer hospitals, dispensaries, sick bays, and other medical units in the Navy.

Dental Corps (DC): Commissioned dentists provide dental services and run dispensaries on board larger ships. The Dental Corps, like the Medical Corps, Nurse Corps, and Medical Service Corps, comes under the Bureau of Medicine and Surgery.

Medical Service Corps (MSC): This corps has specialists in optometry, pharmacy, bacteriology, biochemistry, psychology, sanitation engineering, and medical statistics.

Nurse Corps (NC): Navy nurses are commissioned officers in the grades of ensign through admiral. They serve in a variety of settings, ranging from teaching hospitals to the relatively basic fleet hospitals, and in a variety of jobs, from recruiting assignments to the surgeon general's staff.

Supply Corps (SC): This is the business branch of the Navy; it receives and disburses funds for supply and pay, subsistence, and transportation.

Chaplain Corps (CHC): Officers of the Chaplain Corps are ordained ministers of various denominations; they conduct religious services and promote the spiritual and moral welfare of the Navy and Marine Corps.

Civil Engineer Corps (CEC): This corps is composed of graduate civil engineers, who are normally restricted to shore duty. The CEC supervises the buildings, grounds, and plants as well as all construction of shore stations.

Judge Advocate General's Corps (JAG): Established in 1967, this staff corps is composed of lawyers certified to practice in the Navy.

Warrant Officers

Commissioned warrant officers, who have advanced through the enlisted ranks in various technical specialties, probably have the most detailed practical knowledge of the modern Navy. For the various warrant specialties, see p. 55.

Women in the Navy

Women served in the Navy Nurse Corps as early as 1908 and as enlisted yeomen in World War I, but they did not have military rank and were generally discharged after a conflict was over. They were not formally authorized until 1942, when President Roosevelt signed legislation permitting the enlistment and commissioning of women in the U.S. Naval Reserve. In 1948, the Women's Armed Services Integration Act was passed allowing the enlistment and appointment of women in the Regular Navy as well as in the Naval Reserve. Women have served on active duty continuously since then.

Today, men and women are recruited, trained, and assigned according to the needs of the Navy. While women perform the full range of available assignments, they are prohibited by law from permanent assignment to ships or squadrons that might be engaged in combat missions. Women are assigned to non-

Figure A–4   Women began serving in the Navy in 1942. Today, there are more than 54,000 women serving in a variety of roles. Women serve in 84 of the 102 enlisted ratings and in all but two officer communities, submarine and special warfare.

combatant units and, temporarily, to combatants not on combat missions.

After receiving basic training at the Recruit Training Command in Orlando, Florida, enlisted women specialize in some of the Navy's most technical ratings. Women serve in 84 of the 102 enlisted ratings. Women officers are commissioned through Officer Candidate School, Aviation Officer Candidate School, the Naval Reserve Officer Training Corps, and the Naval Academy. They serve in all officer communities (line and staff) except submarine and special warfare. They also attend senior-service schools and war colleges. In each training program, women study the same subjects and must meet the same academic and military standards as men.

Women have attained the ranks of rear admiral and master chief and are now serving in many demanding positions of responsibility. Women officers have distinguished themselves as lawyers, chaplains, and civil engineers, to name only a few specialties. They command ships and major shore commands as well as remote naval facilities. They are also qualified as surface-warfare officers and naval aviators. Enlisted women have gained resounding approval for their performance in deck forces, intelligence facilities, plane crews, and many other Navy jobs.

Women have earned an excellent reputation as vital members of the Navy Medical Department. Women officers serving in the Nurse Corps, Medical Corps, Medical Service Corps, and Dental Corps provide health care for Navy and Marine Corps personnel the world over. In the hospital corpsman and dental technician ratings, enlisted women provide essential health care ashore and at sea.

At the end of Fiscal Year 1988, women officers totaled 10 percent of officer strength, and enlisted women totaled 9 percent of enlisted strength.

Naval Reserve

The mission of the Naval Reserve, like that of the other reserve components of the armed services, is to provide trained units and qualified individuals for active duty in time of war or national emergency and at other times required by national security.

Since its creation in 1915, the Naval Reserve has been a trained manpower source capable of rapidly augmenting active Navy forces to fill the gap between peacetime capability and wartime requirements. As part of the Navy's total force, the Naval Reserve—in addition to its wartime mobilization mission—is shouldering a greater share of day-to-day peacetime responsibilities. The integration of active and reserve forces ensures that Navy assets are fully utilized.

Its people are the Naval Reserve's most important asset. There are about 420,000 reservists, officer and enlisted. About 233,000 are ready reservists on active duty or on call to active-duty in time of war or national emergency, or when otherwise authorized by law. Another 176,500 are retired reservists, and some 11,000 are standby reservists.

Ready Reserve

The 233,000 members of the Ready Reserve belong to one of three branches: the Selected Reserve, the Training and Administration of Reserves, and the Individual Ready Reserve.

Selected Reserve (SELRES): Selected reservists are the core of the Naval Reserve program, the "active" inactive sailors and officers. They are subject to involuntary recall for war or

Figure A–5   The mission of the Naval Reserve is to be prepared for active duty in the event of war or other national emergency. Here reserves receive firefighting training aboard the USS *Buttercup*, a mock ship at the Naval Reserve Damage Control Training Center, Philadelphia.

**Naval
Reserve**

national emergency, or by the president for up to ninety days to support operational requirements without the declaration of a national emergency. Most selected reservists are Navy veterans who continue their affiliation with the service while at the same time pursuing civilian careers. There are currently almost 130,000 selected reservists, and that number is projected to grow to approximately 137,000 in the early 1990s. Each year these men and women perform inactive-duty train-

ing, typically forty-eight drills, and receive two weeks of training in a pay status.

Training and Administration of Reserves (TARs): Approximately 22,000 TARs serve on full-time active duty in support
of the Naval Reserve. These include approximately 2,300 officers, 1,300 enlisted recruiters, and 18,400 enlisted personnel.
TARs receive full active-duty pay and allowances and the
same benefits as regular Navy personnel. TARs enlist in the
TAR program or convert from Regular Navy or SELRES status. TARs serve in Naval Reserve ships and air squadrons and
join other Naval Reserve activities as well as Regular Navy
commands. Ratings within the TAR program include AC, AD,
AE, AG, AK, AME, AMH, AMS, AO, AQ, ASE, ASM, AX,
AT, AW, AZ, BM, DC, DK, DP, EM, EN, ET, HM, HT, IC,
JO, MR, MS, NC, PH, PN, PR, RM, SK, and YN.

Individual Ready Reserve (IRR): The IRR has approximately 85,000 people, also subject to involuntary recall for war
or national emergency. Members are not required to train,
though many do. Some even train without pay in volunteer
training units established at most surface and air reserve
activities.

To perform its assigned mission most effectively, the Naval
Reserve is structured to significantly increase the Navy's combat capability upon mobilization. This structure is based on the
following SELRES units:

Commissioned units: Composed of ships, aircraft squadrons, or construction battalions, these are complete operational units delivered to an operating force.

Reinforcing units: These augment Regular Navy commissioned units and operating staffs (and some Marine Corps combat commands) with trained personnel so that combat forces
can operate at the highest level of readiness for an indefinite
period of time.

Sustaining units: These reinforce fleet and force support activities with trained personnel to provide a surge capability.

To prepare them for mobilization, the Naval Reserve "horizontally integrates" reservists, providing them with the same
equipment, particularly ships and aircraft, that the active force
uses.

With the addition of six frigates by the end of Fiscal Year 90,
the Naval Reserve is programmed to have fifty-five commis-

sioned ships. The reserve force includes 57 percent of the Navy's special boat units, 100 percent of its mobile-inshore undersea-warfare capability, and nearly 85 percent of its minesweeping force. Fourteen of the Navy's twenty-three fleet hospitals will be staffed by more than 10,000 selected reservists.

The Naval Air Reserve includes fifty-two reserve squadrons with approximately 400 aircraft, including F/A 18 Hornets, F-14 Tomcats, E-2C Hawkeyes, and P-3C Orions. With the introduction of the HH-60H helicopter, the reserve's light-attack and combat-search-and-rescue helicopter squadrons will be consolidated, forming the Navy's only special support squadrons. The Naval Air Reserve modernization program is proceeding on schedule.

Mutual Support

An increasingly important byproduct of Naval Reserve training is the direct support provided to active-duty units of the Navy. The phrase "mutual support" describes Naval Reserve training that also directly assists active-duty units in the performance of their peacetime mission. This mutual support encompasses almost all mission areas.

Mutual support is a preferred method of training, since tasks performed during peacetime are the same as those expected at the outbreak of hostilities.

Training

The primary peacetime task of the Naval Reserve is training to maintain mobilization readiness. Providing reservists for mobilization who are not just trainable, but trained, is the object of the SELRES program.

Many of the hardware-equipped units (ships, squadrons, etc.) of the Naval Reserve have training programs with from four to seventy-two additional paid drills, depending on the criteria established for individual and unit readiness and mobilization requirements.

To train naval reservists, particularly those who live beyond a reasonable commuting distance from their mobilization sites, the Navy has introduced new equipment. At centralized drill locations, the Naval Reserve has established shipboard simulators (SBSs) in essential underway watch stations common to most Navy ships. The SBS consists of seven modules (bridge, combat information center, communications, damage-control central, engineering, damage-control trainer, and problem-generating room). Each module can be used separately or in concert with others, depending on the degree of individual or integrated training required.

The Naval Reserve is enhancing SBS sites with computer-based instructional material such as Navy tactical data system (NTDS) trainers, tactical situations (TACSITS), and Navy tactical gaming (NAVTAG) systems. At the same time, the damage-control trainer (DCT) program will continue to imitate the shipboard environment and allow reservists to practice damage control and firefighting skills.

Annual training (AT), Naval Reserve weekend training, and inactive-duty training travel at mobilization sites provide reserve units with the latest fleet equipment so that they can familiarize themselves with the work they would actually perform in the event of mobilization. An important benefit of this type of training is that the individual reservist is qualified and ready to perform at the time of mobilization.

Today's Navy plays an increasingly important role in strengthening national defense and supporting U.S. foreign policy. Today's Naval Reserve is an integral part of the total-force Navy, essential to the accomplishment of its mission. No longer just a force in reserve, the Naval Reserve provides people and equipment to support the Navy both in peacetime and at times of mobilization.

Naval Reserve Organization

The responsibility for the organization, administration, training, and equipping of the Naval Reserve rests with the CNO. The Naval Reserve force structure that supports the CNO is headed by a rear admiral who holds the positions of director, Naval Reserve (DIRNAVRES), and commander, Naval Reserve Force (COMNAVRESFOR), as well as the title of chief of the Naval Reserve (CNAVRES).

The DIRNAVRES, domiciled in Washington, is the principal advisor to the CNO on all Naval Reserve matters. The functions of DIRNAVRES include the following:

—Acting as the principal advisor to the CNO on all Naval Reserve matters;

—Exercising policy, direction, and control of the Naval Reserve for the CNO;

—Establishing plans, programs, procedures, and standards for the Naval Reserve; and

—Providing budgetary support for the Naval Reserve command, its activities, and its programs.

COMNAVRESFOR, headquartered in New Orleans, is responsible for the administration and management of Naval Reserve programs in accordance with policies prescribed by the CNO, for the management of assigned reserves, and for supervising Naval Reserve activities.

There are three subordinate commands in New Orleans to help carry out this mission: commander, Naval Surface Reserve Force (COMNAVSURFRESFOR), and commander, Naval Air Reserve Force (COMNAVAIRESFOR)—both headed by TAR flag officers—and commander, Naval Reserve Recruiting Command (COMNAVRESCRUITCOM), headed by a TAR captain. The senior of the two flag officers also serves as deputy commander, Naval Reserve Force.

United States Marine Corps

The Marine Corps was founded on 10 November 1775 when the Second Continental Congress passed a resolution authorizing the formation of two battalions of fighting patriots.

Continental marines initially enlisted for duty aboard naval vessels. Then in 1834, separate companies and detachments of marines were formed for service on land. The ground component served under Army command, giving the Marine Corps the unique status of an independent armed service available for assignment in support of both the Navy and the Army.

The evolution of the Marine Corps into an amphibious force began around 1900, a direct result of the Navy's conversion from sailing to steam-powered ships. A steamship's range was limited by the amount of coal it could carry, and the need for a worldwide network of refueling stations became critical. Since the Navy could not build, operate, and defend refueling stations in every part of the world, it had to be prepared to seize and defend advanced bases as required. The task of seizing and defending these bases fell on ships' landing parties, which comprised sailors and marines.

The demand on sailors to operate steamships soon created the requirement for a special organization for landing operations. Because of its naval affiliation, the Marine Corps was the logical choice as the Navy's amphibious arm. Today, the Marine Corps is a separate service under the Department of the Navy.

Figure A–6 A marine aircrewman, manning an M134 7.62-mm minigun aboard a UH-1H Iroquois helicopter stands watch over an RH-53D Sea Stallion on mine-countermeasure patrol in the Persian Gulf.

The current strength of the Corps is approximately 200,000 officers and enlisted personnel. The Corps consists of two fleet marine forces, one in the Atlantic, the other in the Pacific.

The Marine Corps' primary mission is to provide the U.S. Navy with landing forces for amphibious operations. The United States is a maritime nation with worldwide interests; the Corps supports its global national strategy. During peacetime, marines serve as essential elements of U.S. deterrence and project U.S. influence abroad.

The marine philosophy stresses three fundamentals: combat readiness, versatility, and the air-ground team. Combat readiness is a top priority and the cornerstone of the Corps' existence as a fighting organization. Versatility refers to the marines' method of tailoring air-ground teams in size, structure, and striking power to meet specific contingencies worldwide. The air-ground team is a concept pioneered by the Marine Corps. Marine air power does not supplement marine ground

combat elements; rather, the air-ground team is a fully integrated component.

The ability to project sea power ashore is an essential element of a maritime strategy, and the ability to execute an amphibious assault is an integral part of power projection. The
Marine Corps is charged expressly with these tasks.

Marine training exercises emphasize combat readiness, air-
ground coordination, and rapid deployment of forces. Training
takes place in mountain, desert, and coastal areas of the
United States, as well as in Asia, Europe, the Mediterranean,
Africa, and the Indian Ocean. It enables marines to maintain
combat proficiency and to operate with members of other U.S.
services and allies abroad.

To keep its forces at authorized levels, the Corps must recruit and train more than 37,000 new marines each year. Enlisted marines undergo nearly ten and a half weeks of training
at one of the Corps' two recruit-training depots, Parris Island,
South Carolina, or San Diego, California. Women recruits are
trained solely at Parris Island. Officer training is given at the
Marine Corps Combat Development Command (MCCDC) in
Quantico, Virginia. The Officer Candidate School at Quantico
evaluates and screens some 2,500 candidates each year, approximately 2,000 of whom are eventually commissioned.
Newly commissioned officers subsequently complete the 23-
week basic officer training program at MCCDC.

The presence of women in the Regular Marine Corps was
authorized by the Women's Armed Services Integration Act of
1948. Training closely parallels that of male officer candidates,
except that women are not assigned to combat specialties.

An organization unique to the Corps is the Marine Security
Guard (MSG) Battalion. Small, select, specially trained groups
of marines guard posts at American embassies, consulates, and
legations around the world. The MSGs, about 1,400 strong, are
responsible for safeguarding classified material as well as protecting embassy personnel and property. Their duties are de-
fensive, the overall protection of foreign-service missions being the responsibility of the host government.

Marine detachments also serve aboard vessels of the U.S.
Navy, including aircraft carriers, guided-missile cruisers, battleships, fleet flagships, and submarine tenders. These marines
are primarily responsible for protecting the ship's special
weapons and guarding the security-sensitive areas of the ship.
They also perform ceremonial functions and carry out duties
such as damage control.

The Marine Corps Reserve maintains the same high standards of performance and readiness as the Regular Marine Corps. The reserve augments and reinforces the active forces with well-trained units and highly qualified individuals. The strength of the Selected Marine Corps Reserve is about 43,000. The reserve division-wing team consists of the Fourth Marine Division (reinforced) and the Fourth Marine Aircraft Wing, headquartered in New Orleans and supported by the Fourth Force Service Support Group in Atlanta. Units of these commands are located throughout the country.

United States Coast Guard

The Coast Guard is another military service. It operates under the jurisdiction of the Department of Transportation; upon declaration of war or when the president directs, it operates within DON. Coast Guard personnel receive the same pay and benefits as DOD personnel and are subject to the Uniform Code of Military Justice.

The Coast Guard mission encompasses a variety of responsibilities. Primary among them is search and rescue, the saving of lives and property. In a typical year, the Coast Guard receives 80,000 calls for assistance, saves more than 5,000 lives, assists over 140,000 persons, and salvages over $2 billion worth of property.

The Coast Guard operates search-and-rescue stations along America's coasts and inland waters, and stands ready 24 hours a day to dispatch rescue vessels to answer distress calls. It has twenty-seven air stations that assist in searches when rescue by vessel is impossible or speed is essential. A network of rescue coordination centers handles the vital communications necessary to integrate the work of these units.

The Coast Guard operates Automated Mutual-Assistance Vessel Rescue (AMVER), an international program of volunteer merchant vessels that provides the location of participating vessels to any vessel needing help at sea.

The Coast Guard participates in the International Ice Patrol, begun in 1913. Each year, with other nations, it patrols a 45,000-square-mile area in the North Atlantic tracking icebergs.

As the nation's seagoing police force, the Coast Guard is the principal federal agency responsible for enforcing maritime laws and marine safety. Laws cover customs and immigration, fishing, international treaties, the marine environment, and even the protection of endangered marine mammals. To do this job, the Coast Guard uses a fleet of vessels ranging from small utility boats to highly sophisticated 210-, 270- and 378-foot cutters, as well as helicopters and fixed-wing aircraft. When there is an oil or chemical spill, the Coast Guard deploys highly mobile "strike teams" of experts.

The Coast Guard is also responsible for recreational boating safety. It carries out a program that includes research in and development of safer boating practices and equipment, coordination and enforcement of industrial and water safety standards, cooperation with state boating authorities, and education of the boating public.

The Coast Guard maintains a volunteer auxiliary some 40,000 strong. Auxiliarists are trained in boat handling, sailing, rules of the road, marlinespike seamanship, weather, radiotelephone, search and rescue, navigation, meteorology, marine engines, and aids to navigation.

Keeping the nation's 40,000 miles of waterways safe for navigation is another Coast Guard responsibility. It maintains some 45,000 aids to navigation, from small buoys to large, sophisticated navigational buoys; offshore towers; 400 lighthouses (nearly all automated); and more than 13,000 minor lights. It also maintains and operates Loran-C and Omega long-range radio-navigation stations around the world.

The Coast Guard is also tasked with the safety of the nation's merchant marine fleet and ports. From design and construction to eventual scrapping, U.S. flag merchant vessels are under Coast Guard regulation. The Coast Guard approves new vessel designs and examines shipbuilders, prescribes a wide variety of safety and lifesaving equipment, licenses those who sail merchant ships, and investigates serious ship accidents. Each year, through its marine safety and captain-of-the-port offices, the Coast Guard checks out an average of 85,000 shore facilities, boards and inspects more than 54,000 vessels, and supervises some 2,000 dangerous-cargo loadings.

Since its beginning in 1790 as the Revenue Marine, the Coast Guard has played a part in every national conflict. It participates in many DOD activities and in Navy fleet and interservice exercises. The Coast Guard is also involved in NASA launches, the resupply of U.S. stations in Antarctica, the National Narcotics Border interdiction system, and the Navy's maritime defense zone planning and operations in defense of coastal waters, ports, and harbors.

There are nearly 40,000 active-duty men and women on the Coast Guard's roster and some 12,500 selected reservists.

The Coast Guard trains its personnel in naval, aeronautical, and other ratings. It also operates its own academy at New London, Connecticut. Appointments are made on the basis of yearly competitive examinations open to all civilian and enlisted persons ages seventeen to twenty-one. Graduates receive bachelor of science degrees and commissions as ensigns in the Coast Guard.

Coast
Guard

Navy History   **B**

Why History?

History can be dry and dull. But a glance at the history of an organization can give us a good idea of what that organization is, and what it has done. Knowing that, we can more easily figure out our place in it. History can show us where mistakes were made before. If enough of us are aware of those mistakes, we can avoid making them again.

What follows is a bare-bones record of the accomplishments and failures of the U.S. Navy, to help you find out more about this organization to which you now belong. Remember, today is tomorrow's history. You are helping to make it.

The Earliest Years

America was born of the sea. The people who made this nation came from over the sea, and they were sustained by goods exchanged by the shipload. Trade went on for 150 years before the desire to be master of their own destiny led the colonists to strike for independence. The first efforts at sea power were often feeble and fruitless, and yet they had their impact on the course of events. And at the critical juncture, it was the timely actions of the French Navy that resulted in the isolation of British General Cornwallis and his subsequent surrender.

12 Jun 1775	First engagement at sea during the Revolution. Citizens of Machias, Maine, under the command of Jeremiah O'Brien, seized a cargo sloop and with her captured the cutter HMS *Margaretta*. (TB 30 and DDs 51, 415, and 725 were named *O'Brien*.)

| 6 Sep 1775 | The schooner *Hannah* sailed as the first unit of a number of armed fishing vessels sent to sea by the Continental Army to intercept British supply ships during the siege of Boston. |

13 Oct 1775   The Continental Congress authorized the outfitting of a 10-gun warship "for intercepting such transports as may be laden with stores for the enemy"—the start of the Continental Navy. The same act established the Marine Committee, though Congress directed its naval efforts.

3 Dec 1775   The first man-of-war of the Continental Navy, the *Alfred,* was commissioned at Philadelphia. Her "first lieutenant" (XO) was Lieutenant John Paul Jones.

3–4 Mar 1776   A Continental squadron under the command of Commodore Esek Hopkins, composed of the *Alfred* (24 guns), *Columbus* (20), *Andrea Doria* (14), *Cabot* (14), *Providence* (12), *Hornet* (10), *Wasp* (8), and *Fly* (8), successfully attacked the British at Nassau in the Bahamas. (Sailing men-of-war were rated by the number of broadside guns they mounted.) Captured were seventy-one cannon and fifteen mortars. This was also the first amphibious assault by American marines, under the command of Captain Samuel Nicholas. (DDs 311 and 449 were named for him.)

4 Apr 1776   The brig *Lexington* (16), under John Barry, defeated HMS *Edward* (8) in lower Delaware Bay. This was the earliest of Barry's successes. (DDs 2, 248, and 933 were named for him.)

7 Sep 1776   Sergeant Ezra Lee of the Continental Army made the first "submarine" attack on a warship, an unsuccessful attempt to attach a powder charge to the hull of an anchored British ship from the submersible *Turtle*, designed by David Bushnell. Submarine tenders AS 2 and AS 15 were named for Bushnell. (The deep-submergence craft DSV 3 is named *Turtle*.)

11 Oct 1776	A Continental Army squadron of gunboats under Colonel Benedict Arnold fought a British force on Lake Champlain in the Battle of Valcour Island. This caused the British to delay the invasion of the Hudson River Valley for a year, by which time the Continental Army defeated it.	Navy History
15 Nov 1776	Continental Congress set pay rates for officers and men. Petty officer rates were prescribed, though these were not divided into classes until 1885.	
16 Nov 1776	The U.S. flag was saluted for the first time by the Dutch governor of St. Eustatius Island in the West Indies.	
24 Apr 1778	John Paul Jones, in command of the sloop *Ranger*, defeated the sloop HMS *Drake* off Belfast, Ireland. The *Drake* became the first major British warship to be taken by the new Navy.	
4 May 1780	An insignia, adopted by the Board of Admiralty, set up by the Continental Congress to direct naval operations, became the Navy's first official seal.	**649**
23 Sep 1780	John Paul Jones, now commanding the converted merchantman *Bon Homme Richard* (42), defeated the frigate HMS *Serapis* (50) in a night fight off Flamborough Head, England. His ship badly battered (she would sink after the fight), Jones rejected the British surrender question with his defiant, "I have not yet begun to fight!" (DDs 10 and 230 and DDG 32 were named in honor of Jones, and DDs 4, 290, and 353, and CG 19 in honor of his gallant first lieutenant, Richard Dale.)	
5 Sep 1781	The French fleet, under Admiral Comte de Grasse, blockaded Hampton Roads to keep reinforcements from General Cornwallis's British Army at Yorktown, Virginia, under seige by General George Washington's Continental troops and by French forces under General Rochambeau. The *Comte de Grasse* (DD 974) honors this ally.	
17 Oct 1781	General Cornwallis surrendered at York-	Earliest Years

19 Apr 1783	town, thus ending the Revolutionary War. George Washington proclaimed the Revolution officially ended.
2 Aug 1785	The frigate *Alliance,* last survivor of the Continental Navy, sold out of service.

Rebirth and the Second War of Independence

The United States did without a Navy, even without the authorization for one, for nine years. It had been hoped that the world would leave the new country alone. But that was not to be. Barbary pirate states on Africa's north coast captured defenseless American ships, demanding ransom. When the United States finally began reacting to that problem, war broke out between France and Great Britain and U.S. neutral shipping (the United States had one of the largest merchant fleets in the world then) became a target for both sides.

America's miniscule new Navy, whose first units were launched in 1797, first settled the French problem, then that of the Barbary pirates, and finally fought the British. When the last war was over, the United States became a major sea power.

6 Jan 1791	A Senate committee reported that U.S. trade in the Mediterranean was impossible to protect without a naval force.
27 Mar 1794	President Washington signed into law "an act to provide a naval armament," which provided for the building of six frigates: the *Constitution, United States, Constellation, Congress, Chesapeake,* and *President.* The captains were to be paid $75 a month, ordinary seamen, $10. Rations were valued at 28 cents a day.
May–Oct 1797	The frigates *United States, Constellation,* and *Constitution* were launched.
30 Apr 1798	The Navy Department was established. Up to then, the secretary of war, a distant predecessor of today's secretary of defense, had directed both the Army and Navy.
May 1798	The converted merchantman *Ganges,* first warship to fit out and go to sea under the new federal constitution, put to sea to protect shipping off the U.S. east coast.

18 Jun 1798	Benjamin Stoddert, first secretary of the Navy, took office. His salary was $3,000 a year. The first actions in the undeclared quasi-war with France occurred in June. (DD 302 and DDG 22 were named Stoddert.)	Navy History
9 Feb 1799	The *Constellation* (38), under Thomas Truxtun, defeated the French frigate *Insurgente* (36) in 30 minutes. The Frenchmen had 100 casualties, the Americans 4.	
1 Feb 1800	The *Constellation,* still under Truxtun, battered the French ship *Vengeance* (52 guns) for 5 hours, but nightfall and damage to the American vessel allowed the Frenchman to get away. Midshipman James C. Jarvis was lost when the *Constellation*'s mainmast went by the board. (DDs 14 and 229 and CGN 35 were named for Truxton, DDs 38, 393, and 799 for Jarvis.)	
7 Feb 1800	The 32-gun frigate *Essex* became the first U.S. man-of-war to cross the equator.	
31 Oct 1803	The frigate *Philadelphia* (36), under Captain William Bainbridge, ran aground on a reef off Tripoli (Libya) while pursuing Barbary pirate craft; he was captured. The American crew spent twenty months in a Tripolitan prison before being freed.	651
14 Feb 1804	Lieutenant Stephen Decatur, with eighty-three volunteers from the frigate *Constitution* and the schooner *Enterprise*, entered Tripoli harbor at night in the ketch *Intrepid* and destroyed the *Philadelphia* without a single loss. English Admiral Lord Nelson termed it "the most daring act of the age." (DDs 5 and 341 and DDG 31 have been named for Decatur.)	
3 Aug 1804	Commodore Edward Preble in the *Constitution* led the U.S. Mediterranean Squadron in the first of a series of attacks against Tripoli that ultimately ended the Barbary wars and freed Bainbridge and other Americans. The peace treaty was signed 5 June 1805. (DDs 12 and 345 and DDG 46 were named Preble.)	Second War

16 May 1811	In the mistaken belief he was attacking the frigate HMS *Guerriere* (38), which had been conducting some high-handed operations off the American east coast, Captain John Rodgers in the *President* (44) blasted the sloop HMS *Little Belt* (22) in a night encounter begun by the smaller ship. (TB 4 and DDs 254 and 574 remembered him.)
18 Jun 1812	President Madison declared war on Great Britain over "free trade and sailors' rights." The U.S. Navy then had but 17 warships; the British, over 600.
16–18 Jun 1812	The *Constitution,* under Captain Issac Hull, escaped a 5-ship British squadron in a classic 69-hour chase.
3 Aug 1812	The *Essex,* under David Porter, captured HMS *Albert* (16) after one broadside.
19 Aug 1812	Isaac Hull and the *Constitution* defeated the frigate HMS *Guerriere* in a 35-minute slugfest that left the Britisher a hulk. This was the first time an American frigate had defeated a British frigate, and it greatly cheered the nation. As a result of the battle, the *Constitution* received her famous nickname Old Ironsides. (Hull has been remembered by DDs 7, 330, 350, and 945.)
18 Oct 1812	Jacob Jones, commanding the sloop *Wasp* (18), smashed the brig HMS *Frolic* (22) off the Chesapeake Capes. (Jacob Jones was honored by DDs 61 and 130 and DE 130.)
25 Oct 1812	The frigate *United States,* sister ship of the *Constitution,* with Stephen Decatur in command, defeated the frigate HMS *Macedonian* (38) in a 2-hour combat that left over 100 British casualties to 12 American. Taken into the U.S. Navy, the USS *Macedonian* served until 1828.
29 Dec 1812	The *Constitution,* now commanded by William Bainbridge, left HMS *Java* (38) a shambles in a hard two and a half hour fight off Brazil. With this third loss in three frigate-to-frigate actions in five months, the Royal Navy received orders not to take on

	such American 44s as the *Constitution* and the *United States* with less than squadron strength. (Bainbridge has been remembered in DDs 1 and 246 and CGN 25.)
14 Feb 1813	The *Essex* became the first U.S. man-of-war to round Cape Horn and enter the Pacific Ocean.
24 Feb 1813	The sloop *Hornet* (18), under James Lawrence, ruined the brig HMS *Peacock* (2) in two broadsides off Guyana.
30 Mar 1813	Lieutenant John M. Gamble, USMC, took command of the *Greenwich* (10). He was the only marine ever to command a Navy ship.
1 Jun 1813	Rashly responding to a British captain's challenge, newly promoted Captain Lawrence, now commanding the frigate *Chesapeake* (36) and a green crew, was defeated and killed off Boston in a fight with HMS *Shannon* (38), a frigate. Lawrence's dying words "Don't give up the ship!" have lived on as one of the slogans of the U.S. Navy. (Lawrence was memorialized in TB 8, DD 250, and DDG 4.)
13 Aug 1813	The brig *Argus* (20), under William Allen, was captured by the brig HMS *Pelican* (20) in the Irish Sea after her raiding operations had taken 20 British merchantmen. (DD 66 was later named the *Allen*.)
5 Sep 1813	In a bloody engagement, William Burrows's brig the *Enterprise* (14) overcame HMS *Boxer* (14), a brig, off the coast of Maine. Both captains were killed, and they were buried side by side in Portland, Maine. (DD 29 and DE 105 honored Burrows.)
10 Sep 1813	The Battle of Lake Erie. Oliver Hazard Perry, commanding an American squadron of nine ships, defeated a British six-ship squadron to ensure U.S. control of the Great Lakes and the Northwest Territory. Perry carried Lawrence's dying command "Don't give up the ship" on his battle flag,

and the opening phrase of his victory report is still remembered today: "We have met the enemy, and they are ours. . ." (Perry's name has been carried by DDSs 11, 340, and 844, and FFG 7.)

28 Mar 1814   After cruising Pacific waters in a highly successful operation against British whalers, the *Essex*, still under Porter, was trapped and defeated at Valparaiso, Chile, by the frigate HMS *Phoebe* (36) and the sloop HMS *Cherub* (18). (David Porter has been remembered by TB 6 and DDs 59, 356, and 800.)

29 Apr 1814   The new American sloop *Peacock* (22), named after the British unit defeated by the *Hornet* the previous year, defeated the brig HMS *Epervier* (18) off the Florida coast. The Britisher was found to be carrying $25,000 in gold bullion! (Lewis Warrington, the *Peacock*'s captain, was memorialized in DDs 30, 383, and 843.)

22 Jun 1814   The *Independence* (74), first ship of the line in the U.S. Navy, was launched. She served in one capacity or another until 1912.

28 Jun 1814   The second *Wasp* of the War of 1812, a 22-gun sloop commanded by Johnston R. Y. Blakeley, bested the brig HMS *Reindeer* (22) in just 19 minutes in the English Channel. (TB 27, DD 150, and DE 140 have been named for Blakeley.)

24 Aug 1814   British invaders burn Washington, D.C. Sailors and marines under Captain Joshua Barney formed part of the American force defeated at Bladensburg, Maryland, just outside Washington, and fought a stubborn delaying action. (TB 25 and DD 149 bore his name.)

11 Sep 1814   Battle of Lake Champlain. A bloody engagement between Commodore Thomas MacDonough's 16-ship squadron and a British one of like number ended in defeat

for the invaders (this is reminiscent of the Battle of Valcour Island during the Revolution, 11 Oct 1776). (MacDonough has been honored by DDs 9, 331, and 351 and DDG 39.)

16 Sep 1814 — A Navy force, with marines and Army troops, destroys Jean Lafitte's pirate base at Barataria, near New Orleans.

23 Oct 1814 — A "floating steam battery" designed by Robert Fulton was launched for the Navy, which referred to her as the *Fulton* or *Fulton's Steam Battery*. Carrying her paddlewheel between twin catamaran hulls, she had 20 guns and made 5 knots. Never actively used, the *Fulton* was demolished by explosion and fire in 1829.

24 Dec 1814 — The Treaty of Ghent formally ended the War of 1812. Communications were poor in that day, and all the following events occurred because one or both sides failed to receive information.

8 Jan 1815 — The Battle of New Orleans. General Andrew Jackson and an army made up largely of militia defeated a British regular-army invasion force. Jackson's defenses had time to organize because a Navy gunboat force under Commodore Daniel T. Patterson and Lieutenant Thomas C. Jones had fought a successful delaying action at Lake Borgne. (Patterson's name has been carried by DDs 36 and 392 and FF 1061.)

15 Jan 1815 — The frigate *President* (44) was run down and captured by a 4-ship British squadron.

7 Feb 1815 — The Board of Naval Commissioners was established to oversee the maintenance and operation of the Navy under the direction of the secretary.

20 Feb 1815 — Charles Stewart, in the *Constitution*, defeated the frigate HMS *Cyane* (34) and the corvette *Levant* (21) off Madeira Island. The *Levant* was later recaptured by the British, but the *Cyane* served actively in

the U.S. Navy until 1827. (DDs 13 and 224 and DE 238 have borne the name of Stewart.)

23 Mar 1815   James Biddle, in the *Hornet* (18), took the brig HMS *Penguin,* also eighteen guns, in 22 minutes. (Biddle has been honored by TB 26, DD 151, DDG 5, and CG 34.)

30 Jun 1815   In the final naval action of the War of 1812, the sloop *Peacock* captured the brig HMS *Nautilus* (14) off Java, while under the command of Lewis Warrington.

Until the Civil War

In the forty-five years before the Civil War, the Navy fought in a small war with Mexico that gave it experience in amphibious and riverine operations. The Navy also helped pacify Indians, suppress piracy, explore, and experiment. Steam propulsion, iron hulls, exploding shells, rifled guns—all appeared in this period. U.S. men-of-war appeared in all corners of the world, showing the flag and protecting the rights of Americans overseas.

22 Mar 1820   Captain James Barron killed the popular commodore Stephen Decatur in a duel at Bladensburg, Maryland. The resulting public outrage spelled the beginning of the end for duels.

23 Apr 1821   In an experiment typical of this time, the *Constitution* was propelled at 3 knots in Boston Harbor by hand-cranked paddlewheels. The experiment, which sought a way to power sailing ships in close quarters, was not repeated.

16 May 1821   The frigate *Congress* (36) became first U.S. warship to visit China.

31 Aug 1826–
8 Jun 1830   The sloop *Vincennes* (18), under Captain W. B. Finch, became the first U.S. Navy warship to go around the world.

2 Apr 1827   Construction of the first naval hospital was begun in Portsmouth, Virginia.

6 Dec 1830	The U.S. Naval Observatory, the first in the country, was established.
17 Jun 1833	The ship of the line *Delaware* (74) dry-docked in Gosport (now Portsmouth) Navy Yard. She was the first warship to be dry-docked in the United States.
12 Jul 1836	Charles H. Haswell became the first "chief engineer" (of the steam frigate *Fulton II*) in the U.S. Navy.
3 Mar 1837	The rank of sailing master, a senior rank held by warrant officers in charge of ship-board seamanship and navigation, was changed to master. Some masters became commissioned officers, while others held warrants. The rank of master comman-dant—a sailing master in command of a ship—was changed to commander.
1838–42	Commander Charles Wilkes took a 6-ship naval expedition around the world, explor-ing Antarctica and many places in the Pa-cific. (TB 35 and DDs 67 and 441 have borne the name *Wilkes*.)
Feb 1841	The first regulations providing details for enlisted uniforms, including the first spe-cifics on rating insignia, were issued.
1 Sep 1842	The Board of Naval Commissioners was superseded by five technical bureaus, sub-ordinates to the secretary of the Navy. With variations in number and titles, they continue in existence today as the naval systems commands.
5–6 Dec 1843	The *Michigan*, the Navy's first iron-hulled warship, launched herself during the night with no one present! She left naval service 105 years later.
10 Dec 1843	The *Princeton*, the Navy's first screw-pro-pelled steam frigate, was launched.
29 Mar 1844	Uriah Levy, the Navy's first Jewish officer, was promoted to captain. (DE 162 honored his service.)
1845	A captain's annual pay was a maximum of $4,500. The highest enlisted monthly pay was $40 (for a yeoman) and a ship's boy

received $6 to $8 monthly. The rum ration was valued at 20 cents a day.

10 Oct 1845 The U.S. Naval Academy was established in Annapolis, Maryland.

18 Feb 1846 "Larboard and starboard" became "port and starboard" by general order.

11 May 1846 War was declared on Mexico.

11 Jul 1846 The Naval Academy commissioned its first ship's officer, Passed Midshipman Richard Aulick.

20 Jul 1846 The *Columbus* (74) became the first U.S. man-of-war to visit Japan.

1847 "The Kedge-Anchor," by Sailing Master William Brady, USN, was first published. This book was a forerunner of *The Bluejackets' Manual*.

9 May 1847 Twelve thousand Army troops under General Winfield Scott made amphibious landings at Vera Cruz, Mexico. The city surrendered twenty days later, after a siege by Army and Navy forces.

14 Jun 1847 A squadron under Commodore Matthew C. Perry captured the Mexican city of Tabasco after fighting its way 70 miles upriver.

2 Feb 1848 The Treaty of Guadalupe Hidalgo ended the Mexican War, with the United States gaining most of its present southwestern territory.

28 Sep 1850 Flogging—whipping with a cat-o'-nine tails—was terminated as a punishment in the Navy by Act of Congress.

31 Mar 1854 Commodore Matthew C. Perry signed a treaty with the Japanese at Yokohama, opening that country to western trade.

16 Jan 1857 An act of Congress established the rank of flag officer, the first actual rank higher than captain ever established in the U.S. Navy. Before this, commanders of forces and squadrons had held the operational title of commodore but the actual rank of captain.

2 Mar 1859 The first Navy ship to be built on the West Coast, the paddlewheel gunboat *Saginaw,* was launched at Mare Island, California.

The Civil War

The Navy's principal roles in this struggle were to blockade the South's coastline to prevent the export of cotton and the entry of munitions, and to cooperate with the Army in amphibious operations. On Western rivers, the Navy developed specialized craft to dominate the Mississippi and its tributaries, and thus cut the Confederacy off from other supply sources via Texas. In this war, revolving turrets, ironclads, steam power, observation balloons, submersibles, and mines were tried, often for the first time in battle.

9 Jan 1861	The steamer *Star of the West* was fired on by South Carolinians while attempting to resupply Fort Sumter in Charleston Harbor. This was the first in a chain of events resulting in the Civil War.
27 Aug 1861	In North Carolina, a squadron under Flag Officer Silas Stringham bombarded Forts Hatteras and Clark into submission. (*Stringham* was the name of TB 19 and DD 83.)
7 Nov 1861	Flag Officer Samuel DuPont led his squadron to victory over Port Royal, South Carolina (TB 7 and DDs 152 and 941 were named *DuPont*).
21 Dec 1861	The Medal of Honor was authorized by Congress. (It wasn't authorized for award to officers until 1915.)
6 Feb 1862	A squadron under Flag Officer Andrew H. Foote helped take Fort Henry on the Tennessee River.
7 Feb 1862	A squadron under Flag Officer Louis M. Goldsborough captured Roanoke Island, North Carolina (TB 20, DD 188, and DDG 20 all honored Goldsborough.)
14–16 Feb 1862	Foote's squadron again participated in the assault on a Confederate fort, this time helping to take Fort Donelson on the Cumberland River. (TB 3 and DDs 169 and 511 were named for Foote.)
9 Mar 1862	The *Monitor* (Captain John L. Worden), first warship with a revolving gun turret,

met the Confederate *Virginia* (ex-*Merri-mack*) in world's first battle of ironclads. The battle ended in a draw, but the *Virginia* never fought again. (DDs 16, 288, and 352 and CG 18 have been named *Worden.*)

14 Mar 1862   Flag Officer Goldsborough's squadron captured New Berne, North Carolina.

24 Apr 1862   Flag Officer David Glascow Farragut led his squadron past Forts St. Phillip and Jackson up the Mississippi River to a commanding position above New Orleans, which surrendered the next day. (TB 11, DDs 300 and 348, and DDG 37 honor Farragut.)

10 Jun 1862   The *Red Rover,* the Navy's first hospital ship, went into operation on the Mississippi River.

16 Jul 1862   Congress established the ranks of rear admiral, commodore, lieutenant commander, master, and ensign. David Glasgow Farragut was appointed as one of the Navy's first four rear admirals. When the ranks of vice admiral (21 Dec 1864) and admiral (25 Jul 1866) were created, Farragut became the first officer appointed to them.

21 Aug 1862   The *New Ironsides,* the Navy's first *seagoing* armored ship, was completed. (The *Monitor,* mentioned above, was a shallow-draft ship designed for coastal operations.)

31 Aug 1862   The issuance of grog to ship's companies was ended, a year after being terminated for officers and warrant officers. Ship's wardrooms continued to operate "wine messes" until 1914.

16 Feb 1864   The Confederate submarine *H. L. Hunley,* commanded by Infantry Lieutenant G. E. Dixon, sank the Union steam sloop *Housatonic* with a spar torpedo, the first sinking of a warship by a submarine. The *H. L. Hunley* was also lost in the blast. (AS 31 recalls the builder of this craft, H. L. Hunley.)

   19 Jun 1864   The Union steam sloop *Kearsarge* (Captain

John A. Winslow) sank the famed Confederate raider *Alabama* (Captain Raphael Semmes) off Cherbourg, France. (Winslow has been honored by TB 5 and DDs 53 and 359.)

5 Aug 1864   A Union squadron under Vice Admiral Farragut assaulted Confederate forces in Mobile Bay and won a decisive victory. It was here, when mines (then called torpedoes) endangered his forces, that Farragut ordered, "Captain Drayton, go ahead! Damn the torpedoes! Go on!"

27 Oct 1864   A steam launch, commanded by Lieutenant William B. Cushing, sank the large Confederate ironclad *Albemarle* with a spar torpedo. (Cushing was remembered by TB 1 and DDs 55, 376, and 797.)

15 Jan 1865   A squadron under Rear Admiral David D. Porter cooperated with an Army force under Major General A. H. Terry in capturing Fort Fisher, North Carolina (LSD 40 recalls the event.)

Decline and Rebirth

After the Civil War, a combination of war weariness and westward expansion resulted in the Navy's decline. For nearly twenty years the Navy languished. Finally, in the mid 1880s, as nationalism gripped the country, the Navy once again received attention. On this wave of enthusiasm, the nation was swept into the Spanish-American War, the Great White Fleet was built, and the Panama Canal was constructed.

17 Apr 1866   Congress appropriated $5,000 to test the use of "petroleum oil" as fuel for ships' boilers.

1869   New regulations prescribed an enlisted working uniform for the first time. (Before, old dress uniforms were used.)

28 Jun 1869   William M. Wood was appointed first surgeon general of the Navy. (DD 715 was named for him.)

10 Jun 1871	A Navy–Marine Corps assault force made a landing in Korea in a punitive operation against a Korean fort that had fired on a peaceful American ship. Lieutenant Hugh W. McKee was killed in the attack and honored by TB 18 and DDs 87 and 575.
11 Sep 1872	James Henry Conyers became the first black to enter the Naval Academy.
9 Oct 1873	A meeting held by a group of naval officers resulted in the formation of the U.S. Naval Institute, publisher of *The Bluejackets' Manual.*
28 Jun 1874	The *Jeanette,* a supply ship, received the first Navy shipboard electrical system. While proceeding on a mission to the Arctic, she was crushed in an ice pack on 13 Jun 1881.
31 Jul 1874	The *Intrepid,* first experimental Navy torpedo boat to carry self-propelled torpedoes, was commissioned.
3 Mar 1883	The Navy appropriation act for Fiscal Year 1884 authorized construction of the cruisers *Atlanta, Boston,* and *Chicago* and the "dispatch vessel" *Dolphin.* These were the first steel ships built for the U.S. Navy, and thus they mark the beginning of the transition from wood and sail to steel and steam. In these ships, the rank of master was changed to that of lieutenant (junior grade).
6 Oct 1884	The Naval War College was established.
1885	Distinctive first-, second-, and third-class rates were provided in new uniform regulations.
8 Jan 1885	Petty officers were divided into first, second, and third class. For more than a hundred years there had been only the single grade of petty officer.
14 Feb 1885	Congress approved a military retirement act, the first formal retirement program for U.S. armed forces, but an oversight omitted the Navy, and it wasn't until 1899 that sailors were included.
8 Dec 1885	The gunboat *Dolphin,* first steel warship for the U.S. Navy, was commissioned.

24 Sep 1894	The rate of chief petty officer was established by General Order No. 431.	Navy History
15 Feb 1898	The battleship *Maine* was sunk by internal explosion (due to spontaneous combustion) in Havana Harbor. Belief that she had been attacked by Spaniards, encouraged by the press of the day, inflamed American public opinion and resulted in a declaration of war on 25 Apr 1898.	
1 May 1898	Commodore George Dewey's Asiatic Squadron defeated the Spanish in Manila Bay. The battle had been begun by Dewey's order to his flagship captain, "You may fire when ready, Gridley." (DD 349 and DDG 45 were named for Dewey, and DDs 92 and 380 and CG 21 for Gridley.)	
3 Jul 1898	Rear Admiral William T. Sampson's squadron defeated a Spanish force attempting to break out of Santiago, Cuba. Every Spanish ship was sunk or run ashore. (Sampson has been honored by DDs 63 and 394 and DDG 10.)	
13 Aug 1898	Spain asked for peace.	
2 Mar 1899	George Dewey was promoted to Admiral of the Navy, a rank held by him alone. The act creating this rank also abolished the rank of commodore.	

The Twentieth Century

In the last eighty years, the United States has been involved in two world wars, two Asiatic wars, and a variety of lesser incidents. At the end of World War II, the U.S. Navy was the mightiest the world had ever seen. Since then, other calls for national resources have resulted in the Navy living on its accumulated resources until nearly all have been spent; nevertheless, the Navy has managed to accomplish its missions and to be a leader in many areas of science and technology.

12 Oct 1900	The *Holland* (SS 1), the Navy's first submarine, was commissioned.	
19 May 1902	The *Decatur* (DD 5), the Navy's first active destroyer, was commissioned. She was 250	Twentieth Century

feet long and carried two 3-inch guns and two 18-inch torpedo tubes.

16 Dec 1907 The four battleship divisions of the Atlantic Fleet, called the Great White Fleet by the press from the white peacetime color scheme then in use, began its round-the-world voyage, which ended in 1909.

8 Jan 1907 By executive order, President Theodore Roosevelt directed that all U.S.-commissioned ships be called United States Ship (USS). No standard existed before this, and usage varied widely.

6 Apr 1909 Commander Robert E. Peary became the first man to reach the North Pole. (DE 132 and FF 1073 have honored him.)

4 Jan 1910 The *Michigan* (BB 27), the first American "all-big-gun" or dreadnought battleship to enter service, was commissioned.

17 Sep 1910 The *Roe* (DD 24), the first destroyer of the *Paulding* (DD 22) class to enter active service, was commissioned. The ten *Paulding*s, completed in 1910–11, were the first American warships to use oil rather than coal for fuel.

14 Nov 1910 Eugene Ely, a civilian contract pilot, flew a plane off a temporary 57-foot wooden deck built over the bow of the cruiser *Birmingham*—the first aircraft launch from a ship.

18 Jan 1911 Ely landed on a platform built over the stern of the armored cruiser *Pennsylvania* in San Francisco Bay—the first shipboard landing.

Oct 1911 The Navy received its first aircraft. One was built by the Wright Brothers, and two others were built by Glen Curtiss.

5 Mar 1912 The Atlantic Submarine Flotilla, commanded by Lieutenant Chester W. Nimitz (see 31 Dec 1941), was established.

26 Jul 1912 The letter *D*, in Morse code, was sent by a plane to the destroyer *Stringham* a mile away—the first radio message received from an aircraft.

1 Jul 1914 Liquor was prohibited on all ships and stations.

6 May 1916	The first ship-to-shore radiotelephone conversation took place between the *New Hampshire* (BB 25) and Washington, D.C.
6 Apr 1917	The United States entered World War I.
4 May 1917	The first U.S. destroyer squadron arrived in Queenstown, Ireland, to help the British escort convoys. Asked by the English admiral when his ships would be prepared for duty, Commander Joseph K. Taussig replied, in a manner characteristic of "tin can" sailors, "We will be ready when fueled, sir."
17 Nov 1917	Germany's U-58 became the first submarine sunk by the U.S. Navy. She was done in by the destroyers *Fanning* (DD 37) and *Nicholson* (DD 52).
11 Nov 1918	An armistice ended World War I. Celebrated for years as Armistice Day, 11 November is now observed as Veterans' Day.
28 Feb 1919	The *Osmond Ingram* (DD 255), the first Navy ship named for an enlisted man, was launched. Ingram was the first enlisted man killed in action in World War I, lost when the destroyer *Cassin* (DD 43) was torpedoed in Oct 1917.
31 May 1919	Navy flying boat NC-4, under Lieutenant Commander Albert C. Read, became the first aircraft to fly across the Atlantic Ocean.
17 Jul 1920	General Order No. 541 established a system of letter-type symbols for ship designations (CV, DD, BB, AO, etc.). Continually modified to suit changes in the Navy's ship types, the system is still in use.
21 Aug 1920	The first radio message heard around the world was broadcast from a Navy radio station near Bordeaux, France.
20 Mar 1922	The *Jupiter,* a former collier (coal-carrier), was recommissioned after conversion to the Navy's first carrier, the *Langley* (CV 1).
Feb 1923	Fleet Problem I was carried out in the Panama area. Through 1940 the annual fleet problem, an elaborate fleetwide war game,

665

was an important element of the Navy's strategic and tactical preparation for war.

17 Aug 1923 The Washington Treaty went into effect. This post–World War I naval limitation pact placed limits of size and numbers on the battleship and carrier forces of the United States, Britain, Japan, France, and Italy. The later London Treaty, in force 31 December 1930, placed similar limits on cruisers and destroyers. These treaties were attempts to prevent a naval arms race of the sort that preceded World War I.

8 Aug 1925 The first night carrier landing took place aboard the *Langley*.

27 Feb 1928 Commander T. G. Ellyson, the Navy's aviator no. 1, was killed in an air crash.

28 Nov 1929 Lieutenant Commander Richard E. Byrd flew over the South Pole. He had previously flown over the North Pole in 1926.

17 Sep 1936 Squadron 40-T was organized to protect American lives during the Spanish Civil War.

Apr 1937 The first sea trials of an experimental radar were conducted in the destroyer *Leary*.

1 Sep 1939 World War II began as German and Soviet troops invaded Poland. The president proclaimed neutrality and ordered the Navy to form a "neutrality patrol" to track and report belligerent ships near the United States or West Indies.

20 Jun 1940 The Bureau of Construction and Repair (ship design and construction) was merged with the Bureau of Engineering to form the Bureau of Ships, ancestor of today's Naval Sea Systems Command.

19 Jul 1940 President Franklin D. Roosevelt signs the Two-Ocean Navy Act, authorizing 1,425,000 tons of new ships and 15,000 naval aircraft, an unprecedented increase in the size of the peacetime Navy.

3 Sep 1940 The "destroyers-for-bases" agreement was signed. The United States transfers fifty older DDs to Britain in exchange for base

	rights in British territories in the western hemisphere.
7 Dec 1941	In a surprise attack on Pearl Harbor, the Japanese inflicted severe damage on units of the U.S. Pacific Fleet and killed 2,008 navymen.
13 Dec 1941	Guam was captured by the Japanese.
23 Dec 1941	The Marines on Wake Island finally surrendered to vastly superior Japanese forces.
31 Dec 1941	Admiral Chester W. Nimitz took command of the Pacific Fleet. Nimitz commanded in the Pacific through V-J day and later became chief of naval operations.
26 Jan 1942	The Japanese submarine I-173 was sunk by the *Gudgeon* (SS 211), the first enemy naval vessel destroyed by a U.S. submarine.
27 Feb 1942	A combined American-British-Dutch-Australian naval force was defeated by a Japanese force in the Battle of the Java Sea.
1 Mar 1942	Bataan surrendered.
4–8 May 1942	The Battle of the Coral Sea was fought, resulting in the end of Japanese advances in the southwest Pacific. The USS *Lexington* (CV 2) was lost, as was the Japanese light carrier *Shoho*. This was the first battle fought solely by air groups—the fleets never saw each other.
6 May 1942	Corregidor surrendered.
4–6 Jun 1942	At the Battle of Midway, four Japanese carriers were sunk and only one American (the *Yorktown*) was lost, ending the period of Japanese initiative in the Pacific War.
3 Aug 1942	Mildred McAfee was commissioned as the first woman naval (line) officer.
7 Aug 1942	U.S. Marines landed on Guadalcanal in the first American offensive action in the Pacific.
9 Aug 1942	A Japanese cruiser force smashed a similar U.S.–Australian force in the Battle of Savo Island, sinking four cruisers in a half-hour night action.
11-12 Oct 1942	The Americans won a night action in the Battle of Cape Esperance, sinking two Jap-

667

anese warships and damaging two more, while sustaining one loss.

8 Nov 1942	The U.S. Navy and Army participated in simultaneous amphibious landings in North Africa—at Algiers and Oran, Algeria, and Fedala, Morocco.
12–15 Nov 1942	In two furious night actions, U.S. naval forces slugged it out with the Japanese in the Battle of Guadalcanal. The Japanese lost two battleships and three destroyers, the Americans two cruisers and seven destroyers—but the U.S. Navy had begun receiving new units at an increasing rate and so had more muscle left than the Japanese. (Five Sullivan brothers, who died in one of the lost cruisers, were honored by *The Sullivans* (DD 537), the first destroyer named for more than one person. It is now a memorial at Buffalo, New York.)
30 Nov 1942	The Battle of Tassafaronga was the last Japanese try to save Guadalcanal. The *Northampton* was lost and so was a Japanese destroyer. The *Rogers* (DD 876) was named for three brothers lost with the cruiser.
9 Feb 1943	The last Japanese troops were evacuated from Guadalcanal, ending the 6-month battle for that island.
9 Apr 1943	The rank of commodore reestablished (but discontinued again after the war).
5 May 1943	The first antisubmarine hunter-killer group was formed, consisting of the escort aircraft carrier *Bogue* (CVE 9) and destroyers *Belknap* (DD 251) and *George E. Badger* (DD 196). During 1943, hunter-killer groups of jeep carriers, destroyers, and destroyer escorts went into widespread operation and effectively contributed to victory in the battle of the Atlantic. The *Bogue* and her consorts earned a Presidential Unit Citation for their antisubmarine work during 1943–44.
10 Jul 1943	The U.S. Navy participated in the invasion of Sicily.

13 Jul 1943	The Battle of Kolombangara resulted in the sinking of a Japanese light cruiser and the loss of the *Gwin* (DD 433).	Navy History
25 Jul 1943	The *Harmon* (DE 678) was launched, the first ship to be named for a black.	
6 Aug 1943	The Japanese lost three destroyers in the Battle of Vella Gulf. There were no U.S. Navy losses.	
9 Sep 1943	U.S. naval forces landed the Allied Fifth Army at Salerno, Italy.	
2 Nov 1943	At Empress Augusta Bay, U.S. Navy forces defeated a Japanese attack, sinking a cruiser and a destroyer.	
25 Nov 1943	Five U.S. destroyers under Captain Arleigh Burke, commander, Destroyer Squadron 23, defeat five Japanese destroyers off Cape St. George, New Ireland Island, sinking three and damaging another.	
21 Jan 1944	The assault at Anzio was the last amphibious attack on Italy.	
2 Feb 1944	Amphibious assaults were conducted against Kwajalein, Roi, and Namur islands in the Marshalls. The islands were conquered quickly despite fierce resistance.	**669**
18 Feb 1944	Further landings secured Eniwetok and Engebi islands.	
29 Feb 1944	The Navy landed Army forces in the Admiralty islands.	
22 Apr 1944	U.S. landings at Hollandia, New Guinea, met little opposition.	
19 May– 1 June 1944	The *England* (DE 635) sank a record six Japanese submarines during this period. Three were killed in the first four days, and five of the six were downed without assistance! CG 22 is also the *England*.	
4 Jun 1944	The U-505 was captured by a hunter-killer group of destroyer escorts led by the *Guadalcanal* (CVE 60)—the only time the order "Boarders away!" has been passed in this century.	
6 Jun 1944	The Allies invade Normandy. Nearly 2,500 U.S. Navy ships and craft were involved in the largest amphibious assault ever. At one	Twentieth Century

beach alone, 21,328 troops, 1,742 vehicles, and 1,695 tons of supplies were landed in 12 hours.

15 Jun 1944   The Second and Fourth Marine Divisions landed on Saipan and completed operations three weeks later.

19–20 Jun 1944   In the Battle of the Philippine Sea, also called the Marianas Turkey Shoot, naval aviators downed 426 Japanese aircraft while themselves losing only 95 planes.

21 Jul 1944   Marines and Army troops landed on Guam and took complete control of the island by 10 Aug 1944.

24 Jul 1944   The marines landed on Tinian Island against light resistance.

15 Aug 1944   The Navy participated in amphibious landings in southern France, the last ones conducted in Europe.

15 Sep 1944   The Navy-marine team assaulted Peleliu Island in the western Carolines, getting closer to the Philippines.

20 Oct 1944   U.S. forces returned to the Philippines in an amphibious assault on Leyte Island.

23–25 Oct 1944   In three connected sea-air battles, known collectively as the Battle of Leyte Gulf, the Imperial Japanese Navy was virtually destroyed. Lost to the Japanese were three battleships, one attack carrier, three light carriers, six heavy cruisers, four light cruisers, eight destroyers, and a submarine. U.S. Navy losses were one light carrier, two escort carriers, two destroyers, one destroyer escort, a submarine, and a torpedo boat.

14 Dec 1944   The five-star rank of fleet admiral was created. Fleet Admirals William Leahy, Ernest King, Chester Nimitz, and William Halsey have held this lifetime rank.

15 Dec 1944   The U.S. Army landed on Mindoro Island in the Philippines.

9 Jan 1945   Army forces landed at Lingayen Gulf, Luzon.

19 Feb 1945	The marines landed on Iwo Jima. It took twenty-six days to secure the island.	Navy History
1 Apr 1945	In the final major amphibious assault of World War II, Army units landed on Okinawa this Easter Sunday. Navy units were subjected repeatedly to Japanese kamikaze attacks. Thirty-four ships were lost, 288 others were damaged. The Japanese lost 1,228 planes and pilots in the kamikaze effort. Resistance finally ended on 21 Jun.	
7 May 1945	Germany surrendered after losing over 800 submarines to the Allies in the Battle of the Atlantic.	
6 Aug 1945	The first atomic bomb was detonated over Hiroshima, Japan. The weaponeer on the bomber Enola Gay was Navy Captain W. S. Parsons. (DDG 33 bears his name.)	
9 Aug 1945	The second atomic bomb was dropped on Nagasaki, Japan.	
14 Aug 1945	V-J Day. Hostilities ceased in the Pacific, putting an end to World War II.	
2 Sep 1945	Japan formally surrendered on board the *Missouri* (BB 63).	**671**
Oct 1945	The *Stewart* (DD 224) was returned to the U.S. Navy. Damaged early in the war and supposedly scuttled beyond salvage at Soerabaja (Indonesia), she had been in Japanese service as a patrol boat throughout the war.	
2 Jul 1946	A jet aircraft operated from an aircraft carrier for the first time.	
3 Jun 1949	John Wesley Brown became the first black to graduate from the Naval Academy.	
26 Jun 1950	U.S. forces are ordered to support South Korean troops against invading North Korean troops.	
3 Jul 1950	F9F-2 Panther fighter-bombers from the *Valley Forge* (CV 45) attacked Pyongyang, the North Korean capital, in the first strike by carrier-launched jet aircraft.	
15 Sep 1950	Marines landed at Inchon, near Seoul, Korea, in a surprise thrust deep behind the	Twentieth Century

	front lines. This attack compelled the Communist invaders to fall back northward.
9 Nov 1950	The first dogfight involving a Navy jet and an enemy jet was fought. Lieutenant Commander W. T. Amen, in a Panther, shot down a MiG-15, a Russian-built fighter.
28 Aug 1952	First use of carrier-launched guided missiles. Pilotless, radio-controlled (via a TV guidance system) F6F5 Hellcat fighters with high explosives were used against land targets from the *Boxer* (CV 21).
3 Nov 1952	Marine Major W. Stratton, in an F3D-2 Skyknight, scored the first kill by an airborne intercept radar-equipped fighter. He got a Russian-built YAK-15.
27 Jul 1953	The Korean Armistice went into effect.
3 Dec 1954	The *Gyatt* (DD 712) was recommissioned as DDG 1, the first combatant Navy ship with antiaircraft missiles.
17 Jan 1955	The *Nautilus* (SSN 571), the world's first nuclear-powered submarine, began operations.
17 Mar 1958	The Navy's Vanguard I satellite was placed in orbit, where it should remain for 2,000 years. It is the oldest manmade object in orbit today.
3 Aug 1958	The *Nautilus* became the first ship in history to reach the North Pole.
16 Nov 1958	Proficiency (pro) pay went into effect.
1960	The *Triton* (SSN 586) became the first submarine to circumnavigate the world submerged. The voyage covered 41,500 miles in 83 days at an average speed of 18 knots.
20 Jul 1960	The *George Washington* (SSBN 598) made the first submerged launching of Polaris ballistic missiles off Cape Canaveral.
15 Nov 1960	The first deterrent Polaris patrol was begun by the *George Washington*. It lasted 66 days, 10 hours.
5 May 1961	Commander Alan B. Shepard became the first American in space, riding Mercury capsule Freedom 7 on a 15-minute suborbital flight.

9 Sep 1961	The *Long Beach* (CGN 9), the world's first nuclear-powered surface warship, was commissioned.	Navy History
12 Sep 1961	Navy task force carriers on rescue/relief operations off the Texas coast were hit by Hurricane Carla.	
20 Feb 1962	Marine Major John Glenn became the first American to orbit the earth in Friendship 7. Other Navy and Marine Corps officers who have explored outer space include Walter Schirra, James Lovell, Scott Carpenter, Pete Conrad, Richard Gordon, Walter Cunningham, and Alan Bean.	
Oct 1962	President Kennedy gave the Russians a lesson in the use of sea power when he quarantined Cuba with air, surface, and subsurface units and stopped the Russians from sending in shiploads of strategic nuclear missiles.	
10 Apr 1963	The *Thresher* (SSN 593) was lost east of Portsmouth, New Hampshire, because of material failure during a test dive. She was the first nuclear submarine to be lost.	**673**
May 1964	Seventh Fleet carriers deployed off northern coast of South Vietnam (Republic of Vietnam—RVN) in area to be called Yankee Station.	
19 May 1964	The *Kitty Hawk* (CVA 63) began her first period of service off North Vietnam. She was the first American carrier on station in the Tonkin Gulf during the Vietnam war.	
2–4 August 1964	The destroyers *Maddox* and *Turner Joy* engaged North Vietnamese torpedo boats in the Tonkin Gulf. Carrier planes from the *Ticonderoga* and *Constellation* later struck military targets in North Vietnam. On 7 August, Congress passed the Tonkin Gulf Resolution, the legal basis for U.S. armed support for South Vietnam.	
Mar 1965	Combined U.S.–Vietnamese patrol established to counter North Vietnamese coastal infiltration, soon named Market Time. This patrol also provided fire support to land	Twentieth Century

forces, transported troops, and evacuated civilians from combat areas.

8 Mar 1965 Ninth Marine Expeditionary Brigade landed at Da Nang, the first battalion-sized ground combat unit to RVN.

15 Apr 1965 Carriers struck Viet Cong forces in RVN from operating area southeast of Cam Ranh Bay, soon called Dixie Station.

May 1965 Seventh Fleet ships began strike and fire-support missions in RVN.

18 Dec 1965 River Patrol Force (TF 116) established; early in 1966 began operation Market Time on RVN rivers. Patrol craft, helicopters, minesweeping craft, and SEAL teams operated from bases. The Army-Navy Mobile Riverine Force landed and supported ground troops.

Oct 1966 Operation Sea Dragon began. Cruisers and destroyers, aided by carrier spotter planes, struck North Vietnamese military targets; the battleship *New Jersey* joined them for a short while in 1968. The operation ended in October 1968.

28 May 1967 The *Long Beach* (CGN 9) fired Talos missile at North Vietnamese MiG-21 in Tonkin Gulf, making it the first Navy ship to fire a surface-to-air missile at hostile aircraft.

Apr 1968 The battleship *New Jersey* (BB 62) was recommissioned for Vietnam service. After one gunfire support deployment, she was decommissioned on 17 December 1969.

30 Sep 1968 The *New Jersey* fired her first mission off Vietnam, the first battleship combat firing since the Korean War.

Oct 1968 Operation Sealord, concerted U.S.-Vietnamese land/sea/air effort to cut supply lines from Cambodia and disrupt base areas in Mekong Delta, began.

30 Jan 1968 Tet Offensive began as Communist forces threatened most population centers and captured Hue, retaken by RVN troops and U.S. Marines in heavy fighting. North Vietnamese besieged Marine base at Khe Sanh; massive Navy/Air Force air strikes helped

defeat attackers. Communists suffered heavy losses. Large main-force units were pushed toward border areas. RVN control extended.

20 Jul 1969   The lunar module *Eagle* landed on the moon's Sea of Tranquillity after detaching from Apollo 11. The commander of the mission and the first man to set foot on the moon was Neil Armstrong, who had been a Navy fighter pilot in the Korean War.

30 Mar 1972   North Vietnamese Easter offensive began. Defeated by RVN forces with the help of naval gunfire, logistic support, and air/surface strikes on North Vietnam.

18–29 Dec 72   Operation Linebacker II: Navy/Air Force planes conducted major strikes on North Vietnamese military targets in the Hanoi/Haiphong area after peace negotiations stalled and the North Vietnamese strengthened defenses and built up supply lines and stockpiles.

Mar 1973   Last U.S. forces withdrawn from RVN after extended transfer of resources and missions to RV Navy.

22 Jun 1973   The Skylab I team, operating the world's first orbiting space laboratory, completed a 30-day operation. Its members were all naval aviators.

1 Jul 1973   The traditional sailor's white hat, broad collar, and bell-bottomed trousers were superseded by a more conventional, suitlike type uniform.

18 Jul 1973   Operation End Sweep, clearance of mines from North Vietnamese waters, completed by minesweepers and helicopters. Seventh Fleet ships depart Vietnamese waters.

Mar–Apr 1975   Naval ships/aircraft evacuated U.S. allied personnel from Cambodia as that country was overrun by the Khmer Rouge (Operation Eagle Pull). As RVN falls to full-scale North Vietnamese invasion, Operation Frequent Wind evacuates Americans, Vietnamese, and others.

1 Jan 1978   The Navy returned to the traditional bell-

bottom jumper uniform for sailors in grades E-1 through E-4. On 1 May 1980, the Navy began issuing these uniforms to all male recruits, and by 1 October 1983 all enlisted men, E-1 through E-6, had resumed wearing them.

9 May 1980   The *Coral Sea* pulled into Subic Bay, concluding 102 consecutive days at sea.

26 May 1980   The *Nimitz* completed 144 consecutive days at sea, a longer underway cruise than any ship since World War II.

27 Jun 1981   The *James K. Polk* (SSBN 645) completes the 2,000th ballistic-missile deterrent patrol.

15 Sep 1981   The one-star flag rank of commodore was reestablished by an act of Congress. "Commodore" was an operational command title from the earliest days until 1862, when it became an actual officer rank. Abolished on 3 Mar 1899, it was restored on 9 Apr 1943 for use during World War II but was allowed to lapse in 1949.

11 Nov 1981   The USS *Ohio* (SSBN 726), the first of the Trident-firing ballistic-missile submarines, was commissioned.

13 Mar 1982   The USS *Carl Vinson* (CVN 70), the Navy's fourth nuclear-powered aircraft carrier, was commissioned.

2 April 1982   Argentine marines and special forces captured the Falkland (Malvinas) Islands, and nearby South Georgia I., from British defenders. Britain formed a task force to retake the islands; the U.S. announced its support. The islands were recaptured after a land-sea-air campaign in which ships and aircraft were lost or damaged by missiles, and the Argentine cruiser *General Belgrano* was sunk by submarine torpedoes.

28 Dec 1982   The USS *New Jersey* (BB 62), newly armed with missiles in addition to her 5- and 16-inch guns, was placed in commission for the third time by President Reagan.

23 Oct 1983   U.S. forces landed on Caribbean island of

	Grenada, expelling Cuban forces and capturing a quantity of Soviet-supplied arms.
Nov 1985	By act of Congress, the title of the Navy's one-star flag rank was changed from commodore to rear admiral (lower half).
24–25 Mar 1986	In response to terrorist attacks on civilians, a Sixth Fleet force organized around the carriers *Saratoga, Coral Sea,* and *America,* and including the new Aegis missile cruisers *Ticonderoga* and *Yorktown,* engaged Libyan forces in the Gulf of Sidra. Several Libyan·missile patrol craft were sunk or damaged, and a missile battery at Sidra was hit.
14 Apr 1986	In coordination with Air Force F-111s flying from England, Sixth Fleet carrier planes struck military targets in Libya.
10 May 1986	The battleship *Missouri* (BB 63), scene of the ceremony in Tokyo Bay that ended World War II in 1945, was recommissioned at San Francisco.
10 Dec 1986	Kuwait sought U.S. protection for its tankers in the Persian Gulf during the Iraq-Iran war.
7 March 1987	The United States offered to escort Kuwaiti tankers.
17 May 1987	The USS *Stark* (FFG 31), on patrol in the Persian Gulf, was damaged by two missiles fired from an Iraqi aircraft; thirty-seven of her crew were killed.
5 Jun 1987	A contract was awarded to Westinghouse for a prototype airship for fleet airborne early warning (AEW) and communications services (later designated YEZ-2A). The last Navy lighter-than-air craft was operated in 1962.
22 Jul 1987	Kuwaiti tankers, under the U.S. flag, began transiting the gulf under U.S. Navy escort. The tanker *Bridgeton* was damaged by an Iranian mine.
12 Sep 1987	The *Avenger* (MCM 1) was commissioned. A wood-hulled ship designed to locate and sweep contact and influence mines, she was

677

	the first new USN mine countermeasures ship since 1960.
21 Sep 1987	Armed helicopters from the *Jarrett* (FFG 33) and Navy SEALs capture the Iranian craft *Iran Ajr* laying mines in the gulf.
8 Oct 1987	Iranian patrol craft fired on U.S. helicopters. U.S. forces sank at least one of the attackers.
19 Oct 1987	In retaliation for an Iranian missile attack on a U.S. flag tanker, the destroyers *Hoel* (DDG 13), *Kidd* (DDG 993), *Leftwich* (DD 984), and *John Young* (DD 973) bombarded two offshore oil platforms housing military radar and communications gear used in attacks on shipping. Navy SEALs finished the job with explosives, then destroyed a third platform.
14 Apr 1988	The USS *Samuel B. Roberts* (FFG 58) struck a mine in the Persian Gulf; though severely damaged, she was saved by the aggressive efforts of her professional crew.
18 Apr 1988	In response to the mining of the *Samuel B. Roberts*, U.S. ships shelled Iranian oil platforms. Iranian frigates fired missiles at U.S. aircraft. Patrol craft fired on the *Wainwright* (CG 28). Planes and the *Joseph Strauss* (DDG 16) engaged patrol craft and two Iranian frigates. The patrol craft *Joshan* was sunk. The frigates *Sahand* and *Sabalan* were severely damaged. An A-6 from the *Enterprise* (CVN 65) sank one, possibly more, Iranian patrol craft attacking commercial shipping.
Sep 1988	Navy began to scale down Persian Gulf presence after an Iraq-Iran ceasefire of 20 August ended fighting. Tanker escort to be replaced by a general "zone defense."
19 Apr 1989	A powder explosion in Turret II of battleship *Iowa* (BB 61) killed 47 crewmembers. A series of subsequent investigations failed to produce a definite cause for this accident, the first "cold-gun" turret explosion since the Navy began using large-caliber breechloading bag guns in 1895.

16 Sep 1989	*Arleigh Burke* (DDG 51), lead ship of a new class of missile destroyers designed for battle group operations well into the 21st century, was christened at Bath, Maine. Aegis, advanced sonar, LAMPS III, ASW torpedoes, a 5-inch, 54 gun, and a varied battery of missiles give the new ships formidable ability to operate against air, surface, and submarine targets.	Navy History
2 Aug 1990	Iraq invaded and occupied Kuwait. United Nations Security Council condemned the Iraqi invasion.	
6 Aug 1990	The United Nations Security Council voted worldwide economic sanctions against Iraq.	
8 Aug 1990	Iraq declared annexation of Kuwait. President Bush ordered operation "Desert Shield," deploying major U.S. forces to Saudi Arabia to assist in defending that country against possible Iraqi incursion. U.S. land and air forces were ordered in, reserves were recalled to active duty, and additional naval forces were deployed to reinforce those already in the Middle Eastern area.	**679**
9 Aug 1990	The United Nations Security Council declared annexation of Kuwait legally void.	
17 Aug 1990	United States naval forces in Persian Gulf ordered to intercept commercial shipping to and from Iraq and Kuwait to enforce United Nations sanctions.	
25 Aug 1990	The United Nations authorized use of armed force to enforce sanctions.	

Uniform Code of Military Justice

Congress and the Navy have taken steps to keep you informed of the disciplinary laws and regulations most likely to affect your station in the Navy. Article 137 of the Uniform Code of Military Justice (UCMJ) states that articles 2, 3, 7–15, 25, 27, 31, 37, 38, 55, 77–134, and 137–39 must be fully and carefully explained to every enlisted person. This is done when you enter active duty, after six months of active service, and at the time of reenlistment.

In addition, article 137 requires that a complete copy of the UCMJ be made available to every person covered by those regulations. Navy regulations require that the text of the UCMJ be posted in a conspicuous place. You will find a copy of the UCMJ on the bulletin board or in some other prominent place in every naval activity.

Outline of UCMJ, Articles 1–140

684

Article 134, properly known as the "general article," is designed to cover everything detrimental to good order and discipline in the armed forces as well as crimes and offenses not capital in nature.

Beaufort Scale

Beaufort Number	Wind Speed (knots)	Seaman's Term	Appearance of Sea
0	Below 1	Calm	Surface like a mirror
1	1–3	Light air	Ripples that look like fish scales but without foam crests
2	4–6	Light breeze	Small wavelets, still short but more pronounced; crests look glassy and do not break
3	7–10	Gentle breeze	Large wavelets; crests begin to break; glassy-looking foam; perhaps scattered white horses
4	11–16	Moderate breeze	Small waves, becoming longer; fairly frequent white horses
5	17–21	Fresh breeze	Moderate waves, taking a more pronounced long form; many white horses are formed; chance of some spray
6	22–27	Strong breeze	Large waves begin to form; white foam crests are more extensive everywhere; probably some spray
7	28–33	Moderate gale (high wind)	Sea heaps up and white foam from breaking waves begins to move in streaks in the direction of the wind; spindrift begins

	8	34–40	Fresh gale	Moderately high waves of greater length; edges of crests break into spindrift; foam is blown in well-marked streaks in the direction of wind
	9	41–47	Strong gale	High waves; dense streaks of foam in the direction of wind; sea begins to roll; spray may affect visibility
	10	48–55	Whole gale	Very high waves with long overhanging crests; resulting foam is blown in great patches of dense white streaks in the direction of wind; whole surface of the sea looks white; rolling of the sea becomes heavy and shocklike; visibility is affected
	11	56–63	Storm	Exceptionally high waves; small and medium-sized ships might be lost to view behind the waves; sea is completely covered with long white patches of foam lying in the direction of wind; everywhere the edges of wave crests are blown into froth; visibility is affected
	12	64–71	Hurricane	Air is filled with foam and spray; sea completely white with driving spray; visibility seriously affected
	13	72–80		
	14	81–89		
	15	90–99		
Beaufort	16	100–108		
Scale	17	109–118		

Navigational Aids

Aids to navigation are lighthouses, lightships, minor lights, buoys, and day beacons. Aids are located so as to provide a nearly continuous and unbroken chain of charted marks for coast and channel piloting.

Buoys

Navigational buoys are moored floating markers (figure E-1) that guide ships in and out of channels, warn them of hidden dangers, lead them to anchorage areas, and the like. Their location is usually shown by symbols on the area navigational chart. Buoys may be of various sizes, shapes, and colors. Color, markings, and to a lesser degree shape are the main means of identifying a buoy and correlating its location with that of the symbol on the chart.

687

The following are the principal types of buoys used in U.S. waters:

Spar: This is a large floating pole, trimmed, shaped, and appropriately painted. It may be made of wood or metal.

Can and nun: These are cylindrical and conical, respectively.

Bell: This has a flat top surmounted by a framework supporting a bell. Older bell buoys are sounded by the motion of the sea. Newer types are operated automatically by gas or electricity.

Gong: This is similar to the bell buoy, except that it has a series of gongs, each with a different tone.

Whistle: Usually cone-shaped, it carries a whistle sounded by the sea's motion, or horns sounded at regular intervals by mechanical or electrical means.

Lighted: This buoy carries batteries or gas tanks and is surmounted by a framework supporting a light.

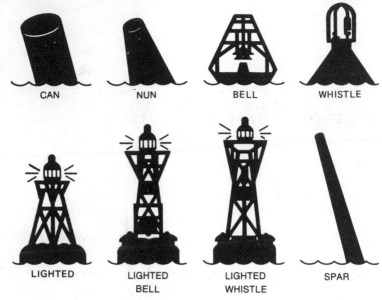

CAN   NUN   BELL   WHISTLE

LIGHTED   LIGHTED   LIGHTED   SPAR
          BELL   WHISTLE

Figure E–1   Principal types of buoys.

Combination: In this buoy (lighted, gong, or whistle), the light and sound signals are combined.

In the United States, red buoys mark the right side of the channel, black and more recently green buoys mark the left side coming from seaward. Remember the saying, "Red-right-returning."

If unlighted, red channel buoys are cone-shaped nun buoys, and black or green channel markers are cylindrical can buoys. If buoys are lighted, it is their color that is most important. Horizontally banded red and black or green buoys mark obstructions. This type of buoy may be passed on either side, but unless you know the dimensions of an obstruction, it is best to give the buoy a wide berth.

If the top band is red, the preferred channel is to the left of the buoy coming from seaward; if the top band is black or green, the preferred channel is to the right. Buoys with red and white vertical stripes mark the middle of a channel or fairway.

Buoys painted all white have no special significance; they are not used for navigation but rather for such purposes as marking anchorage areas or fishing limits. Buoys with black and white horizontal stripes mark fishing areas in some locales.

Buoys are valuable aids to navigation, but you must never depend on them exclusively. They may drag their moorings or go adrift. Lights on buoys are often out of commission. Whistles, bells, and gongs usually sounded by the sea's motion may fail to function in smooth water. Anyone navigating by buoys must be alert to these possibilities.

Numbering: Red buoys marking the right side of a channel bear even numbers, starting with the first buoy from seaward. This is perhaps the only time you'll find anything to starboard with an even number. Black or green channel buoys, to the left of the channel coming from seaward, have odd numbers. Banded or striped buoys are not numbered, but some have letters for identification.

Lights: Red lights are used only on red buoys or on ones that are horizontally banded in red and black or green, with the topmost band red. Green lights are only for black or green buoys, or for black or green and red horizontally banded buoys, with the topmost band black or green. White lights are the only lights used on the red and white vertically striped buoys that mark the middle of a channel or fairway.

Lighting characteristics vary as follows:

A light flashing at regular intervals of not more than thirty flashes per minute may mean either a black, green, or red buoy.

A light with no fewer than sixty flashes per minute—on either black, green, or red buoy—is situated at a turning point or junction where special caution is required.

A light with a series of repeated quick flashes, separated by dark intervals of about 4 seconds, indicates a red and black or green horizontally banded obstruction buoy.

A short-long light, whose flash recurs at a rate of about eight per minute, is placed on a red and white vertically striped midchannel buoy.

Day Beacons

Structural aids to navigation located in or near the water are called day beacons. They usually consist of a piling with a colored and numbered or lettered geometric shape called a day mark near the top, triangular shapes to the right and square shapes to the left (when you are returning from seaward). Their reflective colors and markings correspond to those a buoy would have at the same position. Often a night light is affixed to the top. In U.S. rivers, shallow bays, and estuaries, day beacons are often used in lieu of buoys.

Two day beacons, located some distance apart on a specific true bearing, constitute a day-beacon range. When you can see two beacons positioned in line, your ship is "on the range." Ranges are especially valuable for guiding ships through narrow channels such as the Panama Canal.

Storm-Warning Information

In the United States, information regarding weather and the approach of storms is furnished by the Weather Bureau. The information is disseminated by means of bulletins, reports furnished by newspapers, television and radio broadcasts, and in certain ports, by flags during the day and lanterns at night. Some storm-warning flags are 8 feet square. The pennants have a hoist of 8 feet and fly at 15 feet. Smaller pennants are half this size.

Small-Craft Warning

One red pennant displayed by day, and a red light over a white light at night, indicates winds up to 38 miles an hour (33 knots) and sea conditions dangerous to small craft in the area.

Gale Warning

Two red pennants displayed by day, and a white light above a red light at night, forecast winds ranging from 39 to 54 miles an hour (34 to 47 knots).

Storm Warning

A single, square red flag with a black center displayed by day, and two red lights at night, warns of winds of 55 miles an hour (48 knots) and higher. (If winds are associated with a tropical cyclone or hurricane, the same display refers to winds with a range of 55 to 73 miles an hour [48 to 63 knots].)

Hurricane Warning

Two square red flags with black centers displayed by day, and a white light between two red lights at night, forecast winds of 74 miles an hour (64 knots).

Running Lights

Running lights for steam or other power-driven vessels.

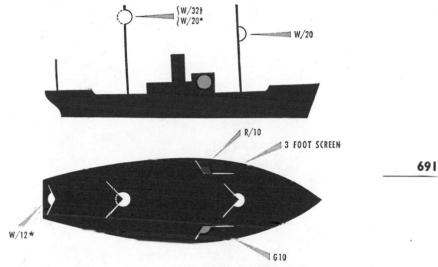

† REQUIRED UNDER INLAND RULES FOR NON-SEAGOING VESSELS
* REQUIRED UNDER INTERNATIONAL RULES FOR SEA-GOING VESSELS OF OR OVER 150'
★ REQUIRED UNDER INTERNATIONAL RULES FOR ALL VESSELS UNDER WAY AND BY INLAND RULES IN CASES WHERE NO OTHER LIGHT IS VISIBLE AFT.

THE NUMBER LISTED AFTER THE INITIAL DESIGNATING COLOR (W FOR WHITE, ETC.) IS THE NUMBER OF POINTS OVER WHICH THE LIGHT MUST SHOW. A POINT IS 11¼ DEGREES.

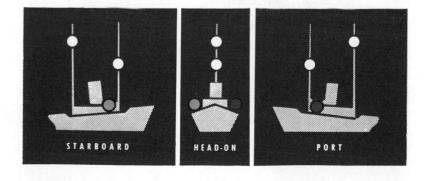

Pennants and Flags

Pennant and Name	Written and Spoken	Pennant	Written and Spoken	Pennant	Written and Spoken
1	PENNANT ONE "WUN"		CODE or ANSWER CODE or ANS		PORT PORT
2	PENNANT TWO "TOO"		SCREEN SCREEN		SPEED SPEED
3	PENNANT THREE "THUH-REE"		CORPEN CORPEN		SQUAD SQUAD
4	PENNANT FOUR "FO-WER"		DESIG DESIG		STARBOARD STBD
5	PENNANT FIVE "FI-YIV"		DIV DIV		STATION STATION
6	PENNANT SIX "SIX"		EMERGENCY EMERG		SUBDIV SUBDIV
7	PENNANT SEVEN "SEVEN"		FLOT FLOT		TURN TURN
8	PENNANT EIGHT "ATE"		FORMATION FORM		FIRST SUB 1st.
9	PENNANT NINE "NINER"		INTER-ROGATIVE INT		SECOND SUB 2nd.
0	PENNANT ZERO "ZERO"		NEGAT NEGAT		THIRD SUB 3rd.
			PREP PREP		FOURTH SUB 4th.

Alphabet and Numeral Flags

Flag	Name — Written / Spoken	Flag	Name — Written / Spoken	Flag	Name — Written / Spoken
	A ALFA "AL·FA"		**M** MIKE "MIKE"		**Y** YANKEE "YANG·KEY"
	B BRAVO "BRAH·VOH"		**N** NOVEMBER "NO·VEM·BER"		**Z** ZULU "ZOO·LOO"
	C CHARLIE "CHAR·LEE"		**O** OSCAR "OSS·CAH"		**ONE · 1** "WUN"
	D DELTA "DEL·TAH"		**P** PAPA "PAH·PAH"		**TWO · 2** "TOO"
	E ECHO "ECK·OH"		**Q** QUEBEC "KAY·BECK"		**THREE · 3** "THUH·REE"
	F FOXTROT "FOKS·TROT"		**R** ROMEO "ROW·ME·OH"		**FOUR · 4** "FO·WER"
	G GOLF "GOLF"		**S** SIERRA "SEE·AIR·RAH"		**FIVE · 5** "FI·YIV"
	H HOTEL "HOH·TEL"		**T** TANGO "TANG·GO"		**SIX · 6** "SIX"
	I INDIA "IN·DEE·AH"		**U** UNIFORM "YOU·NEE·FORM"		**SEVEN · 7** "SEVEN"
	J JULIETT "JEW·LEE·ETT"		**V** VICTOR "VIK·TAH"		**EIGHT · 8** "ATE"
	K KILO "KEY·LOH"		**W** WHISKEY "WISS·KEY"		**NINE · 9** "NINER"
	L LIMA "LEE·MAH"		**X** XRAY "ECKS·RAY"		**ZERO · 0** "ZERO"

694

Decorations and Awards

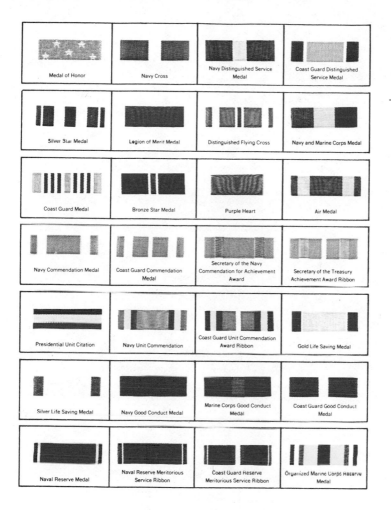

Medal of Honor	Navy Cross	Navy Distinguished Service Medal	Coast Guard Distinguished Service Medal
Silver Star Medal	Legion of Merit Medal	Distinguished Flying Cross	Navy and Marine Corps Medal
Coast Guard Medal	Bronze Star Medal	Purple Heart	Air Medal
Navy Commendation Medal	Coast Guard Commendation Medal	Secretary of the Navy Commendation for Achievement Award	Secretary of the Treasury Achievement Award Ribbon
Presidential Unit Citation	Navy Unit Commendation	Coast Guard Unit Commendation Award Ribbon	Gold Life Saving Medal
Silver Life Saving Medal	Navy Good Conduct Medal	Marine Corps Good Conduct Medal	Coast Guard Good Conduct Medal
Naval Reserve Medal	Naval Reserve Meritorious Service Ribbon	Coast Guard Reserve Meritorious Service Ribbon	Organized Marine Corps Reserve Medal

A decoration is conferred on an individual by name for exceptional courage, bravery, skill, or performance of duty. The Purple Heart is given to members of all military services who are wounded in action. Some minor decorations are not included in this illustration. Service awards are given for participation in designated wars, campaigns, or expeditions, or for service in various military theaters. There are more than three dozen such awards, none of which appears here.

Notes on Sources

The following list contains the principal sources used to prepare this edition of *The Bluejacket's Manual*. All of the official publications are available in every ship and at every station. Most of the Naval Institute Press publications named can be found in ship or station libraries.

All Hands magazine
Bibliography for Advancement Study (NAVEDTRA 10052)
Catalog of Navy Training Courses (CANTRAC, NAVEDTRA 10500)
Enlisted Transfer Manual (TRANSMAN, NAVPERS 15909)
Flags, Pennants, and Customs (DNC 27 [B])
General Military Training (GMT, OPNAVINST 1500 series)
Information Security Program Regulation (OPNAVINST 5510 series)
List of Training Manuals and Correspondence Courses (NAVEDTRA 10061)
Manual of Enlisted Classification Procedures (NAVPERS 18068)
Manual of Advancement (BUPERSINST 1430 series)
Naval Military Personnel Manual (NAVPERS 15791)
Naval Orientation (NAVPERS 10900-83)
Navy Fact File
Navy Pay and Personnel Procedures Manual (PAYPERSMAN, NAVSO P-3050)
Navy Recruiting Manual—Enlisted (CRUITMAN-ENL, COMNAVCRUITCOMINST 1130 series)
Naval Reserve Indoctrination Guide (RAD 716-0257)
Organization of the U.S. Navy (NWP 2)
Rate Training Manuals (RTMs):
    Airman (NAVPERS 10307)
    Basic Military Requirements (NAVEDTRA 10054)

Boatswain's Mate 3 and 2 (NAVEDTRA 10121)
Disbursing Clerk 3 and 2 (NAVEDTRA 10274)
Electrician's Mate 3 and 2 (NAVEDTRA 10546)
Engineman 3 and 2 (NAVPERS 10541)
Fireman (NAVEDTRA 10520)
Gunner's Mate 3 and 2 (NAVEDTRA 10573)
Hull Maintenance Technician (NAVEDTRA 10573)
Personnelman 3 and 2 (NAVEDTRA 10254)
Quartermaster 3 and 2 (NAVEDTRA 10149)
Seaman (NAVPERS 10120)
Signalman 3 and 2 (NAVEDTRA 10135)
Yeoman 3 and 2 (NAVEDTRA 10240)
Replenishment at Sea (NWP 14 [A])
Retention Team Manual (NAVPERS 15878)
Standard Organization and Regulations of the U.S. Navy
    (OPNAVINST 3120 series)
Uniform Code of Military Justice (UCMJ)
Uniformed Services Almanac
United States Navy Regulations
United States Navy Uniform Regulations

Publications by the Naval Institute Press, Annapolis, Maryland

A Mariner's Guide to the Rules of the Road (2d ed., William
    H. Tate, 1982)
Dictionary of Naval Abbreviations (3d ed., Bill Wedertz, 1984)
Division Officer's Guide (9th ed., Captain John V. Noel and
    Lieutenant Commander James Stavridis, 1989)
Engineering for the OOD (Commander Dan Felger, 1979)
Mariner's Pocket Companion (Wallace E. Tobin, 1989)
The Naval Aviation Guide (4th ed., Captain Richard C. Knott,
    1985)
Naval Ceremonies, Customs, and Traditions (5th ed., Vice
    Admiral W. P. Mack and R. W. Connell, 1980)
Naval Institute Guide to Combat Fleet of the World, 1990/1991
    (Bernard Prézelin/A. D. Baker)
Naval Institute Guide to World Naval Weapons Systems (Nor-
    man Friedman, 1989)
Naval Leadership (Karel Montor et al., 1987)
Naval Shiphandling (4th ed., Captain R. S. Crenshaw, 1975)

Naval Terms Dictionary (5th ed., Captain John V. Noel and
    Captain Edward L. Beach, 1988)

Ops Officer's Manual (Commander P. T. Deutermann, 1980)
Service Etiquette (Oretha D. Swartz, 1988)
Shipboard Damage Control (A. M. Bissell, E. J. Oertel, and
   D. J. Livingston, 1976)
Ship Organization and Personnel (Fundamentals of Naval Science Series, 1972)
The Boat Officer's Handbook (Lieutenant David D. Winters, 1981)
The Ships and Aircraft of the U.S. Fleet (14th ed., Norman Polmar, 1987)
Watch Officer's Guide (12th ed., Commander David M. Lee, Lieutenant John M. Brown, Lieutenant Robert Morabito, and Lieutenant H. Scott Colenda, 1986)

699

Official Publications and Directives

While the Constitution, various treaties, and Congress supply the fundamental laws governing the Navy, they are really only broad outlines. The Navy has various publications and official directives setting forth specific procedures for the daily operation of the Navy Department and for the administration of personnel.

Complete familiarity with these publications and directives is required for yeomen (YNs) and personnelmen (PNs), but to help you determine important policies and programs affecting your Navy career, regardless of your rating, all you'll need is a working knowledge.

The most important publication, which affects nearly everything you do—including application for various educational programs, transfers, discharges, and separations—is probably the *Naval Military Personnel Manual* (NAVPERS 15560). Other important publications include pamphlets and brochures distributed by the Naval Military Personnel Command (NMPC) and identified as NAVPERS publications and forms.

Navy Regulations (NAVREGS) outlines the organizational structure of the Department of the Navy and sets out the principles and policies by which the Navy is governed. Its chapters, among many other things, define the responsibility, purpose, and authority of each bureau and office of the Navy Department.

The Manual for Courts-Martial, United States, 1969 (MCM) describes the types of courts-martial established by the Uniform Code of Military Justice (UCMJ), defines their jurisdiction, and prescribes their procedures. It also covers such matters as nonjudicial punishment (NJP) and reviews court-martial proceedings, new trials, and limitations on punishment.

The Manual of the Medical Department (MANMED) (NAVMED P-117) contains general instructions for medical

701

care of personnel; directions for the procurement, storage, issue, and accounting of medical supplies and for training medical and dental personnel; procedures for keeping health records and submitting reports; and special procedures and reports in case of death.

The Manual of the Judge Advocate General (JAGMAN) (JAGINST 5800.7) covers legal and judicial matters that apply only to the naval service. Included among these are instructions regarding boards of investigation and examining boards—their composition, authority, and procedures.

U.S. Navy Uniform Regulations (NAVPERS 15665), or Uniform Regs for short, describes uniforms for personnel in all categories and contains lists of articles worn or used together. It tells you when various uniforms should be worn; how to wear medals, decorations, ribbons, rating badges, and special markings; and how to care for your uniforms.

Joint Travel Regulations (JTR) is issued in two volumes; only the first volume deals with actual travel. JTR interprets the laws and regulations concerning the manner in which transportation is furnished, travel for dependents, the transportation of household goods, reimbursement for travel expenses, and similar information.

U.S. Naval Travel Instructions (NAVSO P-1459) amplifies the rules laid down in vol. 1 of the JTR.

The Department of Defense Military Pay and Allowance Entitlements Manual (DODPM) covers statutory provisions for entitlements, deductions, and collections on military pay and allowances.

The Navy Pay and Personnel Procedures Manual (PAY-PERSMAN) (NAVSO P-3050) contains detailed information about the procedures of the joint-uniform military pay system (JUMPS) for members of the Navy. (The JUMPS system is described on pp. 215–18.)

The Enlisted Transfer Manual (TRANSMAN) (NAVPERS 15909) is the official manual for the distribution and assignment of enlisted personnel; it supplements the MILPERSMAN. TRANSMAN provides quick reference for all matters relating to enlisted distribution.

The Navy and Marine Corps Awards Manual, usually known simply as the Awards Manual, is issued by the secretary of the Navy (SECNAVINST 1650.1) for guidance in all matters pertaining to decorations, medals, and awards, including how they are worn.

The *Manual of Advancement*, published by the Navy Military Personnel Command (BUPERSINST 1430.16), addresses the administration of the advancement system. It explains the basic policies outlined in MILPERSMAN and offers information on eligibility requirements for advancement; the preparation of forms; the ordering, custody, and disposition of Navy-wide exams; the administration of examinations for advancement; changes in rate or rating; and procedures for advancement.

Directives System

In addition to the publications already described, there are certain others that have a bearing on your Navy career. The following commands publish instructional materials governing transfers, educational programs, financial and medical benefits, etc. They are listed as short titles first, since this is the way you will normally hear them described. The full title appears in the righthand column.

BUPERS	Bureau of Naval Personnel
CNET	Chief of Naval Education and Training
COMNAVAIRLANT	Commander, Naval Air Force, Atlantic Fleet
COMNAVAIRPAC	Commander, Naval Air Force, Pacific Fleet
COMNAVCRUITCOM	Commander, Navy Recruiting Command
COMNAVMEDCOM	Commander, Naval Medical Command
DOD	Department of Defense
GPO	Government Printing Office
JAG	Judge Advocate General
NAVAIR	Naval Air Systems Command
NAVCOMP	Comptroller of the Navy
NAVEDTRA	Chief of Navy Education and Training (Command)
NAVMAT	Naval Material Command
NAVMILPERSCOM	Navy Military Personnel Command
NAVSO	Executive Offices of the Secretary of the Navy

NAVSUP	Naval Supply Systems Command
NAVTRA	Chief of Naval Training
OPNAV	Office of the Chief of Naval Operations
SECNAV	Secretary of the Navy
VA	Department of Veterans Affairs

A directive—prepared as either an instruction, notice, or change transmittal—prescribes or establishes policy, organization, conduct, methods, or procedures. Directives either require some specific action or report, or they supply detailed information that is essential. An instruction (INST) contains information that has continuing reference or that requires continuing action. It remains in effect until superseded or canceled by its originator or by higher authority. A notice (NOTE) is a brief, one-time directive.

Say, for example, you look up a certain Chief of Naval Education and Training (CNET) instruction, CNETINST 1560, and discover that there is no CNETINST 1560, but there is a 1560.1. The latter, an update of the basic instruction, is the most current information available on your subject. If it appears as CNETINST 1560.1C, the previous instructions—1560, 1560.1, 1560.1A, and 1560.1B—have been superseded by the new 1560.1C.

If you cannot find the reference CNETINST 1560, do not mistakenly think that 1561 is the newest reference; 1561 refers to a different subject entirely. If CNETINST 1560 is not listed, it probably means that the program has been disestablished. You may have to seek the advice of your resident personnelman to track down a new reference.

One other factor should also be considered. You may find, once you've consulted the reference CNETINST 1560, that certain pages appear as CNETINST 1560 CH 1. This indicates that a change transmittal—which provides specific updated information—has been added. Normally a change transmittal only affects certain pages of an instruction; the remainder of the original instruction is still effective.

If there is some slight—usually temporary—modification in the CNETINST 1560 program, you can locate that information by consulting the current CNET notice (CNETNOTE 1560), which covers the same program.

The same basic rules can be applied to the following command references, which should prove useful during your career:

715

719

Glossary of Navy Terms __K__

A person entering a new trade must learn the vocabulary of that trade. The Navy has a language all its own. In the list below, you will find many commonly used naval terms. Along with those discussed in this manual, they should provide you with a basic naval vocabulary.

Abaft—Farther aft, as in "abaft the beam"
Abeam—On a relative bearing of 90 degrees ("abeam to starboard") or 270 degrees ("abeam to port")
Aboard—In a naval station or on a ship
Abreast—Same as abeam
Accommodation ladder—A ladder suspended over and inclining down the side of a ship to facilitate boarding from boats
Adrift—Loose from moorings and out of control (applied to anything lost, out of hand, or left lying about)
Aft—Toward the stern (not as specific as *abaft*)
After—That which is farthest aft
Afternoon watch—The 1200 to 1600 watch
Aground—That part of a ship resting on the bottom (a ship "runs aground" or "goes aground")
Ahoy—A hail or demand for attention, as in "Boat ahoy"
Alee—In the direction of the wind; downwind
All fast—Tied or lashed down as necessary
All hands—The entire ship's company
Aloft—Generally speaking, any area above the highest deck
Alongside—By the side of the ship or pier
Amidships—An indefinite area midway between the bow and the stern ("rudder amidships" means that the rudder is in line with the ship's centerline)
Anchorage—An area designated to be used by ships for anchoring

Anchor cable—The line, wire, or chain that attaches a vessel to her anchor

Anchor watch—A group of persons available to the officer of the deck during the night for such duties as heaving in or paying out the cable

Armament—The weapons of a ship

Armored deck—A deck, below the main deck, that provides added protection to vital spaces

Ashore—On the beach or shore

Astern—Directly behind a ship

Athwart—Across; at right angles to

Auxiliary—Extra, or secondary, as in "auxiliary engine"; a vessel whose mission is to supply or support combatant forces

Avast—Stop, as in "avast heaving"

Aweigh—Just clear of the bottom, as in "anchors aweigh" (as defined in the Rules of the Road, this means a ship is under way)

Aye, Aye—Reply to a command or order, meaning "I understand and will obey"

Barge—A blunt-ended, scow-type craft, usually non-self-propelled, used to haul supplies or garbage; a type of motorboat assigned for the personal use of a flag officer

Barnacles—Small shellfish attached to a vessel's undersides, pilings, and other submerged structures

Batten down—The act of applying battens to a hatch; the closing of any watertight fixture

Battle lantern—A battery-powered lantern for emergency use

Beam—(1) The extreme breadth of a vessel; (2) a transverse frame supporting a deck

Bear—To be located on a particular bearing, as in "the lighthouse bears 045 degrees"

Bear a hand—Provide assistance, as in "bear a hand with rigging this stage"; expedite

Bearing—The direction of an object measured in degrees clockwise from a reference point (true "bearing" is the angular difference between lines drawn from the observer to true north and to the object; "magnetic bearing" is the direction of the object measured on a magnetic compass; "relative bearing" is the angle between the ship's head and the object)

Belay—To secure a line to a fixed point; to disregard a previous order or to stop an action, as in "belay the last order" or "belay the small talk"

Below—Downward, beneath, or beyond something, as "lay below"; or below the flight deck"

Berth—Bunk; duty assignment; mooring space assigned to a ship

Bight—The middle part of a line, or a loop in a line

Bilge—Bottom of the hull near the keel; to fail an examination

Billet—Place or duty to which one is assigned

Binnacle—Stand containing a magnetic compass

Binnacle list—List of persons excused from duty because of illness

Bitt—Cylindrical upright fixture to which mooring or towing lines are secured aboard ship

Bitter end—The free end of a line

Block—A frame containing a pulley, called a sheave, around which a line (known as a fall) is rove

Board—To go aboard a vessel; a group of persons meeting for a specific purpose, as in "investigation board"

Boat—A small craft capable of being carried aboard a ship

Boat boom—A spar rigged out from the side of an anchored or moored ship to which boats are tied when not in use

Boatswain—Warrant officer in charge of deck work (pronounced *bo-sun*)

Boatswain's chair—A seat attached to a gantline for hoisting a person

Boatswain's locker—A compartment, usually forward, where line and other equipment used by the deck force are stowed

Bollard—A strong, cylindrical, upright fixture on a pier to which ship's mooring lines are secured

Boom—A spar, usually movable, used for hoisting loads

Boot topping—Black paint applied to a ship's sides along the waterline

Bow—The forward end of a ship or boat

Bow hook—Member of a boat's crew whose station is forward

Break Out—To bring out supplies or equipment from a storage space

Breast line—Mooring line that leads from ship to pier at right angles to the ship

Bridge—Area in the superstructure from which a ship is operated (see *Conn*)

Brig—Jail

Brightwork—Bare metal that is kept polished

Broach to—To get crosswise (without power) to the direction of the waves

Broad—Wide, as in "broad in the beam"

Broad on the bow or quarter—Halfway between dead ahead and abeam, and halfway between abeam and astern, respectively

Broadside—Simultaneously and to one side (when firing main battery guns); sidewise, as in "the current carried the ship broadside toward the beach"

Broadside-to—With the side toward something, as in "the ship hit the pier broadside-to"

Brow—Gangplank used for crossing from one ship to another, and from a ship to a pier

Bulkhead—A vertical partition in a ship (never called a wall)

Buoy—An anchored float used as an aid to navigation or to mark the location of an object

Burdened vessel—That vessel required by the Rules of the Road to keep clear of another

By the board—Overboard

Cabin—Living compartment of a ship's commanding officer

Camel—Large timber or rectangular structure used as a fender between a ship and a pier

Can buoy—A cylindrical navigational buoy, painted black or green and odd-numbered which in U.S. waters marks the port side of a channel from seaward

Carry away—To break loose, as in "the rough seas carried away the lifelines"

Carry on—An order to resume previous activity after an interruption

Chafing gear—Material used to protect lines from excessive wear

Chain locker—Space where anchor chain is stowed

Chain of command—The succession from superior to subordinate through which command is exercised; the succession from subordinate to superior through which requests should go

Chart—Nautical counterpart of a road map, showing land configuration, water depths, and aids to navigation

Chart house—The navigator's work compartment

Check—To slow or ease (to "check a line" is to pay out just enough line to prevent its parting under strain); to investigate or examine something

Chip—To remove paint or rust from metallic surfaces with sharp-pointed hammers before applying paint

Chock—Deck fitting through which mooring lines are led

Chow—Food

Collision bulkhead—A bulkhead, stronger than normal, located forward to control flooding in the event of a head-on collision

Colors—The national ensign; the ceremony of raising and lowering the ensign

Combatant ship—A ship whose primary mission is combat

Commission pennant—A long, narrow starred and striped pennant flown only on board a commissioned ship

Companionway— Deck opening giving access to a ladder (includes the ladder)

Compartment—Interior space of a ship

Complete deck—Any deck that extends the length and breadth of a ship

Conn—Station, usually on the bridge, from which a ship is controlled; the act of so controlling

Course—A ship's desired direction of travel, not to be confused with *heading*

Cover—To protect; a shelter; headgear; to don headgear

Coxswain—Enlisted person in charge of a boat

Crow's nest—Lookout station aloft

Cumshaw—A gift; something procured without payment

Darken ship—To turn off all external lights and close all openings through which lights can be seen from outside the ship

Davits—Strong arms by means of which a boat is hoisted in or out

Davy Jones' Locker—The bottom of the sea

Dead ahead—Directly ahead; a relative bearing of 000 degrees

Dead astern—180 degrees relative

Deck—Horizontal planking or plating that divides a ship into layers (floors)

Deck seamanship—The upkeep and operation of all deck equipment

Decontaminate—To free from harmful residue of nuclear or chemical attack

Deep six—To throw something overboard

Dinghy—A small boat, sometimes equipped with a sail, but more commonly propelled by outboard motor or oars

Dip—To lower a flag partway down the staff as a salute to, or in reply to a salute from, another ship

Distance line—A line stretched between two ships engaged in replenishment or transfer operations under way (the line is

marked at 20-foot intervals to aid the conning officer in
maintaining station)

Division—A main subdivision of a ship's crew (1st, E, G, etc.);
an organization composed of two or more ships of the
same type

Dock—The space alongside a pier or in dry dock; any pier or
wharf

Dog—A lever, or bolt and thumb screws, used for securing a
watertight door; to divide a 4-hour watch into two 2-hour
watches

Dog down—To set the dogs on a watertight door

Dog watch—The 1600 to 1800 or 1800 to 2000 watch

Double up—To double mooring lines for extra strength

Draft—The vertical distance from the keel to the waterline

Dress ship—To display flags in honor of a person or event

Drift—The speed at which a ship is pushed off course by wind
and current

Drogue—*See* Sea anchor

Dry dock—A dock, either floating or built into the shore, from
which water may be removed for the purpose of inspecting
or working on a ship's bottom; to be put in dry dock

Ease—To relax, slack

Ebb—A falling tide, as in "on the ebb"

Eight o'clock reports—Reports received by the executive officer from department heads shortly before 2000

Emergency drill—A rehearsal of the action taken by a ship's
crew in an emergency

Ensign—The national flag; the lowest grade of commissioned
officer

Executive officer—Second officer in command

Eyes—The forwardmost part of the forecastle

Fake—The act of disposing of line, wire, or chain by laying it
out in long, flat bights, one alongside the other

Fantail—The after end of the main deck

Fathom—Unit of depth equal to 6 feet

Fender—A cushioning device hung over the side of a ship to
prevent contact between the ship and a pier or another
ship

Field day—A day devoted to general cleaning, usually in preparation for an inspection

Fire main—Piping system to which fire hydrants are connected

First Lieutenant—The officer responsible, in general, for a
ship's upkeep and cleanliness (except machinery and ordnance gear), boats, ground tackle, and deck seamanship

First watch—The 2000 to 2400 watch (also called evening watch)

Flag officer—An officer of the rank of admiral

Flagstaff—Vertical staff at the stern to which the ensign is hoisted when moored or at anchor

Fleet—An organization of ships, aircraft, marine forces, and shore-based fleet activities, all under one commander, for conducting major operations

Flight deck—Deck on an aircraft carrier for aircraft takeoff and landing

Flood—To fill a space with water; a rising tide

Fogy—A longevity pay increase (pronounced *fo-gee*)

Fore and aft—The entire length of a ship, as in "sweep down fore and aft"

Forecastle—Forward section of the main deck, generally extending from the stem aft to just abaft the anchor windlass (pronounced *fok-sul*)

Foremast—First mast aft from the bow

Forenoon watch—The 0800 to 1200 watch

Forward—Toward the bow

Foul—Entangled, as in "the lines are foul of each other"; stormy

Gaff—A light spar set at an angle from the upper part of a mast (the ensign is usually flown from the gaff under way)

Galley—Space where food is prepared (never called a kitchen)

Gangway—The opening in a bulwark or lifeline that provides access to a brow or accommodation ladder; an order meaning to clear the way

General quarters (GQ)—The condition of full readiness for battle

Gig—Boat assigned for the commanding officer's personal use

Ground tackle—Equipment used in anchoring or mooring with anchors

Half deck—A partial deck below the main deck

Halyard—A light line used to hoist a flag or pennant

Hand—A ship's crewmember

Handsomely—Steadily and carefully, but not necessarily slowly

Handy billy—A small portable water pump for general use

Hard over—Condition of a rudder that has been turned to the maximum possible rudder angle

Hashmark—A red, blue, or gold diagonal stripe across the left sleeve of an enlisted person's jumper, indicating four years' service

Hatch—A square or rectangular access in a deck

Haul—To pull in or heave on a line by hand

Haul off—To change course in order to keep clear of another vessel

Hawser—Any heavy wire or line used for towing or mooring

Head—The upper end of a lower mast boom; compartment containing toilet facilities; ship's bow

Heading—The direction toward which the ship's bow is pointing at any instant

Heave—To throw

Heave around—To haul in a line, usually by means of a capstan or winch; to get to work

Heave In—To take in line or cable

Heave out and lash up—Admonishment that originally meant "Get up and lash up your hammocks," once applied at reveille to men sleeping in hammocks, and which now applies to persons in bunks

Heave to—To stop or reduce headway just enough to maintain steerageway

Heaving line—A line with a weight at one end, heaved across an intervening space for passing over a heavier line

Helm—Mechanical device used to turn the rudder (usually a wheel aboard ship, a lever in boats)

Helmsman—Person who steers the ship by turning her helm (also called steersman)

Highline—The line stretched between ships under way on which a trolley block travels back and forth to transfer material and personnel

Hitch—To bend a line to or around a ring or cylindrical object; an enlistment

Hold—Large cargo stowage space aboard ship

Holding bulkhead—The innermost of a series of bulkheads that form the tanks and voids of the torpedo protection system

Holiday—Space on a surface that the painter neglected to paint

Hook—Familiar term for anchor

Hull—The shell, or plating, of a ship from keel to gunwale

Hull down—Of a ship so far over the horizon that only her superstructure or top hamper is visible

Inboard—Toward the centerline

Inlet—A narrow strip of sea extending into the land

Inshore—Close to the shore

Island—Superstructure on starboard side of the flight deck of an aircraft carrier

Jack—Starred blue flag (representing the union of the ensign) flown at the jackstay of a commissioned ship not under way

Jackstaff—Vertical spar at the stem to which the jack is hoisted

Jacob's ladder—A portable rope or wire ladder

Jetty—A structure built out from shore to influence water currents or protect a harbor or pier

Jolly Roger—Banner showing skull and crossbones (the royal standard of His Imperial Majesty Neptunus Rex)

Jump ship—To desert a ship

Jury rig—Any makeshift device or apparatus; to fashion such a device

Knock off—Quit working

Knot—To form an eye in a line, or to tie a line to or around something; nautical miles per hour

Ladder—A shipboard flight of steps

Landing craft—Vessel especially designed for landing troops and equipment directly on a beach

Landing ship—A large seagoing ship designed for landing personnel and/or heavy equipment directly on a beach

Lanyard—Any short line used as a handle or as a means for operating some piece of equipment; a line used to attach an article to the person, as a pistol lanyard

Lash—To secure an object by turns of line, wire, or chain

Launch—To float a vessel off the ways in a building yard; a powerboat, usually over 30 feet long

Lay—Movement of a person, as in "lay aloft"; the direction of twist in the strands of a line or wire; to put something down, as in "lay tile"

Lee—An area sheltered from the wind; downwind

Leeward—Direction toward which the wind is blowing (pronounced *loo-ard*)

Liberty—Official absence from a ship or station for a short time

Life buoy—A buoyant ring or other floating device, except a life jacket or life belt, designed to support a person in the water

Life jacket—A buoyant jacket designed to support a person in the water (a lifebelt fits only around the waist)

Lifeline—In general, the line erected around the edge of a weather deck, specifically the topmost line (from top to bottom, lines are named lifeline, housing line, and footrope); a safety line bent to a person going over the side or aloft

Lighten ship—To make a ship lighter by removing weight

Light Ship—To dispense with blackout precautions

Line—Any rope that is not wire rope

List—Transverse inclination of a vessel

Log—A ship's speedometer; book or ledger in which data or events that occurred during a watch are recorded; to make a certain speed, as in "the ship logged 20 knots"

Look alive—Admonishment meaning to be alert or move faster

Lookout—Person stationed topside on a formal watch who reports objects sighted and sounds heard to the officer of the deck

Lucky bag—Locker under the charge of the master-at-arms and used to stow deserter's effects and gear found adrift

Magazine—Compartment used for the stowage of ammunition

Main deck—The uppermost complete deck

Mainmast—Second mast aft from the bow

Make fast—To secure

Man—To assume a station, as in "to man a gun"

Man-o-War—*See* Combatant ship

Marlinespike—Tapered steel tool used to open the strands of wire for splicing

Marlinespike seamanship—The art of caring for and handling all types of line and wire

Master-at-arms—A member of a ship's police force

Masthead light—A 20-point white running light located in the fore part of the ship, and which may or may not be on the foremast

Mate—A shipmate; another sailor

Mess—Meal; place where meals are eaten; a group that takes meals together, as in "officers' mess"

Messenger—A line used to haul a heavier line across an intervening space; one who delivers messages

Midwatch—The watch that begins at 0000 and ends at 0400

Moor—To anchor with two anchors; to make fast to a mooring buoy; to make fast to a pier or other ship

Mooring buoy—A large anchored float to which a ship may moor

Morning watch—The 0400 to 0800 watch

Motor whaleboat—A double-ended powerboat

Muster—A rollcall; to assemble for a rollcall

Muster on stations—Rollcall taken at work or drill

Nest—Two or more boats stowed one within the other; two or more ships moored alongside each other

Nun buoy—A navigational buoy, conical in shape, painted red and even numbered, that marks the starboard side of a channel from seaward

Offshore—Some distance off the shore

On the Beach—Ashore; a seaman assigned to shore duty, unemployed, retired, or otherwise detached from sea duty

On station—Present (of aircraft); at the assigned location (of ships)

Outboard—Away from the centerline

Overboard—Over the side

Overhaul—To repair or recondition; to overtake another vessel

Overhead—The underside of a deck forms the overhead of the compartment next below (never called a ceiling)

Party—A group on temporary assignment or engaged in a common activity, as in "line-handling party," "liberty party"

Passageway—A corridor used for interior horizontal movement aboard ship

Pay out—To feed out or lengthen a line

Pier—Structure extending from land into water to provide a mooring for vessels

Pier head—Seaward end of a pier

Pigstick—Small staff from which a commission pennant is flown

Pilot house—Enclosure on the bridge housing the main steering controls

Piloting—Branch of navigation in which positions are determined by visible objects on the surface, or by soundings

Pipe—To sound a particular call on a boatswain's pipe

Pitch—Vertical rise and fall of a ship's bow caused by head or following seas

Plane guard—Destroyer or helicopter responsible for rescuing crews during launch or recovery operations

Plank owner—A person who has been on board since commissioning

Plan of the day—Schedule of a day's routine and events ordered by the executive officer and published daily aboard ship or at a shore activity

Pollywog—A person who has never crossed the equator (pejorative)

Port—To the left of the centerline when facing forward

Quarterdeck—Deck area designated by the commanding officer as the place to carry out official functions; station of
the officer of the deck in port

Quartermaster—An enlisted assistant to the navigator

Quarters—Stations for shipboard evolutions, as in "general
quarters," "fire quarters"; living spaces

Quay—A solid structure along a bank used for loading and
offloading vessels (pronounced *key*)

Radar—A device that uses reflected radio waves for the detection of objects

Range—The distance of an object from an observer; an aid to
navigation consisting of two objects in line; a water area
designated for a particular purpose, as in "gunnery
range"

Range light—A white running light mounted in line with, but
higher than and abaft, the masthead light (the two lights
indicate to other vessels a ship's general heading)

Rat guard—A hinged metal disk secured to a mooring line to
prevent rats from traveling over the line into the ship

Reef—An underwater ledge rising abruptly from the ocean's
floor

Relief—A person assigned to the duties of another

Relieve—To take the place of another; to ease the strain on a
line

Replenishment—To resupply a ship or station

Ride—To be at anchor, as in "the ship is riding to her anchor"

Riding light—Light shown by a vessel at anchor

Rig—To set up a device or equipment, as in "to rig a stage
over the side"

Rigging—Lines that support a ship's masts, i.e. standing rigging; lines that hoist or otherwise move equipment, i.e.
running rigging

Rope—Fiber or wire line (fiber rope is usually referred to as
line, while wire rope is called rope, wire rope, or wire)

Ropeyarn Sunday—A workday that has been granted as a holiday for taking care of personal business

Rudder—Device attached to the stern that controls a ship's
direction of travel

Running lights— Navigational lights shown at night by a vessel
under way

Sack—Bunk

Scuttlebutt—A drinking fountain (originally, a ship's water
barrel [called a butt] that was tapped [scuttled] by the

insertion of a spigot from which the crew drew drinking water); rumor (the scuttlebutt was once a place for personnel to exchange news when they gathered to draw water)

Sea anchor—A device streamed from the bow of a vessel for holding it end-on to the sea

Seamanship—The art of handling a vessel; skill in the use of deck equipment, in boat handling, and in the care and use of line and wire

Sea state—Condition of waves and the height of their swells

Seaworthy—A vessel capable of withstanding normal heavy weather

Second deck—First complete deck below the main deck

Secure—To make fast, as in "secure a line to a cleat"; to cease, as in "secure from fire drill"

Service force—Organization providing logistic support to combatant forces

Shake a leg—An admonishment to move faster

Shake down—The training of a new crew in operating a ship

Shellback—A person who has crossed the equator

Shift colors—To change the arrangement of colors upon getting under way or coming to moorings

Ship—Any large seagoing vessel capable of extended independent operation; to take on water unintentionally

Ship over—To reenlist in the Navy

Shipping articles—Enlistment contracts signed by enlisted personnel

Ship's company—All hands permanently attached to a ship or station

Shipshape—Neat, clean, taut

Shoal—A structure similar to a reef, but more gradual in its rise from the floor of the ocean

Shore—Land, usually that part adjacent to the water; a timber used in damage control to brace bulkheads and decks

Sick bay—Shipboard space that serves as a hospital

Side boy—One of a group of seamen who form two ranks at the gangway as part of the ceremonies conducted for visiting officials

Side light—One of a series running lights (the starboard side light is green and the portside light is red)

Side port—A watertight opening in a ship's side, used as a doorway

Sight—To see for the first time, as to sight a ship on the horizon; a celestial observation

Skylark—To engage in irresponsible horseplay

Slack—To allow a line to run out; undisciplined, as in "slack ship"

Small craft—Any less-than-ship-size vessel

Small stores—Personal items, such as articles of clothing

Smart—Snappy, seamanlike, shipshape

Smoking tamp—Period or condition during which personnel are authorized to smoke

Snub—To suddenly check a line that is running out under a strain

Sound—To determine the depth of water; to dive deep (of marine animals); a body of water between the mainland and a large coastal island

Spar buoy—A buoy shaped like a spar, which usually indicates a special area, such as a quarantine anchorage (yellow) or normal anchorage (white), but may be used to indicate a channel (painted red or black)

Special sea detail—Crewmembers assigned special duties when leaving and entering port

Splice—To make an eye, or join lines or wires together, by intertwining strands; the joint so made

Squadron—Two or more divisions of ships or aircraft

Square away—To put in proper order; to make things shipshape

Square knot—Simple knot used for bending two lines together or for bending a line to itself

Stack—Shipboard chimney

Stanchions—Vertical posts for supporting decks; smaller, similar posts for supporting lifelines, awnings, etc.

Stand by—To prepare for or make ready to

Standing lights—Red night lights throughout the interior of a ship

Starboard—Direction to the right of the centerline as one faces forward

State room—A living compartment for an officer, or officers

Station—An individual's place of duty; position of a ship in formation; location of persons and equipment with a specific purpose, as in "gun-control station"; order to assume stations, as in "station the special sea and anchor detail"

Stay—Any piece of standing rigging providing support only

Stem—Extreme forward line of bow

Stern—The aftermost part of a vessel

Stern light—White navigation light that can be seen only from astern to 6 points on either quarter (for a total of 12 points, or 135 degrees)

Stow—To store or pack articles or cargo in a space

STREAM—Standard tensioned replenishment-alongside method

Structural bulkhead—Transverse strength bulkhead that forms a watertight boundary

Superstructure—The structure above a ship's main deck

Swab—A mop

Tarpaulin—Canvas used as a cover

Taut—Under tension; highly disciplined and efficient, as in "a taut ship"

Tender—One who serves as a precautionary standby, as in "line tender for a diver"; a support vessel for other ships

Topside—Weather decks; above (referring to the deck above)

Trice up—To secure bunks by hauling them up and hanging them off (securing them) on their chains

Truck—The uppermost tip of a mast

Turn in—To retire to bed; to return articles to the issue room

Turn out—To get out of bed; to order out a working party or other group, as in "turn out the guard"

Turn to—To start working

Up all hammocks—Admonishment to personnel entitled to sleep after reveille to get up

Upper deck—The first deck above the main deck

Void—An empty tank

Waist—The amidships section of the main deck

Wake—Trail left by a vessel or other object moving through the water

Wardroom—Officers' messing compartment

Watch—One of the periods, usually 4 hours, into which a day is divided; a particular duty, as in "life buoy watch"; to indicate the position of a sunken object (of a buoy or other marker)

Watertight integrity—The degree or quality of watertightness

Weather deck—Any deck exposed to the elements

Weigh anchor—To hoist the anchor clear of the bottom

Wharf—Structure similar to a quay but constructed like a pier

Whipping—Binding on the end of a line or wire to prevent unraveling

Windward—In the direction of the wind

X-ray—Damage-control material condition (a minimum condition)

Yardarm—The port or starboard half of a spar set athwartships across the upper mast (a yard)

Yaw—(Of a vessel) to have its heading thrown wide of its course as the result of a force, such as a heavy following sea, from astern

Yoke—Damage-control material condition (a battle condition)

Zebra—Damage-control material condition (a battle condition)

Photo Credits

Index

739

743